A Military History of Late Rome 284 to 361

"Money is the sinews of war"
Cicero, Philippic 5.2

"Thus, recognizing dangers from afar, the Romans always found remedies for them; and they never allowed them to develop in order to avoid a war, because they knew that war cannot be avoided, but can only be put off to the advantage of others"
Niccolò Machiavelli, The Prince (tr. by Peter Bondanella, Oxford 2005, p.12)

In loving memory of my mother Pirkko.
Your kindness and devotion to the family will be remembered forever.
You found encouraging words even at a time when you fought a losing battle against cancer.
No words can adequately express the sorrow.
You will be sorely missed by all of us.
This book would not have been finished without your help and encouragement and is dedicated to your memory.

A Military History of Late Rome 284 to 361

Dr. Ilkka Syvanne

An officer of the Equites Domestici
(author's drawing inspired by Mattesini)

Pen & Sword
MILITARY

First published in Great Britain in 2015 by
Pen & Sword Military
an imprint of
Pen & Sword Books Ltd
47 Church Street
Barnsley
South Yorkshire
S70 2AS

Copyright © Dr. Ilkka Syvanne 2015

ISBN 978 1 84884 855 9

Typeset in Ehrhardt by
Mac Style, Driffield, East Yorkshire
Printed and bound in the UK by CPI Group (UK) Ltd, Croydon, CRO 4YY

Pen & Sword Books Ltd incorporates the imprints of Pen & Sword
Archaeology, Atlas, Aviation, Battleground, Discovery, Family History,
History, Maritime, Military, Naval, Politics, Railways, Select, Transport,
True Crime, and Fiction, Frontline Books, Leo Cooper, Praetorian Press,
Seaforth Publishing and Wharncliffe.

For a complete list of Pen & Sword titles please contact
PEN & SWORD BOOKS LIMITED
47 Church Street, Barnsley, South Yorkshire, S70 2AS, England
E-mail: enquiries@pen-and-sword.co.uk
Website: www.pen-and-sword.co.uk

Contents

List of Plates

List of Maps

Acknowledgements

First of all, I want to recognize my debt to Professor Geoffrey Greatrex in recommending me to the publisher and to the editor Philip Sidnell for accepting my book proposal.

Perry Gray read two chapters of the narrative and I owe him a great debt for pointing out some mistakes. Professor Armen Ayvazyan helped with the Armenian chapter. I also owe a big thanks to many other friends who know this without saying. My wife also helped me in the finding of some of the sources and also by graciously taking care of the daily chores at home so that I could concentrate on writing. The interest my children have shown towards the books and drawings of their father has also been an inspiration. In particular, the great interest of my firstborn three-year-old boy towards all things Roman is great to see.

In addition, the re-enactors of the Late Roman era have made a very significant contribution to this book in the form of photos of their equipment. I recommend that all readers pay particular attention to this section of the book for the photos give a much better understanding of the types of equipment that the Late-Roman soldiers used than I can possibly hope to do with words or illustrations. I owe particular thanks to the members of *Fectio* and its Chair Robert Vermaat, and to the members of *Comitatus* and its Chair John Conyard for their kind permission to use their photos in this book. In addition, the last but not least of the re-enactors is Jyrki Halme, a fellow Finn, whose contribution to this book is much appreciated. He not only contributed his photos, but also took additional photos with the equipment and poses I suggested. It would have been possible to fill up the photo section of this book with his photographs alone! My warmest thanks to all of the re-enactors! Without their efforts the book would be a lot less colourful.

I owe a particular thanks to Philip Sidnell for his patience when I missed my deadline for three whole months! Thanks!

Introduction

The intention of this book, the first in a series of five, is to present an overview of all the principal facets of Roman military history during the years 284–361. I have included short discussions of all those aspects of the military, economy and culture that I have considered important for the understanding of the military successes and failures. The structure of the book follows the reigns of the emperors in chronological order, and the events and wars are also usually presented in chronological order. However, for the sake of ease of reading some events that took place in one particular sector of the empire are grouped together.

In the following text I will include direct references to the sources only in such cases that need to be argued further, for example because my conclusion can be considered controversial. I have not included footnotes or referrals to sources in such cases where the material is quite straightforward and there exist no significant controversies. I have also not included here a long discussion of the sources used and their problems, because there exists specialist literature devoted to this subject. The uneven survival of information, as well as the different lengths of the reigns, have also meant that some chapters are longer than others. However, there is a need to stress one aspect of the sources that in my opinion has received too little attention in the past, which is that the period authors were not only restricted by their literary models, by their religious beliefs, and by their personal aims (for example to please a patron), but even more so by the fact that they wrote under dictators who had the power over life and death. This is particularly important to keep in mind when reading Ammianus' history, which is by far the most important source for this period.

Ammianus' account has been coloured mainly by three things: 1) his pagan beliefs; 2) his need to please his patron Ursicinus, which has affected his account of the reign of Constantius II; and 3) his need to avoid disclosing such things that could have put him in mortal danger, learnt in the capacity of being a *protector*. In other words, one has to attempt to 'read between the lines' and not to take at face value his more direct statements. Ammianus sometimes includes contradictory information, and he is far too intelligent to have done that inadvertently. He was a career staff officer put in charge of special operations which included spying missions and assassinations. It is clear that he would not have been put in charge of such operations if he was not considered to be a clever fellow. In other words, when Ammianus presents a dark image of Constantius because he had treated Ursicinus unjustly (at least that seems to have been Ursicinus' own view), he still includes contradictory material elsewhere. The Arian Constantius II was also not well regarded in the Catholic courts of Theodosius I and Valentinian II because Constantius II had confiscated the property of Valentinian I's father Gratianus in 351. Valentinian II was the son of Valentinian I and Theodosius was married with the sister of Valentinian II. It is no wonder that Constantius gets bad press from Ammianus. When Ammianus appears to give a positive image of Julian, he also presents evidence to the contrary so that Julian appears as a great failure towards the end of his Persian campaign. In order to please the current emperor Theodosius, Ammianus was also prepared to suppress the successes of Gratian even though he still acknowledges his merits in some places and so forth.

The quality of evidence for the different reigns is very uneven. The most detailed evidence comes from the pen of Ammianus, but unfortunately for the rest of the fourth century we are often forced to rely on very poor and biased sources which consist mostly of epitomes, panegyrics, letters, chronicles, orations etc. This uneven survival of evidence means that there are huge gaps in our knowledge and some of the conclusions are based only on educated guesses.

As regards secondary literature, I have included short referrals to the ones used in this book. When I have included a footnote that refers to the use of some particular secondary source in general terms (for example, 'this chapter is based on', 'the dates are taken from', etc.), it means that my text is in general agreement with the source(s) in question and it would be a nuisance to refer to the same source every time there is, for example, the dating of an event in the text. I have basically grouped these together as one footnote.

I know that I must have also been influenced by other sources for I have read hundreds if not thousands of articles and books dealing with Roman history over the years and did not have time to reread even all of those that I would have liked for this book. Therefore, it is certain that my thinking has been influenced by other historians (and also by university lecturers) and that this indebtedness is therefore not visible in the book, which is a great pity and I apologize for the oversight. I would have loved to include every possible secondary source that I have ever read on the subject. The principal reason for the fact that I was unable to do that is that this book was written during a very short period of time. The lack of time resulted from the many problems that I and my family faced at the time and also from the fact that I had to write the book while doing other work. I and my family have been suffering from 'flu for most of the period, thanks to the diseases brought back home by my firstborn, which has not made it easy to devote time to writing. In addition to this, the very serious health problems of my parents with the resulting angst and things that one has to do in such circumstances have limited my time even further. However, I still hope that the following account proves interesting to read. I also believe that I may in places have struck new ground and have brought to attention overlooked material to back up my argument.

The book includes lengthy analyses of the Roman administration and military matters including the policing of the interior. The reason for this is that it is impractical to point out in every chapter the things that were constantly taking place in the background, namely policing, anti-piracy operations, intelligence gathering, etc. It is easier to group all of these together into one chapter. The same is also true of the enemies and allies of Rome. We know from other sources how their military systems operated and what types of forces, tactics, equipment and ships they used, even if the period sources do not necessarily specify these in the context of their conflicts with Rome. The resulting analysis of the enemies will hopefully give the reader a better understanding of the circumstances in which the Romans had to operate. It would have been impractical to attach these details into each and every chapter, hence their treatment as a separate chapter. In order to shorten the text I have also purposefully left more detailed analyses of some topics to later volumes. These include the analysis of the Roman square formation (2nd volume) as well as analysis of the defences of the Cyrenaican frontier (3rd volume).

As far as the language, transliteration, and titles are concerned I have usually adopted the easiest solutions. I have used the transliterations most commonly used except in the case of Greek military terms which I have generally transliterated, which means that I have maintained the original 'F' of the Greek instead of using the more common 'PH'. I have further adopted the practice of the Oxford University Press and used capital letters for all offices which could be held by only one person at a time. I have also used capital letters for all specific types of troops and military units. However, when I have referred to several office holders simultaneously (e.g. *comites*/counts, *duces*/dukes) I have used small letters.

I have also purposefully adopted the practice of using 'colourful' language of the persons and tribes and their traits, actions and habits. I do not believe that it would serve any good purpose to whitewash history with politically correct language. In other words, I have tried to describe the persons and events with warts and all, and I apologize if this approach causes offense among the more sensitive readers. All illustrations, drawings, maps and diagrams have been drawn and prepared by the author unless stated otherwise. I have used the Barrington Atlas as the principal source for the Maps.

Abbreviations

Com. Dom.	Comes Domesticorum (Count of the Domestics)
CRP	Comes Rei Privatae (Count of the Privy Purse)
CSL	Comes Sacrarum Largitionum (Count of the Sacred Largess)
GC	Georgian Chronicles
Julian1	See Bibliography
Julian2	See Bibliography
LI	Light Infantry
Mag. Eq.	Magister Equitum (Master of Horse)
Mag. Ped.	Magister Peditum (Master of Foot)
Mag. Eq. et Ped.	Magister Equitum et Peditum (Master of Horse and Foot)
MVM	Magister Utriusque Militiae (Master of All Arms of Service)
Mag. Mil.	Magister Militum (Master of Soldiers)
Mag.Off.	Magister Officiorum (Master of Offices)
Or.	Orations
PIPLA	See Bibliography
PLRE1	See Bibliography
PLRE2	See Bibliography
PP	Praefectus Praetorio (Praetorian Prefect)
PSC	Praepositus Sacri Cubiculi (Provost of the Sacred Bedroom)
PVC	Praefectus Urbis Constantiopolitanae (Urban Prefect of Constantinople)
QSP	Quaestor Sacri Palatii (Quaestor of the Sacred Palace)
REF1	See Bibliography
REF2	See Bibliography
SHA	Scriptores Historiae Augustae

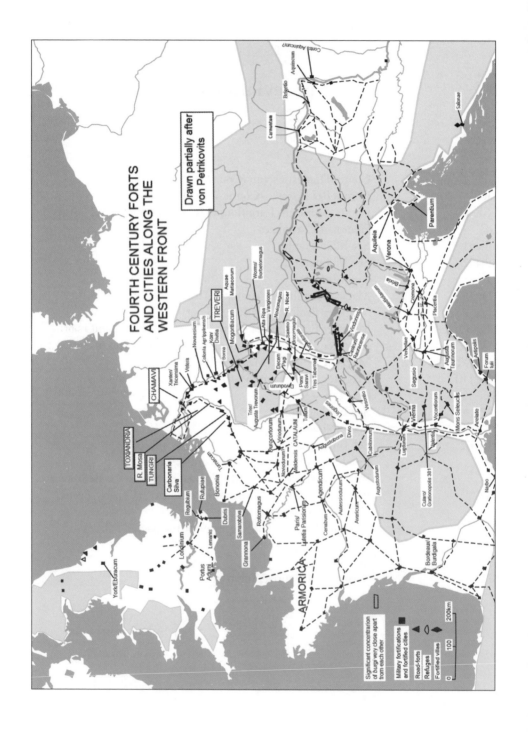

FOURTH CENTURY FORTS AND CITIES ALONG THE WESTERN FRONT

Drawn partially after von Petrikovits

York/Eburacum

Londinium
Portus Adurni
Lemaris
Dubris
Rutupiae
Regulbium

CHAMAVI
TOXIANDRIA
R. Mosa
TUNGRI
Carbonaria Silva

Xanten/Tricensima
Vetera
Colonia Agrippinensis
Novaesium
Koln/Divitia
Bonna
Borea
Mogontiacum
Alta Ripa
Worms/Borbetomagus
Vangiones
Novomagus
R. Nicer
Saleto
Breuccomagus
Drusus/
Rauracense
Altripa

TREVERI
Aquae Mattiacorum

Trier/Augusta Trevorum
Divodurum
Decem Pagi
Pons Saravi
Tres Tabernae

Gesoriacum
Bononia
Samarobriva
Grannona
Rotomagus
Turnacum
Tricensima
Burgcordunum
Virodunum
Noviodunum
Tullum
Nemetis
CATALAUNI
Augusta Trevorum

Paris/Lutetia Parisiorum
Cenabum
Autessiodurum
Agendicum
Americum
Augustobona
Divio
Lingones

ARMORICA

Bordeaux/Burdigala
Augustodunum
Cularo/Gratianopolis 381
Cabiloniium
Lugdunum
Vienna
Valentia
Vocontiorum
Mons Seleucis
Arelate
Narbo

Vesontio
Segusio
Vienna
Augusta Taurinorum
Forum Iuli
Antipolis

Verbeae
Augusta Taurinorum

Cremona
Mediolanum
Placentia
Brixia

Aquileia
Verona
Parentium

Carnuntum
Brigetio
Aquincum
Comb Aquincum?

Salonae

Legend

Significant concentration of *burgi*/very close apart from each other

■ Military fortifications and fortified cities

▲ Road-forts

◆ Refuges

■ Fortified villas

0   100   200km

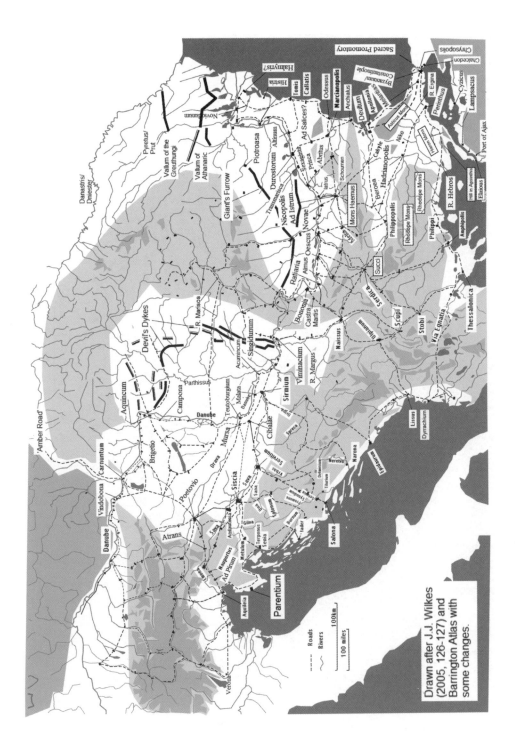

Drawn after J.J. Wilkes
(2005, 126-127) and
Barrington Atlas with
some changes.

Roads
Rivers

100 miles
100km

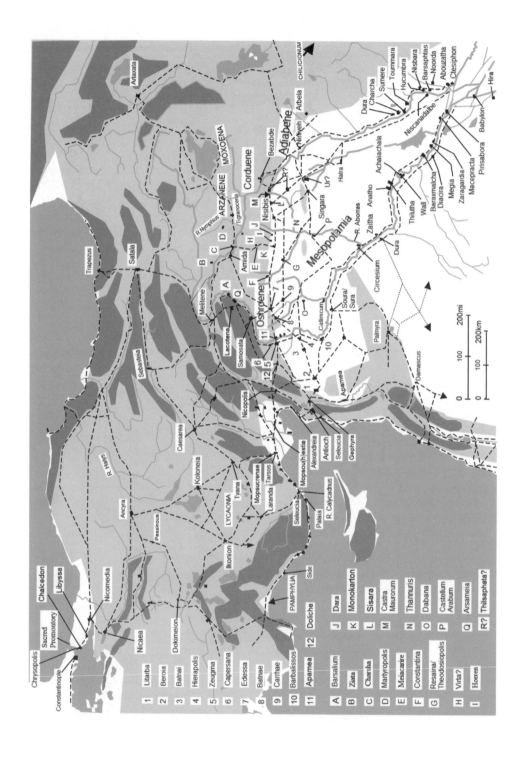

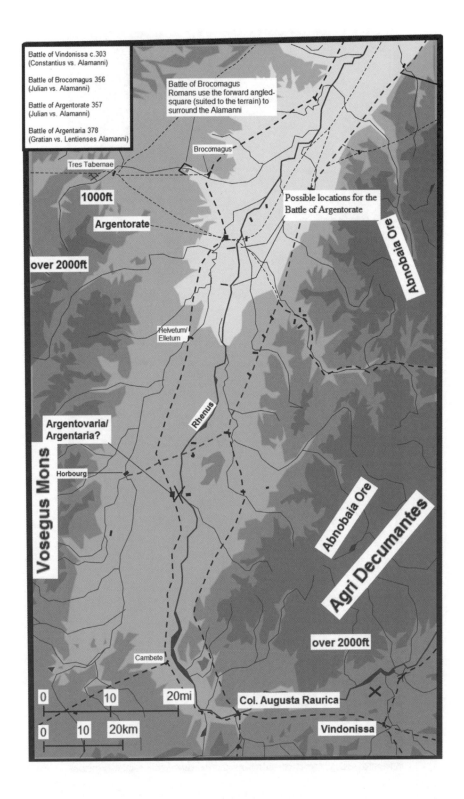

Battle of Vindonissa c.303
(Constantius vs. Alamanni)

Battle of Brocomagus 356
(Julian vs. Alamanni)

Battle of Argentorate 357
(Julian vs. Alamanni)

Battle of Argentaria 378
(Gratian vs. Lentienses Alamanni)

Battle of Brocomagus
Romans use the forward angled-
square (suited to the terrain) to
surround the Alamanni

Brocomagus

Tres Tabernae

1000ft

Argentorate

Possible locations for the
Battle of Argentorate

over 2000ft

Abnobaia Ore

Helvetum/
Elletum

Rhenus

Argentovaria/
Argentaria?

Horbourg

Vosegus Mons

Abnobaia Ore

Agri Decumantes

over 2000ft

Cambete

0   10   20mi

0   10   20km

Col. Augusta Raurica

Vindonissa

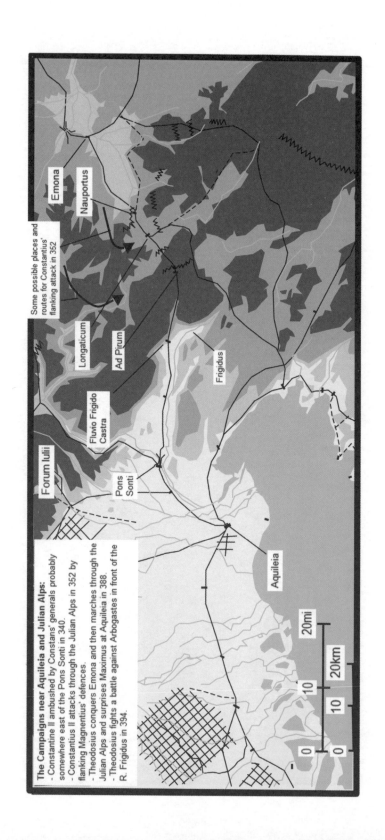

The Campaigns near Aquileia and Julian Alps:
- Constantine II ambushed by Constans' generals probably somewhere east of the Pons Sonti in 340.
- Constantius II attacks through the Julian Alps in 352 by flanking Magnentius' defences.
- Theodosius conquers Emona and then marches through the Julian Alps and surprises Maximus at Aquileia in 388.
- Theodosius fights a battle against Arbogastes in front of the R. Frigidus in 394.

Some possible places and routes for Constantius' flanking attack in 352

Emona

Nauportus

Longaticum

Ad Pirum

Forum Iulii

Fluvio Frigido Castra

Frigidus

Pons Sonti

Aquileia

0   10   20mi

0   10   20km

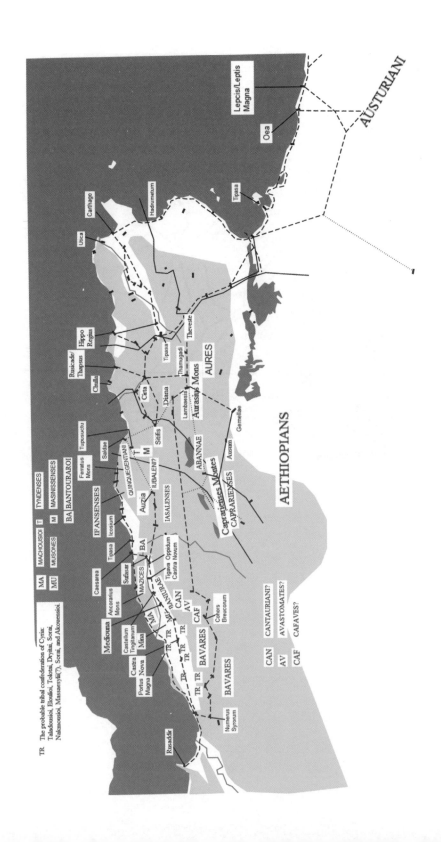

TR The probable tribal confederation of Cyria:
Taladousioi, Eloubai; Tolotai, Dryitai, Sorai,
Nakmousioi, Massaesyloi(?), Sorai, and Akoueisioi

| MA | MACHOUSIOI | T | TYNDENSES |
| MU | MUSONES | M | MASINISSENSES |

BA BANTOURAROI

IF ANSENSES

BAVARES

CAN CANTAURIANI?
AV AVASTOMATES?
CAF CAFAVES?

Medfouna
Ancorarius Mons
Caesarea
Tipasa Icosium
Castra Tingitanum
Portus Mina
Magna

Numerus
Syrorum

Rusaddir

Castellum

MA
MU BAVARUM
CAN
CAF

MAZICES
Tigava Oppidum
Castra Nouum
Cohors
Breucorum

Sufasar

Sidfis
Auzia
QUINQUEGENTIANI
IUBALENI?
IASALENSES
ABANNAE
Ausam
CAPRARIENSES
Capraroienses Montes

Tupusuctu
Saldae
Ferratus
Mons

Rusicade/
Thapsus
Chullu

Cirta
Diana
Lambaesis
Aurasius Mons
AURES
Gemellae

Tipasa
Thamugadi

Theveste

Hippo
Regius

Utica

Carthago

Hadrumetum

Tipasa

Oea

Lepcis/Leptis
Magna

AUSTURIANI

AETHIOPIANS

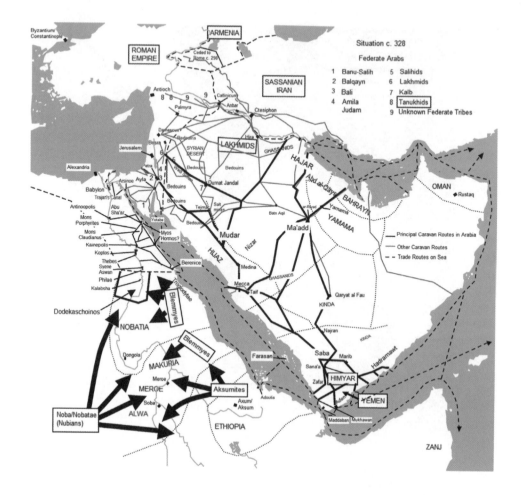

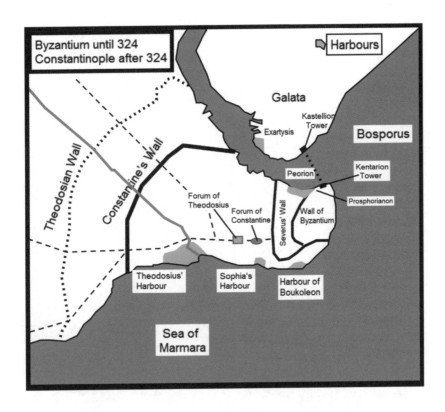

Byzantium until 324
Constantinople after 324

Harbours

Galata

Kastellion
Tower

Exartysis

Bosporus

Theodosian Wall

Constantine's Wall

Forum of
Theodosius

Forum of
Constantine

Peorion

Severus' Wall

Wall of
Byzantium

Kentarion
Tower

Prosphorianon

Theodosius'
Harbour

Sophia's
Harbour

Harbour of
Boukoleon

Sea of
Marmara

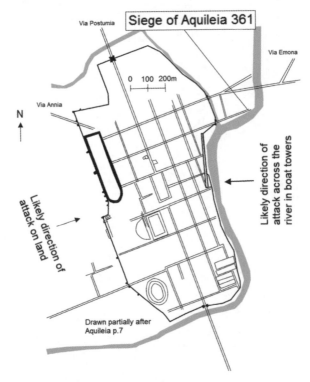

Siege of Aquileia 361

Via Postumia

Via Emona

Via Annia

0   100   200m

N

Likely direction of
attack across the
river in boat towers

Likely direction of
attack on land

Drawn partially after
Aquileia p.7

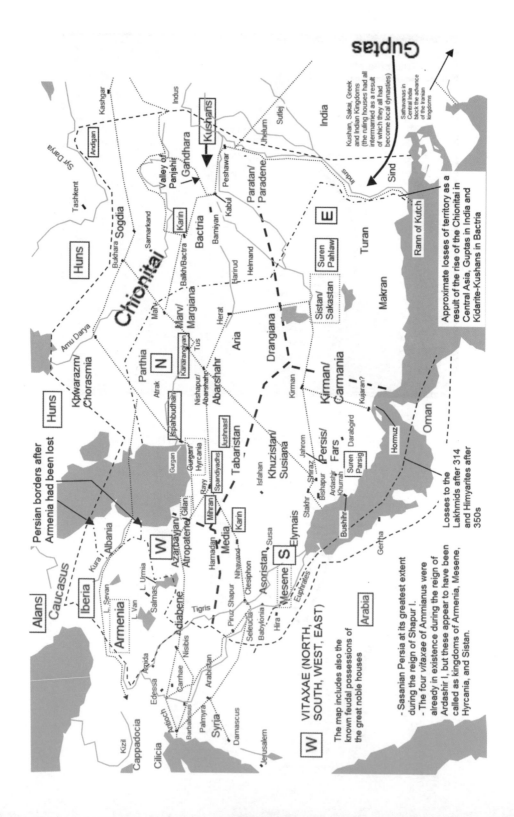

Guptas

Kushan, Sakai, Greek and Indian Kingdoms (the ruling houses had all intermarried as a result of which they all had become local dynasties)

India

Sathavanas in Central India block the advance of the Iranian kingdoms

Sind

Approximate losses of territory as a result of the rise of the Chionitai in Central Asia, Guptas in India and Kidarite-Kushans in Bactria

Kushans

Gandhara

Valley of Panjshir

Peshawar

Paratan/ Paradene

Kabul

Bamiyan

Bactria

Balkh/Bactra

Karin

Helmand

Harirud

Suren Pahlaw

Sistan/ Sakastan

Turan

E

Makran

Rann of Kutch

Oman

Kashgar

Andigan

Syr Darya

Tashkent

Sogdia

Huns

Bukhara

Samarkand

Chionitai

Amu Darya

Marv/ Margiana

Marv

Aria

Herat

Tus

Kanarangyan

Nishapur/ Abershahr

Abarshahr

Drangiana

Kirman/ Carmania

Kirman

Kujaran?

Khwarazm/ Chorasmia

Huns

Parthia

Atrak

N

Spahbudhan

Gurgan/ Hyrcania

Gurgan

Tabaristan

Ravy

Spandyadhs

Mihran

Jushnasf

Azarbayjan/ 'Atropatene'/ Gilan

W

Khuzistan/ Susiana

Isfahan

Persis/ Fars

Jahrom

Shiraz

Darabgird

Suren Parsig

Hormuz

Media

Karin

Hamadan

Nihavand

Susa

Elymais

Stakhr

Bishapur

Ardashir Khurrah

Bushihr

Gerrha

Persian borders after Armenia had been lost

Alans

Caucasus

Iberia

Kura

Albania

L. Sevan

Armenia

L. Van

L. Urmia

Salmas

Adiabene

Piruz Shapur

Ctesiphon

Seleucia

Babylonia

Asoristan

Mesene

S

Euphrates

Tigris

Nisibis

Edessa

Carrhae

Amida

Arbela

Arbayistan

Hira

Hatra

Barbalissos

Palmyra

Syria

Damascus

Kizil

Cappadocia

Cilicia

Jerusalem

Arabia

Losses to the Lakhmids after 314 and Himyarites after 350s

W VITAXAE (NORTH, SOUTH, WEST, EAST)

The map includes also the known feudal possessions of the great noble houses

- Sasanian Persia at its greatest extent during the reign of Shapur I.
- The four vitaxae of Ammianus were already in existence during the reign of Ardashir I, but these appear to have been called as kingdoms of Armenia, Mesene, Hyrcania, and Sistan.

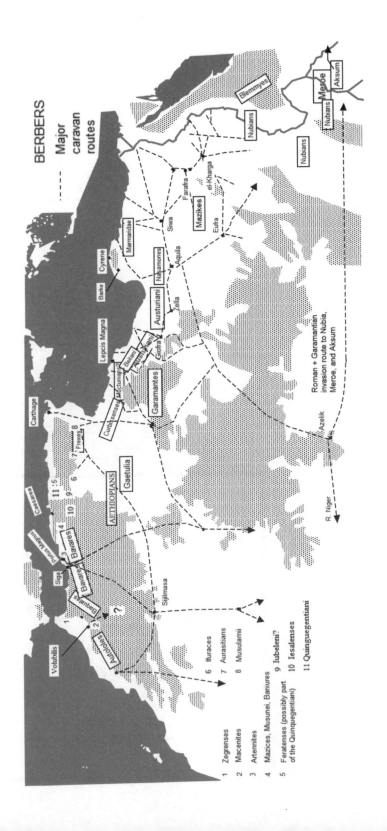

BERBERS

Major caravan routes

- - - - Major caravan routes

Volubilis

Caesarea

Siga

Portus Magnus

Sitifis

Carthage

Lepcis Magna

Barke

Cyrene

Sijilmasa

Sala?

Autololes

Bavares

Bavares

Bavares

AETHIOPIANS

Gaetulia

Curbissenses

Pictunani

Baiani

Austuriani

Giofra

Garamantes

Austuriani

Zella

Marmaridae

Nasamones

Siwa

Aquila

Farafra

el-Kharga

Mazikes

Eufra

Blemmyes

Nubians

Nubians

Nubians

Meroe

Aksum

Azelik

R. Niger

Roman + Garamantian invasion route to Nubia, Meroe, and Aksum

11 : 5

10   9

6

7 Frexes

8

4

3

2

1

1   Zegrenses
2   Macenites
3   Artemites
4   Mazices, Musunei, Baniures
5   Feratenses (possibly part
     of the Quinquegentiani)
6   Ituraces
7   Aurasitians
8   Musulamii
9   Iubeleni?
10 Iesalenses
11 Quinquegentiani

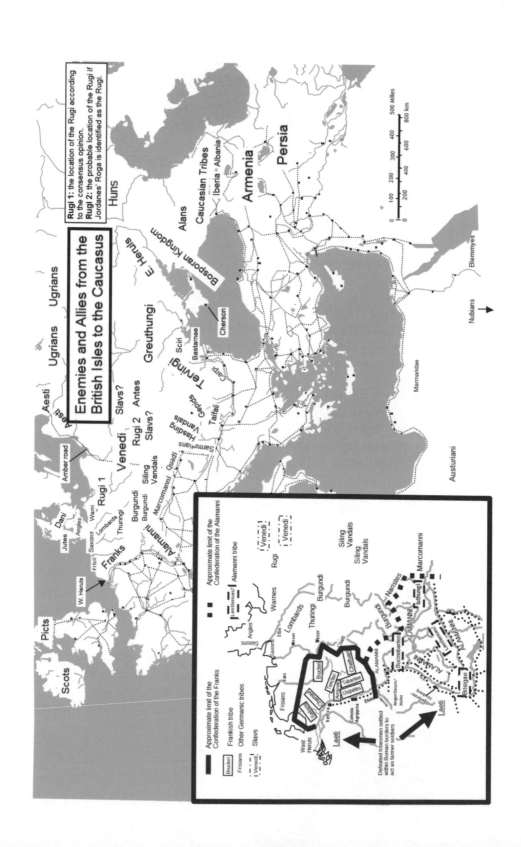

Enemies and Allies from the
British Isles to the Caucasus

Rugi 1: the location of the Rugi according to the consensus opinion.
Rugi 2: the probable location of the Rugi if Jordanes' Roga is identified as the Rugi.

Chapter One

The Early Third Century Roman Empire

Structures

The Emperor

The Principate created by Augustus was essentially a monarchy that retained republican forms and offices and pretended to be a republic, but in practice the *Princeps*/emperor retained all the powers. The judicial basis of a *Princeps'* rule consisted of: 1) the *imperium* of proconsular powers or *imperium maius*; 2) the powers of people's tribune; and 3) the office of *Pontifex Maximus*. The proconsular powers (executive powers) gave the emperor the command of military forces and the administration of most of the provinces. The tribunician powers (legislative powers) gave the emperor immunity from prosecution, rights of veto over any public decision, the right to propose legislation, and the right to hear legal cases. The office of *Pontifex Maximus* made the emperors the official head of state religion and made them the guardians of the Roman calendar and timekeeping. In addition to the formal powers, the emperors possessed informal power over the senators and people, which was publicly recognized under the name *auctoritas* (influence). The *auctoritas* was symbolized with the official surname *Augustus*, which also entailed superhuman powers so that the emperor could in theory perform miracles and would on his death become a god.

When combined these gave the emperor all the executive, legislative and judiciary powers. He controlled Rome's foreign policy and military forces, appointed all civil and military functionaries, proposed and legislated imperial legislation, and acted as the Supreme Court. It did not take long for the republican façade to crumble. The reigns of Tiberius and Caligula had already demonstrated the fact that the *Augusti* were tyrants whose power rested solely on their monopoly of violence, and these emperors did not hesitate to use naked force against their enemies or imagined enemies.

There were several inherent weaknesses in this system. The most important of these was that the Principate did not establish an orderly system of succession. A *Princeps'* power rested on his control of the army which meant that the army could choose its own ruler, and the lack of orderly succession meant that there would always be civil wars fought by different Roman armies. It did not take long for the Praetorians to realize that they could make emperors and after that for the provincial armies to realize that they could also make their own emperors. Since the power of the emperor depended upon his control of armed forces, it became dangerous for any emperor to give control of a large field army or garrison to any capable military commander, which in turn meant that it was practically impossible to defeat two major threats simultaneously. If the emperor was a capable military commander he could deal with one threat at a time, but if he then assigned a sizable army to a capable leader he always took a huge gamble. The emperors sought to minimize the threat of usurpation by limiting the number of legions commanded by each general and by creating the *Frumentarii* and *Peregrini* to keep an eye on the generals. However, the events of the third century prove that this system was neither efficient nor safe enough.

In addition, the effectiveness of the government and its economic, diplomatic and military policies all depended on the personal abilities of each emperor. A bad emperor like Decius or Valerian could overthrow the entire system while a good emperor like Aurelian or Probus could save the empire even from the brink of collapse.

Central Administration

The central administration was effectively created by Augustus as an extension of his own private household. As a result, the imperial palace located on the Palatine Hill became the focal point of the Empire. Its members obviously consisted of the emperor, the imperial family, the *consilium* (private council), and the household staff.

The private council of the emperor was originally created by Augustus as an informal body of advisors which grew to an official body of advisors. The advisors consisted of persons whom the emperor considered competent and loyal and who would give valuable advice. The advisors were known with the official titles *amici* (friends) or *comites* (companions) and had also certain ceremonial and official duties. The *comites* were an inner circle of trusted friends who also accompanied the emperor on his travels and military campaigns. At some point in time during the second century AD (probably during Hadrian's reign) the friends became an official body of permanent advisors who henceforth were also known as the *consiliarii* (counsellors/advisors). The emperor called his advisors together whenever he felt he needed advice on domestic or foreign policy, or in some problematic legal case. Unsurprisingly, the counsellors often included well-known jurists. In the latter part of the third century the newly created *Protectores* (bodyguards and staff-college) became to be considered as part of emperor's *comites*.

The emperor's household staff consisted originally solely of domestics, i.e. of imperial freedmen and slaves dressed in white clothes. It was an imperial chancellery consisting of bureaus/departments/ministries. From the reign of Hadrian onwards the head of each of the departments was an equestrian procurator. The staffs of freedmen and slaves were additionally grouped hierarchically into decuries. The heads of the bureaus of the central government were: 1. *a rationibus* (in charge of the imperial accounts, treasury and finances, which included the payments to the troops in money and in kind etc.), who was assisted by the *magister rei privatae* (in charge of the emperor's personal finances); 2. *a libellis* (in charge of the petitions to the emperor); 3. *ab epistulis* (imperial correspondence) divided into Greek and Latin sections; 4. *a cognitionibus* (hearing of judicial matters); 5. *a studiis* (preparation of files, reports and dossiers for the emperor); 6. *a censibus* (examination of the financial standing of persons seeking to become senators or equestrians); 7. *a commentariis* (archives); 8. *a memoria* (secretarial services).

This chancellery/household of the emperor was effectively in charge of directing all of the resources and forces of the Empire as the emperor saw fit. It should also be noted that the emperor's household included many other functionaries. The most important of these were the *cubicularii* of the imperial bedchamber. The physical closeness to the emperor gave a *cubicularius* (usually a eunuch) the chance of gaining considerable influence and thereby the position of favourite with many official positions.

The Administration

The administration of the Empire consisted of three layers: 1) Rome; 2) Italy; and 3) the Provinces. Rome was the capital of the Empire with about one million inhabitants fed by a huge logistical network controlled by the emperor and his central government. The city was divided into regions controlled by curators who in their turn were under the control of the urban prefect. The urban prefect was in control of the administration of the capital and had the duty of keeping public order. His duties were later enlarged to encompass central and south Italy, and then the whole of Italy. The city of Rome lost its privileged position in the course of the third century as a result of two things: 1) The granting of citizenship to all free persons by Caracalla in 212, together with his father's granting of equestrian status to soldiers which gave the soldiers unprecedented chance of social mobility; and 2) The constant wars waged by the emperors, who were not native Roman senators, meant that in practice the empire was ruled from the marching camp or from the base of operations.

Italy ranked second in the hierarchy. It was formally under the jurisdiction of the senate but in practice the emperor controlled everything through his own representatives, who included members of the emperor's Privy Purse. The principal advantage of Italy over the provinces was Roman citizenship and that Italians were not ruled by (often corrupt) governors. Nor did they have troops billeted, with the exception of the navy and *Legio II Parthica*, but this changed with the granting of citizenship to all free persons by Caracalla in 212.

The provinces were divided into imperial and senatorial provinces. The former were ruled by imperial legates (*legati Augusti pro praetore*), the length of whose term was dictated by the emperor, and the latter by proconsuls (*proconsulares*) who were chosen by lot from among the senators for a one year term. The imperial provinces were further divided into two categories: 1) senatorial legates; and 2) equestrian legates.

Municipal administration

Roman control of people, taxation and movement of goods, valuables and money was based on control of urban settlements and their surroundings. In the east the societies had already organized themselves around cities before the Roman conquests, but in the west the Romans actively founded new cities and settlements in an effort to organize the societies on the Roman model. It was the local Romanized elites who performed the actual administration and taxation of the cities and subjects. Theoretically the municipal administration of all of the cities consisted of three levels: 1) Popular assembly of citizens (no longer functioning in the third century); 2) Municipal council or Order of Decurions (also called a Senate), consisting of the former magistrates and/or wealthy citizens with the unenviable duty of paying the taxes in cases when the taxes fell short of the requirement; and 3) The magistrates with executive powers.

Roman Society, Its Classes and Taxation

Roman society was a class-based society that was divided into judicial and social hierarchies. The judicial hierarchy consisted of the division of the men into freemen and slaves. The slaves were the property of their master and therefore their living conditions were very variable. The possibility of being freed made the slaves work harder and made them less likely to revolt. The freemen consisted of freeborn men and freedmen. The former consisted of the Roman citizens and of the tribesmen of varying rights, unless of course the individual (notable, auxiliary) had obtained Roman citizenship from the emperor. After the granting of citizenship to most of the freemen by Caracalla in 212 it was possible for foreigners to rise to very high positions and even become emperors (for example Maximinus Thrax) to the great ire of the old ruling classes. The freedmen consisted of those who had either managed to buy their freedom or had been granted freedom by their master. The freedmen had no political rights and were usually, but not always, tied to a patron-client relationship with their former master. The position of freedmen was not inherited. The children of the freedmen were freeborn men with full rights.

The three social categories were the senatorial order, the equestrian order, and the plebeians (plebs). The senatorial order was a hereditary order consisting of Roman citizens (senators, wives, and children) with a minimum property of 1,000,000 sesterces. As a sign of their social standing, the senators wore *toga laticlavius* (a broad-brimmed toga). The order was not a closed one, but acceptance into it depended on the goodwill of the emperor, which was one of the means the emperors used for canvassing support. By the third century the bulk of the senators were provincials. However, the senators had an obligation to reside at Rome and to invest one third of their property in Italy. The most important military and civilian offices of the empire were the privilege of the senatorial class until around the 260s.

The equestrian order was a non-hereditary order whose members consisted of Roman citizens who had at least 400,000 sesterces, and had successfully applied to be enrolled into its ranks in order to serve in the imperial administration in the posts reserved for equestrians. Its members consisted of those who had inherited money or who were self-made men. The most successful equestrians could hope to attain the senatorial rank. The equestrians wore the *toga angusticlavius* (a thin-brimmed toga) as a sign of their rank. The role of the equestrians in the imperial administration was constantly on the rise because the emperors recognized that the heterogeneous equestrians were generally more loyal and professional than the senators. In fact the position of Praetorian Prefect, which was the most important position right after the emperor, was the privilege of the equestrian class.

The rest of the free population consisted of the plebs, which included both rich and poor. The rich plebs consisted of the foreign notables and decurions who were allowed to wear the *toga praetexta* (a one-side brimmed toga), and of the rich businessmen and bankers and so on, who did not possess similar *dignitas* as the notables and decurions. The 'middle class' plebs consisted of the artisans, boutique keepers, merchants, bakers, artists, intellectuals/philosophers and so on. The poor plebs consisted of the peasants, carriers, labourers and so on and probably formed the majority of the Roman population.

From about the mid-second century onwards the old judicial and social standings and divisions started to disappear and a new form of class division emerged consisting of the *honestiores* and *humiliores*. The process was accelerated when Caracalla granted citizenship to all freeborn men, which meant that the rich wanted to find other forms of privilege to separate them from the poor, and they were in the position to obtain these. The *honestiores* consisted of the senators, equestrians (including soldiers), veterans, and decuriones, and were separated from the *humiliores* by legal privileges and exemptions from the harsher punishments. In other words, the *honestiores* had acquired both social and judicial advantages. It is symptomatic of the greater trends occurring during this period that this new social order improved the standing of the soldiers vis-à-vis the rest of the society.

Alongside the creation of the *honestiores* came the creation of honorary ranks with judicial privileges. Marcus Aurelius was apparently the first emperor to do this. By about the mid-third century the praetorian prefects had the rank of *viri eminentissimi*, the senators *clarissimus* and the officials of the court the rank of *perfectissimi*.

In the course of the third century the advantages of belonging to the civilian *honestiores* of the decurion class came to be less attractive as a result of the military and economic crisis, which increased their tax burden. The constant wars and upheavals both in the Roman Empire and elsewhere led to the diminishment of trade and caused troubles both for the merchants and artisans. The economic downward spiral caused the decurions to attempt to avoid being put in charge of local administration, for example by placing all of their property in the name of their wife (who was not liable to serve as magistrate).

The position of the *humiliores* was not admirable either as they too had to shoulder an ever-increasing tax burden wherever the troops were billeted or marching or campaigning, and the poorly disciplined troops were not above pillaging their own countrymen. Unsurprisingly, more and more of the peasants chose to flee to the wilderness and become bandits, or to seek the protection of powerful landlords. This in turn caused the tax burden of the rest to rise, leading to a vicious cycle. This in turn caused the military to impose stricter control over the populace and also to increase the payments in kind (*annonae*) for the troops. The soldiers also no longer felt any loyalty towards the native Roman elite but increasingly saw their own commanders as protectors of their interests. The end result was that the Romans could no longer use the varying legal privileges to create loyalty and that the civilians increasingly saw their own army as the enemy. In this situation the Roman Empire urgently needed emperors who would put a stop to the foreign invasions and civil wars, and who would restore public order and thereby respect for the Roman institutions. However, as the events after 284 prove, the Roman Empire remained an economically viable and powerful empire despite all the problems of the third century. In fact, it was economically the most powerful empire on earth thanks to the collapse of the Later Han Empire.

The Roman Empire was an agricultural empire which had significant artisan and merchant classes. Most of the taxes were collected from the peasants through the city councils. It is therefore not surprising that the Romans were quite willing to settle foreign tribes within their borders to till the land and to provide soldiers. Since the income produced through this system was limited and often in arrears the emperors also used other forms of taxation. Since the members of the senatorial class (paid e.g. horses, conscripts, donatives) and the imperial machinery had certain tax privileges, and the richest members of the city councils could force the other members of the city councils to bear to the brunt of the taxes, the bulk of the taxes were paid by the middle class and the peasants. In order to make up the difference the emperors tapped the other resources available to them, which consisted of the produce of the imperial estates, donatives, extraordinary taxes levied when needed, confiscation of the property of the rich, and tolls and customs. In fact, the only way for the emperors to increase their income by legal means other than through tighter taxation was to expand the opportunities for tolls and customs, and this they did. The rich Romans and the wealthy foreigners (in the 'barbarian' lands, and in Persia, India, China etc.) wanted to show off their wealth which created a demand for luxury goods – naturally, the emperors still always wanted to remain the wealthiest person around to separate them from the rest. This created internal trade as goods were transported to the rich, and this was taxed, and it also created demand for foreign goods, that was also taxed. Similarly, Roman exports to foreigners created taxing opportunities. As will be made clear in the following discussion, the emperors actively sought to expand and protect the Roman trade networks so that they could exact tolls and customs from the luxury goods and thereby tax the rich indirectly. This caused less dissatisfaction among the rich than the confiscation of property through fake trials. This also meant that the emperors sought to control the trade networks and movement of peoples so that these could be taxed.

The Armed Forces[1]

The imperial Roman armies of the Principate consisted of the permanent legions, permanent auxiliary troops; veterans called for service when needed; true volunteers or 'volunteers' press-ganged into service; Praetorians and other units posted in the capital; allies/mercenaries; naval forces; and some kind of local militias consisting of tribesmen and urban dwellers. The provinces were divided into those under the emperor's rule and those still under the Senate's rule. The army consisted mostly of volunteers from the less developed provinces and to lesser extent of the conscripts until the third century crisis changed the situation. Thereafter the emperors and officers were forced to force the sons of the soldiers into service and to start using conscription.

The size of the armed forces was slightly more than 350,000 men so that about half of them were legionaries while the other half consisted of the auxiliaries. From the second century onwards the bulk of these forces were stationed along the Danube and eastern frontier. This reflected the Roman analysis of the potential threat posed by the enemies on those frontiers. This analysis must have been made at the highest level of government, because the transfer of troops could only have been done with the approval of the emperor. At the time, the Romans evidently did not face serious threats in Britain or along the Rhine frontier, but the third century wars showed that the coastal areas in the west as well as the defences along the Rhine frontier needed strengthening. This was caused by the emergence of new tribal confederacies, such as the Franks and Alamanni, and also because the Saxons started to raid the coastal areas of Britain and Gaul.

Strategy

Edward N. Luttwak has quite aptly described the Early Roman Empire as a hegemonic empire, which controlled its core territories directly (occupied with garrisons or ruled directly by Roman administrators) and its outlaying territories indirectly.[2] The indirect control of client states and tribes was based on the concentration of armed forces near them in readiness to advance into their territory, if necessary. The legions were grouped together in two-to-four legion camps for this purpose. However, excluding extraordinary or temporary commands, from the reigns of Septimius Severus and Caracalla onwards the legionary commands were split into single or two legion commands for reasons of internal security.

From the reign of Tiberius onwards the strategy was modified.[3] He preferred to keep peace by using barbarians against barbarians, and not initiate new conquests. The goal was to keep the neighbours always weak and divided between those who supported the Romans and those who opposed them. The Roman army was only used to chastise the barbarians when other means of policy had been exhausted. This change of policy also meant the creation of permanent stone-built bases for the legions near the borders, where they acted as deterrents and rapid reaction forces over the border. However, this was not yet the end of the aggressive conquests. There were emperors like Domitian or Trajan or Septimius Severus or Caracalla or Constantine etc. who sought to enlarge the empire. They needed conquests to bolster their own standing. However, there were also those who preferred to stay within the established borders like Hadrian or Antoninus Pius (both of whom, however, did employ the military for operations of punishment), and those who employed both strategies like Claudius I or Aurelian. The choice of strategy depended upon the personality of the emperor and the situation.

The creation of permanent bases along the borders made the legions less mobile than they had been previously with the result that henceforth all expeditionary forces or large scale defensive forces had to be collected as detachments from the existing units, that were then grouped together, which in turn meant that any large scale operations in one sector of the frontier seriously weakened the defences somewhere else. In the absence of seasonal aggressive campaigning, as had been the practice before the reign of Tiberius, this often resulted in enemy invasions along the weakened frontiers. The Roman answer to this was to conduct a campaign of punishment at the earliest possible moment to instil healthy fear of Roman arms. In order for this strategy to work, it needed constant campaigning along the frontiers, which was not always possible with the small expensive professional army in situations in which there were several simultaneous threats. The emperors could not trust large armies to generals, and there were no longer the masses of trained conscripts of the Republican era available that could be employed for aggressive conquests with a small cost (i.e. with a minimal salary), the principal lure being the prospect of military booty. It would have been too risky for the emperor as a dictator to keep in being the Republican era system of universal conscription and training. Augustus recognized this and abolished it.[4]

The third century crisis brought a complete change to this strategy. The civil wars caused the withdrawal of troops from the frontiers to fight the civil wars with the result that significant sections of the frontiers were overrun and that each emerging enemy had to be defeated with the field army operating under the emperor or a general whose forces were therefore constantly moving from one place to another to face each new threat at a time. The goal of practically all emperors, however, was to re-establish the previous frontier system of fortifications and garrisons along the borders with client states/tribes outside.

The Legions

The legions had a paper strength that seems to have consisted of 5,120 heavy infantrymen plus recruits, servants, horsemen and specialists. We do not know with any certainty the exact paper strength of each of the components of the Imperial legion. The legionaries were required to serve about 23–26 years before discharge. According to John Lydus (*De Magistr.* 1.16), when Marius formed his legions the legions consisted of 6,000 infantry and 600 cavalry, and this seems to have served as the model according to which Augustus formed his imperial legions. As regards to the number of 6,000 infantry, it is probable that the figure also includes the recruits and possibly even light infantry. In most cases, the figure of 600 horsemen probably included the servants attached to the cavalry. My educated guess is that the regular fighting (paper) strength of the cavalry detachment was an *ala* of 512 horsemen plus the *supernumerarii* and servants.[5] However, it is possible that there were actually three different types of cavalry units attached to the legions in the third century. Ps-Hyginus (5. 30) doesn't include any *equites legionis* for the three legions, but mentions 1,600 *vexillarii legionum*. This figure is consistent with the 500-man *turmae* of mounted archers, 500-man *vexillationes*, and 600-man *alae* mentioned by John Lydus (*De Magistr.* 1.46). Hence the possibility that the legions could have included three

---

Probable command structure of the legion c. AD 90–260

– 1 Legate (S) until the reign of Gallienus who abolished the office; or Prefect (E) for the Egyptian and Parthian legions.
After Gallienus the commanders were prefects (E); commander of the legion.
– 1 Laticlavian tribune (S) changed by Gallienus into *tribunus maior* (E); in charge of one cohort and second-in-command of the legion.
– 1 *Praefectus Castrorum* (camp, medics, siege equipment etc.) (E).
– 1 *Praefectus Fabrorum* (workmen, construction etc.) (E).
– 5 tribunes (E) each in charge of one cohort of 480 men.
– 1 *tribunus sexmenstris* (in charge of cavalry?) (E).
– 5 centurions of the 1st Cohort (incl. the *primus pilus*, who could act as *praepositus* for the cohort).
– 54 centurions (called *centenarii* by the end of the 3rd century):
　– 5 unattached centurions that could be detailed for a variety of purposes; these could be used, for example, as acting *praepositi* (commanders for the cohorts of 480 men).
　– 9 single centurions, each in charge of two centuries (2 x 80).
　– 9 groups of 4 centurions, each in charge of one century (80 men).
　– 4 cavalry centurions, each commanding 128 horsemen.
– 64 infantry *decani*, one of whom was optio/second-in-command to centurion (each *decanus* part of and in charge of their 8-man file/*contubernium*), in addition to which was a *tiro*/recruit and one servant used for guarding the camp.
– 16 cavalry decurions (each in charge of a 32-man *turma*).
– 1st cohort of 800 men (5 centuries each of 160 men), plus 100 recruits and 100 servants.
– cohorts 2–10, each 9 x 420 footmen (including the *decani* 480), plus 60 recruits and 60 servants per cohort.

– 496 horsemen (including the decurions 512: Vegetius may have been wrong in adding the decurions to the strength of the *turma*, because the Roman cavalry organization was based on the Greek one; however, if Veg. is correct then these should be added to the total for a sum of 512 + 16 decurions) plus around 128 servants/squires.

– at least around 715 artillerymen in charge of the 55 *carroballistae* (cart-mounted bolt/ arrow shooters) and 10 *onagri* (single-armed stone-throwers).

– 10 *speculatores* (formerly scouts, but now couriers, police officers, and executioners).

– *proculcatores* and *exploratores* scouted the roads. It is not known whether these counted as part of the cavalry or were separate from it. In practice the *mensores* could also act as scouts.

– unknown numbers of military police with the title of *stator*, and unknown numbers of guard dogs. Inside each camp there was also a police station called a *statio* under a tribune. Some of the soldiers were also used as sentinels (*excubitores*) and there were also other specific guards for various things.

– in addition, an unknown number of other specialists and bureaucrats consisting of surveyors, *campidoctor* (Chief Instructor), *haruspex* (read the entrails prepared by *victimarius*), *pullarius, actuarii, librarii* (*librarius a rationibus* worked also for the state post and could act as a spy), *notarii* (could act as a spy on the activities of the commander), *commentariensis* (archivist under head curator), heralds, standard-bearers, *draconarii*, cape-bearers, trumpeters, drummers, engineers, workmen, artisans, hunters, carters and cartwrights, doctors, medics etc.

– the legates/prefects were also guarded by a unit of *singulares* (both infantry and cavalry), which consisted of detached auxiliaries. (Confusingly the staff officers in training could also be called *singulares*). These bodyguards were replaced by *protectores* detached by the emperor from his staff at the latest during the reign of Gallienus as a safety measure against usurpations.

– the legion also included beasts of burden (depending on the situation, these could be horses, asses, mules, camels, oxen).

(S) = senatorial office; (E) = equestrian office

different types of cavalry detachments. The only real anomaly is Vegetius who claims that each legion was accompanied by an even greater number of horsemen. He claims that the legions had 726 horsemen plus the supernumeraries.[6] This may represent the strength of the cavalry component after the reforms of Gallienus or more likely by one of his successors.

The traditional infantry component of the legion consisted of ten cohorts. It is usually assumed that after the first century AD the first cohort had 800 legionaries (plus 100 recruits and 100 servants), while the rest of the cohorts from two to ten had 480 (plus recruits and servants). Each of these regular cohorts was divided into six centuries (eighty men plus recruits and servants). In other words, there were fifty-nine centuries per legion. The double-strength five centuries of the first cohort fought as centuries when employing the *pila*-javelins, while the regular centuries were grouped together as maniples (160 men). The smallest unit was the tent-group called a *contubernium*, which fought as an eight-man-deep file in the rank-and-file battle formation. The head of the *contubernium* was a *decanus* (commander of ten) who commanded the seven fighters that formed the file. It included one green recruit *(tiro)* and one servant (with a mule or ass), both of whom were usually left in the marching camp for its protection when the legionaries advanced to fight. The legions also had an inbuilt artillery component that could be used as field artillery or for sieges. The legions further included medical, clerical and logistical services, and various kinds of engineers, architects and artisans to support the operations. See the diagram of the organization based on Bohec (2000).

Despite the fact that there was always upward mobility in the Roman society, it was still very hierarchical and the Roman army was a reflection of the society. The highest commanding positions in the different units were reserved for the men who belonged to the senatorial class (or who had been elevated to that class) and the positions below to the men belonging to the equestrian class. The commanders of the legions almost always belonged to the senatorial class, the sole exceptions being the Praetorian Guard, the 'Parthian legions', and the legions posted in Egypt, which were commanded by equestrians. The officers of the legion consisted, in descending order, of one imperial propraetor legate (senatorial rank, in command of the legion or legions, if governor), one laticlavian tribune (senatorial rank, second-in-command, a young nobleman learning soldiering), one camp prefect (third-in-command, an experienced veteran in charge of the camp), five angusticlavian prefects (equestrian rank, in charge of cohorts etc.), one (?) *sexmenstris* tribune (possibly in charge of the legionary cavalry). The non-commissioned officers of the first cohort consisted of the centurions, in order of seniority: *primus pilus, princeps prior, hastatus prior, princeps posterior,* and *hastatus posterior.* And the rest of the centurions in order of seniority consisted of: *pilus prior, princeps prior, hastatus prior, pilus posterior, princeps posterior,* and *hastatus posterior.* The soldiers were also ranked according to privileges and seniority.[7]

In practice, the actual fighting strength of the legions was usually well below the paper strength figures as a result of injuries, sickness, wounds, deaths and problems with recruiting. However, if there were enough time before campaign, then the units could actually be above their paper strength – but the legions rarely marched out in their entirety. Retired veterans, who had been recalled into service, were sometimes added to the legions as separate detachments or into the 1st cohort, but could also be grouped together separately in their own temporary units.

The Auxiliaries

The regular auxiliaries consisted of various types of ca. 500–1,000 strong units that complemented the legions. The auxiliaries were required to serve for 28 years before discharge. Their principal reason for the joining of the army was that they received Roman citizenship after their service, or already during service if they distinguished themselves. Caracalla's grant of citizenship to all freeborn made service in the auxiliary units including the navy less desirable. The *Auxilia* included: various types of elite cavalry *alae* (wings); medium infantry armed with shields, spears and/or javelins, and a *spatha* (a long double-edged sword); mixed units of cavalry and infantry; foot archers; and slingers. The allies (client kingdoms and tribes) contributed such units that they possessed. The Romans added irregular auxiliary units, called by the generic name *Numeri*, into their army when the regular auxiliaries had become less 'nimble' as a result of their regular attachment into the Roman army. The use of these various tribal *Numeri* gave the Roman armed forces additional flexibility, however, with the result that many of these initially mercenary units also became permanent units of the Roman army. The following list gives the approximate size and organization of the auxiliary units. In practice, the actual size and organization varied greatly. The use of extra-large milliary cohorts enabled the commanders to make their deployment pattern resemble that of the legions. The auxiliary units also included a variety of support personnel, consisting of clerical staff, logistical services, etc.

The smaller auxiliary *cohors quingenaria* units were commanded by prefects, while the larger *milliaria* units were commanded by tribunes. Both the prefects and tribunes belonged to the equestrian class. At least during the early imperial period, the tribune was assisted by a sub-prefect. The *turmae* of the cavalry were commanded by decurions, of whom the most senior was the *decurion princeps*, and groupings of three *turmae* by centurions. The infantry were commanded by centurions.

Approximate size and organization of auxiliary units:

Unit	Foot	Horse	Centuries	Turmae
Cohors Quingenaria Peditata	480		6	
Cohors Quingenaria Equitata	480	128	6	4
Cohors Milliaria Peditata	800		10	
Cohors Milliaria Equitata	800	256	10	8
Ala Quingenaria		512		16
Ala Milliaria		768 (campaign strength?)		24
		1024 (paper strength?)		32
Numeri	varied	varied	varied	varied

The Garrison of Rome[8]

Septimius Severus strengthened the Garrison of Rome considerably. The principal force guarding the capital and emperor were the Praetorian Cohorts (*Praetoriani*) housed in their own camp under the Praetorian Prefects (one to three, one of whom was always a legal expert). After the reign of Severus the Praetorians consisted of soldiers from all over the empire who had distinguished themselves in action. The Praetorians consisted of nine 1,000 men cohorts of infantry (9 tribunes, 54 centurions) for a total of 9,000 footmen, and probably nine *turmae* of cavalry (possibly 192 horsemen per '*turma*'?) for a total of 1728(?) men. The Praetorians were also used for special assignments and security operations, which meant that their members could serve anywhere in the empire as needed. The same barracks housed also 300 *speculatores* (cavalry), whose commander was the *Trecenarius* (centurion in charge of 300) and second-in-command the *Princeps Castrorum*, both of whom were under the Praetorian Prefect(s). These probably acted as the personal guard of the emperor (note the resemblance to the later 300 *Excubitores*) and performed special assignments at his orders. The *Numerus* of *Statores Augusti* was also housed in the same barracks and therefore under the jurisdiction of the Praetorian Prefect. The *Statores* acted as a military police. Their command structure is unknown. The ca. 2,048 *Equites Singulares Augusti* (with a tribune, the *Decurion Princeps* and 32 decurions) were the barbarian bodyguard of the emperor and also served under the Praetorian Prefect, but they were housed in the so-called New Camp.

In addition to this, there were also units that can be considered to have been devoted to internal and external security missions, which consisted of the *Peregrini* and *Frumentarii*, both of which were housed at the barracks on the Caelian Hill. The *Peregrini* were basically the secret police of the emperor, commanded by a *Princeps*, a *Subprinceps*, and centurions. They operated all around the empire as commanded by the emperor. Unfortunately, their overall numbers and organization are not known, perhaps because of the secretive nature of their missions. The *Frumentarii* acted as imperial couriers, in the capacity of which they performed secret missions which included spying and assassinations. Their late Roman successors were the equally notorious *Agentes in Rebus*. Their commander was the *Princeps* of the *Peregrini*.

The Urban Cohorts (*Urbaniaci*) under the Urban Prefect consisted of three 500-man cohorts (three tribunes, 18 centurions) of infantry for a total of 1,500 men. They guarded the city and acted as its principal police force. However, they too could be detached for other duties. The seven 1,000 men Cohorts of Vigiles (sub-prefect, seven tribunes, forty-nine centurions) were under the Prefect of Vigiles, and served as the night patrol, firemen and policemen. They too could be detached elsewhere and at least under Claudius one cohort was stationed at Puteoli and another at Ostia. In addition to this, there were other forces present at Rome. The emperor recruited staff officers from among the *primipilares*; there were permanent detachments from the Ravenna and Misenum Fleets on duty at Rome; and lastly there were always soldiers on leave.

Septimius Severus had also posted the *Legio II Parthica* at Alba, which lay within striking distance of the city of Rome. This enabled the emperor to use this legion as a counterbalance against any units at Rome which showed signs of disloyalty. This also created the complication that when the emperors still resided at Rome, they needed to buy the support of the garrisons at Rome and at Alba.

Intelligence Gathering[9]

The above-mentioned section has already touched upon the matter. The emperor's intelligence gathering network consisted of several overlapping organizations, the purpose of which was undoubtedly to prevent any one of those growing too influential. The principal security apparatus of the ruler consisted of his bodyguard units, most of which operated directly under the Praetorian Prefects. These conducted active intelligence gathering missions as undercover operatives, protected the emperor's person with their presence, and intimidated potential usurpers and assassins with their reputation. The emperor could also use the different units posted in or near the capital against the other units when their loyalty was shaky. The *Peregrini* and *Frumentarii* secured for the emperor an alternative avenue of information that was not under the control of the *PP*. The greatest threat to the emperors was a usurper and therefore the emperor paid particular attention to this aspect. The emperors used the various units involved in intelligence gathering in an effort to expose potential usurpers and they limited the number of soldiers each commander could command at a time. However, as usual with such operations, sometimes these security measures worked while at other times, they did not.

As *Pontifex Maximus* the emperor was kept abreast of the questions presented by the nobility to the soothsayers and astrologers, which enabled him to persecute all who had asked the wrong kinds of question, like how long the emperor would live. The rewards of betraying a 'plot' could also be so great that many persons were ready to become informers even if this entailed interrogation under torture to secure the 'truth'.

The army also conducted active intelligence gathering missions (including spying in disguise) among the enemy under the supervision of the frontier commanders. These missions were performed by select scouting units or by officers with experience of such missions. The above-mentioned *Peregrini, Frumentarii*, staff officers, and members of the bodyguard units and even friends and members of the emperor's household could also be assigned to perform special missions home and abroad, sometimes in the company of some chosen official (e.g. as ambassador or messenger). Other sources of information were prisoners, deserters, and travellers. The Roman practice of using military detachments all over the empire as sentinels (towers, road blocks) and road patrols enabled them to capture suspect persons for interrogation. The control of the state post enabled the emperor's spies to read all the mail that passed through their hands, which meant that anyone who used careless words (and did not use a secure code) was bound to end up on death row. The frontier guard towers were also placed at such intervals that it was possible to transmit information regarding enemy movements by using fire and smoke signals, and by using mirrors.

Equipment[10]

The offensive equipment of the line infantry, both legionaries and auxiliaries, consisted of the spear (*hasta*, called *kontarion* in the sixth-century Strategikon); heavy-javelin *spiculum* (formerly *pilum*), light/medium javelins *verutum* (formerly *vericulum*) and *lancea*; short javelin/dart called *plumbata, mattiobarbuli* or *martiobarbuli*; long-sword *spatha*; short-sword *semispatha* (formerly *gladius*); dagger; and single-edged knife. The offensive equipment of the late Roman soldiers varied according to the type of soldier and mission. The composite type (see later) was equipped simultaneously with melee weapons and bows. According to Bishop and Coulston, from the fourth century onwards the barbarians introduced to the Romans the Germanic weapons the *seax* and the throwing-axe *francisca*. The defensive equipment of the infantry consisted of the helmets, shields, greaves, armour, and padded 'under-armour'.

The c. 2.5–3.74 cm spear was used by the front rankers (in eight rank formation the ranks 1 to 4) as a thrusting weapon mainly against cavalry, but could also be thrown if needed.[11] The *spiculum* was used mainly as a heavy javelin against enemy infantry, but could also be used for thrusting and against cavalry when necessary. The standard size for the *spiculum* was 1.628 m for the shaft and 20 to 22.9 cm for the head, but the length and type of iron head seem to have varied greatly. Maximum effective range for this weapon was about 20m. The *lancea* and *verutum* were medium/short javelins with short shafts (shaft c. 1.03 m and head 22.2 cm) used by the rear rankers (in eight-rank formations, the fifth-eighth ranks) as long-range light javelins. The maximum effective range for this weapon was about 30–40m. The *plumbata* were darts (length about 11.8–15.8 cm) used by all those units that had them placed inside their shields (usually five). The maximum range for these was about 50–60m. There were several variants of this weapon available, some of which had caltrops attached so that even those that missed their targets would at least make movement difficult. The *spatha* was used mainly against the cavalry and the *semispatha* against infantry at close quarters, but both could also be used against either. The daggers and knives were only used as weapons in dire straits when no other weapon could be found.

The offensive equipment of the light infantry consisted of the bow (mainly composite bows, but some self bows may also have been used), *arcuballista* (composite crossbow), *manuballista* (torsion crossbow), light javelins (*lancea*, *verutum*), darts (*plumbatae*), slings, staff-slings, sword (*spatha/semispatha*), and dagger and knife. The bows, slings and staff-slings could be employed from behind the phalanx, inside it, or in front of it as required. The light infantry was very useful for the harassment of the enemy and for skirmishes and sieges. The lead slingshots and the crossbows were particularly effective against armoured opponents because the former caused concussion hits that disabled the armoured men, and the latter had the power to penetrate the armour. The defensive equipment of the light infantry varied greatly depending upon the type of unit, but in general it is fair to say that their equipment differed between those who had no defensive equipment at all to those who had some kind of protective equipment (mail, scale, leather, padded coat) for the torso and head (helmet or hat) and possibly also a small shield.

The standard helmet types of the late-third and fourth centuries were the so-called ridge/segmented-helmets that are variously named after the location in which archaeologists first found them. These include the so-called Intercisa, Berkasovo, Dar al-Madinah, Budapest, and Deurne types. **For examples, see the Photo/Plate Inset which includes photos of re-enactors. See also the accompanying line drawings.**

The standard shield types were round and oval shields of varying sizes and construction. The standard shield bosses were the domed or conical pointed bosses, both of which could be used for 'punching'. The shields were usually constructed of vertical

Roman elite horseman equipped with a ridge helmet and scale armour (source: Arch of Galerius)

Soldiers wearing coifs in the Vatican Manuscript (drawn after Bishop & Coulston)

Adamklisi Trajan's Dacian War

planks of alder (or spruce, aspen, lime, or oak) and covered with painted rawhide. The shields were decorated with unit emblems. The shields had three basic types of grips: 1) the old legionary system of a single handle behind the boss that continued to be used by infantry and which was good for the punching technique; 2) the old hoplite and cavalry style grips in which the shield was held by both hand/wrist and arm along the shield's back (arm with a leather strap and wrist with another or alternatively so that the hand grasped the grip); and 3) shields that had both styles of grip. The single grip shield was particularly useful for use with the *pilum* and *spatha/semispatha*, while the second type of shield was particularly useful for use with the spear and for mass shoving in close infantry formation. The use of the hoplite type of shield grip was not new to this period, because we can detect that type of grip in, for example, Trajan's Column, but its implications have not been taken adequately into account when discussing the fighting techniques employed by the Roman army. There were units that could fight like hoplites in the Roman army!

The standard types of body armour were mail and scale armours of varying sizes. Metallic coifs were also used (see above), but apparently in most cases only when the men didn't wear helmets. Segmented limb defences were also produced at least to serve the needs of the cavalry, but it is also possible that these were also used by infantry when needed as had happened for example during Trajan's Dacian war (see above). The Romans also appear to have always worn a padded garment or coat under their armour for additional protection against enemy missiles. It also protected its wearer's skin from scratches caused by armour. Leather armour continued to be used as ersatz armour or as an under garment. In my opinion, it is also noteworthy that the art works continue to depict men equipped with muscle armour, which can mean either of two things: 1) those were indeed used at least by some units; or 2) the art works reflect artistic taste

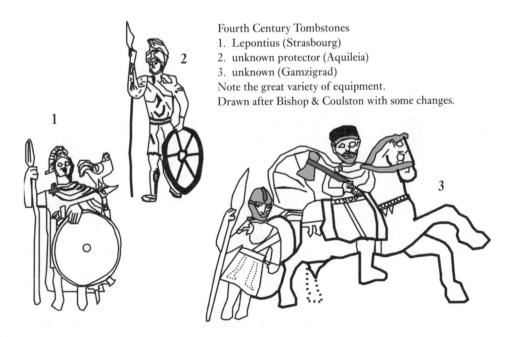

Fourth Century Tombstones
1. Lepontius (Strasbourg)
2. unknown protector (Aquileia)
3. unknown (Gamzigrad)
Note the great variety of equipment.
Drawn after Bishop & Coulston with some changes.

that has nothing to do with reality. However, since the emperors continue to be depicted with muscle armour and it is also depicted for example on Theodosius' column (see the second book in the series), it is possible that it was used at least for parade purposes or alternatively that the elite Imperial Bodyguards wore it. It is also possible that at least some of the officers wore the muscle armour to separate them from the rank-and-file.

The lightly-equipped legionaries (for deployment in forests and mountains) and auxiliaries can be considered to have formed medium infantry. They were equipped with helmets, spears, *spatha* and shields, but usually lacked armour even if they did sometimes use the ersatz armour consisting of padded coats or leather. The lack of armour undoubtedly made these men vulnerable to being hit by missiles or other weapons, but in combat situations the fighting spirit was more important than the amount of armour worn. It was quite possible for the medium infantry to defeat any type of unit in combat.

There were also units of special club-wielders or mace-wielders that were used against the cataphract cavalry.[12] These men were used either in front of the infantry phalanx to break up the enemy charge or behind the phalanx when it was opened up to admit the cataphracts through so that the clubmen could pummel them unconscious. This type of superbly brave warrior could be really lightly equipped as the Germanic clubmen in Trajan's Column prove. They needed the mobility to avoid being trampled by the horses. See the illustration of club-bearer and *lanciarius*, which could also be used in advance of the phalanx to harass the enemy and to break up enemy attack.

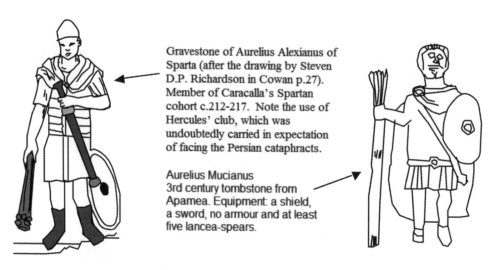

Gravestone of Aurelius Alexianus of Sparta (after the drawing by Steven D.P. Richardson in Cowan p.27). Member of Caracalla's Spartan cohort c.212-217. Note the use of Hercules' club, which was undoubtedly carried in expectation of facing the Persian cataphracts.

Aurelius Mucianus 3rd century tombstone from Apamea. Equipment: a shield, a sword, no armour and at least five lancea-spears.

The offensive equipment of the cavalry consisted of the *contus*-spear, *xyston*-spear, javelins (*lancea*), *spatha*, *semispatha*, axe with a spike, crossbow, composite bow, quivers for missiles, sling, dagger, knife, and possibly also darts (*plumbatae*).

The *contus* had several variants, the heaviest of which, the Sarmatian *contus*, was usable only with two hands for thrusting, presumably because it was a thick spear meant to penetrate the enemy armour. The Sarmatian *contus* was used by specialist *contarii* units for frontal charges. In contrast, the lighter Celtic *contus* (length c. 3.74m) called *kontarion* in the Strategikon could be wielded with one hand and also used as a throwing weapon.

The 'Celtic *contarii*' were the standard type of Roman heavy cavalry. The Roman *xyston* was evidently a heavy thrown spear used to penetrate enemy shields and armour at close quarters. Thanks to its size the *xyston* was also adaptable for thrusting. The short *lancea* was primarily used as a light javelin, but could still be employed as a thrusting weapon. The swords and axes were naturally used only at close quarters fighting. The other standard Roman cavalry type were the *logchoforoi* (*lancearii*) cavalry who skirmished by throwing their javelins and then at the right moment charged and used *lancea* as a thrusting weapon (mainly Moors) or employed their swords and axes at close quarters fighting. All Roman cavalry were trained to use crossbows, spears, javelins, slings and apparently after Hadrian's reign also to use the composite bow, but they were still typically employed only as specialist *contarii* or *lancearii*. Their defensive equipment consisted of the helmet, oval *thyreos/scutum*-shield, greaves, and mail corslet. The Roman cavalry horses wore chamfrons and *parapleuria*/sidecoverings (Arrian, Tact. 34.8) for combat. In addition, the Romans possessed auxiliary, *Foederati* (treaty-bound allies within and outside the borders) and *Laeti* (defeated tribes settled as farmer soldiers inside borders) units of cavalry that included all of the various types of specialist cavalry mentioned by Arrian (e.g. javelin throwers and mounted archers). The cataphracts and spear-bearers were obviously used as shock cavalry and the other types mainly as skirmishers.

The defensive equipment of cavalry consisted of various types of armour (mail or scale) for the men and horses depending upon the type of cavalry, and of the helmets (ridge and segmented types) and shields (oval or round). Regardless of the size and type, the cavalry shields always had a leather strap or straps attached to arm and wrist so that the rider's left hand was free.

The standard military clothing included military style belts and buckles, fittings, long-sleeved tunics, tents, tight and looser trousers, military cloaks (*sagum*-cloak, hooded cloaks *caracallus* and *birrus*, and other types), and studded shoes (a variety of open and closed types). **See Photos Section**. The shoes were a particularly important piece of item for the soldiers. The shoes had to be suited for long marching and also for the needs of hand-to-hand combat in all kinds of terrains and weathers. The military equipment included also all kinds of standard day-to-day items like axes, saws, flasks, cups, spoons, knives, sickles, scythes, brooches, horse harnesses, saddles, etc, but some of the items were obviously specific only to the military. These included military standards, musical instruments, military decorations, caltrops, and various types of staffs used by the centurions and other NCOs. The standard colours for the tunics were yellowish-white and white with purple bands on the hem and cuffs. Red tunics were also quite common, but other colours were used in lesser quantities. The cloaks were usually chocolate or reddish-brown and the trousers dark grey or brown, but as always other colours were also used. The textiles were usually made out of wool.

Roman Tactics and Generalship in General

The standard tactics called for the Romans to find out everything there was to know about the enemy and then plan their campaign accordingly. The availability of good and timely intelligence was of utmost importance and the good generals always also sought out knowledgeable guides and itineraries and maps of the locale in which they were to operate well in advance. The Roman generals expected their army to be better trained and equipped than the forces their enemies could muster and their expectations were usually fulfilled. The Roman army was typically well-drilled and therefore able to perform very complex battlefield manoeuvres. The central position of the Roman Empire and their readiness to borrow what was useful from their enemies had given them readiness to face all kinds of threats and combat techniques. The Empire was also wealthier thań any of its competitors which enabled it to maintain complex machinery to supply and equip their armies. In fact, one of the inherent strengths of the Roman Empire was its good logistical network which enabled its soldiers to starve out the enemies while they themselves lived in relative comfort. The Roman combat doctrine required them to attempt to engage their enemies only in favourable circumstances and in favourable terrain. They also chose their fighting methods to suit the fighting style of the enemy and the situation. Ambushes, stratagems, assassinations and all kinds of other underhand tactics were quite acceptable to the soldiers even if it was not for the civilians.

When conducted by the book, the Roman military operations were therefore usually meticulously planned and performed. The good Roman general always sought to obtain information from his spies, scouts and patrols before doing anything. He also took into account the logistical demands and the necessary safety measures during marching and fighting. If siege operations were foreseen, he also took into account its demands. In friendly areas, the army marched in a column formation, but in unfriendly hostile areas it marched either in a hollow square or in an open half-square or wedge formation which was protected by auxiliary units in front, behind and flanks. When threatened by the enemy, the Romans always used the hollow square/oblong formation or open half-square formations if the terrain allowed it. Contrary to common belief, this was also true when the Romans marched in hilly or wooded terrain. In those places, the units had to use the looser formation that allowed them to pass through difficult places in the terrain. In other words, the units (mainly the centuries) varied their formation (depth, length etc.) and intervals according to the situation, while the units posted as reserves covered up possible ruptures in the array. When threatened by the enemy, the individual units could conduct counterattacks by advancing forward from the square for a short distance. If they advanced too far, the enemy could cut off their route of retreat. In those places where it was possible to use only a column or columns, the Romans posted protective shielding forces in front, behind and on the flanks.

When following the regulations, the army always encamped for the night in a fortified marching camp. The illustration of the fortified camp opposite is based on Pseudo-Hyginus' treatise (drawn after Lenoir), which represents a theoretical field army consisting of three legions, auxiliaries, allies and naval detachments under the emperor.

The following list of qualities that the Romans required from their generals is based on Onasander, whose work was also later copied by later generations of military theorists – for example, his list can still be found in Leo's *Tactica* (tenth century). On the basis of this, the Romans required that their generals were to possess self-restraint so that they would not be led astray; to be vigilant; to be frugal in their tastes, and be hardened by labour; to be alert; not to suffer from avarice; not to be too young or old; preferably the generals were to be fathers, but good childless men were also acceptable; to be good public speakers so that they could encourage the troops; to have good reputation so that the men would follow them willingly; being poor or rich was not considered decisive,

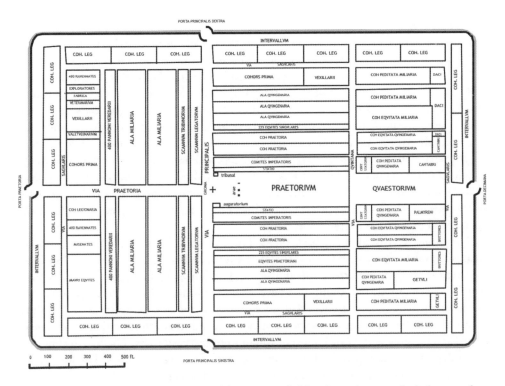

if the person was upright, but men with commercial instincts (petty minded men after profit) were to be excluded; and to have illustrious ancestors if possible, but capable men of low birth were considered as good. In addition, the general was to be trustworthy, affable, punctual, calm, and to have good judgment of character so that he could appoint able and loyal officers to the right posts. Since the numbers of generals were small, the noble candidates were still ranked highest, and after them the rich so that they could keep the soldiers happy by spending money from their own pockets if necessary. This list should be kept in mind when assessing the qualities of the emperors and generals as officers. As will become obvious the standard often fell well short of the ideal, and the military doctrine was not always followed either.

The Romans had a schizophrenic attitude towards the type of strategist and tactician they expected their generals to be. Firstly, they admired the bold risk-taker of the type of Julius Caesar who was ready to risk all and move with alacrity from one place to another and who dealt lightning strikes against the enemy. On the other hand, they also despised this type of general as a risk-taker who endangered all needlessly and favoured the slow and methodological commander who avoided the taking of risks. This type of commander was personified by Pompey the Great, Tiberius and Corbulo. The attitude of the observer decided which of the types was favoured, and this should also be kept in mind when assessing the generalship of Constantine the Great (bold), Constantius II (cautious), Julian (bold failure), Valentinian (cautious) and so forth. It seems probable that the bold commander found favour when he was successful and when he was not, he was despised, and the same is true of the cautious type. If excessive caution led to disaster, it caused general condemnation as happened for example to Pompey the Great in 48 BC.

Cavalry Tactics[13]

During the period under discussion the Romans usually used mixed armies consisting of both infantry and cavalry, but this doesn't mean that they would have neglected their cavalry arm. On the contrary, the cavalry usually decided the battles. Regardless, it is still clear that the importance of the cavalry had diminished after the reign of Gallienus (see Chapter 3), because during his reign the entire army could consist only of cavalry. This doesn't mean that cavalry would not have been deployed independently after that (for example Arbitio versus the Lentienses in 355), but it became rarer. If the cavalry fought separately, it was more usual that this happened because it had been posted in the vanguard of the army, or because it was chasing small detachments of raiders, or because it was used to ambush a careless foe. In the usual circumstances the cavalry was used solely to scout the roads, to protect the wings of the infantry phalanx, to outflank the enemy, and to pursue a defeated foe.

The cavalry consisted of five basic types. The first was the traditional Romano-Gallic-Spanish cavalry armed with a shield, helmet, sword, and javelin(s) or spear(s), but these too were trained to use crossbows and bows. The horses of this type of cavalry were usually unarmoured, but could also have chamfrons and side-coverings. The second consisted of the mounted archers that were mostly recruited from easterners. The third consisted of cataphracts (man and horse armoured, and rider armed with a spear, shield, sword and possibly with a bow), most of whom were also easterners. The fourth consisted of cavalry lancers equipped like the *Sarmatian contarii* or Arabic lancers. The fifth group were the extra-light Moorish cavalry that fought with javelins.

The different types of cavalry also employed different horse breeds supplied by the imperial stud-farms or by taxpayers. Depending upon the type of unit, the cavalry were deployed either as rank-and-file squares/oblongs (the standard formation with depths varying between five and ten ranks according to the quality of the unit), or as wedges, or as rhomboids (at least the Armenian, Parthian and Sasanian units), or as irregular throngs (*droungoi*). In addition, the Roman cataphracts also used a massive 'regimental' wedge for the breaking up of the enemy infantry formation. For additional details concerning the various types of cavalry see Chapter 2.

The standard Roman cavalry formation consisted of two lines, of which one served as a reserve. Before the battle the Romans also used a small separate vanguard to protect the array proper. The actual array could also include ambushers on the flanks if the terrain allowed this. There is evidence for the use of the so-called Italian Drill formation of the Strategikon from the first century AD onwards. The following illustration of the Roman cavalry in the Column of Trajan (drawn by Reinach, but additions by me) provides actually a relatively good picture of what type of formations were used.[14] If the Romans used cavalry forces with less than 5,000 men the second line was to consist of only one reserve division. If the cavalry force consisted of 5,000–15,000 men, it was acceptable to post only two reserve divisions, but during this time period the way in which the reserves were deployed varied greatly.

Each of the larger divisions was divided into units of *koursores* (runners/skirmishers) and *defensores* (defenders). The *koursores* were deployed on the flanks and used for skirmishing and pursuit in irregular order (*droungos*). The *defensores* in the centre maintained close order and protected the former if they needed to retreat and also attacked the enemy with a well-ordered formation. The Romans could also forego the skirmishing phase and attack immediately with their entire line in close order. If they were successful, the *koursores* then pursued the enemy in irregular order. When the Romans outnumbered the enemy, they enveloped its flanks. When the Romans had slightly more men or had equal numbers of men, they usually attempted to outflank the enemy with their right wing. If the Romans were outnumbered, they refused their flanks and sent their centre to the attack first. If the front line or its divisions were forced to flee, the units of the second line were required to support it and attack the enemy.

The different parts of the Italian Array date from different periods. The reserve was already added before the birth of Christ, but we do not know when the other parts of the formation were added. The outflankers and flank guards would have been added when someone noted that the flanks of the first line needed extra protection for it to perform its mission unhindered. The fill-up *banda* ('flags' of men) were added between the divisions of the second line when someone noted that the intervals between them could become too small for the first line division to pass through in retreat. The rear guards were added when someone noted the need for extra rear guards. My working theory since 2008 (found in several research papers since), which I presented in Slingshot in 2011–2012, is that Gallienus put in place the final missing pieces of the array and that the formation received its name from the fact that Gallienus' cavalry *Tagmata* were at least initially

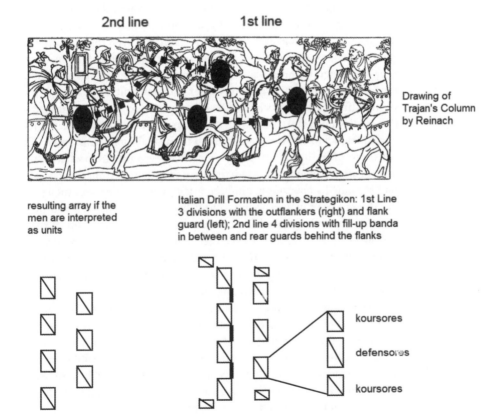

2nd line   1st line

Drawing of Trajan's Column by Reinach

resulting array if the men are interpreted as units

Italian Drill Formation in the Strategikon: 1st Line 3 divisions with the outflankers (right) and flank guard (left); 2nd line 4 divisions with fill-up banda in between and rear guards behind the flanks

koursores

defensores

koursores

placed at Milan.[15] It should be noted, however, that the cavalry was rarely used in this manner during the period under discussion, except when it formed the vanguard of the army. The usual deployment pattern for the cavalry in combat was to be on the flanks of the infantry so that the cataphracts/*clibanarii* were placed next to the infantry and the lighter units further out, or alternatively so that the cavalry wings were also deployed as *koursores* and *defensores*.

Infantry Tactics (see the photo inset for examples of equipment)

The infantry consisted of three basic types: the fully-equipped heavy infantry (legionaries/hoplites); the medium infantry (auxiliaries, *auxilia palatina*, 'peltasts', legionaries in light equipment); and the light infantry (*psiloi*). In addition to these there also appears to have existed a fourth composite type of heavy infantry armed with bows for which there is evidence in Vegetius and Peri Strategikes and in the accompanying illustration; and a fifth group of specialist clubmen/mace-wielders. It should be noted, though, that the Roman regulars were often trained to perform all of these various functions.

Roman tactics had been based on the use of the phalanx formation ever since the turn of the second century AD. The principal phalanx formation used by the Romans was the lateral phalanx with its variants. We can fill the blank spots in our knowledge from the late-sixth century Strategikon, which is likely to have reflected the standard phalanx tactics in use ever since the third century. When the army had less than 24,000 men, it was divided into three divisions (a maximum of 4,000 heavy-armed/2,000 light-armed per division, the rest probably designated as reserves), and if the army had more into four divisions.

These figures also indicate the likely pattern of deployment between the first and fifth centuries, but it should be kept in mind that the figures (unit strengths) given by the Strategikon fit better the structures after Constantine's reforms. However the difference between the 512 men unit of Constantine and the earlier 480 men unit is not that great. It was always a question of uniting the units of various sizes into larger entities that formed up the phalanx. The cavalry units were posted on the flanks of the infantry. The depth of the cavalry units varied from 5 to 10 ranks according to the availability of horsemen. The reserves usually consisted of both infantry and cavalry that were usually posted behind the wings and centre, or where specifically needed. When the baggage train accompanied the army, these were stationed a bowshot behind the infantry force to protect the rear of the formation. The drivers were armed with javelins, bows, slings, caltrops and metal darts to protect the wagons, and some soldiers were usually assigned to support them. They could also throw out a few caltrops to keep the enemy at bay. The wagons were covered by cloth to protect the drivers and the oxen against arrows. The batteries of field artillery on carts were distributed among the wagons to shoot over the head of the army and to protect the rear against possible outflanking attempts by the enemy.

The different sized units and detachments had to be adapted to the phalanx tactics. This means that when the cohorts of or detachments from the 5,120 men legion were deployed as phalanxes and fought with spears (with *pila* or *hastae* depending on the situation) as they did after the turn of the second century, they were probably deployed as double maniples (320 men) with depths of 4, 8 or 16 men behind which were posted the light-armed (160 men for a total of 480), because John Lydus' referral (*De Magistr.* 1.46) to the cohorts of 300 men indicates this (see Chapter 3).

Two variants of lateral phalanx with reserves not in scale (there were also other variants depending upon the size of the army, the placing of the reserves, and deployment of the light infantry):

left: Over 24,000 footmen deployed as double phalanx when the baggage train did not accompany the army. Light infantry shown by the boxes without lines. Light infantry in irregular groups could also be posted on the flanks to make the formation a square.

right: Lateral phalanx with less than 24,000 footmen with the baggage line and artillery carts (the black line). The light infantry posted on the flanks between the heavy infantry and cavalry. This tactic enabled the Romans to use their light infantry against enemy cavalry and infantry simultaneously and also lengthened the line.

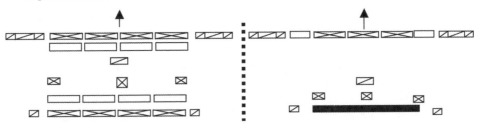

The rear ranks were armed either with *lanceae* javelins or bows and slings. At least during the reign of Diocletian, the Romans appear to have deployed their legionary detachments in such a manner that one 'legion/division' consisted of about 6,000 (6,144?) men, divided into three c. 2,000 (2,048?) -men groups, each of which consisted of about 1,000 (1,024?) men. This bears resemblance to the sixth century practices and may prove that this system predates the reign of Constantine. The Strategikon stated that the *tagmata* were to consist of 200–400 men, the *moirai* at most of 2,000–3,000 men and the *mere* mere (pl. of *meros*, a division) of at most 6,000–7,000 men.

The phalangial heavy infantry was arrayed in ranks and files with varying depths (4, 8, 16 and in exceptional cases 32). The light infantry was deployed either in front, behind, in the middle, or on the flanks as required by the tactical situation. In the ideal circumstance the light-armed could break up the enemy formation even before the lines would make contact. The four-deep array was the shallowest and essentially formed only a single line that could not be divided to form two lines. The other depths allowed the commanders to divide their units to face front and rear simultaneously (*amfistomos phalanx, orbis*) or separate the rear portion into a separate line and form a double phalanx (*difalangia, duplex acies*). The double phalanx could also be achieved by using two sets of separate units one after another, which was essentially the same array as the former double line of legionary cohorts. The double phalanx was used when the army was not accompanied by a wagon train. The Romans also used a phalangial version of the triple line (*triplex acies*).

The principal battlefield tactics of the medium (no armour but melee weapons) and heavy infantry against enemy footmen consisted of different stages, which were the same when the Romans advanced or when they waited for the enemy to approach. The battle began at bowshot range. It was then that the soldiers placed their shields in the 'offensive' *testudo/foulkon* array (tortoise array with a shield roof). This 'offensive' *testudo* was an infantry array used against infantry, cavalry and fortifications in which the men tightened the formation so that their shields interlocked rim-to-boss in front (with file widths of 45–65cm) and the rear rankers placed their shields above their heads. If all men were fully armoured, it was also acceptable to use the less-tight attack formation with shields placed rim-to-rim (c. 80–90cm per man in width) without a shield roof for attack and defence, but for obvious reasons the men preferred the safety of the shield roof even in the looser version. When the soldiers were at the range of the *plumbata/mattiobarbuli*, the *testudo* was opened up under the protective covering fire of the light-armed, and the soldiers threw their *plumbata/mattiobarbuli*. The next stage in combat happened when the lines came within javelin range. At this point, the Romans threw their *pila* or *hastae* with a jump, and then drew their *spathae* or *gladii* and ran forward to attack the enemy with swords by using thrusts and cuts at short range. The *gladius* was more suited to infantry combat while the *spatha* was better against cavalry. The second rank supported the first with spear thrusts and the rear rankers with missiles.

The Roman foot were also taught to employ wrestling, boxing and pancratium moves that could be used at close range combat. The aim of the volley(s) of missiles was to cause casualties among the enemy and to render enemy shields useless, all of which the Roman swordsmen could exploit when they charged forward. At close range, the soldier used his shield and shield boss for bashing and pushing and his sword for thrusts and cuts. The advantage of the attacking version of this system was that it facilitated the aggressiveness of the men and frightened the enemy. The alternative tactic was to stay in place and wait for the enemy to approach. This tactic had two advantages: the combat line would be perfectly aligned and the men were rested. If the battlelines were stationary, sometimes bold individuals also charged out of the formation to engage the enemy and thereby set an example for the rest. If needed the legionaries could also wield axes, mattocks, poles and pitchforks.

Against cavalry the Romans usually adopted the defensive version of the *testudo/ foulkon*, which consisted of the front rankers kneeling and placing their shields rim-to-rim and by placing the butt of their *hasta*-spear (when equipped properly for the situation) or *pilum*-javelin at an angle into the ground so that the spears pointed at the enemy, while the second rank crouched a little and interlocked the bottoms of their shields above the top of the shields of the front rankers, and the third rankers did the same while standing up, as did the fourth rank. The 2nd-4th rankers pointed their *hastae* (or *pila*) towards the enemy while the men behind them threw javelins or darts or shot arrows when the enemy was within range. When the multi-purpose heavies faced cavalry the first three ranks rested their spears on the ground, and the first two ranks aimed their bowshots at the horses and the third shot (and others with bows behind them) at a higher angle so that the arrows dropped on the enemy from above. (See the illustration.) When the enemy approach had been slowed down by the barrage of arrows, the three front ranks picked up their spears and with the fourth rank they formed a wall of spears and engaged the enemy.

The use of the various phalanx arrays enabled the Romans to use various 'grand tactical formations' – even a version of the old triple line with three successive phalanxes. In order to achieve the ability to manoeuvre the units into different formations, the soldiers were taught to thin their lines (spread the formation as every other man stepped to form a new file), to thicken the lines (deepen and shorten the array as files were inserted into other files), to countermarch, to wheel, to turn in place and so forth. If the Romans outnumbered the enemy and/or had longer line, the lateral phalanx was used to outflank the enemy on both flanks. If the Romans outnumbered the enemy only slightly or had

Vergilius Romanus, origin probably western from the 4th or 5th century.

LEFT: Note the hasta-spear, sword, hoplite-shield with protruding shield-boss, scale-armour, pteruges, helmet and the arrow-quiver. The shield with the spike could have been used by front-rankers in phalanx formation. This suggests the use of multi-purpose troops and the phalanx formation later described by Syrianus Magister in the Peri Strategikes/Strategias (16, 27, 36). This type of weaponry would have been chosen for use if the Romans expected to face an enemy force consisting primarily of cavalry. When these men faced enemy cavalry, the three ranks rested their spears on the ground, the first two ranks aimed their bowshots at the horses and the third shot (and others with bows behind them) at a higher angle so that the arrows dropped on the enemy from above. The idea was that the enemy norsemen had to choose whether to protect themselves or their horses with their shields. When the enemy approach had been slowed down by the barrage of arrows, the three front ranks picked up their spears and with the fourth rank they formed up a wall of spears and engaged the enemy. If the Romans had made a mistake and had chosen this type of weaponry and then unexpectedly faced infantry, the front rank used their hastae as if these were pila-javelins and then engaged the enemy with swords while the second rank protected the first with spear-thrusts. The ranks behind them used their spears as javelins, if opportunity for that arose.

RIGHT: A 'Trojan' archer from the same manuscript. Note the use of scale-armour also by the archers.

only slightly longer line, they outflanked it only on one flank. If the Romans had equal or smaller numbers, they attempted to break the enemy's centre with an infantry wedge (formed in middle) while they used various defensive techniques to protect their flanks (cavalry skirmishing, reserves to block the enemy attack, double front by the flank units against outflanking, double phalanx by flank units, light infantry to block outflanking, refused wings etc.).

The Romans could also employ various other forms of phalanx. These included: the use of the oblique formation against one of the enemy flanks to crush it, when the enemy outnumbered the Romans; the lengthening of the phalanx by thinning the depth while one or both flanks advanced against the enemy flanks (variant consisted of the sending of the light-armed in front to protect the advancing wings), which was one of the variant forms of the so-called *epikampios emprosthia* (forward-angled half-square) of Hellenistic military theory; the *epikampios emprosthia* proper to outflank the enemy; the crescent to outflank the enemy; the convex to engage the enemy centre while the wings were refused; the *epikampios opisthia* (rearward-angled half-square); the array deployed against terrain

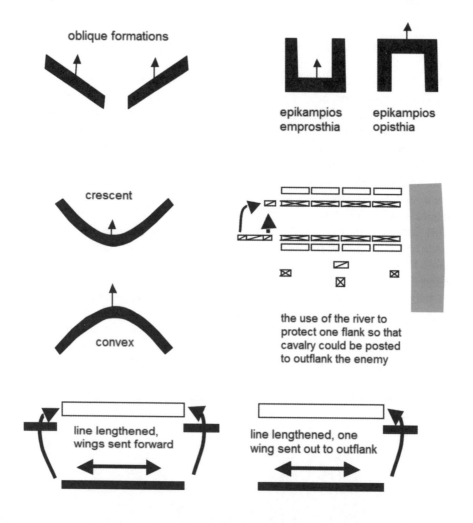

oblique formations

epikampios emprosthia

epikampios opisthia

crescent

convex

the use of the river to protect one flank so that cavalry could be posted to outflank the enemy

line lengthened, wings sent forward

line lengthened, one wing sent out to outflank

obstacles either to prevent outflanking by the enemy or to enable the commander to post all his cavalry on one flank to outflank the enemy; and the hollow square/oblong used as a fighting and marching formation when there was enemy threat from all sides.[16]

The unit/divisional combat manoeuvres consisted of the use of: the line to engage the enemy to its front; the wedge (*cuneus*) to crush and penetrate the enemy formation; the hollow wedge/pincer/scissors (*forceps*) that was used to crush an enemy infantry wedge; the saw (*serra*), which consisted of units advancing and retreating, that was used to harass the enemy; the circle (*orbis*), which was a double-fronted array that was used in defence if the enemy had outflanked the unit; the use of separate and independent cavalry detachments (*globus/droungos*); the use of the *antistomos difalangia* (facing double phalanx) to open up a route for the enemy cavalry wedge to penetrate harmlessly through so that it could be crushed in between. A separate wedge of infantry (probably consisting of club-bearers, *lancearii*, and/or spearmen) could also be sent in front of the phalanx to break up an enemy cavalry charge. For some instances of the use of these, see the narrative.

Campaign Logistics[17]

The Romans stockpiled provisions and equipment in military bases and arsenals in such quantities as they thought necessary. If they planned to conduct a campaign, they stockpiled provisions for the different military units along their planned route of march, and stockpiled further provisions (hardtack, oil, wine etc.) and equipment (arrows, javelins, spare-swords, spare-cords, nails, ropes, boats, leather etc.) at the assembly point for use during the campaign. Sufficient numbers of horses and beasts of burden were also assembled through taxation or from imperial farms, or by purchases. During the second century the officer in charge of the campaign logistics was *praepositus copiarum* (commander of supplies), but his title appears to have been changed into *praepositus annonae* during the third. However, other officials and officers could also be put in charge. For example, the prefects of the fleets could have the responsibility of providing supplies when their fleets accompanied the army. By the fourth century the Praetorian Prefects had the overall responsibility over logistics through their subordinates, and one may assume that they could also have had this responsibility during the third century, especially when they accompanied the emperor on campaign.

Production of Equipment[18]

The Romans produced and supplied material and equipment for their armed forces in different ways depending upon the area and its cultural traditions and circumstances. In the urbanized areas of the Mediterranean, especially in the East, the cities possessed all the artisans and workshops needed for the production of any material needed. However, in those areas where there were not enough cities and local workshops, out of necessity the legions had become self-sufficient in the production of weapons. Certain produce like the clothes, blankets, cloaks, tunics and spear-shafts etc. were probably always bought from civilian producers, but when there was no access to the local producers of specialist military equipment, the Romans appear to have built additional state-controlled *fabricae* (workshops/factories) to manufacture what was needed, at first in the legionary bases and then as separate entities in those cases when the equipment could not be produced by the legions themselves.

It is not known when these *fabricae* were created, and the first time these become visible is in the Notitia Dignitatum, which lists fifteen such centres for the East and twenty for the West. In my opinion, it is probable that at least some were already created during the third century in those sections of the frontier that had been penetrated by enemies, as a result of which the legions had lost control of their home bases and workshops. The organization that is visible in the ND appears to date from the reign of Diocletian because the distribution of the shield workshops appears to tally with the European frontier provinces while the armour factories seem to match up with their dioceses. Most of the factories were located in cities or legionary garrisons, some of which had direct connection with the building program of the Tetrarchs, such as those located at Nicomedia, Thessalonica and Augustodunum. However, the distribution of the more specialized factories doesn't correspond so neatly with the distribution pattern of the provinces and dioceses. For example, all *fabricae ballistariae* and arrow and bow factories are located in the West, but since the Eastern cities possessed skilled guilds of artisans (*fabricenses*) there was no need for them in the East.

There is no reason to challenge the generally accepted theory that the creation of the state factories on a mass scale visible from the ND resulted from the expansion of the army by Diocletian. What is clear is that the mobile forces that were billeted in cities entirely depended on the availability of weapons from the artisans of the cities or from the state factories. They did not have permanent bases with their own workshops. In addition, there is reason to believe that Diocletian created the state woollen mills, linen mills, and dyeworks that were governed by two financial officials, the *Comes Sacrarum Largitionum* and the *Comes Rerum Privatarum*. These mills and workshops were also distributed according to the new administrative divisions. They were probably used to supplement clothing acquired with the *vestis militaris* tax.

As far as the quality of the equipment is concerned, the extant letters from Egypt do suggest that the quality of the standard military equipment provided by the state for their soldiers was not on a par with the best provided by civilian artisans because in those letters the soldiers ask their parents or wives to send to them items that appear to have had superior quality. However, we should not draw too drastic conclusions from this. The equipment provided by the state was undoubtedly good enough for their intended purpose, it was just that with money it was possible to buy equipment of superior quality, just like today it is possible to buy customized weaponry (e.g. customized pistols and rifles) from the private market that are undoubtedly superior to the standard ones. It is clear that a sword, bow, javelin and so on that was customized to the user's hand, strength and height was superior to the standard gear. A good modern parallel to this practice comes from the war in Iraq, during which the families of the American soldiers sent to their loved ones additional protective gear that could be bought from the civilian market to supplement the standard gear, and yet no sane person could claim that the American troops would not have been adequately equipped for the mission they had – the additional gear provided by their families just supplemented this and improved their chances of survival.

Recruitment and Salary[19]

Throughout the Principate the principal source of recruits was volunteers, but conscription was never abolished and was always used in emergencies. The third century crisis meant that the numbers of volunteers diminished with the result that the state resorted to the use of compulsory conscription and started to demand that the sons of the soldiers serve in their fathers' units, and started to use ever increasing numbers of foreigners. These practices were subsequently institutionalized under Diocletian.

During the Principate the soldiers received their salaries in money from which the officers then deducted the amount spent on clothes, equipment, and food, but the third century crisis changed this as well. Now the soldiers received their salary in three forms: salary (*stipendium*); distribution of money for special occasions (*donativa*); and payments in kind (grain, meat, oil, wine, clothes, equipment etc.) called *annona*. This system was institutionalized by Diocletian. The *PP* was placed in charge of the collection of the *annona*. The town and city councils (*curiae*), consisting of the curiales/decurions, had the duty of collecting the produce from the peasantry and then transporting it to local arsenals or military units. The decurions were liable to pay any deficit from their own resources, which naturally made membership in the city council highly undesirable. Since the wealthier classes sought to avoid their duties as decurions by any possible means the state legislated against this and also used military force to compel the decurions to perform their duties.

The donatives were probably the most important source of money for the soldiers because these were always paid in bullion or coin. The donatives were paid when a new emperor assumed the purple and on quinquennial (5, 10, 20 year) anniversaries of his accession. In addition, the donatives could be paid to celebrate other occasions, such as the birth of a child to the emperor, when the emperor or his close relative became consuls, or to celebrate a military victory (real or invented), or on the Calends of January.

In addition, the emperor usually bribed the army with a donative of money just prior to and/or during any military campaign and gave extra large donatives when he or his son/relative became emperor (Caesar or Augustus). The need to bribe the soldiers to fight well during military campaigns created an extra cost to the state, which also played a role when the emperors planned their campaigns. These occasions were funded through special taxes coordinated by the *Comes Sacrarum Largitionum* and paid by the senators, curial elites of the towns and cities, and craftsmen and merchants. The bulk of the burden fell on the 'middle class' artisans and merchants of the cities, despite the fact that the annual cash income of a single senatorial family could be more than the entire donative-tax income of the state. The rich have always had their own means of avoiding the taxes, and that was definitely the case in the Late Roman Empire.

Still another important source of income for the soldiers was the booty obtained during war. In addition to this, some military personnel that managed to acquire local roots could own land or a business from which they could obtain extra income.

Relationship with civilians[20]

Outside their official duties, the soldiers usually came into contact with the civilians only on their furloughs or when they were billeted in cities, towns and villages. During the late Roman period the Roman armed forces consisted of the frontier troops called *Limitanei* and mobile troops called *Comitatenses*. (See the narrative.) In practice this division was not new. Even though the bulk of the Roman armies had always been posted near the border, there had always existed troops that had been detached for duties elsewhere and in the course of the continuous wars of the third century these forces had become semi-permanent so that, for example, by Diocletian's reign his field forces could be called his *Comitatus*. Regardless, Constantine's reform of transferring troops away from the frontier into the *Comitatenses* armies still increased the number of men billeted in cities considerably both in scale and in extent.

The border troops were usually garrisoned in their own forts, but these were typically still located close to towns, cities and villages, which meant that soldiers and civilians were in constant interaction, and the families of the soldiers also lived close by. In fact, cities had usually grown around the garrisons to serve their needs in the West. Since the units on the borders had usually acquired local roots and quite often also consisted of local recruits, their behaviour was usually better towards the locals with whom they had to coexist. Regardless, the soldiers still behaved like soldiers of all ages. They could be drunk and behave quite badly. When on transit to another theatre of war, the border troops were billeted on civilians they did not know with the result that their behaviour could get worse.

The Late Roman *Comitatenses* were always billeted on cities, towns and villages, and their behaviour was notorious. The civilians were by law required to provide *hospitium* or *hospitalitas* for the soldiers. The quartermasters (*mensores* or *metatores*) assigned a third of the civilian property they had chosen to give to the soldiers, and then signalled their decision by writing the names of the soldiers on the doors. The owners were required to provide only shelter, but the unruly soldiers were in the habit of demanding, with the threat of violence, the *salgamum* (pickles). This usually meant olive oil, wood for fireplace, bedding, or even sex. It was actually taken for granted that the soldiers would drink too much wine and attempt to seduce or rape the women. It was also not unheard of that the soldiers would rob their hosts and throw them out of their property. Since the bad behaviour of the soldiers was so well-known some classes of property were exempt from the duty. These included the properties of teachers, doctors, clergy and synagogues. This could also mean that civilians attempted to bribe their way out, which the soldiers were not slow to exploit.

The situation became particularly bad when the troops were campaigning, because the soldiers were then billeted in cities in which they did not normally have to stay. The stress of combat and foreign surroundings made the soldiers restless. The use of alcohol and drinking parties helped alleviate the stress, but with the use of alcohol went bad behaviour. However, there are still some rare instances in which the commanders kept tight discipline and/or the soldiers behaved well, excepting some bad apples that can be expected to be present in any larger organization.

Siege Warfare

Ammianus' description of the standard siege equipment (23.4), together with his descriptions of the sieges, gives us a glimpse of the standard siege practices. Additional information can be found from Vegetius (4.1–4.30), the DRB, and the Greek poliorcetic treatises. The Romans and Persians were the most sophisticated practioners of siege tactics. The rest of the nations did not have any comparable means at their disposal and it can be said with a good reason that both of these superpowers possessed an absolute superiority in all forms of siege warfare against all of their other neighbours.

Offensive Sieges

The standard offensive siege tactics were to prepare the army with adequate provisions, arms, siege-engines and then to proceed against the object of the siege. The first in the list of things to do for the general was to build a fortified camp for the army and conduct a reconnaissance of the defences in person, after which he offered terms of surrender to the defenders. If the defenders did not surrender, the commander ordered an assault. The soldiers would then approach the walls in *testudo*-arrays or under hastily built sheds (if there had been enough time to build these) or behind mantlets, while others brought material to fill up the moat/ditch, and then attempted to climb to the wall by using ladders. This attack was performed under the covering fire of archers and slingers and mobile light-ballistae.

If the place could not be taken with assault, then the attackers usually assembled the siege-engines they had brought with them and attempted to conquer the place through a variety of means. The typical means of assault was to build mounds on top of which were placed towers, ballistae and battering rams. The mounds were built so high that the ballistae placed on the top could force the defenders away from the walls in order that the rams could be brought forward. The rams were usually used against the towers. The attack could also involve the use of siege towers to clear the wall of defenders. When feasible, the attackers could also undermine the walls with mines (*cuniculum*, underground tunnel), or attempt to loose individual stones in the walls with various types of picks, axes and drills (the men working underneath protective sheds). Still another variant was to use a sort of flame-thrower operated by bellows against the stone wall. Fire-darts and fire-bombs could also be employed against the gates and buildings inside. The stone-throwers (*onagri*) and various types of ballistae were used as anti-personnel artillery to enable the attackers to approach the walls or to keep the enemy from making effective sallies. If there was a sea, lake or river nearby, the attackers could attempt to use siege-towers or *sambucas* (counterweight tubes) built on ships to assault the walls. The attackers were always rotated so that while some attacked, the rest rested. The aim was to tire out the defenders by making it impossible to sleep. The lack of sleep (often in combination with hunger) was known to cause the defenders to become inattentive, as a result of which the attackers were often able to surprise them and penetrate the defences.

If the place was unassailable or the assaults and siege-engines had proved ineffective, and the situation allowed (i.e. there were enough supplies, no relief army approaching etc.), the commanders usually resorted to the use of ruses and blockade and famine to bring about the surrender of the defenders.

When the attackers were successful in their attack, the commanders usually let their men kill, pillage, and rape in order to satisfy their men's wishes and lusts. It was only after the men had sated their most immediate bloodlust that the officers would attempt to save the lives of the remaining defenders if these were willing to surrender, and it was also only after this that the men started to think logically what would be valuable enough to be plundered (valuables, prisoners, slaves, and hostages). In some cases the adult males could also be left alive to be taken as slaves, while in other cases, usually as a result of a specific order to do so, the soldiers killed all males older than 12 years and left only the children and women alive. The intention of the latter terror tactic was to scare the enemy and to ensure that there would not be any adults left to take revenge. The booty taken as a result of such sieges could be truly considerable if the place was also a commercial hub or military headquarters.

Defensive Sieges

The standard defensive strategies and tactics were to build strong defences to protect strategically located places. It was preferred to locate such cities, towns and fortresses in places that were already protected by nature's own defences, but this was not always possible. There was one requirement, though, that was always followed. The place had to have easy access to some source(s) of water, as a result of which they were located near a river, springs and/or natural wells, or had to have enough rainfall to fill up water tanks. In addition, the defensive tactics required that the place was to have a large enough garrison that could be strengthened by local civilians, and that there was plentiful supply of arms, provisions, and mural artillery. The defenders' defensive aims were simple. First of all, they aimed to prevent the besiegers from approaching the walls with archers, slingers, and mural artillery. Secondly, if the enemy managed to force their way close to the walls, the defenders could employ several counter-measures. For example, they could use counter-mines to oppose enemy mines, or to undermine the ground below enemy mounds or siege-equipment. The defenders, just like the attackers, could also use screens to hide them from enemy observers and missile attacks. They could use cranes and men to drop heavy objects on enemy personnel and siege-equipment, and they could lift the heads of the enemy rams up with nooses so that those would be useless. And, if everything else had failed, the defenders could make sallies from the postern (and main) gates against the besiegers and their siege-engines and mounds. If the situation appeared hopeless, the defenders also often attempted to negotiate surrender, or attempted some sort of ruse. In addition, if the defending side possessed enough manpower, they usually attempted to end the siege through the use of a relief army and/or guerrilla campaign against the attackers.

Right: Typical *quadriburgus* (small border fort) used by the Romans from the third to fourth centuries.

Below: Sample of some of the types of towers used by the late Romans (after von Petrikovits, 198).

For examples of fortified cities and larger forts, see the narrative (esp. the reigns of Constantius II and Valentinian I)

It should be kept in mind, however, that the Romans varied the style and amount of fortification according to strategic and tactical needs and the type of enemy they faced. The Romans certainly knew how to build sophisticated fortifications that put any attacker at a grave disadvantage, for example because they would face simultaneous fire from several directions, but chose not to use these in those locations that did not need them. They also possessed earlier Greek siege manuals that gave them a theoretical founding on how to build sophisticated fortresses (moats, angled defences etc.) and on how to conduct the defence. However, during this period the Romans did not follow these principles to the letter. For example, instead of using the bastion towers with angles that were the most effective defences against stone throwers, they still experimented with different types of towers, probably with the intention of providing their artillery with as good and wide a range of shooting as possible, rather than making the structure stronger. The same was also true of the gate structures.

Siege-Engines and Equipment
Ammianus' description of the various types of siege-engines and equipment is valuable because he appears to describe the standard equipment in use, but we should not forget that the Romans (and Persians) could, when needed, build all the pieces of equipment described by the poliorcetic treatises.

According to Ammianus (23.4) the standard mural artillery consisted of the ballistae and scorpions (*onagri*). Other standard equipment included the ram, *helepolis* ('city-taker'), and fire-darts. Ammianus' descriptions of sieges make it clear that the Romans typically employed towers, mounds, sheds, mantlets, ships (with possible towers), and ladders.

ballistae carts in Trajan's Column (source Froehner)

onager

Philon's Repeater
(Drawn after Diehl and Schramm, 1918, Tafel 7)

Ammianus describes the ballista as a torsion-shooter, which was operated by young men on both sides, and which shot arrows with such power that they could cause sparks when those left the ballista and flew so far that eyes could not see them. His description of the construction, however, is so unclear that it has allowed many different interpretations.[21] What is certain, however, is that the ballista described was a particularly powerful weapon that had long range and that it required a minimum of two men to operate or even possibly three if a separate loader/shooter was used, but Ammianus mentions only two men in this context. (However, see below.) From Ammianus' own text (see my interpretation of the ballistae during the years 360–361), it is probable that the Romans continued to employ in addition at least the so-called repeating ballistae, and the survival of the technical treatises also proves that other types of ballistae were also used for specific purposes. There were ballistae powered by composite-bows or steel-bows, and there were ballistae that shot two arrows at a time and there were cart- and wall-mounted versions and there were smaller and larger variants of all these.

The one-armed scorpion (*onager* – 'wild-ass') was a torsion weapon that shot rounded stones and was operated by four pullers of the handles on both sides plus a gunner. This weapon presents no problems and an illustration is given above. Ammianus' text assigns nine men for each scorpion, but we do not know whether there were also other men assigned as loaders, for that would have made the loading and shooting faster. In this context Vegetius' referral (2.25) to the use of an 11-man '*contubernium*' to operate each ballista-cart may be of use. The detailing of eleven men for each ballista seems quite excessive, which suggests the possibility that Vegetius either made a mistake or he has included also the recruit and servant in the figure. If he has made a mistake it is possible that the eleven men consisted of the nine users of the scorpion and two users of the ballista. However, I am inclined to believe that Vegetius' figure is to be trusted for the reasons given above and that we should also assign more men than nine (twenty-two?) for each scorpion so that the men pulling the handles could be rotated. It is also probable that, just like in the Middle Ages, there were 'scorpions' of different sizes, even if Ammianus fails to mention this. There is no specific evidence for the use of traction or counterweight trebuchets this early. The first extant evidence for these dates from the sixth century, but it is not impossible that some of the huge stones thrown at the attackers on sieges could have been thrown by counterweight/traction cranes (closely resembling the trebuchet) that had been known ever since Archimedes' times. We do know that the Romans shot rocks/stones as heavy as 181kg during the siege of Nisibis in 350, but unfortunately this cannot be used as evidence for the use of trebuchets because the largest variants of the torsion-ballistae (the huge ballistae were stone-throwers) were able to throw rocks of this size. However, the fact that the Romans had by the fourth century abandoned the use of the traditional ballistae stone-throwers in favour of the scorpions does suggest the possibility that they had also adopted the use of trebuchets to fire the larger rocks that the scorpions could not. What is certain is that the Romans were able to use such powerful stone-throwers that their ability was only to be surpassed in the High Middle Ages when the largest variants of the counterweight trebuchets came into use.

Battering rams had two basic variants: 1) the normal battering ram; and 2) the '*helepolis*' city-taker. The former consisted of a pole at the head of which was a ram's head of iron, which was placed in a shed and operated by men pulling and shoving the pole. It was possible to break up any wall with this engine if the walls had been cleared of defenders. This was the standard piece of equipment. The latter was not the *helepolis* of Demetrius Poliorcetes, as claimed by Ammianus, but a variant of either a torsion-and-man-powered ram/drill, or a variant of Hegetor's ram. What is certain is that the ram was huge, its front consisted of a three-pronged iron-head, and it was protected by a huge *testudo-*

Sample of the various types of siege equipment (sheds, siege towers, *sambuca*, fire-bombs, caltrops, ship-towers, double ram) described by the 10th century Heron of Byzantium most of which are copies of ancient Greek and Roman originals. Source: Wescher.

mantlet covered with mud. It was operated by men guiding the wheels and ropes that were used to add power to the blows. If this piece of equipment was brought against a weaker part of the wall and the defenders were unable to prevent this, then this city-taker was bound to open a great breach in the wall. In addition to these, there were also other types of rams. These included different variants of rams placed on siege towers and rams that were operated using different principles.

Ammianus (23.14, 23.37) states that the fire-darts employed by the Romans were made out of hollowed-out reed with openings held together by bands of iron so that fire (evidently the so-called Medic oil) and inflammable material was placed inside. These were then shot from loose bows so that a swift flight would not extinguish the flames. According to Ammianus, it was impossible to extinguish these darts with water, which only intensified the fire – it was possible to extinguish them only with dust. Other flammable substances used in the fire-darts and bombs included pitch, sulphur, lime, bitumen, naphtha, oil, and so on. As noted above, the Romans and Persians used fire-bombs which consisted of baskets or pieces of pottery filled with flammable substances that were then shot by stone-throwers. In addition, the Romans used flame-throwers powered by bellows to set things on fire and/or they threw incendiaries by hand, or placed flammable substances wherever needed.

The offensive siege equipment included also: *falces* (curved iron-hooks to pull out stones, employed from sheds – sing. *falx*), *vineae* (sheds that could be united to form a line – sing. *vinea*), *plutei* (light sheds covered with hides – sing. *pluteus*), *musculi* (light small sheds – sing. *musculus*), *testudines* (heavy tortoise-sheds – sing. *testudo*); various kinds of ladders (simple, detachable, spy-ladders to observe the defences, etc.), *sambuca* (a counter-balance tube to lift men onto the wall), *exostra* (a bridge to land men on the wall from a siege tower), *tolleno* a (counter-balance crane to lift men onto the top of the wall), and various kinds of siege towers (some with various kinds of rams usable either against the walls or personnel, and some with flails, or hoses to spread hot liquid etc. usable against the defenders on the wall).

Besides the standard mural artillery, bows, slings, javelins, counter-mines, counter-mounds etc., defensive equipment included *culcitae* (cushions/mattresses to absorb hits – sing. *culcita*), *laquei* (snares/nooses/fetters used to snare *falces* and rams – sing. *laqueus*), *lupi* ('wolves', iron grappling jaws attached to ropes used to lift or turn battering rams – sing. *lupus*), and heavy objects and hot liquids dropped from the wall. The illustrations show some of the equipment used by the Romans during this era. Even this small sample should make clear the sophistication of Roman siege techniques.

The Imperial Navy[22]

Background

Just like the army, the imperial navy was also a creation of Augustus and underwent only marginal changes before the third century AD. Around the middle of the third century the navy consisted of the two praetorian 'reserve' fleets (*Classis Praetoriae Misenatium/ Misenatis*; *Classis Praetoriae Ravennatum/Ravennatis/Ravennas*) based in Italy, and of the provincial fleets (*Classis Alexandrina, Classis Syriaca, Classis Nova Libyca, Classis Germanica, Classis Pannonica, Classis Moesica, Classis Britannica,* and *Classis Pontica*).

After the Battle of Actium in 31 BC the period of major naval battles was over and the Romans possessed unchallenged naval supremacy in the North Sea, Atlantic coasts, Mediterranean, Red Sea, and the Black Sea until the emergence of new naval threats in the form of Franks and Saxons in the North Sea, and in the form of Borani, Heruls and Goths in the Black Sea. As a result, the monster polyremes of the Hellenistic age had been abandoned in favour of smaller vessels. The situation did not change in the third century because the ships of the barbarian raiders were even smaller than the Roman *liburnae*.

The fleets were an indispensable part of the Roman armed forces. The navy had the duty of defeating any enemy fleets at sea, the clearing of pirates, the support of the land forces when they besieged coastal cities/towns, and the logistical support of land campaigns. In addition, the coasts also needed protection. The coastal defence consisted of active measures taken by the fleets, and of passive measures, which consisted of the building of forts and towers along the coasts and rivers. In the most threatened areas this last mentioned meant the combining of land forces and fleets under a single command, the most famous of which was the *Comes* of the Saxon Shore. We do not know the exact procedure of how the defence of those coastal areas that did not face any serious threat was organized, but it appears probable that it was the duty of the local civilian and municipal officials to police those with the help of their staff and the civilian police force, which in some cases also included military detachments given to assist them. Their duties would mainly have included the collection of tolls/taxes, and the prevention of smuggling and wrecking. During the early empire special prefects (*praefectus orae maritimae*) were also appointed to guard some sections of the coastline (for example in the Black Sea, Mauretania, Hispania Tarraconensis, Red Sea) when some emergency occurred and one may guess that similar arrangements were also used after the third century.[23] Starr (1943, 69) has proposed that during the later empire the *custodes litorum* (guardians of the coasts), probable descendants of the late-second century *limenarchae*, were given also military functions alongside their civilian duties, which included the controlling of commerce and communications in the ports and harbours.

Organization

The map below shows the principal naval bases after c.324. However, it also shows the principal fleets and naval bases in operation during the third century. The Roman naval strategy was clearly based on four main principles: firstly, the fleets supported the land forces; secondly, they protected the shores against naval raiders and the river frontiers against raids; thirdly, they protected grain and other shipments across the seas and along the rivers into the major cities and military bases; and fourthly, they protected the trade routes and policed the seas against pirates.

The navy was considered part of the auxiliary forces so that the majority of the mariners/soldiers/sailors of the Misenum Fleet were recruited from the eastern provinces and those of the Ravenna Fleet from the Danube provinces, while the personnel of the provincial fleets usually consisted of the locals. A significant number of the seamen were also former slaves with the status of freedmen. The length of service was initially 26 years, at the end of which the men were granted Roman citizenship, but it was changed to 28 years probably during the reign of Philip the Arab or Decius. The granting of

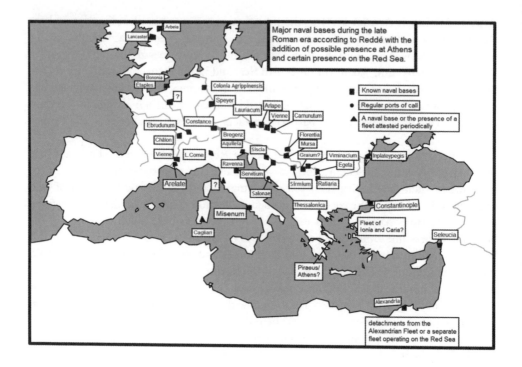

citizenship to all free persons by Caracalla obviously changed the picture and made almost all provincials Romans, but the fleet was still regarded as an auxiliary service used in support of the army. The auxiliary status also meant that the command of the fleets was the prerogative of the members of the equestrian class, but since the fleets just like the army were under the personal control of the emperor anyone whom he would consider fit to serve could do so, including even freedmen and foreigners.

According to Vegetius (4.31), each of the praetorian fleets had a single legion attached to them so that these fleets could transport those troops to any part of the world as needed. Gaul, Spain, Mauretania, Africa, Egypt, Sardinia and Sicily were the responsibility of the Fleet of Misenum, while Epirus, Macedonia, Achaia, Propontus, Pontus, the Orient, Crete, and Cyprus belonged to the sphere of the Fleet of Ravenna.

Modern research has proved this to be an oversimplification of the facts. In normal circumstances the Fleet of Misenum would probably have protected the western shores of Italy and the Fleet of Ravenna those of the Adriatic, but as the Fleet of Misenum was the most powerful fleet in the Mediterranean its services were required all over the empire. As implied by the names, the principal bases of both fleets were located in those coastal cities. However, both fleets could also post detachments wherever needed, and a permanent detachment of the Fleet of Misenum was located in Ostia, the port of the city of Rome. Furthermore, detachments of sailors/mariners from both fleets were permanently garrisoned in the city of Rome, where they operated the canvas awnings of the Colosseum or helped to stage mock naval battles. Detachments could also accompany field armies to operate siege engines.

The principal missions of the praetorian fleets were to act as deterrents against possible usurpers and to support imperial campaigns. This meant that they continued to possess larger ships in greater quantities than the other fleets. Regardless, as noted by Vegetius (4.31), the Roman emperors did not maintain their fleets only to deter possible rebels, but also against foreign foes. As we shall see, this did not make it impossible for competing emperors, or even usurpers, to challenge the emperor's fleets, but it meant that any usurper not already in possession of a fleet would first have to build one. According to a modern calculation, at one point in time the Misenum Fleet appears to have consisted of 1 'sixer', 1 'fiver', 10 'fours', 52 triremes and 15 *liburnae*, while the Ravenna Fleet consisted of 2 'fives', 6 'fours', 23 triremes and 4 *liburnae*. (See the accompanying illustrations of the ships.) Jordanes (Get. 29) claims that Dio stated that the harbour of Ravenna could hold 250 ships, which, if accurate, must also include the naval transport and supply ships.

The principal missions of the provincial fleets were the suppression of piracy and the transport of personnel and supplies. The bulk of these fleets consisted of lighter and more mobile vessels, the 'liburnians', some blue-coloured scouting ships (*scaphae exploratoriae, picati*), and other smaller vessels, plus each fleet had a trireme to serve as a flagship of the commanding prefect.

The principal duty of the *Classis Alexandrina*, with a home base in Alexandria, was to protect the mouth of the Nile and the corn supply from Egypt to Rome (later to Constantinople) with secondary duty to patrol the coasts of Cyrene (permanent base), Egypt and Judaea. In emergencies it could also be employed on the Nile, but the policing of the river was usually performed by a separate river police called the *potamofylakia* (River Guards, presumably civilians). The principal duty of the *Classis Syriaca* appears to have been to suppress piracy along the coasts of Judaea, Syria and Asia Minor (especially the coastline of Isauria, the haven of pirates). When needed the *Classis Syriaca* also provided naval detachments to bolster the numbers of ships posed to protect the North African coastline, as a result of which Syrian ships could be found in Cyrene too. From about 180 onwards the naval base in Cyrene was changed into a new permanent fleet called the *Classis Nova Libyca*, which thereby assumed the former duties of the Egyptian Fleet on that coast. According to the SHA (Commodus 17.7), Commodus created a *Classis Africana*, but it is likely that the author has either confused it with the *Classis Nova Libyca* or with a temporary fleet created by Commodus to alleviate problems of food supply from Egypt. In addition, some researchers have suggested that there existed a *Classis Mauretanica* (consisting of 13 *liburnae*) to prevent attacks of Moorish pirates, but others have either claimed that it consisted of detachments of the Syrian and Alexandrian fleets or of a detachment of the latter.

The *Classis Germanica* operated on the Rhine frontier in support of local military operations and as a river police force with the secondary duty of operating on the North Sea. As a river fleet, the bulk of the German Fleet consisted of the smaller river liburnians, patrol ships (see Chapter 2, Franks) and of even smaller *naves lusoriae*. The *Classis Britannica* supported military operations in the British Isles and protected communications between Britain and Gaul.

The Danube frontier was protected by two river fleets, the *Classes Pannonica* and *Moesiaca*, the latter of which also had the duty of protecting the western side of the Black Sea up to the Crimea. As river fleets, the bulk of their ships consisted of the smaller river liburnians, patrol ships and *lusoriae*. According to the law preserved in the Theodosian Code (7.17.1, January 412), the lower Danube province of Scythia possessed 125 *naves lusoriae* (110 replaced with new ships and 15 repaired) and Lower Moesica 100 *lusoriae* (90 new and 10 repaired), which gives a good indication of the type of ships used and of the manpower required (225 x 45 = 10,125 men).[24]

The southern and eastern side of the Black Sea from the Dardanelles up to the Crimea was protected by the *Classis Pontica* with headquarters at Trapezus. It had absorbed the former Thracian fleet, the *Classis Perinthia*. The raids of the Gothic Costoboci caused the transferral of the headquarters to Cyzicus, probably to protect the traffic passing through the Hellespont and Bosphorus. A detachment was also stationed more or less permanently at Charax in the Crimea.

Reddé (570–572) has noted the principal weaknesses of the Roman naval arrangement. The Hellespont and Bosphorus were relatively lightly defended, which meant that it was possible for the invaders to pass through into the Mediterranean. The detachments based in Cyzicus and Perinthus were just too weak. Gibraltar was also not protected, but as long as the Moors remained relatively peaceful that was not a major problem. Regardless, the example of the Franks passing through in the third century shows the weakness of this solution. The locations of the naval bases of the Rhine Fleet also made it practically impossible for the fleet to intercept an enemy fleet on the North Sea. Consequently, if the enemy then managed to get past the Pas-de-Calais, patrolled by the *Classis Britannica*, it was impossible for the Romans to stop an invasion unless the whole Atlantic coastal line was to be protected. The absence of the fleet on the Euphrates meant that every time the Romans operated there, they also needed to build a fleet from scratch. Contrary to what Reddé claims, the Romans did post naval assests also on the Red Sea during the Principate and Late Roman period. Villeneuve's article based on two Latin inscriptions from the Archipelago of Farasan (in the south of the Red Sea, see relevant Maps) from ca.AD 144 proves that the Romans did not neglect the area during the Principate (a detachment from the *Legio VI Ferrata* was stationed in Farasan), and my narrative will prove that there were some naval assets in the area also during the Late Roman period, probably detachments from the *Classis Alexandriana* posted at Clysma. However, since the naval detachments could not protect each and every ship on the Red Sea, the Romans appear to have continued to post archers on their merchantmen in those cases in which these could not be accompanied by warships. The Roman fleet was very useful, but for reasons of costs it did not possess adequate numbers to protect all of the assets from piracy or large scale naval invasions.

The third-century barbarian invasions caused severe damage to many of these fleets. The Gothic incursions across the Black Sea sapped the strength of the *Classis Pontica* while the Gothic, Getic and Sarmatian invasions across the Danube did the same to the *Classes Pannonica* and *Moesiaca*. Similarly, the Rhine fleet suffered badly from the Frankish occupation of the estuaries of the Rhine. It is not known when the fleet that was based in Byzantium, Greece and Asia Minor was created, but it is possible that at least their core was already in existence during the reign of Gallienus, as it was during his reign that the Roman navy successfully defeated the Goths in the Bosphorus while the Egyptian navy defeated the Heruls.[25]

The Saxons also raided across the North Sea and plundered the coasts of Gaul in the third century, but in contrast to the abovementioned the *Classis Britannica* was not overrun and a new defensive system, consisting of forts and harbours on both sides of the Channel called the Saxon Shore (*litus Saxonicum*) was built and put under the Count of the Saxon shore probably during the third century. The western seaboard of Britain was also raided by Irish pirates with the result that forts and fortified landing places (probably with naval detachments) were also built on the west coast.[26] This lack of success by the Saxons and the Irish in comparison with the barbarians of other frontiers was of course caused by the fact that they did not actually conquer, destroy or occupy the naval bases of the British Fleet.

The fleet was considered part of the Roman military/army with corresponding ranks and hierarchy. Unfortunately, the exact meaning of the naval ranks and their correspondence with that of the army is not known with certainty and even the existence of the correspondence is denied by some eminent historians. The following is my tentative attempt to present a rough overview of the various naval ranks and their corresponding army ranks.[27]

Each of the fleets was commanded by an equestrian Fleet Prefect (*praefectus classis*) who was assisted by an equestrian *subpraefectus*. Even if, as has been suggested, the sub-prefect served primarily as an aide to the prefect, I would not rule out the possibility that he would also have acted as second-in-command (*hypostrategos*) when needed.[28] The prefect obviously held the same position in the hierarchy as the auxiliary prefects on land, while the *subpraefectus* appears to have had the rank of tribune or *primus pilus*. What is certain is that by the fourth century each of the prefects had a tribune or tribunes to serve as their lieutenants. The prefects were assisted by an administrative staff consisting of *quaestores classici* (pay, equipment and supplies), *cornicularius* (officer), *beneficiarius* (appointee), *actuarius* (clerk) and *scriba* (writer).

Immediately below the prefects were the commanders of temporary detachments that consisted of several different ranks of importance. The most important were the detachments consisting of the ships of the two praetorian fleets, the commander of which held the title *praepositus vexillationis*, a position which was usually held by a very high-ranking person. In the third century this person could also be called a *dux* (duke). The common detachments of ships were put under a *praepositus classis/classibus* whose regular rank depended upon the importance of the mission. In the third century there also appeared a new title, *praepositus reliquationis*, who was a temporary commander of the troops left at a naval base when the main fleet was on campaign. According to Reddé (p.549), this position was usually given to a *primus pilus*.

The modern confusion regarding the functions of different naval commanders becomes even more pronounced in the case of *navarchi* and *trierarchi*, both of which have been claimed to be either ship captains or commanders of groups of ships.[29] According to Vegetius (4.32), the two praetorian fleets, each with a legion, were commanded by prefects, below each of whom served ten tribunes each in charge of a cohort, and *navarchi* as captains of individual *liburnae* of varying sizes. The *navarchus* commanded and trained the pilots (*gubernatores*), rowers (*remiges*) and soldiers (*milites*). I would suggest that we should equate the highest ranking of the tribunes (the equivalent of the *tribunus laticlavii*, later *tribunus maius*) with the *subpraefectus*. It should be noted that if Vegetius' description is to be taken at its face value, then the naval legions had more tribunes than land legions. However, we know from other sources that Vegetius' use of military terms is imprecise. Each of the *navarchi* was actually in charge of several ships and can therefore perhaps be equated with the abovementioned tribunes. The most senior of the *navarchi* was called *navarchus princeps* and may perhaps be equated with the *tribunus maius/subpraefectus*.[30] Regardless of the size of the ship, a 'captain' was always called a *trierarchus*. I would equate these *trierarchi*-captains with the fleet centurions (*centuriones classiarii*), *optiones navaliorum* and *suboptiones* depending upon the size of the vessel.[31] In addition, there were officers called as *nonegenarius* (commander of 90 men), but nothing is known of their functions.[32]

The fighting component of a fleet consisted of the soldiers (*milites*), sailors (*nautae*) and oarsmen (*remiges*) led by their officers, which could be bolstered with the addition of land forces, all of which could be expected to serve both on land and sea. Of note is that the sailors and oarsmen were also simultaneously considered to be *milites*. According to Vegetius 4.44, the naval soldiers needed good protective equipment against the missiles and incendiary weapons used on ships. They were expected to wear cataphract-armour or *lorica* (coat of mail?) with helmet and greaves. The *scutum*-shields were also to be stronger and larger than on land to withstand the stones. The fighters included specialist elite *propugnatores* (front-rank fighters), *ballistarii* (users of mounted field artillery, crossbows and torsion *manuballistae*), *sagittarii* (archers), and *urinatores* (divers). Some fleets could also include gladiators and other slaves that were not part of the navy proper.

The men were also classed into pay ranks and ranks of seniority each of which had its own salary and duties. Naturally, the fleets also included other specialists of all sorts, junior officers plus secretarial and headquarters staff. The junior officers on the ships consisted at least of the armourer (*armorum custos*), the standard bearers (*signiferi*) and the trumpeters (*tubicines* and *cornicines*), a helmsman (*gubernator*), a bow-officer/helmsman's adjutant (*proreta/proretus*), a *nauphylax* (supply officer or ship-guard or both?), a man to give timing for the oarsmen (*hortator*), and a musician to give the rhythm to oar movements (*symphoniacus*). In addition, each *liburna* or larger ship had two doctors/ medics (*medicus, subunctor/strigilarius*) and attendants to the sacrifices (*victimarii*) and other attendants. In addition, the fleets included craftsmen (*fabri*), sail-trimmers/makers (*velarii*), rowing masters (*celeustae* or *pausarii*), and bureaucrats (e.g. *scribae* and *libararii*). The fleet paymaster (*dispensator classis*) and clerk (*tabularius*) were freedmen or slaves and were not considered to be on active service.[33]

Modern estimates of the strength of the fleets in both men and ships vary greatly. Courtois' estimate (pp.38–39) is 500 to 600 ships in total and 300 ships for the Italian fleets, while Starr (pp.16–17) gives each of the Italian fleets a minimum of 50 ships and about 10,000 men. Reddé estimates that Ioannes Lydus' figure of 45,562 men (*De Mens.* 1.27) for the fleet of Diocletian would be the minimum figure as that would reflect the situation after Diocletian's reforms in the aftermath of the decadence of the fleet during the third century. Reddé's own estimate is that at the height of the Empire the Italian fleets would have had at least about 125 warships and each of the provincial fleets 62/63 warships, which would give a total (8 x 62.5 +125) of 625 warships. With Reddé's own average numbers for the crews of the warships (200/220 men) this would add up to a total of about 131,250 (125,000–137,500) men for the navy.[34] In fact, what historians have failed to understand is that Lydus' figures refer only to the eastern half of the Empire that was directly under Diocletian's own control. This means that the overall figure for the entire empire would be about 76,000 or slightly less. (See the narrative.)

Ships

As far as the ships are concerned, the third and fourth centuries appear to have formed a watershed during which the old types of warships were gradually replaced by *dromones*. Unfortunately, the exact details of this process are not known with definite certainty. What is certain is that by the time Vegetius wrote his military treatise the transformation was complete despite the fact that he still calls the warships with the traditional name of *liburnae*. The details he provides make it clear that *dromones* are meant. It should be noted, however, that older types of ships may have still been used alongside the *dromones*. There were also other smaller ships for special uses.

According to Vegetius 4.37, the smallest *liburnae* had a single *ordines* (rank) of oarsmen and those a little larger had two ranks, the standard *liburnae* had three or four, and the largest had five ranks. This conforms to the practices of the so-called Byzantine period during which the so-called *pêntekontoros/galea* had 50 or 100 rowers, the *ousiaka kelandia* had a crew of one *ousia* (108 or 110 men), the *kelandia pamfylos* between 120 and 160 men (plus soldiers), and the *dromon trieres/dromon/dromonion* had 200–220/230 rowers plus other crew, including 70 soldiers.[35] It is also probable that this division corresponded with the older division of the ships into triremes and fours and fives and sixes. In other words, there were three basic classes of warships, consisting of small warships, medium-sized warships and large warships, just as there were also in Syrianos Magister's *Naumachica*, which gives us an excellent overview of the pre-liquid-fire naval tactics.[36]

The *pêntekontoros* was a *monoreme* with 25 (one per oar) or 50 (two per oar) rowers on each side and was used, for example, by Constantine the Great. The *ousiaka kelandia* was a bireme with one rower per oar and 25 rowers per row with spare rowers. The *kelandia pamfylos* appears to have had two rowers per oar in the upper deck (20 oars per side = 80 rowers) and one rower per oar in the lower deck (20 oars per side = 40 rowers), and the larger version probably had two rowers per oar on both decks (upper deck 80 rowers and lower deck 80 rowers). The *dromon trieres* (trireme) was also a bireme (two banks of oars per side) the size of which varied slightly but in each of the variants there were three rowers per oar on the upper deck and one to two on the lower, being called a trireme because of the number of rowers on the upper deck. The largest variant had 23 oars per side on each deck so that there were 3 rowers per oar on the upper deck and 2 rowers per oar on the lower for a total of 230 rowers. The second largest variant had 22 oars per side on each deck so that there were 3 rowers per oar on the upper deck and 2 rowers per oar on the lower deck for a total of 220 rowers. The smallest 'trireme' *dromon* appears to have had 150 men on the upper deck (25 oars per side, 3 men per oar) and 50 rowers on the lower deck (25 oars per side, 1 man per oar), but it is also possible that it had 120 men on the upper deck (20 oars per side, 3 men per oar) and 80 men on the lower deck (20 oars per side, 2 men per oar).[37] If there were still sixes in use as flagships, the crew probably consisted of about 300 rowers plus other crew so that there were 150 rowers on the upper deck (25 rowers per side, 3 men per oar) and 150 rowers on the lower deck (25 rowers per side, 3 men per oar).

The following illustration of earlier ships (drawn after Oates) gives a good indication of the size difference between the small *liburnian*, the 'five' (*penteres*) and the 'six' (*hexeres*). The six can be taken to be representative of the largest possible ships (i.e. flagship of the fleet) in use.

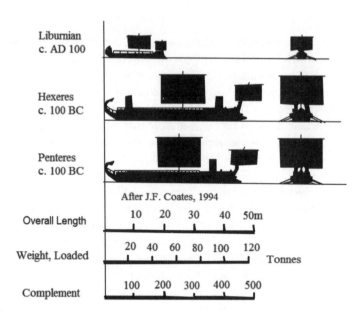

	Overall Length				
After J.F. Coates, 1994	10	20	30	40	50m

The following illustrations of the ships aim to give a general understanding of the types of ships used by the Romans at this time. The reader should keep in mind that this is only a sample of the various types of vessels in use. In truth there were dozens of different kinds of vessels. For example, there were special ships for the transport of horses, rafts and various kinds of merchant ships. The illustrations are based on the drawings of Pitassi but with some very slight changes. The illustrations are not to scale but include measurements.

Scouting and patrolling vessels

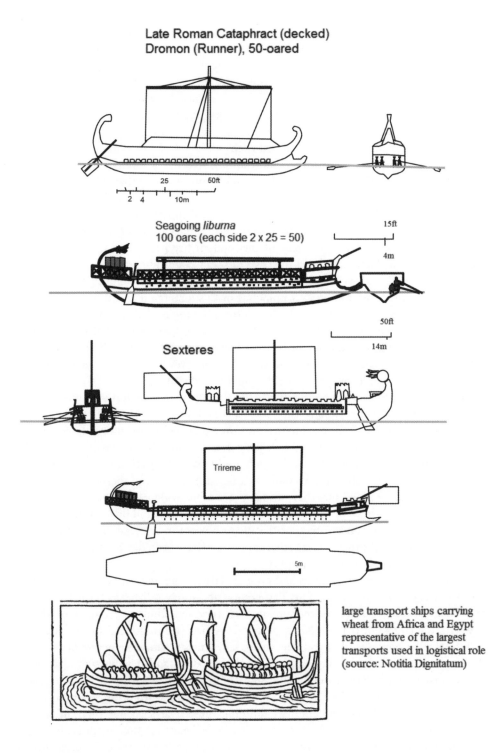

Late Roman Cataphract (decked)
Dromon (Runner), 50-oared

25   50ft

2 4   10m

Seagoing *liburna*
100 oars (each side 2 x 25 = 50)

15ft

4m

50ft

14m

Sexteres

Trireme

5m

large transport ships carrying
wheat from Africa and Egypt
representative of the largest
transports used in logistical role
(source: Notitia Dignitatum)

According to Ammianus (17.4.12–13), when Constantine the Great ordered an obelisk (length 32.5 m) dedicated to the Sun be brought to Rome, he ordered the construction of the largest ship ever to carry an obelisk. The project was put on hold when the emperor died, but was then revived under Constantius II in about 356/7. According to Ammianus, this huge ship was rowed by 300 oarsmen. As is obvious, Ammianus either exaggerated that there had not existed a ship so large (for example, a 'six' would have had 300 rowers), or he meant 300 oarsmen per side, the latter being likelier. I would suggest that this ship was not longer but wider and taller so that each side still had two banks of 25 oars each rowed by a group of six men so that the resulting size was a 'twelve'. This was not a warship, but it shows the maximum size for a rowed transport ship that the Romans could build during the fourth century.

Unlike the later Byzantine *dromones*, the majority of the *liburnae* appear to have still been equipped with rams that were used to puncture holes in the enemy ships in ideal, calm seas conditions.[38] However, most of the modern historians appear to oppose this interpretation and claim, mainly on the basis of some extant illustrations, that the ships were actually equipped with spur-bows designed to be used for running over the oars on top of the ship either to render it immobile or to submerge it by tilting it over.[39] For example, Pryor has proved that the art works from the reign of Trajan onwards suggest the adoption of an early form of spur-bow.[40] However, I would suggest that the earliest form of the spur in evidence from the reign of Trajan onwards was actually a compromise between the traditional bronze ram and spur. In other words it was not yet a true spur such as can, for example, be seen in use during the medieval era.

In short, I suggest that the ram-spur (see the accompanying illustrations) was used for both purposes. If the enemy ship had a low bank and oars were not yet raised or taken inside, the ram-spur could be used to run over the side to submerge it or at least to shear its oars, and if the crew had managed to take their oars inside, the bronze ram-spur could be used to puncture its side. Even if the hole would now be slightly above the waterline, it would still cause the ship to take water as a result of waves and thereby need instant repairs. It should be noted that there also appears to be evidence for the continued use of the real ram-bows in some art works at least until the fourth and fifth centuries, which suggest either artistic conservatism or that there was really a period of transformation when both systems co-existed, just as there appears to have been for the simultaneous use of lateen and square sails in late antiquity.[41]

As regards the number of masts and type of sails for the *liburnae/dromones*, most of the evidence consists of works of art that are not absolutely reliable as the artists could have followed older artistic conventions in their representations of reality. For what it is worth, the largest of the *liburnae* appear to have had two masts and two square sails and the smaller ones one mast and one square sail. Unfortunately, we do not know when the lateen sail (after Latin) was adopted by the warships and it is possible that some of the smaller ships were already employing it. Similarly, it is possible that the largest ships actually had three masts as there is evidence for these from the second century as well as from the Byzantine era.[42] In addition, there is at least one piece of artistic evidence to support the use of several square sails per mast for the fourth century and it is therefore possible that the largest warships and horse transports and merchantmen could have been equipped with several sails per mast.[43] Similarly, the inventory of the

Cretan expedition for the year 949 stated that 100 extra small sails were to be supplied for the 20 dromons, which also suggests a possible use of several sails per ship.[44] Of note is the fact that Procopius (Wars 3.17.5) also mentions the use of small and large sails by the sixth century ships.

The *liburnae* were also equipped with machines and artillery (*tormenta*) consisting of *onagri* (a single-armed torsion stone thrower), *ballistae* (a torsion and/or bow operated catapult), *scorpiones*, grappling hooks, sickle hooks, missiles, arrows, slings, *fustibali* (staff-slings), *plumbatae* (weighed darts), inflammable materials, landing bridges, and the *asser* (a beam/ram attached to a mast like a sail-yard and used like a ram against both personnel and ship). The larger *liburnae* could also have bulwarks and towers.[45]

Vegetius (4.37, 4.46) also mentioned smaller vessels, which included naval scouting ships (*scafae/pictae/picati*), the river patrol boats used on the Danube (*lusoriae*) and the small ship-boat (*scafula*). The *pictas/picatos* was a scouting boat with nearly 20 oarsmen on each side, used on the high seas. The boat received its nickname *pictas* (evidently after the tattooed and painted Picti) from the British because its sails, ropes and wax were all dyed blue and the crew also wore blue clothing for camouflage. The *lusoriae* were also used on the Rhine and elsewhere. In addition, we know that there were also other types of vessels in use ranging from the merchant ships and transports to the specialist ships like the horse transport (*hippagogos*), the Rhine patrol boat, the two-pronged ship, rafts, and various types of small boats like the *musculi* of the Danube.

Tactics

According to Vegetius (4.37ff.), the Roman naval tactics followed certain universal principles. It was not advisable to sail during winter, and there had to be naval experts knowledgeable of winds, tides, seas and signs of weather. The camouflaged scouting boats were used for scouting, spying, surprise attacks, intercepting enemy supply lines, and ambushes. The Roman combat doctrine recognized the utmost importance of having high quality intelligence of enemy activities and plans.

If possible, the Romans sought to use surprise attacks or set up an ambush in the vicinity of islands against careless enemies. Ideally the enemy could be attacked when they were tired after long rowing, and/or they faced adverse wind or tide. If this was not possible and the sea was calm, then the Romans were to form their *liburnae* for battle in crescent formation so that the best ships and men were posted on the flanks. Ideally, the battle was to be fought on the open seas so that the enemy's rear was against land. This made it impossible for the enemy to manoeuvre their ships properly while also increasing the possibility of attempted flight to the shore by the timid persons. The obvious purpose of the crescent was to outflank the enemy.

There were also other formations in use. The typical open sea naval battle would begin at long range, with the *onagri*, *ballistae*, *scorpiones*, bows, slings and staff-slings opening fire at a range of around 300 meters. The *onagri* were used to deliver stones with the purpose of trying to sink the ship and/or kill personnel. The *ballistae* were apparently primarily used for shooting incendiary arrows (flammable oil, hemp, sulphur, or pitch, all set on fire) into the holds of the enemy ships to ignite planks covered in an inflammable combination of wax, pitch and resin. The *scorpiones*, bows, slings and staff-slings were used as anti-personnel weapons.

When the ships got closer together, the Romans also started to employ darts and javelins. Even before this the groups of ships and individual ships had started to manoeuvre themselves into position either for ramming (ideally from an angle), or for grappling, or for keeping their distance from the enemy so that they could continue to pepper them with missiles, or to make an attempt to shear the enemy's oars.[46] At the same time the ships could also launch their boats, manned by men armed with *bipinnis*-axes (two-sided) that they were to use to cut the lines controlling the rudders.

Those ships that sought to grapple the enemy ships placed themselves on either side of the enemy ship and used the *asser*-ram (a double-headed iron beam) against both the enemy personnel and ship while the men continued their missile fire to clear the enemy deck of defenders. Simultaneously, the men armed with the pole-hook (*falx*) attempted to cut the cords holding the sail-yards so that the sails would fall down. In this sort of fighting it was advantageous to have a taller and larger ship with a bigger crew, but it was also possible to do the same advantageously if several smaller vessels gathered around one large ship. After this, if it seemed advisable, the Romans used their landing bridges to storm the enemy vessels and clear the enemy deck in hand-to-hand combat with swords. Alternatively, the Romans could also attempt to cut themselves loose and retreat.[47]

The traditional Roman technique for the larger ships was to use artillery and bows at long range and then collide with the enemy head-on or from an angle, before engaging the enemy ship at close quarters with the larger crew from their taller ship. The lighter galleys relied on their manoeuvrability to avoid head-on collisions and tried to ram the enemy ship from an angle, or they alternatively used missiles to set the enemy vessel on fire, or several of the smaller ships grouped together to engage one bigger galley. Consequently, it was always very important to maintain the correct distances between the ships so that the enemy could not pass between them to ram them from an angle, or to group around one detached ship. All this demanded good maritime skills from the sailors and rowers.[48]

The slightly later- and earlier-sources allow us to reconstruct the details left out by Vegetius. The Roman fleets were usually preceded by three to four scouting ships that could also be left in front to break up the cohesion of the enemy formation. The battle formation was usually divided into three divisions (left, centre, right), each under a separate commander. The Romans used a variety of different battle formations: line abreast; two lines abreast; crescent (used for outflanking); crescent with two lines; convex with one line (used for breaking through the enemy middle); convex with two lines. Each of these formations could also include separate reserve detachments for the left and right wing and for the centre. The lines abreast formations could also employ two different fighting techniques: 1. the *diekplous* (a galley from the centre would rush forward into the interval between two enemy galleys followed up by another; the first would shear the oars and the second ram the immobile ship; the rest of the galleys near the resulting opening would rush to the gap and then attack the enemy line from behind); and 2. the *periplous* (the flank galleys of the wings would try to extend the line to outflank the enemy line).[49] The merchant and transport ships were placed behind the battle line.

In addition, during the Republican era the Romans had used at least once a hollow wedge formation with merchant and transport ships in the middle to break through the enemy centre. It is not known whether this formation was still used, but at least the concept was well known as it was preserved in the Romano–Byzantine historical corpus. The larger and more powerful galleys were usually placed in such locales where the admiral intended to break up the enemy array. The largest ships, used to create such breakthroughs, consisted of the fours, fives and sixes. These ships had also the advantage of height and large crews when it came to fighting at close-quarters ship against ship. There were also more manoeuvrable smaller galleys such as 'thirties' (30 oars), 'fifties' (50 oars), and triremes (three rows of oars), which relied on their manoeuvrability in combat.[50]

Civilians Guarding and Policing the Interior and Borders of the Empire[51]

The upkeep of order in the Empire required that Roman officials would maintain the public order, chase criminals, collect taxes, prevent banditry and barbarian raids and piracy, and would control the movement of people and goods. The threats to the public order were manifold. There were bandits consisting of runaway slaves, impoverished desperate persons, disbanded soldiers and just plain criminals, and then there were bandits/raiders consisting of the tribes that lived both inside and outside Roman territories. The Roman authorities also paid particular attention to apprehending runaway slaves because this constituted a threat to the social order. All classes of people, officials and soldiers were required to cooperate in the search for runaway slaves. Additionally, there were both foreign pirates and pirates living within the Roman territories to deal with. It was primarily the duty of the fleets to deal with these, but it was the duty of the local officials and officers to deal with the pirates wherever they disembarked. There were also the intercity rivalries or rivalries between different religious groups or sport factions. There were riots resulting from famine, religious conflicts or politics. Then there were the regular cases of criminal activity: thefts, forgeries, murders, selling of contraband goods etc. that required normal police work also from the local authorities.

Roman officials controlled the movement of goods in order to levy taxes/customs duties and also to prevent the selling of contraband goods to foreigners. Contraband goods included the trading of weapons and armour to foreigners as well as the selling of iron to such nations (for example Persia) that lacked an adequate supply. The aim was to prevent the enemies of Rome from acquiring enough good-quality weapons and armour.

The Romans sought to control the movement of the goods by using several different layers of control. There were the local administrators in every city/town with a duty to control commercial activity, and then there were specialized officials like Harbour Masters or Guardians of the Coast (*limenarchae*, later *custodes litorum*), along with military and naval detachments and civilian corvées acting as guards, and patrols, which were used to control the movement of the people and goods.

The Roman strategy for the policing of the Empire relied on several different levels of control: 1) community self-regulation; 2) civil law; 3) supervision by local elites; and 4) the threat of Roman military action. The community self-regulation consisted basically of the human psychological tendency to attempt to please other humans. Generally speaking it was and is not desirable to become a social outcast. The punishments included in civil law were obviously meant as a threat against those who transgressed the accepted limits of behaviour in society. The local elites who wanted to maintain the existing social order were eager to employ their own local civilian 'police forces' and when needed also their own slaves and hirelings in support of this. Finally, the threat of Roman military intervention ensured that the locals wanted to do their utmost to avert this.

The Roman approach to civilian police, self-help, posses, and private security reflected the great variety of different peoples and areas encompassing the Empire. Traditionally Roman Law permitted great power for the head of the household to punish slaves, and kill infants or burglars. All members of the household had the right to protect the home with whatever means possible. The rich could also have specialized watchtowers, guards, doormen or gatekeepers, and the great estates could further have a chief slave overseer and slave guards as well as guard dogs. Travellers did carry weapons on long trips for self-defence, but it was not allowed to be fully armed with shields and so forth inside cities. Just like in the Wild-West, the civilians did organize unofficial search parties and posses to hunt bandits and fugitives (for example slaves and criminals) and they did resort to lynching even though the right to sentence someone to death rested with the governor. Roman officials and the local magistrates also used wanted posters with rewards in an effort to find fugitives. This was one form of communal self-regulation and an extension of the right for self-defence on a communal level. In other words, when the local self-help groups were successful against the bandits, there was no need for military intervention by the Roman officials or military.

In addition to these, there existed state-sanctioned militias and watches regulated by magistrates of the cities and towns. The extant sources show once again that there was great variety between the different parts of the Empire, but thanks to the uneven survival of sources it is impossible to say how different the systems were in practice and what sort of police forces were used in those parts of the Empire for which we have no evidence at all. One thing is certain, however, that some sort of local civilian police forces existed everywhere. In the West (and also in Roman colonies in the East) and in Italy there is evidence for the existence of laws that permitted local municipal government to raise a militia or citizen guard if needed. In one case at least these were placed under the *aediles* of the town. In most cases the militia must have consisted of army veterans, and/or the local adult population able to bear arms, and/or local youth groups. Indeed, there is actually evidence for the use of youth groups for the defence of the cities from the Greek speaking East and Latin speaking West. In addition, epigraphic evidence proves that there also existed a municipal official called *praefectus vigilum* (prefect of the watch) in the West and *eirenarchos* (officer of the peace) in the East. This office was probably the same as the *defensor locorum* (defender of the municipality) in Theodosian Code 7.16.3 (18 Sept. 420). This official was a specialized police officer and fire-chief. The variants of the title – *praefectus nocturnae custodiae* (prefect of the night watch) and *praefectus arcendis latrociniis* (prefect defending against banditry) – make it certain that this official was in charge of police operations. The provincial *vigiles* or *nyktofylakes* who served under these officers had the right to bear arms when needed so that they could perform their duties, and they carried bells to raise the alarm. According to Fuhrmann (57–8), there is no definite proof that the local *vigiles* would have been a standing corps. This probably means that they were a civilian patrol raised by the local municipality to act as a sort of armed neighbourhood watch in which the duty to serve was rotated among the male population of the town.

In addition to or instead of the *praefectus vigilum*, most communities in the West organized a local standing police force that operated under the town magistrates. These magistrates were powerful local figures for two reasons. They held the magistracy and they belonged to the local elite, the decurions, with resources of their own: that is, they were members of the town councils that controlled everything in the community from the collection of taxes to the upkeep of the law and order. The two chief magistrates of the town were the *duoviri* or *duumviri* (two men) who served as sort of co-mayors for a one year term. Officially they could not put anyone to death, but during times of upheaval this did happen in practice. Below them served *aediles* who were in charge of public shows, upkeep of roads and buildings, regulating markets (preventing fraud, setting up opening hours and so on), and sometimes the citizen guards. The *aediles* implemented the orders of the two men.

These magistrates had regular attendants known as *apparitores* to assist them in the performance of their duties. The four principal types of assistants were criers, lictors, couriers and clerks, and these included both freeborn men and public slaves. The magistrates could use these servants to enforce the law and the most ruthless of the duovirs were also known to pick up men loyal to themselves and use them to increase their own power.

The two lictors of each *duovir* carried fasces (bound rods) that could be used to beat up men opposing the *duovir*. In contrast the *aediles* employed the public slaves for the upkeep of order and all other duties. Thanks to this monopoly on power, the local magnates could form small oligarchies and rule the towns like their own. Furthermore, like any magistrates, these men were also subject to being corrupted. For example, there exists definite evidence for the bribery of *aediles* by fraudulent merchants.

There exists evidence for the use of the so-called *Burgarii* as watchmen posted on *burgi* (small watchtowers or blockhouses) against low-intensity threats like bandits or tribal raiders from the reign of Hadrian onwards. Since the status of the *Burgarii* was very low – they were classed with the same status as mule drivers and slave workers of the imperial weaving works in CTh. 7.14. – it is clear that they cannot have been regular soldiers. This means that they probably consisted of the levies of townsmen, or barbarian tribesmen like the *Laeti* or barbarian *Foederati*. In fact, the Theodosian Code (7.15) confirms that the barbarians were given control of some of the border fortresses and sections of the frontier. Notably, the *Burgarii* posted to guard the Danube during the reign of Commodus also consisted of some local tribesmen (also *Foederati*?). There also exists evidence for the use of the provincials to man the *burgi* in Thrace, which were used to protect the safety of the roads. The extant evidence supports the existence of this same system also in Africa, Syria, Palestine, Transjordan, Egypt (see below), and the West.[52] The *DRB* 20 also suggests that local landowners were required to build *castella* at intervals of one mile and *vigiles* (i.e. *Burgarii*) were used to garrison these, while the *agrarii* (paramilitary force of peasants?) were used to patrol the countryside along the frontiers. (See the second book of the series.) In sum, the Romans not only used the regular military to guard the borders and roads, but also civilian *Burgarii* and barbarian *Laeti* and *Foederati*.

One should also distinguish the existence of several different types of *burgi*. There were the small installations in the interior manned by civilian levies acting as police stations, guard posts, and guest-houses which were placed in places where there existed low-intensity threats: for example, it is clear that the vast majority of the hundreds of *burgi* in Samaria and Syria were meant to protect the fields and villages from the low-level threat posed by common bandits and thieves. Then there were similar small *burgi* or medium-sized *burgi* in the interior manned by regular soldiers. In these cases there appears to have existed some grave threat that made the presence of the regulars necessary. For example, the roads in Sinai were guarded and patrolled by regular soldiers because of the threat of the Saracens. The soldiers were posted on a chain of *mansiones* which served as halting places and bases for the men. Detachments of soldiers from each mansion acted as escorts for the travellers from their mansion to the next in succession until the travellers reached a safe locale that did not require the attention of the army.[53]

On the surface it would therefore seem logical that the guarding of the most threatened sections of the borders would have been left to the professionals, but this was not the case. In actual fact, the Romans did leave the guarding of some of the most important sections of their frontiers (e.g. parts of the Rhine and Danube) in the hands of irregulars, civilian *vigiles*, and/or barbarian *Laeti* and *Foederati*. This may explain why some sections of the border were less well defended than others, but in practice the picture was more complicated. For example it is well-known that the Rhine frontier collapsed in 406 only after the invaders had managed to defeat the Frankish *Foederati* who defended their section of the border faithfully while there was no real resistance from the regulars.

It seems very probable that the levies of *Burgarii* operated under the same civilian leadership as the other civilian policemen and guards, that is, depending upon the locale under the magistrates, *stratêgoi, praefecti vigilum, nyktofylakes, eirenarchai, archifylax,* and *parafylakes*. (See above and later.) It is also clear that the *Burgarii* cooperated very closely with the local military authorities in the performance of their duty. It can perhaps be said that the *Burgarii* were actually an integral part of the Roman armed forces.

Of particular note is also the existence of *burgi* along the coastal road in Syria (Isaac, 1990, 181), which does suggest also the possibility that these guarded the travellers against the attacks of pirates from the sea alongside their duty to prevent smuggling. If this hypothesis is correct, then the coastal *Burgarii* must have operated under the *limenarchae*, the later *custodes litorum*, and could also alert local naval detachments to the scene. It also seems quite probable that the coastal communities were required to contribute boats and ships to police their waters and to catch pirates and smugglers. In my opinion, the evidence in the Theodosian Code (eg 6.29.10, 7.16, 9.23.1; 13.5.5, 13.5.17, N Val. 9.1) suggests strongly that there existed a civilian organization to guard the coasts so that each section of it was under the local *custodes litorum*. In the normal circumstances the coastal guards appear to have consisted of the *apparitores* and of their superiors who were appointed by the governors (CTh 9.23.1, dated 8 March 356). Since we know that the land-based *eirênarchai* (officers of the peace) were appointed by the governors from the lists provided by local municipalities, it seems probable that these unnamed officials in question, who were in charge of the harbours and shores, were none other than the *custodes litorum*. Since the laws also refer to the existence of possible exemptions for the shipmasters from possible compulsory public service ordered by *custodes litorum*, it is clear that the shipmasters could also be ordered to perform patrolling duties and so on by the custodians of the shores. The laws contained in CTh 7.16 (10 Dec 408 to 18

Sept. 420) prove that in extraordinary circumstances the emperor could order the entire coastline to be protected by guards, which must have also included the use of civilian levies to be effective. As stated above, on the basis of the existence of guard towers along the coastal roads, it is probable that at least in some areas this was already performed by the local levies of civilians.

In Greek Asia Minor the city councils (*boulê*) also chose chief magistrates, *prytaneis*, *archontes* or *strategoi*.[54] Below them served the *agoranomoi*, *logistai*, *sitones*, *astynomos* (town guardian), and *grammateus* (scribe), which were the equivalents of the *aediles*. There was great flexibility within this organization because any of these magistrates could be ordered to restore public order. There exists definite evidence for the existence of specialized police officers for the East. The cities of Asia Minor had a great variety of specialized police forces. Some cities had also special night *stratêgos*.

In Lycia the provincial council appointed an *archifylax* (chief of the guard) and a *hypofylax* (under-guard) to operate on a provincial level in the upkeep of law and order. In the rest of Asia Minor there were *eirênarchai* to uphold public discipline. The *eirênarchai* were all members of the local elites, because this office required them to contribute their own money to support the armed force, but the office was still much sought after. The eirenarchs had a permanent police force to support them called *diôgmitai* (chasers or pursuers) and they did perform some spectacular operations against the bandits, that also put them in real danger. The best proof that the *diôgmitai* were a true permanent police force somewhat akin to the Texas Rangers or the Mounties is that these men could also be ordered to accompany the Vicar of the Diocese, as happened for example in 368.

The *diôgmitai* could also be put under the command of local city police officers called *parafylakes* (sing. *parafylax*). This office was held simultaneously by two wealthy local citizens of the town. The *parafylakes* appear to have organized patrols to patrol the surrounding areas while the eirenarchs organized more spectacular operations deeper into the wilderness, often in cooperation with the local Roman governor. In fact, the governors chose the eirenarchs from a list of nominees submitted by the city. The eirenarchs served for a year, but could also have a colleague, and could also serve for a number of years if found to be good in the job. Eirenarchs hunted brigands and outlaws in the rural territories of the city. When they caught a criminal, the outlaw was delivered to the jail with a report of the action, after which the eirenarch acted as a witness for the prosecution in a trial conducted by the governor or magistrates, depending upon the situation. This did lead to abuses of justice when the governors blindly trusted the testimony of the flashy 'bandit-hunter'. The same was true of the *diôgmitai*, who could also abuse their position against other civilians. Indeed, the eirenarchs and *diôgmitai* were also charged with the duty of persecuting Christians when this was required by the state. *Eirênarchai* and *parafylakes* and their armed followers were also known to have acted as ruffians for the magnates against other urban dwellers and peasants, and to have extorted gifts from their hosts. In short, the ancient police forces were subject to the same sort of problems as modern ones. However, the effective policing offered by these police forces made it possible for the Romans to avoid having to commit their armies for internal security functions.

Cilicia and Isauria were special regions within Asia Minor for the reason that the Isaurian mountaineers formed a particularly formidable opposition to the local authorities.

The policing of the area was usually left to the local city councils, but thanks to the scale of the problem the Romans were also forced to post some military units permanently in Isauria and in the surrounding regions. When the civilian policing failed and the various groups of Isaurian mountaineers combined their actions, they could pose a formidable threat even to the imperial authorities. They could even steal local boats and ships and become pirates. Just like elsewhere in the area, the counter-insurgency and counter-banditry operations were led by eirenarchs and *paraphylakes* who had at their disposal *Diogmitai* (pursuers) and sometimes also the local youths of the curial class (the *neaniai*, undergoing military training in the local gymnasium) led by a *neaniskarches* (commander of the youth). The local police and their Hellenized officials also interrogated the captives by torturing them like animals, which naturally led to further troubles. Specifically, the Hellenized lowlanders abused the mountaineers – who spoke a different language – and treated them like animals, and like animals they also threw them to the beasts in amphitheatres at least from 353 onwards.[55]

The extant evidence suggests that Egypt was a special case and that it had more police forces than any other province in the empire. The administrative structure of Egypt also differed from the rest of the provinces. Most of the communities lacked town councils and related magistracies. When the Romans annexed Egypt in 30 BC it had very long traditions of institutional policing, but not even this satisfied the Romans. The Romans increased the number of compulsory services for the populace and added numerous types of liturgies and levies for the civilians. At the top of the administration were the *stratêgoi* of the *nomes*, who, despite being civilians, commanded all irregular paramilitary forces and policemen of their districts. The most important police forces in Egypt were the town watches which consisted of a huge variety of guards designated with the *–fylax* compounds: field guards, guards of the threshing floor, sluice guards, crop guards, prison guards, day guards, night guards, watchtower sentries, harbour guards, estate guards, river guards, guardians of the peace and the eirenarchs, bandit catchers, and guards without any specification. Most of these varieties were created by the Romans, which does confirm as true the image of Egypt as a place which was innately disordered as claimed by ancient authors. The religious violence between the pagans and Christians and between the different Christian sects during the fourth century also proves that Egypt remained an unstable place despite all the policing. The probable reason for this was that most of the actual police and security work was conducted by civilians who had been assigned to this duty. It was possible for the local civilian leaders and also bishops (through agitation) to use these forces for their own purposes.

Most of the guarding and security duties in Egypt were performed by civilians as *nyktofylakes* (night guards) or as other guards. They were required to be reasonably wealthy because the duty lasted for a period of one year. There were usually one to twenty night watchmen per village. They may also have worked as watchmen during the days so that their night and day duties were rotated. Thebaid was a special case. It was less Hellenized and poorer, with the result that the peasants were organized as small groups that were required to perform police and guard duties one month at a time. These groups were led by a *dekanos* (leader of ten), who took orders from the local Roman authorities (usually detachments of soldiers). The Roman army used these peasants to man the watchtowers posted on the roads: that is, their purpose was to prevent banditry both by the local bandits and by the nomadic populations, such as the Blemmyes, bordering Egypt. Optimally the sentinels could warn the towns and military garrisons of the approach of raiders and bandits in a timely fashion. The guards could also be used to arrest individuals and to summon them before the magistrates. The liturgical policemen who performed this duty in Egypt were known as the *archefodos* (head-inspector), or *kômarchos* (village-chief), or eirenarch. The *strategoi* gave them arrest warrants which they then sought to fulfil.

We should not, however, forget that the civilians did not perform their guard and police duties alone without either the support of or control exercised by the Roman army. The units in the provinces did post their own separate guards at road blocks, guard towers, and patrolled roads and rivers. In addition, detachments were detailed to assist Roman officials and imperial magistrates in the performance of their duties, and to maintain peace. Consequently, when the civilian authorities failed to protect the inhabitants against riots, revolts and banditry, the Roman armed forces were close by to interfere when needed.

Indeed, there were groups of people that could cause this to happen. Firstly, there were the food riots in which the commoners demanded to be fed. Secondly, the religious factions and gladiatorial factions rioted occasionally which demanded the attention of the army proper. However, the religious groups and factions could also be used by the civilian or military authorities against other factions. Thirdly, there were peoples and tribes such as the Jews, Samaritans, and Isaurians that could start a full-scale war, which

The Geneva silver missorium depicting Valentinian, which leaves open who of the three Valentinians was meant. Of note is the shape of the formation in which the emperor on the pedestal is placed at the apex of a wedge. He is clearly speaking to the troops after a victory. The different shield-emblems (unfortunately mostly erased) belong to the different units of the imperial bodyguards.

Auxilia Palatina
Heruli Seniores
(Author's drawing
inspired by Mattesini)

once again demanded the attention of the army because the civilian police was far too weak to oppose them. However, by Roman standards these groups were poorly equipped and organized, which meant that the Romans could always defeat them, if they just decided to delegate enough troops to the task. In the case of the Isaurians, who were lightly-armed mountaineers equipped with javelins (with a potential to become pirates as well), the Romans also stationed garrisons in the area in case the civilian authorities proved incapable of dealing with the bandits. In most cases military intervention in Isauria meant just the restoration of the status quo. The army simply forced the Isaurians back to their mountain holdouts and did not interfere as long as the Isaurians maintained only low-level banditry in the area. The reasons for the large-scale Isaurian revolts appear to have been poor harvests or opportunistic behaviour when the Persians invaded. The Jews appear to have revolted only when they were persecuted more than usual by the imperial authorities, which did not happen too often during this era.

In sum, the civilians performed an often unrecognized role in the policing and guarding of the empire. As a result of this, a significant portion of the male population learned rudimentary weapons skills which enabled them to defend the cities and towns against attackers and which also made them dangerous foes if and when they rioted. Excepting Judaea, Sinai and Isauria, the civilian policemen freed most of the regular army to the duty of protecting the frontiers against enemy invasion.

Chapter Two

Enemies and Allies

The Extreme West

The Picts and the Irish[56]

The British Isles lay at the westernmost edge of the Roman Empire. The Romans had conquered Britannia, but both Caledonia and Ireland remained free. The Romans had made two attempts to conquer Scotland, one in the first century AD under the leadership of governor Agricola and then a more serious attempt under the emperor Septimius Severus in 211. Septimius Severus' goal was nothing less than the total extermination of the Caledonians and the conquest of the entire island. Only the death of Septimius saved the remnants of the population, but the campaign of extermination had been so successful that the northern frontier of Britain remained at peace for almost 100 years after this. In fact, the destruction had been so complete that the next time we hear of troubles it is an entirely new people called the Picts that causes it.

The Picts made their first appearance in the books of history in 297, but it is quite probable that the Picts filled up the power vacuum created by Severus' campaign very soon after it. According to Bede 1.1, the Picts traced their ancestry to 'Scythia' from which they supposedly first arrived in Ireland in a few longboats and from whence they then sailed to northern Britain. It is usually assumed that this is just a legend that bears no connection with truth, but just like Paul Wagner (pp. 4–10) I see no compelling evidence not to take Bede's account at its face value. It is entirely plausible that relatively small numbers of young warriors could have formed the core group around which the tribe was formed.

Pictish society was a matrilineal tribal clan society, which was divided into seven kingdoms each ruled by a king (later known as *toiseach/mormaer*, i.e. great steward). The kings were the war leaders and judges of their societies. Each of the kings had a designated heir, as second-in-command (*tannist*). The Picts, just like the Maetae and Caledonii before, were also divided into two peoples, Verturiones and Dicalydones, in other words into northern and southern Picts, the latter of which was probably the senior branch. Both of these areas were ruled by High Kings, but there were also periods in which there was only one High King. Below the kings were the tribal chieftains each in charge of their own clan. Each of the clans could consist of several sub-clans. The so-called 'higher-men' formed the top of the clan hierarchy and the bulk of the warriors. The middle class of the clan consisted of the freemen who tilled the land and could be called upon to perform military service when needed. After them came the so-called 'commoners' (subjected people?) who were forbidden to carry weapons, and below them were the slaves who formed the most lucrative part of the booty for the raiding and pillaging warrior class.

The size of the Pictish forces was significantly smaller than that of the Maetae and Caledonii had previously been, which reflects the almost complete destruction caused by the military campaign of Septimius Severus, combined with the adverse climate changes associated with the marine transgression that had started at about AD 230. I would suggest on the basis of their ability to overcome the Roman garrisons and cities that the Picts must have had at least 20,000–30,000 young warriors and 10,000 older ones.

The Pictish military consisted of the military retinues of the kings and nobles, and of the general levy of the population. As regards to military equipment, the Picts appear not to have used armour or helmets. In fact, the name Picti means the painted or tattooed ones. Indeed it was typical for the Picts to fight naked so that their tattooed bodies could be seen by the enemy. This had a dual purpose: 1) it demonstrated to the enemy and friends their utter determination to fight to the death; and 2) the tattoos had talismanic purposes that supposedly protected their wearers. The only form of protection was a shield that was either round, rectangular or 'H'-shaped. The vast majority of warriors were armed only with spears, javelins or pikes, but the warrior elite, consisting of nobles and their retinues, employed in addition short swords or seaxes. Some of the Picts also used the crossbow, simple wooden bow and axes in combat.[57]

Unfortunately, the only real pieces of evidence for Pictish military tactics are the stone slabs dating from the seventh and eighth centuries. By that date the Picts appear to have abandoned the habit of appearing naked on the battlefield and had started to wear clothes. The probable reason for this is their adoption of Christianity. Their tactics still show continuity by being clearly based on a mix of their own native practices and local Celtic traditions. As regards battle tactics our best piece of evidence is the so-called Aberlemno stone slab. It shows that the Picts used the typical ancient battle array consisting of the infantry phalanx and cavalry wings. It, just like the other extant stone slabs, shows that the cavalry was equipped with spears, swords and shields, and that the cavalry spear was used for both thrusts and throwing. The slabs show the infantry phalanxes deployed with depths of either three or four, the former being more common, but there are also some other variances. For example, in the Aberlemno slab the Pictish infantry is shown facing the enemy cavalry with an array consisting of three ranks: 1) the front rank armed with sword and small shield; 2) the second rank armed with a pike held with a two handed-grip plus a larger shield hanging from the shoulder; and 3) the third rank being armed with a shorter spear and shield. The second-rank man appears to have protected the first by pointing his long pike in front of him and the first-rank man protected the second with his sword if the enemy managed to get past the spearhead. The third-rank man either threw his javelins over the two front rank men or acted as a reserve. The actual formations may have had more ranks organized in this way. In another slab, the Pictish infantry is once again facing cavalry opponents, but in this case in front of the three ranks of spearmen there is one rank of crossbowmen to shoot at the enemy cavalry. There is no doubt that this method, just like the previous one, was a very effective countermeasure against cavalry forces like those employed by the Romans. The other stone slabs prove that the abovementioned methods were particularly designed to be used against cavalry forces, since whenever the enemy consisted of infantry forces the Pictish infantry consists only of spearmen.

The Picts were also quite adept in the use of raids and guerrilla tactics and even continued to use war chariots at least until the sixth century, and the Picts also used circular forts placed on hills and promontories. These forts were strategically placed to control choke points on the routes of travel both on land and sea. With regards to the defensive structures, these did not pose any serious difficulty for the Romans if the latter were determined to take the strong-points. The Romans possessed far too-sophisticated siege methods for these simple structures to withstand.

However, the Pictish military methods were not restricted to fighting on land, which is not surprising in light of their maritime origins. In fact, the Picts did possess quite respectable naval forces and appear to have employed similar types of ships to the Irish and the Saxons (see below). Every group of 20 houses was required to provide 2 seven-benchers (meaning a minimum crew of 14 rowers and 1 steersman). The northern and southern Picts maintained separate fleets each of which consisted of 150 'longboats' and curraghs. When the Picts launched a major naval raid their force amounted to probably not more than some hundreds of men and at most to 2,100–4,500 even with full conscription. It is noteworthy that the Romans were also using scouting boats with the nickname *picatos*, *pictas*, *picti* and *picots*, which were painted Venetian blue. There are three possibilities for the use of this name: 1) the Roman scouting boat may have been modelled after those used by the Picts; 2) the boat may have received its nickname from the Pictish boat; and 3) the boat may have been named after the Picts as a pun.[58]

During the late-third century, the Irish [the *Scotti* and probably the *Attacotti* and others] also appear to have started raiding the coastal lowlands of Wales. One may hazard a guess that the reason behind this sudden raiding activity was the same adverse climate changes that were behind the Frankish and Saxon raids. The naval raiding forces of the Irish are unlikely to have possessed more than a few hundred men. Fortunately for the Romans the political structure of their Irish enemies was fragmentary. Ireland consisted of about 150 tribal kingdoms which were grouped together into 5–7 provinces called Fifths. Each of these kingdoms had a tribal army called a *Tuath*, consisting of family groups of nobles and their clients. The highest ranking nobles acted as leaders of the war-bands. There were three ranks of kings: king of one *Tuath*; king of several *Tuaths* (including his own); and king of a Fifth. During the seventh century AD, Ireland also had a 'High King', but there is no certain evidence for its existence in the Roman era. During later periods the average strength of one *Tuath* appears to have been about 700 men. The King of a Fifth usually commanded an army consisting of 2–3 bands of 700 men each. According to one source, in the third century Cormac had created military retinues called *Fiana* that were the equivalent of the German *comitatus*.[59]

The ability of the Irish to raid Roman Wales suggests that they possessed seaworthy vessels. The Irish seem to have employed several different types of vessel, ranging from small coracles (round, curved-bottomed vessels for one person) and logboats (hollowed-out single trunks of oak) to the seagoing currachs/curraghs (wooden- or wicker-framed vessel covered with pitched animal hides giving them a black appearance) and longboats (clinker built with overlapping planks, high curving bow and stern) that acted as true warships. It appears probable that the Irish longboats resembled those employed by the northern Germans and therefore had crews of about 30–50 men per ship. Considering the Roman response of building forts in Lancaster and Cardiff (and possibly also elsewhere) the numbers of raiders were significant enough, but probably not nearly as threatening as those raiding the 'Saxon coast'.

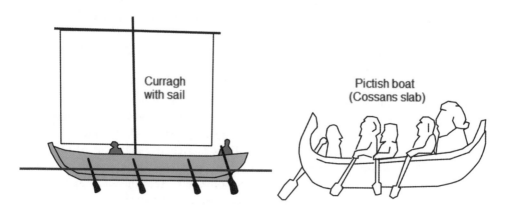

All in all, the Picts and Irish did not pose any serious threat to the Roman Empire. It was only when the Irish and Picts united their forces with others like the Saxons and Franks, as happened in 367, that they could challenge the Romans. Their military methods were simply too archaic to withstand the techniques of the sophisticated Roman army, but regardless the threat still required the building of some coastal defences south of Hadrian's Wall and the posting in them of small garrisons and naval detachments.[60] It is probable that the Romans did make their own naval raids against both as punishment even if the sources fail to mention this. In favourable circumstances (ambushes and surprise attacks) the Picts and Irish could of course inflict some local defeats to Roman arms, but they simply did not possess enough population, wealth and military sophistication to challenge the Roman Empire. In fact, their best defences against the Romans were their inhospitable terrain and general poverty. Excluding some periodic seeking of easy military glory, the Romans rather protected their existing territory with relatively small numbers of men. In the end, it was simply just too costly to try to conquer and occupy Scotland let alone Ireland. The Romans could not stomach the costs both in manpower and money.

From the English Channel to the Caucasus: The Germanic Peoples[61]

General Description

The Germanic peoples can be divided into: 1) the Scandinavian tribes; 2) the western Germanic tribes who spoke western dialects (Saxons, Franks, Alamanni, Suevi/Suebi/Iuthungi, Marcomanni, Thuringians, Lombards, the western branch of the Heruls etc.); and 3) eastern Germanic tribes who usually spoke eastern dialects (Goths, the eastern branch of the Heruls, Burgundi, Vandals, Gepids, Taifali, Rugi, Sciri, Bastarni etc.).[62] The first mentioned does not concern us here, but the last two do. As a clarification this division doesn't imply the origins of the tribes in question, but the situation during the third century. Many of these tribes originated in Scandinavia, the 'womb of nations', from which the core groups had travelled south-west, south, or south-east, and just like Vikings later these tribes formed new nations or empires where they settled.

The narrative, artistic and archaeological sources all prove that the Germanic ways of fighting war remained much the same between the first and sixth centuries. There is not much difference between the accounts of Tacitus and the Strategikon. Basically the only real differences were the increased importance of heavy cavalry among the 'western Germans' after the Goths had proved its worth, and the creation of vast confederacies of tribes. However, even this was not a new phenomenon, but had also happened in the ancient past. For example, the Teutones and the Cimbri had operated together and so had many tribes under Arminius and Maroboduus. The sources are unanimous that the Germanic peoples were bold and fearless in combat. All of these peoples were also very good at hand-to-hand combat either on horseback or on foot. The Germanic societies also resembled each other.

At the very top of the hierarchy of a tribal confederacy there was a single High-King or temporary war-leader or even High-Kings. The tribal confederacy could get such a High-King as a result of the great military successes of one of the kings so that the other kings recognized him as their lord, or when at the time of war the other tribes nominated one recognized war-leader as such. The situation in which there were several high-kings could result from the division of the empire between brothers. In a confederacy of equally powerful tribes, each of these tribes was led by a regular king (*rex*) who was required to follow the orders of the high-king (when the confederacy had such) during periods of war. In the case of a single tribe, there was naturally only one king (*rex*). The tribal confederacies always, and the individual tribes at least sometimes, included lesser kings/princes (*reguli*) that were leaders of the lesser tribes or sub-groupings. All of the tribes included wealthier nobles (*optimates*) and regular warriors (*armati*). The entire free male population of each of the tribes was required to serve in the tribal army. The entire populace was divided into 'hundreds' that were required to contribute a hundred warriors for the army when called for. The male population was also divided into age-groupings so that when men reached a certain age they were required to prove their manhood in either combat or hunting in order to be considered eligible to marry a woman and sire children. This youth of the tribe was the section of the society (alongside the military retinues of the nobles) that would usually fight the wars. The older men were required to fight only in emergencies.

The wealthier nobles possessed military retinues called *Comitatus* or *Truste*. The nobles and their retainers were bound to each other so that each noble was required to provide food, shelter, arms and booty for his followers while his followers were required to fight to the death if necessary to protect their lord. The membership of the retinue was not restricted to the members of the tribe. The tribal armies could also include hired mercenaries.

The Germanic armies were provisioned through three means. Firstly, all men were expected to carry as many supplies as they could; secondly, the king(s) could obtain additional supplies but these did not last for long; and thirdly, by living off the land. In short, the Germanic armies were vulnerable to the denial of supplies.

The armament varied slightly from tribe to tribe (see below), but the basic panoply of the common warriors consisted of a spear and/or javelin(s), shield, and some sort of sword or knife. The poorest were equipped with a bow. These men fought usually on foot. The nobles and their retinues wore the full panoply of equipment consisting of a long-sword, short-sword, knife, spear, javelin(s), shield, and could also include armour and helmet. The wealthiest fought as horsemen, but their readiness to dismount in emergencies and fight to the death made all Germanic tribes particularly dangerous enemies. The Germans often attempted to avenge their dead comrades disregarding all else, and on top of this the Germanic tribes also included berserks. It was with a good reason that the Romans feared the *furor teutonicus*.[63]

According to the Strategikon, the Germans still formed their battle lines according to tribe, kinship, and common interest during the sixth century which makes it clear that very little had changed since Tacitus. The front of the Germanic battle line consisted of densely packed ranks and files. Their attacks on horseback and on foot were almost always wild, undisciplined and impetuous. The Germanic nobility and warriors had to be handled with care because they were known to be disobedient. The Germans also despised complicated manoeuvres so that they usually favoured the straightforward charge.

Their cavalry units employed both the close and irregular (*droungos, globus*) formations, both of which were used for impetuous attack at a gallop. The Germanic cavalry's close order was not as tight as the Roman (about 2m per file, and 4–5m per rank). The wild Germanic cavalry charge at a gallop required good nerves from those who faced this frightening sight. Most of the Germans also exploited their stallions' aggression to make their charges more effective.

The Germanic infantries all used the same basic fighting formations (irregular, open, close, *testudo/foulkon*) as the Romans, which enabled them to fight as phalanxes in the open terrain and as irregular formations in difficult terrain. When the Germans faced an enemy using missiles, they used the tortoise formation. When their enemies used cavalry, they used a hedgehog of spears (if available) and bows to oppose them.

The German battle formations were not limited to the use of just one battle configuration. (See below.) The tribes that used large numbers of horsemen posted their cavalry either in front or on the flanks of their infantry. When the battle line was longer than the enemy line, the flanks were used to outflank the enemy. When employed separately, the cavalry formation included usually only a single line behind which could also be placed a reserve of cavalry or ambushers and infantry. The principal offensive infantry formations were the deep infantry column and the wedge. The wedge, however, was also highly useful for the breaking of the enemy's cavalry charge and also as a marching formation in the woods and forests.

The phalanxes were divided into units and divisions (left, centre, right) according to tribe, kinship, and common interest. It is also clear that all of the Germanic tribes had their own martial arts traditions, mostly in some form of ritualized wrestling. The Germans employed several different defensive formations. The standard defensive and offensive infantry formation was the phalanx/shield wall, but the Germanic peoples also employed the hollow-square and the circle. The eastern Germans in particular employed the wagon laager (*carrago*) as their defensive base, but earlier accounts prove that the same practice was also followed by the western Germans when they migrated as families. The Germans could also raid enemy territories in small war-bands, which their enemies often found difficult to counter and they could also use guerrilla warfare against invaders when they had advance warning of an invasion. Finally, they were ready to conclude truces and treaties with the Romans and other tribes as needed.

Typical Germanic battle arrays and tactics (each of the arrays could also include a wagon laager behind):
1. Cavalry formation with the retinue of the commander behind it as a reserve. However usually the commander fought in the front ranks. 2. Infantry centre, cavalry wings. 3. Single cavalry line with possible reserve of the commander and possible infantry support to the rear. 4. Probable method of outflanking enemy flanks by longer line. 5. Infantry circle or square used by the dismounted cavalry and infantry when surrounded; could also include the wagon laager. 6. Infantry wedge used for attack, defence and for marching.

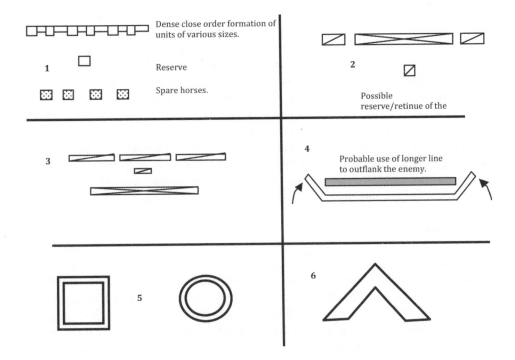

The *furor teutonicus* earned the Germans so fearsome a reputation in pitched battles that the sixth-century Strategikon recommended the avoidance of pitched battles in the initial stages of conflict and the use of guerrilla warfare to lower their ardour before fighting a battle. However, this was not the approach during the third and fourth centuries. Then the Romans almost always sought to engage the Germans in pitched battles. The principal reason for this difference was that in the third and fourth centuries the bulk of the Roman forces consisted of infantry that was more effective against the infantry-based armies of the western Germans in pitched battles than the sixth-century cavalry armies were. If one had a cavalry army, it was not wise to engage well-ordered infantry forces and the sixth century Romans recognized this. The average Roman soldier was also better trained than the Germanic warrior as a result of which the Romans usually expected to win – obviously this did not ensure victory, but it did still give the Romans a realistic expectation that they would win. However, this doesn't mean that the Romans would not have used guerrilla tactics against the Germanic invaders during the fourth century. The tactics were always the same when the commanders deemed their army too weak to face the invaders in a pitched battle – they almost always resorted to the use of guerrilla warfare.

The Roman strategy against the Germans can be characterized as aggressive. The Roman objective was always to force neighbouring Germanic tribes into an alliance in order to form buffer states against nations further away. In return for this the clients were rewarded with trading rights. The standard Roman strategy was based on the use of defensive fortifications and garrisons on both sides of the Rhine and Danube and on alliances with the tribes (both inside and outside the borders) so that enemy invasions would be stopped near the border. When such alliances faltered, the Romans would force allies back into the fold by using retaliatory raids and invasions. In these cases the Romans would always attempt to surprise the enemy, for example by invading earlier than usual or by using allies or several invading forces simultaneously so that the enemy could not evacuate their civilian population and could not concentrate their forces. It was only in exceptional cases that the Romans departed from this strategy, but this may have been forced upon them by the multiple threats they were facing simultaneously. It is perhaps best to say that the Romans always acted opportunistically. If there was a real chance of conquering new territory, as there was during the reign of Constantine, they did that. The Romans could also attack friendly tribes if the emperor needed military glory. In the end the Roman strategy always depended upon the personality, personal abilities and political needs of the emperor.

'West Germans'

The Saxons[64]

Haywood (25) considers the origins of the Saxons even more obscure than that of the Franks. What is known is that they were a confederacy of closely related coastal tribes of the North Sea littoral. The earliest reference to the Saxons is in Ptolemy's Geography, which dates from c.150. The book places the Saxons next to the Chauci on the North Sea coast. The Saxons were presumably a confederation that originally included at least the Reudingi and the Aviones in the second century. In the third century, when these tribes spread westward to the Ems, parts of the Chauci and Frisians probably joined the confederation. In my opinion, the Saxons were probably originally tribal warriors who carried *seaxes/scramasaxes* (short single-edged swords) that had gathered around some specific chieftain who then managed to achieve a dominant position first in his own tribe and then among the neighbouring tribes.

The first recorded Saxon naval raid occurred in the 280s, later than the first known Frankish piratical raids. However, this is probably a mere reflection of the poverty of sources for the third century, because the rise in sea level resulting from the marine transgression was sure to ruin their agriculture and serve as inducement to raid their more prosperous neighbours. In support of this Haywood (32) has noted that the archaeological record demonstrates that the coastal areas of Britain and northern Gaul were definitely suffering from piracy already during the 270s. He has also speculated that the Franks began their naval raids already during the 250s and that the Saxons were almost certainly active already during the 270s. In fact, the best evidence for the seriousness of the naval threat comes from the great extension of the coastal fortification system in c.250–280 on both sides of the English Channel. Haywood (36) considers it probable that most of the forts in this sector were built only after the collapse of the Gallic Empire in 273, but that some of the defences were already built before that.

The new chain of fortifications came to be known as the 'Saxon Shore Forts'. Structurally these fortifications were a departure from earlier Roman practice. The builders clearly stressed the defensive aspects over offensive ones. The fortifications had semi-circular external bastion towers, thick walls, massive gatehouses and well positioned wall-mounted ballistae. However, the defensibility of the site was not the decisive factor, but rather the suitability of the site to serve as a base of naval operations. The fortifications were concentrated in the Straits of Dover, because it formed a natural bottle-neck through which the pirates had to go if they wanted to raid the coasts of southern Britain, Gaul or Spain. The Straits gave the Romans their only real chance of regularly patrolling the seas. The system of forts and naval bases made it relatively difficult for a large fleet to pass through undetected, but it did not provide any real security against individual or small groups of raiding ships that could easily evade detection at night or in a fog or rain. However, once the raiders landed, their presence was no longer a secret and they could be intercepted on their way home by sea, or on land. Despite the fortification programme, the situation worsened. In 280, unknown barbarian raiders destroyed the Roman Fleet of the Rhine while it was laid up for the winter. Consequently, during the 280's the Franks, Saxons and even the Heruls of Denmark raided the coasts of the Roman Empire. The Roman response was not long in coming. In 285 the Menapian Carausius was appointed as overall commander of the Roman naval forces of the Channel. (See Chapters 3–4.)

The extensive building program of coastal defences and the appointment of Carausius proves that Roman military authorities considered the Franks, Saxons and their allies capable of mounting large scale amphibious military operations that posed a very serious threat to the Romans in Britain and Gaul. The motives behind the raiding were undoubtedly the typical ones: the glory-seeking of young warriors and chieftains; the lure of booty; and the periodical bad harvests. The need for the youths to prove themselves in combat may have been quite an important motivator behind the raids.[65]

Despite the quite sizable Roman countermeasures, the numbers of the Saxon raiders are likely to have been small.[66] Even after the conquest of England, the Anglo-Saxon genes in Britain amount to only about five per cent of the total population. In the Saga of the Jómsvikings (9), the naval forces of the Danish king Harold consisted of a mere 50 ships (a minimum of c.1650 men) and of the rebel Svein of 30 ships (a minimum of c.990 men). The maximum numbers of ships and men for the Saxons, when all of the chieftains cooperated, can also be gauged from the saga. The naval force of the Danish Jómsvikings consisted of 120 large ships (possibly c.100/ship equals not more than 12,000 men) and that of the

Norwegian Earl Hákon of more than 360 ships (possibly c.100/ship equals not more than 36,000 men). This means that in the ideal circumstances, when all of the Saxon chieftains and their allies cooperated, one can hazard a guess that the Saxons could achieve a temporary local military superiority against the Romans, as seems to have happened during the years 367–370. However, it would have been far more typical for the naval force to have consisted of a few raiders ranging from 3 to 10 ships. A fleet consisting of 30–50 ships (perhaps about 50 men per ship making altogether about 1,500–2,500 men) would already have been a major incursion. In other words, when the Roman forces occupying Britain already had their hands full in dealing with the tribes of northern Britain and the Irish (Scotti) raiders, even relatively small naval forces could seriously threaten the security of the more peaceful and prosperous and less well defended parts of the island.

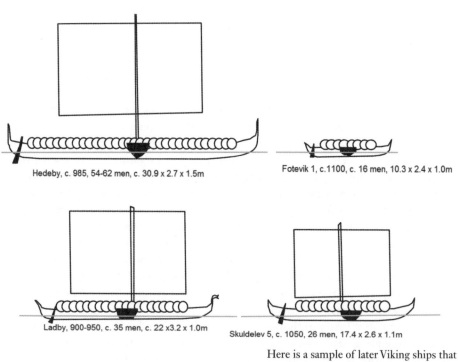

Hedeby, c. 985, 54-62 men, c. 30.9 x 2.7 x 1.5m

Fotevik 1, c.1100, c. 16 men, 10.3 x 2.4 x 1.0m

Ladby, 900-950, c. 35 men, c. 22 x3.2 x 1.0m

Skuldelev 5, c. 1050, 26 men, 17.4 x 2.6 x 1.1m

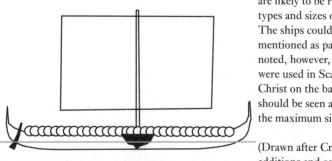

Skuldelev 2, c. 1060, c.60-70 men, c. 30 x 3.8 x 2.1m

Here is a sample of later Viking ships that are likely to be representative of the various types and sizes of ships used by the Saxons. The ships could carry more than the crew mentioned as passengers. It should be noted, however, that even bigger ships were used in Scandinavia already before Christ on the basis of extant carvings so this should be seen as a conservative estimate for the maximum size of the ships.

(Drawn after Crumlin-Pedersen with additions and one correction to the information regarding Skuldelev 2)

The Saxon (and Herul ships) probably resembled closely those of the Anglo-Saxons and Vikings.[67] The clinker-built ships were powered by both sails and oars. (See above.) The typical crew on board a raiding ship was about 30 or 50–60 men. For example, according to Haywood, the Herul ships that raided Lugo in 455–7 had crews of about 55 men. The largest ships of some major figures like kings or chieftains had probably about 100 to 120 men crews on board. If one can judge from the results of Roman countermeasures, these fleets and ships were not able to oppose the Roman fleets if the Romans concentrated their naval forces to defeat the raiders.

Roman galleys had many advantages over the Germanic vessels. The largest Roman war galleys had bigger crews, were taller and had towers, ballistae and catapults. Most importantly, the Roman war galleys also had rams or spur-rams.

As regards to armament on board, the Saxon raiders appear to have used a combination of bows, thrown stones, spears, shields and *seaxes/scramasaxes*. As regards to the last mentioned weapon, the *seax/scramasax*, from which the Saxons got their name, was undoubtedly used by Saxon heroic champions/berserks when they boarded enemy vessels and fought in close quarters combat. The shortness of the sword/long-knife helped during close quarters fighting and stood as a proof of its user's manhood. As regards to the use of missiles, the Saxons were clear underdogs. The Romans used far more effective artillery and (composite) bows than the Saxons and in much greater quantities. In fact, it is quite probable that the principal missile weapons of the Saxons on board their ships were stones thrown by hand or by sling. The later Viking Saga of the Jómsvikings (15, 21) contains a good description of the use of thrown stones in a naval battle. It also describes how the clinker-type of ships were often tied together to form a continuous fighting platform behind which could be deployed the reserves and how in naval combat the attackers aimed at outflanking the enemy so that they could bring groups of ships against smaller numbers of ships, and how in boarding the berserks spearheaded the attack.

From later sources we learn that on land the Saxons employed typical Germanic battle tactics based on the use of shieldwalls and infantry wedges. The Saxons could ride to the site of battle, but they usually fought on foot using only spears, seaxes and shields. Only the elite wore armour and helmets and used true two-edged swords. The combat naturally began with challenges to single combat, followed by a short exchange of missiles that was followed by attack. Just before contact was made, those who had javelins threw them and then the men fought with spears and shields. The swords, axes and seaxes were only used when the spear had become useless.[68] As is obvious, the Saxons were not numerous enough to pose any real threat to the Roman Empire, even if they could cause considerable economic damage. The location of the Saxon territories also posed a problem for it was possible for the Romans to conduct punishing raids only by naval raids, which they undoubtedly did even though the sources fail to mention this.

The Franks

The Franks first appear in Roman sources in the middle of the third century AD, when they invade the Roman territory.[69] In my opinion, this makes it likely that the Frankish confederation had been formed during the second century AD as a result of intertribal warfare in the course of which other tribes grouped around the Chamavi. According to Gregory of Tours, the Franks originated from Pannonia, from whence they moved to inhabit the banks of the Rhine. The story as such is not impossible. The core group may indeed have originated from Pannonia. The word Frank meant originally 'bold, fierce, courageous, protected' but it came to mean the free man: i.e. the Franks were the 'freemen' belonging to the tribes living on the free side of the Rhine in what are now called the Netherlands and the north-western part of Germany.

The Frankish confederacy consisted of several tribes and remnants of scattered tribes. The tribes included the Chamavi, Bructeri, Tencteri, Chatti, Chattuari/Chasuarii, Salii/ Salians, Angrivarii/Amsivarii, Usipi/Usipetes and Tubantes. In addition, when the Saxons broke up the Chauci, some groups evidently fled to join the Franks. Some groups belonging to the Heruls and Frisians may also have joined the Franks. However, during this period the Frankish confederacy was a loose coalition of tribes that had grouped around the Chamavi.

Reconstruction of the equipment worn by the Frankish king Childeric I (died c. 481/2) on the basis of equipment found from his tomb. For an analysis of the archaeological finds, see Brulet. Note the similarity of equipment with the first century AD German (see the photo of the German at the Museum of Kalkriese). The basic Germanic equipment had remained the same. They did not wear armour or helmets, but used shields, spears and swords. The only addition to the older type of equipment is the pointed shield-boss which enabled its user to use shield bash with greater efficiency. Note the simultaneous use of the scramasax and spatha.

(Drawn after Lebedynsky, 2001, 98 which is based on the reconstruction of P. Pellerin)

It is probable that there had been some Frankish king who had formed the confederation, but whose name is lost in time. After his death, the confederation had become a loose organization of tribes that were still known with the common name even if only small sections of the tribes still cooperated together when threatened. The Franks were once again united under one king towards the end of the fourth century, but it was only the famous Clovis of the tribe of Salii that accomplished the final unification of the Franks at the turn of the sixth century AD, and even then the tribes maintained their separate identities in some cases even until the ninth century. This meant that the

Romans were still in a position to use diplomacy to break up the unity of the Franks. On top of this, the Franks became a very important source of recruits for the *auxilia* and Imperial Bodyguards and the Federate Frankish tribes became an indispensable part of the Roman defensive system in the north of Gaul. One can say with good reason that there existed a Frankish faction/mafia within the Roman army during the fourth century.

Unfortunately, the sources do not describe the military strategy and tactics used by the third- and fourth-century Franks, but fortunately the later sources do. The names of the tribes provide important clues, as do the situations in which the raids and invasions occurred. We can also compare the information provided by the earlier and later sources. The names of the tribes show that the Frankish confederacy included tribes that specialized in the use of cavalry (the Tencteri), infantry (Chamavi, Amsivarii, Chatti), and ships. Consequently, the Franks were in a very rare position to exploit all possible avenues and ways of attack against the Roman Empire. The situation in which the raids and invasions began tells us a lot about the Frankish strategy.

Around the year AD 230 marine transgressions began that brought about great changes in the geography of the lower Rhine and North Sea coasts. The sea level rose in places over 4 meters in the lands around the mouths of the Rhine. This meant the destruction of the agricultural economy of the Low Countries and its depopulation. This in turn led to the reduction of the Roman military presence, and by c. 250 the Romans had withdrawn most of their garrisons. The Franks exploited the situation by moving in to fill up the vacuum, and pirate raids soon followed. The Franks now had direct access to the open sea and Roman defensive structures had been ruined, with the result that the sea routes also lay open to exploitation.[70] In other words, the Franks were opportunistic predators just like other tribal confederations. Whenever the Romans showed signs of weakness, the Franks exploited this. The chieftains and warriors needed military adventures and booty to secure their positions in tribal society, and the richest pickings were in the Roman Empire.

From later sources like Procopius and Agathias we learn that the Franks proper (i.e. not the remnants of Roman military units) did not usually wear any armour or helmets. The nobility and their mounted retinues were usually equipped with only round shields, spears, javelins and swords. The Frankish armies were based upon the king's personal following, war-bands of the Frankish chieftains and general levy of the tribesmen. Kings and nobles had small retinues of elite cavalry, but the overall numbers of horsemen remained small. There appears not to have been any overall high king for the whole confederacy during this period.

There was a great variety of equipment among the Franks, because the different tribes forming the confederacy used their own 'national' weaponry. However, there were still some common elements among the tribes making up the confederacy. The Frankish weaponry consisted mostly of weapons intended for close range combat, combining short-range missile attack with close quarter melee with short swords. During the fifth and sixth centuries the Franks were especially famous for the *francisca*-throwing axe. Unfortunately, we do not know when this weapon was introduced. My suggestion is that some of the Frankish tribes (possibly including the Chamavi) used it from the very start and continued to do so. A realistic throwing range for the throwing axe was about 10–12 meters. In combat, the throwing axe was used to break up the enemy shield wall just before the charge into close-quarters combat.

Some of the Frankish tribes seem also to have used a harpoon-type javelin, which was the immediate ancestor of the famous *angon*, a barbed short javelin encased in iron. The harpoon javelin was used for throwing and as a close-quarters combat weapon. When thrown at the shield of a footman, the Frankish soldier could step on the butt of the javelin and bring down his shield. The maximum throwing range for the harpoon javelin was about 30 meters. The Frankish tribes also used round (and less often oval) shields with a protruding boss that was used for shield-bashes, wooden clubs, swords, short swords (*scramasaxes/seaxes*), daggers, spears or javelins other than the harpoon-javelin, bows, and different types of helmets. The cavalry typically used lances and swords in wild charges. The most common type of bow was a simple one-piece wooden bow (a self bow) and the Franks used a two-finger (thumb and forefinger) grip. The net result was that their archery was less powerful than the Romans' archery with the composite bow, but they compensated for this by using poisoned arrows.

As noted, the majority of the Frankish forces consisted of infantry using the tactic of first throwing the axe or javelin or spear to disrupt the enemy ranks before engaging in hand-to-hand combat. In essence, this resembled the Roman *pilum* tactic. Their battle formations appear to have consisted mostly of the unarmoured infantry that was arrayed as a dense phalanx or as a wedge, or so that the infantry formed the centre and cavalry the wings. The cavalry was deployed in close order, but due to poor discipline Frankish cavalry formations had a tendency to break up before the attack reached its target. The Franks were also very skilled users of small raiding bands, ambushes, feigned flights and surprise attacks. Most importantly, the Frankish cavalry could cross rivers by swimming (especially the Tencteri) and were therefore very dangerous foes for the Romans. Consequently, the Romans could not rely on the use of river-lines in defence. The Frankish tactics were archetypically Germanic.

When the whole Frankish confederacy with allies was collected for an invasion, the sheer size of their army made it dangerous for the Romans to face in the open battle except with equally large forces. The armies invading Italy during the sixth century are said to have consisted respectively of 100,000 and of 75,000 men. These figures can be taken to be representative of the military potential of the entire Frankish confederacy, if the Romans failed to divide them with bribery. However, it was far more typical that the Frankish armies consisted of raiders that could be counted in hundreds rather than in thousands. Even when some of the Frankish tribes invaded simultaneously it was typical that they would immediately spread out in the countryside in small raiding bands because they lacked siege skills, which enabled the Romans to destroy the raiders piecemeal. In the middle of the third century, this was actually the most efficient way of collecting booty and causing damage, because once the Franks had broken through, they did not face military reserves or fortifications in the rear. However, since the Franks were very inept as besiegers, the Roman response, the building of fortifications and the posting of garrisons in them, proved very efficient. The solution of Gallienus to increase the numbers of cavalry also had the benefit that the Romans could then concentrate their cavalry fast to engage and defeat the small Frankish raiding bands one or two at a time, always with superior numbers of horsemen.

The principal offensive siege tactics of the Franks were actually surprise attacks, intimidation and city investment. These were quite inefficient against the Romans. As regards to the Frankish defensive strategy, they still seem to have followed the age old

The abatis of the 16th century Finns (Olaus Magnus, History of the Northern Peoples, 1562) shows well how the forest and archery could be used to defeat would be invaders. This is exactly the same method as was used by the early Germans.

tactics of using swamps, woods/forests with *abatis*, guerrilla warfare, and ambushes so familiar to us from the ambush/battle of Teutoburg in AD 9. The Romans in their turn countered these tactics by attacking them during the winter or early spring.

The Franks began their piratical raiding of the Roman Empire during the 250s and continued to make them thereafter. The reason for the attacks was simply the desire for loot and the Roman weakness. In fact, the naval exploits of the Franks assumed epic proportions when their pirate fleets roved around the Mediterranean and Atlantic. (For the Roman countermeasures, see the section on Saxons.) Nothing is known of the Frankish ships during this period, but Haywood (45ff.) speculates that Frankish warships may have resembled Roman warships such as those discovered at Mainz. The Mainz ship was probably the *lusoria/scafa exploratoria* used by the Romans as a light fast scouting ship. It had a crew of 20 to 26 oarsmen. It was c.18.6 m long and 2–3.1 m wide, and had a shallow draught. It was a seaworthy and very manoeuvrable craft with a small cargo capacity. (See my reconstruction – based on Syvänne, 2004.) The Franks may also have used the so-called Bruges boat (see below). This boat was a very seaworthy vessel, but not suited to facing Roman ships in combat. However, it still gave the Franks the capacity to sail past the Romans (for example in fog) and then land their forces somewhere in Gaul or Spain.

In sum, Frankish battle tactics did not differ in any significant way from typical German tactics. The better military organization, better command structures and combined joint arms tactics still ensured that the Romans retained tactical superiority over the Franks. The principal weaknesses of the Franks were their inability to cooperate effectively, inability to stay in the field for long periods of time in large numbers, their comparably weak missile arm and their small numbers of horsemen. In spite of these comments, the Frankish tribes were still very formidable enemies that caused the Romans many a defeat. Frankish military strategy and tactics were based on the use of great mobility afforded by light equipment. Whenever the Romans showed any signs of military weakness, the Franks invaded, either in strength or in small bands, or raided the coasts with pirate fleets. Both types of threats were dangerous at times of internal and external troubles, because the Frankish confederation was large enough to cause major disruption.

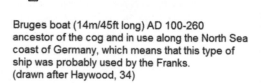

Carved stone slab from Hornhausen, variously dated from c. 100-700 and attributed either to a German or western Slav. Note the use of the lug/flange/cross-bar ('stopper') behind the spear-head. It is usually associated with infantry warfare, but this is a mistake. Note the use of the 'stopper' also by Constantius II and by the Franks in the Leiden Ms. (Maccabees) c. 924.

Bruges boat (14m/45ft long) AD 100-260 ancestor of the cog and in use along the North Sea coast of Germany, which means that this type of ship was probably used by the Franks. (drawn after Haywood, 34)

The Alamanni

The origin of the Alamanni (All Men) is not known and many theories have been forwarded, which have been conveniently collected by Drinkwater (2007). His book is a must-read, even though I disagree with him at times. According to one theory, the Alamanni consisted of the Suebi who migrated to the Agri Decumantes after c.261/2. According to another theory that has gained currency recently the Alamanni emerged in situ through enthnogenesis from the people or warriors inhabiting the area. Drinkwater has developed this theory further by suggesting that several war-parties consisting of mainly young males bent on plunder, or larger groupings of such young males (and their females, children and slaves) who were bent on seeking their fortunes elsewhere, gradually created the Alamannic confederacy through enthnogenesis.

My own view is that the core of the Alamanni probably gathered around the Suebian Semnones (or some other tribe belonging to the Suebi) so that its principal chieftain/warlord in the late-second century created a confederation of tribes, through conquest and warfare, that recognized his suzerainty, and that the Iuthungi ('Young Ones'), later one of the Alamanni tribes, were an early-third century offshoot of the Semnones consisting of the young warriors who had gathered around some charismatic member of the Semnonian royal house.[71] The Iuthungi prided in being pure-bred first class fighters and their principal striking force consisted of their cavalry, as befitted a tribe which had as neighbours eastern Germanic tribes. The name Alamanni was applied to the new grouping of tribes because the resulting conglomeration of tribes also included tribes that did not belong to the Suebi.[72]

The progress of the original group of the Alamanni can be detected from the spread of the so-called 'Elbergermanic' artefacts from the lands on and to the east of the Elbe to the area of the Main and Neckar Rivers and the *Agri Decumantes*. I would suggest that the Alamanni and Iuthungi still operated as a unified force during the 250s and 260s and that the cause of the collapse of the unified rule resulted from the series of defeats that they suffered during the reigns of Gallienus, Claudius, Aurelian, and Probus. Of particular note is the fact that at the time the Alamanni and Iuthungi were able to raid deep into Italy and that the Romans had been forced to abandon the *Agri Decumantes* to the Alamanni in about 261/2 (the evacuation had been ordered by Postumus). This suggests the probability that we should assign to the Alamanni the huge numbers of warriors as claimed unanimously by all the extant sources. This was also the first time since the time of the Cimbri and Teutones that Italy had been invaded by a powerful barbarian enemy that even inflicted a serious defeat on Aurelian.

Ammianus' (28.5.9) text also proves that the Alamanni were a very populous nation that always recovered its youthful strength (i.e. the women and men were very fertile) from the defeats inflicted upon them by the Romans. I would also suggest that there was another reason for the ability of the Alamanni to recover so quickly. Even after their confederacy had lost its unified leadership and had settled in the *Agri Decumantes*, the tribes still seem to have cooperated on several levels in the defence of their territory or when raiding foreign lands. Since we know that the Romans successively burned and destroyed fields and houses along the right bank of the Rhine and the Alamanni were able to inhabit those places immediately the Romans had retreated it is practically certain that the Alamannic tribes must have had some sort of 'social security' as a result of which those families who had lost their properties were first given a roof and shelter and subsistence in the interior and then given enough food and other help to rebuild their lives along the Roman frontier. This suggests a system in which the settlements in the safer locales were always required to help other settlements along the frontiers. It is not known whether this system operated only on a level of a single Alamannic tribe or whether the other tribes were also required to contribute to the upkeep of the frontiers when needed. What is certain is that such a system must have existed for otherwise it would be impossible to explain the ability of the Alamanni to recover their strength immediately. One may also speculate that similar systems must have existed among the Franks.

This brings up the question of how the Romans sought to counter this at times of hostilities. It should be stressed that the Alamannic tribes were more often allies and sources of recruits than enemies, but when hostilities did occur the Romans usually resorted to three standard practices. Firstly, they attempted to surprise the Alamanni, because when the Romans managed to kill or capture the inhabitants along their border it was not so easy for the enemy to recover quickly. Secondly, the Romans could assassinate the enemy leader and replace him with their own candidate. Thirdly, they subjected the enemy territories to a continuous attack and invasion so that they would be able to cause such economic damage that the communities further in the *barbaricum* would not be able to sustain them.

The goal in all cases was to bring about a peace treaty favourable to the Romans and to increase the prestige of the emperor. This brings up another reason for the war against the Alamanni which was to prove to the soldiers that their emperor was a successful warrior: I agree with Drinkwater that the Romans sometimes started wars against the Alamanni just to increase the prestige of the ruler. We should remember, however, that for the Romans this was an acceptable reason for a war. The Romans expected their rulers to be warriors.

Yet it should not be forgotten that this does not rule out other rational reasons for the waging of wars. The Romans always sought to limit the power of the warlords on their borders, and whenever there was a real danger that some barbarian ruler and ally of Rome would obtain an empire of his own the Romans sought to prevent this either by invading or by using other tribes for an attack. The Romans knew that the barbarians posed a real problem only when they had managed to assemble overwhelmingly superior numbers of troops. It was then that the Romans were in trouble. It was dangerous for the emperors to entrust large numbers of men to one able general, on top of which their professional forces could not be assembled quickly unless the Romans had prior knowledge of the impending invasion because these forces were spread out in many different cities, forts and garrisons.

After the collapse of their unified leadership the Alamanni consisted of several different tribes. The three major groupings that we know are the Bainobaudes (north of the Main), Lentienses (Raetia, with a sub-tribe, the Raetovarii) and Iuthungi (Raetia-Danube). These three tribes appear to have operated separately from the rest and may have had their own High-Kings. In the 350s the military organization of the rest of the tribes (one of these was the Brisigavi) along the Rhine frontier consisted of two high kings ('*exelciores ante alios reges*'), five regular kings (*reges*), ten lesser kings/princes (*reguli*), nobles (*optimates*) and 35,000 warriors including mercenaries (*armati*). These tribes followed the standard Germanic tactics, which consisted of the use of infantry wedges and cavalry mixed with infantry. In offence these tribes usually employed only raiding bands except when they intended to settle in an area. In defence these tribes either posted their forces along the Rhine, or attempted a pre-emptive strike, or they withdrew to the interior and subjected the Romans to a guerrilla campaign while attempting to defend hill refuges/forts. The Lentienses and Iuthungi employed mostly cavalry.

All in all, when the Romans were well led and had enough soldiers to face the Alamanni, they could expect to win their encounters. The events of the 350s prove that most of the Alamanni cooperated against the Romans. The forces of the two high kings cooperated against the Romans along the Rhine, while the Lentienses and Iuthungi, composed mainly of cavalry, conducted their own separate wars against the Romans. The only exception was the tribe of the Bainobaudes, who were Roman allies. The division of these forces into two to three separate armies enabled the Romans to engage each of these armies separately, and the looseness of the confederacy enabled the Romans to break it.

The Marcomanni

Germanic shield-wall behind a river on Aurelius' Column (drawing by Reinach), which demonstrates the good order of the Marcomannic infantry phalanx. The Germans were not a bunch of disorderly barbarian pushovers, but a real threat to the Romans unless taken seriously.

The Marcomanni of the late-third and fourth centuries were no longer the serious threat they had been in the second. The Romans fought two campaigns against the Marcomanni in 294/5 and 299, after which the Marcomanni appear to have stuck to their part of the treaty. This proves that the Marcomanni cannot have posed any serious threat to the Roman interests in the area and, just like the neighbouring tribe, the Quadi, they too preferred to maintain peace with Rome. It is therefore probable that just like the Quadi the Marcomanni had also become partially Romanized (the existence of Roman style buildings north of the Danube are the best proofs of this) and were unwilling to disturb the profitable cross-border trade with the empire. We do not know the military practices of the Marcomanni during this period, but it is probable that the influence of the Iuthungi to the west and the Quadi to the east had increased the importance of cavalry among the Marcomanni, but that does not mean that they would have neglected their infantry. It is still probable that their infantry fought as shown in the Column of Aurelius (note the rank-and-file formation).

'East Germans'

The Burgundians

The origin of the Burgundi is not known with certainty. According to one theory, they came originally from the Island of Bornholm from which they settled west of the Vistula. At some point in time, the Burgundi also appear to have become divided so that part of them joined the Goths in their trek to the Black Sea. According to Ammianus (28.5.11) and Isidore of Seville (Etymologies 9.2.99), the Burgundi and Romans both thought that the Burgundi were descendants of the Roman settlers of the Elbe. In my opinion, this is not at all impossible. It is plausible that the Romans left behind would have formed their own warrior band that could have achieved supremacy over some sections of the

Burgundi living in the area so that the rest of them joined the Goths. A good later example of this phenomenon is the formation of Medieval Russia around the core group of the Rhos: i.e. the original small group of Romans would have become fully Germanized within a couple of generations just like the Rhos became Slavs. The root of the name *Burgundiones/Burgundii/Bourgoundoi* is probably indo-European *brghus* (Latin *burgus*) which meant grand, high and fort.[73]

Ammianus' (28.5.14) ethnographic description of the Burgundi states that they called their king with the title *Hendinos*. He was chosen to act as the tribe's representative to the gods, just like the Egyptian pharaohs, so that he was deposed if the Burgundi were defeated in war or the crop failed. The chief priest was called *Sinistus*, but unlike the kings he was chosen for life.

On the basis of the archaeological finds all of the freeborn Burgundians possessed at least one knife, or long knife or *scramasax*, shield and probably also some sort of javelin or spear. No bows have been found, but it is certain that those were also used. Consequently, the basic equipment of the Burgundian infantry consisted probably of some sort of knife, spear and shield in addition to which some men probably used bows. The nobility wore a full panoply consisting of longsword, small axe, spear, javelins, shield, and helmet. The armament suggests a tendency to fight at close quarters.[74]

Unlike other East German tribes, the Burgundians appear not to have changed their fighting tactics to resemble those of their Sarmatian neighbours. In fact, the infantry seems to have been their principal fighting force at least until the later sixth century, if we use the exploits of Mummolus as our guide. When the Longobards invaded Gaul, Mummolus moved his army, consisting mainly of Burgundians, against them. He surrounded the Longobards in a forest where he blocked their way with felled trees and thereby utterly defeated the invaders. In other words, the Burgundian method resembled the traditional German fighting tactics in wooded terrain that was also followed by the Franks in defensive warfare. In short, they were the least Sarmaticized of the eastern Germans. Regardless, this does not mean that the Burgundians would have neglected their cavalry. On the contrary, they took pride in their horsemanship and horses and practised horse-breeding. They may have introduced the so-called 'horse of *comtois*' into France (Katalin, 268).

The Burgundians were the neighbours of the Alamanni, which was close enough for them to invade Roman territory. However, it was equally possible for the Romans to use them as allies against the Alamanni – as Valentinian's diplomacy proves. The facts that the Burgundi considered themselves descendants of the Romans and that they had border disputes over salt-pits with the Alamanni made them natural allies of Rome. The salt-pits were clearly a major source of income.

The Quadi (see also the chapters on Alans, Sarmatians, and Goths)
The Quadi appear to have consisted of several Germanic sub-tribes, as well as of a foreign Sarmatian client tribe, after the reign of Constantine the Great. Ammianus' account proves that the Quadi were at least sometimes ruled by a single *rex* below whom served the *subregulus*, *optimates*, and *iudices* (judges). The Quadi were fully 'Sarmaticized' as far as their fighting methods are concerned (see below) and according to Ammianus were no longer considered a major threat in the fourth century. In fact the Quadi appear to

have favoured the maintenance of the status quo and good relationships with Rome and only acted when they considered that their rights had been violated (see the 2nd book in the series). The probable reason for this is that the major commercial route, the so-called Amber Road, passed right through their territory to Carnuntum. They clearly did not want to disturb this trade. The Quadi rather enjoyed the civilized Roman lifestyle afforded by the presence of Roman artisans just across the Danube.

The Quadi and Sarmatians along the Danube according to Ammianus
Ammianus' text (17.12.1–16) shows that the Sarmatians and Quadi fought in the same manner. Warriors employed two to three geldings to increase their mobility and in combat put their trust in the use of very long '*hastae*'-spears and scale armour of horn. He also mentions shields alongside the spears, but this is inconsistent with the employment of long spears in combat. It is not impossible that the same warriors carried different pieces of equipment for different situations. In fact, it is possible that some of the *kontoforoi* may have employed shields during the approach, when it would have been held in front of the rider and horse, after which it would have been either thrown behind the back or left hanging on the left side on its straps. Ammianus' treatise implies that the Sarmatians and Quadi both divided their battle array in three divisions (*agmina*), but which could also include a separate reserve. Each of the divisions in their turn consisted of separate wedges (*cunei*).

Basically, this confirms what we already know from other sources. Both peoples also gelded their horses to make them obedient, so that the sight of mares would not make them excited, and so that the horses would not become unruly when hidden in ambush. These tribes were also known to be able to ride over very great distances either in pursuit of fugitives or in retreat. Each warrior had one or two swift and obedient spare horses to make this possible. They could also exchange their horses while galloping to speed up their progress. In Greek military theory this type of cavalry was called the *amfippoi* (Byz. Interpolation of Aelian, Divine ed. 38.3; Dain C3). In addition, both peoples used infantry, which must have consisted largely of the poor.

The Vandals
According to Wolfram (2005, 42), the Vandals (Lugian-Vandal community) originally formed one large ethnic group just like the Suevi. Another theory is that the core group of the Vandals had migrated from Scandinavia. The first certainly-known grouping of Vandals with client tribes lived in the Oder region in Silesia. This grouping was broken up when first the Longobards (Long-Beards) and then the Gutones (the Goths) arose against the Vandals. The separation of the Gutones from the Lugian-Vandal community occurred at the turn of the first century AD when they migrated from Pomerania to the Vistula. The Silesian Siling Vandals also began to expand southward from central Poland. The Sudeten Mountains came to be called the Vandal Mountains. However, the majority of Silings remained on the other side of the mountains. At the time, the Hasdingi (long-haired) Vandals lived east of the Silingi, but by the time of the Marcomannic wars Hasding groups had already crossed the Carpathian Mountains. The Hasdingi were accompanied by another Vandal tribe called the Vitufali/Victuali.

It is very difficult to estimate the potential armed strength of the Hasding or Siling groups that could join the other tribes to invade Roman territory. The later sources, however suggest that the male population of both probably consisted of about 80,000 males of whom about 50,000 were able-bodied warriors. It is unlikely, however, that when either of the Vandal groups joined the other tribes to invade Roman territory their forces would have exceeded the figure of 20,000 (their youth), and it is more than likely that their numbers on such occasions were in actuality closer to 5,000–6,000 men.

Unfortunately, the meagre period sources do not describe the Vandal fighting methods in any great detail. However, most if not all of the Hasdings entering the Roman Empire appear to have been cavalry armed with lances and swords, because the later sources make it clear that the vast majority of the Vandals were cavalry lancers and swordsmen. Their close contacts with the Quadi and Sarmatians had affected their tactics. However, it is uncertain whether the Hasding Vandals had maintained their German cavalry traditions and kept their shields and shorter spears or had adopted the Sarmatian *contus*. The latter appears more likely because Procopius shows that, despite being fully armoured, the Vandals were at a grave disadvantage when they could not charge into contact with an enemy using bows and javelins. The Vandals did not dismount to fight on foot. All this suggests that, just like their fifth- and sixth-century Alan allies, they did not use shields that could have enabled them to fight on foot.

Some of the later sources also imply that the Vandals employed at least small numbers of mounted archers that used poisoned arrows. This is entirely plausible, but one suspects that these mounted archers were drawn from the ranks of allied tribes such as the Alans and Sarmatians. The vast majority of the Hasding Vandals appear to have been lancer cavalry that at least on occasion was even ordered to use only swords so that the men would be forced to come into close contact with the enemy. The principal battle formation appears to have been the single cavalry line that could on occasion include a separate reserve under the king. The later sources suggest that at least part of the Hasding forces would have consisted of infantry armed with shields, spears, swords and bows. These appear to have accompanied the army at least on those occasions in which the families accompanied the army. When the families and infantry accompanied the army, the Vandals appear to have fortified their camps with wagons. Procopius' text shows that the smallest Vandal cavalry units had 20–30 men. There were also 1,000 men cavalry units (chiliarchies) that were arrayed together to form larger battlefield divisions (*lochoi*) of about 5,000 men. Perhaps one can also hazard a guess that there would also have been about 100 men strong 'hundreds'.

The place of habitation – mountains and woods – suggests that the role of the infantry remained more important among the Silingi Vandals during the third century. However, during the later period there appear to have been no major differences in tactics between the different groups of Vandals, which suggests that the Silingi also primarily employed cavalry just like their southern brethren. In this context, it is important to note that all of the neighbours of the Vandals were subsequently famous for their cavalry lancers. Therefore, it appears probable that the Vandals also belonged to the eastern Germanic groups that specialized in the use of lancers. It is notable that subsequently the Vandals were to form the most dangerous naval threat to the Roman Empire. Consequently, it is likely that the Vandals and the Silingi in particular, had already had some experience in the use of boats, long boats, rowing and sailing while they lived in what is modern-day Poland. The territories of the Silingi and Hasdings did not touch the borders of the Roman Empire, but their presence was taken into account in Roman diplomacy.

The Goths[75]

The original homeland of the Goths was in Scandinavia, from which they had migrated first to north Germany or directly to Pomerania in Poland, and from there to the shores of the Black Sea in the course of the second century AD. The principal Gothic tribes were the Greuthungi and Tervingi, but there were also other smaller Gothic tribes. The Goths did not migrate alone, but were accompanied by other tribes which included at least the Vandals, the Heruls and the Taifali. The Heruls appear to have accompanied the Greuthungi so that they advanced furthest east opposite the Alans on the Don, while the Taifali accompanied the Tervingi and in like manner formed a buffer between the Tervingi and the Romans along the Danube. Modern archaeologists have identified the resulting Scythian-Gothic Empire with the *Sântana-de-Mureş/Černjachov* culture. The Romans started to recruit the Goths into their auxiliary units almost immediately after their arrival in the late-second century AD. The Goths in their turn started to raid Roman territory probably very soon after this.

The Scythian Goths

The Gothic armies the Romans faced had adopted the Sarmatian way of fighting. Each third century Gothic 'knight' was equipped as a lancer/archer with at least two to three spare horses (Syvänne, 2004, 2010; Jordanes, *Get*. 103; Sidonius, *Epistulae* 1.2.5; *Chronicon Paschale*, Olymp. 311). In other words, the Goths resembled their allies/client tribes, the Sarmatians and Alans, who also used *kontoforoi/contarii* and cataphracts. The primary weapon of this type of cavalry was the heavy and thick ca.3.74m long *contus*-spear, which was usually used with a two-handed grip and less often with a one-handed grip, while the bow served as their secondary weapon. Book 11 of the late-sixth century Strategikon proves that the cavalry lancers could be very effective against mounted archers in open terrain. The Goths recruited their lightly-equipped mounted archers and *contarii* from the ranks of the Sarmatians and Alans, and the bulk of their light cavalry 'swordsmen' from the ranks of the Heruls and Taifali (both, however, employed lancers too). The numbers of the mounted archers and multipurpose troops remained so low that the Goths still needed infantry archers. The third-century Goths resembled nomads so closely that some classical authors started to call the Goths Scythians, and with a good reason.

The military organization of the Goths was based on the retinues of the nobles and the levy of free men. At the top of the command structure was the king and his advisors, and below him served the other lesser kings and nobility, in addition to which came the forces provided by subject tribes and allies. The Gothic army was divided nominally into units of 10, 100, 500, 1000, 3,000 and 6,000 men. The 3,000-man unit was called an army (*harjis* = Roman *moira*).[76] It is not entirely clear whether we should add to this figure an additional 3,000 squires so that the actual strength of the *harjis* would have been the equivalent of the 6,000-man *caterva* (Roman *legio* or *meros*). This conclusion does receive support from the late Roman practice of employing squires among the Federate units.

A horseman (*contarius* with lamellar armour) employing his *contus* (lance) with a two-handed grip against a footman. A Goth, Lombard, or Gepid in the Roman army? (adapted from the Isola Rizza dish, c.600).

The same rider shown here as a cataphract (with frontal armour for the horse and a bow in a bowcase) employing the favourite lancing technique used against horsemen, but the *contus* could also be used on the right side as needed.

The conquests had increased the numbers of Gothic nobles/knights (*optimates*) with the result that the Goths possessed more heavily-equipped elite lancers than any other Germanic people. All of these elite troopers fought on horseback and possessed retinues of warriors and servants/squires. We know that the most important of these families were the House of Amal, the royal house of the Greuthungi, and the Balthi (after *Baltha*, i.e. Bold) the royal house of the Tervingi, but other powerful families ruled by their chieftains must have existed too. The Tervingi overthrew their kings in the early fourth century so that their realm was organized into subdivisions ruled by chiefs (*reiks*) that decided matters in tribal councils, but they could still nominate a judge (*iudex*) to lead the tribe in times of crisis (Wolfram, 1990, 94).

Thanks to their great wealth the tribal nobility could devote most of their time to military pursuits (hunting with bows and weapons training). In combat each noble wore chain mail or scale armour, a helmet, a round shield, a lasso, a *spatha*-sword, a *contus*-spear, a composite bow, and possibly also javelins. The bulk of the Gothic heavy cavalry were equipped as cataphracts – or at least all of their *optimates* and front-rankers.[77]

The common people were not as good fighters as the nobles and their retinues. In order to earn a living they had to till their fields and/or herd their cattle. The wealthier commoners, who could afford a warhorse, were designated to the cavalry to serve either as lancers or as javelin throwers, while the poorer were designated to the infantry to serve either as spearmen (armed with a spear, sword, and a shield) or as archers (armed with a long bow, sword, and possibly a shield).

Thanks to the lack of extant evidence it is very difficult to establish how many *optimates* the Goths had during the third and fourth centuries. However, we can make some estimates on the basis of later evidence. In AD 406 the Romans enrolled the 12,000 surviving *optimates* of the Ostrogothic king Radagaisus into their Roman army (Olympiodorus *frg.* 9), which represents the approximate paper strength of two *catervae*. Considering the fact that these men were battle survivors, their initial strength must have been greater, perhaps something like 18,000 men. We should also remember that the Ostrogoths had suffered a series of disasters between c. 375 and 406 that had diminished their numbers, which means that at the height of their power in the fourth century they must have had at least 24,000 *optimates*.

In sum, the Gothic cavalry and infantry was equally well-adapted to fighting at long distance with bows, and at close quarters with spears and swords. Just like the other Germanic peoples, the Goths were also ready to dismount and fight as footmen even if it meant certain death. The Goths were dangerous foes when encircled. It was always costly to destroy desperate men in close quarters fighting.

Considering the fact that the bulk of the Gothic forces must have consisted of the common Goths, it is plausible to use Procopius' (Wars, 5.16.11) figure of 150,000 men for the Ostrogothic army in the sixth century as evidence for the probable strength of the Greuthungi army. I would divide this figure so that the cavalry forces consisted of at least 100,000 cavalry (mostly lancers and cataphracts) and 50,000 infantry (mostly heavy infantry). In my opinion, this is a very conservative estimate because even the less powerful Hasding Vandals had 80,000 warriors. When considering the entire military potential of the Greuthungi at the height of their power under Hermanaric we should not forget their allies: the Tervingi (until 330s), Taifali, other Goths, Sarmatians, Alans, and Heruls. The Tervingi must have had at least 80,000–100,000 men most of whom would also have been horsemen; the Taifali had perhaps about 30,000 or more cavalry; the Heruls had at least about 40,000 horsemen; the Sarmatian and Alan client tribes also at least about 40,000 horsemen. It is possible that the totals were even greater, because it is difficult to believe that even 40,000 lightly-equipped Heruls would have been enough to oppose the c.100,000 Alan mounted archers.

What is clear, however, is that the Goths and their allies could not put their entire armed strength into the field at the same time for logistical reasons, which means that it is unlikely that the maximum size of their field armies would have been much in excess of 70,000–100,000 men. Theoretically the Goths and their allies could field more men than this when they migrated with the civilians, but even then the actual fighting force would probably not have been greater, because the children, young, infirm, old, sick, and the women were left in the wagon laager(s).

Gothic Warfare

As I noted in my article (2010a), Gothic warfare consisted of four distinct types: 1) the *Optimates* under the king or some nobleman conducted cavalry raids, which also included a baggage train and servants when the intention was to take the loot back home; 2) the kings conducted wars of conquests on the steppe and forests with their cavalry and/or tribal levy and baggage train; 3) the whole populace could migrate to escape insufferable

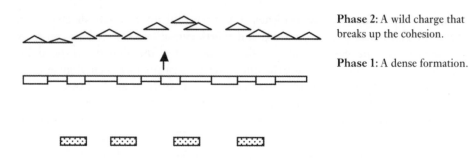

Phase 2: A wild charge that breaks up the cohesion.

Phase 1: A dense formation.

conditions, or because they could obtain better pastures and fields elsewhere; and 4) the individual chieftains and petty kings were also in the habit of serving as mercenaries.

A Gothic marching formation usually included scouts, a vanguard, a rearguard, and wings, which made it difficult for enemies to surprise their main marching formation. Their principal combat formation was the single cavalry line in which each unit was under its own lord. The standard tactic was for the king or commander to lead his cavalry forward so that the whole force charged at a wild gallop. This attack was to be repeated until either the enemy gave up or the Goths had no more spare horses. The Goths expected their leader to lead from the front which meant that it was rare that the king/commander and his retinue stayed behind as a reserve. As steppe cavalry the Goths were also adept users of the feigned flight and ambush (see Syvänne 2011a), and also in the use of outflanking detachments. The Goths appear to have employed two cavalry unit orders: the rank-and-file oblong array well-suited to frontal charge with cataphracts; and the irregular order (a *droungos*/throng that resembled a wedge with the commander at the apex) that was the most manoeuvrable of the formations and the one that was used when the charge had to be repeated or when the army was deployed for ambush. (See the mechanics of Gothic cavalry charge above – source: Syvänne, 2004.) The Gothic infantry (dismounted cavalry or infantry) used all the typical Germanic arrays (phalanx, wedges, hollow square), and also the wagon laager (*carrago*), plus all the standard unit orders (close, open, irregular, tortoise). The Gothic infantry was usually delegated the duty of serving as a defensive bulwark for the cavalry.

Carrago

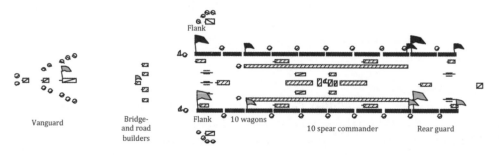

Vanguard   Bridge-and road builders   Flank   10 wagons   10 spear commander   Rear guard

The Hussite marching order according to Jan Durdík, 158.

The Gothic wagon laager (*carrago*) formed the last line of defence. The only pieces of information we have of the way in which the Goths formed their wagon laager is that when they had enough time they added a double moat and stakes around it, and rigged their wall of wagons with ox-hide (to serve as protection against arrows). Our best clue to the likely structure of the laager, the fifteenth-century Hussite wagon laager, is late, but

The closing of the wagons by the flanks and rear: Durdík, 161.

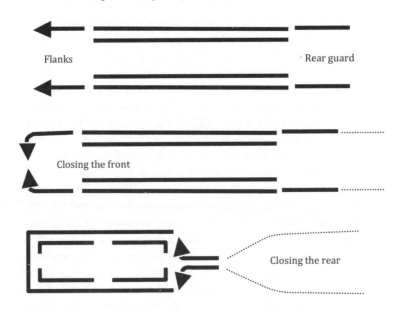

The closing of the wagons according to the lay of the land: Durdík, 161.

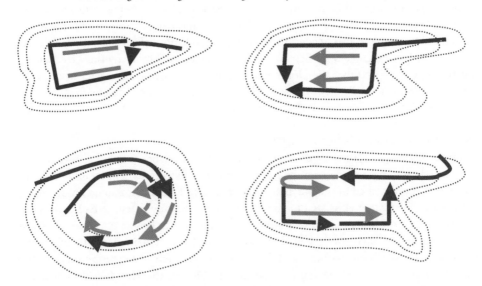

at least it does give us a chance to understand how complex a procedure it was to move thousands of wagons around and then park them in a predetermined order according to the lay of the land. The accompanying diagrams, published earlier in Desperta Ferro and which I have drawn after Jan Durdík, demonstrate these difficulties well.

Gothic Siege Warfare

The Goths had one major weakness which they did not entirely overcome in the existence of their nation, which was that they were inept as besiegers and equally inept as besieged. Their forte was their fearsome cavalry charge, which made other peoples tremble. This weakness enabled the Romans to weather out the Gothic invasions even after they had lost their field armies – as the events after Adrianople prove.

Goths vs. Romans

The Goths were probably the greatest threat to the Romans after the Sasanians, but in normal circumstances, that is when well led, the Romans could expect to defeat the Goths with their disciplined infantry forces because they did not have to face the entire armed strength of the Gothic nation on their borders, and the events of the years 267–270 also prove that the Romans could defeat even the migrating masses of the Goths. The principal reasons for this were that at the time the Roman infantry was disciplined enough to withstand the Gothic charge, the Roman cavalry was well led, the Goths were inept as besiegers, and the Gothic fleets could not challenge the Roman navy.

The Roman policies towards the Goths varied, but in general after 270 the hostilities between the two peoples were rare in comparison with most other neighbours of Rome. There must have been reasons for this. In my opinion, the likeliest reasons were the profitability of good relations and trade between the nations. The Goths served as one of the conduits of goods to the Romans from the east when the Romans and Persians were at war. Similarly, the grain produce of Ukraine, and the fur and amber from the north, passed at least partially through their hands. One should see the conquests of Hermanaric in light of this. It is probable that he attempted to bring under his control all of the trade routes passing north of the Caucasus and from the north towards Roman territory. The Romans also needed these products and most of all they appreciated the value of the Gothic lancers in their wars against Persia, which is why their treaties with the Tervingi stipulated that the Goths were required to provide auxiliaries in return for payment whenever the Romans needed. This situation lasted until Valens foolishly made a mockery of it.

Herul-Berserks, and the 'Beastly' Taifali

According to Jordanes, the Heruls originated from Denmark or the south of Sweden. The Dani had driven them away from their homeland. The Heruls were not a unified people. Some of them remained in the north near the mouth of Rhine while some groups moved to the east. The former consisted mainly of infantry while the latter were of cavalry.

One can find the best description of the Herulian society in Procopius' Wars. Procopius is a late source, but, fortunately, Herulian society had clearly remained true to its roots and maintained its barbarian character and therefore one can safely use Procopius' description with great confidence. According to Procopius (6.14–15), the Heruls maintained close contacts with Thule (Scandinavia) even during the sixth century. Procopius considered the Heruls a barbarous people who observed many customs that were not in accord with those of other men. Before the sixth century, the Heruls were pagans who even practised human sacrifices. It was also not permissible for the men to live when one grew old or fell sick. If one was overtaken by old age or sickness, the person affected was required to ask his relatives to kill him. After this, the relatives piled wood and laid the man on its top and then sent one of the Heruls, who was not a relative, to kill him with a dagger. Then they lit the funeral pyre. In addition, if the man had died, it was not permissible for the wife to live. She was to kill herself or be considered an outcast. Herulian society was also hierarchical. It was ruled by a king below whom were the nobles, warriors and squires.

In the opinion of Procopius, the Heruls were also the basest of all barbarians. According to him, their warriors mated in an unholy manner with both males and asses. This has led some scholars to suggest the ritualistic practice of homosexual pederasty in connection with the initiation rituals between the young and adult warriors in all of the early Germanic men's societies. This may be taking the evidence a bit too far, but there are still very strong reasons to believe that this would indeed have been the case among the Heruls and also with the Suebian Taifali (Amm. 31.9.5) and possibly also among some other tribal warriors. The behaviour of the Heruls and Taifali was mentioned with such abhorrence only because the other barbarian tribes did not follow similar practices. Ammianus mentions that when the young Taifali man caught a boar single-handed or killed a bear, he became exempt from the approaches of the adult males. It appears probable that the Herul youths reached full manhood and acquired similar exemption from the lusts of adult males when they had killed their first enemy.

The above makes it absolutely clear that Herulian society was a pure warrior society of males. Even the old and sick were killed. But this is not the whole picture. Even the Herulian way of waging war, including their equipment and tactics, were a reflection of their male-dominated warrior society. The Heruls, who under their own nobles and kings seem to have accompanied the Goths in their southward march, were primarily lightly-equipped sword-wielding horsemen.[78] The fact that the Heruls who had remained behind and the Heruls who had reached the Black Sea were both skilled pirates demonstrates that the Heruls also possessed quite remarkable nautical skills.

The Heruls did not use helmets or armour. Their only protective equipment consisted of shields and thick jackets. The young squires/servants did not even use shields until they had proved themselves in combat. Basically, the Heruls were warrior berserks! However, just like other Germans during this period, the Heruls also fought on foot. And like the Goths, they were also ready to embark on ships to raid the coasts of the Black and Mediterranean Seas. The lack of armour made the Heruls particularly vulnerable when the enemy employed bows. Unfortunately, we do not know what type of fighting formation they used. The only text describing their array dates from the sixth century and even it allows two different interpretations: loose fighting order; or alternatively a scattered battle formation that consisted of close order units with wide intervals. The latter option would appear more likely. In sum, the Heruls excelled as light cavalry and were particularly dangerous at close quarters fighting where they could employ their superb swords or spears to a great effect.

Procopius' description (Wars 6.14.10–32) of the war between the Heruls and Longobards demonstrates another aspect of Herulian warrior society, namely that it was fully geared towards the waging of wars. How else could the young squires prove their manhood except by waging war against their neighbours? This is the principal cause behind the constant troublemaking of the Heruls. They could not be trusted to keep peace. The Herulian youth needed their first kill in order to reach full manhood and freedom from the lusts of adult males. It was a disgrace to be the passive partner with other males, but not to be the active partner.[79] The behaviour of the Gepids also demonstrates that the youth of other Germanic tribes needed their chance of proving their manhood, which in the case of the Gepids evidently meant the killing of enemy warriors, raping of their women and looting of their cattle and other property. It is no wonder that the Germanic societies were in a constant state of turmoil.

The origin of Taifali is disputed, but in my opinion Ammianus' view that they were Suebi Germans should be considered conclusive. The Taifali were allies and clients of the Tervingi Goths and operated alongside them in most operations. As noted above, the Taifali were like the Heruls in their warrior ethos and expected their youth to prove their manhood in order to escape the punishment of being forced into submissive sex with the elder males. Just like most of their eastern brethren, they also fought as cavalry and were known for their bravery, hence the readiness of the Romans to recruit them into their armies. There may have been at least a temporary break in the alliance between the Taifali and Tervingi in about 357–377, because they served independently as allies of Rome during those years while Athanaric failed to protect them in 376 against the Huns.

The Bastarni/Bastarnae (Peucini) and Sciri

At the time of Tacitus, the Bastarnae and Sciri seem to have lived within the territory of modern Poland possibly somewhere near the Masurian lakes. The Bastarnae (Bastards) were an ancient mixed Celtic-Germanic people, but they also became more mixed as a result of contacts with Sarmatian and Thracian bloodlines. Their neighbours, the Sciri contrasted themselves with them through their name which meant the pure-ones or clean-ones: that is, they boasted of their pure Germanic blood. Of note is the fact that some of the other Germanic peoples also held pure bloodlines in very high esteem: for example, the third-century Iuthungi (Young-ones) contrasted themselves from their neighbours the Alamanni (All-men). The Bastarnae and Sciri had already reached the Danube region by about 230 BC, but after they had been defeated by the Dacians they returned north. However, some of the Bastarnae stayed on the island of Peuce on the Danube and were therefore called the Peucini.

The migration of the Bastarnae and Sciri back to the Black Sea either occurred simultaneously with the migration of the Goths or predated it with a few years. It is usually held that both of these peoples were crushed and scattered about as a result of the arrival of the Goths. In actual fact, the Bastarnae and Sciri were the first pirates raiding the coasts of the Roman held Black Sea, which is suggestive of their desire to seek new lands when pressured to do so by the Goths.

It is likely that the military methods of both the Bastarnae and Sciri were heavily influenced by their neighbours the Sarmatians, and they therefore fought as cavalry. However, the Bastarnae and Sciri were small tribes that were not a major threat to the

Romans. They could threaten the empire only in conjunction with other tribes. In fact, one part of the Bastarnae was even settled inside the Roman Empire by the Emperor Probus.

The Gepids

The Gepids were still another eastern Germanic tribe in the area. The Gepids arrived in the Carpathians in around 290/291 (Wolfram, 2005, 47). The Goths considered them to be hostile relatives of theirs. According to Jordanes (Get. 261), in 454/5 at the Battle of Nedao against the Huns, the Gepids on horseback raged among the enemy with their swords, which suggests that their warrior culture may have resembled the Heruls' ways excepting the pederasty part. The use of swords demonstrates that they too valued above all else the show of bravery in melee. However, Ennodius' Panegyric (28ff.) of Theoderic the Great proves that at the Battle of the River Ulca in early 489 the armament of the Gepid forces consisted of all of the typical steppe equipment. The Gepid cavalry was armed with swords and missile weapons (i.e. with spears/javelins, and bows) and used wedges as combat formations. This probably means that the Gepids varied their tactics according to the situation. Against the Huns, who possessed superior numbers of archers, the Gepids charged into close quarters and used swords, while against the Goths they preferred to use the river as a defensive line behind which they used missiles to break up the momentum of the Gothic charge. The account of the Ulca also makes it clear that the Gepid armies were accompanied by a train of storage wagons that could undoubtedly be used as a *carrago*.

The Gepids did not pose any problem for the Romans during this era. It is in fact possible that the Romans may have had a treaty with the Gepids of which we know nothing because the Gepids were suitably positioned for the Romans to attempt to use them in diplomacy against their neighbours bordering the Roman Empire.

Other Germanic Tribes

There were other Germanic tribes such as the Thuringi, Rugi, Warni, Longobards etc. that inhabited areas further away from the Roman borders that do not really feature in our sources until later. This does not mean that the Romans would have been unaware of them (note for example their decision to use the Burgundi against the Alamanni). It is possible that the Romans did conclude treaties with such tribes against their neighbours, of which we know nothing, or that members of these tribes invaded Roman territories as mercenaries of other tribes, but if they did we again know nothing about it.

Other Peoples between the Rhine and Caucasus

The Dacian Carpi

The origin of the Carpi is disputed, but most scholars consider them to be Dacians and probably the descendants of the Free Dacians who had simply changed their name. Nothing much is known about them, except that they fought several wars against the Romans from 238 until about 318. The Carpi were a sedentary people and therefore the bulk of their forces appear to have consisted of light infantry, which the Romans seem to have been able to defeat with relative ease. During the Tetrarchy, the Romans fought a long war against them as a result of which most of them were transported to Roman territory. Despite the prolonged wars, the Carpi cannot be considered to have been a major threat to the Romans, and it is possible that most of the wars against them were fought solely to improve the standing of the ruler among the army by providing them with loot and pride.

The Sarmatians and Alans[80]

The Sarmatians were an Iranian speaking group of nomads, who in the course of the third and second centuries BC achieved a dominant position on the European steppes. The early Sarmatians appear to have consisted of four major tribal groupings. The armed strength of the easternmost of these groups, the Aorsi (Aurs- 'White'), gives a good indication of how powerful the steppe confederations could be.[81] The Aorsi were also divided into two separate major groupings, one living close to the Black Sea and another living close to the Caspian Sea. The former, the 'Superior Aorsi' were able to field 200,000 mounted archers.

In the course of the first century AD the Alans, another Iranian speaking Sarmatian tribal grouping, achieved a dominant position among the Sarmatians. In the late-second and early-third century AD the arrival of the Gothic confederacy of tribes (Goths, Heruls and others) ended the Alan domination of the Ukrainian steppe and pushed the remnants of the Sarmatian Roxolani to Pannonia (Hungary), where they joined the Sarmatian Iazyges, and the Alan-Ossetians towards the Caucasus. The Gothic victory led to the fragmentation of the Sarmato-Alans and the emergence of new coalitions of tribes. Along the Danube, opposite Roman Pannonia, the Iazyges and Roxolani were replaced by the Argaragantes (Free Sarmatians) and Limigantes (their 'slaves'), and along the Danube, opposite Roman Moesia and Thrace, the remnants of the Sarmatians and Alans became client tribes of the Tervingi Goths. The remnants of the Alans also formed their own state in the northern Caucasus which either through marriage contracts between the ruling houses or through force formed a union with the Bosporan Kingdom by about 285. The division of the Sarmatians and Alans in half meant that their different halves moved in different directions. The *kontoforoi* traditions grew in importance among the Sarmatian peoples north of the Danube, because they were in constant contact with the Germans and Romans, while among the Alans east of the Don, archery traditions grew in importance as a result of their closer contacts with the central Asian nomads and the Huns, plus the Armenians, Parthians and Sasanians. I would also suggest that the collapse of the Alan confederacy eventually led to the emergence of a confederacy of Huns (consisting of a mix of Huns/Xiongnu, Alans, Ugrians and Turks) between the Black Sea and Caspian Sea.

Sarmatian Society

The Sarmatians and Alans did not form a unified empire or confederacy, but consisted of separate confederacies of tribes within which there was a hierarchy of tribes, the leading tribe being the 'royal tribe' and the rest its 'slaves'. However, all men were born free and if there were any actual slaves these were prisoners of war. Each of the tribes within these confederacies had their own king chosen from the ranks of the 'royal family' and possibly also petty kings each in charge of his own clan or sub-tribe. Each of the tribes had a nobility/aristocracy which the Romans called with the name *optimates*. These *optimates* also had a hierarchy, some of them being 'magnates' (possibly with herds of up to 4,000–5,000 horses) while others were just nobles. It is also very probable that each of the clans had an elder who was the head of the clan and who took part in the senate of 'seniors' that advised the king mentioned by Ammianus (17.13.21) in the context of the Limigantes. The *optimates* formed the main striking force of the tribe as *katafraktoi* while the ordinary freemen fought as *kontoforoi*.

The society was also divided into age classes so that the 'young ones' had the duty of waging war and conducting raids to prove their manhood. The elders fought only in major wars in which the fate of the whole tribe was threatened. Sarmato–Alan society was entirely geared towards waging war. The fact that the Sarmato-Alans consisted of separate tribes meant that the Romans could face the Sarmatian tribes or tribal confederacies as independent armies both along their Danube frontier and in the Caucasus, and also as allies or subjects of some other enemy.

The Sarmatians and Alans of the third century were the archetypical nomadic 'heavy' shock cavalry consisting of the cataphracts (*catafracti/katafraktoi*) and of the *contus/kontos*-bearers (*contarii/kontoforoi*) both of which were famous for the use of the heavy long lance called in Latin the *contus Sauromatus* (Sarmatian *contus/kontos*) that was wielded with a two-handed grip in combat. The Sarmatian *contus* was heavier than the Celtic or Germanic *contus* employed by Roman cavalry. The equipment of the former consisted of scale or mail armour for both the man and the horse, a helmet, a *contus*, a long-composite bow and arrows/quiver, longsword on the left, a short *akinakes*-sword on the right, and a dagger. The equipment of the *contus*-bearers consisted of the *contus*, longsword, shortsword, bow/quiver/arrows, and dagger. Their horses were unarmoured, but the man could be either unarmoured or armoured depending upon the wealth of the individual. The only difference between the '*kontoforoi*' and the super-heavy '*katafraktoi*' cavalry was that the latter type of cavalry was always more fully armoured, both man

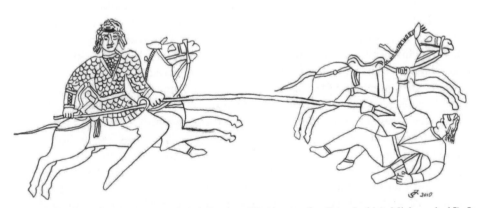

The so-called Kossika vase (Russia) 1–3rd Century AD (drawn after Brzezinski & Mielczarek, 15). It is usually thought that the men represent duelling Sarmato-Alans, but I would suggest the possibility that the *contus*-bearer on the left would represent a Goth while the man on the right would represent a Sarmatian mounted archer. However, it is impossible to be certain for both used the same tactical systems. Of note is the fact that the *contus*-bearer had shot at least two arrows before he charged.

and horse. The Danubian Sarmatians appear to have adopted the use of the shield and possibly also a lighter version of the *contus* from the Germans by the end of the third century. Some of the poorer Sarmatians and Alans appear to have been equipped as traditional nomadic light cavalry mounted archers (*hippotoxotai*) equipped with both bows and swords and possibly also with short spears and/or javelins, the use of which is suggested by archaeological grave finds. There is some evidence to suggest the possible use of infantry by the Sarmatians of the Danube. It is indeed feasible that they had some small numbers of footmen (poorest of the poor or allies) after the populace at large became more and more sedentary in their habits. (See also the chapter on Goths.)

Alano-Sarmatian warfare was based on their abundant stock of horses. Their breeding program was a great success and used horses with superb endurance. The heaviest stock could carry full cataphract equipment and still perform long endurance riding to achieve a military surprise. It was not without reason that both Hadrian and Probus rode captured Sarmatian horses. According to the SHA (Probus 8.3), Probus' 'Alan' could run about 150km/day for up to eight or ten days! This distance could be increased even further by taking along several horses, as they often did. The horses were marked with *tamgas* (a *tamga* is heraldic symbol) which not only showed the ownership but also the origin of the horse. The different Sarmatian breeds were highly valued! The Sarmatians may also have employed proto-stirrups like the Scythians before them. (See also the Chapter on Quadi.)

Alans of the Caucasus according to Ammianus
According to Ammianus (31.2.12–25), the various Alan (Halani) tribes consisted of two groups, the East and West Alans, which were widely separated [the East and West Alans, sometimes the Black and White Alans]. This would suggest that there were also Alans further east or that some of the Alans had moved further west, but this does not concern us here. Ammianus claims that all Alans followed similar customs. They dwelled in wagons covered with rounded canopies of bark which they drove together with their flocks of cattle and horses over the boundless wastes. When they reached a place rich in pasture, they parked their carts in a circle and fed their beasts. They were also justifiably famous for the high quality of their horses, because they paid particular attention to the breeding of horses. This implies that the Alans possessed better horses than the other nomads. All those who were unfit for war (young, old, and women) stayed close to the wagons while the young men were taught riding and fighting skills. Ammianus described the Alans as tall and handsome men with blond hair. He also claimed that the Alans resembled the Huns in their manner of life and habits, except that they were less savage. This suggests the probability that the Alans also used scattered cavalry wedges and archery equally well to harass the enemy before they galloped to close range where they used their long pikes, swords and lassoes against the enemy, but that they did not employ the same style of strategy of terror and devastation against their enemies as did the Huns. This implies that the role of the archery was more important among the Alans than among the rest of the Sarmatians, which is confirmed by the other accounts (for example, Armenian and Georgian Chronicles and later by Procopius). By the late-third century the Alans employed both the nomadic archery tactics in scattered groups/wedges and the Persian shower-archery tactics with stationary close-order lines.

Ammianus states that the Alans of the Caucasus directed their plundering and hunting expeditions as far as the Maeotic Sea and the Cimmerian Bosporus, and also to Armenia and Media. He further noted that the Alans enjoyed a life of danger and warfare, and considered such a man happy who died in battle. They also took heads as trophies, stripped off the skins of the dead as horse trappings, and worshipped a naked sword fixed in the ground as their god of war. The Alans also did not know the meaning of slavery, because all were born free, and they chose their chiefs on the basis of their military abilities. In sum, Ammianus praises the military qualities of the Alans highly.

Sarmato–Alan Tactics

The Sarmatians and Alans fought wisely. They adapted their tactics to the circumstances. The most typical form of warfare was raiding by the young ones in which the endurance and speed of horses was of great benefit. If the whole force was lightly equipped (*kontoforoi* and *hippotoxotai*) for this purpose, they could be gone before the enemy could mount a response. The Sarmatians did not consider flight a disgrace. They would rather survive and fight another day.

The accounts of Aelian and the Strategikon give us a relatively good chance of reconstructing the cavalry battle formation used by the Sarmatians and Alans. According to the 'Alan Drill Formation' in the Strategikon, the Alan array consisted of a single line of cavalry which was divided into units of *koursores* (runners/skirmishers/assault troops) and *defensores* (defenders). The *moirai* (at most 2,000–3,000 men) were arrayed 2–400 hundred feet (a Roman foot = 29.6cm, therefore c.60–120m; a Byzantine foot 31.23cm, therefore c.62–125m) apart from each other. The Alan Drill had two variants, both of which were based on the use of feigned flight and skirmishing. In the first, the *koursores* charged out of the formation at a gallop as if in pursuit (in irregular order), and then turned back and retreated into the intervals and reformed themselves. Next the reformed *koursores* (by now

The Roman Alan Drill.
(Not to scale! Shows only the principle and not all of the units)
The cavalry arrayed in one line consisting of *moirai* of *koursores* and *defensores*. The *moirai* (at most 2,000–3,000 men) were arrayed c.60–120m apart. The *moirai* would have consisted of the *tagmata/banda* (c. 200–400 men). The *koursores* (initially deployed as rank-and-file oblongs) were used as pursuers or skirmishers (now in irregular order) in front of the array. If the enemy attacked, the *koursores* turned and feigned flight by performing a sudden about turn, or by counter-galloping through the files or by having the unit wheel right. The use of the irregular order/loose wedge would have enabled the use of all these variants. After the feigned flight, either the *koursores* together with the *defensores* attacked the pursuers frontally, or the *koursores* attacked the pursuers' flanks.

definitely in irregular order) turned around and together with the defenders charged against the (pursuing) enemy. In the second variant the *koursores* turned around in the intervals and charged out against the flanks of the pursuing enemy unit.

The use of *koursores* and *defensores* doesn't necessarily imply the use of two different types of troops (light and heavy), because in the Roman version of the Alan Drill both were equipped similarly, but rather implied two different ways of using similarly-equipped men: that is, both the *defensores* and *koursores* could consist of similarly equipped men so that the cataphracts (nobles) of each tribe would be posted in front and the less well equipped men behind. Regardless, if the tribal unit did not possess enough cataphracts to form the front rank this system still facilitated the simultaneous use of light and heavy cavalry so that the lightly-equipped units could be deployed as *koursores*.

The information in the Byzantine Interpolation of Aelian (Devine 38.1–39.4; Dain C1–D4) suggests that the Alans and Sarmatians used deep oblong shaped formations and long spears in combat. The information in the Strategikon provides some support for this while also noting the use of irregular order. The Alans and Sarmatians were initially deployed as deep oblongs consisting of ranks and files, but when these units were used for skirmishing or pursuit, these adopted the *droungos*-irregular order. In short, the Sarmatians and Alans seem to have employed two different unit formations.

On the basis of the information in the Strategikon and Tacitus (History 1.79) the Sarmatian force appears to have consisted of 'divisions' (perhaps about 6,000–10,000–12,000 horsemen), *'moirai'* (regiments of c. 2,000–3,000 horsemen), *'banda'* ('flags' of c. 200–400 horsemen), and *'turmae'* (troops of c. 32–36 horsemen?). The information in Ammianus suggests that the entire force was divided into three sections/divisions (left, centre, right) while the information in the Strategikon and Trajan's Column suggests that every other *moira* was almost always deployed in front as a line of skirmishers.[82]

In addition to their standard tactics the Sarmatians and Alans could also use the standard nomadic tactics of loose and mobile wedges and archery to pepper the enemy with arrows, together with the use of ambushes. The Alans also employed the Sasanian style of archery with close-order units, but this tactic was apparently not employed by the rest of the Sarmatians.

The Roman Response

The Sarmatians and Alans and their tactical systems did not pose any significant problem for the Romans even if the threat was still taken very seriously as the plentiful garrisons and fortifications along the Danube show, because: the Sarmatians along the Danube had settlements that could be targeted, which made them vulnerable; the tribes were so divided that the Romans could engage them separately; the Romans could divide their enemies further through the use of diplomacy as well as by employing other tribes as their allies; the Danube with its forts and fleets gave the Romans a significant advantage as long as it did not freeze; the use of infantry gave the Romans advantage over their enemies in pitched battles; by the mid-third century the Roman cavalry also appears to have held the upper hand over its enemy; and the Iberians and Armenians usually took care of the Alans. However, the fact that the Romans copied Alan cavalry tactics still proves that they appreciated their cavalry tactics highly.

The Greek Cities of the Black Sea and Bosporan Kingdom[83]

The Greek colonies/cities of the Black Sea had been Roman client states/protectorates ever since the first century BC, but in the course of the third century the situation was changed as a result of the arrival of the Gothic Confederacy on the Ukrainian steppes. The Goths and their allies either subdued or destroyed most of the cities, leaving only a small number of cities like Cherson (Chersonesus) and probably also Olbia as Roman protectorates. In the meantime, the native royal house of the Bosporan Kingdom friendly to the Romans had passed away and was replaced by a 'Sarmatian' one with the result that the kingdom abandoned their former friendship with the Romans and provided shipping for the Goths. The importance of the Crimea and Ukraine to the Romans arose from their importance as suppliers of grain and as middlemen in trade, and it was these that were most badly affected as a result of the Gothic onslaught. With Bosporan support the Goths and their allies were able to prey upon Roman shipping and pillage the coastal areas of the Caucasus, Asia Minor and the Balkans. In some cases they even penetrated into the Roman interior or to the Mediterranean.

Ballistae wagons/carts. Sources: Syvänne, 2004; 1–3) De re militari, Vatican Library, Cod.Gr.1164, f.238v, Rome (G.T Dennis, *Three Byzantine Military Treatises*, CFBH 25, Washington D.C. (1985), 241ff, under the title Campaign Organization and Tactics, 261); 4) De rebus bellicis Tabula III (Latina Monacensis) Ballista Quadrirotis (DRB 7), in *Anonymi auctoris, de rebus bellicis recensuit*, Robert J. Ireland, Teubner (1984), Tabula 3; Syvänne, 2004. The numbers 1, 3–4 are definitely arrow shooters, but in contrast to my previous guess in my doctoral dissertation, I now believe that it is possible that number 2 is a stone thrower of the *onager* type. These figures show that it was possible to form a truly effective wagon fort by using the ballistae wagons, if there existed enough time for that. Similarly, the use of wagons to protect the rear was undoubtedly a very effective means of protecting the rear since (even excluding the use of missiles) the above wagons would have created a serious obstacle to any enemy force.

The situation changed after the Romans had managed to destroy the mass migration of the Gothic Confederacy in 267–271. The Goths were forced to withdraw temporarily from the Black Sea back to the steppes while the Romans themselves managed to regain some of the lost territory, but not all of it, as the Sarmatian Royal House of the Bosporan Kingdom managed to retain their freedom of action, which meant that the Romans could no longer post a detachment of their fleet in their waters.

The military organization of the Greek colonies still under Roman rule and of the Bosporan Kingdom was a mix of Greek, Sarmatian and Roman influences, but the exact details are unknown. All that we know is based on some extant pieces of art and archaeological finds and a few scattered references in the narrative sources. In both Olbia and Cherson there appears to have been a council of six *strategoi* under the chief magistrate and primate (*stefanêforountos* and *prôteuontos*, i.e. president). In addition, it is likely that there were officers called *chiliarchoi*, *tagmatarchai*, and *lochagoi* just like there were in the Bosporan army. The military seems to have consisted of the levy of the male populace including the Sarmatians living in the area together with variable numbers of Sarmatian mercenaries. The army consisted of the Sarmatian light and heavy cavalry and of the infantry either armed in Roman manner or as light infantry. In addition, the Greeks also used war-chariots/wagons of the type later used by the Hussites inside which they posted soldiers armed with *cheirobalistrai* (torsion-powered crossbows). It is quite possible or even probable that the Greeks had copied the use of the war-wagons from the Sarmatians and Alans or Goths, but with the addition of their own native torsion-crossbows and ballistae (see previous page). This combination proved highly effective against Sarmatian cavalry forces. The fleets of these cities seem to have consisted of the local shipping, probably under a *navarchos*, and of the Roman naval detachments posted in these cities.

At the top of the military hierarchy in the Bosporan Kingdom stood the king and below him either a *strategos* or a council of *strategoi*. Unfortunately, all our evidence is based on some extant inscriptions that allow many different interpretations. Consequently, it is also possible that the *strategoi* could have been commanders of military districts or cities, and in the case of Gorgippia there may even have been several *strategoi* in the city. On the basis of the epigraphic evidence there were also officers called *chiliarchoi*, *tagmatarchai*, and *lochagoi*, but these appear not to have had the same meaning as their equivalent ranks had in the Hellenistic military or later in the Byzantine military. For example, the *lochages Tanaeiton* implies that there was only one *lochagos* in the city of Tanais rather than several as one would expect if the *lochagos* had been the equivalent of a file leader as in the Greek and Byzantine military theory. In addition, there is an inscription from Panticeum that mentions *speirarchos* Gattion, which suggests that there may also have been separate commanders for infantry units of cohort size. Further, there were separate commanders of fortifications and men with ranks of '*o epi tes nesou*', whatever that means. The commander of the Bosporan fleet was called *navarchos* (admiral).

The army of the Bosporan Kingdom consisted of Sarmatian-style cavalry, mainly provided by Sarmatian and Alan settlers, and Roman style infantry with its light infantry components. After about 270 the army also included some Goths and other Germans. There is also some evidence for the adoption of Gothic style equipment, in particular

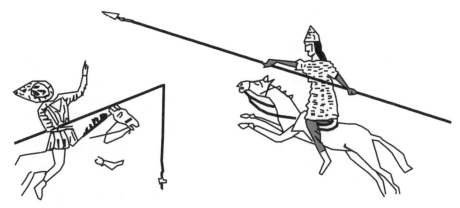

Drawn after a tomb painting in Panticapaeum (c. 2nd century AD)

the adoption of the round umbo (shield boss). It appears likely that the whole free male population was liable to perform military service just like it was among the Sarmatians. Among the Sarmatians the nobles were required to contribute five to ten horsemen – or more – to the army depending upon their wealth. The cavalry was equipped either as 'heavy cavalry' cataphracts/*kontoforoi*, or as light cavalry archers. The cataphract was equipped with full scale armour (both man and horse), helmet, long sword, short sword (sometimes), dagger (sometimes), bow, and *contus Sarmaticus*. The quivers consisted either of the *gorytus* (bow and quiver) or of separate quivers. Such quivers could have up to 300 arrows. The equipment of the *kontoforos* was alike except that he did not necessarily use any armour or helmet (see above). The light cavalry did not necessarily use armour or helmets and was equipped with a long sword, short sword, bow and javelins, and possibly also with a shield. The infantrymen were equipped with large oval or medium-sized round shields, long swords, short spears, javelins and bows depending upon the type of unit. The principal striking force of the late-third century Bosporan army consisted of its Sarmatian style cavalry, which could, when well led and in large numbers, cause serious problems for the Romans. The Bosporan campaign against Constantine in 323 may imply that the Bosporans used at that date large numbers of ships able to transport their entire army to the Danube. They may also have had a Gothic royal house.

Caucasus and Armenian highlands
The peoples of the Caucasus consisted of several different nations, tribes and language groups. The most important of these were the Iberians, Colchians/Lazicans, and Albanians and even these kingdoms included different tribes with different languages. To the south of them were the Armenians in the Armenian Highlands, who occupied a strategic position between Rome and Persia. Even though all of them had their own cultural peculiarities and native traditions, their administrative structures and culture still owed much to Iranian influence and all of these kingdoms were ruled by the members of the Arsacid house. Their position between the two superpowers of the age, the Romans and Parthians/Persians, ensured that neither the Romans or Persians could dominate them entirely.

Depending upon the time period, the Roman encroachment into this zone enabled them to make some or all of the states into their client kingdoms. The Persians were obviously not prepared to tolerate this and pushed the Romans away whenever they could do so. The other side of the coin was that all of these kingdoms could also use either of the superpowers against the other in order to gain some semblance of independence. However, thanks to their sizable military establishment the Armenians were a special case. When united under able leadership, the Armenians could defend themselves effectively against either of the superpowers. Regardless, the feudal nature of these societies, Armenia included, also meant that those who were dissatisfied with the current ruler could always seek help from one or the other of the superpowers, which the superpowers eagerly exploited to their own advantage.

In addition to these came the multitude of local tribes of the Caucasus and the (semi-) nomads of the Northern Caucasus. All of these could act independently or as part of a larger coalition of tribes, feudal lords, or states, which complicated the politics in the area.

The strategic location of the Caucasus and Armenian Highlands ensured that the superpowers would not leave the kingdoms alone, but would always pay close attention to their affairs. The most significant of these reasons were: 1) Both sides could invade the territories of the other through Armenia; 2) The possession of the passes through the Caucasus gave the ability to block the invasion routes of the northern nomads or to let them through as needed; 3) If the Persians were able to conquer Colchis, they could threaten Byzantium/Constantinople from the sea; 4) There were gold mines in Colchis, Svania, Iberia and Armenia (in Sper); and 5) The fact that one branch of the Silk Road also passed through this area was not unimportant either.

Of these areas Colchis/Lazica, despite being ruled by native kings, was in practice almost continually under direct Roman control thanks to the Roman naval supremacy in the Black Sea. The Romans lost control of Colchis only for brief periods of time. The control or allegiance of the other areas was more heavily contested, but the conversion of these areas into Christianity tilted their situation slightly in favour of the Romans.

Most of the Caucasus was and is covered by mountains and forests, which has meant that the permanent occupation of any part of it has demanded an inordinate amount (or wastage) of resources and manpower for any aspirant conqueror to achieve. Whenever the enemy forces have advanced in strength against the population centres, at least part of the population and especially its arms-bearing male population have been in the habit of seeking refuge in the mountains.[84]

The hardy mountaineers could put up a spirited fight, but could also prove to be ideal recruits and allies for the armies of the superpowers. It was and is cheaper for the superpowers to exercise their influence/power in the area either through alliances or by employing local warlords to keep order. Once again Armenia was a special case. The sizable and effective army ensured full independence of action for Armenia when it was internally at harmony with itself.

Armenia[85]

Background

Armenia had been ruled by an Armenianized branch of the Parthian Royal family the Arsacids ever since the reign of Tiridates I (AD 53–75), whose position had been confirmed by a treaty between Rome and Parthia during the reign of Nero in 66. The overthrow of the Arsacids of Iran by the Sasanians changed the situation. The Arsacid king of Armenia, Khosrov, had the duty of exacting revenge and henceforth there existed a blood feud between the rulers of Armenia and Persia. The situation changed temporarily when Khosrov was murdered by a Persian assassin in ca. 256–257 – who was actually Khosrov's distant relative, Anak from the House of the Surens.[86] According to the Armenian tradition, when the Persians invaded in ca.258–261, the regent Artavasdes Mamikonean managed to take Khosrov's underage son Trdat/Tiridates to the safety of Roman territory, where he was raised in the house of the count Licinius.

After this, Armenia was ruled by a member of the Sasanian family who had the title of the Great King of Armenia. The first of these was Shapur I's son Hormizd who subsequently also became the Persian 'King-of-Kings' in ca.270/1–272. His brother Narses replaced him and ruled Armenia (and Iberia) and acted as a sort of viceroy of the western front between 270/1–292/3. Narses became the king of kings of Persia in his turn in 292/293.

Trdat/Tiridates proved his loyalty to the Romans and valour beyond any doubt during the Gothic war of 276 as a result of which Probus gave Trdat some Roman forces to bolster his Armenian followers and sent him back to Armenia to reclaim the crown in about 277/8. Thanks to the fact that the Persians were facing other problems (see Chapter 3), Trdat managed to inflict a crushing defeat on the Persians. The situation changed when Narses, who had also received reinforcements from Persia, returned. Trdat had to resort to the use of guerrilla warfare along the western borders of Armenia, until the crushing victory of Galerius over Narses (now the 'King-of-Kings') in 298 resulted in a peace treaty in 299 that gave the throne of Armenia to Trdat (ca. 298–230). At the same time the grateful Trdat was forced to concede a part of the Armenian kingdom to the Romans in return for the help he had been given. However, as a sort of compensation for this loss of territory, Trdat was also able to subject Iberia as a client state of his.

Society[87]

Armenian society was roughly divided at least into three estates: nobles (magnates and lesser nobility), priests, and the third estate consisting of the non-noble (*an-azat*) *ramik* (which included people of the towns, traders and the peasant *shinakan*). At the top of the hierarchy was the Arsacid king with his queen (*bambishn, tikin*) and below him were the magnates consisting of the *nakharars* (*vitaxae*, princes/dukes; *nahapets/tanuters/*heads of *nakharar* families; and *sepuhs/*members of the nobility) that were further classed as seniors (*awag, barjereck, gahereck, mecameck*) and juniors (*krtser*). These magnate families possessed hereditary autonomous domains and the most important of them also held hereditary offices. There were at least 120 autonomous families, but only a minority of them could be considered true magnates, i.e. seniors. The senior magnates could also be *ashkharhakai* (administrator of the area), or *ashkharhater* (native-lord), the former of which was an office that could also be hereditary. The most powerful of the magnates often had significant domains and dwelled in remote and inaccessible fortresses, which made their position vis-à-vis the king relatively strong. The magnates were the dominant class of the period and it was necessary for the king to obtain their support.

The lesser nobility *azats* (the free, some of which may have served as *dasapet/dehkan/* head-of-village) usually held their land conditionally as grants from the magnates. Below the nobles ranked the clergy, which before the conversion led the people in worship of Armenian-Greco-Iranian-Semitic Gods, but the role of the Zoroastrian gods was on the rise during the Iranian occupation after ca. 262. The shrines of the major gods, each served by hereditary priests, consisted of vast estates and could also include fortifications and guards.

At the bottom of the hierarchy were the townspeople and peasants who, besides paying their taxes, could also be required to perform military service. The king was advised by the council of the realm consisting of the representatives of the nobles (magnates and lesser nobles), clergy, and the third estate (*ramik* and *shinakan*).

The principal offices of the realm, the military commands included, were hereditary in certain *nakharar* families and the removal of the office from the member of such a family could result in trouble for the king. The office of *sparapet* (Pl. *spahbed*), commander-in-chief of the army, was hereditary in the Mamikonean family from the reign of Trdat the Great onwards. The office of *aspet* (Master of the Horse, Commander of the Cavalry) was hereditary in the Bagratuni House. The Bagratuni were also the royal coronants (*tagakap*). The office of *hazarapet* (Chancellor; acted probably as a sort of PP) was originally hereditary in the family of Anjit/Angeltun, but they lost the position to the Gnuni at the beginning of the reign of Arshak II (Arsaces) in ca.350. Unlike in Persia, this office appears to have been a purely civilian one with the duty of overseeing the peasantry, economic activity and collection of taxes needed for the upkeep of the state and its army.[88]

There were also two separate *mardpets*: 1) the *hayr-mardpet* (grand chamberlain), who was originally a eunuch who supervised the royal household, and so was not hereditary; 2) the hereditary *mardpet*, the commander in charge of a section of the south-eastern border. In the fourth century the *hayr-mardpet* was a royal official in charge of the royal fortresses. The title *malkhas* appears to have been hereditary in the family of Khorkhoruni and may have signified the commander of the royal bodyguard. Others, however, think that the commander of the royal bodyguard was the *nuirakapet* (master of ceremonies). It is possible that both were commanders of the bodyguards, in which case the former was the senior position. The four Toparchs/Viceroys of the realm (the *Vitaxae of Aljnik, Gugark, Korduk* and *Nor-Shirakan*) were also hereditary positions and holders had the duty of guarding the frontiers.[89]

The position of *shapstan takarapet* (chief-cupbearer), the equivalent of the Persian *takar-bagh* (master of the court), was one of the most important positions in the court and was often held by a eunuch (i.e. it was not hereditary). Hübschmann (Faustus/ Garsoïan, 556) has suggested that the word *shapstan* should be identified with council, secret council, which, if true, may in my opinion suggest possible connection with spying with the implication that the *shapstan* was the so-called Eye of the King (see below). The exact functions of the palatine office of the *senekapet* (chamberlain) are not known except that it had some military functions, had the responsibility of guarding the royal treasure, and was not hereditary.[90] *Vardapet* meant a teacher and instructor, which in my opinion may also suggest some other more important official function, possibly as an instructor of soldiers etc. The position of *akhorapet* (chief-stabler, head of the stables) was also important, but we do not know whether it was hereditary. The position of the chief-executioner may also have been important and hereditary.[91]

The office of the *datawor* (judge) belonged to the clergy just like in Iran, which suggests that some of the clerics may have been used for the maintenance of internal security as some sort of religious security police, which not only investigated but also judged and may even have executed. Just like the Romans and Persians, the Armenian king must also have had other intelligence gathering organizations besides his religious police. It is obvious that the commander of the bodyguards (*malkhas? /senekapet?*) with his men must also have had intelligence gathering functions, but we do not know for certain whether the Armenian king also had professional spies and the so-called 'Eye of the King' as their boss, but we may make the educated guess that at least some men of the king's inner circle must have acted as his spies. The parallels between the Persian and Armenian systems definitely suggest that the Armenians must also have had a separate civilian intelligence chief (see the Section on Persians). If nomads like the twelfth-thirteenth century Mongols possessed their own effective intelligence gathering organization, it is practically certain that the much better organized Armenians had one too. Otherwise, they would have been operating in the darkness when basically all of their borders were threatened by enemies of various types.

The Armenian Military

The best evidence for the defensive structure of the realm comes from the Armenian Military List, the *Zoranamak*, which has been studied in great detail by Adontz and Toumanoff, who have pointed out probable discrepancies in this list. Both claim that the fourfold division is anachronistic and has been added to the list after the reforms of Khusro I Anushirwan divided the frontier defences of Persia between four *Spahbeds*. The approach adopted by Adontz and Toumanoff has been accepted by the vast majority of historians, but contrary to this view, I have accepted the Four Gates and Four Marches and Four *Vitaxae* (*Bdeshx*, Viceroys) to reflect actual historical reality. It is still clear as both Adontz and Toumanoff have argued that the extant list does contain duplicates (including cadet branches) and misspellings, and can place commanders in charge of Gates that were not part of their own feudal domains, leave out noble houses, contain dubious names, and so on. However, in my opinion there is still plenty of evidence to support the fourfold division of the army (most sources mention this in one form or another) and the differences in the names and places as well the differences in the rankings in the list (and other sources) simply reflect the fact that the list described the situation at one particular point in time. At other points in time the rankings would have been different.

The earliest and original fourfold defensive system consisting of the four *Vitaxae* (viceroys) was meant to defend the approaches from which enemies probably came at the time when both Persia and Armenia were still ruled by the Arsacids, making it unnecessary to post a separate force against Parthia. Consequently, it is quite probable that the first reorganization of the Armenian defences occurred soon after fall of the Parthian Empire during the reign of the king Khosrov the Great. The viceroys may have been reinstated when the Persians conquered Armenia in ca.261 because there was once again no need for the defensive system against Persia. The final blow to the *Vitaxae* as a defensive system came when Trdat handed over to the Romans the territories in 299 that traditionally formed the *Vitaxae* of Aljnik and Korduk. The offices of *Vitaxae* were still kept as feudal titles, but the actual defensive structure of the realm was now rearranged/reorganized according to the Four Gates system (North, South, West, East). Of note is the fact that during Trdat and his son's reign the general of the Northern Gate was the king of Iberia.

The following map lists the armies of the Four Gates and the Royal Reserves, as well as the armies of some individual noble houses that can be located:

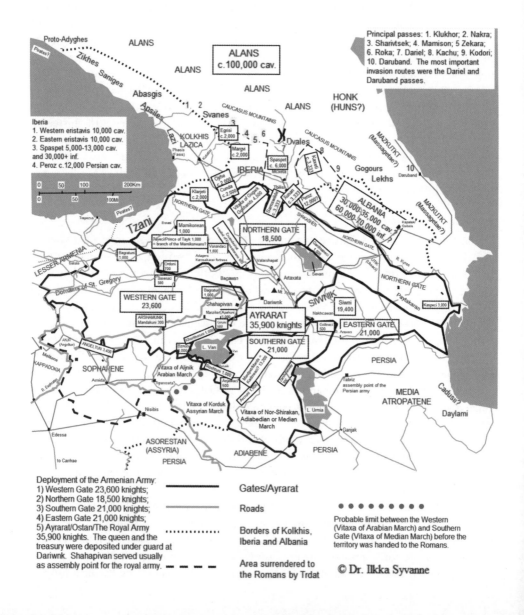

© Dr. Ilkka Syvanne

The following Armenian Military List (*Zoranamak*), on the next page, is based on the translation of Adontz/Garsoian (1970, 193–195), but I have made some changes in the transliteration to make the text simpler, and I have also added my own comments to the text in square brackets. The list makes it abundantly clear that the defence of the Armenian realm was based on the fourfold division of the frontiers, while the forces at the king's disposal formed the central mobile reserve. It also makes abundantly clear that the main striking force of the Armenian army were the *azat*-knights. When reading the list (which is also close in content to the Throne List, the *Gahnamak*), it should be kept in mind that there were two separate ranking systems in use, one based on the number of knights contributed to the military (reflected in *Gahnamak* and *Zoranamak*) and one based on the nobility of birth. The former may mislead the researcher to assume that, for example, the Kamsakarans would not have been very powerful with their mere 600 retainers, whereas from the narrative sources we learn that as relatives of the Arsacids (they were originally Parthian Karin Pahlaw), they could wield considerable power.

It is clear that thanks to this feudal system, the Armenian kings had at their disposal an abundant supply of horses together with large reserves of first rate cavalry, on top of which they could also call to service the irregular *gugaz*-levies from the estates of the nobles.[92] In sum, the Armenian army was divided into four sections to defend the different frontiers that could be bolstered with the Royal Army and general levies, or alternatively the different Gates could bolster the numbers of the Royal army when needed. The overall size and quality of the Armenian army was truly awe inspiring. The army of the Western Gate encompassed 23,600 knights, the Eastern Gate 21,000, the Northern Gate 18,500, the Southern Gate 21,500, and the Royal Reserves 35,900 knights (in Ayrarat), making altogether 120,000 knights.

It is obviously clear that the Armenian king could not usually put to the field the whole army simultaneously for three reasons: 1) It was impossible to supply the entire force during the campaign; 2) He could not leave other areas of the kingdom undefended; and 3) When enemies invaded, some Armenian nobles often sided with the invaders. However, there were still some rare occasions in which the king/*sparapet* was able to assemble almost all of the feudal forces (Royal Army, princely retinues and others) for a single campaign. This united army was called the Army of Armenia (*Hayastan Gund* or *Hayotz Gund* or *Hayastan*).[93] In addition to this there were also the forces provided by the client kingdoms like Iberia and by the allies.

Of note is also the fact that outside the immediate system of feudal service described by the *Zoranamak*, there were noble houses on the Roman side of the border after 299, who also professed loyalty to the king of Armenia. Therefore, the overall size of the Armenian army could be even greater than implied by the *Zoranamak* and the narrative sources. The reason why the Princes of Siwni (Siunik) ranked high among the nobles is apparent from their huge personal retinue. Basically, the size of their contingent made them semi-independent rulers that all tried to woo to their side.

The Armenian army was a feudal army, the core of which was formed of the retinues of the various noble houses. The armies on campaign consisted of these feudal units/ divisions (*gunds*) each of which had its own standard that were then grouped together to form larger entities like regional armies (the Gates, *Vitaxae*, lesser frontier governors called *kolmakals*, and lesser governors of the interior called *kusakals*), or the Royal

Western Gate

[According to Stephen Orbelean, when Trdat established military commanders, he appointed the Prince of Korduk (Corduene) in charge of the West, while another source claims that the commander was the Vitaxa of Aljnik/Angeltun, the position of which was the senior one of the Vitaxae. The assignment of the Western Gate variously to the Princes of Angeltun and Korduk results from the unification of the two Vitaxae to form the Gate. The position of the Vitaxa of Aljnik could also be transferred to a member of another family, if the person revolted (BP 3.9: Valinak Siwni replaced the rebel Bakur/Pacorus) or fell from favour. In sum, the commanders of the Western Gate came from different families at different periods of time.]

Eastern Gate

[According to Stephen Orbelean, when Trdat established military commanders, he appointed the Prince of Siwni in charge of the East]

Angeltun	3,400	Siwni	19,400
The Bdeshx (Vitaxa) of Aljnik	4,000	Amaskoni (=Amatuni?)	200
Baznunakan [Bznuni]	3,000	Awacaci	200
Manawazean	1,000	Varjawuni	200
Bagaratuni	1,000	Tamraraci	100
Khorkhoruni	1,000	Mazazaci	100
Copaci	1,000	Colkepan	100
Vahuni	1,000	Grzchuni	50
Apahuni	1,000	Varnuni	50
Gnuni	500	Bakan	50
Basenaci	600	Kchruni	50
Paluni	300	Gukan	50
Ancaki (Anjakh?)	4,000	Patsparuni	50
Mandakuni	300	Gazrikan	50
Salkuni	300	Vizhanuni	50
Varazhnuni	300	Zandalan	50
Aycenakan	100	Sodaci	50
Arwenean	300	Akaceci	50
Varzhnunean	100	Ashchshnean	50
Spanduni	300	Kinan	50
Rapsean	100	Tagrean	50
[Total	23,600]	[Total	21,000]

... and certain others in other lands; and the number of men from these nations was 84,000 [in truth 84,100 knights] in addition to those who serve the royal court, the Ostan [Ayrarat], who go forth to war with the king, and the *Mardpetakan*, who are the guard of the queen and the treasure, and in altogether the number of the Armenian forces is 120,000. ... © Dr. Ilkka Syvänne

---

Army (the Ayararat/Ostan plus reinforcements) that in their turn consisted of wings (left, centre, right) and sometimes also of other groupings like reserves, outer wings, scouts, ambushers, infantry specialists (for example, mountain troops) etc. The chosen elite of the army was called the *matenik gund* (elite division/unit), that meant selected

Northern Gate		Southern Gate	
[According to Stephen Orbelean, when Trdat established military commanders he appointed the Vitaxa of Gugark in charge of the North, who would have also been its original commander]		[According to Stephen Orbelean, when Trdat established military commanders he appointed the Prince of Angeltun in charge of the South. The original commander would probably have been the Vitaxa of Noshirakan or the Mardpet.]	
The Bdeshx of Gugark	4,500	Kadmeaci	13,200
Kamsarakan	600	Kordwaci	1,000
Kaspeci	3,000	Arcruni	1,000
Uteaci	1,000	Roshtuni	1,000
Cawdeaci	1,000	Mokaci	1,000
Tayeci	1,000	Goltneci	500
Mamikonean	1,000	Anjewaci	500
Vanandaci	1,000	Haruzhean	100
Garmaneci	1,000	Trapatuni	100
Orduni	700	Mehnuni	100
Arweleank	500	Akeaci	300
Ashocean	500	Zarehwaneay	300
Dimaksean	300	Erwantuni	300
Gantuni	300	Hamastunean	100
Bokhayeci	300	Artashesean	300
Gabelean	300	Sagratuni	100
Abelean	300	Abrahamean	100
Hawnuni	300	Truni	300
Saharuni	300	Buzhuni	200
Jewnakan	300	Kajberuni	100
Ashkhadarean	100	Boduni	100
Varazartikean	100	Muracan	300
[Total	18,500]	[Total	21,000]

contingents or royal bodyguards similar to the Persian Immortals or simply the centre (or reserve?) of the army. The Armenian army on campaign had a clear command structure, which included the overall commander (*sparapet* – and/or the king), a commander of the cavalry (*aspet*), generals (*zoravars*, in charge of the wings?), and commanders of the *gunds* (*gundapets/gamapets*), below whom served the lesser officers all the way down to file leaders and rearguards.[94]

Armenian military methods were very flexible and adaptable, and one should not make the mistake of concluding that the Armenian army was poorly organized on the basis that it was feudal. On the contrary, when the Armenians were united under a respected and powerful monarch or *sparapet*, their feudal army could defeat practically any opponent. Similarly, contrary to the popular image of the feudal armies, the Armenian army was well organized, supplied and paid (note the central bureaucracy). The only serious weakness of the Armenian army was the relative independence of the princes, which at times of discord could cause some of them to defect and/or to fight their own personal wars against the other princes. The independent and free spirit of the knights made their charge much feared on the battlefield, but at the same time it made the control of the army difficult.

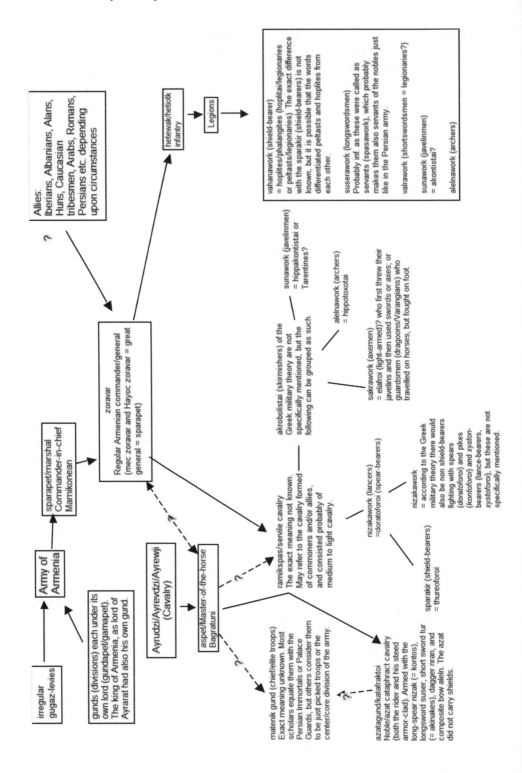

Allies:
Iberians, Albanians, Alans, Huns, Caucasian tribesmen, Arabs, Romans, Persians etc. depending upon circumstances

hetewak/hetiotk infantry

Legions

vahanawork (shield-bearer)
= hoplites/phalangites (hoplitai/legionaries or peltasts/legionaries) The exact difference with the sparakir (shield-bearers) is not known, but it is possible that the words differentiated peltasts and hoplites from each other.

suserawork (longswordsmen)
Probably inf. as these were called as servants (spasawork), which probably makes them also servants of the nobles just like in the Persian army.

valrawork (shortswordsmen = legionaries?)

sunawork (javelinmen)
= akontistai?

alelnawork (archers)

sparapet/marshal
Commander-in-chief
Mamikonean

zoravar
Regular Armenian commander/general
(mec zoravar and Hayoc zoravar = great general = sparapet)

Army of Armenia

gunds (divisions) each under its own lord (gundapet/gamapet). The king of Armenia, as lord of Ayrarat had also his own gund.

irregular gugaz-lewis

akrobolistai (skirmishers) of the Greek military theory are not specifically mentioned, but the following can be grouped as such.

sunawork (javelinmen)
= hippakontistai or Tarentines?

alelnawork (archers)
= hippotoxotai

sakrawork (axemen)
= elafroi (light-armed)? who first threw their javelins and then used swords or axes; or guardsmen (dragoons/Varangians) who travelled on horses, but fought on foot.

AyrudzilAyrevdzilAyrewji (Cavalry)

aspet/Master-of-the-horse
Bagratuni

ramikspas/servile cavalry
The exact meaning not known. May refer to the cavalry formed of commoners and/or allies, and consisted probably of medium to light cavalry.

nizakawork (lancers)
=doratoforoi (spear-bearers)

nizakawork
= according to the Greek military theory there would also be non shield-bearers fighting with spears (doratoforoi) and pikes (kontoforoi) and xyston-bearers (lance-bearers, xystoforoi), but these are not specifically mentioned.

sparakir (shield-bearers)
= thureoforoi

matenik gund (chief/elite troops)
Exact meaning unknown. Most scholars equate them with the Persian Immortals or Palace Guards, but others consider them to be just picked troops or the center/core division of the army.

azatagund/katafraktoi
Noble/azat cataphract cavalry (both the rider and his steed armor-clad). Armed with the long-spear nizak (= kontos), longsword suser, short sword tur (= akinakes), dagger nran, and composite bow alein. The azat did not carry shields.

The elite knights consisting of the *azatagund*-cavalry were equipped as cataphracts (rider and horse armoured). These knights wore *zrah*-armour (mail, scale, lamellar, plate or their mixture depending upon the wealth of the individual) from head to foot, a *salawart*-helmet, and carried the *nizak*-spear (probably *kontos*), *suser*-longsword (double-edged Iranian style longsword), *tur*-shortsword (Iranian *akinakes* = single-edged sword), *nran*-dagger, and *aleln*-bow (long and powerful composite bow). In general, the knights appear not to have used the shield, but one cannot rule them out categorically as there are probable instances of their use. For example, the shields would have been needed whenever the knights were besieging or defending fortresses and cities. The rest of the cavalry forces consisted of the non-noble *ramikspas* and allied horsemen, which appear to have consisted of lancers (with shields and without) and skirmishers (mounted archers, javelinmen, axemen). (See diagram on previous page.) The infantry consisted of legions of footmen that were divided into heavy (shield-bearers, long-swordsmen?/ short-swordsmen?) and light foot (javelinmen? and archers).

When campaigning the Armenian army followed the standard military safety protocols which included the posting of scouts and patrols around the marching army (*karawan/ karewan* = military column/caravan), the securing of adequate supplies, and the use of fortified marching camps. The fortified camps included three varieties: 1) the home camp (*bun banak*) which was the assembly point of the Royal Army; 2) The ordinary fortified marching camp (*banak*); and 3) The elaborately fortified camp in an inaccessible place (*lakis*).[95]

The Armenian arsenal of tactics included the whole spectrum of military methods: the use of ambushes, surprise attacks, night attacks, assassinations of enemy leaders by special operatives, targeting of enemy leaders in combat, attacks against enemy camps, raiding, guerrilla warfare, regular warfare with pitched battles, and variable methods of siege warfare. The principal arm of service was the super heavy cataphract cavalry and the use of infantry was usually restricted to supporting roles in defence of the fortified marching camp or for use in sieges. The Armenians had a very well-developed military doctrine to deal with a great variety of circumstances, which allowed them to choose the most appropriate response to any situation.[96]

Since the main striking force of the Armenian army was its heavy cavalry, it is not surprising that the Armenians favoured open plains where their lancers could operate unhindered and in which the route of retreat for the enemy was blocked by terrain. However, when the Armenians were outnumbered, they could choose to retreat to difficult terrain well known to them, use the scattered formation for fluid cavalry warfare, and then concentrate their elite cavalry forces opposite the enemy commander to kill him with a precision strike.[97]

The Armenian pre-battle routines were elaborate: before each battle, the commander held a council of officers to form a battle plan; religious sermons/ceremonies and speeches to the troops were used to encourage the men; troops were equipped according to the circumstances; religious shouts were used during combat, and so forth. The cavalry attack with *contus*-lances was conducted with closed ranks as fast as possible. However, it is still important to keep in mind that the use of the super heavy cataphract cavalry did not mean that the Armenians would have used their *azatagund* only for frontal charges. The same cavalry could also be used for long distance archery combat and with the removal of some pieces of armour it could also be used as light cavalry. For example, the sources mention the use of *azat*-cavalry as a skirmishing force in open order in which the spears were thrown rather than used as lances. Regardless, the *contus*-lance was still the primary weapon of the Armenian *azat*-cavalry. The Armenian knights could even gallop back to the rear to obtain a spare lance if they had shattered or lost theirs, which means that when the first Armenian line re-grouped behind the reserves, they usually re-arranged their line for a new lancer charge.[98]

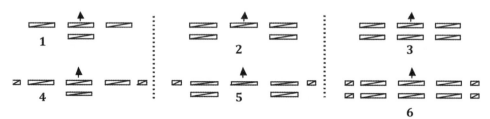

Probable Armenian cavalry formations
I have here given two alternatives, three arrays (1–3) without outer wings and three arrays (4–6) with outer wings.

Unfortunately, we can reconstruct only the most important features of Armenian battle tactics and formations. What we know is that Armenia possessed a very long cavalry tradition and could defeat the Sasanians and Romans when well led and unified. We also know that the Armenian battle formations differed from one battle to another according to the size of the army and the circumstances, and that in most cases they seem to have deployed cavalry reserves and sometimes also ambushers. The most common version had two reserve divisions. The above diagrams give just some possible examples of the different formations in use.[99] When looking at the diagrams, it should be kept in mind that even when the sources fail to mention the use of separate wing units (the outermost wings in the Indo-Persian five-division array or the outflankers/flank-guards of the Roman army) outside the threefold front (left, centre, right), it is possible that those were still used. The two typical unit orders used by the Armenian cavalry were the square and rhombus formations, both of which could have been employed as needed by the Armenian *azat*-cavalry.[100] The rhomboids were usually employed by the flank units (a rhombus faced all directions) and the squares/oblongs by the rest.

All of these different units and divisions, each under their own lord, were placed under their lord's banner (*droshm*, after *drafsh*) which showed his coats of arms. The most important banner was the national banner which was carried only when the *sparapet* (or *aspet*?) or king was present. The troops were commanded either by using these banners, or by verbal commands, or by employing musical instruments. The banners were particularly useful as visual objects around which the men could be regrouped when needed.

The third- and fourth-century military successes of both Khosrov (ca.211–256) against Ardashir and Shapur I and the successes of his son Trdat (ca.276/8–330/2) against Narses and his successors prove that the Armenians, when united and well led, were easily able to keep Sasanid Persia in check and inflict grievous losses on them.[101] Consequently, it would have been in the interest of Rome to prop up the Armenian kingdom as a buffer state against Iran. However, the constantly recurring problems with Armenian kings and nobles after the reign of Trdat convinced the Romans to think otherwise, yet the subsequent division of Armenia between Rome and Persia proved even costlier for the Romans. Instead of having a medium-sized Christian buffer state to bear part of the cost of the defence, the Romans had to take the responsibility of the defence entirely into their own hands.[102] The uneven division of Armenia between the empires also meant that the bulk of the Armenian forces were given on a silver plate to the Persians. In fact, excluding their periods of revolts, the Persarmenians became one of the elite branches of the Sasanian armed forces and on several occasions even saved the Sasanian Empire from collapse.

Iberia/Kartli[103] and Colchis

The structure of Iberian society was basically the same as in Parthia, Armenia and Albania, which is not surprising considering the long Iranian cultural influence on the area. Some of the noble houses even had domains in both Armenia and Iberia. It should be noted, however, that these systems were not exact carbon copies of each other as each had its own peculiarities, just like there were some minor differences in the duties of the same officials between Armenia and Iran.

The highest echelon of the society after the king (*mepe*) consisted of the royal family (*sepe*), and supreme judge of the land who was also the chief of the army (*spaspet*). Right below them were the magnates/aristocrats (heads of family *mamasakhlisi* with the regular *mtavarni/sepetsulni*), followed by the second estate consisting of the pagan priests/magi (later Christian clerics). The free agriculturalists and soldiers formed originally the third estate, which at this time had effectively become two estates, consisting of petty nobles with lands who performed military duty as feudal mounted warriors (*tskhentartsani*), and of the petty people who performed military service as common foot (*mkvirtskhlebi*). The former were called, as noble cavalry, *azaurni* (Armenian *azats*, *azatagund*) and the latter as *tadzdreulni* (free agriculturalists/petty people) with a duty to serve as infantry. The fourth estate consisted of the semi-dependent agriculturalists/peasants (*glekni*) who were basically tenants with no military obligations.[104] In short, society was basically organized to support its military forces.

As regards the ruling house of Georgia at the time, the Chosroids, I would suggest that its supposed founder, king Mirian/Mihran/Mihrshah, who is said to have been a son of Shapur I (240–271), is most likely indeed his unknown son whose career the GC has utterly confused with those of Shapur's better known sons Hormizd and Narses, and that the current consensus regarding the beginnings of his rule and his supposed Mihranid origins among the historians is utterly wrong. The family connection with the Sasanians made the Chosroids susceptible to seeking help from their relatives whenever needed, while the conversion of Mirian into Christianity made them equally ready to ask for help from the Armenians and Romans whenever needed. In fact, Mirian had domains both in Iberia and in Armenia and served as the general of the Armenian Northern Gate under Trdat and Khosrov and was therefore a client king with feudal obligations towards his lord.

According to the Georgian Chronicles (pp. 34–36), the Iberians modelled their military organization after the Parthian model so that the king appointed all eight regional *eristavis/ pitiaskhshi* (generals, governors, dukes, viceroys/*vitaxae*), and the commander-in-chief *spaspet* (*erismtavari* = Armenian *sparapet*), whose forces (the royal army/central reserve) were located in the Inner Kartli (around Tpilisi/Tbilisi and Mcxeta/Mtskheta).[105] The eight *eristavis* were further divided into Eastern *eristavis* (Kaxeti, Xunan, and Samshwilde) and Western *eristavis* (the two *eristavis* of Egrisi – Egrisi and Margvi; Ojrhe; Klarjeti; and Cunda).[106] A ninth Persian *eristavi* was added to the Eastern *eristavis* in ca.280.

The original domains of the *eristavis* included also the Black Sea coastline as well as part of Greater Armenia. However, the Black Sea coastline was already lost to the Romans before the birth of Christ and the parts belonging to Greater Armenian similarly. Furthermore, a ninth *eristavi* was added to the number in about 280. As a result, it is impossible to locate their exact domains at the beginning of our period of research. The accompanying map presents my educated guess of the situation in c.300 after Tiridates/ Trdat (276/8–330/2) had been reaffirmed as king of Armenia. The ninth *eristavi*, Peroz, was Mirian's relative and he was given territory from Xunan (Xunan may have been divided in two) in return for his military support, which was later (ca.332?) changed into that of Samshwilde, which had until then been ruled by the crown prince Bakar. In this place and other places, the GC also makes clear that the domains ruled by the *eristavis* could be changed and transferred, which further complicates matters. Therefore, the locations of the *eristavis* in the accompanying map should only be considered indicative of their likely place in ca.300.[107]

Of particular importance is the fact that Peroz was a Persian and his forces consisted similarly of Persians. The strategic location of Peroz' (and also the crown prince's) forces opposite the Albanian frontier just east of the major road leading into Tpilisi and Mcxeta is no coincidence, and in fact, considering the attention given to Peroz in the GC, it is possible that he did indeed possess about 12,000 Persian horsemen as his successor in the same area was claimed to have. The size of his cavalry contingent would have made him the third most important man after the king and *spaspet*.

Below the *spaspet* and *eristavis* served *spasalarni* (generals) who commanded divisions and *khliarkhni/atasistavni* (quartermaster?) who collected taxes and gathered the troops. Under them served the lesser officers (usually magnates) each in charge of his own contingent of *azaurni*-cavalry (fully-armoured cataphract cavalry) and/or *tskhentartsani* (regular cavalry consisting of *kontoforoi*, spear-bearers, javelin-throwers, and mounted archers) and/or infantry (*mkvirtskhlebi/tadzdreulni* consisting of spearmen, swordsmen, and light infantry). The *azaurni*-cavalry (rider and steed armour-clad; equipped with a lance, axe, sword, bow, and, at least during the fifth century, also with a shield) formed the elite component of the army, but the vast bulk of the cavalry consisted of the common less well-equipped troops. The infantry formed by far the most numerous part of the armed forces, but it was usually only used for duties of secondary importance, such as garrisons of cities and forts. However, we should still not downplay its significance, because its services were necessary in difficult terrain and sieges and its continued importance was recognized by its continued existence alongside the so-called elite forces.[108]

Unfortunately we possess even less information of the Iberian military than we do of the Armenian. Consequently, one has to resort to the use of the evidence provided by the narrative sources (especially the GC), which are notoriously unreliable. When listing the combined forces of the *Eristavis* of the East, the cavalry of the *spaspet* , and the infantry of the city of Mcxeta, the GC (Georgian version/Leonti Mroveli, pp.65–66) claims that there were, besides the warriors (i.e. probably those posted outside the gates), a total of 30,000 infantry, and another 10,000 cavalry. The totals in the Armenian version are 16,000 cavalry and 30,000 infantry, a total implying that the 'warriors' outside the gates consisted of 6,000 cavalry, which must have been the cavalry contingent of the *spaspet*.

This would tally well with the number of elite cavalry given by the Persians to Mirian when he assumed the throne. According to the GC (p.76), in ca.262 the Persians gave Mirian/Mihran a force of 40,000 elite Persian cavalry of which 5,000 (Armenian version) or 7,000 (Georgian version) were to be used as the king's bodyguards. However, since the GC has mixed Mirian with Hormizd and Narses, I would suggest that the larger number of troops (35,000 or 33,000) were the troops posted in Armenia as an occupying force under its king, while the smaller figure (5,000 or 7,000) was the force given to Mirian for use in Iberia. If the original Iberian contingent of the *spaspet* remained in existence, then the size of his force was increased to around 11,000–13,000 men.

If one makes the assumption that the forces of the East and West must have been approximately equal in size, then the *Eristavis* of the West also had 10,000 cavalry. These figures would give us a realistic estimate of the overall size of the Iberian armed forces, which would then consist of about 20,000 cavalry of the *eristavis* and at least of about 5,000–7,000 cavalry (reaching possibly the figure of 11,000–13,000 horsemen?) under the *spaspet*. To this figure one should also add the 12,000 Persian horsemen of Peroz, but strictly speaking these men were not part of the Iberian army proper. Their loyalty was solely towards their own lord. (See the Map of Armenia above.)

The overall numbers of infantry are less easy to estimate, because we do not possess reliable figures for the other cities or the countryside. Perhaps the figure of 60,000 infantry given by Juansher would be the best educated guess, but in truth most of these would have been used to protect the cities, towns and forts. Consequently, my educated guess would be that the infantry contingent of the field army would have been about 30,000 men at most.

The Iberians could also sometimes employ allied forces provided by the tribes of the Caucasus (mostly lightly equipped infantry with some cavalry forces), Ossetes (Alans), Armenians, Romans, Albanians and Persians. The size of the contingent provided by the allies, especially by the more powerful ones, obviously depended upon the circumstances and cannot be generalized.

The Caucasian kings were a special case as for most of the time these appear to have been in a client relationship with their more powerful southern neighbour. Juansher claims that they were able to provide 50,000 cavalry for service, but this figure seems fantastic and one may perhaps take one zero off and make the educated guess that the Caucasian kings under Iberia/Kartli could contribute about 5,000 cavalry for service while their entire arms-bearing male population would have consisted of the ca.50,000 men. It seems probable that as allies they kept the bulk of their forces, consisting mainly of light infantry, behind to protect their homes.

The figures provided by Juansher (History of King Vaxtang Georgsali) in the GC are too fantastic to be taken seriously, except perhaps as estimates of the overall male population capable of bearing arms. Juansher informs us that in the fifth century all of the forces of Kartli (Iberia) consisted of 100,000 cavalry[109] and 60,000 infantry in addition to which came the 12,000 men of Varaz-Bakur (*eristavi* of Ran, possessor of Peroz' old domains) and the 50,000 cavalry contributed by the kings of the Caucasus against the Ossetes (Alans). At another place Juansher claims that the combined forces of Kartli and the Caucasian kings consisted of 200,000 men to which were added the 200,000 men (Persians) of Varaz-Bakur, Adarabagan and Movakan; and still later Vaxtang supposedly had 240,000 men.[110] In fact, the early account of Strabo (ca. 7 BC) seems to confirm my educated guess that the figure of 200,000 men could have some relevance if interpreted to refer to the entire arms-bearing male population of Iberia and its client kingdoms in the Caucasus.

According to Strabo (11.2.19–11.4.5), the Soanes (also called 'Iberians'), who were masters of the country around them and occupied the heights of the Caucasus, could assemble an army of 200,000 men, because all of their people were fighting men. Strabo has here clearly confused two different tribes, the Iberians and Soanes/Svanes with each other because the latter were clients of the former with the duty of providing warriors for the former. Strabo also noted that the Iberian field army was still smaller than that of the Albanians (see below).

The mountainous terrain determined what tactics could be used. It was not well-suited to cavalry warfare except in the plains and valleys, but this still did not prevent cavalry's prevalent role in the warfare. The difficult terrain with few roads also hindered the use of large armies, and if such were used their supply routes could easily be cut. Warfare in the area still varied from the more typical small scale raiding and cattle wrestling to the large scale warfare of surprise attacks, battles and sieges.

The Georgian Chronicles give us some instances of Iberian battle formations and tactics, some of which are early in date while others are late in date. Unlike the Armenians, the Iberians usually used both infantry and cavalry together. A good early example of the use of combined forces is the battle of King Mirvan (ca. 159–109 BC) against the Durjuks who inhabited the area around the Dariel Pass. The Durjuks blocked the route, as a result of which the king dismounted and marched with his infantry while the cavalry followed. The enemy was defeated after a hard fought battle and pursued past the pass.

Similarly in the 'fifth century' the Alans occupied a cliff and shot volleys of arrows. The king's response was to place his cataphracts in the vanguard to act as a shield for his infantry, behind which was posted the majority of his cavalry. The use of cataphracts in front of the infantry suggests that the infantry did not wear any armour. Behind them all was the king with his select cavalry. The cataphracts forced their way to the level ground after which the army was deployed for battle, which is unfortunately not described. Juansher tells us only that the king with his reserve was forced to steady the situation on both flanks until the enemy fled. Just like most of the ancient peoples, the Iberians also attacked enemy camps from three directions while leaving one side open to induce the enemy to flee rather than fight.

The Iberians were not powerful enough to defend themselves against either of the superpowers, but this doesn't mean that they would have been militarily inefficient. They were just too small a people/nation to withstand a major invasion, and in the history of their nation, their territory was ravaged either by the Romans or Persians or Armenians or nomads on several occasions. It was only in conjunction with Armenia that they could hold their own against either of the superpowers, and even then the situation would not last long.[111] The Iberians feature in the events of the fourth century usually only in the capacity of being allies or clients of one of the bigger players (Rome, Persia, Armenia, Alans) in the area.

Nothing much is known about Colchis-Lazica during this era, but on the basis of later evidence the Lazi-Colchian nobility appear to have provided both infantry (fought as a phalanx) and cavalry forces (fought as heavy cavalry) to their Roman overlords when needed. The organization of these feudal forces is likely to have resembled the organization of the better known Iberian ones.

'Mountaineers' of the Caucasus

Unfortunately, the information provided by the narrative sources regarding the mountain peoples of the Caucasus is very sparse, but fortunately it can to a certain extent be expanded upon by archaeology. During the third century from west to east the mountain peoples consisted of the proto-Adyghes (Adyghes, Tcherkesses), Zikhes, Saniges, Abasgis, Apsilis, Svanes, Dvales, Gogours, Lekhs and Massagetae.[112]

At the time Strabo wrote (c.7 BC: 11.2.12–14), the westernmost of the tribes (Achaei, Zygi, Heniochi: that is, probably the proto-Adyghes) were pirates of the Black Sea. They used slender and light boats carrying about 25 men or rarely 30 men, which the Greeks called '*kamares*'.[113] They equipped fleets of these and then attacked merchant ships, or raided enemy territory and cities. The Bosporans sometimes assisted them. When the pirates returned to their country, which lacked suitable mooring places, they placed the boats on their shoulders and carried them up into the forests where they cultivated the poor soil. With the arrival of the new sailing season, they brought the boats down to the coast for another session of raiding. When raiding poorly guarded enemy coasts, the pirates landed, carried the boats on land and hid them, after which they marched on foot to capture prisoners for slavery or for ransoming. It is not known what happened to these pirates subsequently. It is of course possible that the sources just fail to mention their ongoing piracy, because piracy just like banditry was an endemic phenomenon but not militarily significant. The same could also be true of the Sannoi (neighbours of the Trapezuntines) who Arrian (Periplus 11.2) claims to have been practising piracy in the second century AD. It is possible or even probable that the proto-Adyghes took part in the major naval raids and invasions of the third century in which the Bosporan fleets and/or their own makeshift transported the Borani, Heruls and Goths to the Roman shores.[114]

The next tribes in the western half of the Caucasus were the Saniges (area around modern Sotchi), Zikhes (area around Sebastopolis), Abasgi, Apsili and Lazi. All of these were Roman client states that protected the coastal trade and the passes of the Caucasus, and all of these also possessed small Roman forts and garrisons plus veteran settlements in their respective areas.

As one progressed towards the east along the Caucasus range the central portion was controlled by the Svanes and the Dvales, and the easternmost by the Lekhs, the Gargarees/ Gogours (Garrhi) and the Maskouts/Massagetae (Mazkukt). If one is to believe Strabo's referral to 200,000 warriors of the Svanes (Soanes, Suanes, Svanokolkhi) tribe, then they were by far the most powerful of the tribes of the Caucasus as far as manpower was concerned. However, Strabo's statement (11.2.19) that some called them Iberians suggests that he has probably mixed the two with each other for the reason that the Svanes were likely to be a client tribe of Iberia/Kartli. On the basis of this it is reasonable to suggest that the overall size of their army was probably about 20,000 mountaineers. After the Svanes, came the Dvales who occupied a particularly important position in the Caucasus because the Dariel Pass (i.e. the Caucasia Gate, Gate of the Alans) lay in their territory. In normal circumstances they too seem to have been clients of Iberia and probably possessed about 20,000 mountaineers. The Gogours and Lekhs formed the sedentary population of what is today Dagesthan while their neighbours (Massagetae/Huns? and Sarmates) belonged to the semi-nomadic groups. Unlike the other major tribes of the area they appear not to have controlled any major passes. Regardless, they still had an important role to play in many of the invasions on both sides of the Caucasus, and one may guess that each would have had about 20,000 warriors. The semi-nomadic Massagetae 'Huns' seem to have controlled the Daruband Pass, which meant that they had a very important role to play in the Caucasus until the pass was conquered by the Sasanians. Their army probably consisted of about 30,000 armoured horsemen plus the elders.[115]

The Romans considered the passes of the Caucasus to be impassable during the winter months. The locals did use spiked/studded snowshoes to move around in the snow and ice.[116] The Roman strategy in the area consisted of the posting of garrisons along the coast of Colchis as well as of the use of diplomacy to secure the passes controlled by the Zikhes, Saniges, Abasci, Apsili, Svanes and Dvanes. The methods how the Romans achieved this consisted of the simultaneous use of the stick and carrot. The former consisted of the threat posed by the Roman armed forces plus clients and/or allies, while the latter consisted of the payment of gifts to the kings (who could therefore secure their position with Roman support) and of access to the Roman trade network.

The client states of Rome and Persia (Armenia, Iberia and Albania) and the northern nomads also sought to use the same methods to promote their own interests, while the mountain kingdoms attempted to extort as much money as possible from each side for their support. Militarily the small mountain kingdoms were too small to resist the superpowers or their clients, but since the actual conquest and occupation of the mountains would have been way too costly they were still able to maintain some semblance of independence.[117] Basically, what the Romans or the other players in the area did whenever a tribe or tribes in the area opposed their will was to invade the area of the recalcitrant tribe and pillage and kill until the enemy submitted to their will.

Albania

It is very unfortunate that there is very little information regarding the early history of the Albanians and we have to rely on very few scattered references by foreign historians. Albania consisted of a multitude of tribes who spoke twenty-six languages or dialects over which the Arsacids had imposed unity under a single king. Originally the Albanians appear to have been nomads and shepherds, but it did not take long for urban centres to appear. As a result, just like their neighbours, Albanian society appears to have been modelled after Iranian/Parthian structures.

The Albanian army appears to have been similar to that of Armenia and consisted of both cavalry and infantry, both in light and heavy varieties. According to Strabo (11.4–5), at the time Pompey invaded Albania, its field army consisted of 60,000 infantry and 22,000 cavalry, which he claimed to have been stronger than the Iberian field army. These figures could be bolstered with nomadic allies. According to Strabo, the Albanians used javelins, bows, armour, shields, and helmets to which may be added the same equipment as was used by the Armenians. One may make the educated guess that at the time the Sasanians ruled Albania (after ca.262), the size of the field army would have been stronger as a result of the presence of Sasanian garrisons and military settlers (feudal cavalry). My own educated guess is that there would have been about 60,000–70,000 infantry and 30,000–35,000 cavalry of which the latter in its entirety or its part was usually fighting alongside as allied forces either with the Armenians, Persians or Romans or against them.

Of the areas south of the Caucasus, Albania belonged quite securely to the Persian sphere of influence and it was only rarely that the Armenians or Romans could challenge this. However, there was one thing that made the Albanians occasionally ready to turn against the Persians, which was their conversion to Christianity after Armenia under Trdat had adopted it as its state religion. Whenever the Persians were persecuting Christians and the Armenians or Romans had enough resources in the area, the Albanians were quite willing to change the sides. Regardless, it was much more common that the Albanian feudal forces fought alongside their Persian overlords.

Sasanian Empire (see also the Maps Section)

Ammianus' Description of Persia

The best place to start the discussion of the Sasanian Empire is to begin with Ammianus' description of the Persian Empire (23.6). Of particular importance for the understanding of the Persian defensive and offensive organization is Ammianus' referral (23.6.13–14) to the existence of the four *Vitaxae* as Persian *magistri equitum*. According to him, there was a *Vitaxa* or king or satrap for each direction of the compass (i.e. for the *'regiones maximae'*), who were essentially early equivalents of Khusro's four *spahbeds*, but with much greater powers because their position appears to have been based on their standing as magnates of the empire. This also implies that each of the appointed *vitaxae* could be simultaneously a king and/or satrap of his own feudal domain.

The *Vitaxa* of the North faced the Caspian Gates (a mistake, the right area is in Gurgan/Hyrcania where Khusro I subsequently built a wall), and the Cadusii (another mistake), 'Scythians', and Arimaspae. In this case Ammianus has confused the two sides of the Caspian Sea with each other, but it is clear that the *Vitaxa* of the North faced the nomads east of the Caspian Sea. The *Vitaxa* of the West faced Armenia, the 'Asiatic Albani', the 'Red Sea' (a mistake for east of the Caspian Sea), and the Scenitic Arabs called Saracens (in this case the Arabs of Northern Mesopotamia just south of Armenia). The *Vitaxa* of the South looked down on Mesopotamia (i.e. its southern portion with Arabia). The *Vitaxa* of the East faced the Ganges River.

The lesser regions consisted of Assyria, Susiana, Media, Persis, Parthia, Greater Carmania, Hyrcania, Margiana, Bactria, Sogdia, Sacae (Sakastan = Sistan?), 'Scythia' at the foot of the Himalayas, and 'beyond it' Serica (probably a mistake for China, which

Ammianus describes as a neighbour), Aria, the Paropanisadae, Drangiana, Arachosia, and Gedrosia. It is clear that Ammianus' account refers to the greatest extent of the Sasanian Empire during the reign of Shapur II, because the Sasanians lost control of at least Bactria, Sogdiana and Scythia at the foot of the Himalayas after the rise of the Guptas in India and the resurgence of the Kushans as Kidarites.

Of importance are also Ammianus' referrals to the importance of the magi as a social class in Persia, and that the Medians were the best soldiers after the Parthians. That is, he implies that the Median cavalry with their Nisaean horses, and the Parthian cavalry were the best troops of the Persian Empire. The Persians also did not practise pederastry. It was considered beastly. They did not have fixed hours for eating with the implication that it was difficult for the Romans to surprise them when they were hungry. The Persians were also extremely cautious when invading so that they did not touch anything in enemy gardens or vineyards because they feared poisoning (note the use of hellebore etc. to poison the terrain and water recommended by Julius Africanus) or magic arts (i.e. the spreading of diseases in the manner described by Julius Africanus in his *Kestoi*).

The Persians were also very brave, cruel and crafty warriors who punished ingrates and deserters very harshly. If one person was found guilty, all of his relatives were put to death. This undoubtedly made all men eager to ensure the loyalty of the relatives to the state. Further, the Persians excelled in the arts of siege warfare and field battles. The flower of their army was the cavalry, which consisted of the nobles. The infantry was armed like *murmillones* in the Gallic manner with small oblong shields and swords, and followed obediently behind the cavalry like servants or slaves. This description is slightly inaccurate for we know that some of the footmen also carried bows and spears, but at the same time it proves that Ammianus considered the Persian foot to be quite prepared to fight it out at close quarters like gladiators. In his opinion, the Persians would have been able to conquer an even larger Empire had they not been plagued by constant civil and foreign wars that had prevented them from concentrating their forces on one front. In short, Ammianus clearly held the Persians in very high esteem as soldiers and enemies.

Sasanian Society[118]

At the very top of society was the *Shahanshah* and below him were four ranks of nobles: 1) the local kings and the sons of the *Shahanshah* who held important posts (*sahrdar*); 2) the members of Sasanian family who were not direct descendants of the ruler (*waspuhragan*); 3) the heads of the most important noble families most of whom consisted of Parthians (*wuzurgan*); and 4) the rest of the nobles (*azadan*). All of the higher ranking offices and military commands were the privilege of the first three categories while the lesser positions were reserved for the *azadan*. According to the *Kohan-Nameh*, which formed part of the *Ain-Nameh* (Book of Regulations), there were altogether 600 different grades of dignitaries in the Sasanian Empire. Each of the ranks, positions and offices also entailed the use of particular types of clothing and colour schemes that distinguished the higher ranking nobles from the lesser ranks. In addition, the females of the royal family received a significant amount of respect.

The first Sasanian ruler of Persia, Ardashir I divided the populace according to the Zoroastrian religious doctrine into four estates (*peshag*: class division): 1) *asronan* (clergy, priests, judges, ascetics, temple-guardians, and teachers), with the most important fire-temple *Adur Farrabay*; 2) *arteshtaran* (warriors/soldiers, cavalry, infantry), with a special fire-temple *Adur Gushnasp* at Shiz near Ganzak (Ganjak); 3) *dahigan* and *wastaryoshan* (common peasants and husbandmen), with a fire-temple *Adur Burzenmihr*; and 4) *hutuxshan* (artisans, merchants, traders etc.), with no fire-temple.[119] At least from the conquests of Shapur I onwards the society was also further divided into Iranians and non-Iranians, the latter of which was ruled by satraps appointed by the ruler.

As noted above, the entire society revolved around the 'magi' (clergy). The judicial system was entirely based on Zoroastrian religion, which meant that all transactions within the society were controlled by religion and priests. This class provided the rulers with councillors, judges, religious police, internal security apparatus, etc. We do not know the exact organization of the priestly class except that it was organized hierarchically into separate branches, each of which had its own duties, and that there was also a 'High Priest' who was one of the most powerful persons of the empire. Thanks to the importance of religion and the clergy to the Sasanians, their enemies always considered the religious establishments, temples and members of the clergy as prime targets.

The warrior class was led by the supreme commander, *Iran-spahbed*. The warriors consisted of the forces provided by the local kings; princes related to the king; the grandees; and the gentry. This estate provided the main striking forces of the empire. The location of the fire-temple of the warriors was vulnerable to attacks from Armenia and it is therefore not surprising that both the Armenians and Romans looted this temple whenever possible. It was one of the principal targets of attack, because the looting and destruction of this temple was always a very serious blow to the prestige of the Sasanid ruler and could even result in his downfall.

The peasants and husbandmen provided the empire with its main source of income and provided subsistence for the other estates. The Chief of Husbandmen, *wastaryoshan salar*, represented the interests of this estate in court. As befitted Zoroastrian rulers, the Sasanians paid particular attention to this estate and created large state controlled projects to enlarge or improve cultivated lands. The goal was to provide a base upon which the Sasanians could build the rest of their projects. The enlarged agricultural produce enabled the Sasanians to support the artisans and merchants inhabiting the new cities built by them, and provided them with taxes to support the state structures. The principal agricultural areas were Iraq and Khuzistan. The former, which also included the Persian capital Ctesiphon, was vulnerable to Roman raids and invasions, which meant that the bulk of the Persian fortresses and defences were located in this area.

The Sasanian policy towards the artisans and merchants was schizophrenic. On the one hand, with the exception of slaves, the fourth estate was considered the lowest of all with the result that most of its members consisted of the religious minorities. In other words, most of the trade was in the hands of the Sogdians and Christians. On the other hand, the Sasanians actively sought to enlarge this class by creating new cities and by importing prisoners from the Roman and Armenian territories into them. This meant that the Sasanians did not actively attempt to open up new markets to their traders, but left it to private enterprises, while they still conquered new territories through which the trade routes passed in order to exact toll road taxes. Sasanian policies also increased the domestic and international trade by protecting the roads, by minting standardized silver coins, and by providing a safe environment for the trade. All commercial transactions were governed by law. The Sasanians also created royal workshops to produce high quality products for the court, and they did import Roman prisoners in an effort to end their reliance on Roman produce, but not in such quantities that the demand for Roman produce would have stopped.

The largest silver mine of the Sasanians lay in Panjshir (in Khurasan, the responsibility of the *Vitaxa* of the North) and it can be said with some justification that their monetary economy depended on it. Consequently, whenever this area was under threat from the various Central Asian powers the Sasanians were forced to react, which in turn limited their ability to take the initiative against the Romans. The loss of this area to the Kidarite-Kushans in the latter-half of the fourth century was a very serious blow to the Sasanians. In my opinion, it can be said with some justification that the silence on the Roman eastern front from ca.384 onwards had more to do with the loss of the eastern territories than with any peace deal that divided Armenia. The loss of Bactria not only caused the loss of the most important silver mines, but also control of the Silk Road, which made it all the more important for the Persians to regain control of the sea route. (See the narrative and the next books in the series.)

The Sasanians also formed alliances and conquered fortresses on the Arabian side of the Straits of Hormuz in an effort to control trade in the Persian Gulf and on the India Ocean, but they did not build a large enough navy to challenge the Arabic or Roman traders, let alone the Roman navy. The most important commercial ports were Bushirh, Siraf, Hormuz, and Guzeran/Kujaran. Unsurprisingly, the Arabic pirates targeted in particular Persis, because Bushihr was located there. The protection of the trading ships was basically left to the traders themselves. The merchant houses, however, were up to the task and created their own trading stations in India, Ceylon, East-Africa and even in China, with the result that at least in the sixth century they were often in the position to buy all of the trading goods available in India before their competitors could even arrive. However, this seems not to have been the case during the fourth century. Rather, the extant evidence suggests that the Romans were able to bypass the Persians with their own trading vessels and with those of their allies, the Aksumites and Himyarites.

The Silk Road was the other major commercial route that the Persians used as their milk cow. The principal trading hubs for the Indian and Chinese produce were located in Armenia and Mesopotamia. The Roman and Armenian merchants paid the eastern merchandice either with produce of their own or with money. At times of war, both of these routes were blocked with the result that those who were in control of the sea routes from India and/or of the land route north of the Caspian Sea were in a position to benefit. It is therefore not surprising that the Romans considered it in their interest to wage war or form alliances in both areas during the fourth century. The Persians did try to control the tribes of the Arabian Peninsula, but Ethiopia and north of the Caucasus lay beyond their grasp. The almost continuous state of war between Rome and Persia is the principal reason for the increased wealth of the Arabs and Aksumites during this period. In short, the Romans could impact the Persian economy also through control of the trade routes north and south of Persia, which they usually sought to achieve through alliances.

We should not be misled into the belief that the strict division of the Sasanian society into classes would have led to stagnation. On the contrary, the Sasanian era saw a rise in urbanization and prosperity and it was thanks to the state controlled expansion that this was possible: that is, the greater centralization and control of society enabled the Sasanian rulers to expand the economic base which in turn enabled them to build cities, fortresses and pay for the upkeep of permanent military units and garrisons. However, despite all the efforts of the rulers, the Sasanian economy remained weaker than the Roman one, which meant that the rulers still had to rely on their 'feudal lords' to provide the bulk of the cavalry and infantry.[120] Despite the fact that the feudal horsemen provided mainly by the Parthian lords were superb soldiers, this created an inherent weakness within Sasanian society: the rulers were always dependent upon their magnates which meant that they always had to negotiate their policies.

Sasanian Administration[121]

The most important offices were actually the hereditary privilege of the seven most important families of the realm (Arsacids/Sasanians?, Surens, Mihrans, Karins, Ispahbudhans, Spandiyadhs/Isfandiyar, Andigan?, Ziks?), most of whom were Parthian by origin.[122] According to Theophylact, the first of the seven great families placed the diadem on the king (hereditary in the Suren family), the second acted as commander-in-chief, the third led the administration (the *Hazarabed/Chiliarch/*Chancellor/Prime Minister), the fourth acted as Chief Judge (*Dadwaran Dadwar*, and also as head of the *mowbeds/*priests), the fifth commanded the cavalry (hereditary in the Ispahbudhan family), the sixth levied the taxes and controlled the royal treasuries, and the seventh was the custodian of arms and military uniform (*hambarakapet/ambarakapet*, overseer-of-stores, quartermaster[123]). Excluding the ones I have delegated to one family, the rest of these offices were held by different families at different times, but the Surens and Mihrans dominated the military appointments.

The Persian administration was highly organized with different grades and rankings, which was based on the abovementioned class divisions. The civilian administration of the ruler included '*Hazarabed*', counsellors, High-Priest, priests, the Master of Servants, Master of Ceremonies, Chief Scribe, Treasurer, Palace Superintendent, Chief Physician, scribes, accountants, etc. The scribes included writers of official communications, accountants, recorders of verdicts and registrations and covenants, writers of chronicles, physicians, poets, astronomers, etc. Most of these offices had equivalents in the Roman administration. The local kings possessed a councillor, a priest, a scribe, knights/nobles, messengers, and chiefs.

The administration of the empire was based on the abovementioned four quarters, each under a *Vitaxa*. Note the similarity with India, Armenia, Georgia and Rome. The *vitaxae* in turn consisted of provinces called *shahr*, administered by a *shahrdar*, that were divided into districts also known as *shahrs*, each under a *shahrab* (satrap) and *mowbed* (chief priest). The district was divided into *rustags* (several villages), and the smallest unit was the *deh* (village) under a *dehgan* (lesser nobility). This administrative hierarchy enabled the Sasanians to tap all available resources for their use when needed, and the presence of priests enabled them to exercise control over various members of this hierarchy.

Just like the Armenian kings, the Sasanian rulers also had their own feudal lands called the *ostan* that were headed by the *ostandar*. These lands produced both income and personal feudal levies for the ruler. It should be noted that the Roman emperors also possessed private property farmed by tenants that provided income and recruits to the army. In contrast to the late-Roman practices, the Sasanian *vitaxae*, *shardar* and *shahrabs* controlled both civilians and the military in their regions. It should also be noted that Sasanian control over the feudal territories of the magnates and kings was limited. In short, it is absolutely certain that the Sasanian administrative apparatus was an effectively organized hierarchical structure, the purpose of which was to collect resources for the upkeep and expansion of the empire.

The Sasanian Military[124]

The Sasanian military organization resembled a pyramid. At the very top was the *Shahanshah* (king of kings), who was assisted by the supreme commander of Iran, the *Iran-spahbadh*. The *Sparapet* (Commander of Cavalry, hereditary in the Ispahbudhan family), the *Vitaxae*, the thirty local kings, the *Kanarang*, the *Paygan-salar* (Commander of the Infantry), and the various other officers, such as *spahbadhs* (generals) and *marzbans* (governors), all served under the *Iran-spahbad*.

The position of the *Kanarang* was a special regional command that belonged to the family of Kanarangiya. Thanks to the presence of the strong position of the *Kanarang* in the *Vitaxa* of the North, all persons nominated to head the North had to take into account the opinions of the *Kanarang*. Therefore, it is not surprising that the *Kanarang* could also serve as the *Vitaxa* of the region. The *Hazarbed/Chiliarch* (Commander of the Thousands) was apparently some sort of 'Prime Minister', but the title also implies some kind of role in the military hierarchy. The commander of the bodyguard was probably the *Pushtigban-salar* (Commander of the Royal Guard). Several of these positions were hereditary in the great noble families. The military also included special functionaries: the senior vet, officers in charge of supply and arsenals, commanders of forts, cavalry instructors, infantry commanders, commanders of bodyguard units, commanders of foot archers, commanders of elite cavalry, and so on. Thanks to their well-organized administrative and military system, the Persians were able to organize, collect and train armies to rival the Romans.

According to the late source, the *Karnamag* of Khusrov I (9), the Persian military hierarchy consisted of seven ranks, which corresponds with the seven grades of *as-Siyasa al-ammiya*: 1) the *sahib al-liqa* (Lord of the Battle = *Iran-spahbed?*); 2) *batriq* (*patricius/ patrikios*, a Roman dignitary = the four *vitaxae*, possibly with the *Sparapet?*); 3 *amir* (general = *spahbeds?*); 4) *qa'id* (senior officer, deputy of the commander = *marzbans?*); 5) *mubariza* (champion, duellist); 6) *arif* (commandant of a squadron); and 7) *al-gund* (soldiers).[125] I have included the probable equivalent rankings for the third and fourth centuries within the brackets.

The army (*spah*) consisted of the bodyguard units, heavy cavalry (*asvaran/savaran*), the light cavalry provided by mercenaries and tribal forces, the elephants of the royal house, the foot soldiers (*paygan*), the navy, and the logistical services.

The Sasanians were also interested in the theoretical side of war and wrote several military manuals. True to their habit, the Sasanians wrapped military teachings into their religion so that the *Denkard* also contains a military section entitled the *Arteshtarestan* ('warrior-code'). The military manuals ensured that military knowledge passed unaltered from one generation to another while new treatises were also written and old ones improved.

It is commonly assumed that the Sasanian army was based on the decimal system, but it is possible that the Sasanian practice resembled the Roman system so that the figures also included recruits and servants who were not usually required to participate in combat except in the defence of the camp. The smallest unit attested was a 'company' (*washt*), which consisted of 100 men so that 10 companies made up a 1,000-man 'regiment' (*drafsh*), and ten regiments constituted a 10,000-man 'division' (*gund*). However, other sources suggest that in practice the Persians used divisions of 6,000 men (*caterva*/legion) and 12,000 men.

The Sasanians were able to put into the field as many men or even more than the Romans when they did not face serious hostilities on their other fronts. The rulers expected that the seven families would each contribute 10,000 horsemen to the army plus infantry when asked. This would mean that the rulers were always entitled to receive 70,000 feudal horsemen. However, since it was in practice impossible to collect the entire force on one front, the usual figures were lower, or, when high, included allies, mercenaries and/or infantry. A typical large army had a maximum of about 30,000–50,000 men, but when the ruler had collected forces from all over his vast domains he could put into the field armies of about 90,000–120,000 men including infantry, on top of which came the servants or other workers pressed for service. Thanks to the demands of supply, this kind of super-large force was employed against the Romans only in the sector of the *Vitaxa* of the West, while the other *Vitaxae* were protected by skeleton forces.

The Persians were always taking a gamble when they left the other fronts thinly defended. It should be noted that this was rare and that such large forces included many soldiers of poor quality and that such forces could not stay in the field for long periods of time except when very close to their supply depot located in their own territory. It was therefore usual that the Persians divided their forces when they invaded. Consequently, the Romans with their professional soldiers could expect to be able to withstand the Persian invasions unless they had been forced to transfer a very significant portion of their own forces elsewhere.

The flower of the Persian army was its 'knightly' heavy cavalry, which consisted of the members of *aswaran* and *azadan* who fought as cataphracts. It is not known with certainty whether the *Sparapet* commanded the knights, or allied cavalry, or all cavalry, or some specific unit, or was just responsible for the equipping, training and supplying of the cavalry. During Khusro I Anushirwan's reign the martial equipment of the knight consisted of the helmet, hauberk, breastplate, mail, gauntlet, girdle, thigh-guards, shield, *contus*-spear, sword, battle-axe, mace, bowcase, two bows and bowstrings, a quiver with thirty arrows, two extra bowstrings, a lasso, a sling and stones, and horse armour (either metal or leather).[126] The only places left unprotected during this period were the eyes and nostril holes in the mask worn with the helmet. The Persian cataphracts were superb horsemen who could even fight hand-to-hand with the Roman infantry for hours (lulls in combat included), which was not a mean feat considering the advantage that the footmen generally had when fighting against cavalry at close quarters. The *Shahanshah*'s bodyguard consisted of the so-called 10,000 Immortals that formed the elite corps of the cavalry. The Armenians, when fighting for the Persians, were also considered to be elite heavy cavalry. The light cavalry consisted mostly of allies or mercenaries and during this period included the Sagestani, Albani (which could also include cataphracts), Chionitai, Kushans, Arabs, Kadiseni, and Armenians.

The infantry consisted of the 'heavy infantry' and of the 'light infantry', drawn mostly from the ranks of the peasants. The *Paygan-salar* was the commander of the infantry. Their primary function was to act as servants to the knights and as 'cannon-fodder' in sieges. In fact, the Persians usually used infantry only for sieges or for the protection of the camps. The 'heavies' carried either wattle mantlets or huge shields that were covered with wickerwork and rawhide, and fought with spears and swords. In combat the 'heavies' usually formed the front ranks of the phalanx and the light infantry archers the rear. The standard tactic for the 'heavies' was to form a wall of shields, together with a hedgehog of spears, towards the enemy, while the archers, deployed behind, shot arrows.

According to Ammianus, at least some of the Persian infantry were equipped like gladiator *Murmillones*. The Dailamite/Dilemnite/Daylami tribesmen formed an elite corps, which carried shields, spears, pikes, swords, and dirks tied to the left arm. Despite being officially part of the Persian Empire, the Daylami had not been fully subdued, which meant that they fought as mercenaries. The Daylami also employed small quantities of archers and could fight as heavy or light infantry as needed.

The Sasanian elephant corps seems to have consisted mainly of the beasts kept in the royal parks. These elephants were used for a multitude of military purposes. Firstly, they served as beasts of burden. Secondly, they were used as a workforce to clear roads etc. Thirdly, they were used in combat as 'tanks' to create openings in the enemy line. Fourthly, they were used behind the troops, to induce the men to go forward, as observations posts, and as archery platforms. Fifthly, the elephants served as archery platforms, siege towers and battering rams in sieges. The pachyderms were divided into these different duties according to the amount of training received and according to their natural inclinations. Only the most highly trained beasts were usable in sieges and battles and could carry towers. In pitched battles the beasts were posted in front, or behind or on the flanks of the army as required by the situation. The war elephants were at their best as weapons of terror against men and horses unaccustomed to facing them. The Romans knew how to counter this threat and always sought to isolate and surround individual beasts (in particular the leaders of the pack), because even the wounding of individual beasts could cause the defeat of the entire elephant corps. The Romans knew how to open up their phalanx formations to provide intervals for the beasts to charge into while using missiles to enrage the elephants, and they also knew that elephants were particularly vulnerable to field artillery fire. Consequently, the Persians did not achieve any decisive advantage from the use of elephants, even if they still performed invaluable service.[127]

The Sasanians did possess a navy of some sort and/or they forced their merchant houses to provide ships whenever needed. The details are not known, but we do know that the Sasanians conducted naval campaigns across the Persian Gulf, for example during the reigns of Ardashir I, Shapur II and Khosrov I. During the reign of Khusro I the Persian ships (*kashtig*) carried 100 passengers each on top of the crew across the Gulf, which may be representative of the capacity of the vessels. The admiral of the navy was probably called *navbed*.[128] The probable ship type used by the Persians was the dhow, which did not stand a chance against Roman warships. (For diagrams of dhows, see the illustration pages in the section on the Arabs.)

The Sasanian approach to military conflict was very sophisticated and involved all kinds of calculations and the making of alliances, or they employed proxies such as the nomads or Arabs to fight on their behalf. The Persian armies always used spies, scouts, and took captives; used safe marching formations and fortified camps (with a separate cavalry detachment outside the camp, just like the Romans used during this era); and employed stratagems, ambushes and night attacks. Their marching formation consisted of the vanguard, the rear guard, the wings, and the centre. The commanders used standards, trumpets, drums and verbal commands to control their forces. The national standard was used only on special occasions to encourage the men. The troops were encouraged with religious ceremonies and pre-battle speeches. The traditional Persian machismo was evident in their eagerness to seek single combats before the battle. The outcome of such battles could decide the entire conflict in cases where both sides agreed to abide by its result, or because the outcome of such fight(s) affected the morale of the superstitious soldiers.

The Persians sought to position their forces in the most advantageous way, which usually entailed the positioning of the entire force or at least its centre on higher ground so that the army had the advantage of the wind and sun behind them. The Persian aim was to facilitate their ability to shoot arrows from their advantageous position and only then to charge. However, when the Persians considered it advantageous or necessary, they could still charge immediately. When they attacked they attempted to lower the enemy morale with loud shouting and war cries and loud drumming.

The cavalry battle line had two basic formations (see below) and several variants, which could also consist of specialized sections with differing equipment. This resulted from the use of allies. In such cases the Persians often placed their (preferably left-handed) mounted archers on the left wing and the lancers on the right wing. The two principal cavalry battle formations were the single-line and double-line formations. The single-line array placed the light cavalry vanguard and rear guard alongside the cataphracts so that the formation consisted of five parts (outer left, left, centre, right, outer right).

The position of the light cavalry depended upon the tactic chosen. If the light cavalry was placed on the outer wings, then the purpose was to outflank the enemy, and when they were placed between the cataphracts, the purpose was to harass the enemy frontally, so all used archery. The second variant of this array was that the entire line consisted only of the cataphracts. In such situations most of the Persian units were deployed as rhomboids that allowed the units to face threats from all directions.[129] It is possible, however, that only the flank divisions used rhomboids (just like it was with the Macedonians), while the cataphracts in the centre used the square/oblong formations.

The standard double-line formation consisted of the light cavalry in front (used to soften up the enemy with arrows) and cataphract reserves that charged at the right opportunity. The second variant of this array was that both lines consisted only of the cataphracts. The standard tactic even with this array was to withdraw the first line to replenish ammunition after they had run out of arrows, while the second line moved forward to pepper the enemy with arrows. The intention was always to destroy the enemy with arrows rather than through fighting at close quarters if at all possible.

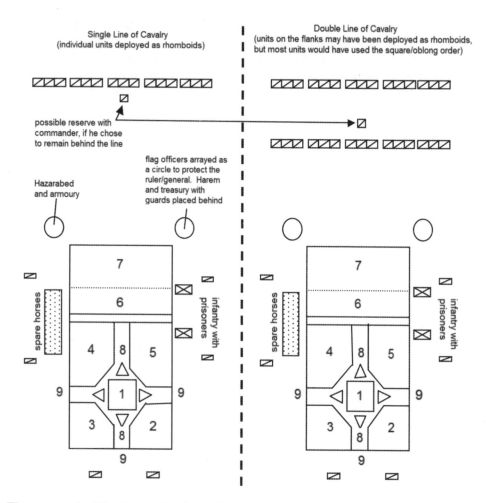

The two standard Persian cavalry formations with infantry and camp placed behind (not to scale)

– the probable structure of a Persian marching camp based on the supposition that later Muslim practices mirrored those of old Persia: 1) King or general, his entourage, guards, war chest etc. 2–5) Officers, officials, doctors, elephant keeper, entourages, guards, servants etc. 6) Cavalry. 7) Infantry. 8) Roads. 9) Gates. The Persians also posted a strong guard unit on one side of the camp to act as ambushing and guarding forces against any army trying to surprise them in their camp.

– the rear half with the ruler's entourage (1–5, 8–9) was the camp proper; and the front half (7) with infantry, wagons and hospital (could also include a trench and caltrops) was the portion facing the enemy (with no gates) that served as a bulwark against attackers. The cavalry advanced from the camp proper (6) to form the cavalry battle array. When the camp was built behind the battle line to protect the army in battle, it could include separate cavalry detachments to protect the flanks and rear, which I have added to the illustration on the basis of later practices. The reason for this reconstruction is that the Tafrij, which includes these detachments, includes several borrowings from the earlier Persian treatises as a result of which it is possible that these were also used by the Sasanians.

After Syvänne (2004, 2009) based on the Strategikon (11.1), Tarfij (the 5-lines formation), Gotha (square formation), and the illustration of the ancient Persian battle array by Fakhr-i Mudabbir.

The Persian, Parthian and Armenian rhombus (Aelian, Devine 18.4 and Byzantine Interpolation 45.1–2) typically consisted of mounted archers. The paper strength for the rhombus was 128 men.[130] The Persians' square/oblong order appears to have consisted of ranks and files with a frontage of eight and depth of four for a total of thirty-two men. In addition to this, Persian cavalry forces did include tribesmen that employed the skirmishing version of the small wedge array. The heterogeneous composition of the Sasanian forces ensured that there were variations in the unit orders and equipment of the troops.

When the infantry and other forces accompanied the army, these were placed in the rear so that the footmen with wagons were usually deployed in front of the camp proper to form a defensive bulwark for the cavalry. Occasionally, however, the infantry was also used as part of the battle formation and in these cases it was either deployed behind the cavalry (and elephants), or between the cavalry wings. The elephants could also be deployed with infantry.

The standard tactics with all formations was to outflank the enemy on both flanks (crescent), if the Persians possessed numerical superiority; to outflank the enemy only on one flank (preferably on the right because of the needs of archery), if only slightly superior; to destroy the enemy centre with a charge (convex), if outnumbered; and to place the entire army on higher ground and use archers, if the commander considered it unwise to deploy in the open. In desperate situations, the Persians formed a defensive circle on the spot.

The type of bows employed and the shooting technique varied according to the nationality and region of the force. Some employed the so-called Sasanian bow (long composite bow with long ears), while others used the so-called Hunnish bow (long composite bow that could be asymmetric) and still others a variant of the Scythian short

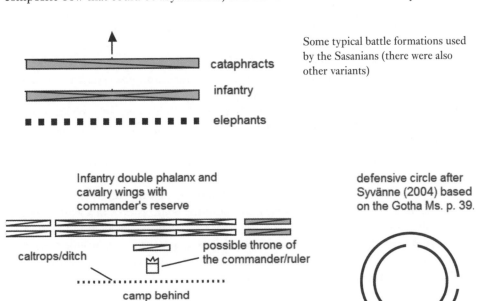

cataphracts

infantry

elephants

Some typical battle formations used by the Sasanians (there were also other variants)

Infantry double phalanx and cavalry wings with commander's reserve

defensive circle after Syvänne (2004) based on the Gotha Ms. p. 39.

caltrops/ditch

possible throne of the commander/ruler

camp behind

composite bow. As can easily be seen the names of the bows are quite misleading. The 'Sasanian bow' was best suited to delivering rapidly shot volleys of arrows either with the so-called 'Sasanian draw/lock' or with the 'thumb/Mongolian draw/lock'. The 'Hunnish bow' was best suited to delivering powerful long range shots with the so-called 'thumb draw/lock'. Both of these bows enabled the use of a prolonged archery barrage at long range and the avoidance of having to make contact with the enemy.

However, this is a simplified version of the facts. The length and the stiffness of the bow depended upon the user's height, muscle-power and length of arms. There were also several different variants of the thumb lock each of which had its advantages (and supporters), in addition to which the size of the hand and the lengths of the fingers affected which of the locks the archer could use. Furthermore, the archery tactic did not depend only on the type of bow and lock used. The bow's materials and the quality of the construction, as well as the type and material of the cord, all affected the performance of the bow. Similarly, the length, weight, and material of the arrow and the type of arrow-head all affected the performance. As a general statement one can say that the longer and heavier the arrow, the shorter its range and the greater its penetrative power, while the lighter the arrow, the longer its flight range would be at the cost of penetrative power.[131] The length of the arrow also had to be suitable for the length of the bow and its user. That is, within the limits stated above, the Sasanians and their allies could change the type of arrow employed according to the distance and type of protective equipment worn by the enemy. It was possible to pick and choose the best tactic and combination to the situation by varying the type of arrow, bow and lock.

The Parthians and Sasanians were famous for their archery and in particular for their 'shower archery' technique. The Persians were also ready to dismount to increase the effectiveness of their archery. We know from extant Muslim treatises that were based on Persian practices that, for example, Ardashir I invented a thumb lock/draw which was named after him. This suggests the possibility that the use of the thumb lock of Ardashir may have given his troops a slight advantage in archery over that of the Parthians, which later disappeared as they too adopted Ardashir's version as one of the locks in use. The Muslim archery treatises, all of which were based on Iranian originals, state that Ardashir I and Shapur I both paid a lot of attention to archery and after them archery declined until it was revived by Bahram Gur in the fifth century.[132] This 'decline' probably resulted from the increased use of armour by the cavalry which is in evidence from the year 328 onwards.

According to the Arab Archery (pp. 151–155), there were five (if Bustam's version is counted as one) versions of 'shower shooting': 1–3) a maximum of six arrows is placed on the right hand with varying gripping techniques; 4) a bundle of arrows is placed in the left hand, which in the opinion of the author of the book resulted in a weak grip (this was definitely used by the Parthians, for which see the illustration below); and 5) Bustam, who lived during the reign of Khosrov Anushirwan, appears to have invented the most effective version of the shower/successive shooting with five, ten or fifteen arrows.

The favourite tactic of the Sasanian Persians and most of the peoples of the Middle and Near East after them was shower-archery, as can be read from Procopius, Strategikon and Arab Archery (e.g. p.112). In sum, considering the fact that Ardashir was himself an expert archer and had invented one of the locks, it is more than likely that he had invented at least one of the versions (1–3) in which the arrows were gripped with the right hand, and this invention would have given his forces a slight advantage over the Parthians.[133]

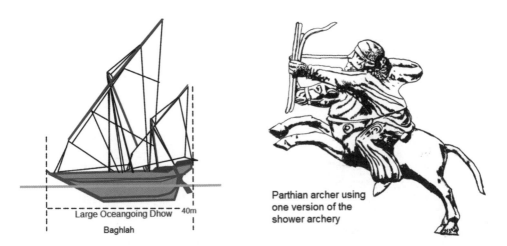

Large Oceangoing Dhow   40m
Baghlah

Parthian archer using
one version of the
shower archery

Unfortunately, it is impossible to make any definite comparisons regarding the capabilities of Roman mounted archers and the Persians beyond the general statement that the Persians usually had an advantage over the Romans in the sheer amount of arrows shot. This advantage could have resulted from the greater numbers of archers among the Persians but the archery techniques used by the Romans may have contributed to this. During the sixth century the Romans favoured the slower Hun-technique and bow, but powerful bows and thumb-locks were not unknown before the arrival of the Huns. Similarly we do know that the Romans used at least one version of the Persian 'shower-archery' technique, but we do not know which one, and it is possible that the Romans also changed their practices as they copied their enemies. However, we do know that at the Battle of Mursa in 351 the commander of the Armenian mounted archers fitted three arrows at a time to his bow, which does suggest the probability that the Romans and Armenians still used the slower variant and not the one invented by Ardashir or his successors.

Unlike the Roman sources would lead us to believe, the Sasanian melee techniques were very sophisticated and quite varied. The Sasanian cataphracts and *contus* -bearers employed their long spears with different types of two-handed grips that enabled them to vary their attack technique according to the situation.[134] The Sasanians were also using famous Indian-steel (two-edged straight) long swords with the sophisticated 'Italian grip' as well as pick-axes and maces against armoured and helmeted opponents, and at really close quarters various martial arts techniques. In short, the principal weapon of the Sasanians was their bow, but they were still very well trained for close quarters fighting if the situation was favourable.

If imitation is the highest form of flattery, then it can be said with good reason that the Persian cavalry equipment, archery, and tactics were superb. The Romans copied much of their cavalry tactics and equipment from the Parthians and Sasanians. Regardless of this, it is still clear that the Romans had the advantage in close quarters combat thanks to

Here is a sample of Sasanian cataphracts in action. Note the simultaneous use of the long *contus*-spear together with the bow. The only exception to this rule is the graffito from Dura Europus, which may actually imply that this *clibanarius* was actually Roman or Arabic rather than Persian or that the gorytus-quiver was placed on the left. Drawn after von Gall.

their cultural inclination to fight that way, while the Persians had the advantage in long range combat. The Persians rather fled and fought another day.

The Sasanian siege techniques were basically the same as those of Rome with the exception that they excelled in archery. Their offensive siege tactics included the use of surprise attacks, treachery, bribery and intimidation, blockade, assault, and use of siege equipment. If the enemy could not be surprised or taken through treachery, the Persians first offered terms and if these were not accepted they resorted to the actual siege. The siege techniques included the use of battering rams, ballistae, ladders and fire, mining, fire-bombs/explosives (see the narrative of the years 359–361), stone throwers, mantlets and wicker screens, elephants as siege towers, regular siege towers, and siege mounds. The Persians were more prepared to risk heavy casualties in offensive sieges and assault the walls regardless of the cost in lives than the Romans, probably because the rulers considered the peasants and allies as expendable 'cannon fodder'.

Defensive tactics were basically the same as those employed by the Romans, except that the Persians were more prepared to sally out and endanger their lives. The Persians were more stubborn as defenders than the Romans thanks to their patriotism and especially thanks to the fact that those who surrendered were considered traitors with the result that their families and relatives would face capital punishment. It was therefore with a good reason that the sixth-century Strategikon regarded the Persians as formidable when laying siege, but even more formidable when besieged. On the basis of the fact the Romans were still using an abandoned gigantic Persian battering ram from the 250s, the Persians probably possessed better and bigger battering rams that the Romans. It should be noted, however, that Julian's Persian campaign shows that the advantage held by the Persians in this field was only slight. (See the next book in the series!) By contrast, the Romans appear to have had better field and siege artillery, which enabled them to suppress Persian archers during sieges. Consequently, the Persians always captured Roman artillery pieces after a successful offensive siege and employed those in the subsequent sieges against the Romans.

Persian Ways of Intelligence Gathering

In order to be able to react fast to any emerging trouble Ardashir I also established an efficient network of informers and spies, probably in accordance with the Achaemenid model. According to the Letter of Tansar (24–26), Ardashir had informers and spies everywhere with the result that all men were trembling in fear.[135] However, according to the text, innocent and upright men had nothing to fear, because only those who were trustworthy, obedient, pure, devout, learned, religious and abstinent in worldly things were made the 'eyes' and informers of the Kings. As a result of this everything was supposedly reported accurately. The effectiveness of this system becomes apparent for example during Julian campaign when the Persian high command was clearly aware of every action committed by the Persian troops and commanders.

Similarly, according to Mirkhond (p.281), who refers to the final form of the system already in full operation, Ardashir increased the vigilance of the government with the introduction of a system of inspectors who had the duty of reporting to him every morning what had happened in the preceding day. With this in mind, he appointed intelligence officers for each part of his empire to provide him reports on common and particular matters of interest. In this way he was kept abreast of the general mood of the populace and of particular events taking place everywhere within the empire. The most impressive point of this was that even after Ardashir had enlarged his empire to encompass territory from the Euphrates to Indus, he still expected to be able to learn of events taking place in the farthest corners of his empire within twenty-four to forty-eight hours. It was the duty of the local postmasters to forward the relevant information for the Head Postmaster and King of Kings. The value Ardashir put into the gathering of intelligence is also apparent from the fact that the first thing he did every morning was listen to the intelligence reports.

Unfortunately thanks to the secrecy surrounding the system we do not know the exact details of this organization, but some educated guesses can be made. Firstly, the sources make clear that the royal postal service was used for internal security purposes, as were the inspectors/judges/counsellors of the clergy that were attached to each province, court and larger unit of the army. Secondly, one can speculate that the same was also true of the scribes (the Persian equivalent of the *notarii*) that were attached to every organization in the realm. Notably, the scribes were taught the so-called 'secret script', which would have enabled them to communicate secretly (Daryaee, 2009, 53). In addition to this, the Persians also appear to have had a foreign intelligence service of some sort that included (depending on the time period) at least Zoroastrian priests, Manicheans, and traders. The former probably operated as separate branches of the priestly class. On the basis of the events of 359 it seems probable that the merchant spies were controlled by the governors of the frontier regions. The same is obviously true of the scouts detached from military units. The governors in their turn must have reported any suspicious activities to their *Vitaxa*, and he in turn to the *Iran-spahbed*. Since Ardashir modelled most of his administration after the Achaemenid model, it is perhaps best to speculate that he also divided the intelligence services into separate organizations[136] 1:) the king's bodyguards under the *Pushtigban-salar* (who also performed spying/security functions around the court); 2) the eyes and ears of the king (i.e. the informers and probably also professional spies) operating under the mysterious 'King's Eye'[137] 3;) couriers/spies operating under the director of the royal post; and 4) the religious police consisting of the various branches of the clergy. It is also likely that seers and astrologers etc. were required to inform the ruler of what the nobles had asked, just like they were in Rome.

It is obvious that the extent to which the king would have been expected to take charge of matters in person has been exaggerated, but the all-encompassing nature of this police state system is still apparent. It is clear that such a large network of spies and informers had to be centrally directed so that only the most important pieces of news were brought to the king's attention while the less important decisions were left for the local authorities to decide. For example, the priests as judges would have been expected to carry out punishments for common crimes on behalf of the state at the local level.

Of note is also the great care that Ardashir took to ensure that his ambassadors were loyal and honest, and reported accurately what had been said. In his opinion this was very important because it was possible that if the messages were not reported accurately this would have resulted in unwanted wars and calamities. According to him, many armies had been defeated and many alliances broken as a result of the disloyalty and perfidy of the ambassadors.[138] Ardashir was clearly a man equipped with exceptional foresight, perception and intelligence.

The Sasanian spy organization seems to have worked relatively well against the Romans. The Persians appear to have usually been well informed of the activities that took place deep in the Roman territories. It is also important to understand that the Persian rulers always learnt of a Roman invasion within twenty-four to forty-eight hours from the time the invasion occurred regardless of where they were in the vast empire. If they had reserves available they could send orders for the troops to assemble and proceed towards the invaders within forty-eight to ninety-six hours. However, just like any modern spy organization all of the Sasanian security systems could fail, especially in the case of internal security. The best proofs of this are the frequent revolts of the princes and magnates. The system could work only when the King of Kings could retain the loyalty of his subjects. When the magnates and priests considered the ruler to be a tyrant they did not forward the necessary information to the king and did not hesitate to take action against him.

Sasanians vs. Romans

The Sasanians were by far the most sophisticated and dangerous of the enemies the Romans faced. The Persians possessed superior numbers of cavalry that the Romans could only match by strengthening their forces with Armenian and/or Gothic allies. The Persians also possessed superior numbers of archers, but thanks to Roman defensive armour and battle formations, this was not decisive. In fact, whenever the Romans had enough men available, they could expect to win their pitched battles. The Romans knew this and always sought to force the Persians to fight pitched battles while the Persians usually avoided these unless the situation demanded it. Since the Romans knew that Persian cavalry armies usually suffered only light casualties even when defeated, the Romans always sought to surprise the Persians or force them against an obstacle that prevented or hindered flight.

The Roman strategy against the Persians depended upon the situation and personality of the emperor. Some emperors (for example, Galerius, Constantine I, Constantius II – initially and at the end – Julian, and Valens from 369 to 377) were ready to take the offensive and were even ready to dream of the conquest of Persia. The idolization of Alexander the Great and Trajan had a role in this, but the exploits of Septimius Severus, Carus, and Galerius were also remembered. On the other hand, there were also emperors (Augustus, Tiberius, Nero, Diocletian, Constantius II between c. 344 and 360, Valens in 377, and Theodosius) who were readier to conclude peace or retain the status quo. Some emperors (Hadrian, Philip, Jovian, or Theodosius) were even ready to concede territory in return for peace. In short, Roman strategy towards Persia varied, but with the exception of Julian there is one common feature for all of the emperors, which was that they all sought to form alliances against Persia in order to isolate it and to fortify the borders and interior to improve the defences.

Deserts from Mesopotamia to Egypt (See the Maps Section)

The military tactics of the desert peoples of Africa and the Near/Middle East were quite similar. Their tactical methods arose from the place of their habitation, the desert, and from the lifestyle it forced upon them. They employed armies that consisted principally of lightly-equipped horsemen and footmen. They raided the lands of the settled peoples from within the safety of the desert. The mobility of their camels and horses allowed them to surprise their enemies and to escape before being caught. In addition, the use of camels to protect the camps provided them with a barrier which they used effectively against enemy cavalry. Despite the similarities, there were also differences that arose from the weapons which they used. The similarities and the differences are dealt with below.

The Arabs
There were a great variety of Arab/Saracen tribes from Mesopotamia to Arabia. Some of these were urbanized and/or sedentary while others were semi-nomadic or entirely nomadic. In addition, some of these tribes were located within the Roman borders (inner *limes*) while others were located just outside them (outer *limes*), or travelled between the areas, and still others further away (these included independent tribes and clients of Persia). Some of the tribes within Roman territory were Romanized and sedentary and employed as regulars while others had retained their tribal structures, even when sedentary, and were therefore treated as barbarian federate tribes. The former had received Roman citizenship in 212, but the latter had not. The tribes of the buffer zone, that is the outer *limes* (included sedentary, semi-nomadic and nomadic tribes), were also subsided to act as federates against the semi-nomadic or nomadic tribes still further

away. The loyalty of these tribes depended upon their treatment and ultimately on the existence of adequate regular military forces in the area. The primary motivators of the Arab *Foederati* and Bedouins were subsidies and the prospect of booty. The only way the Romans could control the Bedouins was with the help of some powerful Arab federate phylarch.[139]

The dominant federate group of the northern sector along the Euphrates were the Tanukhids who had migrated across the Euphrates at the time when Ardashir I overthrew the Parthians. After their arrival and after the fall of Palmyra, the Romans appear to have concluded a treaty with them and promoted them to become the dominant group in the area. The other tribes of Mesopotamia and northern Syria remain unknown. The Tanukhid military camps (*hadir/paremboles*) appear to have been located outside the cities of Chalcis, Beroea, Hiyar, Anasartha, Maarrat al-Numan, and possibly Zabad and Sawwaran, all of which were located in Northern Syria. The case for the cities of Epiphania and Laodicaea is less certain. They may also have had a military camp just outside Callinicum. After the fall of Palmyra, the Tanukhids appear to have occupied a similar dominant position among the federate tribes as the Salihids and Ghassanids later, which means that it is likely that the Romans had already appointed its king as phylarch of all Arab tribes.[140]

In my opinion there is a strong case for a marriage union of the Great Houses of the Tanukhids and Lakhmids for the fourth century so that these two Great Families eventually became mixed up in the sources. The best evidence for this comes from the fifth century when the rule of the then pro-Persian Lakhmids in Hira was protected by two groups of soldiers, the Tanukhids and the Sasanian Savarans, which suggests the presence of two 'foreign' contingents to support the rule of the Lakhmid King in the city – that is, when the Lakhmid King had regained the possession of Hira, he had brought with him his own personal retinue. It is very probable that the union of the two tribes had already occurred during the reign of Imru al-Qays, the 'King of All Arabs', who apparently became the Roman federate Phylarch of the Arabs in c.313/4.

The *Foederati* of the central section of the frontier undoubtedly consisted of several tribes, but we have information regarding only three of them that had dominant position over the lesser tribes: the Kalb, the Salihids, and the Lakhmids. I would suggest that after the desertion of the Lakhmids to the Roman side, which was probably sealed with a marriage contract with the Tanukhids, the Romans promoted their chieftain Imru to the dominant position (phylarch) among the tribes of Northern, Central, and Southern Arabia (including the Provincia Arabia). The Lakhmids were certainly present near Namara where their king Imru al-Qays was buried. The Salihids appear to have occupied the area just east of the Dead Sea near the Wadi Sirhan. They were to become the dominant tribe during the fifth century. The Kalb were located south of the Lakhmids and occupied the strategically important Dumat al-Jandal in the north of the Arabian Peninsula. They and the southern Federates (see below) protected the important trade routes from Arabia and stood later as bulwarks against attacks by the Arab allies of Persia.[141]

The Federates of the southern portion of the frontier consisted of Judam, Amila, and Balqayn, and possibly of the Banu-Salih and Bali. The Judam and Amila were considered sister tribes and occupied the area in the Hisma region in the northern Hijaz, east of the Araba and the Jordan. The Balqayn (Banu-al-Qayn) were located within the Roman limes in Sinai and Trans-Jordan. The Banu-Salih were likewise located within Roman territory near Mt. Sinai. The Bali lived south of Judam, but possibly still within the borders of Provincia Arabia. Collectively these tribes together with the Kalb protected the Roman frontiers against the Arab allies of Persia.[142]

The armies of the Federate Arabs, the Bedouins bordering the Roman Empire, and the Arab allies of Persia usually used camels for the transport of men and supplies. Horses were used for fighting. It was rare that the camels were used as mounts in combat. The use of camels as beasts of burden provided the sedentary Arabs and Bedouins with the ability to move in the deserts from one oasis to another, unless this was blocked by the enemy. To put it simply, the Arabs used the desert as their cover from which they launched surprise attacks, after which they retreated back to the desert. These surprise attacks were typically directed either against Arabs of the oases, or against sedentary settlements. The cavalry consisted mostly of light cavalry lancers (spears, javelins, sword, shield, and possibly some armour and helmet) and to a lesser extent of mounted archers, but it was also possible that both long-range and melee weapons were carried simultaneously. In addition to these, there were small numbers of cataphracts armed with bows and melee weapons, but their numbers had diminished after the fall of Palmyra. The armies of central Arabia appear to have consisted mostly of camel mounted infantry, who fought with short swords, long spears, and bows, but spear-armed horsemen were also employed. The standard marching array of the Arabs and Bedouins was a *khamis*, a tribal army of five components: centre, two wings, vanguard, and rearguard that could readily be deployed for combat in various ways.

The typical cavalry attack consisted of a charge at the gallop in loose and irregular formation, which, if successful, was followed up by pursuit. The charge could also include the use of archery to disorder and disorient the enemy. If the charge was unsuccessful, the lancers retreated and possibly tried to repeat the charge. Some of the Bedouin tribes (just like their 'cousins' in the cities) had also learnt in Roman and Persian service how to employ their cavalry in tight and well-ordered formations. In contrast to their cavalry, the Arabic infantry almost always fought as tightly arrayed phalanxes. The open terrain made this a necessity, but when needed they still knew how to fight in looser formations in difficult terrain. If they faced strong opposition, the Arabs and Bedouins did not consider it shameful to flee, but when they decided to engage the enemy in combat, they were absolutely fearsome as light cavalry lancers just as they were justifiably famous for their handling of the sword at close quarters. In 378 the Goths in front of Constantinople had a taste of how fearsome the Arabs could be when they wanted. The Arab commanders often led from the front, but this depended upon the situation.

The Arabs who lived along the coasts of the Red Sea could also seek to enrich themselves by piracy, but their sewn ships (dhows) posed no serious naval threat to the Romans. It sufficed for the Romans to place archers on board their merchantmen and use their allies (depending upon the time period the Lakhmids, Himyarites, and Aksumites) to police the coasts and waters. However, there were periods in which the Romans also posted warships in the Red and Arabian Seas to support military operations undertaken in support of their ally in the area (see the narrative).

A procession of Palmyran nobles about AD 100-150
Note the bow-cases and quivers attached to the rear of the saddles as well as the ends of the spears between the legs (shown with the darker colour). This group was clearly equally well adapted for long and short range combat. The equipment is clearly copied from the Parthians. This is how the Arab/Bedouin armies (when lightly-equipped) would have looked like when they came out of the desert to assail the settlements of the sedentary peoples. The wealthier Arab and Bedouin tribes could also bring armour with them (placed in saddle bags carried by the camels) so that they could then put on their armour when needed.

The Arabian Limes

The Roman strategy in the southern sector of provincial Arabia consisted of the use of diplomacy, a show of force, and the integration of various tribes into the economic system through trade and treaties. With these means the Romans sought to ensure that there would always be a friendly tribal chieftain at the head of a tribe or tribal confederation. The Roman position remained strong in the area.[143]

The defences in the area consisted of the Federate Arabic tribes (both within and outside the border), strategically placed guard towers, forts, fortifications, and garrisons. These defences had many purposes: 1) the Federate tribes provided intelligence of the activities occurring in the desert and also policed the desert areas and when necessary were used to supplement the regular forces that also included Arabic units; 2) the forward-posted towers and forts gave the Romans an early warning of an approaching enemy force; 3) the forts placed to guard the oases denied an enemy access to these; and 4) if necessary, the larger concentrations of forces in the garrisons gave the Romans the ability to assemble substantial numbers of forces via their road network at the chosen assembly point to engage the enemy. Regardless of the network of roads and fortifications, this system was still heavily reliant on the loyalty of the Arabic allies, because it was only through their services that the Romans could obtain accurate and timely information of the events taking place in 'Arabia', and it was also thanks to them that they could police the desert. When the Arab allies were in revolt, the Romans could only react to the invasions or raids after they had already taken place.

The Yemeni [144] (See Maps Section)

By about 210 Yemen was dominated by three states Himyar ('Homerites'), Saba, and Hadramawt. The history of the third century was dominated by the wars these three waged against each other, or against their neighbours, or against or with the Aksumites against each other. Eventually the Himyarites emerged on top with the result that in 272 the Aksumites joined the Palmyrenes in a vain attempt to take control of the trade network. By about 275 the Himyarites had conquered Saba and with it its desert vassals the Kinda. This was followed up by the conquest of Haramawt with the help of the Sabaeans and Kinda in about 290. By about 295 the king of Himyar used the title of King of Saba, Dhai-Raydan, Hadramawt, and Yamanat. After this, the Himyarites turned their attention towards Central Arabia and the Persian Gulf, which eventually brought them into conflict with the king of Hira. However, the Himyarites seem to have recognized the Aksumites as their overlords by at least about 296–298, which suggests a defeat, but the situation fluctuated.

The change in the balance of power away from the desert based tribes to the tribes occupying the mountains and coast in the third century resulted from the Roman transferral of their trade away from the traditional caravan routes dominated by pro-Persian tribes to the sea routes controlled by the Romans. There are several indications of this. Firstly, the spread of the power of pro-Persian tribes (especially the Lakhmids) to central Arabia effectively blocked Roman trade routes; secondly, the Aksumite king Endubis and his successors modelled their monetary system on the Roman model, which does suggest strong trade links. However, the situation was volatile and alliances changed.

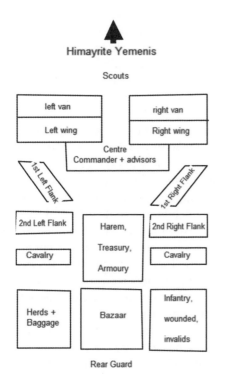

Himyarite 'Knight' and Axeman
Drawn after Yule and Robin Fig. 159 with the
reconstructed lower half of the relief (below dotted line).

At least from about 270 onwards to about 328 the Aksumites were enemies of Rome. The Himyarites appear to have been clients of the Aksumites at least until about 298 and therefore enemies of Rome, but they appear to have thrown off the Aksumite yoke at least temporarily after that, or at least their independent embassy to Persia in about AD 300 would seem to suggest this, but, as said, the alliances were unstable (see the narrative).

The ancient Yemeni military structure consisted of four different elements:[145] 1) the national troops called the *Khamis* under the king, or one of his generals; 2) levied troops from the highland communities; 3) cavalry (light and heavy); and 4) Bedouin allies/mercenaries. It is not known whether the *Khamis* consisted of professional soldiers or peasant conscripts, but the king's bodyguards certainly did consist of professionals. As is evident from the ancient battle formation of the Himyarites preserved in the thirteenth-century Persian treatise (illustrated above), the vast majority of the Himyarite army consisted of infantry, and this is also confirmed by other sources. The main weapons of the infantry were dagger and spear, but true swords were also used by the wealthy. There is probably some racial pride in the claim by al-Kindi (1.8–9) that the best swords were the ancient Yemeni steel swords, but at the same time it must be said that many of his contemporaries in the ninth century seem to have shared this view.[146] This implies that the Himyarites favoured fighting at close quarters and were evidently very good fighters with the dagger and sword, but there is still enough evidence to prove that bow, sling and axe were also used, which naturally lends support to the educated guess that that infantry consisted of specialized heavy and light forces, even if there is also evidence for the use of multi-purpose footmen. For the duration of the march, the infantry was usually mounted on camels and then dismounted for combat. The poor who could not afford a camel rode pillion.

The cavalry appears to have constituted at most about 10–25 per cent of the army, but their importance should not be underestimated. It too appears to have consisted of the specialized heavy and light contingents, the former consisting mainly of the Yemenis (see the 'Knight' relief) and the latter of the Bedouins. The baggage train of the army consisted of the camels and asses and their handlers.

By Roman standards the sizes of the Sabaean and Himyarite armies were modest, but at the height of its power Himyar still possessed enough men to conquer most of the Arabian Peninsula, which suggests that at least it, as the most populous tribe, possessed thousands of men at its disposal. Most of the evidence (mainly inscriptions with some scattered literary evidence) suggests that the typical size for the army in Yemen was less than one thousand men. The inscriptions mention raiding forces or armies of 40, 50, 203, 250, 270, 670 (20 of which were 'regular' cavalry and 50 other cavalry), 1026, and 2500, but there is also evidence for the use of larger armies. According to one inscription, the Hadramawt army suffered 2,000 casualties on one occasion, and still another mentions 4,000 defenders for Shabwa. One source mentions that 1,500 men and 40 cavalrymen defeated 16,000 non-regular Himyarites. This last mentioned piece of evidence is considered unreliable, but in my opinion there is plenty of circumstantial evidence to support it. From later evidence, including the military treatises, we know that the Muslim military organization (16, 32, 64, 128, 256, 512, 1024, 2048, 4096, 8192, 16284) was based on Hellenistic Greek practices and it is therefore quite possible that the 16,000 men in question consisted of the Himyar tribal levy/phalanx. The various figures (600; 150;

750 camel-mounted and 70 horse of which 30 camel-mounted and 4 horse were detailed as scouts) given by the inscriptions (E.12.4; C.350.4–6; J.662.6–23) for the size of the vanguard of the Sabaean *Khamis* also suggests figures of about 3,000–4,000 men for the standard *Khamis* of Saba, but we should take into account the facts that Himyar had the largest population and, after the conquest of the other kingdoms of Yemen, the Himyarites had access to the entire military pool of the area. Similarly, the thousands of warriors (for example in Tabari i.2218–2221 for the battle of al-Qadisiyyah: 3,000 Yemenis reinforced later with 2,000 Yemenis) required from Yemen by the Caliphs suggests a sizable pool of both professionals and conscripts. In short, the combined army consisting of the three *Khamis* (Saba, Himyar, Hadramawt) would have had about 9,000–12,000 men in addition to which came the feudal forces, levies and Bedouins. The full potential of the Himyarite forces in Yemen alone cannot have been much lower than 30,000–40,000 men in addition to which came the forces of the various client kingdoms (60,000?).

The battle formation illustrates nicely how well-ordered and disciplined the Himyarite battle formation was, especially its infantry divisions. The battle array provided an all-round defensive perimeter for the commander/king and his retinue while also presenting a solid front against enemies to the front. It also provided several layers of reserves as well as forces for the outflanking of a careless enemy. In fact, the cavalry was posted so far back that the horsemen could almost be seen as ambushers who would have suddenly burst forth from behind the many divisions of infantry to take the enemy in the flank.

The Himyarite navy appears to have consisted of the dhow merchant ships meant either for trade in the Red Sea, Arabian Sea or Indian Ocean, and small numbers of pirate vessels. The dhow was and is an easily manoeuvred sewn boat or ship that was powered by one to two lateen sails. There were several different classes and types of dhows meant for a great variety of specialized uses that at least in modern times are classified according to the type of hull. The larger ship types include the following: *baghlah, batil, boum, ghanjah, jalibut, sambuq/sambuk/sanbuq*, and *zaruq*. Some of these are illustrated below.

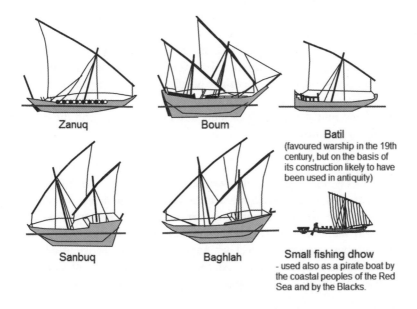

Zanuq

Boum

Batil
(favoured warship in the 19th century, but on the basis of its construction likely to have been used in antiquity)

Sanbuq

Baghlah

Small fishing dhow
- used also as a pirate boat by the coastal peoples of the Red Sea and by the Blacks.

On the basis of nineteenth-century practice and ancient origins of the *batil*, it is perhaps justified to speculate that this was the principal ship type used by the Arab pirates of the Red Sea. The bulk of the Himyarite naval assets lay in the ports of Mukhawan, Aden, Qana, and after its conquest also in Oman. These ports could house truly significant numbers of these ships. For example, on one occasion in the third century the Sabeans destroyed forty-seven cargo vessels/*sambuccas* in one of the Hadramawt ports (ry.533.9–10, Beeston, 17, 50) and if these are to be identified with the *sambuqs/sanbuqs* (1 to 3 masts) favoured by the modern inhabitants of Yemen, it is clear that each of the ports had respectable numbers of large vessels.

The merchant houses in these areas indeed possessed true oceangoing ships that could carry, when loaded wisely, about 100–150 men on board and when badly overcrowded up to 400 men. The best proof for the former is that six dhows carried 100 Persian soldiers each across the Persian Gulf during the sixth century, while the best proof for the latter is Buzurg's referral to such in AD 919, admittedly late but undoubtedly true also for the earlier period, because the Romans required even elephants to be carried in ships from India.[147] The merchant houses exploited the monsoons in their trade so that they carried their wares from Arabia to India in the winter and from India to Arabia in the summer. The principal or sole naval tactic employed by the users of the sewn ships was the boarding of an enemy vessel after its crew had been subjected to a rain of missiles. Despite their great size, these ships with their sewn hulls were still vulnerable to being sunk by the oar- and sail-powered Roman warships with their nailed hulls during those periods of time when these were deployed in the area.

The inscriptions also prove that the Himyarites employed a relatively efficient intelligence gathering organization, consisting of spies and agents that provided the commanders with timely information on enemy actions. The Himyarites were part of the international trade network and therefore it is not surprising that their diplomats could be found in Roman territory, Aksum, Ctesiphon, and in India. Their military campaigns were also well organized. If needed, supplies were deposited in advance to supply depots after which the king summoned his vassals, levies, and allies and set a date and place to assemble for a campaign. After this, the force was divided into units for the campaign. The Himyarites appear to have favoured the use of raids (wells and fields destroyed, booty taken, people killed or captured) and show of force (battles and conquest of cities through hunger or assault) to compel their neighbours to accept their rule. Wars were fought for a great variety of reasons, but the most important ones were the maintaining of control of trade routes, gathering of booty and military glory, and the punishment of disloyal subjects or clients.

Egypt (See Maps Section)

Life in Egypt was entirely based on the periodical floods of the Nile. Egypt was basically one long oasis around which were some scattered oases in the desert. In addition to this, the Red Sea provided fish and a commercial sea route to India. Most of the cities, towns and villages were naturally built along the Nile, just like the Roman fortresses.

After the conquest of Egypt by Octavian Augustus, the initial encounters with Egypt's southern neighbours, the Kingdom of Meroe, were hostile, but both sides soon found out that it was more beneficial to conclude a mutually beneficial alliance because this entailed greater profits from commercial traffic going through the hands of the Meroites. In contrast, the permanent conquest of Meroe would have been a very costly enterprise. As a result of this solution the Romans were able to post only a small and insignificant number of soldiers south of the first cataract, because they could rely on the city state of Meroe to maintain the equilibrium. The tactics of the nomadic tribes of the Nile Valley bore close resemblance to those of the Moors (see later).

The strategic significance of Egypt arose from the fact that it was one of the three principal breadbaskets of the Empire, the other two being North Africa and Aquitania. The principal purpose of the garrisons of the North of Egypt was to secure these vital grain shipments both to Rome and to Byzantium/Constantinople. It is also not a surprise that Egypt possessed more civilian police forces and guards than any other part of the empire, most of which were used to guard each part of the process of farming, from the use of sluices to the guarding of the fields. Egypt also lay between two important commercial routes: 1) the Nile route through which the merchants brought merchandize from Africa and Red Sea (through Myos Hormos and Berenice); and 2) the Red Sea route through Trajan's Canal that brought merchandize from Arabia, Africa and India. The latter of these was particularly important.

In addition to these, Egypt also possessed some very important gold and emerald mines in the eastern desert (between the Nile and the Red Sea) as well as quarries of building stone. Egypt possessed the only quarry that produced porphyry, the favourite stone of the emperors. The harbours of the Red Sea were also important transport routes for the produce coming out of the desert.

The Romans faced three potential threats and the placing of the garrisons reflected this. The most typical threat facing the Roman administration was urban unrest in the city of Alexandria, which is the reason why the bulk of the troops were placed right next to it, and naturally there were also civilian police forces in the area. In an emergency these very same troops posted in the north were also used to quell disturbances in the south, as well as in Libya. This problem caused Diocletian to put the entire region under one commander, the *Dux Aegypti Thebaidos utrarumque Libyarum*. Before his reforms the size of the force posted in the north was not large (one legion plus auxiliaries), because the urban dwellers and the neighbouring *Marmaridae* of Libya did not pose any significant military threat. The situation was about to change with the migration and creation of the Austuriani/Laguatan League that required greater concentration of forces.

The most significant threat was the threat of usurpation, but the smallness of the garrison made it relatively easy for the authorities to quell these. This caused Firmus to seek support from the nomadic tribes of the south. The small size of the Roman army in the north also meant that whenever a significant unforeseen threat arose from the east (for example, the Palmyrans and the Muslims), the army was unable to stop it.

The nomadic and semi-nomadic tribes of the Western Desert, Eastern Desert and the south (mainly the Blemmyes and Nubians, but in the Western Desert also the smaller tribes of Goniotai, Mastitai, and Mazikes) and the well-organized Kingdom of Meroe formed the third threat to Roman rule. The Roman response was to protect the choke point of the Nile at Syene just north of the 1st cataract. The rough terrain of the cataract forced all attackers to leave their boats and march on land making them vulnerable to attack. The Romans also posted another garrison at Philae ('the gate of Nubia') above the cataract to act as a staging point for attacks into Nubia. These two cities together with Elephantine contained three cohorts of soldiers and formed the hub of the army of Upper Egypt.

The occupation of Nubia south of Philae was considered to be of secondary importance and was therefore left to detachments whose mission was to collect intelligence, back up friendly tribes and rulers, and to police the Dodekaschoinos and its temples.[148] The policing of the Dodekaschoinos, however, proved very costly and as we shall see Diocletian adopted a new strategy in the area. The deserts were guarded by small mobile detachments, garrisons and forts that were placed to protect the oases (which provided tax income) and other economically important places like mines or roads or crossroads.

The events of the latter half of the third century proved that these defensive arrangements were insufficient in the face of the new threats that arose mainly in the south. It is quite probable that the Palmyran invasion in combination with the usurpations in Egypt (Aemilianus c.260–261; most importantly that of Firmus in c.272, who appears to have been aided by the Blemmyes, Arabs and Aksumites;[149] and the usurper Saturninus was also recognized in Egypt in c.280) created the whole problem. Firstly, as a result of the usurpations and Palmyran invasion the defeated Egyptian forces suffered very heavy casualties, which weakened the defences against local threats. Secondly, Firmus appears to have brought the Blemmyes to the north to act as his allies and thereby destroyed the Roman defensive arrangements. On the basis of his friendship with the Aksumites (Ethiopians), he may also have received support from them. The policies of the Palmyrenes and then of Firmus appear to have been to support the Aksumites and Blemmyes against the Meroites (if they were not already clients of Aksum), which appears to have upset the delicate balance of power in the region leading eventually to the downfall of the Kingdom of Meroe in the next century. The second of the goals may have been to bypass also the Himyarites with the help of the Aksumites, if they were independent and not clients of Aksum at the time. The goal of the Palmyrenes and Firmus appears to have been to facilitate the international trade network from the Red Sea to India in an effort to bypass the Sasanians.[150] The revolt of Aemilianus, on the other hand, seems to have been behind the migration of some Egyptian/Berber tribe that came to form the core of the Austuriani Confederation.

The account of Rufinus also proves that the Aksumites and Romans were enemies at the turn of the fourth century. According to him, at the time the custom dictated that, if the Aksumites had learnt from the neighbouring tribes (implies that these were vassals of Aksum) that the *foedus* with Rome had been broken, they had the right to kill the Romans. Accordingly, in the late-third or early-fourth century, on one occasion the Aksumites boarded a Roman ship that carried the philosopher Merobius, killed its crew and captured two Tyrian and Christian boys, Frumentius and Aedesius, and enslaved them.[151]

The important quarries and mines of the eastern desert and the harbours of the Red Sea also needed protection. The Roman solution was to build a series of desert outposts and forts along the roads from the Nile to the coast, each manned by small numbers of soldiers. The Mons Porphyrites continued to be important also in the fourth century, the best evidence of which is that Diocletian extended the road to Abu Sha'ar and had a fort built there. The desert terrain made it unnecessary to post large numbers of troops in the area. The principal threats were the bandits and the Blemmye raiders, which usually required only policing and only in very exceptional circumstances was it necessary to deploy sizable armies in the region. (For further details, see Breeze, 129–132.)

The Meroites (See Maps Section)

The Kingdom of Meroe (Kushites) upheld the old Egyptian civilization in what is modern Sudan. Meroe was wealthy and urbanized thanks to its agricultural produce and international trade. Meroe was a hierarchically organized society, which was also probably reflected in its military administration. There is some evidence that the members of the royal family led armies, and for the existence of a 'general of the land', 'general of Meroe', '*strategos* of the water' (commander of the Nile fleet?), commandants of fortresses, and 'chief of the bowmen'. The officers appear to have usually combined military and civilian duties.[152]

However, as regards the fighting methods, they were inferior in the face of Roman aggression. According to Strabo the 'Ethiopians' (Meroites) and Meroe were not numerous because they inhabited only a narrow track of land along the Nile. They were also badly commanded and badly armed. Therefore it is not surprising that they eventually fell victim to their neighbours. The Meroites used cavalry, but the bulk of the troops consisted of infantry organized for combat as an infantry phalanx. These men used large oxhide shields, and were equipped with axes, spears, and swords. The weapons of choice, however, were spears and bows equipped with poisoned (iron-tipped or stone-tipped) cane or wood arrows. The principal tactic was to pepper the enemy with arrows from a great distance, which was done with great efficiency. Archaeological evidence proves that the Meroites were using thumb-rings and the so-called Mongolian release. At least part of their army also appears to have continued to use bronze weapons. The Meroites also employed local small African elephants both for ceremonial and military purposes. There also exists evidence for the use of forts to protect strategic locales.[153]

Since the only extant accounts of the fighting between the Romans and Meroites date from the Principate I will give a summary of those. It is clear that the Romans and Meroites must have also fought after that. The first hostile encounter between the Romans and the Kingdom of Meroe occurred when the latter invaded Egypt and attacked the cities of Syene, Elephantine and Philae in 25–21 BC. The Romans had imposed on Meroe a heavy tribute with the result that they now exploited the absence of Roman troops that were campaigning in Arabia under Aelius Gellius. The Roman response was swift and brutal. The governor of Egypt, Petronius, with 10,000 foot and 800 horse crushed the enemy army of 30,000 men, after which he conquered several of their cities. The end result was that the Meroites begged for peace, which was granted. According to Strabo, thereafter the three below-strength cohorts posted at the 1st cataract were enough to stop any attempts by the Meroites. This suggests that contrary to the common opinion the relationship between the Romans and the Meroites was not always amicable. This seems to be confirmed by reference to two Roman military expeditions against the 'Ethiopians' during the late-first and early-second century in Ptolemy's Geography 1.8.1–7, which also suggests that similar hostilities may have been left out from the extant sources.[154]

According to Ptolemy, Septimius Flaccus led his troops from Leptis Magna across the Sahara to Garama (the capital of Garamantes, see later) and from thence the march against

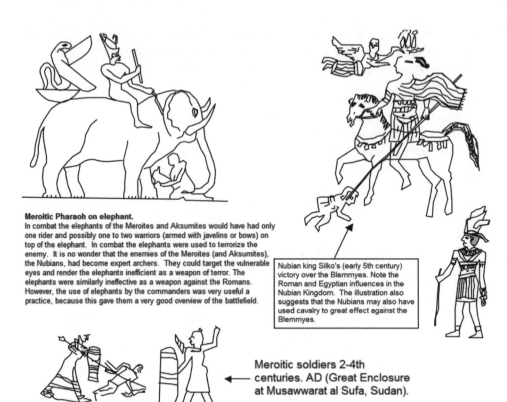

Meroitic Pharaoh on elephant.
In combat the elephants of the Meroites and Aksumites would have had only one rider and possibly one to two warriors (armed with javelins or bows) on top of the elephant. In combat the elephants were used to terrorize the enemy. It is no wonder that the enemies of the Meroites (and Aksumites), the Nubians, had become expert archers. They could target the vulnerable eyes and render the elephants inefficient as a weapon of terror. The elephants were similarly ineffective as a weapon against the Romans. However, the use of elephants by the commanders was very useful a practice, because this gave them a very good overview of the battlefield.

Nubian king Silko's (early 5th century) victory over the Blemmyes. Note the Roman and Egyptian influences in the Nubian Kingdom. The illustration also suggests that the Nubians may also have used cavalry to great effect against the Blemmyes.

Meroitic soldiers 2-4th centuries. AD (Great Enclosure at Musawwarat al Sufa, Sudan).

the 'Ethiopians' took three months to accomplish. The second campaign under Julius Maternus started at Leptis Magna from which he advanced to Garama. After joining forces with the king of the Garamantes, he marched for about four months to Agisymba (Aksumia?), the country of the Ethiopians, where the rhinoceroses gathered.[155] There are three things that suggest that the campaign was really directed against either the 'real' Ethiopians (Aksumites) or against the Meroe 'Ethiopians': 1) the word 'Ethiopian'; 2) the length of the journey – three to four months; and 3) the presence of rhinos.[156] There is no definite certainty whether the Ethiopians were the Aksumites (Agisymba) or the Meroites. The only things that definitely speak for the Meroites is that they were the neighbours of Rome; and that Meroe shielded the Aksumites. The intention of the Romans was clearly to surprise the enemy with the help of an allied kingdom.

It is feasible that the Romans were also simultaneously attacking Meroe from the north to make the surprise even greater. It is quite possible that similar expeditions took place about which we know nothing because of the poor survival of the sources from the third to fourth centuries. Notably, the extant portions of Dio fail to mention the expeditions from Leptis Magna to the deserts. We know of these only because Ptolemy chose to mention them as curiosities. This suggests there is a possibility that the late Romans also tapped the resources of the Garamantes at times when they conducted operations in the area. What is certain, however, is that the Romans did fight occasionally against the Nubians,

Blemmyes, and Aksumites, which does suggest the probability that the Meroites were involved either as allies of Rome or as allies or subjects of the others.

The decline of the Meroites started when the Aksumites and Romans were able to bypass them. This resulted from two things: 1) the Romans were increasingly using the Red Sea route; and 2) the Aksumites conquered territory in the second-half of the third century as a result of which they were able to build a road to the Roman territory bypassing the Meroites (Burstein, 101–104). The primary purpose of this military road was to control the client tribes of the eastern desert (Hatke, 59ff). However, it is still not known when the Kingdom of Kush/Meroe ceased to exist as an independent unit.[157] The last recorded king lived c.AD 283–300, but there is evidence for the existence of kings after him possibly even up to the second half of the fourth century. There is also evidence for the building of fortresses during the early-fourth century, which does suggest some military urgency, and there is evidence for the occupation of Meroe by the Aksumites from the reign of Ezana onwards. It has often been suggested that Ezana actually destroyed Meroe in about 360 when he punished the Nubian clients who had revolted (Burstein, 115–119), but the truth may never be known for certain. There are still signs that the locals continued to practise their old habits into the second half of the fourth century and that there were also some kings. This may mean that the Aksumites may have used client kings to rule the area. There are also signs that the Kingdom simply broke up into parts, some of which may have been taken over by the Nubians, while the heartland was at least initially overtaken by the Aksumites or it could be that these two groups ruled those areas through client kings. Consequently, it is possible that the Meroites took part in the wars of the fourth century against the Romans as clients of some of the Nubian kingdoms or as clients of Ethiopia.

The Blemmyes (See Maps Section)
The home of the Blemmyes (modern Beja) lay in the eastern deserts of Nubia from which they raided their neighbours and the Roman territories. The Palmyrenes and Firmus appear to have brought them further north in 271–272 and may have possibly even handed over to them the Dodekaschoinos. As a result, the Romans were forced to fight a series of wars to oust them even after the revolts of Zenobia and Firmus had been crushed. The balance of power, however, had been upset beyond recovery and the Romans were constantly attempting to find new solutions to the problem posed by the Blemmyes in the course of the next 300 years.

We should not make the mistake of considering the Blemmyes as unskilled nomadic barbarians. For centuries they had been under the influence of Egyptian civilization and the Hellenistic Ptolemies both of which were reflected in their culture and administration. At the head of the Blemmyes were kings and below them phylarchs (chiefs of separate tribes) and tribal dignitaries called *hypotyrannoi* ('under tyrants'). They also appear to have had a navy, consisting mainly of sewn ships or boats (dhows), which was placed under a *navarchos* (admiral). The threat posed by the Blemmye 'navy' to the Romans was not militarily significant and belonged to the sphere of anti-piracy operations. As nomads the Blemmyes specialized in the use of camel-mounted infantry armies and circular camel ramparts. Otherwise the camels were used as beasts of burden. The infantry fought as a phalanx behind which was placed the circular camp. If they faced cavalry, they could also send forward 'horse-stabbers' who ducked underneath to stab the horses' chests or bellies open in order to break up the enemy attack. In practice, however, the Blemmye infantry proved incapable of stopping the Roman cavalry let alone their infantry. The only real advantage of the Blemmyes was their ability to flee into the desert if they were in trouble. The Blemmyes were armed with spears, bows (they used poisoned arrows), and sometimes with short swords, but wore very little armour, if at all. As besiegers the Blemmyes were very inept, which ensured that even the most unsophisticated and insignificant Roman fortifications were enough to frustrate them.[158]

The Nubians[159] (See Maps Section)

The nomadic Nubians (ancient Noba/Nobatae) were not a unified tribe, but consisted of several sub-groups that appear to have on occasion worked together as a confederation. This lack of unity was later reflected in the creation of three different kingdoms (Nobadia, the X-Group, in the North; Makuria in the middle; and Alwa in the south) on the ruins of Meroe. It is possible that these tribal groupings existed already during the fourth century (there were definitely several different Nubian tribes), which could have formed tribal confederacies that came to be represented later as the Kingdoms of Alwa, Nobadia and Makuria. In the fifth and sixth centuries Alwa and Nobadia maintained usually cordial relations with each other, but Nobadia and Makuria fought several wars, which may have been the case also beforehand. Archaeologically Nobadia formed the so-called X-Culture while the other two maintained traces of the former Meroitic culture. This does suggest the probability that the Kingdom of Nobatia as Roman *Foederati* had the duty of fighting against their other southern neighbours and not only against the Blemmye.

At the root of Nubian life lay a tribal society, but as they came into contact with their more developed neighbours they readily borrowed from them whatever seemed useful. At the top was the king and below him the sub-kings. Unfortunately, we do not know how the Nubian armies were organized, but some guesses can be made. It seems probable that there was originally some sort of bodyguard and Royal Army (the tribe of the king) under the king and that the other divisions of the army consisted of the forces of the sub-kings. The king held absolute power and the succession passed through the matrilineal line. Most of the evidence regarding the administrative organization comes from the Kingdom of Makuria from the eleventh to the fourteenth centuries (at that time 'Nobatia' formed also part of Makuria), which in my opinion can be used to shed light on the earlier period thanks to the fact it is clearly copied from the late Romans.[160]

The Makurian sources attest the existence of a 'Great King' with absolute power and below him at least thirteen 'kinglets'. The kinglets were priests without military power who lost their right to perform liturgies if they killed someone. Below them was the *Eparch*, the Greek equivalent of the Latin *Praefectus* (*Praetorio*). The Arab and Old Nubian sources indicate that the *Eparch* could have the titles of 'Lord of the Mountain' (*Magister Officiorum*?), 'Lord of the Horses' (*Magister Equitum*?), 'Lord of the King's Horses' and so forth. The powers of the *Eparch* also varied so that under King David (c.1268–1275/6) the *Eparch* ruled half of the kingdom and had a court similar to that of the king. There are also references to the simultaneous existence of two *eparchs* for different territories. The *eparchs* controlled all military forces in their territory, received all visitors who entered the kingdom for the purpose of trade or diplomacy, and controlled the distribution of grain from the public stores. Each *Eparch* also had a *vice-eparch* (i.e. *vicarius*) to assist him. Further, some of the *eparchs* held several offices simultaneously and could pose a threat to the Great King.

Just like the above, the rest of the officials were clearly copied from the late Romans. These included the *primicerius*, *promeizon*, *protodomesticos* of the palace (*Comes Domesticorum?*), *domesticos*, *tetrarchos* (no details known), *Tricliniaris* of the *Domesticos*, *Tricliniaris* of *No*, *Domesticos* of *Pachoras*, *Potentiary* (?) of *Nan-Nokko*, *Meizoteros* (?) of *Adouou*, *Silentiary* (?) of *Nobatia*, *Ness* of *Nobatia*, *Ness* of the *Domesticos*, plus *Tot* of *Michaêlk(l)* and (?) *Motiko(l)* of *Ibrim*. The exact functions of these are not known with definite certainty regardless of the fact that the offices were clearly copied from the late Romans, but what these do suggest is that the Nubians possessed a relatively well organized administration which they had copied from the Romans.

In addition to the above there is evidence for the existence of two *navarchoi*, and for the existence of a Great Admiral (*Meizonanavarchos*) for the year 1069, all of which proves the existence of a fleet. The towns along the Nile obviously possessed boats.

In my opinion, it is possible to make educated guesses regarding the time period when the Nubians adopted these titles. Since the armed forces, supplies and diplomatic activities were controlled by the Prefect and his Vicar, it is probable that the Nubians copied the organization after Diocletian had introduced his Dioceses with vicars, but before the Prefects became civilian officials and before the *Mag. Off.* took over control of diplomatic activities. In short, the likeliest date for the adoption of the late Roman administrative system is the date when the Nubians became Roman *Foederati*, i.e. in about 298. It seems probable that it was then that the 'Great King' stripped the powers of the lesser kings, the chieftains of the tribes, and placed the Eparch in charge of the military. That is to say, the Roman administrative system was used to diminish the power of the traditional tribal nobility and to replace it with officials.

It is notable that even the Nubians who lived further south followed the same model. The influence of the Greek and Roman administrative systems was paramount in the area. The Blemmyes, Nubians, and even the Aksumites all copied their administrative system from the Romans and used Greek names for their officials. It seems probable that the *Eparch* received the further titles (definitely 'Lord of the Horses') after the Romans changed their system under Constantine the Great. Considering the use of Greek/Roman titles for the officials and naval officers and the use of Roman military dress by King Silko (c. 410–450, see above), there are plenty of reasons to believe that the Nubian military organization had also been copied from the Romans or at least that the Nubians copied what they thought useful.

The Nubians were famed infantry archers. They employed both wooden self bows and composite bows. The use of the archer's loose suggests the use of the 'Mongolian release' which enabled a faster shooting rate with great power. Indeed, the very high quality of the Nobades/Nubian foot archers is evident from two facts: 1) the Romans recruited entire units of Nubian archers; and 2) the Muslims gave the Nubians the nickname 'archers of the eyes' because they were crack shots. According to al-Baladhuri (vol. 1, pp. 379–382), the Nubians were so accurate that they would scarcely miss and were able to shoot out the eyes of the Muslim attackers.

Archaeological finds also suggest that the Nubians used spears, halberds, small spears or javelins, and single-edged swords. The finds of body armour are rare, which may result from the wide-spread use of rigid leather armour. The wealthiest used chain mail armour. In general, however, the Nubians were lightly-equipped. The most important protective piece of equipment was the shield made out of leather.

The Nubians used significant numbers of horsemen, and apparently also camel mounted troops. At the Battle of Old Dongola in 652, the Nubians may have protected their horses with breastplates, but their use in the fourth century is uncertain. Just like the Persians the Nubians used rows of small bells on their horses. The bells were decorative items that could scare the Blemmye camels with their sound. The Makurian horses were known to be very small, the size of an ass, but the so-called Dongolawi Horse, which was/ is bred in the Dongola Reach – the area of ancient Kush – was particularly well suited for military use. It was bigger than the Arab Horse, had excellent stamina and was very obedient. It was a true warhorse much sought after by all peoples in the region. In fact, Heidorn suggests that there is plenty of evidence for continued interest in horse breeding and handling from ancient times onwards in Sudan. The painted horses on the walls of Christian Churches in Nubia show that the same breed was already in use hundreds of years ago. The Dongolawi horse is closely related to the Barb horse of North Africa and belongs to the Occidental breeds. There is also another smaller horse breed in Sudan in the area of Kordofan – just to the east of Darfur – that would probably be representative of the smaller horse used by local cavalry. The Dongolawi horses would probably have belonged to the wealthy Makurians. In sum, there is plenty of evidence for the existence of first class cavalry forces among the Nubians.

The above discussion should have made it abundantly clear that we should not underestimate the administrative and military sophistication of the Nubian kingdoms. After all, their bureaucracy was modelled after the 'Byzantine' model, and one may speculate that their military was also but for this we do not possess definite evidence. What is certain, however, is that the Nubians possessed superb archers and cavalry forces that were subsequently able to inflict severe defeats on the Muslims. This was not easy to achieve. This makes it all the more remarkable how well the Roman armed forces performed against this powerful foe.

The Aksumites (Ethiopians)[161] (See Maps Section)
The Aksumites were one of the major players of the Red Sea and Nile trade routes and therefore important for Roman diplomacy in the area. The second thing that made the Aksumites very important for the Romans was their gold, which they obtained in return for various commercial items from the tribes in the interior of Africa so that the trip to the gold miners and back lasted six months. They were apparently one of the principal sources of gold for the Romans.[162]

The Aksumites were originally settlers from the Kingdom of Saba in Yemen, and therefore culturally very close to them. The Aksumites could either be cooperative or they could block Roman interests in the area. In fact, the ability of the Aksumites to effectively block both routes (overland and sea) made them particularly important. It was in the interest of the Aksumites to facilitate the trade contracts with Rome as most of their wealth derived from trade, but the complex political map consisting of the Garamantes (see later), Blemmyes, Nubians, Meroites, Yemenites, coastal Arabs, and Romans ensured that there were periodical troubles. In 271–272 the Aksumites had supported the enemies of the legitimate Roman government, with the result that at the turn of the fourth century the Nobatians served as allies of the Romans against the Meroites, Blemmyes, and Aksumites, but this situation was not to last.

The Aksumite Empire was a loose structure in which the core of the Empire consisted of the Aksumite kingdom which was surrounded by the kingdoms that recognized the supremacy of the Aksumite King of Kings by paying tribute. The Aksumites placed only the strategically important areas, such as the port of Adulis, under their direct control. At its largest the Aksumite Empire encompassed Ethiopia, Eritrea, Sudan and the Arabic coast from Leuke Kome to Yemen, but this loose structure was also its greatest weakness. The subjects were not happy to pay tribute, which meant that, especially after the death of an Aksumite King of Kings, the outlying areas always initiated revolts that required military campaigns to pacify. It is, in fact, probable that some of these revolts had been encouraged by the Romans who usually wanted to ensure that none of their neighbours grew too powerful. The Aksumites, with their allies, could and did pose a periodical threat to Roman Egypt, and they did occasionally threaten Roman alliance structures as well as their trade routes to Africa, Arabia, and India.

The Aksumite Empire possessed a well-organized central government, army, and navy, all under their absolute monarch, which ensured that in general they maintained more efficient military forces than any of their tribal enemies. Only the Meroites and Yemeni had similarly well-organized states, but by the beginning of the fourth century the former was already too weak to oppose the Aksumites and had effectively become a client state.

The King of Kings (*negusa nagast/basileus basileon*) was the supreme commander of the Aksumite armed forces and often led the armies in person.[163] If he chose not to lead the campaign, the army was usually placed under some close relative. The army consisted of the permanent Imperial Guard, and of the 'corps/regiments' (*sarawit*, sing. *sarwe*) of unknown size, each with its own name. The names of the known corps include Hara, Halen, Damawa, Sabarat, Hadefan, Sabaha, Dakuen, Laken, Falha, Sera, Metin, and Mahaza. 'Kings' (*nagast*, sing. *negus*) served as commanders of the regiments. This suggests that the subordinate kings led their own tribal contingents.

The military campaigns were well organized with preset muster-points, garrisons and supply magazines. The supplies, especially the important water supplies, were carried by camels and partially by human porters. Additional supplies were obtained by living off the land. The army consisted primarily of infantry equipped with javelins, swords, and round shields, but some of the regiments were probably cavalry forces. The Aksumites were particularly famed as javelin throwers. The Aksumites rarely trained their elephants, which means that usually only small numbers of those served in the armies.[164] However, one cannot entirely preclude the use of even larger numbers, because one Roman ambassador saw 5,000 elephants grazing. It is possible that the wild elephants were also used for combat just like those were in India. The trained elephants would have been used to goad the wild ones into the desired direction. On the basis of the inscriptions and Procopius, the size of the Aksumite army was not large by Roman standards. The enemy casualty figures (758 killed, 629 prisoners; 705 killed, 205 prisoners; more than 400 killed etc.) mentioned by inscriptions suggest that the typical size for the army could not have been more than about 3,000–4,000 men, and on the basis of another inscription that claims the capture of 10,000 prisoners the probable upper limit for a major army being in the neighbourhood of perhaps 30,000–50,000 men. The later Muslim writers claim that the Aksumites sent 4,000-, 70,000- and 100,000-man armies to Yemen, but Procopius' figure was more modest at 3,000. However, on the basis of the fact that the medieval Ethiopian kings moved about with an army of 50,000 one cannot entirely rule out the possibility that similar strengths could have also been used by the Aksumites when they assembled all of their forces.

The Aksumite navy consisted of sewn ships or boats of the dhow type. These posed no threat to the Roman ships, but were effective enough to threaten the similarly equipped Blemmye, Arabic and Persian fleets and occupy their harbours, which meant that the Aksumites could effectively control the access of Roman ships to the ports when in control of them. In fact, the Aksumite fleet was probably the largest and most efficient navy in the Red Sea area, which the Romans had to take into account in their plans even if these could not face one-on-one with Roman warships. However, whenever necessary the Romans were still able to defeat the Aksumites with forces that were relatively small by Roman standards.

From Libya to Tripolitania

The Berbers[165] (See Maps Section)

The populace of Roman northern Africa from Libya to Mauritania Tingitana consisted of a mixed population. It included natives of the coast, descendants of the Punic population, Greeks, Jews, Blacks, Roman colonists and others. There were also entire Moorish/Berber tribes inside Roman provinces as well as outside, in some cases even on both sides of the 'border'. In addition, there were individuals who had 'dual' citizenships: that is, they were simultaneously Roman citizens and members of their own tribe. The *Constitutio Antoniana* did not grant full Roman citizenship to all of the Moors. The privilege was granted only to the tribal chieftains and such persons who had proved their loyalty to the Romans. Essentially, this means that the Romans granted citizenship only to such persons whose support they needed to control the tribes. This also means that there were several potentially hostile Berber tribes within the borders of the provinces that needed to be controlled just like there were on the outside.

The situation was made more difficult by the enlargement of the Roman territories by the Severans because this brought ever more potentially hostile tribes within the Empire. The problem with this solution was that even the highest ranking military commanders with tribal backgrounds could pick and choose where their loyalty lay.[166] The same was also true of the Rhine and Danube frontiers. There was however one significant difference between Roman Europe and Roman Africa, which was that in the former most of the people had been granted citizenship and in the latter most were not. This meant that the latter were more prepared to abandon their loyalty to Rome and join a Moorish tribal confederacy, which left only the Roman colonists, garrisons and others with no local tribal connections to defend Roman territory.

The first time the Romans made acquaintance with the Moors/Berbers of North Africa resulted from the Punic Wars. At first the relationship was based on an alliance pact which was conducted with the famous Masinissa, the king of Numidia, and his successors, but eventually the Romans annexed also this client kingdom. At first the Roman interest lay in the ability of the Numidians to provide auxiliary forces, especially light cavalry javelin throwers, and this was also to play an important role throughout Rome's involvement in North Africa. It was only gradually and later that they also became very interested in the agricultural produce of the rich coastal areas. In fact, North Africa became one of the principal breadbaskets of the Empire, and after the creation of Constantinople, the city of Rome became entirely dependent upon Africa's supply of corn.

The Berber tribes were further divided into 'mountain' tribes, who tilled the land and fought mainly on foot and used fortified towers as places of refuge, and into 'desert' nomads, who fought as light cavalry. The basic social unit of the Berbers was the *ikh* (people) which consisted of several families. In the case of the settled Berbers two to three of these often formed a village and several villages a tribe. In the case of the nomads, the equivalent would have been a wagon and camel caravan of people, several of which in combination would form a tribe. The smaller tribes were led by tribal elders while the larger ones were ruled by 'kings'. When the tribes united as a confederation, they also chose a temporary military chief to lead them.[167]

For the most part warfare in this area consisted of endemic banditry that was of minor interest to the Romans, requiring only policing, but when the Berbers managed to form a confederation or one tribe achieved supremacy over its neighbours, the Berbers could pose a serious threat. The most difficult situation arose when the sedentary Berbers of the provinces joined their nomadic brethren. In this case the Romans also faced enemies inside their own provinces while they were attempting to cope with an outside invasion. In such situations it was also typical that the Berbers had a very significant numerical superiority over the Romans. Regardless, it was still more typical for the Berbers to avoid pitched battles and use guerrilla warfare, which involved raids, ambushes, and feigned retreats, than attempt to engage the heavy Roman units in pitched battles. It was indeed the general inability of the various Berber tribes to work together for long periods of time as well as their very rudimentary siege skills that enabled the Romans to control the whole of North Africa with some veteran colonies that were protected by fortified villas, forts, fortified towns and cities, one legion (*III Augusta*) with detachments spread around widely, and some auxiliary units. The Berber siege tactics consisted only of surprise attacks, and the use of treachery and blockades. Therefore it is not at all surprising that the Romans did not build truly strong and sophisticated fortifications in Africa. They had no need for them.

The Romans controlled the various parts of Africa through the use of a combination of methods. The strategic locales like oases or cities were protected by fortifications and garrisons. The presence of military installations and garrisons served to cow the people into obedience. The forts placed to guard the oases were meant to control the movement of people, just like the *Fossatum Africae*, the linear defences consisting of mud-brick walls 1.5–3m wide, at least 2.5 m high and fronted by a ditch 4–6m wide and 3m deep. These barriers had small gates and towers. During peacetime the principal purpose appears to have been to direct the movement of the people to openings in the barriers so that the people could be controlled and taxed. Of equal importance was obviously the military purpose. The barriers both limited the ability of the external Berber tribes to conduct fast raids into areas located behind the barriers, and contained the internal tribes in their own territory.[168]

The most important means of control, however, was the use of diplomacy and the network of alliances with the various Berber tribes. The tribes or rather the tribal elites that acted as the Romans wished were rewarded with various privileges and could also expect to receive Roman military support against their enemies, while the tribes that did not were subjected to Roman military reprisals and the denial of privileges. In order to be fully aware of the developments within these tribal groupings, the Romans employed a network of tribal spies who gave their reports to the intelligence officers posted to the outposts and garrisons of the tribal frontiers.[169]

The size of the Berber armies varied from a tribal army of a few thousand men to the massive armies of the tribal confederacies. The latter typically had at least about 20,000–30,000 men. In very exceptional circumstances there could be even about 100,000 persons or more probably including the non-combatants. Any threat posed by such a confederacy would be short-lived as the tribes forming the confederacies were unable to cooperate for long periods of time and in most cases the Romans were usually able to obtain deserters immediately the enemy suffered their first setback. Furthermore, the Roman habit of recruiting Berbers into their army not only provided the Romans with superb light cavalry but also channelled the energy of the restless youth into something useful. There was obviously also a downside to all this. The Berbers learnt how the Romans fought and knew therefore how to counter their tactics.

The nomadic or semi-nomadic Moors/Berbers were famous for their light infantry and light cavalry, both of which used light javelins or spears and small circular shields constructed of reed. Their light cavalry was particularly famous for the use of unbridled horses and very effective use of an amorphous irregular order in combat. The Berber light cavalry was especially valued and sought after by the Romans for use as auxiliary irregulars/scouts and also as elite cavalry units. The Berbers used camels as beasts of burden and as emergency bulwarks for their camps. In addition to rings of camels the camps could also include similar barriers of oxen/cattle, donkeys, sheep and goats all of which were hobbled together to form a significant obstacle. The use of massive numbers of camels made it possible for the nomadic Berbers to emerge from the desert all of a sudden and flee just as fast. The attack, however, was conducted from horseback.

Unfortunately, the best sources for the Berber military are either early or late, but fortunately their military methods appear to have remained much the same throughout the antiquity, the only significant difference being the abandonment of the use of elephants after the fall of the well-organized Numidian Kingdom. According to Procopius' generalized account of the Berber military, the Moors wore no armour, had small shields, carried two to three javelins and used terrain or palisaded camps as bases of attack. This is a good summary of the most typical military facts, but fortunately Corippus provides us with a more detailed expose. In actuality, the fighting methods of the Moors varied considerably from one tribe to another depending upon their mode of living and it was only when they fought as a confederacy that they showed the usual tendencies of using light cavalry in front, infantry phalanx behind and a circular camp behind them. Corippus states

(1.85ff.) that the Marmaridan tribes (i.e. the Laguatan Confederacy of the sixth century) consisted of the following types: 1) the Frexes employed both infantry and cavalry; 2) the Austur (a sub-tribe of the Austurians from Libya) specialized in the use of the camp and the camel; 3) The Llaguas were hardy bloodthirsty warriors employing cavalry lancers; 4) the Ifuraces were noted for their shields and powerful swordplay while their charge was characterized by leaping up and down for dramatic effect; 5) the Muctunians from the wastes of Libya fought in the front; 6) the lake tribes employed boats; and 7) the Barcaei (probably neo-Berbers/inhabitants close to the Barca/Barke) tied their shields to their left hand and their swords to their right with bracelets. And then there were still other tribes that also had their own peculiarities. These included the mountaineers such as the Aurasitians (tribes of the Aures) who employed only cavalry armed with a two-ended spear and shield. Berber ploughmen who had joined the confederacy fought as infantry. In addition, some tribes used poisoned arrows while others did not.

The lightness of the Moorish equipment compelled them to avoid hand-to-hand combat in the open with the Romans, which translated into an avoidance of direct pitched battles and the use of guerrilla warfare. If threatened by the Romans, the mountain tribes and their nomadic cousins were in the habit of retreating into their mountain holdouts. However, if the Romans managed to surprise the nomadic Moors in the open, the Moors formed a defensive circular palisaded camp by tying together their camels and other domesticated animals, outside which they would scatter caltrops or place stakes. They could also form a second inner barrier in similar manner. When the enemy had been brought to a standstill in front of such barricades, the tribesmen would burst out of their encampment to attack the enemy. If not surprised, the Berbers always sought to use the terrain to their advantage by placing their camp on slopes, or on the top of a mountain while groups of men hid in suitable locales to ambush a careless enemy.

The Berbers placed their women, children, and baggage in the middle of the camp. The perimeter and 'gates' of such a circle were protected by spear or pike-bearers while the slingers and archers were placed behind them. The women and youth could also take part in the defence of their families. We should not make the mistake of underestimating the military potential of women and youths. They did contribute to the defence of their fortified places by using slings, stones and improvised weapons. The famed Berber light cavalry was either deployed as a single irregular line in front of such a camp or it was used for sallies against the front or flanks of the enemy when it had been brought to a halt in front of the camp. There is a strong possibility that the African Drill in the Strategikon (6.3) reflects the Berber cavalry tactics – for which see the accompanying diagram. Alternatively, the Berbers could also use a battle formation which consisted of infantry placed in front as a phalanx behind which was the light cavalry. The latter was used for the making of harassing attacks against the enemy. If the situation allowed, the cavalry or a part thereof, was placed in ambush.

The mobile nomadic tribes posed a greater threat to Roman interests than the mountain tribes or sedentary tribes because the sedentary populations had dwellings and fields that made them static targets. The Romans could always bring them to submission by destroying their fields and, if necessary, by bringing to bear their overwhelming technical superiority in siege warfare. The wooden fieldworks or stone towers and rudimentary defensive siege skills posed no serious obstacle for the sophisticated Roman siege

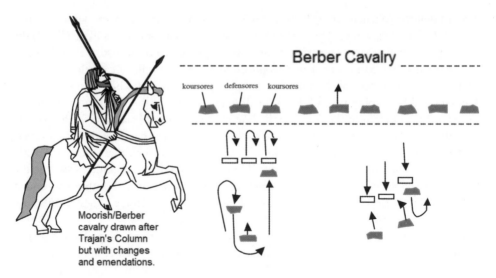

Moorish/Berber cavalry drawn after Trajan's Column but with changes and emendations.

According to the Strategikon 6.3, in the African Drill the cavalry was arrayed as a single battle line evidently still with long intervals (200–400 ft.) in between *moirai*. The middle *moira* (c.3,000 men) formed the defenders (*defensores*) while the wings (also *moirai*) formed the runners/skirmishers (*koursores*). Each of the '*moirai*' naturally consisted of smaller irregular units. All of the *moirai* attacked simultaneously and, when the enemy had been defeated, the pursuit was performed by the flank *moirai* in irregular formation while the middle one maintained its close order. When the enemy made an about turn, one of the wing units would stay in place while the other galloped back to the defenders, after which the one that had stayed in place started its retreat. When this happened the one that had already retreated back rode to the same side and came face-to-face with the one that was fleeing. The above illustrations/diagrams show one possible confederate cavalry array (c. 27,000 horsemen).

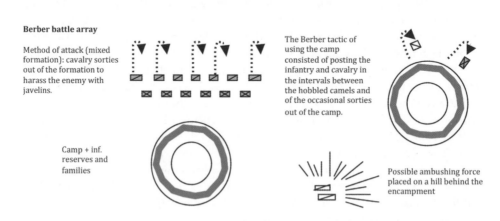

Berber battle array

Method of attack (mixed formation): cavalry sorties out of the formation to harass the enemy with javelins.

Camp + inf. reserves and families

The Berber tactic of using the camp consisted of posting the infantry and cavalry in the intervals between the hobbled camels and of the occasional sorties out of the camp.

Possible ambushing force placed on a hill behind the encampment

techniques. In contrast, one of the methods used by the nomads was to retreat before the advancing Roman force into the desert and to let the lack of food and water take their toll while they themselves found subsistence from their herds of animals. The Roman countermeasure against this was not to go too far south but only so far as their supply routes allowed. The Roman aim was to isolate the Berbers away from rich farmlands of the north, which would eventually force the Berbers either to fight or negotiate.

The Laguatan/Marmaridae/Austuriani[170]

The principal enemy facing the Romans between Cyrenaica and Tripolitania were the Laguatan/Marmaridae/Austuriani Confederation of tribes. The original Llaguas/ Laguatan tribe appears to have been neo-Berbers who migrated from Egypt to Libya through the chain of oases from el-Kharga to Dakhla, Farafra, Bahariya and to Siwa, the centre of the Libyan *Ammon* cult. From Siwa the Laguatans advanced to Aquila, the centre of the Nasamones and an oracular centre of *Ammon*, and from there to Zuila, Zella and Giofra. At some point after this it is likely that Ghirza, which was a local tribal centre and focus for the *Gurzil* worship, also joined the confederacy. The *Gurzil*-deity was the bull-headed offspring of *Ammon* that was carried into battle by the priests of the sixth-century Laguatans.

Each of the oases was controlled by a populous tribe and the Laguatans became ever more powerful as they incorporated these into their confederation. When the Laguatans had reached the area just south of Cyrenaica they seem to have incorporated the Marmaridae into their Confederacy with the result that they came to be called Marmaridae. The other alternative is that the Marmaridae incorporated the newcomers. After this, the Laguatans seem to have incorporated the Austur with the result that the name of the confederation became Austuriani, which name stuck until the fifth century, or more likely it was the Austur who incorporated the Marmaridae/Laguatans into their league until the Laguatans overthrew their superiors in the fifth century. After the confederacy came to be called the Austuriani, they moved on to the territory of the Nasamoneans, which was also duly incorporated into the new league of tribes. Nasamonean just like the Marmaridae and Austuriani, was later used as a synonym for Laguatan.

The Muctunians and other Libyan tribes were soon to follow in their footsteps. The confederation was so successful that many of the local sedentary tribesmen and semi-Romanized populations joined them even if they publicly maintained their formal allegiance towards Rome. The ability of the fierce fighters of the confederacy to crush all opposition created a snowball effect. With every new success the less likely it was that the next tribe would refuse to follow the will of the leading tribe. In normal circumstances each of the tribes was ruled by its own chieftain that together formed a council of chieftains that chose one supreme leader (tyrant) to act as their war leader when needed.

I would suggest that we should associate the migration of the Laguatans with the revolt of Aemilianus in Egypt in c.260–261. It is likely that the Laguatans were a Federate tribe that had supported the usurper with the result that, when he was overthrown, the Federates thought it best to change scenery. It was probably because of this that the new governor of Egypt, Probus, immediately marched to Cyrene when the news of the invasion of the Marmaridae in 269–270 had reached his ears. He was in haste to put an end to the rebellious tribe that had escaped his clutches before.

As far as the military tactics of the Marmaridae are concerned before the birth of the tribal confederacy, it is likely that the *Marmaridae* fought like the other North Africans as lightly equipped infantry and cavalry. However, for what it is worth Silius Italicus' Punica (2.56ff.) claims that the *Marmaridae* army consisted of cavalry and two-horsed chariots and that their forces included women. He claims that at the time the *Marmaridae* were led by Queen Asbyte, who was the child of the king of the Garamantes. Indeed there is a possibility that the two tribes were occasionally united against the Romans and at least for the latter there is some evidence for the continued use of chariots. In fact, the Garamantes too may have become part of the Austuriani Confederation after the collapse of the Roman defences in the fifth century.

The Austuriani/Laguatans fought like the archetypical nomadic Berbers. They employed vast amounts of camels as beasts of burden, and attacked as cavalry lancers. They worshipped and fought under the guidance of the oracles and priests of Ammon and Gurzil, both of which were used to encourage the warriors to do their utmost. Behind their line of battle was placed the circular camp with its ramparts of camels and other domesticated animals. Since the Laguatans are later described using close order in combat, it appears probable that this was learnt in Roman service as either auxiliaries or Federates.

The Kingdom of the Garamantes[171]

The Kingdom of the Garamantes is the great unknown mercantile empire of the Sahara. Their culture was based on the exploitation of a subterranean water-extraction system which consisted of a network of tunnels. The water enabled them to cultivate the land and create an urban culture. They had eight major towns and plenty of other lesser settlements. Their capital was the town of Garama (now the Jarma Oasis) and it had a population of about 4,000 people, and around it an additional 6,000 people within a 4.8km radius. The city temple may have been associated with the desert god Ammon. The population expansion resulting from agriculture allowed the Garamantes to conquer their neighbours and acquire vast numbers of slaves to work in the tunnels and to build more tunnels. Silius Italicus claims in his poem (2.56–63) that at the time of Hannibal the king of the Garamantes controlled an area from the Nasamones to the Syrtic coast. It is difficult to verify this claim, but at least after the Roman conquest of North Africa the coastline belonged to the Roman sphere of influence, as did the Garamantes themselves.

An archaeological team led by Mattingly has come to the conclusion that the regular and orderly layout of the towns must have come about as a result of strong political control. In the second or third century Garama received an impressive stone-and-mud wall which suggests a need for additional defence. The petroglyphs suggest that the kingdom was an aggressive warrior society in which the males hunted ever more slaves to work in the tunnels and to enlarge the network of tunnels. The most common representations show men brandishing weapons, riding, and dashing along in two-wheeled chariots. The Garamantes were famous for their light cavalry, but they did also employ infantry armed with spears and shields, and may also have continued to use bow-armed infantry. The Garamantes seem to have employed small numbers of chariots alongside their cavalry that they could take apart and reassemble as needed. Silius Italicus (2.56ff.) also connects the use of chariots and cavalry with the Garamantes. Just like their neighbours, the Garamantes also appear to have used camels for transport and horses for combat. On the other hand, Arrian (Tac. 19) does refer to the existence of chariots among the Cyrenaicans, but claims that their use had stopped. This, however, is not conclusive because there exist so many depictions of chariots in art from this period that these were undoubtedly also employed.[172]

The initial contacts between the Garamantes and Romans were hostile as the former were in the habit of raiding Roman territories. In 21–20 BC governor L. Cornelius Balbus the Younger defeated the Gautuli and conquered Garama. He may even have reached the Niger if the river *Dasibari* can be identified with the '*Da Isa Bari*' (Great River of the *Da*), a Songhai name of the Niger, but it did not take long for the Garamantes to resume their raids.

After several conflicts in which the Garamantes were defeated, they once again interfered in Roman affairs by supporting the city of Oae (Tripoli) against Lepcis Magna in 69 AD. The governor Valerius Festus intervened, defeated them, and once again conquered Garama.

As a result the Garamantes were finally forced to come to terms with reality and conclude a treaty (*foedus*) with Rome. This resulted in the abovementioned joint expeditions against the 'Ethiopians'. The fact that the Garamantes and Romans were able to conduct three- to four-month long campaigns in the desert suggests strongly that both were employing camels, even if it were precisely the two Garamantian caravan routes across the Sahara that allowed the use of horses.[173]

Unfortunately due to the poor survival of literary sources we do not know how well the treaty between the Romans and Garamantes held, on the basis of which it is possible that the Garamantes may have occasionally joined forces with the Berbers or Marmaridae against the Romans or raided on their own. Since during the reign of Septimius Severus warlike tribes threatened Tripolitanian Limes and new forts were built under the Severans, one can presume that the Garamantes may have once again joined the other tribes for opportunistic raids. Similarly in the third century the fortress of Bu Njim (Gholaia) is attested to have been engaged in keeping an eye on the Garamantes and on one occasion is attested to have sent soldiers to Garama. It is not known whether this referred to a campaign or that soldiers were sent as an escort for someone. Regardless, there is plenty of evidence for the Garamantes to have acted like the other peoples of the desert. For example, there are strong reasons to believe that they usually joined the Austuriani against the Romans every time that it seemed to offer them a good chance of gaining booty, and this held true also for the fourth century. The Garamantes continued this throughout their existence: John of Biclar mentions that the Garamantes requested peace from the Romans as late as 569.[174]

In my opinion this proves that the Romans were able to operate in the deserts even at times when it is usually assumed that their control was limited only to the coastal areas. It is very probable that the Romans were conducting similar operations also during the fourth century as they were during the third and sixth, even if we lack any knowledge of those thanks to the lack of detailed sources interested in the events of the periphery.

In comparison with Roman might, the Garamantes were a small player even if they still controlled the caravan routes of the central Sahara. Their only real protection against Roman aggression were the maintenance of peace and commercial relationship as well as the long distance (about 30–40 days' journey) separating them from each other. The Garamantes transported black slaves, precious stones, ivory, elephants and possibly West African gold to Roman territory while they themselves bought glassware, pottery, lamps, olive oil and wine. It was not in the Roman interest to crush the Garamantes. The long distance was not a hindrance for the Romans if they were really determined to punish them, but financial loss was. If needed, the Romans just raided and pillaged the settlements in order to force the Garamantes to renew their treaty.

The Berber Tribes from Byzacena to Mauritania Caesarensis, and the 'Ethiopians'

There is not much to say about the other Berber tribes for this era (e.g. the Quinquegentani, Bavares, Baquates etc.) except that as far as the sources allow their tactics resembled those already described. The same is also true of the so-called Ethiopians inhabiting the area south of Numidia. The fighting methods of the tribes of the Aures differed slightly because these included mountaineers such as the Aurasitians (tribes of the Aures) who employed only cavalry equipped with the two-ended spear and shield. The Berber ploughmen who lived in the areas occupied by the Romans fought as infantry while the tribesmen beside the lakes employed boats when they joined forces with the semi-nomadic Berbers.

However, one particularly important development took place in the provinces of Mauritania. It was in these provinces that in the course of the second and third centuries the Romans started to rely on the use of Federate Berber tribes that either lived within the Roman borders, or as semi-nomads moved their livestock from outside the borders to inside the borders according to the seasons. The chieftains of these tribes were granted Roman citizenship and eventually the official status of being Roman officers. The Romans also evacuated part of their forts and gave the possession of these to the tribal Federate forces under these chieftains. In other words, the *foedus* with the Goths in 382 was not without precedents, and it could also result in similar troubles – as the revolt of Firmus proves. However, at the same time this experiment can also be considered a success, because it saved money and because the chieftains of the Federate tribes came to consider themselves as Romans even while retaining their tribal affiliation.

The chieftains are also considered to have derived their legitimacy as rulers of their tribes from the Roman emperor with the result that they were eager to confirm their legitimacy from the emperor even as late as the sixth century, immediately after Belisarius had reconquered the area.

Mauritania Tingitana[175]

Mauritania Tingitana was a troubled and isolated peripheral province of the Roman Empire. The Rif and Atlas Mountains effectively separated it from *Mauritania Caesarensis* and dominated its outlook. The semi-nomadic Baquates and Macenites, who inhabited the most central position on the Atlas Mountains province, were populous and troublesome tribes and required the use of a combination of military means and diplomacy. On the one hand the mountains provided the tribesmen a safe refuge with enough fertile land from which to obtain subsistence, the occupation of which was just too costly for the Romans. It was from these safe havens in the mountains that the tribesmen conducted their periodic raids into the Roman occupied lowlands. On the other hand, the periodic twice annual movement of the tribes down from and up into the mountains made them vulnerable to Roman strikes. In combination these facts meant firstly that practically all agricultural land was located in close proximity to the Roman cities and garrisons that provided adequate protection against the mountaineers. Secondly, the vulnerability of the tribes during their twice-annual movement meant that the Romans could at those times compel the tribal *Princeps* (the first among the *primores*/leading men) to sign a treaty. The Romans sought to encourage this treaty aspect by supporting their own candidates to the positions of *principes* and by granting to them Roman citizenship. Regardless, the mountain tribes Baquates and Macenites were effectively autonomous and did not pay any money to the Roman treasury.

What was particularly problematic for the Romans was that the lowland tribesmen under their direct control were less numerous than the mountaineers and remained largely un-Romanized, as a result of which only the top echelons of their society had received Roman citizenship to enable them to better control their peoples. The Autololes whose territory lay south of the province were also fully independent of Rome, because the name of these tribes appears to have been a corruption of the word *autoteleis* (self-tributary) peoples. The name, though, appears to signify some sort of tribal confederacy, which means that they too could potentially pose a threat to the Roman province. The most significant threats were still the Macenites and Baquates who were also occasionally united under one *Princeps/Rex*. On occasion even the Bavares from Mauritania Caesarensis belonged to this same confederation, making them a really significant threat on both sides of the Atlas. The inability of the Romans to prevent raiding in small groups meant that the forts were spread across the province to protect the agricultural land and peasants, but the bulk of Roman forces and forts were concentrated in the area of Volubilis, which appears to have been the main highway into the province and a commercial crossroads: one of the Roman strategic aims appears to have been to secure the trade route.

Consequently, there was a continuous but delicate balance between the treaty relationship guaranteeing some semblance of order between periodic bouts of banditry and actual large scale warfare, but this came at a great cost. *Mauretania Tingitana* was one of the smallest provinces of the Empire (only the Alpine provinces were smaller) but it still required about or over 10,000 auxiliaries to control, which was only slightly less than the much larger province of *Mauretania Caesarensis* needed. This cost was inordinate in relation to the strategic significance of the southern portions of the province (in contrast with the north) when one takes into account the small tax yield produced by the province. Some researchers have even claimed that it was abandoned during the reign of Diocletian, but nowadays, on the basis of archaeological finds, most researchers are of the opinion that this was not the case. What actually appears to have happened was that the Romans delegated the defence of the south of Tingitana to the Federate tribes in order to save costs.

The sources provide us with too little evidence to make any certain conclusions regarding the composition of the enemy forces beyond some generalities. The fact that the Baquates and Macenites fought alongside the Bavares in the late-third century and with the Laguatan in the sixth makes it likely that their tactics resembled each other. The territories of the Baquates and their neighbours the Bavares also included part of the Mediterranean coast and it appears probable that both possessed some naval resources that had enabled them to raid the coasts of Spain and Sardinia during the reigns of Marcus Aurelius and Septimius Severus (SHA M. Aur. 21, Sev. 2; Reddé, 328, 422–423). If this happened later, as is very probable, the sources are silent about this. The same was also true of the other tribes of *Mauretania Caesarensis*.

As result of the threat of Moorish pirates, there were *praefecti orae maritimae* in Spain and elsewhere. Their mission was to protect the coast. One prefect was also posted for the coast of *Mauretania Caesarensis* with an *ala* of cavalry and supporting naval detachments/ patrols (Reddé, 423, 565–569): that is, the cavalry was used to police the coastline for possible pirate bases/bays while the naval patrols tried to intercept their vessels. It is quite probable that this was also the case during the latter half of the third century and later, but it should be kept in mind that the naval threat posed by the Moorish pirates was not significant. It was only a nuisance.

As regards the Autololes, there is even less information. For what it is worth Silius Italicus (first century AD) in his highly unreliable poem of the Second Punic War (2.63, 3.306–309) claims that the Autololes lived in forests and fought as highly mobile light infantry, but the problem with this is that he placed them on the Syrtic coast. Had they migrated west after that? He also claimed that no horse or flooded river could keep up pace with their speed. In other words, if there is any truth to his claims, it is easy to see why the Romans with their small more heavily equipped forces were able to contain the threat posed by the numerous Autololes. Regardless, the referral to the speed of their light infantry in the same context would still suggest that even the Roman cavalry *alae* posted in the area had had significant difficulties in coping with their mobility.[176] In some respects they would have been the ancient equivalents of the nineteenth-century Zulus. If so, it is quite probable that their fighting methods would have remained much the same except perhaps that it is likely that the numbers of horsemen would have increased gradually.

Chapter Three

The Third Century Crisis

The Beginning of Troubles

The beginning of the late Roman period is usually dated to the beginning of Diocletian's reign in 284, which reign is considered to make a clear break with the past. In truth many of the changes that become visible to us for the first time during his reign had already taken place between c.212 and 283. The reason for the false impression is the better survival of sources from Diocletian's reign onwards. In truth, despite the reforms Diocletian instituted, like the new administrative organization of provinces and the Tetrarchy, his reign still represents in many respects a conservative counter reform.

Diocletian inherited an Empire in a state of chronic and prolonged crisis. The professional Roman army had lost its aura of invincibility and its defensive structures along the frontiers had been overrun by enemies. The core of the army still consisted of the legions and auxiliary units, but this is as far as the resemblance goes. The combat tactics had already been altered during the reign of Hadrian, and Gallienus had changed its organizational and administrative structures.[177] The role of the cavalry had also grown in importance from the reign of Trajan onwards so that Severus Alexander had created a new cavalry army out of Easterners, which was destroyed by Decius and then recreated by Gallienus (Syvanne, 2011a). The following gives a brief summary of the third-century background to Diocletian's difficult inheritance.

The fortunes of the Roman Empire began an ever accelerating downward spiral after the murder of Caracalla in 217. Septimius Severus and Caracalla had both showered their soldiers with money and privileges in an effort to maintain their support, as a result of which their successors found it increasingly difficult to maintain the army's trust. Septimius Severus allowed the soldiers to marry and made them all equestrians by allowing them to keep a ring, which opened up the opportunity to hold equestrian offices even to the lowest ranking soldiers. The soldiers came to be considered as *honestiores*, men of highest rank. The soldiers were about to take full control of the empire so far ruled only by the Roman upper classes, and even more importantly, after the granting of citizenship to all free persons – except the so-called *dediticii* (defeated enemies settled within the Roman Empire as 'allied' troops), *laeti* (probably similar to the above, but may imply the settlement of tribesmen of a single tribe on one selected area as farmer-soldiers under their own leaders with Roman citizenship), and *foederati* (treaty-bound allies who lived both within and outside the borders) – in the Roman Empire by Caracalla in 212, the soldiers seeking to rise to dominance also included men who had previously been considered foreigners.

Caracalla's intentions were probably manifold: 1) with this measure he made the auxiliary troops and other non-citizens indebted to him personally; and 2) by giving the citizenship to all, he gained more money to pay the military pay rises instituted by him and his father. In the short term, this created an army and populace that felt loyalty towards Caracalla, but in the long term the *constitutio Antoniniana* worsened the military situation by making service in the auxiliary units and navy less attractive in comparison with the legions.[178] The emperors needed to find supplementary sources of manpower, which often meant the recruiting of foreigners as *laeti* and *foederati* as the emperors were unwilling to increase the number of better-paid legionary troops.

Caracalla's cowardly murderer and successor, the praetorian prefect Macrinus, was a Moor with equestrian rank. However, the Romans in general were not yet ready to accept a man of so lowly a rank, but even more importantly he was incompetent as a general and it was this that sealed his fate in the eyes of the soldiers. Macrinus' successor, the eccentric Heliogabalus, rose to power only by claiming to be the son of the beloved Caracalla, but it did not take long for the soldiers to become fed up with his eastern eccentrics and bisexual behaviour. Alexander Severus, who also owed his position to his supposed descent from Caracalla, together with his mother and advisors, tried to restore the situation and stop the increasingly erratic behaviour of the soldiers, but to no avail. Alexander and his mother were both murdered by soldiers in 235. The first consequences of the *constitutio Antoniniana* had already made themselves felt during Alexander's reign. The discipline of the soldiers was deteriorating and the difficulties in obtaining recruits for the navy started to tell. For the first time since the suppression of piracy by Pompey the Great, it was necessary to appoint one person in charge of suppressing piracy in the Mediterranean.[179]

From the point of view of military history Alexander's reign is also significant for the reason that it was during his reign that a new and more menacing enemy, the Sasanid Persians, appeared in the east and because Alexander created a large cavalry army out of Parthian refugees and Oshroenian mounted archers, Moorish light horse plus detachments of Roman cavalry, a part of which was equipped as cataphracts. It was this cavalry force that his successor Maximinus Thrax used to great effect against the Germans. This was not the first great Roman cavalry army – for example Augustus had employed one against the Germans – but it was the first semi-permanent or permanent (?) mobile cavalry force consisting of several auxiliary units and legionary detachments, all at the disposal of the emperor.[180] Alexander Severus and his mother were also the first Roman rulers who showed significant interest in Christian religious doctrine, a question which was to dominate the religious policies of the Empire during the latter half of the century.

The SHA (Alex. Sev. 58.4) mentions the existence of the Limitanei (frontier soldiers) for the reign of Alexander Severus, which has led some historians to speculate that those were created during his reign or that the referral is anachronistic because the Limitanei were supposedly created under Diocletian or Constantine. Notably, the SHA (Pesc. 7.7, Prob. 14.7) mentions the existence of the Limitanei also for the reigns of Pescennius Niger and Probus, which precludes that. However, what modern historians have failed to understand is that the frontier forces had actually already been created during the first century AD and that the word Limitanei was just a new apt term for those. Essentially historians have been chasing something that has always been under their nose. It doesn't really matter what the frontier forces were called.

It is also possible that some of the famous late Roman bodyguard units date from the period of ca. 180-249, because the Chronicle Paschale (ed. Dindorf, pp.501-2) and Cedrenus (ed. Dindorf, pp. 451) claim that Gordian and Philip the Arab created two groups of Candidati (dressed in white) out of the sixth and seventh scholae to act as personal bodyguards for the emperor. Further support for this claim comes from the SHA (Gall. 8), which shows Gallienus surrounded by white uniformed soldiers. See also Frank (128ff.). In addition, the SHA (Sev. Alex. 23.3) names an unknown bodyguard unit Ostensionales (Paraders = the later Armaturae?) dressed in bright clothes for the reign of Severus Alexander and notes (Maximini 3.5) the existence of 'corporis in aula' as personal court bodyguards for Septimius Severus. It is also possible that Septimius Severus created the legionary structure visible in Vegetius' text for his new Parthian legions, because Dio (76.12.5) refers to a 550 men group (cohort?) of soldiers for his reign. See the Chapter Four. Furthermore, the SHA (Max. et Balb. 13.5ff.) states that during the short reign of Maximus and Balbinus in 238 there were three groups of bodyguards: the milites (i.e. the Praetorians), Germani (i.e. the Equites Singulares Augusti and other Germans), and the aulici ('Court-troops', Palatini: possibly precursors of the Scholae/ Candidati, and/or Protectores).

We also know that Caracalla created a new personal bodyguard unit which he called with the name Leones (Dio 79.6.1ff.). It consisted of Scythian (mainly Goths) and German (Germans from the Rhine) freemen and slaves. Speidel (1994, 64ff.) has suggested that the Leones belonged to the Equites Singularis Augusti, but this is contradicted by their command structure and recruitment. The SHA (Car. 6.6ff.) states that Triccianus, the prefect of Legio II Parthica, also commanded the equites extraordinarii who were also called with the name of protectores. Since during the Republican period the auxiliary alae extraordinarii formed the bodyguard of the commander, it seems incontestable that these must have been Caracalla's cavalry guard known as Leones or Protectores. See also Speidel (1975). In short, since the Equites Singularis Augusti had been under the PP (it is of course possible that these were transferred to the commander of the Legio II) and Dio implies the raising of a new unit, it seems very probable that Caracalla created a new bodyguard unit for himself. There is also evidence for the existence of equites itemque pedites iuniores Mauri for the reign of Caracalla, which suggest the existence of seniores-unit and also the possibility of new Moorish bodyguard units (Handy, 176). Notably, Commodus' bodyguards also included both Parthian archers and Moorish javeliners (Handy, 176; Herodian 1.15.2). In short, it is possible that the precedent for the seniores-iuniores units was also created much sooner than usually suggested.

Speidel (1994, 69-71) has also noted the creation of unit ala Celerum Philippiana by Philip the Arab as his personal cavalry guard on the basis of the fact that the Celeres (Swift-Ones) had served as Romulus' bodyguards, but speculates that it is possible that the unit had originally been raised by Maximinus Thrax as his bodyguards. Unfortunately, we do not know what happened to this unit.

Then there is the problem of the units of Scholae mentioned by the Chronicle Paschale and Cedrenus. It would be easy to dismiss these as anachronisms, but we have evidence for the existence of colleges/clubs of under-officers called scholae (schools) from the reign of Septimius Severus onwards (Bohec, 2000; Speidel, 1994). It is quite probable, that because the Protectores and Domestici were organized as scholae, that the term scholae was sometimes used colloquially as a name of the new guard units already during the third century. Similarly, it seems probable that the cavalry scutarii (sing. scutarius) referred to bodyguards that were associated with the scholae and from which one progressed to the 'protectores' units.

The new emperor Maximinus Thrax (235–238) was a very competent military leader, but as a man of humble birth and of Gothic and Alan descent he failed to gain the support of the Roman upper classes and people, with the predictable results. Yet his reign still marked the next step in the direction of the loss of control by the traditional Roman upper classes. His reign was a watershed. It marked the beginning of the military anarchy and era of usurpations and civil wars. He was the first barbarian and 'Illyrian' to assume the purple. He was also the first emperor of the century to begin to persecute the Christians, which eventually led to the alienation of a significant portion of the population, especially in the east. Henceforth there was to be a constant struggle between the religiously tolerant and Christian emperors (Philip the Arab, Gallienus, Constantius Chlorus) and the persecutors (Decius, Valerian, Aurelian, Diocletian) until Constantine the Great unleashed a new era.

After a period of civil wars, the situation was briefly stabilized under Gordian III and his upper class Roman supporters, but after he had suffered a defeat in the war against the Persians in 244, he too was murdered at the instigation of his praetorian prefects Philip the Arab and Priscus. Philip the Arab (244–249) was probably the first Christian emperor, but as an Arab Christian he naturally failed to gather the loyalty of the more conservative members of the Roman upper classes, as a result of which he was overthrown by the ultra-conservative Decius in 249. Decius was also the first 'Illyrian' of true Roman origins and his reign marked the first bout of conservatism that originated from Illyria, the populace of which was more Roman than the Romans themselves after they had received full citizenship from Caracalla.

Not only was the Roman Empire divided within, but it was also facing more dangerous enemies than before. During the late-second and early-third century there rose new and more powerful Germanic tribal confederacies (Franks, Alamanni, Burgundi, Vandals, Goths) that threatened the whole length of the Rhine and Danube frontiers. Similarly, the Sasanians overthrew the Parthians in Persia and initiated a new more aggressive foreign policy towards Rome than was the case before.

The military situation became acute after the Goths killed the emperor Decius (249–251) and annihilated his army at the Battle of Abrittus in 251, and the Persians defeated and captured the emperor Valerian (253–260) near Edessa in about 259. The ultra-conservative irredeemable pagans had led the Roman Empire to the brink of extinction. Therefore the reigns of Decius and Valerian mark another watershed. After Decius had destroyed the imperial *comitatus* with its very substantial cavalry army that had been in existence since the reign of Alexander Severus, the Roman frontier defences (including the fleets) in Europe and Asia were effectively destroyed by a succession of invasions.

The Low Point of the Third Century and Reforms of Gallienus

The prestige of Roman arms was at an all time low and the situation was made even worse by the fact that the power-hungry Roman generals everywhere rose in revolt against Gallienus (253–268), the son and co-emperor of Valerian. With prestige low and civil wars being fought, the enemies of Rome seized their opportunity and broke through the frontiers everywhere. In Gaul Postumus created a separatist Gallic Empire, which weakened Gallienus' position even further and led to the development of separate military organizations in the different parts of the Empire. And this was not the only revolt Gallienus was facing. It was symptomatic of the situation that Gallienus had to grant Odaenathus, the Arab prince of Palmyra, the command of all loyal Roman forces in the east with the title *Corrector Totius Orientis* against the Roman forces of the usurping family of the Macriani in Asia, while his own forces engaged their main army.

Gallienus could not trust any native Roman with the command of an army against Roman usurpers, but his emergency measure led to further troubles. Its by-product was the short-lived Palmyran Empire, and one can say with very good reason that the father of the Palmyran Empire was Gallienus. Odaenathus' role in the defeat of Shapur I in 260 and in subsequent events has been overstated. Odaenathus had merely raided Shapur's personal retinue in 260 while the divisions of Shapur's army were actually defeated by the Roman forces which consisted of those sent by Gallienus (the fleet under Ballista) and those who had survived the fall of Valerian. It was this army that the Macriani then turned against Gallienus.

In the West, the Dunkirk II marine transgression beginning in c.230 had led to the abandonment of the forts at the mouth of the Rhine, which the Franks had exploited by beginning to conduct piratical raids alongside their land operations. In 260 the Franks penetrated all the way to Spain before being defeated by Postumus, who then duly usurped power. The earliest recorded piratical raid of the Saxons occurred slightly later in the 280s, but it is possible that they too had started this activity earlier because a new set of fortifications was built on both sides of the Channel between c.250–285 that we today know with the name of the Saxon shore.[181] The Roman coastal defences and fleets had proved incapable of protecting the coasts of Britain, Gaul and Spain.

Elsewhere, the Alamanni had been able to march into Italy before being defeated by Gallienus; the Goths and Heruls had ravaged Asia Minor, the Balkans and even the Mediterranean before being defeated through the combined efforts of three successive emperors – Gallienus, Claudius II and Aurelian; the Persians had ravaged Asia Minor and Syria; and the Berbers had raided Mauritania Tingitana. Similarly, further east other Berbers (Quinquegentanei, Bavares and Faraxen/Frexes) had ravaged the North-East of *Mauritania Caesariensis* and the North-West of Numidia from 254 to 259.[182]

During Claudius II's reign the Blemmyes had ravaged Egypt and the Marmaridae had ravaged Cyrenaica, and the Palmyran Arabs and their Roman auxiliaries had been able to conquer most of the east. Even the Isaurians had revolted and started raiding.

Gallienus did not only fight these enemies, but concluded treaties with the Franks, Marcomanni and Heruls. He was desperately short of manpower, and was therefore ready to use a combination of force and diplomacy. This policy allowed him to pacify whole sectors of the frontier and it also gave him access to a pool of auxiliaries and *Foederati* that he could employ against other foreign or domestic enemies. It was highly symptomatic of the situation that foreigners were needed for the fighting of civil wars.

However, eventually after many years of fighting, Gallienus managed to stabilize the situation partly thanks to the many reforms he made, partly thanks to his own superb generalship, partly thanks to the efforts of others (Postumus, Odaenathus, generals), partly by treaties, and partly thanks to the temporary abandonment of terrain to the enemy. Gallienus was faced with an unenviable situation, and therefore instituted many changes and reforms to save the situation: for example, he granted religious freedom to the Christians to gain their support, especially in the east.

It should be stressed, however, that the reforms of Gallienus concerned only that part of the empire which was ruled by him. For example, in the Gallic Empire the usurper Postumus had to bolster his military strength by employing a great number of auxiliary troops consisting of 'Celts' (Germans or Gauls?) and Franks (SHA Gall. 7), who may have been the precursors of the Late Roman *auxilia*. In contrast, Gallienus created a personal field army *comitatus* consisting of a mix of new recruits and existing units and their detachments. The core of this army was based on cavalry that Gallienus grouped together. Foreigners did play a role in his army too, but mainly as allied forces.

The most famous of Gallienus' reforms was the creation of the first separate mobile cavalry army, the *Tagmata*, in Milan as a rapid reaction force against threats from Gaul, Raetia and Illyria.[183] The evacuation of the *Agri Decumantes* by Postumus opened Italy to invasions through Raetia.[184] What was novel about the *Tagmata* was that the legionary cavalry forces had been separated from their mother units and joined together with the auxiliary cavalry units to form the first truly separate and permanent cavalry army (that is, it was not a temporary grouping) under its own commander. This army consisted of cavalry units/legions about 6,000 strong, the equivalent of infantry legions. But this was not the whole extent of the reform. Gallienus also separated the infantry units and detachments into their own separate 6,000-man 'legions'. It is unlikely to be a coincidence that John Lydus (*De magistratibus* 1.46, p.70.3–4) also refers to the existence of separate 6,000-man infantry legions, and 6,000-man cavalry legions (i.e. the equivalent of later *mere/meros*) in the past, the practice of which I date to Gallienus' reign.

According to the sixth-century author Lydus (*De Magistr.* 1.46), the professional Roman army consisted of units (*speirai*) of 300 *aspidoforoi* (shield-bearers[185]) called cohorts; cavalry *alae* (*ilai*) of 600 horsemen; *vexillationes* of 500 horsemen; *turmae* of 500 horsemen and legions of 6,000 footmen and the same numbers of horsemen. On the basis of the fact that this list fails to mention the *limitanei* or *comitatenses* and includes the *praetoriani*, it is clear that the names must predate the reign of Constantine. However, Lydus' referral to the cohorts of 300 *aspidoforoi* should be seen as a referral to the use of the legions as phalanxes consisting of 320-man units. It is of course possible that this is a mistake resulting from his misunderstanding of the structure of the republican era manipular legion of *principes*, *hastati*, and *triarii*, which Marius had changed to include the light-armed *velites* for a total of 480 men. If Lydus is correct then the 'cohort' in question could be a second- to third-century detachment that consisted of only the four centuries of shield-bearers (à 80) for a total of 320 men (depth four to eight men), in addition to which came the light-armed (*lanciarii, sagittarii, verutarii, funditores, ferentarii* for a total of 160 men, deployed two to four deep). That is, with the inclusion of the light-armed this cohort retained the old strength of 480, but it was still smaller than the 'old cohort', because it had included in addition to the 480 legionaries 240 light-armed troops. This alternative receives support from the fact that the units would not have marched to war in their entirety, which would have made necessary the use of the abovementioned smaller cohorts. The other alternative is that we should identify the 300-man cohorts with the 256-man *tagmata* of the former legions mentioned by the *Strategikon* (12.B.8.1) so that each detachment (1024 men) consisted of four such and 256 light-armed men grouped separately. However, this seems to refer to the situation after the reforms of Constantine.

Lydus also provides the following list of various types of troops encompassing the army, which is very useful for the purpose of seeing how many different types there were. It should be kept in mind, however, that the same men could be used for a variety of roles with different equipment and not all of the types were specialists. Of note is also the inclusion of the *primoscutarii/protectores*. After Gallienus, each of the armies included *protectores*, such as the historian Ammianus, who acted as staff officers and intelligence officers. Another noteworthy inclusion is the referral to the *ballistarii* as artillerymen rather than as crossbowmen. The inclusion of *ocreati*, *hastati/doryforoi*, *pilarii/akontistai*, *lanciarii*, and *verutarii* in the list implies the use of different pieces of equipment by the different ranks in battle formation. The heavily-equipped footmen of the front ranks, the *aspidoforoi*, (depending upon the depth of formation ranks, 1–2, or 1–4, or 1–8 deep) would have varied their equipment according to the needs of the moment: 1) against cavalry as *doryforoi/hastati*; and 2) against infantry as *pilarii/akontistai*. Regardless of the other pieces of equipment, the first rank would have always consisted of the *ocreati*, while the rear ranks behind the 'heavies' would have always used some kind of javelins as the various names (*lancea*, *verutus*) imply. Basically, this list agrees with the information that we have of Roman infantry and cavalry tactics. The list is based on the edition and translation of Bundy (Lydus, pp.69–75) with some changes. The underlining is to highlight important types of troops.

Lydus' Legions:

alai apo ch hippeôn	alae of 600 horsemen (former auxiliary cavalry)
vexillatiōnes apo f hippeôn	vexillationes of 500 horsemen (former legionary cavalry)
tourmai apo f toxotôn hippeôn	tourmae of 500 mounted archers (new type of cavalry created by Alexander Severus?)
legiōnes, legiones apo hexakischiliôn pezôn	legions of 6,000 infantrymen
tribounoi, dēmarchoi,	tribuni, tribunes
ordinarioi, taxiarchoi, ordinarii	ducenarii and centurions?
signiferai, sēmeioforoi,	signiferi, standard-bearers (during Vegetius' day called draconarii)
optiōnes, optiones	chosen men (centurion's deputies/vicars) or registrars
vēxillarioi, doryforoi,	vexillarii, spear-bearing men belonging to vexillationes, i.e. legionary cavalry
mēnsōres	mensores, camp-surveyors
toubikines, salpistai pezōn	tubicines, infantry buglers
boukinatōres, salpistai hippeôn	bucinatores, cavalry buglers

kornikines, keraulai	cornicines, horn-blowers
andabatai, katafraktoi	andabatae, cataphract cavalry
mētatōres, chōrometrai	metatores, land-surveyors
archytēs kai sagittarioi, toxotai kai beloforoi	arquites and sagittarii, archers and arrow-bearers
praitōrianoi, stratēgikoi	praetoriani, praetorians, general's men
lagchiarioi/lanchiaroi, akontoboloi	lanciarii, lance-throwers
dekemprimoi, dekaprōtoi	decemprimi, heads of 10 horsemen, decani
benefikialioi, hoi epi therapeia tōn beteranōn tetagmenoi	beneficiales, those giving medical aid to the veterani/veterans.
torkouatoi, streptoforoi, hoi tous maniakas foreuntes	torquati, torc-wearers who wear necklaces (rewarded for bravery and segmented arm-guards (manicae)).
brachiatoi, ē toi armilligeroi, pselioforoi	brachiati or armilligeri, bracelet-wearers (rewarded for bravery). It is possible that the brachiati should be united with the following term.
armigeroi, hoploforoi	armigeri (armour-bearers), arms-bearers (hoplon-bearers)
mounerarioi, leitourgoi	munerarii, servants or soldiers (munifices) doing fatigues and services
dēputatoi, afōrismenoi	deputati, deputies appointed for a specific task
auxiliarioi, hypaspistai	auxiliarii, auxiliaries (note the use of hypaspistai/shield-bearers for foreign troops which is suggestive for their later use as a term for bucellarii)
kouspatōres, fylakistai	cuspatores, gaolers
imaginiferai, eichonoforoi	imaginiferi, imaginarii, image-bearers, i.e. bearers of the emperor's image
okreatoi, pezoi sidērōi tas knēmas peripefrakmenoi	ocreati, infantry with iron greaves to protect the calves
armatoura prima, hoplomeletē prōtē	armature prima, first arms service
armatoura sēmissalia, hoplomeletē meizōn	armature semissalis, advanced arms practice
hastatoi, doryforoi	hastati, spearmen
tessarioi, hoi ta symbola en tōi kairōi tēs symbolēs tōi plēthei perifēmizontes	tesserarii, who announce the watchword to the soldiery at the time of encounter
dracōnarioi, drakontoforoi	draconarii, the bearers of the dragon standard
adioutōres, hypoboēthoi	adiutores, adjutants
samiarioi, hoi tōn hoplōn stilpnōtai	semiarii, the polishers of arms
baginarioi/vaginarioi/thēkopoio	vaginarii, scabbard-makers
arkouarioi, toxopoioi	arcuarii, bow-makers
pilarioi, akontistai	pilarii, javelin throwers
beroutarioi, veroutarioi, diskoboloi	verutarii, throwers of verutum/spiculum javelin (Veg: shaft 3.5 ft, iron tip 5 in.
founditōres, sfendonētai	funditores, slingers
ballistarioi, katapeltistai (katapeltēs de estin eidos	ballistarii, catapult-men. A catapult is a kind of city taker/siege engine; it is called
helepoleōs, kaleitai de tōi plēthei onagros	by the soldiers/multitude onager (wild ass)
binearioi, vinearioi, teichomachoi	vinearii, wall-fighters or men who fought with the siege sheds
primoskoutarioi, hyperaspistai, hoi legomenoi protēktōres	primoscutarii, shield-bearers who are now called protectores
primosagittarioi, toxotai prōtoi	primosagittarii, first archers i.e. mounted bodyguards or LI commanders?

klibanarioi, holosidēroi. kēlibana gar hoi Rhōmaioi ta sidēra kalummata kalousin, anti tou kēlamina	clibanarii, the horsemen who wear iron armour, for the Romans call iron coverings celibana, that is to say celamina
flammoularioi, hōn epi tēs akras tou doratos foinika rhakē exērtēnto	flammularii, who bear at the end of their spears scarlet banners
expeditoi, euzōnoi, gymnoi, hetoimoi pros machēn	expediti, well-girt, lightly clad and mobile, ready for battle (i.e. non-encumbered with baggage train and lightly equipped for ease of movement)
ferentarioi, akrobolistai	ferentarii, skirmishers
kirkitōres, hoi peri tous machomenous periiontes kai chorēgountes hopla mētō epistamenoi machesthai adōratōres, beteranoi, teirōnes	circitores, who go about the fighters and give them arms adoratores, honourably retired soldiers; veterani, those who had grown old while in service; tirones, recruits not yet permitted to fight.

The creation of a separate independent cavalry *Tagmata* and commander (Aureolus in Zonaras 12.25: '*archôn tês hippou*') can be seen as a precursor for the later division of the armed forces under a *Magister Equitum* and a *Magister Peditum*, as the title 'Commander of the Cavalry' also implies that there must have been a separate commander for Gallienus' infantry forces. In fact, it is obvious that Gallienus' infantry detachments, drawn from all over the Empire – including the areas under Postumus – required a new administrative system at the head of which must have been some commander for the infantry. It should be kept in mind, however, that on the basis of a papyrus dating from 302 the cavalry was not yet regarded as fully independent. That is, each legionary cavalry unit retained its connection with their infantry unit for administrative purposes until the reign of Diocletian (Parker, 1933, 188–9), but it is also possible that one of Gallienus' successors reattached the cavalry back to the legions. Unfortunately, we do not know the title of the infantry commander that is likely to have existed for the infantry detachments. He may have been *Comes* or *Magister Peditum*, or *Comes Domesticorum Peditum*, or *Praefectus Praetorio*.

I would still suggest that the Tribunus et Magister Officiorum was actually the overall commander of all Protectores, because according to Aurelius Victor 33, Claudius II, who was the most important man right after Gallienus in 268, had only the title of tribunus in 368. I would equate this with the title of Tribunus et Magister Officiorum (note also SHA Elagab. 20.2). Gallienus was quite prepared to create large military commands for his trusted men. Of note is Gallienus' creation of regional commands in the same manner as Philip the Arab had done. For example, the former '*Hipparchos*' Aureolus served as *Dux per* Raetias in 267–268 with command of all of the forces facing Postumus and Alamanni in Italy and Raetia. The largest command was granted to Odaenathus who held the position of *Corrector Totius Orientis*, with the powers to command all of the forces of the East, but in this case Gallienus probably had little choice. It should be noted, however, that for the creation of the supreme command of the eastern armies there were also precedents, for example from the reign of Philip the Arab and even before that from the early Principate.

One of Gallienus' more important reforms was the exclusion of senators from positions of military leadership (*tribuni*, *duces*, *legati*) in order to limit their possibility for usurpation. Obviously this did not concern every senator, only those who did not have Gallienus' trust. Gallienus' favourite senators still continued to hold on to and to receive new military appointments. Similarly, this exclusion did not concern the position of governorship. Gallienus' reform meant that henceforth Roman generals would consist of *duces* (dukes), *comites* (counts) and *praefecti* (prefects), all appointed by the emperor, and no longer of the senatorial legates as before. Unsurprisingly, it was during this period that the senatorial *legati* stopped being commanders of legions. Henceforth the legions were commanded by professional military men of equestrian rank who had risen to higher commands through service in the ranks.

The *dux* (leader, duke) was originally a temporary command, but thanks to the fact that temporarily-created forces like Gallienus' *Comitatus* and *Tagmata* were constantly operating together, the position became a regular one. Besides his command duties, the *dux* was also in charge of recruiting, training, and supply. The *comes* (companion, count) was originally a member of the emperor's entourage, which now became a permanent title for a great variety of offices. Militarily the most important offices were the *Comes Domesticorum* (commander of the *Protectores Domestici*) and *Comes rei Militaris* (general). The inscription (PLRE 1 Marcianus 2) AE 1965, 114 Philippolis (Thrace) confirms the existence of comes or magister as military commander for the reign of Gallienus. It runs as follows: "ho diasêmotatos, protector tou aneikêtou despotou hêmôn Galliênou Se(bastou), tribounos praetôrianôn kai doux kai stratêlatês". Dux and stratelates (comes or magister) are clearly two separate posts. The closeness of the *comites* to the emperor ensured better chances of promotion, just like with the *protectores* (see below). The importance of the temporary position of *praepositus* also increased and became semi-permanent in many cases. The significance of the tribune also increased, the highest ranking of them being in charge of the units of bodyguards and the lesser in charge of the cavalry vexillations, legions and auxiliary cohorts.

Further, Gallienus increased the importance of the institutions of *Protectores/ Protectores Domestici* (protectors/ protectors at home/court), which may have been created by him or by Caracalla, and the *Frumentarii* (postmen/spies/assassins) as instruments of imperial security.

The exact status of the *protectores/domestici* is not known. There were also three or four types of *protectores*: those who had been posted in the provinces and whose origin probably lay in the governors' bodyguards (*equites* and *pedites singulares*); those who stayed with the emperor and came to be called *Protectores Domestici* or *Domestici* (these latter were also later sent on missions as *deputati*); and those who had received the honour of simply being given the title. According to one view the *protector* was originally an honorary title that was then extended to men who acted as the emperor's bodyguards/ staff college from which the men received appointments to other higher positions, and/or the title was given to all officers who had reached a certain rank to make them more loyal to the emperor. According to this view the *protectores* were not really a military bodyguard unit, but simply men with the officers' rank that acted simultaneously as the emperor's bodyguards and staff-college and from which they could be seconded to special missions or for duty in the generals' staffs.

According to another view there were two separate entities of *protectores*, the first of which was the staff-college/military intelligence staff and the second of which was an actual imperial bodyguard unit. According to this version, the latter *protectores* were formerly called either *speculatores* (300 'scouts' stationed in the same camp as the Praetorians) or they consisted of the former *equites singularis Augusti* (c.2000 horsemen).[186]

My own tentative suggestion is that there were 'three' bodyguard units of *protectores/domestici*: 1) the former *speculatores* who performed simultaneously the functions of bodyguards, military intelligence gathering, acted as sort of political commissars who kept their superiors in check, and acted as a staff-college for the emperor who could then use these officers for special missions; 2) military units like the *equites singulares Augusti* and *Scholae/Aulici* commanded by these *protectores* and which were also collectively called *protectores*; and 3) the former bodyguards of the governors and were now only renamed as *protectores*.

There are several reasons for this conclusion. The *protectores* were later used as commanders and officers of (for example) the *Scholae* of Constantine, which points to the likelihood that the *protectores* probably commanded different units under each different emperor. Many of these units would also have consisted of barbarians or other ethnic groups, just like the case with the *equites singulares Augusti* or Caracalla's *Leones*. Consequently, during Gallienus' reign the cavalry *protectores* probably consisted of the *Equites Singulares Augusti, Scholae, Equites Dalmatae* (and possibly also of the *Comites, Equites Promoti* and some other units) while its infantry counterparts would probably have been some palatine units like those later known as the *Ioviani* and *Herculiani*.[187] Notably, the *Equites Dalmatae* formed Gallienus' retinue at the time of his murder.

It is further important to note that besides being bodyguards, just like the praetorians and all those garrisoned at *castra peregrinorum* in Rome, the *protectores* were also used as spies and imperial assassins, and it is also known that Gallienus sometimes even spied upon people in person in disguise at night. As Frank has pointed out it is probable that the *protectores* also served as the military equivalent of the civilian *agentes in rebus* (successors of the *Frumentarii*) in the staffs of the period commanders. That is, the *protectores* performed military intelligence gathering missions which included spying on superiors and on foreigners. The messenger/inspector *Frumentarii* were by no means the only imperial special agents. It is not known whether Gallienus also used priests, astrologers and fortune tellers as informers just like the earlier emperors, but one may make the educated guess that such practices were also continued alongside the other systems.

Among the greatest successes of Gallienus can be counted that in his own portion of the Roman Empire he created and trained a highly efficient and mobile army commanded by equally gifted men of lowly Illyrian origin all of whom had risen through the ranks. It was this army and its leaders that breathed new life into the Roman Empire. It is true that the final mopping up of the Gothic and Herulian invading forces was left for Claudius and Aurelian (Aurelianus) to complete during the years 269–271, but it was still primarily thanks to the valiant efforts of Gallienus in 267–268 that the terrible migration/invasion of the Eastern Germans was stopped. The destruction of the Gothic and Herulian fleets, together with a sizable portion of their manpower and population, caused a temporary collapse of Gothic power in the Black Sea region with the result that, for example, the Sarmatians were able to regain control of the Bosporan kingdom. The same victory also

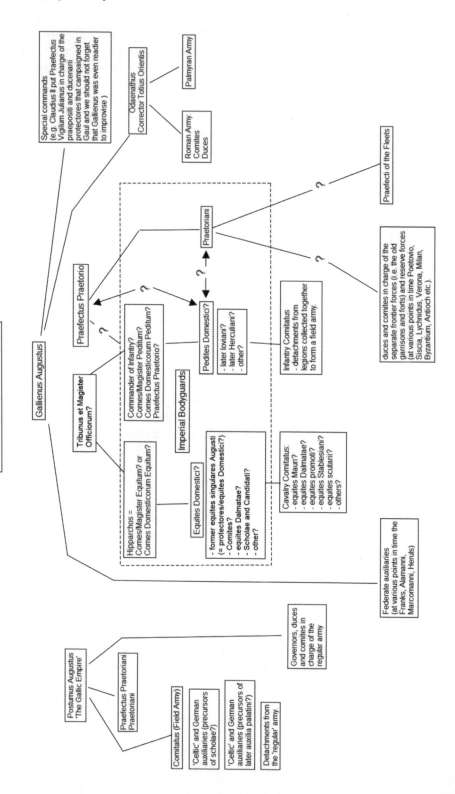

secured to the Romans the control of the allied Greek cities of the North Black Sea such as Olbia and Chersonesus, the latter of which proved instrumental in warfare against the Bosporans. It is of course possible that the Romans never lost the control of these cities, but the crushing defeat of the Goths in 267–271 certainly secured these for the Romans. It is also probable that it was then at the latest that the 'Huns' moved westward to occupy lands north of the Caucasus previously under the control of the Goths, unless of course the reason for the Gothic invasions/migrations had not been their attack to begin with rather than the arrival of the plague with the lure of easy booty – additional details are included later in the narrative.

Despite all the frantic efforts of Gallienus, at the time when he was murdered by his own officers the Roman Empire was still effectively divided into three parts: 1) the Gallic Empire under the usurper/emperor Postumus; 2) the Roman Empire under the legitimate emperor Gallienus; and 3) the Palmyran Empire, still nominally ruled by Gallienus but already in practice by Zenobia, the widow of the murdered Odaenathus. The revolt of Aureolus and the murder of Gallienus had also meant that the mopping up of the Gothic invaders had been left unfinished, as a result of which Claudius' short reign was entirely spent on dealing with the Goths, while the Palmyrenes rose in revolt against him. The Palmyrene takeover of the East and Egypt caused serious but not permanent damage to the *classes Syriaca/Seleuca* and *Alexandriana* both of which, however, appear to have managed to survive by fleeing to Roman territory. The end result of this was the resurgence of the problem of Isaurian piracy. The fleets as such survived and took part in the reconquest of the East during the reign of Aurelian.

Thanks to the fact that Gallienus' almost only available recruiting area was Illyricum, he had brought the Illyrians to the dominant position among the military. The Illyrians were tough soldiers but only semi-civilized in Roman eyes. It was largely thanks to this that, after the murder of Gallienus by Illyrian officers, the Empire was effectively ruled by the 'Illyrian Mafia', at least until the downfall of the Constantinian Dynasty.

The Empire Restored 270–275

Aurelian was deservedly called the 'Restorer of the Roman Empire'. In 270 he defeated Claudius' brother at Aquileia and marched to Rome to secure his position. In 271 Aurelian defeated invaders in Pannonia, and returned to Italy to fight the invading Alamanni and Iuthungi. This time, however, he made a serious blunder: the Alamanni ambushed him and decimated his cavalry force with the result that there was a revolt in Rome. As an able soldier he swiftly resorted to the use of guerrilla warfare and then defeated the invaders in two battles which he followed up by crushing the revolt in Rome. Aurelian defeated the Goths also in 271 after which he evacuated Dacia either in 271 or 274. This evacuation worked in the short run because it shortened the frontier, but at the same time it made it necessary for the Romans to build a new line of fortifications in the area, which was probably begun by Aurelian and then continued by Probus and his successors. In spring 272 Aurelian marched to the East where he defeated the Palmyrenes, capturing both Palmyra and Zenobia while also defeating the Persians and Armenians (who deserted undoubtedly because the legitimate ruler of Armenia Trdat/Tiridates was accompanying the Roman army[188]) sent in support of Zenobia.[189] It was probably then that Constantius, the father of Constantine the Great, met Helena, the mother of Constantine, at Drepanum in Bithynia.[190] Aurelian's successful campaign against the Arab queen of Palmyra formed a culmination point for the history of the Arabs. First of all, thanks to the fact that Zenobia had killed the king of the Tanukh, whose nephew was the Lakhmid king Amr, the latter chose to abandon his alliance with the Persians and join the Romans against the Palmyrenes and Persians.[191] The destruction of Palmyra also signified the transfer of Arabic mercantile power and activity away from the traditional caravan cities of Northern Arabia to the Lakhmids of Hira and to the Himyarites of Yemen.

In the course of his eastern campaign Aurelian attempted to undermine Christianity by introducing the worship of the Sun, with Apollonius of Syane as its Messiah. Aurelian spent the winter in Byzantium and then in the spring defeated the Carpi. It was then that the future emperor Constantine was born at Naissus on 27 February (Barnes, 2011, 38). In the meanwhile the Palmyrans and Egypt had revolted forcing Aurelian to return East. Palmyra was recaptured and destroyed, and the revolt in Egypt crushed, both in 273.

In 274 Aurelian invaded Gaul and returned it to the fold of the Roman Empire. It is not known whether Aurelian at this time attempted to unify the administrative and organizational structures of the various parts of the Empire, but one can make the educated guess that at least some of the changes that had been instituted either by Gallienus or Aurelian were extended to the West.

In 274/5 Aurelian held a spectacular triumph in Rome. Of note is the fact that the prisoners included Aksumite captives, which suggests that the Ethiopians of Aksum had fought alongside the Blemmyes in support of the Egyptian revolt.[192] (For further details, see Chapter 2.) This was the sign of further troubles to come.

After having demonstrated his power in Rome, Aurelian had to return in haste to Gaul in the spring of 275 to nip a revolt in the bud. Now Aurelian was finally free to turn his attention towards the East where he had unfinished business with the Persians. Consequently, he began his trek towards Persia, but was murdered en route by a conspiracy of officers brought about by a ruse of Aurelian's secretary. It is also possible that Aurelian was murdered in a Christian conspiracy (the secretary may have been a Christian), as he was said to be about to launch a persecution of them. However, the intended timing of Aurelian's invasion of Persia had been very opportune, because the Persian empire was in a state of turmoil.

If Modestus' treatise (supposedly written for Tacitus) is accepted as genuine and not a fifteenth-century forgery based on Vegetius, then either Claudius II or Aurelian had reattached the cavalry to their legions. This conclusion receives support from the resulting strength of the legionary cavalry detachment, which was 726 horsemen plus supernumeraries. The increased cavalry numbers would have resulted from the distribution of Gallienus' enlarged cavalry army back into the legions. In light of the subsequent diminished role of the cavalry under the Late Roman emperors, this seems quite probable. See also chapters 1 and 4.

Empire Fights Back 275–284: The Setting of the Stage for the Tetrarchy

At this point in time, the soldiers felt disgusted by the behaviour of their officers who had murdered so successful an emperor as Aurelian, as a result of which they delegated the choosing of the new emperor to the Roman Senate. The Senate was afraid of the army, as a result of which there was an impasse of six months, after which the Senate finally gathered enough courage to appoint an elderly senator named Tacitus as the new emperor. His reign signified a break in the line of Illyrian emperors for he seems to have had Italian roots with estates in Italy, Numidia and Mauretania.

According to the SHA, Tacitus considered his first duty as an emperor to be the punishment of the officers who in their drunken state had murdered Aurelian, and this he set out to accomplish. However, I would consider this claim to be at most only partially true. Tacitus was in no hurry to punish the officers of the army assembled in the East. Rather his first priority seems to have been to try to gather some military glory by butchering the allied Goths who had disembarked their troops in Asia Minor to assist the Romans against the Persians. The SHA (Tac. 13) claims that the Goths used as their pretext for the invasion a supposed command of Aurelian to take part in the forthcoming Persian war, but it is more than likely that Aurelian had indeed concluded an alliance with the Goths that the Romans now failed to respect because the consolidation of the new emperor's position required military successes.[193] The Goths responded by raiding Pontus, Cappadocia, Galatia, and Cilicia, but unsurprisingly the new emperor Tacitus, who took charge of one army, and his brother and praetorian prefect Florianus, placed in charge of another army, both defeated the 'invaders' with relative ease.

However, in the meanwhile, or so the story goes, Tacitus had appointed Maximianus, his kinsman, as governor of Syria, and in this position Maximianus had started to behave in a high-handed manner with the result that the soldiers, who notably also included Aurelian's murderers, killed him. I would rather suggest that the real reason for the revolt was the anger felt by the commanders of the Eastern army who were expecting to march against the Persians only to learn that the new emperor had betrayed their hopes. Even more importantly, the Goths had been let loose on the families of some of the Eastern troops based in Asia Minor, who would have been assembled closer to the frontier in anticipation of the forthcoming Persian war. The killers of Aurelian and other plotters, who undoubtedly also included the future emperor Probus, naturally feared punishment and before the emperor could react they had sent their own men to assassinate him.[194] Tacitus had left his brother in charge of mopping up the remnants of the enemy forces and was already on his way home, but the assassins reached him before he was able to cross into Europe and killed him. As a result, the Eastern forces chose Probus as their new emperor, while the imperial army chose Florianus as his brother's successor. At first, Florianus continued the unfinished campaign against the invaders and he did achieve a considerable victory before he learnt of the usurpation of Probus, as a result of which he was forced to march to crush the upstart.

Despite the fact that Probus was the more experienced of the two as military commander, his position was still precarious. He had at his disposal only the forces of Syria, Phoenicia, Palestine, and Egypt, while Florianus controlled all the rest of the empire. In this difficult situation Probus was forced to rely on the support of the murderers of Aurelian, unless of course he had done this already from the very start. Probus' only advantages were his reputation and that he controlled the Egyptian grain. Consequently, Probus opted to prolong the conflict by blocking the Cilician Gates while using guerrilla campaign in combination with efforts to undermine the loyalty of the enemy troops. One can perhaps include in this latter category the (possibly) fictitious letter of Probus to the praetorian prefect Capito (otherwise unknown) in which he assured that he would have no other prefect than Capito if he administered all things well.[195]

When Florianus reached Tarsus and billeted his forces in the city in the midst of a summer heat wave, his mostly European troops, who were unaccustomed to the climate, fell ill. When Probus learnt of this he began skirmishing with the enemy forces in front of the city. It was now that the fame of Probus and his propaganda behind the scenes paid off. Some of Probus' men were admitted into the city where they imprisoned Florianus. However, some of Florianus' men apparently came to other conclusions and claimed that it was not Probus' will to depose Florianus, which encouraged the latter to don the purple again – but only with the result that Probus' men killed Florianus probably in August 276.[196] The 'Illyrian Mafia' had regained power. Just like Aurelian's reign, Probus' reign was marked by constant fighting on all fronts, with the result that he was always on the move as befitted a soldier emperor.

The reason why the Persians did not bother the Romans amidst all this chaos was that the new King of Kings Bahram/Wahram II was facing the revolt of his cousin Hormizd in the east. The revolt of Hormizd was particularly dangerous as it was also supported by the Kushans and other eastern states and tribes. Narses, the son of Shapur I and Great King of Armenia (and uncle of Bahram II), was also opposed to the accession of Bahram II, but chose not to revolt out of patriotism at a time when the Romans threatened the western border. In fact, the new king appears to have left Narses in charge of the defence of the western frontier. In addition, according to the Georgian Chronicles, which has mixed up Mihran and Narses with each other, Narses was at the time facing nomadic problem.[197]

As new emperor, Probus needed to secure his position. This meant that he needed the approval of the other Roman armies as well as the approval of the Senate (i.e. the old nobility). He also needed to decide how to deal with Aurelian's murderers, and he needed to secure the frontiers that had once again been breached by barbarian hordes after the death of the feared Aurelian. Consequently, he was just as eager to avoid having to fight a war against the Persians as the Persians were, and in fact neither made a move against the other at the time. After having announced his assumption of sole power, Probus duly received the approval of the Senate. Next he invited the killers of Aurelian to a banquet and had them killed, and then received the submission of all of the armies of Europe who had recently made Florianus emperor.

In the latter half of the year 276 Probus appears to have fought against the Goths as a result of which he was able to take the title *Gothicus* in 277. It is possible that the Goths he defeated were the last remnants of the Gothic force still tarrying in Asia Minor, or that the Roman civil war and the need to revenge the wrongs suffered at the hands of Tacitus encouraged even more of the Goths to join their brethren in Roman territory (suggested by Agathangelos). According to Agathangelos (37) and Moses (2.79), the exiled Armenian king Trdat/Tiridates had been educated in the house of count Licinius (the future colleague of Constantine the Great) with the result that when the ruler of the Goths had assembled an army to wage war on the Romans, Trdat and his men formed part of the Roman army. The Armenian version can be considered credible because the Goths would have been eager to send a new army to ravage Roman lands after they had learnt of the Roman betrayal.

According to Agathangelos (39–47), the Gothic king challenged the Roman emperor to single combat. Probus faced a problem. He was bodily too weak to accept the challenge in person and he also had too few men to challenge the enemy in a pitched battle. Consequently, he sent messages to his commanders and troops to come to him immediately, regardless of where they were. Licinius was one of those who followed the order and he came with Tiridates (Trdat). En route, however, they had faced a problem. They arrived before a locked gate of some city at midnight and could not find enough fodder for their vast cavalry army in the middle of the night. They saw in a walled pen a great pile of hay, but it lay on the other side of the wall. The energetic Tiridates took the matters into his own hand and climbed over. He threw back heaps of hay together with the guards and donkeys, and then climbed back. Licinius was amazed by this great feat of strength and then when in the morning his army was able to enter the city he immediately went to see the Roman emperor with all the magnates, generals, officers and nobles and suggested that Tiridates should be used as their champion. Tiridates was brought before the emperor, after which it was agreed that the challenge would be accepted.

Next morning Tiridates was robed with the imperial garb and sent to fight the duel. When Tiridates and the Gothic king then whipped the flanks of their horses and charged at each other, Tiridates tilted the king on the ground, took him prisoner and brought him before Probus. Unfortunately, the story doesn't tell us what happened next, but we can presume that the Tervingi Goths, who were settled on the Danube, is the group meant here, and that Probus struck a deal with the captured king and settled him and his followers as Federates on the Danube to protect the frontier. The last remnants of the fleeing Gothic forces were actually destroyed by Tejran, the king of Bosporus, who intercepted and massacred the survivors, enabling Probus to strike coins with '*Victoria Pontica*' and '*Victoria Gothica*'.[198]

The grateful emperor entrusted Tiridates with a great army with which he invaded Armenia and faced the Persians successfully on the battlefield in 278(?). Many of the Persians were killed and many had to flee back to Persia.[199] The success achieved by Tiridates is not that surprising when we remember that the Persians were simultaneously also facing Hormizd's revolt in the east and a nomadic invasion through the Darubend/Darbend Gate (see below). It was the success of Tiridates that then enabled Probus to claim the title *Persicus Maximus* on 21 October 279.[200]

The version provided by the Georgian Chronicles (pp.80–81) is even more illuminating. According to this chronicle, at the time the Goths had invaded the Roman territory, the 'Khazars' (either proto-Turks, proto-Huns or 'Massagetae', or some other nomads[201]) again tried to take Derbend as was their custom and Mihran (Mirian with Narses) went against them as was his custom. In the meanwhile, the Roman emperor had gathered his army and marched to meet the Goths. The king of the Goths proposed a duel, but the emperor was not ready to fight him in person. Instead, he dressed Trdat, the son of Khosrov, in the emperor's clothes and sent him to fight the Gothic king. Trdat captured his opponent, and the Romans routed the Goths. Consequently, in recognition of his services, Trdat was crowned king of Armenia, given Roman troops, and sent to Armenia. Trdat expelled Mihran's soldiers and Persian governors from Armenia. According to the timeline provided by Moses (2.91), Trdat was crowned as king of Armenia in about 278, which means that the invasion would have taken place slightly before probably in very late 276 or in 277.[202] However, when Mihran (Mirian and Narses) returned from fighting the Khazars in c. 278–279(?) the situation changed. Narses received reinforcements from Persia commanded by Persian nobles that included a relative of his named Peroz. Mirian (the king of Iberia) gave Peroz his daughter as wife and land in western Iberia. With these reinforcements Narses advanced against Trdat. Trdat was compelled to avoid battling with superior enemy forces and was therefore forced to conduct a guerrilla campaign against the Persians that lasted years. During these years Trdat gained great renown because no one was able to defeat him in single combat.

In 277, Probus marched with a huge army to Gaul, which, following the death of Aurelian, had been partially occupied by the Franks, Alamanni, Burgundi, and Vandals. In fact the whole Roman defensive system had been overrun, which is not surprising considering the fact that the abandonment of the *Agri Decumantes* alone had left a gaping hole in the defences. After his arrival Probus is said to have fought several great and successful battles, as a result of which he was able to take back from the barbarian invaders sixty Gallic communes and all their booty. According to the SHA, Probus slew about '400,000' Germanic invaders on Roman soil and drove all the rest back over the Niger (Neckar) and the Alba (Elbe).

Zosimus' account makes it clear that Probus gave the command of the war against the Franks to his trusted general (Proculus?) while he defeated the Alamanni in person in the South of Gaul and Raetia and pushed them back over the Neckar while his general did the same to the Franks. After having defeated the Alamanni, Probus faced the Burgundians and Vandals (Zos. 1.67–8), but he had too few men to engage them. Consequently, he withdrew his army behind an unknown river and enticed part of the enemy force to follow after and then attacked before the entire enemy force could come across. The survivors sued for peace on condition that they returned their booty and prisoners, but when they did not do that Probus pursued and crushed them. The enemy prisoners were transported to Britain.

The first stage of the fighting, the clearing of Gaul of invaders, appears to have lasted for the whole summer of 277 after which Probus and his generals appear to have launched an invasion of enemy territories across the Rhine and Neckar as far as the Elbe, following which Probus built *castra* on the right bank of the Rhine and left garrisons in them. The borders facing the *Agri Decumantes* in particular needed a whole new series of forts. The soldiers were given farms, store-houses, homes and rations of grain to support them.

The war against the barbarians, with a price set for the head of each killed barbarian, was continued until nine kings (*reguli*) of different tribes surrendered and prostrated themselves at Probus' feet. Probus demanded and got hostages, grain, cows and sheep. He also demanded the return of all booty and punished those who did not comply, as the above makes clear. In addition, he demanded and was given 16,000 barbarian recruits (Alamanni?) that he distributed among the provincial garrisons in groups of 50 and 60. It is probable that at the same time Probus also reorganized the defences in Raetia, because the abandonment of the *Agri Decumantes* made this necessary. Reddé (p.630) has suggested that the creation of the so-called *barcarii* (ND Occ. 35.32) on the Lake Constance was undertaken by Probus for this very reason at this time. It is possible that the Fleet of Lake Como was also created at this time for the very same purpose.

Probus' trusted commander also captured significant numbers of Franks that were then resettled on the Danube frontier probably as *Laeti* (?) with the requirement to provide troops when needed. Probus' strategy along the Rhine frontier can be seen to have set a precedent for his successors to follow. The hostile barbarians were first forced to become clients by the use of offensive warfare until they surrendered. Probus' goals was not to enlarge the empire, but to fortify both banks of the Rhine so that the forts on the barbarian side acted as outposts in front of which were barbarian allies as a first line of defence.

It is very probable that most of Probus' new forts along the frontiers followed the so-called Tetrarchic model: that is, these forts would have been smaller and usually square in shape (*quadriburgia*) with thick walls and ramparts, and projecting corner and interval towers. The barracks were also placed against the walls. In short, these forts were more defensible than had been the earlier larger rectangular fortresses with more modest defensive structures. Indeed, modern research has proved that the Romans had already adopted the so-called Tetrarchic square forts by the late-second and early-third century (Le Bohec, 2006, 98ff.), which makes this conclusion very likely.

In the meantime, the Baquates had revolted in Mauritania Tingitana (continued until c.280), the Sarmatians and their allies, the tribes of Getae (this could mean any or all of the following: the Getae, Goths, Carpi, and Bastarnae) and Isaurians appear to have exploited the absence of the emperor – on top of which Saturninus the Moor usurped the power in the East. Probus had left Saturninus in charge of the east with the title variously reported as Magister Militum (Jordanes, Rom 293) or Magister Excercitus (Jerome, Chron. 281) or Dux Limitis Orientalis (SHA Firmus etc., 7.2: appointed to this post by Aurelian and possibly promoted to the previous by Probus). It is possible that these terms are anachronistic, but it is equally possible that Probus may have attempted to keep Saturninus loyal with a grandiose title. What is certain is that Saturninus had a large command for which there were earlier precedents too – only the title would have presaged what happened later. Consequently, in 278 Probus was forced to turn his attention East. He defeated the Sarmatians in Illyricum (Upper Danube) and then marched to Thrace (Lower Danube), where he defeated all the 'Getic tribes' (Goths, Carpi and Bastarnae), after which he left the crushing of the Isaurian rebels to his general and continued his march against the usurper.

The usurper had taken with him most of the Egyptian forces, with the result that the Blemmyes had invaded Egypt. When Probus' army approached the usurper's army, his frightened soldiers killed him (Zos. 1.66, Zon. 13.29), or he was first forced to fight a series of battles after which the usurper was killed by Probus' assassins (SHA Probus 18.4, Firmus 11.3). In the meanwhile in 279(?), two generals Proculus and Bonosus appear to have usurped power jointly in Gaul. According to the SHA, the usurpers controlled Gaul, Britain and Spain. Modern historians consider the revolt of Britain to have been separate from that of Gaul, but I am inclined to follow the SHA. There were several reasons for the revolt in Gaul. Proculus was a brave soldier, but he was very depraved as a person. He used to brag only about the number of women he had been able to mate or rape. Bonosus, who was a hopeless drunkard 'born not to live but to drink', feared Probus' punishment for his failure to prevent the burning of the galleys of the Rhine fleet by the barbarians – Probus like his compatriot Aurelian was a known disciplinarian. Consequently, both men had serious personal weaknesses that united them and made them also liable to turn against their master.

Probus was unable to advance against them immediately, because he had two problems on his hands. Firstly there was the ongoing war with Persia that he was fighting by proxy via the good services of Trdat, and then there was the Blemmye invasion to solve. However, when the Persians sued for peace, Probus with a superb poker face rejected the gifts and threatened the Persians with an invasion. The frightened Persians had by now learnt that Probus had defeated Saturninus and that his generals had defeated the Blemmyes (but they had evidently not learned of the usurpations in Gaul) and believed that Probus was therefore free to invade. Consequently, the Great King of Armenia Narses, as acting regent of the West, signed the peace on Roman terms. Neither side appears to have entertained any plans to respect the terms of the contract, but had rather just bought time.

After this, Probus marched to Thrace where he received huge numbers of barbarian fugitives that included 100,000 Bastarnae and an unknown number of Gepids, Greuthungi and Vandals from the other side of the Danube and settled them alongside the Franks. When Probus continued his march against the usurpers, the Gepids, Greuthungi, Vandals and Franks revolted and at least the Franks built a fleet and pillaged Greece, after which they sailed to Sicily and attacked Syracuse. They then sailed to Africa, where they were defeated by the Roman army near Carthage, but were still able to sail through the Straits of Gibraltar and reach their homes. The Roman fleets were clearly unable to cope with the threats they were facing simultaneously on several fronts. Of note is also the fact that Probus appears to have sought to establish the same strategic principles (fortified borders, alliances and revitalization of local economy) in operation along the Danube frontier as he did along the Rhine. (See above and below.)

In the meanwhile, the usurper Proculus had scored a significant victory over the invading Alamanni that had endeared him to the troops, which in turn made the job of defeating him more difficult for Probus. The following is my reconstruction of the likely sequence and course of events. First, Probus defeated Proculus in Raetia and forced him to flee. After this, Probus marched against Bonosus, but Bonosus fought back with greater skill than his co-ruler. Consequently, the war became prolonged. Bonosus' resistance gave Proculus a chance to attempt to bring the Franks to their assistance, but Proculus was betrayed by them and therefore defeated and killed by Probus. Now the situation had become hopeless for the surviving usurper with the result that he fled to Britain. Another possibility is that Bonosus hanged himself in Gaul immediately after Procolus' demise and that one of the usurpers' trusted officers then usurped power in Britain.

What is certain is that Probus sent Victorinus the Moor against the remaining usurper in Britain rather than attempt an invasion in person. The reason for this was that Victorinus had recommended the nomination of the officer in question and therefore had the responsibility of correcting his mistake. Victorinus pretended to be a fugitive and managed to gain his friend's trust with the result that he was able to remove him. It appears to have taken the entire campaign season of 281 for Probus to defeat the usurpers. After this Probus pacified the locals by allowing the Britons, Gauls and Spaniards to make as much wine as they wanted without any restrictions. Notably, he had already followed a similar policy in the Balkans, had planted chosen wines near Sirmium, and had apparently given the same permission to the populace of Illyricum. These measures increased the economic viability of the areas in question while obviously weakening the prominence of the Italian wine producers.

In late 281 Probus celebrated a triumph for his successes in Rome after which he intended to march against the Persians and begin the war that Aurelian had already planned. The situation was still very opportune. The Persian *shahanshah* was still fighting in the East while Narses faced the skilled Trdat in Armenia. Then once again disaster struck. Probus' *Praefectus Praetorio* Carus launched a very well-prepared coup. While Probus was spending his time in Sirmium in the spring and summer of 282, he kept his army busy by making them drain a marsh and by making a canal. He had apparently overworked his men and had not let them enjoy the fruits of their great victories, because they betrayed him. Consequently, when Probus sent an army against the usurper it deserted. After this, Probus' soldiers, including his guardsmen, revolted and he was forced to flee to an 'iron tower' where he was killed on 29 August 282 by his guards (probably the Praetorians). The sources are in disagreement regarding the origins of Carus. Most claim that he was a native of Narbonensis, but the SHA suggests three different alternatives: Rome, Milan or Illyricum. Consequently, there seem to be strong reasons to suspect that the 'Illyrian Clique' had now lost power.

Despite his sad end Probus' career had proved to be a success for the empire. According to the SHA (Probus 22.3), Probus had trained the most illustrious *duces* of the era: Carus, Diocletian (Diocles/Diocletianus), Constantius, Asclepiodotus, Hannibalianus, Gaudiosus, Ursinianus (Ursinus?) and others. It is no surprise that these men followed the precedents set by Probus.

Carus made his sons Carinus and Numerian his co-rulers. Carus left Carinus in charge of the West and took Numerian with him. In the autumn of 282 the new ruler Carus was immediately forced to fight against the Sarmatians and Quadi who had exploited the civil war by invading. After Carus had defeated them, he launched the long planned invasion of Persia. Carus conquered Mesopotamia without opposition and conquered Ctesiphon, after which he took the title *Persicus Maximus*. After this, urged on by his *Praefectus Praetorio* Aper, Carus continued his march past Ctesiphon, but then he died in mysterious circumstances in June 283. When he was bedridden as a result of some illness, a thunderstorm hit the Roman camp and it was claimed that lightning hit the emperor and killed him, or that he had already died of disease before that, after which some of his *cubicularii* burned the tent, or that the tent was burned as a result of the lightning.

Obviously, it was suspected that the emperor had been assassinated, the act being covered by the burning of the tent. There are only two possible culprits for such an assassination: the *Praefectus Praetorio* Aper, the father-in-law of Numerian, or the *Comes Domesticorum* Diocles. The former could hope to rule through the weak Numerian while the latter could hope to usurp power himself as the most deserving man.

Aper is the likelier of the two, but it is impossible to say with certainty what happened. It is quite possible that Carus had indeed died after being struck by lightning. Whatever the cause, after the death of Carus the Roman army began to retreat northwards along the Euphrates. In the course of their retreat the Romans suffered a defeat that I would connect with the incident in which the King of Armenia Trdat was forced to swim across the Euphrates to safety. In other words, it is likely that the Persians attacked the Roman army when it was making a crossing of the Euphrates and that they managed to annihilate the entire force still on the eastern side of the river.

As noted above, many of the typical features of the so-called Late Roman era had in all probability been introduced during the third century. This means that the break between the Late Roman and earlier period was not as great as has often been claimed. The real break with the past occurred during the reigns of Alexander Severus and Gallienus – and the first steps to cancel these had in all probability been taken by Claudius II and Aurelian – and Probus had started the process of refortifying and strengthening the border defences and garrisons. All that was left for Diocletian to do was to finish the process begun by his Illyrian predecessors.

A member of the *Schola Armaturarum Seniorum*.
The golden helmet, shield and muscle breastplate   © Dr. Ilkka Syvänne 2012
adapted from the various illustrations describing
the imperial units of bodyguards and Notitia
Dignitatum. The horse drawn after Mattesini.

Chapter Four

The Rebirth of Rome: the Tetrarchy

Diocletian the Tyrant vs. Carinus the Rapist, 284–285

The Inauguration of the New Era in 284–285[203]

On 20 November AD 284 there was nervous excitement in the ranks of the expeditionary Roman army that had encamped near Nicomedia.

In the morning when the Roman army was approaching the city of Nicomedia, there had occurred an incident that had left the soldiers in a state of confusion. They had not seen their emperor Numerian for days and now there was a strong stench coming out from the litter carrying the emperor. Aper, the Prefect of the Praetorian Guard and father-in-law of the emperor Numerian, tried to reassure them that everything was OK, but the soldiers (probably the *Protectores Domestici*) forced their way through the guard set up by Aper and found Numerian dead inside. Aper was arrested on the spot and a marching camp and a tribunal were built for a general assembly/council of the army. Aper was then dragged before the tribunal to await judgement. The different units of the army were gathered around the tribunal in anticipation for the appointment of the new emperor and the punishment of Aper. At the same time, the soldiers also expected to be bribed with the donative that their new emperor would grant to them.

In the meanwhile, the officers had held a meeting in which their choice fell on Diocles, the commander of the *Domestici*. When the meeting was over, the officers came out of the imperial tent and took their seats on the tribunal. Then one of the men, the highest ranking officer on the tribunal, took charge of the proceedings and asked for the acceptance of the men for their and gods' choice as new emperor, Diocles. The men responded with shouts of 'Hail Augustus!', which served as a cue for Diocles to step onto the tribunal, which was followed by repeated rhythmical shouts of 'Hail Augustus!' by the tens of thousands of soldiers present. On signal the men stopped their shouting, after which one of the officers theatrically asked 'How had Numerian been killed?' which Diocles answered by drawing up his sword and pointing it at Aper, who he then stabbed with the sword while shouting aloud that 'It is he who engineered Numerian's murder!' Diocles ridiculed the dying, gored man further by shouting: 'You may well boast Aper that you have died in the hands of mighty Aeneas!' So began the rule of Caius Aurelius Valerius Diocles (later called Diocletianus/Diocletian) Augustus, 'the second Aeneas or founder of Rome', who was not even satisfied with this but preferred to be called 'lord/master and god' (*dominus et deus*) and likened himself with the supreme god Jupiter (*Iove*). To commemorate the event Diocletian later built a column with a statue of Jupiter on the top, on the very same spot where he had been chosen as emperor. His rise to power signalled the beginning of the era which is today called Late Antiquity or the Late Roman Empire.

The above story of Aper's guilt concocted by Diocles and his supporters seems quite far-fetched. It is difficult to see what Aper could have gained from the killing of his son-in-law Numerian in contrast to Diocles. It is inherently more likely that Diocles as *Com. Dom.* was behind the murder and that it had been Aper's praetorians who had failed to prevent this. When Aper had learnt of the death of Numerian, he had undoubtedly hidden the truth so that he could gain time to secure supporters from the ranks, while Diocles was undoubtedly aware that his assassin had poisoned/killed Numerian days ago and had grown ever more restless in the meantime, with the result that he finally had to urge his *domestici* to force their way to the emperor's litter and expose the death. He could wrest power from Aper only after Aper could no longer claim to act on behalf of Numerian. Diocles and his Illyrian Mafia had now regained the dominant position.

Eutropius' (9.26) characterization of Diocletian seems apt. He stated that Diocletian was a cunning, shrewd and intelligent man, and that he was able, diligent and hardworking as emperor. His lowly origins showed in his sumptuous dress (he dressed like an eastern tyrant) and in the demand to be worshipped like an eastern despot (*Dominus et Deus*). This is not surprising. Just like his Illyrian compatriot Aurelian, who had adopted similar practices, Diocletian had risen from the ranks and had therefore a real need to establish himself above the nobility and commoners through ritual and dress. Diocletian was also well aware of the dangers of being secluded from reality in the imperial palace – the gilded birdcage – which enabled the courtiers (friends, attendants, eunuchs) to mislead the emperor to do something wrong (SHA Aurelian 43). This suggests that he made a conscientious effort of not being too reliant on courtiers.

When Diocletian assumed the purple on 20 November 284 his power was restricted to the Eastern provinces which included at least Asia Minor, Syria, and probably also Egypt. Most of the Western half of the Empire stayed loyal to Carinus. Carinus was a skilled commander, and he had not been idle while his father had campaigned in the East. In 383 Carinus had restored the Rhine Frontier and may also have defeated a revolt in Britain. Regardless, he was still facing trouble both in Italy and the Balkans, mainly thanks to his own behaviour. Carinus had either seduced or raped the wives and daughters of several high ranking senators and officers with predictable consequences, and Diocletian was not slow to exploit this through the network of contacts he had built as *Comes Domesticorum*. The various Imperial security organs (Praetorians, *Frumentarii*, *Protectores-Domestici*) were full of the supporters of Diocletian, their comrade in arms. A good example of this is Constantius, the governor of Dalmatia and father of Constantine the Great. He was an Illyrian and former *protector* like Diocletian, as a result of which he immediately declared his support for Diocletian without any hesitation. As *Com. Dom.* Diocletian was well aware of how the intelligence apparatus operated.

I would also suggest that one of his first actions as emperor was actually the abolishment of the *Frumentarii*, which took place during his reign (Aur. Vict. 19.44). This measure would have served multiple purposes. Firstly, it is likely – even though the immediate commander of the *Frumentarii* was the *Princeps* of the *Peregrini* – that the *Frumentarii* were subordinated and reported to the Praetorian Prefect, which in this case meant that they could have been considered to have been Aper's collaborators and also potential spies for the Praetorian Prefect Julianus (see below). Secondly, the abolishment of the *Frumentarii* sent a positive message to the governing classes: Diocletian promised to rule justly and not use the *Frumentarii* as his eyes, ears and assassins. The truth is obviously the opposite. Despite the fact that the successors of the *Frumentarii*, the *agentes in rebus*, are for the first time attested during the reign of Constantine, it is clear that Diocletian did not abolish the imperial courier system, but only changed the name of the organization. The only real change was that he removed potentially disloyal elements from the organization. It is not known whether the *agentes in rebus* still continued to operate under the Praetorian Prefect (now Diocletian's own), as they are known to have done in about the mid-fourth century, or whether they operated under the *Tribunus* (*et Magister*) *Officiorum* as they did by the end of the fourth century. This office was already in existence (see below) and must predate Diocletian. In fact, it is quite probable that the various emperors changed the organizational structures according to the needs of the moment, as a result of which it would be foolish to claim that Diocletian's organizational structure would have been the same as some later one.

Despite Carinus' military talent, his subjects could not feel any love or loyalty towards such a ruler. We know for certain that after the death of Numerian there was at least one usurpation by M. Aurelius Iulianus against Carinus in Italy and Pannonia (Barnes 1981, 5) between 383–385, but thanks to discrepancies in the sources it has been postulated that there were two usurpations, one by the *Corrector* Sabinus Julianus in Italy (*PLRE1* M.Aur. Sabinus Iulianus 24) who was defeated near Verona and another by the *Praefectus Praetorio* Sabinus Julianus in Italy (*PLRE1* Sabinus Iulianus 38) who was defeated in Illyricum. The former alternative appears likelier, and I would suggest that it took several months for Carinus to crush the revolt, so that he defeated the usurper first near Verona in 384 and then again in Illyricum in 385 where the usurper was killed. I would also suggest that Julianus' usurpation was organized and supported by the *Praetoriani*, whose position was threatened by the rise of *Comes Domesticorum* Diocletian: that is, the Praetorians created their own competing emperor.

Diocletian had used the intervening time well. He had courted the Italian senators with the naming of Bassus as his consular colleague and made similar overtures towards other power brokers. While Carinus had been fighting against Julianus, Diocletian had marched to the Balkans. Diocletian hoped that the other two would destroy each other so that he would have to face a weakened foe, and he intended to engage the winner before he was able to obtain reinforcements. However, when the armies came face-to-face across the River Margus in Moesia in the spring of 285, between the Mons Aureus and Viminacium, Carinus' army still outnumbered him, probably because Diocletian was facing troubles of his own in Asia Minor (see below). In fact, Carinus won the battle and would have crushed the usurper had he not been assassinated during the pursuit by the officers whose wives he had ravished. One may suspect that Diocletian's messengers and these officers had held secret discussions before the battle and that the officers in question belonged to Carinus' unit of bodyguards. After Carinus' death his men surrendered and were duly pardoned by Diocletian. Of particular note is Diocletian's treatment of Carinus' Praetorian Prefect Aristobulus, who not only kept his office but was also nominated as consul with Diocletian for the year 285. This if anything suggests cooperation between the two men prior to the Battle of Margus and that it had been Aristobulus and his Praetorians who had killed Carinus. The imperial bodyguards had once again betrayed their emperor.

The Diarchy 285–393: Diocletian the Autocrat and Maximian the Serial Rapist

The Empire Secured 285–293

After this Diocletian marched to Italy, where he visited Rome to secure the goodwill of its governing classes (Zon. 12.31). Diocletian was in a hurry. The withdrawal of forces from Gaul by Carinus had once again led to the collapse of the defences as well as to the rise of the *Bacaudae/Bagaudae*, who were led by the usurpers Amandus and Aelianus. The *Bacaudae* appear to have been some kind of unauthorized militia or paramilitary group that the Gauls had created in the absence of any order or official authority, and one may speculate that it is possible that they may also have had some sort of religious/cultist background (followers of the doctrine of Mary Magdalene?; see later). The *Alamanni* and *Burgundi* had invaded across the southern Rhine, and so had the *Chaibones* (an unknown tribe) and *Eruli* (Western Heruls); the *Franci* and *Saxones* were ravaging the coasts of Gaul and the mouth of the Rhine; and the Sarmatians had invaded the Balkans and possibly also Asia Minor (see below). Diocletian could not be everywhere at the same time and he also needed to make certain that the commander he chose to conduct the operations in his stead would be happy to remain in his position and not be encouraged to usurp power, as had happened practically every time since 235. Consequently, he decided to make the new commander of forces in the West *Caesar*, which entitled the future promise of imperial powers as *Augustus* because Diocletian had no sons. Therefore, Diocletian Augustus invested his old and trusted friend Maximian (Maximianus) as Caesar and his son (*Filius Augusti* = Augustus' son) at Milan, probably on 21 July 285, and sent him to Gaul. The appointment of Maximian proved to be a double-edged sword. Maximian appears to have been quite capable as military commander, but his poor understanding of the finances as well as his sexual behaviour seem to have undermined many of his achievements on the battlefield.

Maximian's – or more likely Diocletian's (Diocletian was at Milan and Maximian is known for his ignorance of naval warfare) – first order of importance appears to have been the creation of what was called the province of *Gallia Riparensis* in the ND, which encompassed the Alpine areas between Italy, Raetia and Marseilles, for the war against the *Bacaudae* and against the Alamanni. This also meant the creation of several new river fleets to assist Maximian in his operations (both for the movement of supplies and of troops). In short, Diocletian appears to have created the following offices with their accompanying fleets that were later known as (ND *Occ.* 42, 17–20–23): *Praefectus classis Fluminis Rhodani, Viennae sive Arelati; Praefectus classis barbariorum, Edruduni Sapaudiae; Praefectus militum musculariorum*, and *Massiliae Graecorum*. In addition, he probably also created the office of *Praefectus classis Araricae, Caballoduno* in the Province of *Lugdunensis* for the same reasons. The Fleets for the Lakes Constance and Como may also have been created at this time, or in 288 (see below), for service against the Alamanni, if these were not already created by Gallienus, Aurelian, or Probus.[204]

Maximian was indeed an able general. He quickly crushed the *Bacaudae* in the interior and then marched against the invaders, probably establishing his headquarters at Mogontiacum (Mainz). Since Maximian's forces were too small to engage the large army of the Alamanni and Burgundians, he decided to employ scorched earth tactics and guerrilla warfare against them, as their size made them susceptible to being defeated through such a strategy, while he himself marched against the smaller enemy force consisting of the Chaibones and Eruli.[205] The latter Maximian annihilated completely in a single battle with a small force consisting of only 'a few cohorts' while the former were engaged by his generals. Maximian let the Alamanni and Burgundians fall victim to the 'plague' after which he obtained the surrender of the scattered remnants.[206]

Maximian gave command of the operations against the Franks and Saxons to Carausius, of Menapian birth, because he had distinguished himself against the *Bacaudae*, after which he returned to Milan for the winter. This means that Carausius was appointed at least commander of the *Classis Britannica* (main bases at Dover and Bologne) and probably also of the so-called Saxon shore. Carausius proved highly successful and defeated the raiding fleets of the *Franci* and *Saxones* during the last months of 285. However, he made the mistake of not returning all of the recaptured booty. He kept part of it for himself and his men, which caused his enemies to accuse him of imperial plans. Maximian was all too ready to believe this story, but there were also friends of Carausius among Maximian's men who warned Carausius of the threat. In the meanwhile, Diocletian promoted Maximian to the rank of *Augustus* on 1 April 286.[207] Now the two rulers were publicly considered 'brothers', but Diocletian was still in practice the senior emperor. To demonstrate this difference Diocletian instituted the use of allusions to the gods, in which he was to be called *Iovius* after *Iove Iupiter* while Maximian was to be called only *Herculius* after *Hercules*.

Then the not-too-bright Maximian learnt from supposedly reliable sources that Carausius was intercepting enemy raiders only after they were already returning laden with booty so that he could then capture the booty, supposedly in collusion with his Frankish friends (the invaders), and embezzle large portions of it for himself. The report also accused Carausius of trying to canvass the support of the British legions with the ill-gotten booty. The accusation is at least partially unfounded. It would have been quite impossible for anyone to intercept all enemy fleets in a timely fashion. Carausius simply had no option but to wait for the arrival of news of the invasion before he could send his fleet to intercept.

The accusation of planned usurpation is equally likely to be unfounded. It is more likely that Carausius was simply keeping his men satisfied by distributing money liberally as any good commander should have. Of course, one cannot entirely preclude the possibility of planned usurpation, because Carausius' revolt progressed so smoothly. In spite of this, it is likelier that the accuser or accusers had their own agenda and Maximian was known to be a simpleton or at least a person who did not understand the intricacies of naval warfare and intrigue at court. Whatever the truth, Maximian ordered Carausius to be arrested and killed. However, the person(s) who carried the message or the person(s) who received the command were clearly disloyal because Carausius was informed of the order with the predictable result that he revolted in the autumn of 286. This in fact suggests that the persons who were expected to carry out the order considered it unjust. Carausius took control of the fleet with its stations in both Britain and in Gaul, and thereby created the *Imperium Britanniarum*. According to Stephen Williams (47), Carausius' first coins declared, following Virgil, *Expectate Veni* ('Come, expected one'), which recalled Aeneas' escape from Troy to found Rome. If this allusion is correct one may also suspect that it

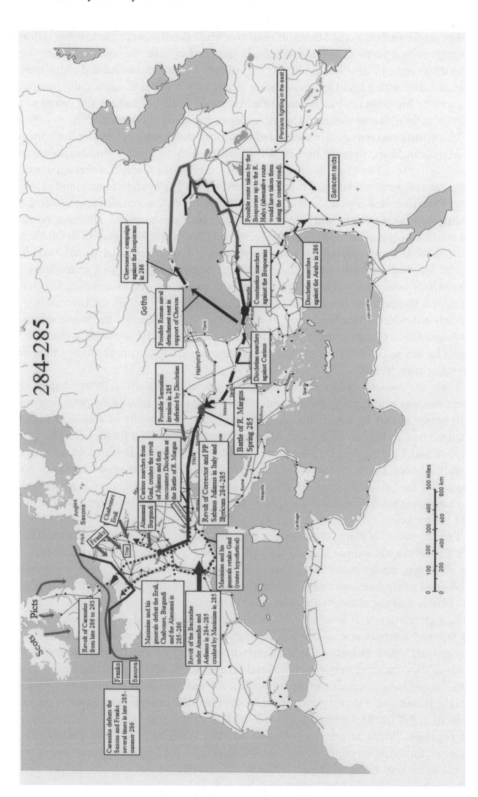

also referred to Diocletian's own allusions to being a second Aeneas in a mocking manner. Now Diocletian and Maximian faced a serious problem.

Maximian appears to have advanced against the usurper immediately and inflicted a defeat on him on land, as a result of which Carausius had embarked the bulk of his troops on ship and sailed to Britain (*Pan.Lat.* 10.11.7, 8.12.1), but the question whether Carausius abandoned Gaul in its entirety at the same time is contested. The numismatic evidence can be used to support either a total abandonment in 286 (followed up re-conquest in 290), or the continued rule over the north-west Gaul.[208] In my opinion the referral to the seizing of a legion (presumably not part of Carausius' command), some *peregrinorum militum cuneis, mercennariis cuneis barbarorum*, and especially the levy of Gallic merchants, is conclusive (*Pan.Lat.* 8.12.1, 8.16.2). There is no doubt that Carausius ruled north-west Gaul until 293. The core of his army consisted of detachments from six 'continental' legions and one kidnapped legion and auxiliaries, in addition to which came the three British legions and their auxiliaries. In addition, as the above makes clear, he had barbarian mercenaries and Gallic levies. The most important part of his force, however, was his fleet that effectively controlled both the British and Gallic coasts. Maximian faced a daunting task.

Maximian undoubtedly planned to crush the Menapian upstart in 287, but immediately following 1 January 287, when he was celebrating the taking of the consular *fasces* in Milan, he had to march to combat some invaders (probably the Alamanni), which he defeated, but this was not the end of his troubles. Maximian also faced the invasion of some 'Germans' in Gaul, which demanded the fighting of countless battles. The 'Germans' undoubtedly consisted either of the Franks and Saxons who had allied themselves with Carausius and/or of the abovementioned Alamanni. Maximian's war against the 'Germans' was also made more difficult by the fact that Maximian had lost part of his army when Carausius had usurped, on top of which he now also needed to detach still another part of his force against the usurper. In the course of this campaign season Maximian crossed the Rhine and invaded enemy territory to chastise the enemy into obedience. As a result, Maximian's panegyrist could claim that the barbarian side of the Rhine was also Roman.[209] Since no barbarians were settled within Roman territory, it appears probable that the barbarians had simply fled before Maximian's army. Later circumstantial evidence also suggests that, just like Diocletian, Maximian began to recruit and levy new troops from the very start of his reign for the forthcoming campaigns, as well as occupy the new and old forts he had built or repaired along the frontier.

In the meanwhile Diocletian had returned to the East in 285. He advanced slowly along the Danube to improve its defensive arrangements while also fighting against the Sarmatians who had taken advantage of the Roman civil war by invading. Diocletian was a pragmatist who sought to re-establish the frontiers with a combination of measures. We do not know the exact sequence of his measures and reforms, and we do not know when the fleets that are later attested to have been in the Danube area came into existence. It is possible that he had already reorganized the defensive structures of the Danube frontier in 285–286, and so had united the Danubian fleets (*Classis Pannonica, Classis Moesica*) as a single Danubian Fleet (*Classis Histrica*) as suggested by Reddé, and after the revolt of Carausius divided it up into smaller commands that were then placed under the direct command of the *duces* in charge of the different sectors of the frontier. If this is the case, then the reason for the division would have been to prevent usurpations by naval commanders. On the other hand, the reigns of Aurelian and Probus would also be equally suitable dates for the creation of a single Danubian Fleet, because both emperors reorganized the Danubian defences. What seems to be clear, however, is that by the end of Diocletian's reign the Danubian fleets had been divided into smaller fleets just like the frontier provinces. The exact dates and nature of Diocletian's reforms are not known and they may have taken place at any time between 285 and 303, and may also have been introduced in stages. (See below.)

What is certain is that Diocletian started immediately the process of raising new legions and auxiliaries to increase the size of his existing but depleted force. The process of building this enlarged army, however, was gradual and lasted until the end of his reign. It was marked by a policy of continuous reassessment of the defensive and offensive needs of the army regardless of the fact that it also included certain uniform characteristics, such as uniform unit and garrison sizes for the new formations. Diocletian was a conservative by nature and his reform of the defences reflected this. The bulk of the army was to be posted on the borders in fortified garrisons to act as visible deterrents to the enemy. However, Diocletian still retained a number of elite units and detachments as imperial armies with the result that by about 295 these were considered to be personal retinues (*Comitatus*) of each ruler. The size of the legion was set at the traditional 6,000 fighting men and the new legions were also once again to include their own integral cavalry contingents, or at least that is the impression given by Vegetius' referrals to the ancient legions.[210] We should not forget that with the complementary cavalry, squires, artillerymen, workmen, artisans, servants, medics etc. the legion encompassed about 8,000 to 10,000 men. (See the Introduction.)

However, if the basic structure of the legion remained traditional, there were still some important reforms in armament and organization that took into account the developments of the third century. If Vegetius' figures are to be used as our guide, the numbers of horsemen per legion were kept at 726 men. The continued existence of such cavalry units as the *promoti* suggests that the separation of legionary cavalry and infantry that had taken place under Gallienus continued to be true in practice at least for some units, even if the administration of the cavalry units may have been carried out through the mother legions. The extant remains of the period legionary garrisons suggest that the size of the legionary garrisons was now set for 2,000–2,500 men, because in practice the men were constantly being rotated between service in the base and in the field.[211] Those serving in the garrisons were essentially resting between assignments. The numbers of infantry archers were also increased, and new types of equipment like the *mattiobarbuli/plumbata* (five throwing darts placed behind the shield) now became standard equipment for the new legions.

The following list presents the legionary organization according to Vegetius. It should be kept in mind, however, that it is possible that his version may include his own ideas on how to reform the legion of his day. On the other hand, Vegetius' referrals (1.17) to the two 6,000 strong legions *Iovii* and *Herculiani* of Diocletian in this context, as well as the new hierarchy of officers without senatorial members and the change in armament does strongly suggest the possibility that Diocletian's legions served as his models.

Vegetius' Legion (Epit. 2.6ff.) with additional comments in brackets.

- 1 *praefectus legionis* formerly *legatus*; commander of the legion.
- 1 *tribunus maior*; appointed by the emperor in charge of one cohort (probably the 1st) and second-in-command of the legion.
- 1 *Praefectus Castrorum* (camp, medics, siege equipment etc.)
- 1 *Praefectus Fabrorum* (workmen, construction etc.)
- *tribuni minores* from the ranks (6 tribunes? put in charge of the cohorts and cavalry alongside with *praepositi*).
- 5 centurions of the 1st Cohort (Vegetius' list differs from the other known lists of officers and is also 100 men short of the 1100 men he gives for the 1st Cohort):
  primus pilus, in charge of 4 centuries/400 men (probable standard organization and deployment was 320 heavy infantry deployed 8 deep and 80 light infantry deployed 2 deep)
  primus hastatus, 'now called *ducenarius*' in charge of two centuries/200 men (probably 160 heavies and 40 light)
  princeps, 1.5 centuries/150 men (probably 120 heavies and 30 light)
  secundus hastatus, 1.5 centuries/150 men (probably 120 heavies and 30 light)
  triarius prior, 100 men (probably 80 heavies and 20 light)
- 45 centurions of the 2nd – 10th Cohorts, each in charge of 100 men 'now called *centenarii*'; 5 cavalry centurions.
- 1st Cohort: 1105 footmen (990 footmen, 110 *decani* and 5 centurions; possible organization behind the numbers could be 800 legionaries incl. the *decani* deployed 8 ranks deep, 200 light infantry deployed two ranks deep and 100 recruits, or 880 legionaries and 220 light-armed and recruits).
132 horsemen (128 horsemen and 4 decurions; in truth the decurions may have been part of the 128 horsemen in addition to which came one centurion, 2 musicians and one standard-bearer; when trained to do so the 128 horsemen could form up a rhombus so that one decurion stood at each apex).
- 2nd – 10th Cohorts: 9 x 555 footmen (495 footmen, 55 *decani* and 5 centurions; possible organization behind the figures could be 400 legionaries inc. the *decani*, deployed 8 ranks deep, and 100 light infantry 2 ranks deep and 50 recruits, or 440 legionaries and 110 light-armed and recruits).
9 x 66 horsemen (64 horsemen and 2 decurions; as noted above the decurions should probably be included as part of the 64 horsemen; formed in combat either two 32 men units or one 64 men wedge).
- artillerymen (55 *carroballistae* each with 11 men and 10 *onagri* per legion), squires servants and various kinds of standard-bearers and musicians and other specialists like clerks, medics, wood-workers, masons, carpenters, blacksmiths, painters, siege-equipment builders, armourers etc. (*aquiliferi, imaginarii/imaginiferi, signiferi/ draconarii, tesserarii, optiones, metatores, librarii, tubicines, cornicines, buccinators, mensores, lignarios, structores, ferrarios, carpentarios, pictores* etc.)

It is possible that this organization was already in use during Septimius Severus' reign for the newly created legions, because Dio (76.11.5) refers to a group of 550 men (cohort?).

On the basis of my above hypothesis regarding the organization behind Vegetius' figures, this suggests that a possible overall fighting strength of Vegetius' legion may have been: 4,400 heavy infantry; 1,100 light infantry; 726 cavalry; at least 660 artillerymen with 55 *carroballistae* and 10 *onagri*; at least 550 recruits left to defend the marching camp alongside the servants and workmen. The extra men on top of the older paper strengths may actually represent the recruits not normally included in armed strengths. The obvious problem with Vegetius' information and my reconstruction based on it is that we have practically no evidence to corroborate it, but at least if one presents the info in this manner it does make sense and is therefore plausible. Vegetius notes that the legion could also include several milliary cohorts, which probably refers to the Praetorians or refers to the practice of his own day to group together different units to form 'temporary legions' that were later called *mere* by the East Romans (sing. *meros*/division).

The first new legion formed by Diocletian,[212] *Legio I Pontica* with a base at Trapezunt, is attested for the year 288 and its main purpose must have been to protect the naval base in the city of Trapezunt against the piratical raids of the Bosporans, as well as to act as marines for the fleet.[213] The implication is that the process of recruiting and training must have begun already in 287 or 286 or 285. The creation of the legion must be connected with the campaign of Constantius in Asia Minor (see below) against the Sarmatians of the Kingdom of Bosporus that can be dated between 285 and 287, because Constantius is attested to have moved to Gaul by 288. Consequently, the most likely date for the creation of the legion is 285. The Bosporans would simply have taken advantage of the absence of the Roman field army during the civil war. When one takes into account the facts that Diocletian did receive the title *Sarmaticus Maximus* in 285 and was in Nicomedia by January 286 (see below), it becomes even more likely that Constantius' campaign took place in 285 – for which Diocletian received the title – and that the new legion was also formed in 285 for the protection of the fleet, Pontus and Colchis. It is quite probable that Diocletian had been forced to divert important resources against the Sarmatians already before his decisive battle against Carinus (see above).

Two new legions for the Armenian frontier (see later) are attested for the first time in 300, but this is too late for the campaign of Constantius, because by that time he was already in the West, unless of course these two legions were also formed before their first attested date of existence. Similarly, since we know that another new legion, *Legio I Iovia Scythica* with a base at *Noviodunum* in the new province of *Scythia Minor*, was created between 285 and 293, it seems probable that its creation should also be connected with Constantius' war against the Bosporans.[214] It is clear that this legion was posted at *Novidiunum* to block the western invasion route from the Bosporan Sarmatians. In short, it appears very probable that the Bosporans under their Sarmatian rulers posed a serious threat to Roman interests in the Black Sea area at the very beginning of Diocletian's rule and that he created two-to-four new legions to counter this. I would suggest, however, that while Constantius was fighting against the Sarmatian Bosporans and their Alan allies in Asia Minor Diocletian was also fighting against the Sarmatians in the Balkans, which resulted in the reform of the military structures of the Danube frontier in the very first years of Diocletian's reign. The creation of the *Legio I Iovia Scythica* would also be part of this reform, not as a response to Diocletian's own Sarmatian campaign but to the Bosporan problem.

According to the fragment preserved by Constantine Porphyrogenitus (*De admin. imp.* 53.1ff.), during the reign of Diocletian the Sarmatians under the leadership of 'Sauromatus the Bosporian' invaded Roman territory, conquered Lazica, and advanced as far as the Halys River. It is probable that the Sarmatians did this in collusion with the Georgians and Persians. Diocletian responded by sending Constantius (father of Constantine the Great) the 'tribune' (= probably *Tribunus et Magister Officiorum* and the overall commander of all '*protectores*' including the *Comes/Comites Domesticorum*) to the scene.[215] He managed to prevent the Sarmatians from crossing the Halys River, but was unable to defeat the invaders. (See Map 284–286.) The Sarmatians had penetrated truly deep into Roman territory and may have even overrun several legionary garrisons and possibly also the naval base at Trapezunt en route to get there.

This part of the campaign must have taken place in 285 and may even have taken place before the decisive Battle of Margus River. As a result, Constantius was compelled to ask Diocletian to order the Chersonites to make a diversionary invasion and attack the homeland of the Sarmatians so that they would be able to use their families and cities as bargaining chips. The chief magistrate and primate Chrestus, son of Papias, complied. It is possible that the remnants of the Pontic Fleet and the new *Legio I Pontica* were sent to support the Chersonese. The Chersonites assembled men from the neighbouring forts, constructed military wagons and placed in them the so-called arbalests (*cheirobolistrai*). After this they advanced against the city of the Bosporans. They decided to take it through a stratagem. The Chersonites placed an ambush during the night and then sent a handful of men against the city. After having fought from dawn till the third hour, they feigned flight and led their foolish pursuers up to the ambush. The pursuers were then brought to a halt with concentrated volleys of crossbow-bolts shot from the fort formed out of the war wagons, while the ambushers surrounded and annihilated them. After this, the Chersonites returned, and captured both Bosporus and the rest of their forts on the Maeotic Lake, together with the families. This part of the campaign must have taken place in 286. The Sarmatians had no other alternative than to do whatever the Romans wanted if they wanted to see their families, and they complied and withdrew. The negotiations may have taken place at the same time as Diocletian negotiated with the Persians in 287 or earlier during 286. This campaign stands as a good piece of evidence for the effectiveness of the combination of wagon forts and the salvos (arrows or spears or darts or pebbles/lead balls depending upon the construction of the machines in question) shot from the crossbows/ballistae against nomadic cavalry. The superior range and striking power made the crossbow a weapon to be feared.

Diocletian is attested to have returned to Nicomedia by January 286 and stayed there until 3 March. I would connect his stay in Asia Minor with the abovementioned Bosporan invasion of the Caucasus. It is probable that Diocletian and Constantius met in Nicomedia to discuss the defensive needs against the Bosporans and decided to create new legions to protect the borders. The removal of forces from the East also seems to have led to a revolt in Asia and possibly also in Palestine, because Diocletian seems to have visited Palestine during the summer of 286 and he is also attested to have transferred Saracens from Asia to Thrace to inhabit the deserted farmlands.[216] I would connect the revolt of the Saracens with the change of the ruler that would have made the previous *foedus* void. Saracen violence against the Romans was undoubtedly meant to convince the new emperor of the necessity of placating them, but if Diocletian's reaction to that was the transferral of their populace to Thrace, as seems probable, the Saracens failed.

It is also probable that the Saracens had been aided by Amr, the Lakhmid King of Hira. He had previously, during Aurelian's reign, changed sides, but had once again become an ally of Persia. The Romans knew fully well that the alliances with the Arabs lasted only as long as the Arab sheiks considered it advantageous to them. Amr died in about 291/2 and was succeeded by his son Imru al-Qays who just like his father stayed loyal to the Persians for a while before renouncing it.

It is also probable that Diocletian fought a campaign against the Persians at the same time as he engaged their Arab allies in 286 and 287 because the ruler of Persia sent ambassadors bearing gifts in 287 with the result that a peace favourable to the Romans was concluded in the same year. The Persians acknowledged Roman claims to the territories west and south of the Tigris, and dropped their claim to Armenia at the same time accepting Trdat as King of Armenia. One may suspect that Trdat's own campaign against the Persians had also played its part in the achievement of the favourable outcome, just as did the other troubles facing the Persians.

After the peace of 287 Diocletian reassessed the defensive needs of the area and started the building of the so-called *Strata Diocletiana*, which was basically a road with forts and garrisons between Damascus, Palmyra and Soura/Sura. Its primary purposes appear to have been to stop the Saracen raids from the desert that Diocletian had already faced once after having taken the throne. The garrisons along the road, as well as the mobile contingents behind it, made it possible to move forces wherever needed relatively quickly. Additional reasons for the project would have been to control nomadic transhumance and the caravan routes for tax purposes, to protect the farmers, and to control the Arabs living on Roman soil behind this road. This also meant the raising of new units to garrison some of the forts. In addition to this, Diocletian analyzed why the Persians had managed to penetrate deep into Syria and had even conquered Antioch in the 250s and 260s. As a result of this analysis, he fortified at least Circesium (Amm. 23.5.1–2) and probably also some other places in the inner *limes* (frontier zone).

Diocletian's fortification program and increasing of the number of soldiers seem to have been great successes. Firstly, the Persians were no longer able to penetrate deep into Roman territory even when they subsequently defeated Galerius. The presence of fortified cities and reserve forces prevented this. Secondly, the presence of Roman forts and garrisons deep in the desert zone put pressure on the Arabic tribes which subsequently brought tangible results in the form of alliances. The small Roman forts placed on top of the oases effectively prevented the Bedouins from raiding Roman territories, because they lacked siege skills. This forward-based defensive zone and alliances brought unprecedented security for trade and agriculture. As a result, during the fifth and sixth centuries Palestine and north-west Negev both flourished as no time in history before the twentieth century (Isaac, 1990, 215).

After his Persian victory Diocletian was ready to help his troubled co-emperor Maximian. He met Maximian probably at Mainz during the winter of 287–288 to discuss how to organize the rule between the two *Augusti* and how to conduct next year's joint campaign against the Alamanni. Diocletian also brought with him his trusted lieutenant Constantius, because Maximian clearly needed someone to assist him. Constantius became Maximian's Praetorian Prefect (henceforth PP) (that is, he was promoted to that position having previously been *Tribunus et Magister Officiorum*) and was required to divorce his current wife (mother of Constantine the Great) and marry Maximian's daughter Theodora.[217] The subsequent duties of Constantius suggest that the PP had command of the frontier armies in the sector of the frontier assigned to him. The forthcoming campaign against Carausius was also planned, and Maximian started to build a fleet on every river which could be used to transport soldiers across the Channel. It is possible that it was at this time that the *classis Anderetianorum, Parisiis* was created, together with the Rhine Fleets attested to have existed on the Rhine during the fourth century.[218] Another possibility is that the former was created only after the reconquest of Britain. After this, the rulers made a successful pincer attack against the Alamanni, with Diocletian advancing from Raetia, and Maximian probably from Mainz. Following this Diocletian returned to his domains and left Maximian to fulfil his part of the plans. Maximian dispatched Constantius against the Franks, the allies of Carausius. Constantius once again proved himself an exceptionally gifted commander and slaughtered the Franks all the way up to the shores of the North Sea, with the result that their king Gennobaudes sued for peace and was settled on deserted land near Trier – possibly as *Laeti* or *Foederati* with the duty to farm the land and provide soldiers.[219] The stage was now set for a campaign against Carausius.

It is not known when the *Classis Venetum* in Aquileia, and the *Classis Comensis* and *Classis Histrica* mentioned by the ND (Occ. 32.52, 33.58, 34.28, 47) were created, but the time when Diocletian operated in Raetia stands as the likeliest alternative.[220] The previous campaign by Diocletian against the Sarmatians in 285 would have brought to his attention the need of securing supplies for his Balkan campaigns through Aquileia via Nauportus either to the Sava River, or via Nauportus to Poetovio and the Drava River – and he did campaign against the Sarmatians once again in 289. The division of the *Classis Histrica* into smaller entities would fit well with the circumstances, but it is possible that this reform took place only after the provinces were also divided into smaller ones after ca. 293. On the other hand, the logistic, defensive and offensive needs of Diocletian's stay in the Balkans could also have made the change necessary. If the Como Navy was created by Diocletian the reason would have been the same, the threat of the Alamanni and the operational needs of the Raetian theatre of operations. As noted above, the division of the Danube Fleet into smaller fleets would also have made sense from another standpoint. Carausius had recently usurped power and Diocletian may have felt it necessary to prevent the possibility of a similar usurpation by another fleet commander. (For additional discussion of the fleets, see the analysis of the reform of 293.)

In 289 Maximian launched his naval operation against Carausius, but with disastrous consequences. We do not know the exact details. The panegyrist blamed the sea and weather for the destruction of the entire fleet, but it is possible that if Carausius had scored a significant naval victory that the panegyrists of Maximian and Constantius would still have blamed the sea rather than the incompetence of the commanders. Similarly, we do not know what Constantius' role was in these events, but it seems probable that the fleet had been under the personal command of Maximian and that he had left Constantius in charge of the defence of the Rhine frontier. Eutropius (9.22) claims that the emperors concluded a peace with Carausius, but this is not accepted by all modern historians (e.g. Barnes). On balance, considering that from this date onwards Carausius represented himself as the legitimate colleague of the *Augusti* rather than their enemy, it seems preferable to accept Eutropius' claim. The *Augusti* had no other alternative than to buy a temporary peace because they were facing a multitude of troubles.

The evidence points to the probability that Maximian now left the command of his armies entirely to Constantius, while he himself spent his time in the most degenerate way imaginable. The only excuse for Maximian's behaviour was that he was also gathering money from the wealthy Gauls to pay for the increased size of the army. In order to do this he fabricated charges, confiscated property and then raped (if attractive) and killed the unfortunate victims, but he went even further than this. He raped every beautiful woman and attractive male who was unfortunate enough to be spotted by him or by his henchmen (Lactantius 8.5–6).

Maximian was not your average lovable character. He was a wild, despicable and depraved person – a serial rapist and murderer – and excluding his military talents he was otherwise a mediocre man with limited intellectual capacity. This had undoubtedly made him initially suitable to be Diocletian's partner. With his limited skills and abilities there was no chance of Maximian ever being able to govern the Empire on his own.[221] Regardless, I would still suggest that Diocletian had probably been unaware of the true scope of Maximian's underlying depravity when he had appointed him as a ruler. It is likely that Maximian had managed to keep his vices within tolerable limits before he became emperor, and that it was the supreme power that had gone to Maximian's head and had brought the worst in him to the surface. It was acceptable for military commanders to rape pretty enemy captives while on campaign, but according to Aurelius Victor (39.46–7) Maximian could not even keep his hands off hostages (children, men and women), and was therefore becoming an embarrassment for Diocletian. According to Victor, Diocletian feared that enemies would learn of Maximian's treatment of their hostages and the result would be war. In fact, it is very likely that this happened and that most of the wars fought against the Franks and Alamanni under Constantius had been caused by Maximian's raping of the hostages and that Constantius had been put in charge of these campaigns for that precise reason. It would have been impossible to conclude any new treaties between Maximian and the tribesmen whose relatives he had raped. According to Victor (39.47–8), some even claimed that Diocletian subsequently resigned because of Maximian's behaviour and persuaded him to resign with him. Maximian was undoubtedly an able general, but all the same he was a disaster as a ruler. Indeed, according to the SHA (Aurelian 44.1–2), Diocletian was acutely aware of his mistake. Maximian should not have been promoted to any higher positions than *dux*, but it was now too late.

Lactantius accuses Diocletian of the same greed as Maximian. He claims that Diocletian also fabricated accusations after which the wealth of the person in question was confiscated and the unfortunate noble killed. It is probable that this may indeed have happened on occasion when there was an urgent need for money, but at the same time this claim seems not to reflect Diocletian's general policy, which included good relations

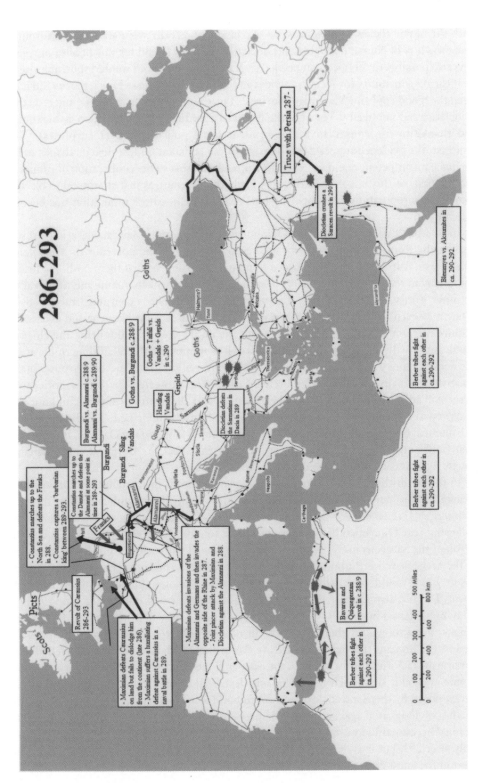

286-293

Picts

Scots

Revolt of Carausius
286-293

Franks

Goths

Goths

Gepids

Sarmatians

Quadi

Burgundi Siling
Vandals

Burgundi

Harding
Vandals

Alamanni

Alamanni

Alamanni

Mat. command

Siscia

Sirmium

Truce with Persia 287-

Diocletian crushes a
Saracen revolt in 290

Diocletian defeats
the Sarmatians in
Dacia in 289

Blemmyes vs. Aksumites in
ca. 290-292.

Berber tribes fight
against each other in
ca. 290-292

Berber tribes fight
against each other in
ca. 290-292

Berber tribes fight
against each other in
ca.290-292

Berber tribes fight
against each other in
ca.290-292

Carthage

Bavares and
Quiquegentani
revolt in c.288-9

Goths + Taifali vs.
Vandals + Gepids
in c.290

Goths vs. Burgundi c.288-9

Burgundi vs. Alamanni c.288-9
Alamanni vs. Burgundi c.289-90

- Constantius marches up to the
North Sea and defeats the Franks
in 288.
- Constantius captures a barbarian
king between 289-293.

- Constantius marches up to
the Danube and defeats the
Alamanni at some point in
time in 289-293

- Maximian defeats Carausius
on land but fails to dislodge him
from the continent (late 286).
- Maximian suffers a humiliating
defeat against Carausius in a
naval battle in 289.

- Maximian defeats invasions of the
Alamanni and Germans and then invades the
opposite side of the Rhine in 287.
- Joint pincer attack by Maximian and
Diocletian against the Alamanni in 288.

0   100   200   300   400   500 Miles

0   200   400   600   800 km

with the upper classes – in contrast to Maximian who really went after the rich Roman senators. It is of course possible that Diocletian used his friend for this precise purpose. It is also possible that Diocletian needed cash from the West, but wanted someone else to bear the responsibility for illegal practices and killings. In this case Diocletian would have been the 'good cop' and Maximian the 'bad'. The extant evidence, however, suggests that Diocletian did not need to resort to the use of extraordinary means as often as Maximian did thanks to his conservative and prudent fiscal policies (budget surpluses).[222] In contrast, the evidence suggests that Maximian ran constant budget deficits thanks to his financial incompetence, and was therefore forced to resort to the confiscation of property. On the basis of this it is inherently more likely that Lactantius just attempted to blacken Diocletian's reputation by comparing him to Maximian, whose reputation was beyond redemption.

In 288 or 289 the Bavares and Quinquegentani appear to have made a joint revolt against the Roman authorities with the result that in 289 the governor of *Mauretania Caesarensis*, Aurelius Litua, was forced to fight a campaign against them both. He forced the enemy to retreat into their places of refuge in the Hodua Mountains and Sekel valley. In other words, he achieved only a partial success. Both tribes continued their raids.[223] They may even have raided the coasts of Spain as pirates. This revolt would eventually require imperial attention. Maximian spent the entire year of 290 touring the cities of Gaul, supposedly to secure their loyalty as well as money for the rebuilding of his army. He needed money and was ready to concoct any accusation to achieve his purpose. In the meanwhile Maximian's Praetorian Prefect Constantius protected the Rhine frontier with great skill and at some point in time between 289 and 293 captured a barbarian king who had prepared 'an ambush for Constantius but was himself ambushed'. He also devastated 'Alamannia' from the 'Rhine Bridge' (Mogontiacum/Mainz) to the Danube. It is possible that Constantius timed his invasion at the same time that the Burgundi and Alamanni fought against each other. (See the Map 286–293.)

In the meanwhile, in 289 Diocletian was also facing his own troubles in Dacia which demanded his personal attention. He was once again successful and took the title *Sarmaticus Maximus* to celebrate this, but Diocletian could not rest on his laurels. In the following year Diocletian had to march to Syria (on 10 May 290, CJ 9.41.9) to quell the revolt of the Saracens in Syria, which he accomplished with celerity. His harsh treatment of the Arabs as well as the building of the *Strata Diocletiana* had not yet brought the desired result, but it would eventually – but only after a lot of money, blood and effort had been spent. I would also suggest that the Lakhmid King Amr had once again supported his Arab brethren against the Romans. Diocletian was not only fighting against the Saracen clients, but also against their Arab ally. In other words, the Persians kept up pressure against the Romans through their satellite. According to Malalas (12.38), Diocletian built three arms factories for the army in the east, and one factory in Edessa for local use, and a mint was built at Antioch to replace one destroyed by an earthquake. In addition, the threat posed by the Saracens caused him to build arms factories at Damascus to supply the forces designated against them. The process of building these factories was probably gradual because these were situated according to the new division of the provinces made only after 293, but it is likely that the arms factories (*scutaria et armorum*) of Damascus were at the latest created in 290, if not already in 287.

However, on other fronts Diocletian and his co-emperor could breathe a momentary sigh of relief. There was a temporary peace on the Danubian front in 290, because the various barbarian tribes or tribal alliances were fighting against each other. It is in fact possible that Diocletian's successive victories over the Sarmatians had caused them to retreat away from the Roman border, which had set in motion a domino effect among the peoples behind them. According to Panegyric 11.17, the Goths (Greuthungi or other Goths) defeated the Burgundi (probably in 288 or 289?) who were thereby pushed against the Alamanni. The Burgundi in their turn at a great cost defeated the Alamanni, who had already been weakened as a result of the Roman campaigns, and obtained land from them. The Alamanni not unnaturally attempted to regain their lost land in about 290. In the meantime the Tervingi Goths and their allies the Taifali fought against the Vandals and Gepids. There was also temporary peace in Africa because the different Moorish tribes fought against each other. The Panegyric doesn't state which Moorish tribes were involved, but on the basis of the subsequent campaign in the area by Maximian it is easy to guess that the tribes in question were probably the neighbours of the Bavares and Quinquegentiani in Mauretania and the neighbours of the Austuriani in Libya. As usual the end result of such intertribal fighting was the rise of one tribe or tribal confederacy to such a position that it could challenge the might of Rome, which each of those did soon enough. The situation in Egypt was also peaceful for the moment because the Blemmyes were fighting against the Ethiopians (Aksumites), but this was not to last. The peace on the eastern front held because Bahram II was still fighting against Hormizd, on top of which he was also facing an irritating rebellion by *mobed* Guprashnasp near Arbela (Chron. 10). The *mobed* appears to have formed a religious society reminiscent of the later assassins. Guprashnasp was holed up in a tower on a mountain with his 560 expert archers, which he used to terrorize the surrounding areas that in turn made it impossible for the merchants or farmers to practise their trades. The revolt was only ended when the Persian commander managed to lure the *mobed* to a parley where he was captured.

In short, thanks to the mishandling of the situation in Gaul and raping of hostages Maximian was facing a series of troubles in the north west which once again required the personal intervention of Diocletian. On top of this Maximian had also angered the Gallic upper classes with his personal behaviour. Consequently, Diocletian travelled to meet Maximian in Milan in late December 290. We do not know what was discussed, but since Maximian was at Durocortum on 18 February 291 and north west Gaul was held by Carausius until 293, it is possible that Diocletian had ordered Maximian to make another equally unsuccessful attempt against Carausius (Barnes 1981, 8).

It also seems probable that now at the latest Diocletian had become aware of the consequences of Maximian's sexual behaviour and that he took the precautionary step of reducing the numbers of Praetorian cohorts and citizens bearing arms at Rome available to Maximian, which Aurelius Victor (39.47) stated to have happened when Diocletian learnt of Maximian's deeds. Another possible date for the latter would be the year 293 when Diocletian introduced the Tetrarchy, undoubtedly at least partially in an effort to control Maximian and to remove him permanently from Gaul which together with the tribes beyond the Rhine was steaming in anger against Maximian.

As far as the *Augusti* are concerned the next two years appear to have been quiet. The next time we have information of Maximian's whereabouts is from March 293, which does suggest that he had spent the time following his crushing defeats in the lap of luxury and debauchery that he was so famous for. In the meanwhile, Diocletian had continued his reorganization of the Danube frontier, but most importantly he had been making plans for the future. Diocletian was now able to enjoy the fruits of his labour, because his past military successes in the area and the resultant intertribal wars had pacified the Danube frontier for the time being.

Tetrarchy I: 293–305
Augusti: Diocletian the Autocrat; Maximian the Serial Rapist
Caesars: Constantius the Prude; Galerius the Beast

Creation of the Tetrarchy, 293
In early 293 Diocletian considered the time ripe for the implementation of his new plans – the end result of this was the creation of the Tetrarchy. From his personal experience he knew that he could not be simultaneously both in the East and Balkans at the same time, and he also knew that he needed to strip down Maximian's powers and duties in order to balance the situation in the West. In particular he had come to the conclusion that his loyal friend Maximian was not as good a soldier as he had expected on the basis of his rough military outlook. An emperor and military leader also needed other qualities besides generalship. He also needed to be an able diplomat and administrator and Maximian the Serial Rapist had none of those qualities. Diocletian needed to give Maximian a *Caesar* who had proved himself to be an able soldier and administrator. Fortunately, he had one such man at his disposal, named Constantius Chlorus ('the Pale' – not used at the time). Consequently, Diocletian decided to nominate two *Caesars* to act as deputies for the *Augusti*. The intention was to institute an orderly system of succession. The imperial positions would be hereditary (either through adoption or by birth) so that each member of the imperial college would be satisfied to await his own turn in the order of succession.

Diocletian conferred his plans to Maximian who duly dominated his Praetorian Prefect and son-in-law Constantius as his *Caesar* while Diocletian nominated Galerius Maximianus (possibly Praetorian Prefect and probably only about 30 years old) as his *Caesar*. However, on the basis of the name Galerius Maximianus it has been suggested that he was chosen as Diocletian's *Caesar* by Maximian (Maximianus) himself, quite possibly as a sort of revenge, or that the name was meant to serve as a consolation for the outmanoeuvred Maximian. Both Caesars were appointed either jointly on 1 March, or Constantius' appointment (1 March) predated that of Galerius (21 May) as claimed by the Paschal Chronicle and suggested by Constantius' precedence. Modern researchers are divided on this question, but I am inclined to support the latter alternative so that Diocletian's initial intention would have been to weaken Maximian who had then demanded that Diocletian also adopt a *Caesar* with the result that Diocletian did and also added the name Maximianus to console his friend.[224]

The new Caesars were opposite personalities. Constantius was a physically frail but disciplined, temperate, moderate and wise ruler who favoured the Christians, while Galerius was a large and bulky ox with a cruel streak who hated the Christians intensely. Both were able military commanders. The fact that Diocletian raised to high position such men as Maximian and Galerius begs the question: why? Did he take the thugs as his colleagues for the reason that they were his fellow Illyrians and thanks to their brutish behaviour very unlikely to be able to attract enough support to overthrow him? It is in fact very probable that Diocletian did indeed use these brutes as scapegoats for his own unpopular decisions. We should not forget that Stalin was loved by his people who thought that all of the evil deeds had been committed by his brutish officers without his knowledge.

Now the order of precedence was that the *Augusti* were considered to be brothers but in such a manner that the *Iovius* Diocletian held the senior position. The *Augusti* adopted the two new Caesars as their sons, but in such a manner that Constantius, despite being Caesar of the Junior Augustus, was considered senior of the two Caesars. The new rulers were also linked to their 'parents' through marriage. Constantius had divorced his first wife and married Maximian's daughter Theodora probably in 289, while Galerius had married Diocletian's daughter Valeria, probably also before his promotion. Subsequently, Galerius also managed to marry his only legitimate daughter to Maximian's son Maxentius.

Just like most of their recent predecessors, the four men were Illyrians. The Empire was effectively ruled by an Illyrian Mafia. The principal reason why Diocletian resorted to the use of adoptions and marriages was that he had no son of his own to succeed him. However, Maximian had a son Maxentius and Constantius had Constantine, as a result of which both could now hope to see their offspring succeed them. Both, or at least Constantine, appear to have been sent to Diocletian's court to be groomed for the throne and also to act as hostages.

The Empire was also physically divided into four quarters so that each of them had his own court, Praetorian Prefect (or prefects), bodyguards (the names of the units appear to have varied and only the *Augusti* had Praetorians), *comitatus* (imperial field army), administration, frontier army, and navy. Now the people of each area had an emperor who they could expect to defend them, but this reform didn't have only good consequences. The multiplying of courts, administrations and armies obviously increased the costs and therefore increased the taxes, and even more importantly each new high ranking officer cost huge amounts of money. We do not know the exact pay-scale, but if one works one's way through backwards from the Byzantine era as Treadgold does, it is clear that the salary of each new *comes* and their equivalents must have represented the salary/cost of more than 2,000–2,500 legionaries.[225] Consequently the multiplication of high offices was very costly. Lactantius (7.1) in fact claims that each of Diocletian's colleagues sought to have more troops than the previous emperors had had. It is also important to understand that the aim was not to create an elite army, but a large army that had enough soldiers to protect the entire length of the borders – the goal was quantity over quality. The Roman army became a mass army. Now both the Romans and their enemies were prepared to employ any man able to bear arms, which means that henceforth generalship, amount of training, discipline, organization, availability of supplies, and the quality of equipment would decide the outcome of a battle. The Romans would have no advantage as far as the quality of soldiers was concerned, but thanks to the regular drill and training their men were still better prepared for combat than the so-called barbarians.

According to John Lydus (*De Mensibus* 1.27), Diocletian's army consisted of 389,704 soldiers and navy of 45,562 men. The usual interpretation is that these figures refer to the overall size of the Roman armed forces, but this is an error. Lydus refers to the size of the forces of the Eastern half of the empire, in addition to which one should include the armed forces of the Western half. When one remembers Agathias' (5.13.7) claim that the size of the Roman army had dwindled from 645,000 men to a mere 150,000 men under Justinian it becomes quite apparent that the overall size of the Roman army at the end of Diocletian's reign was about 645,000 men of which about 390,000 men served in the East.[226] This leaves about 255,000 men for the Western half of the empire. If the size of the fleet followed the same proportions, there were about 30,000 men in the Western fleets. If one takes into account the diminished size of the Roman army at the time Diocletian took power, it is entirely possible that he quadrupled its size when one takes into account the fact that not only new units were added to its strength but also the ranks of the old units were filled with new recruits.

One of Diocletian's greatest achievements was the revitalizing of the Roman naval forces, which secured for the Romans full control of their river frontiers and coastal areas and mastery of the seas for the next century. The fleets appear to have consisted of the 'frontier' and river fleets on the one hand and of the seagoing fleets on the other hand. The former were tied to the defence of their local section of frontier, while the latter acted as mobile 'reserve fleets'.

In the West the 'frontier fleets' came to consist of the fleets posted in the provinces (ND Occ. 42, 17–20–23): *Praefectus classis Fluminis Rhodani, Viennae siue Arelati; Praefectus classis barbariorum, Edruduni Sapaudiae; Praefectus militum musculariorum, Massiliae Graecorum*; the Rhine Fleet or fleets; the *Praefectus classis Araricae*, Caballoduno; the Fleet of Lake Constance; the Fleet of Lake Como; and the *classis Anderetianorum, Parisiis* (may have been created after the reconquest of Britain in 296). The seagoing mobile fleets consisted of the Praetorian *Classis Misenatium* and *Classis Ravennatium* and of the *Classis Venetum* (at Aquileia). After the reconquest of Britain in 296, its naval forces were divided into (at least) two commands: the *dux tractus Nervicani et Armoricani* on the continent; and the *comes litoris saxonici per Britanniam* in Britain.[227] It seems probable that the Praetorian fleets under their respective prefects served under the Praetorian Prefect(s),[228] while the provincial fleets and their prefects served under their respective superiors, the *praepositi*, or *duces*, or *comites*, depending upon the situation.

The evidence for the Eastern fleets is poor. There remains only circumstantial evidence in the form of references to the existence of navies in the narrative sources and the incomplete list of fleets in the ND. The evidence that we have suggests that the Eastern fleets were also organized as frontier fleets and seagoing fleets, but unfortunately it is almost impossible to reconstruct the actual organization at the time of Diocletian.

It is clear that the Flavia fleets were created by some member of the Constantian dynasty and the earliest plausible date for that is after 316 when Constantine gained possession of the area in question, the likeliest date being between 316 and 324, but one cannot rule out the possibility that these fleets would have been created later. We do not know whether Constantine just renamed existing fleets already created by Diocletian or created new ones, but considering the fact that Diocletian did reorganize the Danubian defences and created new legions also for Sirmium, it is quite likely that he also posted new ships to support his army, which may have included the creation of new fleets as well. According to Reddé, there is no information that would allow one to reconstruct the dates of creation for the other fleets in the list, but, in my opinion, the reign of Diocletian still stands as the likeliest alternative in light of his policy of dividing the provinces into

Danubian Fleets according to the extant text of the Notitia Dignitatum (after Reddé, 632).

Fleet	Base	Duchy	Source
Classis Histrica	Carnuntum	Pannonia I	ND Occ. 34.28
	Vindobona	Pannonia I	ND Occ. 34.28
	Florentia	Valeria Rip.	ND Occ. 33.58
	Mursa	Pannonia II	ND Occ. 32.52
	Aegeta	Dacia Rip.	ND Occ. 42.42
	Viminacium	Moesia I	ND Occ. 41.38
Classis Pannonica I	Seruitium[1]	Pannonia II	ND Occ. 32.55
Pannonica II	Siscia	Savia	ND Occ. 32.56
	Aegeta[2]	Dacia Rip.	ND Occ. 32.56
Classis Flavia I	Sirmium	Pannonia II	ND Occ. 32.50
Classis Flavia II	Graio[3]	Pannonia II?	ND Occ. 32.51
Classis Arlapensis	Arlape	Norique Rip.	ND Occ. 34.42
Classis Maginensis	Commagenae	Norique Rip.	ND Occ. 34.42
Classis Lauriacensis	Lauriacum	Norique Rip.	ND Occ. 34.43
Classis Stradensis	Margum	Moesia I	ND Or. 41.39
Classis Germensis	Margum	Moesia I	ND Or. 41.39
Classis Ratianensis	Ratiaria	Dacia Rip.	ND Or. 42.43
Classis musculorum Scythicorum[4]	Inplateypegis	Scythia Min.	ND Or. 39.35
Naves amnicae	Transmarica	Moesia II	ND Or. 40.36

1) Unknown location on the R. Save. 2) The name of the fleet *classis Aegetensium sive secundae Pannonicae, nunc Siscia* means that it was originally part of the Pannonian fleet and then transferred to Aegeta (near the Iron Gates) and then transferred to Siscia by the time the ND was written. The location of Aegeta in Pannonia is not known and the dates of the changes are similarly not known. 3) Location unknown, but probably either on the R. Save or on the R. Drave. 4) ND has '*Praefectus ripae legionis primae Ioviae cohortis… et secundam Herculiae musculorum Scythicorum et classis, Inplateypegiis*', emended by Mommsen '*et classis musculorum Scythicorum*' according to Reddé (p.632). The location is unknown.

smaller entities and most importantly because he is attested to have increased the size of the army and the fleet. However, Reddé's suggestion that the *Transmarica* fleet was probably created after Constantine had reconquered *Dacia Malvensis* seems valid.[229]

The evidence for the seagoing fleets is even worse, but it is practically certain that Diocletian would have drawn at least some detachments from the Italian fleets to serve him as his 'Praetorian Fleet'. However, considering the size of Diocletian's navy it is probable that he also created a new Imperial Fleet probably based at Nicomedia and other ports in the area, but there is no definite contemporary evidence for this, only later circumstantial evidence.

Indeed, Zosimus' account (2.22) of the naval forces employed by Licinius against Constantine suggests that there were several fleets in existence in the East that must have been created by Diocletian. According to Zosimus, Licinius' fleet consisted of detachments from Egypt (80 triremes; *Classis Alexandrina*), Phoenicia (80 triremes; *Classis Syriaca/ Seleucena*), the Ionians and Dorians in Asia (60 triremes; withdrawn elements of the Greek Fleet or part of the Imperial Fleet?), the Cyprians (30 triremes; A New Fleet?), the Carians (20 triremes; withdrawn elements of the Greek Fleet or part of the Imperial Fleet?), the Bithynians (30 triremes; the Nicomedian division of the Imperial Fleet?), and the Africans (50 triremes; the Libyan Fleet?). In addition, since Constantine's fleet was anchored at Athens, which was one of the naval bases in Greece, it is likely that Constantine was in possession of at least part of the former Fleet of Greece created during the reign of Gallienus. Consequently, there is enough circumstantial evidence for the continued existence of at least the *Classis Alexandrina, Classis Syriaca* now renamed as *Classis Seleucena, Classis Pontica* (note Constantius' campaign in the area and the creation of the new legion for the port city of Trapezunt), and also probably for the continued existence of some African Fleet.[230] In addition, one can postulate the existence of new fleets and/or a new Imperial Fleet that was later transformed into the Imperial Fleet based at Constantinople. It is impossible to make a secure educated guess regarding the establishment strength of the new Imperial Fleet on the basis of the figures given, because it is possible that some of the locations were separate new fleets, some of the fleets may have included reinforcements from the *Classis Pontica*, and it is likely that Licinius would have built additional ships to strengthen his navy against Constantine. My best educated guess based on the sizes of the Imperial Fleet in Constantinople from the sixth to the tenth centuries is that it had between 100 and 150 'triremes' (see Syvänne, 2004).

On the basis of information dating from 335 and 358–9 the *Classis Seleucena/Syriaca*, based at Seleucia, the port of Antioch, had a special role in the Eastern defensive system. It was commanded by the *Comes Orientis* at the latest by 335, who also had a duty of organizing supplies for the garrisons and armies operating in Mesopotamia.[231] Consequently, it was the fleet of Antioch that secured the sea lanes to Antioch from which the supplies were then transported to Mesopotamia in wagons and carts and it was the *Comes Orientis* who organized the transport fleets, when necessary, for the armies operating along the Euphrates and Tigris. I would suggest, however, that there was nothing new in this arrangement. Antioch had always served as a logistical hub for the eastern theatre of war, which means that the *Classis Syriaca* and its commanders had always performed these duties. The only new thing about this system was that after Diocletian had reorganized the provinces, the *Comes* organized the supply of the armies with the assistance of the *Vicarius* of *Oriens*.

The armed forces were recruited from four sources: 1) volunteers; 2) sons of serving or former soldiers who formed the bulk of the recruits; 3) citizens conscripted as a tax from landowners' estates; and 4) barbarians recruited as auxiliaries. It has been suggested that Diocletian introduced hereditary service into the army to ease the problems of recruiting (Lee, 2007, 81). In return for service soldiers and veterans received certain benefits in order to make the occupation more lucrative, but in practice thanks to corruption, poor pay caused by inflation, and harsh discipline, the natives were less and less enthusiastic of the prospect of having to serve. This meant that in future the ranks of the army came

Plate 1: Coin of Gallienus. (British Museum: photo by the author)

Plate 2: Coin of Aurelian. (British Museum: photo by the author)

Plate 3: Coin of Probus. (British Museum: photo by the author)

Plate 4: Coin of Carus. (British Museum: photo by the author)

Plate 5: Gold Aurei of Diocletian. (British Museum: photo by the author)

Plate 6: Coins of Diocletian. (British Museum: photo by the author)

Plate 7: Coin of Maxentius. (British Museum: photo by the author)

Plate 8: Coin of Licinius. (British Museum: photo by the author)

Plate 9: Solidus (27) and medallion of Carausius (28). (British Museum: photo by the author)

Plate 10: Medallion commemorating Constantius I's victory over Allectus. (British Museum: photo by the author)

Plate 11: Constantine the Great. (Source: Wikipedia Commons)

Plate 12: Constantine's coin with the *Labarum*. (British Museum: photo by the author)

Plate 13: Coin of Constantius II. (British Museum: photo by the author)

Plate 14: Coin of Constantine the Great. (British Museum: photo by the author)

Plate 15: Coin of Constans. (British Museum: photo by the author)

Plate 16: The four Tetrarchs in embrace. (Source: Maailman Historia)

Plate 17: Constantine the Great. (Source: Wikipedia Commons)

Plate 18: Either Constantine the Great or Constantius II. In the past this bust was unanimously considered to be Constantius II, but now some researchers attribute it to his father Constantine the Great. (Source: Wikipedia Commons)

Plate 19: Julian. (Source: Maailman Historia)

Plate 20: Statue of Constantine the Great (Constantinus Magnus). (Source: Bernoulli J.J (1894), *Römische Ikonographie*. Stuttgart, Berlin, Leipzig)

Plate 21: Roman elite soldier in readiness to fight on the frozen surface of a lake. The shield presents an adaptation of the ND shield patterns. Colour-scheme takes some artistic liberties. It should not be forgotten that Roman soldiers were sometimes required to fight during winter time. (© Jyrki Halme)

Plate 22: A Roman elite soldier shouting insults to the enemy, or calling help from the God or gods. (Colour scheme takes artistic liberties) (© Jyrki Halme)

Plate 23: Berkasovo-helmet, *spatha*-sword, and angon-javelin. (© Jyrki Halme)

Plate 24: Roman front-ranker (shown by the use of the shin-guards). Note the plate-armour guard for the sword-hand, and the handle of the shield just behind the shield-boss. (With permission of www. fectio.org.uk)

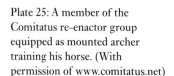

Plate 25: A member of the Comitatus re-enactor group equipped as mounted archer training his horse. (With permission of www.comitatus.net)

Plate 26: Members of the Comitatus re-enactor group in light equipment. Two guards escorting an officer. (With permission of www.comitatus. net)

Plate 27: Roman military equipment after Piazza Armerina mosaic. Note the *Draco*-standard used by most Roman forces at this time. It served even as an imperial banner for Julian. Note also the *pilleus Panonicus* hat. (© Jyrki Halme)

Plate 28: Light–armed officer scouting the road. Note the *pilleus Panonicus* hat. (© Jyrki Halme)

Plate 29: A fully equipped (*hasta*-spear, *spatha*-sword, *lorica squamata*/scale-armour, Deurne-helmet, shield, shin-guards) front rank elite soldier in readiness to fight. Colour-scheme takes some artistic liberties. (© Jyrki Halme)

Plate 30: Berkasovo–helmet. (© Jyrki Halme)

Plate 31: The re-enactor group Comitatus giving a demonstration of Roman cavalry manoeuvres. (With permission of www.comitatus.net)

Plate 32: Roman cavalry on exercises. (With permission of www.comitatus.net)

Plate 33: Members of the Comitatus re-enactor group practicing archery. The basic Roman archery training consisted of this type of training on foot with three different types of draw depending upon the unit: the Mediterranean, the 'Mongolian', and the Persian. The members of the cavalry progressed to the use of the bow on horseback only after they had demonstrated sufficient skill on foot. (With permission of www.comitatus.net)

Plate 34: Members of Comitatus giving a demonstration of the use of the spear on horseback. (With permission of www.comitatus.net)

Plate 35: A Roman light infantry archer. (With permission of www.comitatus.net)

Plate 36: A Roman officer with the *Draco*-standard and lamellar armour. (© Jyrki Halme)

Plate 37: The Deurne-helmet which combines elements from the Berkasovo II helmet. (© Jyrki Halme)

Plate 38: A Roman soldier in light equipment without a shield to show the different pieces of equipment. (© Jyrki Halme)

Plate 39: Equipment of the first century AD Germanic warrior. By the third century, the shape of the shield changed, but not much else. (Kalkriese, Museum of the Battle of Teutoburg, photo by the author)

Plate 40: Germanic field fortifications at Kalkriese (Battle of Teutoburg Forest AD 9) also used during the third and fourth centuries. (Photo by the author)

Plate 41: Womenfolk of the soldiers. One of the reasons why the young men soldiered was to obtain wives. (With permission of www. comitatus.net)

Plate 42: Ancient Danish warriors according to bog finds. These also roughly represent West Germanic warriors. (reconstruction 1917, Maailman Historia)

Plate 43: *Draco*-standard with wind blowing through. (© Jyrki Halme)

Plate 44: Front-ranker equipped with shin-guards, scale-armour, *spatha*-sword, shield (colour scheme takes artistic liberties), and Deurne-helmet. The cloak is from the Piazza Armerina mosaic. (© Jyrki Halme)

Plate 45: A Roman marine in light equipment as reconstructed by Comitatus (With permission of www.comitatus.net)

Plate 46: Roman soldier attacking with the *spatha*-sword. (© Jyrki Halme)

Plate 47: Roman front-ranker (shown by the use of shin-guards). Note the plate arm-protection and the guard tower in the background. It should not be forgotten that the Romans also fought in the cold and nasty winter weather. (With permission of www.fectio.org.uk)

to contain an ever increasing number of barbarians. In addition, in order to increase military capacity even further, veterans and barbarians were also settled on abandoned land both to farm it and to act as a sort of local militia: for example, the barbarian *laeti* were expected to provide auxiliary units in return for their land.

According to Lactantius, the increased size of the army and taxes led to the abandonment of farmland by the taxpayers who wanted to avoid having to pay the taxes. This in turn caused Diocletian to divide the provinces into smaller entities (from about 50 to about 100 by 303) and he grouped a number of these into dioceses, each under a *vicarius* or *vices agens*, and the dioceses in their turn operated under the Praetorian Prefects. Northern Italy was also regarded as a province for tax purposes. Diocletian needed money to pay for the upkeep of his mass army, and it was easier to gather the taxes when the provinces were smaller. However, in order to diminish the costs created by the enlarged army, Diocletian appears to have established the *annona militaris* (payment in kind of grain, meat, oil, and wine) as the principal form of payment. The equipment and clothes were also issued by the state. Some of the provinces like Italy (under a *Corrector*), Asia and Achaea continued to be governed by senators for the glory it entailed, but by now the division into equestrians and senators was almost meaningless and entirely replaced by the '*noblesse de robe*', who owed their position to the emperor.

Of note is also the fact that modern research has attested two legions per frontier province. We do not know when Diocletian decided on this reform, but he must have taken this decision at the latest at the same time that he started to divide the provinces into smaller entities for tax purposes. The practice of posting two legions per province was not new, but what was new about this was that the same practice was now also extended to cover the new smaller provinces, which naturally resulted in the strengthening of the frontier forces.

The civilian and military authority of these frontier provinces was also divided so that the military forces of each province were placed under a *dux*, while the civilian administration and legal matters belonged to the governor. This approach was not new but Diocletian's long reign ensured that this solution would become permanent. The division of the civilian and military duties made it more difficult for generals to usurp power. There were some exceptions to this rule, however. The governors in various African provinces did retain command of the troops at least until the 350s and were also briefly given those back later (Mattingly, 1995, 171ff.). The *duces* in their turn were subjected to the authority of the *comites* (counts, sing. *comes*) who ruled longer sections of the frontier. These in their turn were under the command of the praetorian prefects, Caesars and Augusti.[232] The diagram shows the likely new military organization (c. 295).

The Verona List dated to about 303 shows the complete extent of Diocletian's famous administrative reform that had divided the provinces into smaller entities for tax purposes, and which were then grouped together as dioceses. The military organization mirrored the civilian one so that each of the frontier provinces had two legions and auxiliaries under a *dux*. The *duces* in their turn served under a *comites* or *praefecti praetorio*. The process obviously took some time to complete, because the borders of the provinces had to be adjusted to the needs of the taxation and defence, Britain was not even part of Diocletian's Empire at the time the reform was started, and the African provinces were only divided in about 303 (Mattingly, 1995, 171ff.).

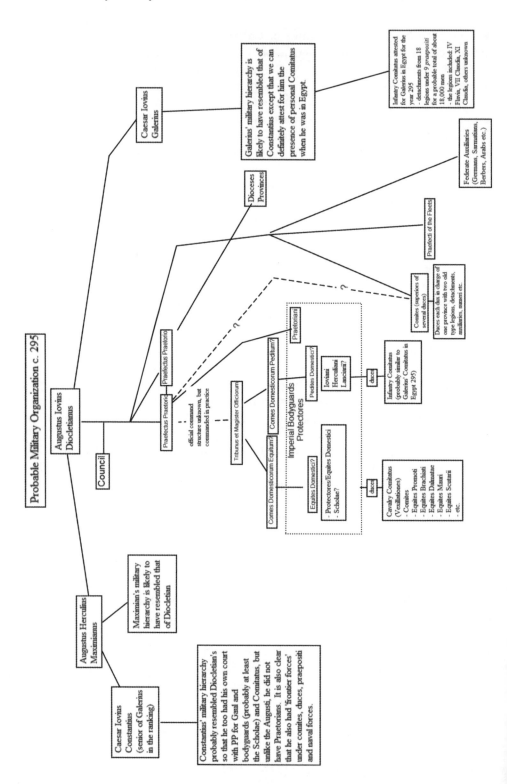

Probable Military Organization c. 295

Augustus Iovius
Diocletianus

Council

Caesar Iovius
Galerius

Galerius' military hierarchy is likely to have resembled that of Constantius except for him the presence of personal Comitatus when he was in Egypt.

Infantry Comitatus attested for Galerius in Egypt for the year 295
- detachments from 18 legions under 9 *praepositi* for a probable total of about 18,000 men
- the legions included: IV Flavia, VII Claudia, XI Claudia, others unknown

Dioceses
Provinces

Federate Auxiliaries
(Germans, Sarmatians, Berbers, Arabs etc.)

Praefectus Praetorio

Praefectus Praetorio

official command structure unknown, but commanded in practice

Tribunus et Magister Officiorum

Praefecti of the Fleets

Comites (superiors of several duces)

Duces each dux in charge of one province with two old type legions, detachments, auxiliaries, numeri etc.

Comes Domesticorum Peditum?

Pedites Domestici?

Praetoriani

Iovaini
Herculiani
Lanciarii?

duces

Infantry Comitatus (probably similar to Galerius' Comitatus in Egypt 295)

Comes Domesticorum Equitum?

Imperial Bodyguards
Protectores

Equites Domestici?

- Protectores/Equites Domestici
- Scholae?

duces

Cavalry Comitatus
(Vexillationes)
- Comites
- Equites Promoti
- Equites Brachiati
- Equites Dalmatae
- Equites Mauri
- Equites Scutarii
- etc.

Augustus Herculius
Maximianus

Maximian's military hierarchy is likely to have resembled that of Diocletian

Caesar Iovius
Constantius
(senior of Galerius in the ranking)

Constantius' military hierarchy probably resembled Diocletian's so that he too had his own court with PP for Gaul and bodyguards (probably at least the Scholae) and Comitatus, but unlike the Augusti, he did not have Praetorians. It is also clear that he also had 'frontier forces' under comites, duces, praepositi and naval forces.

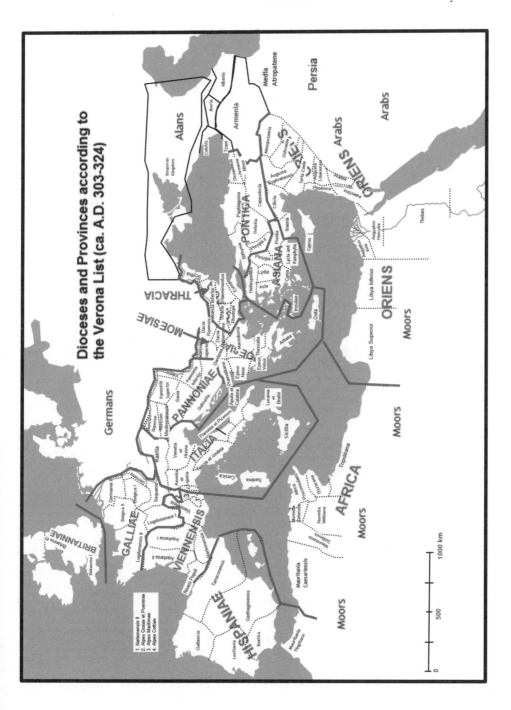

Dioceses and Provinces according to the Verona List (ca. A.D. 303-324)

The military forces posted in the provinces (legions, *equites*, cohorts, *alae*) continued to be commanded by *duces*. According to Malalas (12.40), these frontier armies were deployed in such a manner that some of the forces were stationed on the border in permanent camps while the *duces* with a large number of men were deployed behind them to act as local reserves. Since the new legionary garrisons were designed for about 2,000 to 3,000 men, it is quite apparent that Malalas' statement is correct, despite the suspicions aroused on the basis of Zosimus' claim that Diocletian guarded the empire by stationing the entire army in cities, fortresses and towers on the frontiers and that Constantine then 'ruined' this system by withdrawing troops from the frontier to the cities. The remainder of the new legionary forces (3,000–4,000) would have indeed been deployed behind their garrisons with their *duces* or detached to some other duty (policing, tax collection, outpost duty etc.) and then periodically rotated with those left in the garrisons. In fact, if one looks closely at what Zosimus says there is no contradiction. Even he admits that some of the 'frontier troops' were stationed in cities. It was only a matter of how many troops were posted behind and how far.

Diocletian's reforms naturally added new layers of administration and increased the number of accountants, directors and deputy governors, but it worked. The system was also fairer than the previous one, because if the decisions of the governor were found to be unsatisfactory, it was possible to make a complaint to the vicar who was his superior. Henceforth, taxes were collected more effectively. In truth the increased taxes were a small burden for the taxpayers in comparison with the devastations caused by foreign invasions even if the populace did not understand it. It was thanks to the increased size of the army that the borders were eventually secured which in its turn led to the general improvement of the economy. It was not Diocletian's fault that this vast bureaucratic apparatus he had created eventually mushroomed and became ever more ineffective and corrupt. Each new office created new opportunities for patronage, corruption and inefficiency. This just followed the natural laws of a mushrooming bureaucracy, so well explained by Parkinson's Law.

At this point Maximian ruled Italy, Spain and North Africa, with his headquarters/capital in Milan. Constantius ruled Gaul and Britain, with his headquarters/capital at Trier. Diocletian appears to have initially chosen to rule the Balkans, while Galerius ruled the East. During this time Galerius' de facto headquarters/capital lay in Antioch, but it is difficult to pinpoint a single headquarters for Diocletian because he travelled constantly. One can perhaps still say that his principal administrative centres were Sirmium and Nicomedia. It should be kept in mind that this division of territories was not meant to be permanent. The emperors could and did change places when there was a need, they also sent reinforcements from one territory to another when necessary, and the different administrations also coordinated their activities through messages, messengers and meetings.

Diocletian's reforms didn't include only army, judiciary system (governors, vicars and Praetorian Prefects acted as judges) and administration, but also legislation and its interpretation. The judges were provided with up-to-date legal guidance in the form of handbooks (c.293), the *Iuris Epitomae* after 293, and the *Codex Gregorianus* (c.295 with later additions). In the West the compendium *Senteniae Pauli* was published.[233] This obviously improved the workings of the judicial system and improved the good governance of provinces and financial matters. A well-working judicial system meant less need for military intervention against those who felt themselves cheated, and it also secured more money for the upkeep of the new defensive system. The system was not perfect, as Maximian's actions prove, but at least Diocletian had made an effort to improve it. Diocletian, just like his Illyrian predecessors Aurelian and Probus, was more Roman than the Romans themselves. Notably, similar ultra-nationalistic tendencies have also been demonstrated by the modern tyrants Stalin (Georgian) and Hitler (Austrian). Diocletian sought to establish Roman Law as the only law in the Empire, just as he sought to make Latin the only official language even in the East. It is as such quite noteworthy that Roman Law was not yet followed everywhere, despite the fact that Caracalla had already spread it into the entire Empire in 212. Local practices had persisted and imperial officials had been unwilling to change those. It was difficult to rule the Empire by imperial edicts and laws alone if the men whose duty it was to implement those failed to do so.

At the same time Diocletian also set about to reform the monetary system by introducing new high-grade silver coins that were put in circulation in 294 to accompany his high-grade gold coins already introduced in 286. He also reformed the other denominations and created new mints throughout the Empire. The mints were located in such a manner that these would serve the needs of the army. The intention was to increase the buying power of the silver coinage so that it would be easier to pay for the upkeep of the increased army and administration. The new coins were circulated alongside older low-grade coins with the result that the people started to hoard the high-grade coins, especially the gold ones, which resulted in inflation. The exact mechanisms of how this happened are contested, but it is clear that the resulting inflation made it more difficult for the government and soldiers to obtain even their daily necessities.

Just like the mints, Diocletian also created new arms factories to serve the needs of the enlarged army. As discussed earlier (see Introduction), the distribution pattern of the imperial arms workshops listed by the ND suggests strongly that these had been created by Diocletian. Diocletian clearly distributed the factories rationally so that the local needs and divisions of provinces and dioceses were fully taken into account. The imperial arms workshops were only built where local production could not meet the needs of the army.

Empire Consolidated 293–299

It was also in 293 that Diocletian completed the reorganization of the defences along the Danube by fortifying or refortifying places along it while at the same time making preparations for the forthcoming campaign against the Sarmatians. With this in mind two new bridgeheads were built opposite Aquincum (Budapest) and Bononia to serve as launching points for the campaign. At least three new legions (*Legio V Iovia*, *Legio III Herculae*, and *Legio VI Herculea*) were formed prior to the following year's campaign. The last one may have been sent to the East with Galerius at the same time as he took other new and old legions (at least *Legio I Maximiana Thebaeorum*) with him to Egypt. Galerius crushed the revolt of Busiris and Coptos in Egypt during 293–295.[234] It appears quite probable that in this case the Egyptians once again received help from the Aksumites (Ethiopians with their subjects the Meroites and Blemmyes), and probably also from the Himyarites ('Indians') as their ally. On the basis of the fragmentary papyrus P. Oxy. 43

(dated to Feb 295) analyzed by Parker (1933), Galerius' expeditionary army (*Comitatus* or *Sacer Comitatus*) consisted of 18 legionary detachments (*IV Flavia*, *VII Claudia*, and *XI Claudia* being mentioned in the extant text) under nine *praepositi* (temporary commanders) for a likely total of about 18,000 men (that is, about 1,000 men per detachment) in addition to which came the cavalry *vexillationes*. This number of units divides itself nicely into three 'legions' of 6,000 men each of which would have consisted of three 2,000 men 'regiments' each under a *praepositus*. We don't know whether we should include among the detachments the bodyguard units, but probably not. If one adds to this figure at least three legions that accompanied Galerius, then the overall fighting strength of the infantry would have consisted of about 36,000 men (the equivalent of 3 legions and 18 detachments) plus some bodyguards and perhaps about 12,000 horsemen. This is a very conservative estimate, because I have not included any auxiliaries in the numbers. With them the infantry could easily have numbered about 50,000 and the cavalry about 20,000. After his victory Galerius appears to have stationed the *Legio I Maximiana Thebaeorum* at Pilae (Arguin, 145), and he may also have garrisoned the *Legio III Herculae* in what was later called the Province of *Aegyptus Herculia* (the province was probably created by Diocletian in c.298) even if it later served under Maximian in Mauretania in 298 (Arguin, 145).

In 294 Diocletian launched his Sarmatian campaign while Galerius continued his campaign in southern Egypt. Diocletian appears to have crushed the Sarmatians severely with a pincer movement launched simultaneously from Aquincum and Sirmium/ Bononia. Diocletian took the title *Sarmaticus Maximus* once again. Aurelius Victor (39.43) claims that Diocletian crushed the Marcomanni before his campaign against the Carpi, which may be a separate campaign that took place between 291 and 295. After his 294 Sarmatian Campaign Diocletian seems to have progressed from Sirmium down the Danube in the course of which he reorganized the defences and made preparations for the following year's campaign against the Carpi. He was in Singidunum from 8 to 12 September and by mid-November he was in Nicomedia where he wintered.[235]

Two of the new legions (*Legio V Iovia* and *Legio VI Herculea*) were stationed at Sirmium, probably with the purpose of acting as imperial reserves in the area. However, it is still likely that detachments of both were used by Diocletian in the coming campaigns. Diocletian continued his military campaign/strengthening of the defences of the Danube frontier for two more years and fought a successful campaign against the Carpi in 295 and/or the summer/autumn of 296 that enabled him to claim the title *Carpicus Maximus*. According to some sources (for example, Ammianus), Diocletian settled some of the defeated Carpi in Pannonia. Jerome dates this event to the year 295, but this has been contested by some modern historians on the basis of conflicting information (for example, Eutropius 9.25 claims that the settlement of the Carpi and Bastarnae took place after the Persian war).[236] It appears probable that it was now at the latest that the *Legio II Herculae* was stationed in Troesmis in the province of Scythia Minor. The year 296 saw heavy fighting on almost every frontier facing the Roman Empire.

In the meanwhile in 293 Constantius had marched so fast to north-west Gaul that he managed to besiege Gesoriacum/Bononia before the news of his elevation as Caesar reached its defenders. He built a mole to block its harbour so that the defenders could not flee by sailing away nor their helpers reach them from the sea. (See the Map below.) The garrison had no alternative than to surrender and join Constantius' army. Even though the panegyric doesn't mention it, it is clear that Constantius' army also took the other cities and ports still held by Carausius' forces either at the same time as Bononia or at the latest by the next year. After Constantius had accomplished this, he started the rebuilding of the forts and harbours as well as the building of a fleet in preparation for the conquest of Britain. The loss of Bononia caused a loss of confidence in Carausius' abilities that his *rationalis summae rei* Allectus exploited to his advantage. Allectus was suspected of embezzlement, but in this situation he managed to have Carausius murdered and take his place.

Constantius followed up his success by marching against the barbarian supporters of the rebel government in order to secure his rear before the conquest of Britain. He defeated the barbarians (Franks, Chamavi and Frisii) near the mouth of the Rhine and the Scheldt between 294 and 295, and then settled them south of the Rhine as farmers with the duty to answer the call to come to arms when necessary. In other words, they became so-called *laeti*. I would suggest that it was now at the latest that Constantius began the process of increasing the size of his army with Frankish and other barbarian recruits that were enrolled into units later known as *auxilia palatina*. The fact that Constantius was able to resettle barbarians on Roman soil proves that his campaign had been a great success. They had not been able to flee away and fight another day. It should be kept in mind, however, that the emptying of sections of the frontier would eventually lead to the migration of new enemies into the area.

In 296 Constantius launched his invasion of Britain while Maximianus secured the Rhine frontier.[237] Constantius had divided his fleet into two. He sailed from Bononia while his Praetorian Prefect Asclepiodotus sailed from the mouth of the Seine. In addition, he seems to have had a third fleet that consisted mainly of troop transports that sailed probably from Samobriva and/or from the mouth of the Rhine to join his fleet – an alternative is that the troop transports had just embarked their troops so slowly that Constantius' warships had already sailed away. It is possible that Constantius' fleet was only a decoy that allowed Asclepiodotus' fleet (and the fleet of transports?) better chances of making a landing. Allectus with the bulk of his forces and fleet stood opposite Constantius probably in Dubris (Dover) while another fleet was stationed near the Isle of Wight against Asclepiodotus (see Map 'British Campaign').

Constantius and Asclepiodotus embarked on their ships in bad weather, which suggests that their intention was to attempt to bypass the enemy fleets unobserved and effect a landing without having to fight a naval battle. Asclepiodotus managed to avoid the enemy fleet in the fog and disembark his troops, after which he burned the ships to encourage his men and began to march towards London. In the meanwhile, Constantius' fleet approached the Kentish coast, but could not make a landing because the transport fleet sailed past them to the North in the fog. The frustrated Constantius sailed back.

In the interim, Allectus had learnt of the landing of Asclepiodotus and decided to engage and defeat him first and then return to the Kentish coast to defeat Constantius. He marched to London and ordered his troops to assemble for battle and then started to march towards Asclepiodotus. The speed of Asclepiodotus' march seems to have surprised Allectus, because he met the former's army on the road without having put his army into fighting formation. Furthermore, the reinforcements he had called had not yet arrived and he had to fight a battle against Asclepiodotus' crack forces with a force consisting only of his Frankish allies and fellow conspirators. Allectus lost his life and his army was routed. The Frankish mercenaries withdrew to London and began to make the most of their time left in Britain by starting to pillage the city before returning to their homes. Unfortunately for them a significant proportion of Constantius' fleet of transports had lost their way and had disembarked the men on the coast and then marched to London. When these forces came across the looting Franks, they attacked and massacred the remnants of Allectus' army, to the great joy of Londoners. It was after this that Constantius with the rest of his forces sailed to Britain where he was greeted as a liberator and saviour.

This was not even the whole scale of the troubles facing the Tetrarchs in 296. It is possible, but not certain that the Franks raided through the Channel as far as the Spanish coast in support of Allectus in late 296.[238] If true, then it is easy to see that one reason for Maximian's subsequent campaign via Spain also included the clearing of Frankish

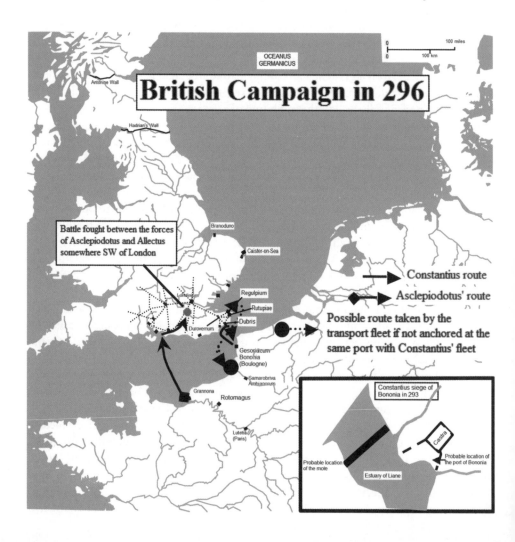

pirate bases in the area. The whole of Roman Africa was also engulfed in fire. The Roman military commanders had been unable to dislodge the Bavares and Quinquegentiani from their strongholds and in particular the Libyan tribal confederation of Austuriani appear to have exploited the Roman troubles in North Africa, Egypt and the East by pushing ever closer to the vital Roman possessions in coastal areas. The situation had become so grave that it required the personal attention of the emperor Maximian. Otherwise there was the possibility that the Egyptian rebels and their Aksumite, Blemmye, Meroitic (?), and Himyarite allies could receive support from the Austurians while the Persians threatened the eastern frontier, making the task really daunting.

Therefore, after Constantius had conquered Britain and had returned to Gaul, Maximian marched to Spain where he fought (against Moorish raiders or Franks or local rebels or all of the above?) while Constantius assumed responsibility for the defence of both Britain and Gaul. Maximian took with him a large army, consisting of detachments drawn from the legions posted in the West together with new Thracian recruits, and auxiliaries. Of particular note is the fact that according to Aurelius Victor (39.22) the Moorish enemies consisted of Julianus and the Quinquegentani. This appears to imply that the enemies consisted of a large confederation of tribes that had been formed as a result of intertribal wars. The family name *Iulii* (if one interprets *Iulianus* to mean *Iulius*) implies that the Baquates, who were occasionally united with the Bavares, had probably subjected the Quinquegentani and had created a North African state encompassing most of Mauretania Caeserensis.[239] Consequently, after having defeated the enemies in Spain, Maximian, at the head of a large army, crossed to Africa where he began the long campaign to crush the revolt of the Moorish/Berber tribes in Mauretania in the spring of 297.

In the interim, Maxentian's hunger for beautiful women to rape had caused unforeseen consequences in the East. According to Agathangelos, in the beginning of his reign Trdat was intensely hostile towards the Christians. The reason for this was that Gregory, the son of the murderer of his father, was a devout Christian.[240] Trdat had in fact issued an edict that ordered his subjects to worship the national gods, and later still another edict that promised rewards to those who exposed Christians. After Trdat had ruled for thirteen or fifteen years Maxentian (Agathangelos has Diocletian, but this is clearly a mistake) sought a 'wife' (or rather beautiful women to rape) with the help of painters. These found a 'wife' for Maximian in a nunnery in Rome and the Emperor could not contain his lust after seeing the portrait. This maiden was Rhipsime, supposedly a daughter of a pious man of royal lineage, who was a protégée of abbess Gaiane. Maximian's men entered the nunnery by force, but the women resisted and part of them managed to flee to the city of Valarshapat, a residence of the Armenian kings, where they earned a living by glassmaking.

Maximian sent search parties and it was soon found out that the women had fled to Armenia. He clearly had nothing better to do! According to Agathangelos, Diocletian (or more likely still Maximian) sent a letter to Trdat that stated that he was either to send the women back or keep them for himself. Trdat duly obeyed and the women were found. He then forcibly had Rhipsime brought to his quarters, where he tore off her clothes to rape her, but, according to Agathangelos, Rhipsime still managed to resist and flee with the result that the king's nobles and the chief-executioner roasted her alive. After this, the chief-executioner killed thirty-seven Christians, but when Trdat learnt of the whole extent of the carnage the next day – he had probably been drunk when he was attempting to fulfil the imperial request – he became ashamed and depressed and half-mad. He had a very bad conscience. It was only after Trdat's sister released Gregory from the prison and brought him before Trdat that he was able to regain his senses. The king, princes and magnates all begged forgiveness, which was duly granted after certain conditions were fulfilled. After this, the king gave an edict to obliterate the pagan religion. The king and his army advanced from Valarshapat to Artashat to destroy the altars of Anahit. This had the additional benefit of destroying the magi secret service, the fifth column working for Persia. However, Trdat was no fool. He also attempted to placate the Persians and negotiate a lasting peace with Persia. It was because of this that he recognized Narses as the new King of Kings and as his overlord in 293/4. (See below.)

The conversion of Armenia to Christianity was to have truly long lasting consequences, and one can therefore state with good reason that Maximian's lust changed the course of history. Even if it is actually quite probable that Trdat converted mainly because of his bad conscience, it is still clear that it did not take him long to understand that the conversion was simultaneously a statement of independence from both Rome and Persia. He had thrown away the faith of his fathers and adopted a religion ostracised by the Roman elites. When Constantine became Christian this brought the two nations together, but in the long run the conversion deepened the already deep divisions among the Armenian elites. Henceforth, it would be the Zoroastrian and pagan feudal lords who yearned for cooperation with Persia and it would be the Christian lords who would seek help from the Romans.

And this was not even the whole extent of the consequences resulting from Maximian's perverted desires![241] The group of refugees accompanying Rhipsime to Armenia had also included St. Nino, who subsequently converted the Georgians in about 325–6. What follows is of greatest interest to those who have read the *Da Vinci Code*. St. Nino's father 'Zabilon' of Cappadocia had served as a military commander in Gaul against the 'Branj' (Franks) and had defeated them, capturing their king and chieftains, and had then converted them to Christianity. This event cannot be dated securely, but the likeliest date would be Probus' reign. After this, he had retired to Jerusalem and married the sister of a local patriarch who then gave birth to the daughter Nino. When Nino was 12 years old, her parents sold everything and devoted their lives to God. They left their daughter in the loving care of the Orders of Christ of Mary Magdalene and the Sisters of Lazarus. Nino was then instructed in Christian doctrine according to Mary Magdalene. When Rhipsime and her friends asked to be baptized by the Christians of Jerusalem, Nino eagerly took the mission and travelled to Ephesus where the women were staying. She then accompanied the fugitives to Armenia where she survived the massacre of the refugees and managed to flee to Iberia. It was there that she started to spread the teachings of Mary Magdalene and eventually in about 325/6 converted the queen, the king and the court. Note especially the connection between her father's stay in Gaul and her version of Christianity, which was based on the teachings of Mary Magdalene! There may indeed be at least a germ of truth behind the beliefs that Mary Magdalene had moved to Gaul to spread her version of Christianity. Maximian's lust had far reaching religious, political and military consequences.

In about 292/3 the Persian *Shahanshah* Bahram II had died and had been succeeded by his son Bahram III. His uncle Narses, the Great King of Armenia, had not accepted this but had started a civil war as a result of which Bahram III had been deposed after having ruled for only four months. The Paikuli Inscription set up by Narses describes these events.[242] Narses mentions that at the time of his accession the Romans maintained peace. His text also seems to imply that the Kings of the Kushans, Chawarezmia, Makuran, Turan, Gurgan, Iberia, Sigan etc. obeyed him. Narses was now free to start a war. Of note is the fact that this list also includes King Tirdad who must be Tiridates/Trdat of Armenia as well as Amru (Imru) King of the Lakhmids. This list therefore suggests that Trdat had recognized Narses as his overlord and had thereby obtained temporary peace, but as former Great King of Armenia Narses would not let Trdat enjoy this state of affairs for long. Similarly, the list also suggests that at least part of Diocletian's problems with the Saracens had been caused by the Lakhmids.

We do not know the exact date, but it was soon after this that Narses launched his campaign against Armenia and Rome. He invaded Armenia first to oust his archrival Trdat. The Georgian Chronicle (81–2) appears to give the correct version when it states that the king of Iberia joined forces with Narses and attacked Trdat who was unable to oppose the combined strength of the two kings. Faustus (pp.235–41) adds that the Persian king had incited all the northern peoples against Trdat and that the Slkuni betrayed him, but then claims that Trdat defeated the northerners in a bloody battle after which he felt unable to oppose the Persians without Roman help. This obviously betrays the fact that Narses had defeated Trdat and forced him to resort to the use of guerrilla warfare until the Romans could arrive to help him. I would date these campaigns to the years 294–295. Now the road lay open for the invasion of the Roman Empire.

Consequently, in 295 Galerius returned in haste from Egypt to oppose Narses' invasion of Roman territory.[243] He defeated Narses and all four emperors took the title *Persicus Maximus*, but the situation in Egypt had not yet been fully pacified and Narses was not about to give up. Narses renewed his offensive against Syria in the early summer of 296 and things started to go from bad to worse. The vast majority or at least a significant portion of the Persian army appears to have consisted of the heavy cataphracts, each rider holding a bow and a spear and riding a Nisaean horse. According to Orosius (7.25), Galerius, heavily outnumbered, fought two inconclusive battles, the first of which must refer to the year 295 and the latter to the early summer 296. As a result of the latter battle, the Persians were able to push Galerius' force aside and conquer a number of Roman fortresses, which in turn led Galerius to ask for help from Diocletian.

When Diocletian learnt of this, he was still in the Balkans. Now he had no other choice than to march to Antioch, which he reached in late 296. He probably brought with him five new legions (30,000 men) that were subsequently garrisoned in the East. After this Diocletian gave Galerius a force which he deemed sufficient for him. In the following spring 297 Galerius advanced against the dreaded Persian cavalry on the plain between Carrhae and Callinicum with predictable results. He suffered a humiliating defeat in which he appears to have lost most of his troops. Considering Diocletian's reaction it seems probable that Galerius had been in charge of a cavalry vanguard and had engaged the enemy prematurely without waiting for the arrival of Diocletian. Whatever the cause of the defeat it is still clear that the presence of Diocletian's sizable *Comitatus* plus the reinforcements made it impossible for the Persians to exploit their victory and they retreated.

Unsurprisingly, Diocletian was very angry with the poor performance of Galerius and when the humiliated warrior came into his presence he made Galerius feel his displeasure in public by making the overly proud Caesar run on foot in front of Diocletian's chariot. The public humiliation was meant to chastise the failed commander and make him the scapegoat. It was not Diocletian who had failed but his Caesar.

Diocletian dispatched Galerius to the Balkans to gather a new army while he secured the borders. However, there followed another piece of bad news. Egypt had revolted again after troops had been transferred to Syria. If the tax edict of the Prefect of Egypt Aristius Optatius/Optatus is dated to March 296 as Williams (81) and Barnes (1981, 17) do, then it is possible that the cause of the revolt was the new uniform tax system introduced by Diocletian, but if it is to be dated to March 297 as Roger Rees (158) does then the purpose of the new tax edict would have been to reconcile the locals to the government. The edict actually claims that it corrects injustice so it is possible that the revolt was just a continuation of the previous one. It is in fact probable that Galerius had failed to pacify Egypt before having to march to Syria in 295. At any rate it is clear that the uprising was very popular among the Egyptians. Lucius Domitius Domitianus was declared as the nominal emperor, but the real power was in the hands of Achilleus, who as *Corrector* of Egypt was the de facto ruler. The new regime was entirely Hellenic in nature and even issued coins imitating the old Ptolemaic coins.

Consequently, when the military situation had stabilized as a result of the winter weather setting in and the arrival of new reinforcements from the Danubian frontier, Diocletian marched to Egypt to crush the revolt. Two new legions, *Legio II Flavia Constantia*, and *Legio III Diocletiana Thebaeorum* are attested for the first time in 296, but in my opinion it is likelier that these had already been created by Diocletian well before this for Galerius' Egyptian campaign and that the legions just become visible when they are garrisoned for the first time. Another possibility is that these were indeed created by Diocletian for his Egyptian campaign so that he would not have to withdraw any more troops from the eastern frontier than was necessary. It was wiser to take the new legions (probably formed with a core of veterans) against the Egyptian militias rather than use those against the dreaded Persians.

It should not come as a surprise that the senior monarch chose to march with the bulk of the forces to Egypt at a time when the Persians held the upper hand. The Romans practically always saw usurpations as more serious threats than foreign invasions. Egyptian grain undoubtedly played its role too. Therefore, in practice, the division of the army meant that Galerius was once again left with too few men to deal with the Persians, but this time Galerius opted to engage the enemy through subterfuge. He had no other alternative. He did not have enough men to engage the Persians in the open.

In the meantime Diocletian and his *Comitatus* crushed the Egyptian rebels easily in the open and forced its remaining supporters to seek shelter from Alexandria, where Aurelius Achilleus managed to defend the city probably until March 298. But this was not the end of the war. Zonaras (12.31) and Aurelius Victor (39) both claim that Diocletian was fighting against the Ethiopians in Egypt when Narses invaded Syria. Consequently, Diocletian still needed to punish the allies of the rebels, the Ethiopians (Aksumites) and their clients the

Blemmyes, and probably also the Himyarites (Yemenis). The inclusion of the Ethiopians and Indians (Himyarites rather than real Indians) as enemies in the Panegyric (*Pan.Lat.* 8.5.2) definitely implies this. It is probable that the Meroites were also clients of the Aksumites and thereby fellow enemies of Rome, but this is not known with certainty. Diocletian's solution to this problem proves his ingenuity. In 298 he concluded a treaty with the Nubians against the Blemmyes, and then also another treaty with the Blemmyes. Both of these were paid money in return for peace.[244] In return for their help, the Nobatae received the *Dodekaschoinos* (south of Egypt) which was to serve as a buffer zone between Egypt and the Blemmyes and Meroites, and their overlords the Aksumites. Diocletian's decision to use the Nubians against the Blemmyes and Aksumites further undermined the relative position of the Kingdom of Meroe among the kingdoms of the area. Henceforth, the Meroites would be surrounded by the Nubians on three sides. If they were to survive, they needed help from their overlords, the Aksumites, who were not their friends either. The conclusion of the treaty with the Blemmyes in turn may have signified Roman support for the Blemmyes against the Aksumites with the result that the relative power of the latter diminished, but this is less certain because it is possible that the treaty could also have included the overlords of the Blemmyes as well. We simply do not have enough extant evidence to exclude that possibility, because at a later date the Aksumites followed a hostile policy against the Romans only when their subjects did not have a treaty with Rome.

In addition, Diocletian fortified and garrisoned the Island of Philae close to the city of Elephantine and constructed temples and altars on it to serve as places of pagan worship for the Nobatae, Blemmye and Romans. These sanctuaries remained in use until the reign of Justinian, who tore them down. In other words, Diocletian used religion successfully to connect the Roman and tribal interests in the area and thereby set a precedent for the Christian emperors to emulate.

It was after this or during these operations that Diocletian made a complete overhaul of the imperial and local administration in Egypt and posted garrisons in the strategic locales with an eye for both internal and external threats. We know that *Legio II Flavia Constantia* was stationed in Thebaid with *I Maximiana Thebaeorum*, and that *Legio III Diocletiana Thebaeorum* was stationed in Andaro (Schabur) in the province of *Aegyptus Iovia* from 297 onwards (Arguin, 145). *Legio III Herculae* (attested in 293) in its turn formed part of the garrison of *Aegyptus Herculia*, one of the three provinces into which Diocletian divided Egypt. Notably, we also know that *Legio III Herculae* or its detachment was stationed in Mauretania in 298 (Arguin, 145), which means that in the midst of all his own problems Diocletian was also forced to send reinforcements to his beleaguered colleague Maximian so that he could defeat the Berbers in Mauretania. (See later.) It seems as if Diocletian had to be everywhere all at once – except Gaul, where Constantius was performing well – despite having three colleagues.

In 298 Galerius decided to use the reinforcements, which included Gothic Federate cavalry (who served in return for tribute) he had brought from the Danube frontier to make an invasion of the Armenian territory held by the Persians. In fact, it may actually have been Narses' plan to advance through Armenia to Satala and from there either towards Syria or Nicomedia, because according to Faustos 3.20 (who misplaces the event by ca.40–50 years) Narses' camp was at Oschay in the District of Basean. This would mean that Galerius merely reacted to Persian actions.

However, this time the Persians' actions actually helped the Romans. Galerius was able to add to his numbers the remnants of the famed knights of Trdat who, with the Gothic Federates, formed a truly frightening force of cavalry lancers at a time when Galerius probably had way too few horsemen left after his disastrous defeat. Galerius left his army at Satala and reconnoitred in person with the assistance of two Armenians. Having assessed the strength and dispositions of the enemy camp at Oschay, he returned and led his 25,000 men army (probably cavalry vanguard) forth. He managed to surprise the enemies in their camp at daybreak, destroy the Persian army, and capture Narses' family and his treasures. The *shahanshah*, however, was able to flee despite having been wounded. According to the GC (82–3), the Persian King of Kings fled to Persia, while the Iberian King Miriam/Mihran fled to his capital Mcxeta. All the Iberian and Persian elite soldiers had died. Consequently, Miriam decided to conclude a separate peace. He sent messengers to both Galerius and Trdat. The son of Miriam, called Bakar, was given as hostage to the Romans, Trdat gave his daughter Salome in marriage to Bakar, and both sides were reconciled. However, the Persian-Iberian lord Peroz still opposed the policy of Miriam, but could do very little in the circumstances.

Galerius exploited his victory to the tilt and advanced from Armenia to Media and then to Adiabene and defeated the Persians in two pitched battles after which he captured Nisibis before October 298. Narses had sent an envoy very soon after his disastrous defeat to negotiate the release of his family, but had got a stern refusal. In response Galerius had noted how Shapur I had treated Valerian and had then skinned and stuffed him for public display. Following the capture of Nisibis, Galerius marched down the Tigris and captured Ctesiphon, after which he continued his march at least up to Babylon before returning back home along the course of the Euphrates. Both future rulers of Rome, Constantine the Great and Licinius, served under Galerius during this campaign and thereby gained invaluable military experience.

When Diocletian returned back from Egypt in the spring of 299 and met Galerius at Nisibis the situation changed and serious negotiations began. Diocletian sent his *Magister Memoriae* Sicosius Probus to present terms that were non-negotiable: 1) Persia was to hand over territory so that the Tigris was to be the border between the Empires; 2) Armenia was to be a Roman protectorate; 3) Iberia was to become a Roman protectorate and its king was to be nominated by Rome; 4) five Armenian satrapies were to be handed over to the Romans; and 5) Nisibis was to be the only place for commercial transactions (that is, it limited the possibilities of spies posing as traders and also secured customs duties). Narses had no alternative other than to agree, and both emperors were able to return in triumph to Syria.[245] The five Armenian satrapies became a separate Roman bulwark in the area. Their feudal lords were required to contribute their feudal contingents to the Roman army and defend the area.

In 297 Maximian had begun his campaign against the Bavares and Quinquegentiani (and probably also against the Baquates) in their mountain strongholds. Unlike the local Roman generals, Maximian was ready to waste manpower on a campaign fought in the most difficult of conditions. He was a harsh warrior who had brought with him a sizable army. Consequently, regardless of the cost in sweat and losses, he defeated the Bavares and Quinquegentiani by the end of the year and was able to celebrate a triumph at Carthage on 10 March. It appears probable that Maximian re-established the old system of using *foederati* to control the borders and interior. The commanders of these forces, the *praepositi*, were simultaneously Roman officers and tribal chieftains with fortified headquarters *centenaria* (Liebeschuetz, 2007, 480). But the celebrations proved premature. The fact that the reinforcements (*Legio III Herculae*) sent by Diocletian were posted in Mauretania in 298 proves that it had not yet been fully pacified, on top of which there was also the even more difficult problem of the Austuriani to solve. This is clear from the referral to these events in Corippus' *Iohannis* (7.530ff.). He states that Maximian had marched across the 'entire Punic state' victoriously in a bitterly fought war before facing the Austuriani/Laguatan Confederacy in Tripolitania and Libya in 298–299.

Contrary to the older view proposed, modern historians do not think that Maximian would have abandoned Tingitana or Mauretania either in part or in their entirety when he campaigned in the area. There is plenty of evidence in the form of inscriptions and archaeological finds to suggest that this was not the case. There may have been some adjustments made in the defensive structures (for example, some territory granted to *foederati* to defend), but no real abandonment of territory: the Notitia Dignitatum still places units deep inside the desert.[246]

The references to Maximian's campaigns in Corippus' *Iohannis* (1.480–483, 5.178–180, 7.530–533) make it abundantly clear that the war was not the great success subsequently claimed by Maximian. According to the different versions preserved by Corippus, Maximian had had a taste of how mighty the Laguatans (i.e. the Austuriani) were as warriors; the Laguatans had defeated the Romans and Maximian could not defeat them; and Maximian was not able to engage the Laguatans in battle. All of this suggests that Maximian had either felt unable to face the considerable enemy army even with the large numbers of men at his disposal, or that the Laguatans had simply retreated into the desert and had then inflicted a defeat on Maximian through the use of guerrilla warfare. The latter alternative appears to be the likeliest, because that would have still enabled Maximian to claim a victory as he did. After all, the enemy had refused to fight him in the open and had chosen to flee! It was obviously a distortion of the truth. It was the emperor who chose to stop the fighting before his own position could become untenable. Had his troops continued to suffer similar numbers of casualties in the years to come as they did in 297 and 298, and with no end in sight, they would have overthrown their leader.

In short, regardless of his difficulties, Maximian still managed to regain at least nominal control of the whole of North Africa (from Tingitana to Libya) from the hands of the Berber Confederacies, even if it had cost him plenty of men and money. He was an able tactician despite his other failings. However, Corippus makes it quite clear that at least the latter war against the Austuriani was ended through negotiations rather than fighting. This means that it was Maximian's show of force that restored the old network of treaties in the area, according to which the Romans paid money to the Berber Federates for the upkeep of the peace. Consequently, despite the fact that Maximian had failed to achieve actual military victory and had been forced to ask for reinforcements from Diocletian, it is still fair to say that Maximian's African campaign had been a great success. He had managed to restore the status quo through a combination of force and negotiations as a result of which the multiple enemies facing the Romans in Africa and Egypt had not been able to join forces.

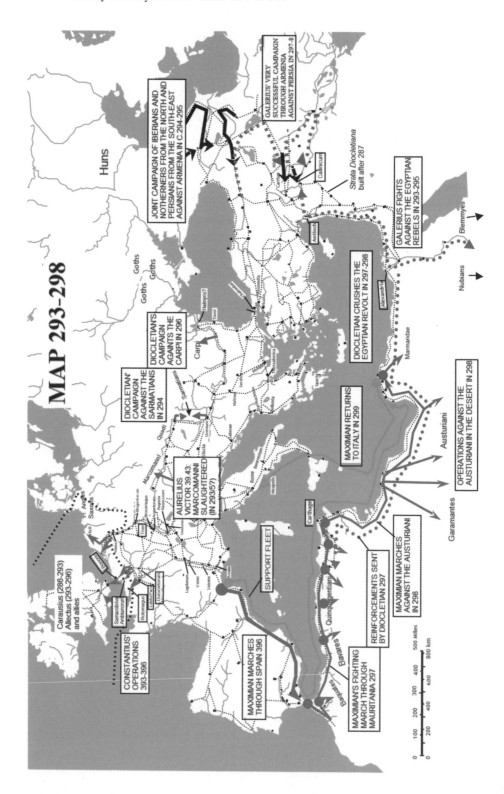

MAP 293–298

HUNS

GALERIUS' VERY SUCCESSFUL CAMPAIGN THROUGH ARMENIA AGAINST PERSIA IN 297-8

JOINT CAMPAIGN OF IBERIANS AND NOTHERNERS FROM THE NORTH AND PERSIANS FROM THE SOUTH-EAST AGAINST ARMENIA IN C.294-295

GALERIUS FIGHTS AGAINST THE EGYPTIAN REBELS IN 293-295

Strata Diocletiana built after 287

DIOCLETIAN CRUSHES THE EGYPTIAN REVOLT IN 297-298

DIOCLETIAN'S CAMPAIGN AGAINTS THE CARPI IN 296

DIOCLETIAN' CAMPAIGN AGAINST THE SARMATIANS IN 294

AURELIUS VICTOR 39.43: MARCOMANNI SLAUGHTERED (IN 293/5?)

MAXIMIAN RETURNS TO ITALY IN 299

SUPPORT FLEET

OPERATIONS AGAINST THE AUSTURIANI IN THE DESERT IN 298

Austuriani

Garamantes

MAXIMIAN MARCHES AGAINST THE AUSTURIANI IN 298

REINFORCEMENTS SENT BY DIOCLETIAN 297

MAXIMIAN'S FIGHTING MARCH THROUGH MAURITANIA 297

MAXIMIAN MARCHES THROUGH SPAIN 396

CONSTANTIUS' OPERATIONS 393-396

Carausius (286-293) Allectus (293-296) and allies

Goths

Goths

Goths

Huns

Blemmyes

Nubians

Quinquegentiani

Bavares

Bavares

Carthage

Rome

Naples

Quadi

Marcomanni

Sarmatians

Carpi

Marmaridae

Alexandria

Antioch

Callincum

Angli

Saxons

Frisii

Saxons

0   100 200 300 400 500 Miles
0 200 400 600 800 km

The Fruits of Victory: Persecutions 299–305

Maximian was able to return to Italy in 299 where he celebrated a triumph in Rome. It is not known when the provinces of northern Africa were reformed according to Diocletian's scheme, but his new administrative organization was definitely in place by the time the Verona List was written in about 303. It is therefore probable that the reorganization of the provinces of Africa took place at the same time as Maximian was there. After this Maximian's vices took over and he spent his remaining years in power in idleness. During this time he managed to alienate the Italian upper classes by terrorizing the Senate. He concocted false charges and sentenced the leading senators to death, confiscated their property, and in the process of doing that he raped whomsoever caught his lusty eyes. In contrast to Diocletian, whose money coffers were always full, Maximian's fiscal policies continued to be a mess. According to the period sources, he spent more than he earned with the result that he had to resort constantly to extraordinary means to obtain money, which meant stealing from the rich. We have no reasons to suspect that this was not the case. The sources are unanimous regarding Maximian's personality traits. He was unsuited to be ruler of anything and on top of it all he was not really a good commander because a good general also needed other qualities besides tactical acumen. The raping of hostages that secured peace was something that not even the harsh warriors of Illyria accepted. The hostages were sacrosanct and it was fortunate that Maximian left Africa immediately after he had pacified it and did not linger in the area.

In the meanwhile Constantius had continued his good rule. We have no reasons to suspect this despite the fact that the extant sources would have had every reason to flatter Constantius and his descendants. The sources are quite unanimous regardless of whether these were written by pagans or Christians. Constantius maintained good relations with the leading classes and thereby secured their support for his continued rule. According to Eutropius (10.1), Constantius used to say that private individuals were better guardians of the state's money than a single imperial vault. One of Constantius' underlying goals must have been to stress the contrast between his rule and that of Maximian. Constantius' previous successes enabled him to consolidate his position during the years 297–299, which he seems to have spent well. His next order of things was to take the offensive against the Franks either in 300 or 301, after which he fought off three enemy invasions of the Upper Rhine region between 302 and 304. The Picts definitely raided Britain in 305, but may already have done so in 304 or even before, which also eventually brought a response from Constantius.

According to Eutropius (9.23), at one point in time, which Barnes (1982, 61) dates to the year 302, Constantius was near the city of Lingones (Andematunnum/Langres) when he came across the Alamanni, and was forced to flee into the city but had difficulty in getting inside because the gates were shut and he had to be lifted onto the wall by ropes. After this, Constantius' army advanced against the Alamanni and killed almost 60,000 enemies within 5 hours. It is clear that the Alamanni had invaded deep into Roman territory and that Constantius had been forced to march either from Durocortum or Trier to Lingones, but there are two probable explanations for the rest of the story. Firstly, it is possible that Constantius had stationed his army inside the city of Lingones and had advanced from there to reconnoitre in person. Secondly, it is possible that Constantius' army was still on the road and he had advanced past Lingones to reconnoitre the area south of it. In both cases the Roman army would have then attacked the Alamanni in front of the city walls. It is impossible to know which of the alternatives is the correct one.

The Panegyric (*Pan.Lat.* 6.6.3–4) states that after the victory in the territory of the Lingones, Constantius covered the fields of Vindonissa with enemy corpses, which means that Constantius managed to catch the invading Alamanni after they had crossed the Rhine with their backs against the River. (See the Map.) Barnes (1982, 61) dates this campaign to the year 303. According to the same source 'a huge multitude of Germans from every nation'[247] exploited the freezing of the Rhine and crossed to an island on foot between its different branches, but were then cut off when the weather suddenly warmed up with the result that Constantius was able to send boats (*lusoriae ?*) to besiege them. The barbarians were allowed to go in return for handing over captives drawn by common lot for service in the Roman army. Barnes (1982, 61) dates this event to late-winter 304.

The great victory over the Persians had made Galerius feel himself all puffed up and one of its first fruits was to be the beginning of the first persecution of Christians since the dark days of Decius and Valerian. Despite being an uneducated bore, Galerius was still wily enough to know that he had achieved a great victory over the Persians and that the army loved him for that – and he knew how to use that to his own advantage. Just like the other Illyrian emperors he was more Roman than the Romans themselves, but unlike most of them he could not tolerate any deviants. He was the least willing of the emperors to compromise. For some unknown reason he felt a particularly intense hostility towards the Christians. He wanted to destroy them. I would suggest that the most likely reason for this particularly strong hate would be that Galerius' victory over the Persians had resulted from the help provided by the Christian Trdat who had then had the audacity of claiming Divine Help from the Christian God. It is similarly quite probable that Constantine, who had accompanied Galerius on this campaign, had also demonstrated his solidarity with Trdat and his beliefs. If this is the case, then it is possible to argue that one of the reasons for Galerius' hostility could be his effort to undermine Constantine's position as successor, as suggested by Barnes (1981, 25). Barnes also suggests that Maxentius may also have been sympathetic towards Christianity and that Galerius also sought to undermine his position. Another possibility is that Diocletian, who was also hostile towards the Christians, was just using his old trick of making someone else bear the blame for the persecution, but in this case at least it seems likelier that the originator of the first persecution was indeed Galerius and Diocletian just played along to keep him happy. Until now Diocletian had been quite tolerant towards Christians. He could even see a church from his palace in Nicomedia, and it seems probable that his wife Prisca and daughter Valeria were also sympathetic towards them (Lact. 15.1).

Whatever the reason, Galerius and his accomplices made their first move immediately after Diocletian and Galerius reached Syria in 299. When both emperors were performing pagan sacrifice and divination, some members of their households who were Christians made the sign of the cross to ward off demons. It is in fact possible that these included members of the Imperial *Comitatus* , because there were Christians even among them.[248] After this the *haruspices* could not find the normal marks on the entrails and their *magister* Tagis accused the Christians of interfering with the sacrifices. As a result, the emperors ordered all the members of the imperial court to make sacrifices to the gods. It is clear that the *haruspices* had been instructed to do what they did. Whether it had been Galerius alone or both who had instructed them to do that is not known with certainty. It depends on whose *haruspices* were performing the sacrifice.

Both emperors then sent letters to all the military commanders in which all soldiers were instructed to perform sacrifice or resign. This if anything seems to connect the hostility of Galerius towards the Christians with the war he had just fought, even if Lactantius (11.1–2) claims that Galerius had got his hatred of Christians from his mother's milk. In Galerius' eyes his army had undoubtedly included a dangerous number of Christians who had rather joined Trdat's Christian ceremonies than taken part in the public pagan sacrifices performed in Galerius' presence. It is clear that the traditionalist Diocletian would not have accepted this sort of behaviour either and readily issued the order for his soldiers to perform the sacrifice. He wanted to follow the ancient practices to the letter.

After this Galerius and Diocletian changed places. The Caesar had the responsibility over the Danube frontier while the Augustus ruled the entire East. Galerius made Thessalonica his place of residence and built a propagandistic triumphal arch in which he celebrated his victory over the Persians. However, Galerius was a man of action who did not rest on his laurels. In late 299 or 300 Galerius conducted a successful campaign against the Marcomanni, and then probably in late 301 he fought a campaign against the Carpi. Next year, in 302, Galerius fought successfully against both the Carpi and Sarmatians.

Diocletian seems to have completed his reorganization of the defences of the eastern frontier in 300. Five new legions are attested for the year 300 (Arguin 145–6): 1) *Legio IIII (IV) Parthica* stationed at Besaira in Oshroene; 2) *Legio V Parthica* stationed at Amida; 3) *Legio VI Parthica* stationed at Cefae in Mesopotamia; 4) *Legio I Armeniaca* stationed at Claudiopolis in Cappadocia; and 5) *Legio II Armeniaca* formed in Armenia for the defence of the north-east sector of the Persian frontier. It is quite probable that these legions were actually created for the Persian war in c.295–7 and that the existence of these legions just comes visible in the record (inscriptions) for the first time when they are garrisoned after the conclusion of the peace. What is certain, however, is that Diocletian strengthened the defences of the eastern frontier significantly as regards the number of men, the quality and number of the fortifications, and the mileage of roads.

In addition, according to Arguin (145–6), three other legions were created by Diocletian (that is, are attested for the first time) in 300. These are: 1) *Legio IIII (IV) Iovia* stationed in Pannonia Inferior; 2) *Legio I Noricum* recruited for service in Noricum with a base at Favianis (Mautern, Austria); and 3) *Legio I Martia* stationed in Castrum Rauracensis in Germania Superior (Kaiseraugst). It seems probable that these legions had also been formed prior to the date when first attested and it seems quite likely that at least the last two were recruited by Constantius and Maximian. The same policy of increasing the numbers of soldiers and fortifications can be attested to have happened throughout the Empire.

By 301 Diocletian's monetary reforms had led to the situation in which rampant inflation had made it impossible for the government and soldiers to obtain even the daily necessities. In a manner typical to him, Diocletian sought to resolve the situation by imperial Edict. He artificially doubled the value of silver and bronze coins on 1 September 301 and then in late-November or early-December 301 issued the Price Edict, with maximum prices that the government would pay for the goods, work and services named. The problem with the last mentioned was that it was not circulated in the West for some reason, with the result that all products disappeared from the marketplace in the East despite the shedding of blood by Diocletian's officials. The sellers would not come to sell their wares or foodstuff when they would receive less money that it had cost to produce them. Furthermore, it was easy enough to transport the goods to the West. Diocletian had no other alternative than to back down. In his old age Diocletian, the autocrat, seems to have expected to be able to solve all problems just by the issuing of Edicts and this proved to be an absurd idea when others failed to implement them. The timing of the Edicts in the winter undoubtedly played its role also in the lack of cooperation by the Western rulers. The Edicts were already overturned by the time these could have been implemented in the West.

Diocletian visited Egypt in the winter of 301/2, probably to make certain that his army would obtain the supplies and services at the prices decided by him. The other alternative is that he issued the Price Edict to cover the costs of providing free food for Alexandrians. However, since we have no evidence for the latter it is safest to assume that the Edict was meant to serve the needs of the army. The edict would then have caused a shortage of foodstuffs and another bout of urban unrest in Alexandria, which Diocletian then tried to calm down by granting to the Alexandrians the right to the delivery of free bread. What is almost certain is that Diocletian's Edict had caused the famine in question.

While Diocletian was still in Alexandria he also issued a re-script to the proconsul on 31 March 302 in which he ordered the Manichean leaders to be burned alive, together with their scriptures. This ruling is not surprising because Manicheans could be considered to have been fifth columnists working for the Persians – this in fact appears to have been their intended purpose in the eyes of Shapur I, who had supported their proselytizing especially in the Roman territories. The publication of this Edict makes sense only if the Romans at the time were threatened by the Persians, and this seems to have been the case. At about the same time, in 301/2, Narses the ruler of Persia died and was succeeded by his son Hormizd. It is probable that the Persians activated their Saracen allies to raid Roman territory after this, because Malalas (12.48) claims that it was during 'Constantius Chlorus' reign' that Licinius was sent with a large army against the Persians and Saracens because they had disturbed the peace as far as Egypt. It is not safe to draw too many conclusions on the basis of Malalas' text because he has confused too many things in the same context, but it is still plausible that the change of ruler in Persia had made the previous treaty void with the result that the new ruler fought by proxy by reactivating the allied Arabs. This could also have caused Diocletian's presence in Egypt together with the abovementioned Edict.

I would also connect the embassy of the Himyarite king to the Sasanian court that took place in about 300 with these events.[249] The likeliest reason for such an embassy would have been an attempt by the Himyarites to conclude an alliance with the Persians against the Aksumites. Diocletian's war in the south of Egypt and the conclusion of the treaties with the Blemmyes and Nubians would have weakened the Aksumite Empire and provided a suitable opportunity for the Himyarites to overthrow the Aksumite grip on Yemen. If this line of reasoning is correct, it is quite possible that Diocletian had come to Alexandria in 301/2 to negotiate with the Aksumites who had expressed their readiness to conclude a treaty with the Romans now that the Blemmyes had a treaty with the Romans and the Himyarites had concluded a treaty with Persia. Unfortunately, there is no definite evidence for this and as far as we know the Aksumites remained hostile towards the Romans until about 328. Regardless, the Persian-Himyarite alliance had at least one certain consequence: when the Persian client kingdoms, the Lakhmids and Himyarites, subsequently collided in Central Arabia this resulted in the desertion of the former to the Roman side. (See later.)

In the autumn of 302 Diocletian was back in Antioch and, just when he was performing the normal preliminary sacrifice before official business, the Christian Deacon Romanus from Caesarea burst into the court and committed an inexplicable provocation by interrupting the imperial ceremony and denouncing it in a loud voice.[250] Unsurprisingly, he was seized and Diocletian ordered his tongue cut out. Romanus was also imprisoned and then executed next year. Galerius was not the only fanatic around. Romanus had clearly done his best to make the Christians hated. The autocratic Diocletian was duly incensed and provoked. Diocletian proceeded to Nicomedia where he assembled a council consisting of his counsellors, which included Galerius, in the winter of 302/3. There was only one issue on the table: what to do with the Christians. Galerius urged persecution and so did most of the counsellors. When Diocletian still 'hesitated' Galerius supposedly advised that the oracle of Apollo at Didyma should be consulted. Unsurprisingly, the rulers got what they desired and the persecution began.

It had been the audacity of Romanus that had pushed Diocletian over the edge, but regardless Diocletian was still astute enough to involve his advisors in the decision so that they would share the guilt. It is not at all surprising that the counsellors advised Diocletian as he wished in light of the fact that it included such persons as Hierocles, who had written a treatise against Christianity. The oracle simply sanctioned their wishes. Diocletian acted just like another Pontius Pilatus and washed his hands. What Constantine did at the time we are not told. All of this is confirmed by Lactantius (11.5) who clearly states that whenever Diocletian was intent on committing some outrageous decision, like in this case the persecution of Christians, he always sought to involve his councillors in the same decisions and use them as his scapegoats, and whenever he had decided to do something good, he did not consult anyone but took the entire credit of the decision for himself.

It was decided that the festival of the *Terminalia* on 23 February 303 would mark the day of the termination of Christianity. The first act of the persecution was an attack against the Christian Church in Nicomedia at dawn led by the *Praefectus Praetorio*, *duces* (clearly generals of the *Comitatus* and possibly also Counts of the *Domestici Protectores*), *tribuni* (commanders of the bodyguard units) and *rationales* (financial officials in this case taking care of the needs of the Guards and in charge of the confiscation of property). Of note is the fact that the group of military forces assigned for the destruction was led by the Praetorian Prefect and below him served the generals (*duces*) of the *Comitatus*. The fact that the force included *duces* proves that it included members of other units (for example of the *Comitatus*) besides the Praetorians, despite Lactantius' statement (12) that the Praetorians levelled the church with axes and iron tools. The Latin authors and official texts continue in an archaic manner to call the imperial bodyguards 'Praetorians', even after their official abolishment by Constantine – as a further example, Stilicho could still be called officially *tribunus praetorianus militis* as late as 383.

This account, as well as Constantius' previous role as PP of Maximian and Asclepiodotus' role as Constantius' PP, proves that the PPs were the highest ranking military commanders right after the emperor during Diocletian's reign and could be given charge of the bodyguards, *Comitatus* and frontier armies. Diocletian also seems to have had several PPs serving under him in the old manner so that only one of those was the man in charge of the military operations while the other took care of legal matters (that is, Dioceses and Provinces). According to the PLRE1, Verconnianus Herennianus 6 (284/305) and some others served as PPs simultaneously under Diocletian. These included at least Asclepiades 2 (PP at Antioch) in 303 and Flaccinus (PP East) in c.303 and other anonymous persons, as a result of which there may even have been three PPs with different duties serving simultaneously under Diocletian himself. In addition, Afranius Hannibalianus 3 (286/92) may also have served under Diocletian, but there are also strong reasons listed in the PLRE1 to assume that he may have served under Maximian.

The church at Nicomedia was destroyed and the Edict against Christianity was publicized on the following day. Christian worship was made illegal; churches, books and scriptures were to be destroyed; cult objects were to be confiscated; Christians who refused to disavow Christianity were to be expelled from office; and Christians were made outlaws without any rights. This was not to be the last of the edicts of persecution. Diocletian issued a series of edicts against the Christians in the coming months. However, before this a strange incident occurred. Earlier, in February, the imperial palace in Nicomedia had burned to the ground and both the pagans and Christians had accused each other. Constantine later claimed that it had been lightning and fire from heaven, and Lactantius accused Galerius and his staff. Galerius in his turn accused the Christians and eunuchs, and investigations began. Unsurprisingly, the emperors took personal interest and several members of the imperial household were tortured, killed and roasted alive. This was not the end of the fires, however. A second fire occurred fifteen days after the first and Galerius fled from the city (c.14 March 303[251]) and soon after Diocletian followed his example, but not before intensifying the purge to a full-scale pogrom. It was then that Diocletian forced his wife and daughter to make sacrifices to the gods. After this Diocletian decided to celebrate his *vicennalia* and Persian victory in Rome.

It is impossible to determine with certainty whether the Christians of the court had attempted to kill the persecutors, or whether Galerius had committed arson to urge Diocletian on, or whether the whole thing had just been caused by lightning. However, in light of the subsequent execution of several members of the court, the first option actually appears to be the likeliest despite the denials of Christian sources. Romanus' outrageous provocation against Diocletian stands as the best piece of evidence for the audacity and stupidity of the fanatic Christians at the time.

The extent of the resulting persecution depended upon the personal initiative of the emperors and governors, and in all cases required the active participation of military forces. The pro-Christian Constantius demolished only the churches, but didn't allow actual persecution of the followers of Christ. Maximian, however, launched a real persecution, but his proconsul of Africa and governor of Numidia went even further and required all Christians to perform sacrifice, which naturally caused plenty of martyrs as well as apostates, the latter of which were to be the cause of many troubles in the area. The fanatic Christians would later prove unwilling to accept the apostates back into the bosom of the Church with predictable results. The Edict was also forcefully put into effect in the East with the result that there were riots in Melitene and Syria. The Christians were becoming militants. This in turn caused the publication of a new Edict, which ordered all clergy – the 'provocateurs' – arrested, and this in turn caused the prisons to overflow and on 20 November Diocletian ordered all released on condition that they sacrificed to gods. In practice most of the clergy were thrown out of the prisons with one excuse or another to make room for the real criminals.

In early 304 the Fourth Edict was issued that required all city-dwellers to perform collective sacrifices to the gods, but Constantius and Maximian did not put this one into effect. Considering the subsequent revoking of the Edicts of Persecution by Constantine, Maxentius and even by Galerius on his deathbed, it seems very probable that this persecution did not meet with the general approval of the populace. We shouldn't forget that many of the pagans also had Christian friends and relatives, and they cannot have been indifferent to Christian suffering. They simply did nothing because their own lives were also at stake. In essence the persecution of Christians was a waste of valuable military resources that only created discord among the populace.

After having left Nicomedia in March 303, Galerius proceeded to fight still another successful but inconclusive campaign against the Carpi in the autumn of that year. We do not know what Diocletian did at the time, but he is attested to have visited Durostorum on 8 June and then Sirmium in the summer/autumn of 303.[252] This probably means that he also campaigned in the area, as suggested by Eutropius' account (9.25), which claims that Diocletian and Galerius campaigned together and separately against the Carpi, Bastarnae and Sarmatians after the Persian war. The locations of Diocletian's stay suggest that he may have fought against the Carpi and Bastarnae with Galerius and then moved against the Sarmatians while Galerius continued to fight against the Carpi and Bastarnae. It is possible that at this time Diocletian and Galerius built the so-called Devil's Dyke and Giant's Furrow (massive earth ditches) in the Balkans to serve as the borders of the Roman 'outer *limes*', but it is still likelier that this took place during the reign of Constantine. (See later.)

In about 303(?) there was a strange usurpation by one Eugenius, who commanded a 500-man strong 'taxiarchy of hoplites' put on harbour work at Seleucia. According to Libanius, the same men were also required to do night fatigues and could therefore get no sleep. This naturally angered the men and they forced their commander Eugenius to assume the purple or be killed. He agreed reluctantly to save his life. While Eugenius was trying to find a way to save his own skin, his men gathered all the wine from the surrounding farms and started drinking. Then, the men marched to Antioch in a drunken state. Once inside they faced the citizens, that included even women who had armed themselves with poles and crowbars. The civilians killed easily the drunken throng of men. This resistance appears to have been organized by the city council, but when Diocletian learnt of the usurpation, he executed arbitrarily the highest ranking and innocent members of both city councils (Seleuceia and Antioch), and the victims also included Libanius' grandfather.[253] Perhaps what really angered Diocletian enough to do this was not the usurpation, but the independence shown by the councils.

Diocletian and Maximian celebrated their *vicennalia*, together with the *decennalia* of their Caesars and Galerius' triumph against the Persians, in Rome in late-November 303. In his old age Diocletian had become a grumpy old autocrat who could not stomach being considered as one of the citizens, as was expected in Rome. Consequently, he had left Rome in the winter before his ninth consulate and assumed the consulate in Ravenna on 1 January 304. Thanks to the nasty winter conditions Diocletian contracted an unknown illness, but still continued his inspection of the Danube frontier during the spring and early summer. He and Galerius may have also fought a joint campaign together against the Carpi.[254] Despite all his failings Diocletian was a conscientious ruler who put his own health at risk to perform his duties, but he was no longer a young man. Unsurprisingly the illness became worse because Diocletian refused to rest. He was forced to use a litter. Diocletian reached Nicomedia by 28 August, and on 20 November he collapsed in public view. On 13 December it was rumoured that he had died, and it was believed that he had died until he made his next public appearance on 1 March 305, but he was visibly too weak to rule.

Galerius met Maximian first at some unknown location and convinced him of the necessity of forcing Diocletian to resign after which he came to meet Diocletian at Nicomedia in March. Galerius wanted Diocletian and Maximian to resign and appoint new *Augusti* and *Caesars*. The most obvious candidates as new Caesars would have been Constantine and Maxentius, who had been groomed as such, but Galerius managed to force his will on Diocletian, who was now physically and mentally too weak to resist his bulky and strong Caesar. Galerius put forward as candidates his own men, Severus, who was a hard-drinking soldier and close friend of Galerius, and Maximinus, Galerius' own nephew, who was also suitably born on the same day as Diocletian had become emperor. These two men were now appointed as *Caesars* on 1 May 305 while Constantius and Galerius became *Augusti*. This proved to be a great mistake and the undoing of Diocletian's heritage. Maximinus' career from *scutarius* (probably in the *scholae*), to *protector* (*schola* of protectors), to *tribunus* (commander of one of the bodyguard units), to Caesar is indicative of the organization of the imperial bodyguards under Galerius.

At the same time Diocletian convinced his old friend Maximian to resign with him, but this was only a formality because Galerius had already sent his trusted lieutenant Severus to be beside Maximian, undoubtedly with instructions to kill Maximian if he refused to comply. Galerius had effectively organized a coup. Diocletian retired to his homeland where he lived at his palace in Spalato, while Maximian retired to Lucania. The retirees became honorary members of the college of rulers as senior *Augusti* and fathers of the new *Augusti*. Diocletian knew all too well that Maximian could not be left in office after he had resigned. He was just too mad. Despite being *Herculius* Constantius was considered to be the senior *Augustus*. The empire was also divided. As Augustus, Constantius received Spain in addition to his former domains; Galerius held the Balkans and Asia Minor; Severus received Italy and Africa and possibly also part of Pannonia; Maximinus got the Diocese of Oriens.

On paper Galerius' position was now very strong. He and his appointees ruled most of the empire, he could entertain the hope that the frail Constantius would soon die,

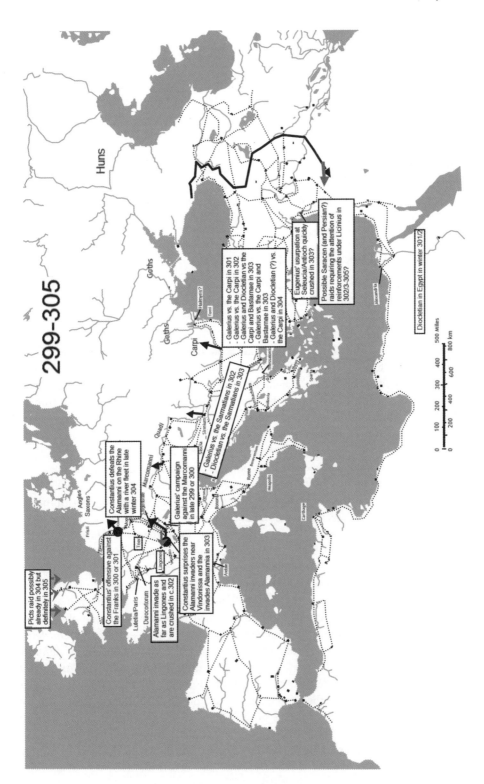

299-305

Huns

Goths

Goths

Carpi

Angles
Saxons

Frisii

Picts raid possibly
already in 304 but
definitely in 305

Constantius' offensive against
the Franks in 300 or 301

Lutetia/Paris

Duocortorum

Alamanni invade as
far as Lingones and
are crushed in c.302

Constantius surprises the
Alamanni invaders near
Vindonissa and the
invades Alamannia in 303

Constantius defeats the
Alamanni on the Rhine
with a river fleet in late
winter 304

Galerius' campaign
against the Marcomanni
in late 299 or 300

Marcomanni

Quadi

- Galerius vs. the Sarmatians in 302
- Diocletian vs. the Sarmatians in 303

- Galerius vs. the Carpi in 301
- Galerius vs. the Carpi in 302
- Galerius and Diocletian vs. the
  Carpi and Bastarnae in 303
- Galerius vs. the Carpi and
  Bastarnae in 303
- Galerius and Diocletian vs.
  the Carpi in 304

Eugenius' usurpation at
Seleucia/Antioch quickly
crushed in 303?

Possible Saracen (and Persian?)
raids requiring the attention of
reinforcements under Licinius in
302/3-305?

Diocletian in Egypt in winter 301/2

Rome

Neapolis

Carthage

0   100   200   300   400   500 Miles

0   200   400   600   800 km

and he still held Constantine as a hostage. Constantine understood that he had to leave court at the first opportunity he got – and he did. When Constantius had for the third time asked Galerius to send Constantine back to him, Galerius complied but stated that Constantine should begin his journey back next day. Constantine realized that he had to use his opportunity immediately, because he guessed, correctly in my opinion, that Galerius would prevent it on the following day by using some excuse. Consequently, Constantine fled and hamstrung the horses of the public post. This had two purposes: it prevented pursuit by Galerius' men; and it prevented the sending of a message to Severus to block the route of his flight. Constantine reached his father when he was in Bononia, about to cross the Channel to fight against the Picts. In the meanwhile, the other heir apparent, Maxentius, decided to take up residence in a villa just outside Rome. All the pieces of the game of 'Last Man Standing' were now in place.

Assessment of Diocletian's Reign

Diocletian's twenty-one years at the helm had been a great success. Diocletian had been a conscientious ruler who had sought to rule justly. Diocletian had secured the Roman frontiers. He had accomplished this by increasing the size of the army and navy; by fortifying the borders; by creating the Tetrarchy that had put a stop to the endemic civil wars; by improving the administration and legal system; and by creating an effective system of tax collection to support the vastly-increased state apparatus. Diocletian was truly a new Augustus or Aeneas. The borders of the Empire were now so secure that it could withstand years of civil war of the kind that had led to the collapse of the frontiers in the 260s. In addition, the navy that Diocletian had rebuilt after years of neglect secured for the Romans control or even mastery of the seas bordering the Empire for over 100 years. It was thanks to Diocletian that Rome ruled the waves.

Unfortunately, Diocletian had also made a series of mistakes during his last years at the helm. The persecution of Christians had created a situation in which the religion could be (and was) used as a weapon against the other rulers. The last and the most important of Diocletian's mistakes was the abandonment of the intended order of succession in 305, which was to undo his heritage. This was not entirely Diocletian's own fault. At the time he had just been too ill to oppose his physically strong and ruthless Caesar Galerius.

The associated map gives the known dispositions of the Roman legions at the time Diocletian resigned his office in 305. According to Bohec's calculation, there were at least 51 legions in existence at the time of Diocletian's death, which means that the following list should be seen as only indicative of the likely locations of most of the known legions. Other estimates range from 50 legions (17 new legions created by Diocletian) to 69/70 legions (36/7 legions created by Diocletian).[255] It should be kept in mind that the legionary dispositions do give a slightly misleading picture as in truth the legions did post detachments outside their main garrison. Further, the *duces* took detachments from those legions to act as their mobile reserves, and similarly the emperors also took detachments from the legions to serve in their field armies. In addition, there were also imperial reserve armies and bodyguards as well as auxiliary troops and barbarian *foederati* and *laeti* both inside and outside the borders that are not shown on the map. In addition, when needed civilians like the youths (*iuventes*) and urban dwellers were able to form

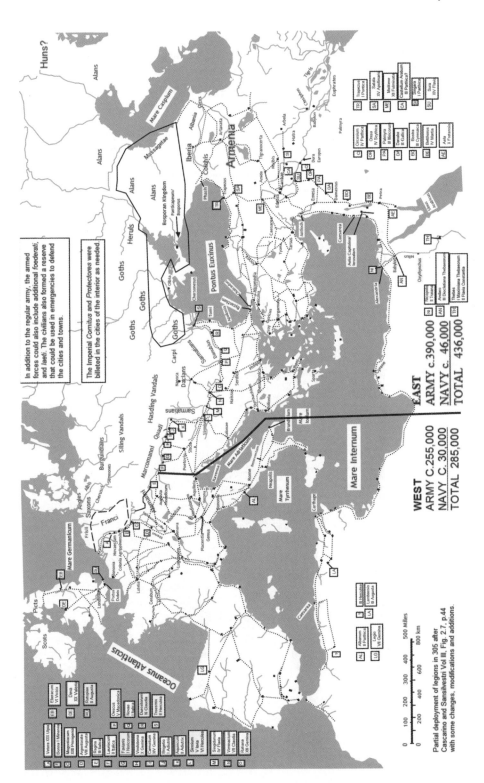

In addition to the regular army, the armed forces could also include additional *foederati*, and *laeti*. The civilians also formed a reserve that could be used in emergencies to defend the cities and towns.

The Imperial *Comitus* and *Protectores* were billeted in the cities of the interior as needed.

EAST
ARMY c.390,000
NAVY c. 46,000
TOTAL 436,000

WEST
ARMY C.255,000
NAVY C. 30,000
TOTAL 285,000

Partial deployment of legions in 305 after Cascarino and Sansivestri Vol III, Fig. 2.7, p.44 with some changes, modifications and additions.

paramilitary groups that could even defeat foreign invaders and Roman elite forces. Regardless, the positioning of the legions shown on the map still gives a good overall view of Roman strategic priorities. Most of the forces were posted to guard either the Danube or the eastern frontier where the greatest threats were, but this situation was not to last.

A soldier of the *legio palatina Ioviani seniores*. The shield and shield emblem have been taken from the ND. The helmet is a segmented helmet known as Spangenhelm/Der el-Medineh. He wears the scale armour similar to that shown in Galerius' Arch at Thessalonica, and is armed with a *spatha* sword and *hasta* spear.

© Dr. Ilkka Syvanne 2012

Chapter Five

The Age of Constantine the Great[256]

Tetrarchy 2, in 305–306:
Augusti: Constantius the Prude; Galerius the Beast
Caesars: Severus the Drunkard; Maximinus the Ogre

As noted above Constantine reached his father in Bononia just when he was about to cross the English Channel to fight against the Picts. After the reunion of father and son, they crossed the Channel and defeated the Picts somewhere north of Hadrian's Wall. One of the purposes of the presence of Constantius' heir apparent was to form a strong bond between Constantine and the senior officers and the soldiers. Constantius knew that he had not long to live and he needed to secure the throne for his eldest son. Constantius died at York on 25 July 306. All of Constantius' children were by his bedside at the time of the death, but it was Constantine who was destined to be his successor. The orderly succession of emperors was about to stop.

The Heirs to the Throne Claim Their Inheritance 306–311

Constantine Proclaimed by the Army

Immediately after the death of Constantius, with Crocus, the King of the Alamanni in Roman service taking the lead, the imperial entourage and army proclaimed Constantine as Augustus on the spot. The legitimate sons of Constantius were bypassed in favour of the more experienced Constantine. According to Zosimus 2.9.1, the soldiers responsible for the proclamation of Constantine were the soldiers of the court. When one combines this information with the role of the Alamannic king and presence of the Alamanni units in the army, this suggests the probability that Constantius I had appointed Crocus as his *Comes Domesticorum* (or something similar) in the same manner as Mallobaudes would later be simultaneously a King of the Franks and *Comes Domesticorum* for Gratian. This also suggests that Constantius had already increased the importance of the Germanic element in his army and his son Constantine merely followed the example set by him.

Constantine was now de facto ruler of Britain, Gaul, and Spain, but he still needed to secure his position because he had essentially usurped power without the prior approval of Galerius. It is not surprising that the officers and soldiers were willing to proclaim their own Augustus, because they knew that by doing so they would gain better prospects of future advancement. Furthermore, all the men also knew that Constantine had been groomed as a successor and had a distinguished military career behind him.

Constantine knew that it was important for him to gain the support of the soldiers through successful military campaigns and the support of the magnates and populace through enlightened religious and taxation policies. He also knew that it was important to gain official recognition for his new position from Galerius and the other emperors. Consequently, Constantine's first actions as emperor were the ending of the persecution of the Christians, the sending of an embassy to Galerius in which he informed him of his accession and asked for his confirmation, and the crossing of the Channel to Gaul to fight against the Franks who had invaded.

The Franks had exploited the absence of the Roman field army. As noted by Barnes, with the ending of the persecution of Christians Constantine had claimed for himself the right to legislate his own laws without any consultation with the other emperors. Constantine, in fact, went so far as to return to the Christians the property they had lost, which does suggest that both Gaul and Spain must have had a sizable and influential population of Christians.

Constantine's reaction to the Frankish invasion was swift. He needed to prove himself both as a commander and protector of Gaul. Consequently, Constantine transferred his army immediately across the Channel in 306 and crushed the Franks in pitched battle. Constantine ordered the two captured chieftains, Ascariscus and Merogaisus, and the other captives to be fed to the beasts in the amphitheatre at Treves. He wanted to instil a healthy fear of Roman arms in Rome's enemies, and according to one Panegyric this worked at least for a while. For the ensuing years the barbarians stayed on their own side of the Rhine, even when the Rhine dried up in the summer or froze in the winter. As I noted in my article, courageous, swift, bold and decisive military action were to become the trademarks of Constantine's military operations. On the basis of this it seems probable that Constantine was temperamentally inclined to act fast and attack furiously whenever there was a need for a military campaign. He had already demonstrated these traits as a young cavalry officer. Constantine's personal bravery, his solid understanding of strategy and tactics, his generosity towards soldiers, and his good looks, soon translated into universal admiration by the rank and file. The soldiers simply loved him. Constantine was also a very ambitious person who at every opportunity sought to enlarge his domains and power.

Galerius, however, was not happy. Fortunately for Constantine Galerius had in the meantime made a serious blunder. As senior Augustus Galerius had ordered a universal census to be conducted in all urban areas throughout the Empire, including the city of Rome. This move was very unpopular and caused unrest. The Romans and Italians south of the Apennines were angry because Galerius had now removed their exemption from provincial taxation. In these circumstances, Galerius decided to make a compromise. He was ready to accept Constantine only as Caesar while Severus was promoted as new Augustus, and in order to show that the real power rested with him he sent a purple robe to Constantine which indicated that he had received his rule from Galerius and not from Constantius. Constantine accepted the demotion. He knew that he needed to consolidate his position first.

Maxentius Usurps the Power

Maxentius was jealous of Constantine's recent promotion and decided to exploit the anger of the Roman and Italian magnates and populace over Galerius' tax policy. When Galerius' commissioners arrived to register the populace, Maxentius put his plan into effect. With the help of three tribunes of the Urban Cohorts, whose support Maxentius had gained, he killed the Vicarius who had been placed in command by the superior Urban Prefect. As a safety measure Galerius had removed most of the Praetorian Cohorts away from their home base, but some remained behind and these joined Maxentius and together with the others proclaimed Maxentius *Augustus* on 28 October 306. Now Maxentius, like Constantine before him, needed to secure his new position. Consequently, he called himself only *Princeps* instead of *Augustus* or *Caesar* and sent envoys to Galerius to ask for recognition. Similarly, soon after his elevation Maxentius proclaimed toleration of Christians, but unlike Constantine he did not yet return their property to them. He apparently also needed to placate the opinion of the pagan senators. Unlike Constantine and despite being Galerius' son-in-law, Maxentius failed to obtain Galerius' recognition. Galerius simply hated Maxentius too much.

Now Maxentius had no other alternative than to fight back while leaving the door open to a possible reconciliation. Consequently, he refused to accept Galerius' nomination of Severus as consul for the year 307 (he named Galerius instead) while still accepting Maximinus as a consul. In addition, he asked his father Maximian to don the purple again as Augustus. Maxentius needed both his support and advice. Maxentius' position was not strong. He did gain the support of Alexander, the Vicarius of Africa and former nominee of Maximian and therefore secured grain from Africa for Rome, but he did not possess an army or the money to raise one. Consequently, Maxentius was forced to resort to emergency measures. In order to gain the support of the Roman magnates, the senators, which he sorely needed because he also needed money, he made the position of the Senate stronger than it had been for over 100 years. He appointed a senator as *PP* (this office had been from the start prerogative of the equestrians) and he also appointed senators as commanders of the troops, the last of which had not happened since the reign of Gallienus. Regardless, he was never able to gain the full support of the senators because at the same time he was forced to tax both the Italians and Romans to allow him to strengthen his army and then pay for its upkeep. The need to obtain money also worsened Maxentius' relationship with the common populace.

Galerius was unable to intervene in person because the ongoing war against the Sarmatians demanded his attention. Therefore, he ordered Severus, who was at Milan, to depose the usurper. Severus started his march against the usurper even before the winter had ended and on paper he should have easily won the contest, but since his men had formerly served under Maximian most of them voluntarily changed sides when Maxentius offered bribes. The deserters included even Severus' Praetorian Prefect. Severus was forced to flee to Ravenna. Maximian besieged Severus and then offered terms with the result that Severus foolishly surrendered. Now Maxentius and Maximian had an army and a hostage, but this did not bring about reconciliation with Galerius with the result that Maxentius gave up all hope of settlement and Severus was either killed or forced to commit suicide. Galerius, however, was still unable to move against Maxentius because he was fighting against the Sarmatians.

At this point Maximian and Maxentius sought either alliance or neutrality from Constantine. Maximian offered the hand of his daughter Fausta in marriage to Constantine. Constantine's first wife Minervina, who bore him a son Crispus in about 305, had either died very recently or Constantine now divorced her to marry again.

Constantine, however, drew a hard bargain before agreeing to this. He demanded that Maximian would officially promote him to Augustus. Maximian eagerly grasped this opportunity, but got in return only neutrality from Constantine, because the latter wisely stayed aloof of the power struggles. Constantine was in no hurry to become embroiled in wars for the empire before he was ready. Instead, he sought to secure his own power base. This undoubtedly entailed the making of some changes to the administration and defensive systems. It is also likely that Constantine removed some persons from office and replaced them with his own appointees. Constantine visited Britain in 307 while the other emperors fought a civil war. It is probable that Constantine's visit so soon after the war against the Picts in 305–306 was caused by renewed hostilities and that the war had been left unfinished at the time when Constantius I had died. Thanks to Maximian's support Constantine felt free to assert his independence from Galerius. He proclaimed his own consuls in 307 with the result that Galerius also stopped considering him as a member of the collective imperial college. However, Constantine still maintained the pretence that nothing had happened.

Galerius was finally free to begin his invasion of Italy in late-August or September 307. Maxentius and Maximian did not attempt to face Galerius in battle, because they were fully aware of Galerius' reputation. He was known to be a superb tactician. On top of this, he fielded a sizable field army which was used to winning. Father and son decided to use the same strategy that had previously worked so well against Severus. In fact, Galerius played right into their hands. He had never visited Rome and he did not have any understanding of the magnitude of the opposition he faced. The size of the city of Rome and its walls took him by surprise. He did not possess enough men to put the city under proper siege. When his army reached Rome, Maxentius' agents immediately started to undermine Galerius' standing among his troops. Maxentius the High Priest also used pagan ceremonies to encourage the defenders. After having seen the size of the city Galerius decided to attempt a negotiated settlement and sent Licinius and Probus to offer Maxentius the throne in return for first making formal submission. Maxentius refused, probably because his position was strong and he did not trust the man.

Soon after this, several of Galerius' legions deserted and he was in danger of losing more. Galerius managed to maintain the loyalty of the rest only by humbling himself before them and by promising huge rewards. After this, Galerius led his army north in complete disarray. He was forced to reward his men by giving them permission to ravage and pillage Italy. This had the added benefit of making pursuit difficult. The great Galerius had been brought to his knees before Maxentius, as a result of which Maxentius' fame as a great sorcerer began to grow among the superstitious.

Constantine's Military Reforms and Early Campaigns

In the meanwhile, Constantine's decision to concentrate his attention on the defence of Gaul proved its worth. We should not forget that the soldiers and officers had their families and personal possessions located in Gaul. Most importantly, this policy also endeared him with the Gallic merchants who were his financial backers. Constantine's initial strategy was based on the concept of defence in depth created by Diocletian, and the alliances with the Alamanni. The latter gave Romans additional resources for use against the Franks. Constantine also continued the program of fortifying the cities, the repairing and building of border forts, and the project of providing patrol boats for the whole length of the Rhine. Constantine changed his strategy after he had secured the defences of the left bank of the Rhine. After this, Constantine adopted a more pro-active defence, which meant the building of forward bases on the opposite river bank, and the use of punitive raids and invasions to subject the neighbouring tribes to client status. As a reflection of this change of strategy Constantine launched a very successful surprise attack against the Bructeri in 308 with the result that they could not flee to the safety of the marshes and forests as they usually did. Constantine continued his terror campaign by feeding the prisoners to the beasts in the amphitheatre.

Constantine inherited from his father a well functioning military system. Constantine's Edict (CTh. 7.20.4) from 325 proves that at that time his armed forces consisted of: the mobile armies known as the *Comitatenses* (i.e. the former *Comitatus*); the frontier armies, the *Ripenses Milites* (the 'river soldiers', that is, the later *Limitanei*); and of the imperial bodyguard units known collectively as the *Protectores*. The last mentioned was used as a generic term for all bodyguards commanded by Count(s) of Domestics and not only as a referral to the *Protectores* proper. The best proofs of this are that the Counts of the Domestics were clearly in charge of the bodyguards protecting the emperors (for example, Magnentius for Constans, and Barbatio for Gallus), and the *Protectores* consisted of so many troops that they were able to protect the Euphrates frontier in 359 (Amm. 18.7.6). What is certain is that the *Protectores* as imperial bodyguards certainly included the *Protectores* and *Protectores Domestici* proper and the *Scholae* (note Lydus' *primoskoutarioi/protektores* and *Schola Scutariorum Prima*, etc.), but unfortunately we do not know for certain the names of the other units that must have already served in this capacity under Constantius I. One may make the educated guess that most of these must have consisted of units later placed at the top of the hierarchy of the palatine troops in the ND and may have also included the Moorish Horse Guards that were executed in 388. (Note especially the legions commanded by Magnentius.) In addition, even the *Protectores Domestici* included more men per *schola* (school/barracks) than was the case later because Julian (CTh 6.24.1) sacked all men above fifty, and forced the rest to return to their own peoples and lands. The fact that the *Protectores Domestici* included foreigners who were expelled does also suggest the possibility that the *Protectores* as bodyguards included some units later known as *Auxilia Palatina* (and/or as *arithmoi/numeri* based at Constantinople). (For further details, see the second book in the series, together with Syvanne (2011b).)

It is not known with certainty when Constantine reformed the military structure (a reform he is famous for), by withdrawing detachments from the *Ripenses* to form the more sizable version of the *Comitatus* known as the *Comitatenses*. This also entailed the separation of the cavalry units from their mother legions. Note, however, that there is a possibility that some of the units that had belonged to the *Comitatenses* of the Tetrarchs retained their cavalry contingents even after Constantine's reforms (see the next book in the series). The cavalry units of the *Comitatenses* were then put under the command of the *Magister Equitum* and the infantry units under the *Magister Peditum*.

The units would also become progressively smaller in the course of the century as new detachments were always drawn from the older units.

One possibility is that this system resulted from the collection of forces by Constantius for his British campaign and that Constantine made it permanent for two reasons: 1) he would have wanted to keep the sizable field army in existence in order to ensure that nobody could attempt to rise against him; and 2) the billeting of the troops in the interior was cheaper for the exchequer than the keeping of forces near the border. Considering Zosimus' claim that it was Constantine who withdrew forces from the frontier into the cities it is probable that he bolstered the size of this campaign army by attaching to it even more forces from the frontiers. The downside with the billeting was that it did not endear the ruler with the inhabitants of the cities, but it is possible that Constantine would have lessened the burden by extending exemptions to important persons (i.e. whose help he needed) and by lowering the other forms of taxes for the rest. It is unfortunate that we do not know the date and details of Constantine's reform, but is still probable that he would have made most of the reforms early on or at least would have experimented with those and then extended them to the rest of the empire as he conquered it.

There are also compelling reasons to believe that Constantine raised at least some of the so-called *Auxilia Palatina* units mentioned by the ND consisting of Germanic recruits for his forthcoming war against Maxentius, as stated by Liebeschuetz (1990, 7ff.). The large scale recruiting of barbarians (especially into the *auxilia*, but also into the *scholae*) by Constantine and Constantius ensured that barbarian elite units would have a significant role to play during the fourth-century military campaigns. The *auxilia* units formed part of the *Comitatenses* that Constantine must have already formed during the years 306–312.

We know that after Constantine's reign there were in existence new unit ranks for some units that are not attested before his reign. Unfortunately, we do not know when these new units and ranks were created. The following emended version of St. Jerome's list of cavalry ranks (by Bohec, 2006, 84–7) describes the 'new' cavalry *bandon / tagma / vexillatio* of Jerome's era that probably resembles closely also the organization of Constantine's new units, because it includes the exact same numbers of ranks as the 'old' cavalry 'regiment'. The probable fighting paper strength of such a cavalry unit would have been about 512 horsemen plus officers and *supernumerarii* as before. Treadgold (1995, 89–91) and Bohec (2006, 84–7) both suggest that the new infantry 'cohorts' would also have had similar ranks. Bohec's additions to Jerome's list are shown with Italics while my own additions and comments are placed inside parentheses:

---

tribunus (or Comes in the Strategikon)
primicerius (former highest ranking cav. centurion/ilarchês/vicarius; primus pilus
    of the 1st CO of inf.)
senator (former number 2 of the cav. centurions; princeps prior of the 1st CO)
ducenarius (commander of 200, former number 3 of the cav. centurions; hastatus
    prior of the 1 CO)
centenarius (former lowest ranking cav. centurion; princeps posterior and hastatus
    posterior of the 1st CO)

centenarius protector (former legionary 2–10 COs pili/triarii centurions)
centenarius ordinarius (former legionary 2–10 COs principes centurions)
centenarius ordinatus (former legionary 2–10 COs hastati centurions)

biarchus (former optio and highest ranking Decurion in the cav. and Decanus in the infantry and commander of a double file of 16 men.)
circitor (former cav. decurions or inf. decani or distributor of arms.)
semissalis (pentarchês, commander of five; or decanus commander of a file; the latter likelier)
eques (horseman)
pes (footman)
tiro (recruit)

If the 'new cohorts' were organized similarly, this would mean that they too now had 512 fighting men instead of the 480 fighters that conforms better with the Hellenistic phalanx tactics used by the Romans ever since the days of Hadrian. In fact, Maurice claims in the Strategikon (12.B.8.1) that in the past the infantry *tagmata* had been formed uniformly of 256 men. However, in my opinion, the same list of officers would rather imply the number of 1024 footmen for the infantry 'regiment' rather than 512 men. I would suggest the following tentative theory for the paper strengths of the new units. The *tribunus* (*chiliarches*) would have been in charge of the whole 'new heavy infantry regiment' of 1,024 men plus officers and *supernumerarii*; the *primicerius* (*pentakosiarches*) would have led 512 men; the *senator* (*syntagmatarches/tagmatarches*) would have led 256 men; the *ducenarius* (*taxiarches/hekatontarches*) would have led 128 men; the *centenarius* (*centurion/tetrarches*) 64 men; the biarchus (either dilochites or lochagos) 32 or 16 men; a higher ranking circitor (lochagos?) 16 men, if not a distributor of arms; a regular circitor or semissalis (decanus/dekarches) 8 men. It should be kept in mind, however, that each 16-man *lochos* had two recruits and two servants in addition to the fighting strength. The presence of the recruits enabled the officers to use them to replace sick, wounded, or injured men of the regular fighters so that each file posted in the battle formation would consist of the same number of men.

The fact that the equivalent cavalry 'regiment' would have had only 512 men is consistent with the same Hellenistic practice. The equivalent light infantry (*levis armaturae* units) would have had 1,024 men or a pair of 512 men. If the new system followed closely the Hellenistic principles, then the 'new legion' would actually have had 2,048 men under *comes* consisting of two units of 1,024 men each under a *tribune*. In fact, Ammianus' text seems to support the probability that in the new system each pair of imperial *Auxilia* (later called *Auxilia Palatina*) or legions were always placed under a *Comes*, which to me suggests the probability that the new legions had paper strengths of 2,048 plus supernumeraries and the *Auxilia* 1,024 men plus supernumeraries. In other words, the infantry *moira* of the sixth-century Strategikon (2,000–3,000 men) would have consisted of 2,048 heavy-armed men (see below), or, for example, 2,048 heavy-armed and 1,024 light-armed. We should not forget that the division of the old legions also created specialist units like artillery regiments, which the new type of army needed if they wanted to besiege places. For combat purposes all of the various types of units cavalry and infantry were still grouped together as needed in about 6,000–7,000-man legions or *mere*-divisions (sing. *meros*). That is, the infantry *meros* probably usually had about 4,096 heavy-armed and 2,048 light-armed plus the supernumeraries.

What is remarkable about this structure is its close resemblance to the army structure of the expeditionary army of Galerius (consisting of detachments from legions) in 293, which does suggest the probability that the change in actual combat organization was not significant or that it had actually taken place before (between 255–284?). After all, there is not much difference in size even between the standard 480 men (plus 60 recruits) cohort and 512 men (plus 64 recruits) 'new cohort'. All of these units were divided into files of four, eight or sixteen plus the light-armed as needed. It should be noted that the increase from 480 to 512 men meant a very slight increase in the size of the units posted in the field army. It should be remembered that most of the above are educated guesses.

These figures are consistent with the unit sizes based on the Hellenistic phalanx that all of the subsequent military treatises after Vegetius describe, which does suggest that the author of the reform was aware of Hellenistic military theory. The sixth-century authors Urbicius, Syrianus Magister, and Maurice all give details that are consistent with Hellenistic military theory and the use of the infantry phalanx. Vegetius' figures and information are the only anomaly in the information we have. Even Arrian had deployed the legionaries as a phalanx. However, we do not know for certain when this change took place, but in light of the existing evidence the reign of Constantine seems to be the likeliest alternative.

What then happened to the old units? The usual and best assumption is that these either retained their older establishment strengths or were weakened by the amount of troops drawn from them to form the new '*Comitatenses*' units of Constantine. There is also evidence for the continued existence of cavalry attached to their mother legions or at least that each 'legion' or division had 726–800 horsemen.[257] That is, the old units of the field army and imperial guard such as the *Ioviani* and *Herculiani* (we do not know whether Constantine actually possessed these two, but he certainly possessed some legions which were later called *Legiones Palatinae*) retained their old establishment strengths while the old legions and other units posted along the frontiers were reduced in size by the same amount of men as they had been forced to contribute to the *Comitatenses*. It is also possible that some of the field army units were similarly divided to form new units. The old diminished units left along the frontiers maintained their original structures. In contrast, all of the units belonging to the *Comitatenses* or *Protectores* were reorganized according to the new system so that each 512 or 1,024 men 'regiment' was commanded by one tribune. In the case of the Scholae, the Domestici/Protectores held the ranks from circitor to the tribune (see also Frank).

The best evidence for this is the existence of several tribunes simultaneously – for example, for the *Ioviani* (see the second book in the series) – while the whole unit or two such units were under a *Comes*. Contrary to popular belief, I do not believe that Constantine would have created all of the new auxiliary units that were later given the name *Auxilia Palatina*. There is plenty of evidence from the reign of Postumus onwards that the emperors in Gaul recruited barbarians across the border and it would be unbelievable if none of these units survived. Consequently, I would suggest that there is a strong probability that these older *auxilia* maintained their original size, whatever it was. Regardless, their structures were also reorganized to follow the new system.

And how did the old units then work together with the newer units? Since the actual combat tactics (and organization of the files) had remained the same at least from the turn of the second century onwards and detachments had constantly been united together for campaigns, it is clear that this did not pose any significant problem. The different sized units and detachments were just grouped together to form larger entities. For example, the sixth-century Strategikon makes the strength of the basic cavalry unit, the *bandon*, vary between 200 and 400 men so that the various units could be combined to form these either by dividing the over-sized units into smaller entities or by combining the below-regulation-strength units into larger entities. The same requirement held true also for the infantry. These were then grouped together to form about 2,000–3,000 strong *moirai* and the *moirai* in their turn were grouped together to form about 6,000–7,000-man *mere* (divisions = legions). It is quite obvious that this had always been the case even though the Strategikon is the first extant treatise to make these recommendations. The width of the unit could be adjusted either by making the units deeper or shallower.

The creation of a permanent and enlarged *Comitatenses* by Constantine resulted in increased dependency by these units on the availability of weapons and other equipment from state factories and the private artisans of the cities. They did not possess permanent bases with their own workshops, which meant that their needs had to be supplied from other sources. Furthermore, the division of the legions into smaller entities meant that most of the units did not have access to the artisans of the original legion. These units had to be supplied from other sources.

One of the greatest advantages of the existence of a permanent large field army, which was billeted in cities and towns, was that henceforth the units of the field army were closer to their actual paper strengths than had been the case with the garrison armies. The garrison forces were almost always forced to leave a portion of their fighting strength behind to protect local forts while the new field army units were expected to march in their entirety to a new location. Furthermore, it was more difficult for the officers to 'cook up' the roster books with 'dead souls' when the emperor was close by and able to conduct inspections in person, which also ensured that the field forces were closer to their establishment strengths than the frontier armies. The greater privileges and salaries granted to the field armies also made the officers less likely to steal money from their subordinates. In sum, the creation of the new larger privileged elite force made the Roman army under Constantine more efficient as long as discipline was maintained.

The creation of the new central army consisting of the *Comitatenses* and *Protectores* also entailed the reorganization of the top level structures. The *Ripenses* continued to be commanded by *duces*, but the *Comitatenses* obtained new commanders. The highest ranking military commander was the *Magister Equitum*, who was in charge of the cavalry, and the second-in-command after him was the *Magister Peditum*, in charge of the infantry. The lesser commands were still held by *comites*. Depending upon the unit, the *Protectores* were probably placed under the *Comes Domesticorum* (the *Protectores / Domestici*) and / or *Tribunus et Magister Officiorum* so that the *Mag. Off.* was probably the overall commander. Since Constantine did not have any Praetorians it is uncertain whether his Praetorian

Prefect had any specific units directly under his command. However, it is still probable that the *PP* continued to be used as military commander even if he did not have his 'own' units.

Similarly it is not known when Constantine changed and reformed his civilian administration, but it seems probable that the change of the titles for most of the civil servants happened only after 324, as usually assumed, and I will deal with that part of the reform only then. However, it is possible that Constantine started to make changes to his administrative structure immediately after having taken power: for example, the fact that the *PP* did not have any Praetorians may already have led Constantine to assign to him charge of the provinces, taxes and supplies without any military commands.

Galerius' Last Attempt to Restore the Tetrarchy and the Rise of Licinius

In the meantime, the desperate Galerius begged Diocletian to intervene and abandon his retirement. Galerius needed his help and authority to solve the difficult situation he had got himself into. Galerius also made Diocletian consul for the year 308 in an effort to force him to come out of retirement. In April 308 Maximian made the fateful mistake of attempting to usurp power from his son. Maximian called an assembly of soldiers and then accused his son of all the ills and ripped the purple from his son's shoulders, with the result that Maxentius jumped off the platform to the safety of the army, which then demonstrated its unanimous support for Maxentius. Maximian had no other choice than to flee Rome, and he fled to Constantine who owed him a favour. Maximian had not understood that thanks to his eccentric sexual behaviour he was not as popular among the soldiers as his son. Maximian fled and Constantine had no other choice but to welcome his father-in-law Maximian and give him a place of refuge.

Galerius was once again forced to spend the entire summer of 308 fighting, this time against the Carpi, as a result of which he was once again able to take the title *Carpicus*. He is attested to have been at Serdica in October 308, at Carnuntum on 11 November 308, but he had returned to Serdica before the end of November 308 (Barnes, 1982, 64). Consequently, Galerius was able to convene a grand meeting of emperors only in the autumn. Diocletian abandoned his retirement temporarily and Maximian came to meet his old senior colleague. On 11 November 308, with the approval of both Diocletian and Maximian, Galerius nominated Licinius as Severus' successor. Maximian was once again forced into retirement and Constantine demoted to Caesar.

The emperors gave Licinius the mission to crush Maxentius. Licinius took up residence at Sirmium while Galerius returned back to his favourite capital Thessalonica. According to Barnes (1981, 32), Constantine had been hoping that the emperors would accept him as Augustus and there is no evidence that Constantine ever accepted the demotion. Now Maximinus was also displeased because he had been sidelined in the promotion. He thought that he should have been promoted instead of Licinius. Consequently, he demanded that he be proclaimed Augustus too. Galerius had no other choice but to attempt to make him abide by the agreement and pay respect to Licinius' greater age and grey hair. This did not satisfy Maximinus, as a result of which Galerius invented a new title, 'Sons of the Augusti', for both Constantine and Maximinus in an effort to placate them. Maximinus was apparently ready to accept this for the moment.

In the summer or autumn of 308 Maxentius' position suddenly took a turn for worse. The *Agens Vicem Praefectorum Praetorio* (i.e. *Vicarius*) of Africa, Valerius Alexander, revolted and proclaimed himself *Augustus*. The immediate cause appears to have been the mistrust Maxentius felt towards Alexander, possibly because he knew that Alexander had been loyal to his father Maximian. When Alexander refused to send his son as hostage, Maxentius sent assassins to kill him but the plot was betrayed. This naturally led to the revolt of Alexander. Alexander apparently possessed a sizable naval force, because he was able to seize Sardinia and stop corn deliveries to Rome, not only from Africa, which is unsurprising, but also from Egypt, which suggests that he possessed naval supremacy in the area. Alexander also sought to form an alliance with Constantine against their mutual enemy, but as far as we know got no actual help from Constantine. When the Roman populace started to suffer from hunger and rioted, Maxentius responded by sending his Praetorians into the streets to crush the uprising, which they did with much bloodshed. Maxentius had saved his regime with violence, but it did not endear him to the populace.

Alexander's Achilles' heel was the smallness of his regular army, which made it necessary for him to start enrolling Gaetulians and Berbers into his army. Maxentius sent his *PP* Rufius Volusianus (senator) with a small and well-trained army to Africa in 309. Volusianus defeated Alexander's forces with ease and then marched through Carthage and other cities, all of which were pillaged. Volusianus' men pursued Alexander to Cirta, which they stormed and pillaged. The usurper was captured and then strangled. After this, Maxentius' henchmen purged all known supporters of Alexander, together with many innocent people. The surrendered rebel forces were sent to the north of Italy to bolster its defences.

In 309 Hormizd II (Hormisdas 302–309/10) with a large army launched an invasion of Roman territory, as a result of which he was able to plunder many cities (Chron. Arb. 11), but then luck smiled on the Romans. Hormizd had angered the great men and the Zoroastrian priests with his high-handedness and disrespect. The official cause of his sudden death was an accident while hunting, but in truth he was assassinated. The conspirators acted quickly to keep power in their hands. They killed Hormizd's eldest son Adhar Narseh, blinded another son, and then declared the still unborn child of the murdered ruler as successor by placing a crown on the queen's womb. However, since the conspirators didn't know the sex of the unborn child, they imprisoned Hormizd's third son, Hormisdas (he would later flee to the Roman territory), just in case they would need him as their puppet. When Hormizd's son Shapur II was then born, the conspirators immediately dispatched letters and couriers of the postal/security service to the farthest corners to secure the situation. Now the magnates and magi were free to exercise their powers at least as long as Shapur was underage.

This usurpation of power by the magnates and priests had far reaching consequences. Firstly, it secured Roman frontiers because Persia remained weak under the caretaker government. Secondly, it ensured that Shapur II would be brought up by the Zoroastrian priests, which ensured that he would become a religious bigot with far reaching consequences later. It is not surprising that it was during Shapur II's reign that the

Zoroastrian creed consolidated its grip even further under the Chief Priest Aturpat (Pourshariati, 334).

Maximinus Daia spent the year 310 well. The chaos in Persia enabled Maximinus to exploit the situation and inflict a defeat on the Persians, as a result of which all emperors hypocritically took the title *Persici Maximi*. In essence, Constantine and Licinius stole part of the fame achieved by their mortal enemy.[258]

Licinius appears to have exploited the troubles Maxentius was facing in Africa by invading Istria (Histria) in 309, because the Istrian town of Parentinium honoured Licinius as its ruler in 310. Licinius' purpose would have been to secure an alternative route to Italy that bypassed the usual route from Emona to Aquileia. This operation seems to have caused Maxentius to close the mints of Ticinum and Aquileia so that these would not fall into enemy hands. However, before Licinius could proceed any further, the Sarmatians seem to have created a distraction. It is quite probable that the Sarmatians had invaded immediately after they had noted that Licinius had withdrawn garrisons on the border to attack Maxentius. Since Galerius' health was already failing, Licinius had no other alternative than to defend his base of operations and return. Licinius was able to claim victory over the Sarmatians on 27 June 310. This distraction may have enabled Maxentius to transfer troops from Africa and then reconquer Istria.[259]

The spring of 310 was also significant for other reasons. It was then that Galerius' health suddenly and unexpectedly took a turn for worse thanks to the cancer that apparently affected his bowels or penis. His doctors desperately attempted to save his life, and when they failed they paid for it with their lives. Galerius lost his ability to act vigorously and therefore his ability to lead armies in the field. It is possible that it was because of this that Maximinus was emboldened to allow his troops to salute him as Augustus on 1 May 310. Galerius was beginning to lose his grip on power thanks to his failing health, just like Diocletian had. Galerius' failing health meant that Licinius started to make preparations for the period after Galerius' demise. Maxentius had also nothing to fear from Constantine, because Constantine was busy fighting against the Franks and making himself loved throughout his domains. In these circumstances it was not wise to invade Italy, with the result that Maxentius was able to strengthen the defences in the north of Italy.

In 310 Constantine was planning to continue his offensive against the Franks, and in preparation for this he built a bridge over the Rhine at Colonia Agrippina. He had foolishly left his father-in-law Maximian, who was now a private citizen and Constantine's trusted advisor, with a part of the army to secure the south of Gaul against a possible invasion by Maxentius. Maximian, who was always more ambitious than his mental abilities allowed, attempted once again to usurp power at Arles. This time he claimed that Constantine had died while fighting against the Franks. He confiscated all public funds and paid a donative to the troops on condition that they proclaim him Augustus, but only part of the army accepted this. Constantine's response was swift. He marched his army from Colonia to Cabillunum, embarked the men on boats of the local fleet, and then rowed along the Saône and the Rhone. Maximian panicked and fled to Massilia (Marseilles), which possessed strong walls. When Constantine reached Massilia, he ordered his men to assault the city immediately. This ended in disaster, because the soldiers (that is the engineers) had miscalculated the height of the walls and the ladders were too short.

Constantine had no other alternative than to order his men back. After this, Constantine resorted to the use of negotiation. The troops inside surrendered – after all they had been duped by Maximian. Constantine spared Maximian initially, but had him executed later – or alternatively Maximian hanged himself. This campaign betrays one feature which was typical of the Gallic troops and their engineers. They were not as skilled in siege warfare as their Eastern counterparts. Constantine's military engineers were clearly quite incompetent at this stage. However, as I noted in my article in 2006, Constantine improved standards considerably after this debacle. In other words, Constantine was a man ready to learn from his own mistakes.

After he had crushed his father-in-law, Constantine marched his army with forced marches back to the north (Constantine is attested at Treves in August) before the Franks could exploit his absence from the border. Since there was apparently no fighting, it is probable that Constantine made a treaty with the Franks and enrolled them into his *auxilia* units. In very-late 310 Constantine visited Britain once again, which probably implies some sort of troubles because he was ready to cross the Channel that late. The best guess is that the Picts had once again invaded.

The conspiracy and death of Maximian caused Constantine to attempt to strengthen his position through propaganda. He also knew that his legitimate brothers posed a potential threat to his own position, if they wanted to attempt usurpation. Consequently, Constantine wanted to stress his own legitimacy by proclaiming through an orator that he was a descendant of the emperor Claudius II, that he was the eldest son of Constantius I who had been sired when Constantius was at the prime of his life, and that he was a superb general and soldier. At the same time Constantine also replaced Mars on his coins (which he had used from the beginning of his reign) with Sol, the patron god of his father. The same orator also stressed Constantine's connection with the local Gallic cult of Apollo in Autun.[260] The situation was not yet ready for the public conversion to Christianity, even though it is very likely that Constantine's entourage already included Christian priests and bishops: I do not believe that Constantine would have been a follower of Sol or Apollo. Yet Constantine needed to proceed with caution in order not to alienate his supporters.

… And Then There Were Just Two…

Preparations for war

Since all emperors knew that the death of Galerius would result in a civil war, they spent the entire year of 311 in strengthening their own positions vis-à-vis the other emperors. Galerius died in late-April or early-May 311, but before his death Galerius revoked all persecution edicts against the Christians. However, he did not return the confiscated buildings or property. This raises the possibility that on his deathbed Galerius started to have regrets regarding his own cruel policies. He was a desperate man and may even have secretly attempted to seek a cure from Christian faith. Before his death, Galerius had entrusted his wife and bastard son Candidianus to Licinianus.

Now Licinius faced an uneviable situation. His predecessor's census had affected Licinius' standing among the troops, which Maximinus now exploited to his own advantage. Maximinus cancelled the census throughout his domains, as a result of which he gained immense popularity, and invaded Asia Minor. Licinius was still at Serdica on 9 June 311 and in order not to lose his position he also exempted all his soldiers five *capita* from the census and tax payments, and allowed all discharged soldiers the exemption of two *capita*. This was significant for the soldiers because they also owned property as private citizens. After this, Licinius marched against his enemy, but both sides decided on a compromise. The emperors met on board a ship and came to terms.

Maxentius was also attempting to strengthen his own position by heavily garrisoning the two invasion routes to Italy. The principal garrisons were located at Segusio/ Segusium (Susa) and Augusta Taurinorum (Turin) in the West, and at Verona and Aquileia in the East to hold the Alpine passes against a possible attack. He also sought to pacify the Christians, and allowed them to choose a new Bishop of Rome (later Pope). In order to distract 'domestic' opposition to his rule, he also hypocritically declared war on Constantine during the summer of 311. We do not know what Constantine's response was, but we do know that Maxentius was unable to conquer any territory from Constantine.

In the meanwhile, Constantine had increased his own popularity among his populace by lowering taxes. He had also made a tour of his areas, probably in an effort to secure the loyalty of all for the forthcoming war. In addition to this, Constantine wisely offered the hand of his sister in marriage to the elderly Licinius. Licinius accepted the proposal, which meant that they formed an alliance against Maxentius and Maximinus. This did not escape Maximinus' attention. He sent an offer to recognize Maxentius as emperor, which the latter grasped eagerly. Maximinus had also prevented the implementation of Galerius' policy change regarding the Christians and six months after that had initiated a new persecution. Maximinus also made an innovation. He created a new state-sponsored pagan religion, the organization of which was modelled after the Christian Church. He established state-sponsored pagan high-priests in each city and above them pontiffs in each province. The pagan priests were also empowered to ensure that the Christians did not possess any buildings for worship, to force them to sacrifice to the gods, and to arrest the Christians and take them to the magistrates. In essence, Maximinus created a religious police to guard the 'morals' of the populace, which had taken influences from both the Christian and Zoroastrian Churches.

In the meantime, Candidianus, Valeria the daughter of Diocletian, and Severus' son Severianus appear to have fled to the relative safety of Maximinus' court because they all feared Licinius. Valeria was under the false belief that she would be safe at Maximinus' court because Maximinus was a married man. This proved a grave mistake. Maximinus was in the habit of raping all women who caught his fancy, and after he had satisfied his own urges, he gave them as wives to his own slaves. His *comites* imitated his behaviour and also raped the women of their hosts. When Maximinus learnt of Valeria's arrival he immediately started to lust after her for political reasons – she had previously been his 'mother'. Consequently, he asked her hand in marriage, but his wishes were rebuffed. As a result, the arch-adulterer exiled Valeria and her mother, confiscated her possessions, condemned all her associates with trumped-up charges of adultery, and tortured all her eunuchs to death. Valeria managed to send a letter to her father, who duly demanded that the women were to be returned to him, but with no result. At the same time as this happened, Diocletian also learnt that the statues and paintings in which he was portrayed together with Maximian had been destroyed when Constantine had ordered the damnation of the memory of Maximian. All of this proved too much for the old man to bear. He was powerless to save even his wife and daughter and his memory was also being destroyed alongside Maximian's. Diocletian starved himself to death, which finally came on 3 December 311. *Sic transit gloria mundi*.

Maximinus' Armenian Campaign in 312

As noted above, Maximinus Daia had renewed the persecution of Christians and had also been foolish enough to extend this policy to Roman Armenia, where he attempted to compel the local Christian Armenians to sacrifice to idols and thereby alienated the local lords and populace. Unsurprisingly, the Armenians revolted and sought to gain their freedom by rejoining the Armenian Kingdom. This also meant an alliance with Persia. Consequently, the Armenians and Persians began to raid Roman territory, but Maximinus' response was decisive. He invaded Armenia in August or autumn and defeated all of the enemy forces he encountered. These operations made it impossible for Maximinus to intervene on behalf of his ally Maxentius during the year 312.

The Persians made a diversionary invasion into Oshroene and burned the city, but this did not prevent Maximinus from completing his war successfully. As a result of his military success Maximinus was able to detach additional districts from Armenia as a punishment of the Armenians for their intransigence. Then he returned to home territory and rebuilt Oshroene (Edessa) and renamed it Maximianopolis.[261] The Iberians also appear to have joined the Persians and Armenians in their campaign against Maximinus at this time. After this, in about 313/4, King Mirian gave the Christians religious freedom, probably in an effort to placate the rulers of Rome, Constantine and Licinius (GC, p.110). It is unsurprising that following this war both Armenia and Iberia would have sought good relationships with Licinius. In particular, it is unsurprising that Trdat saw Licinius as his best friend, as they must have been friends from childhood, having lived under the same roof.

We should remember, however, that Maximinus' successes against the Armenians and Persians do not prove him to have been anything but a competent general. The Persians in particular were distracted by other enemies. According to Tabari (i.836), when the Turks (Kushans?) and the Romans learnt that the Persians were ruled by the child Shapur II, they cast their eyes on Persian territory. He obviously means the Roman invasions of 310 and 312 by Maximinus and later by Licinius, but the 'Turkish' invasion is otherwise unknown. He also mentions that the Arabs from Abd al-Qays, Bahrain, and al-Kazimah (on the coast of Bahrain), exploited the situation by crossing the sea and landing on the coastlands of Fars. They seized and looted everything and set up military encampments against the town of Abruwan (unknown) in the province of Ardashir Khurrah. The Arabs apparently continued to loot and pillage for years, because the Persians could not agree amongst themselves who would be put in charge of the operation. I would suggest that the Arabic invasions took place mainly after Imru had become a Roman client in about 313/4.

Constantine Invades Italy in the spring of 312 (See Maps Section)

Constantine knew that he had to conquer Italy first if he wanted to obtain a strong enough position to challenge Licinius later. He also knew that Maxentius had placed the bulk of his forces at Verona in the mistaken belief that he would be able to invade

Licinius' territories. Consequently, after having completed his preparations Constantine invaded Italy at the first opportunity in the spring of 312. Constantine did this contrary to the advice of his generals, who undoubtedly looked only at the comparative strengths of the forces. Constantine's generals did not realize what Constantine did: Constantine's geographic position was far stronger than that of his fellow emperors. The Germans across the Rhine consisted of several different tribes that did not possess adequate offensive siege skills, as a result of which their threat could be ignored for a short period of time. In contrast, Maxentius had to worry about both Constantine and Licinius; and Licinius about Maxentius and Maximinus and the barbarians across the Danube; and Maximinus about Licinius and Armenians and Persians.

When planning the campaign Constantine had undoubtedly followed the following procedure:

> When intending to go on an expedition, Constantine the Great was accustomed to take counsel with those who had experience in the relevant matters, such as where and when the expedition should be undertaken. When he had ascertained from this advice the place and time for the expedition, he was also accustomed to enquire as to which others knew about these matters, particularly those with recent experience. And when he had found whether any others were knowledgeable, he summoned these also and asked each one individually how long the route was which ran from home territory to the objective, and of what sort; and whether one road or many led to the objective, and of what sort; and whether the regions along the route were waterless or not. And then he enquired as to which road was narrow, precipitous and dangerous, and which broad and traversable; also whether there was any great river along the way which could not be crossed. Next he enquired about the country; how many fortresses it possessed, which were secure and which insecure, which populous and which sparsely populated, what distance these fortresses were from one another; and of what sort were the villages about them, large or small, and whether these regions were level or rough, grassy or arid. He asked this on account of fodder for the horses.
>
> Then he enquired as to which army was available to support these fortresses in time of war, and at what distance they lay from them, when they were ready to go on campaign, and when dispersed and at rest at their homes, not anticipating war, further, in which place they campaign and when, or whether they never campaign, but remain always in the same region. But he asked the same questions also about other lands, so that no one would know definitely in which region he intended to campaign. For often, being given information from among such advisers, the enemy secured their borders or prepared themselves for battle.
>
> *Constantine Porphyrogenitus, Three Treatises B.1–25, tr. by J. Haldon, 83.*

I would suggest that Constantine had done precisely what the treatise attests. Since we know that Maxentius had posted the bulk of his forces against Licinius it is clear that Constantine had managed to surprise him. It is therefore quite likely that Constantine had made similar preparations along the Rhine frontier to fool Maxentius' spies among his army. Constantine's plan was a great success. Despite having left most of his soldiers behind to protect the Rhine, he is likely to have achieved – at least initially – a local numerical superiority over his enemy thanks to the fact that Maxentius' forces were divided into several corps.

According to Zosimus, Maxentius had 170,000 infantry and 18,000 cavalry in total, while Constantine, even after levying soldiers from the barbarians (Germans, Britons and Gauls), had only 90,000 infantry and 8,000 cavalry, but most of his troops were battle hardened veterans. Zosimus' figures should be interpreted to mean the entire armed strengths of these two emperors, 260,000 infantry and 26,000 cavalry for a total of 286,000 men, was the strength of the entire western half of the empire. This figure is in agreement with the totals achieved during the reign of Diocletian, but we should remember that 285,000 for his reign included about 30,000 naval personnel, which means that both Constantine and Maxentius had increased the size of the army after Diocletian's death. As regards the actual numbers of men who took part in the campaign, Zosimus' figures are contrasted by Panegyric 12, which states that Constantine invaded Italy with less than 40,000 men, which was scarcely a quarter of his total strength, while Maxentius had 100,000 men in arms, all armed with every weapon in the manner of the first rank. The reference to the full panoply of equipment for Maxentius' forces suggests that Constantine's forces probably lacked similar (see later) and that only the front rank soldiers in his army wore the full panoply of equipment. In fact, this was to become the standard practice later on. (See Syvänne (2004) and the forthcoming books in the series.)

It is also important to note that Panegyric 12, in fact, implies that Constantine's total armed strength was at least 160,000 men instead of the 98,000 mentioned by Zosimus, with the implication that the totals for the western half of the empire now exceeded 348,000 men. If Panegyric 12 is accurate in its figures, as is probable because it was presented to Constantine, then Constantine's fleet consisted of approximately 50,000 men. We do not know how large a portion of his fleet Constantine used against Maxentius, but we do know that his navy was able to blockade the ports of Italy and was also later used for the invasion of Africa. This does suggest a very sizable force, because the Praesental Fleets of Italy had at least 1-sixer, 3-fivers, 16-fours, 75 triremes and 19 *liburnae*, and this is a very conservative estimate because according to Jordanes (Get. 29), Dio stated that the harbour of Ravenna alone could hold 250 ships. In short, even with the minimum figures Maxentius' navy consisted of about 33,000 men, which should be added to his armed strength. If Constantine committed the same number of 50-oared *liburnae* as he did in 324, this would mean a navy of about 200 *liburnae* and 21,600 men (200 x an *ousia* of 108 men so that there were 50 rowers plus 58 others on board). It is quite probable that Constantine did not need any more ships to destroy the Praesental Fleets because his fleet consisted of greater numbers of more manoeuvrable ships than his enemy, and it is probable that Maxentius' fleet was not assembled together. In addition, it is probable that, in contrast to Maxentius' men, Constantine's sailors and marines were experienced naval fighters thanks to the wars that had taken place during the reign of Constantius I.

The above obviously still begs the question of why Licinius did nothing. The likeliest answer is that it was because Licinius was uncertain of Maximinus' intentions. Maximinus invaded Armenia only in the autumn as a response to their invasion, which means that Licinius did not know what Maximinus intended to do before July. (See above.) However, this still begs the question why Licinius did nothing while Maximinus was fighting against the Armenian king Trdat, his former comrade-in-arms. Perhaps Constantine's operations in Italy caused Licinius to wait and see what Constantine would do next, or Licinius did not want to appear to support the enemies of Rome.

The Assault on Segusio in the Spring of 312

Constantine marched from Treves to Vienna and then through the Alps via the Mt. Cénis pass. This route was blocked by the garrison posted at the fortified town of Segusio/Segusium. He ordered an immediate assault of the town. The light-armed infantry provided covering fire with their slings and other missiles, and the rest brought ladders against the walls and applied torches to the gates. The defenders did not put up much of a fight, but the fire spread into the buildings inside with the result that Constantine had to order his men to extinguish the raging fires. Constantine's army was a disciplined elite force and thanks to this Constantine was able to order his men not to kill the surrendered populace and garrison. Constantine's army was no longer the incompetent bunch that had assaulted Massilia. The men and engineers had clearly received additional training after that incident. Constantine's method of attack resembles the one recommended by the sixth-century Strategikon. The Strategikon advocates that stone throwers be used to throw fire bombs inside the city so that the defenders would be preoccupied with putting out the burning buildings while the soldiers would take the city by using ladders.

The Battle of Augusta Taurinorum (Turin) in the Spring of 312

This defeat did not discourage Maxentius' forces posted at Taurinorum. The garrison marched out to meet Constantine's army. Maxentius' general deployed the men on a hill in a wedge formation with the flanks turned back downhill. The *clibanarii* were deployed in the middle to cut Constantine's infantry phalanx into two pieces. This appears to imply the use the *epikampios opisthia* with the centre consisting (of the wedge?) of *clibanarii*. Lactantius' text 40.5 provides an example of this formation and shows how the *clibanarii* and mounted archers (*sagittarii*) escorted and protected the women to their site of execution by assuming the wedge formation. There are strong reasons to suspect that the *clibanarii* were deployed like the tenth-century Byzantines as a huge wedge with front and edges consisting of the *clibanarii* and the interior of the *sagittarii*. Unfortunately, the sources do not state the strength of Maxentius army or the strength of the *clibanarii* corps. The tenth-century Sylloge (46 with Syvanne, 2008) proves that the size could vary greatly. This treatise gives the following possible strengths for the wedge: 1504, 504, and 384. In light of the fact that the *clibanarii* formed the principal striking force the figure 1504 seems likeliest.

In this context it is important to understand how the *clibanarii* were to be used. According to Nazarius (22.3ff.), the *clibanarii* horsemen were covered in iron mail and the chest and forelegs of the horses were covered by a corselet. The *clibanarii* were taught to maintain their course of assault even after they had charged into the enemy line so that they would break through it. Lactantius' inclusion of the *sagittarii* among the *clibanarii* makes it probable that when the assault began the mounted archers were used to disorder the enemy with volleys of arrows before the wedge charged into the enemy formation. In this context it is also of great importance to note the type of protection used by the horses of the *clibanarii*. Nazarius' account implies that the Roman horses usually wore only frontal covering, which makes it certain that Constantius II's reform of cavalry in ca. 336/7 meant the introduction of additional pieces of armour for the horses in imitation of the Persian practice.

In sum, Maxentius' general adopted a variation of the mixed formation that could be used in two ways: the *clibanarii* wedge to crush the centre of Constantine's army; and the wings to encircle Constantine's army in the same manner as Hannibal had done to the Romans at Cannae in 216 BC. However, Constantine was not a rookie, but a general with long experience. He knew his techniques. Constantine sent ahead both flanks (apparently his cavalry) against the wings of the enemy formation in order to frustrate any encircling attempts (Pan.Lat 12.4), and opened up the infantry formation in the middle to induce the enemy cataphracts to attack (Nazarius 24). In other words, he used the opening (*antistomos difalangia*) in the middle to frustrate the enemy cavalry wedge (Byzantine

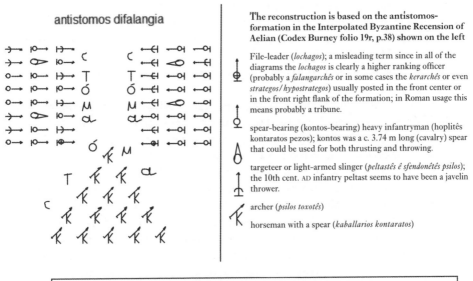

antistomos difalangia

The reconstruction is based on the antistomos-formation in the Interpolated Byzantine Recension of Aelian (Codex Burney folio 19r, p.38) shown on the left

File-leader (*lochagos*); a misleading term since in all of the diagrams the *lochagos* is clearly a higher ranking officer (probably a *falangarchês* or in some cases the *kerarchês* or even *strategos*/*hypostrategos*) usually posted in the front center or in the front right flank of the formation; in Roman usage this means probably a tribune.

spear-bearing (kontos-bearing) heavy infantryman (hoplitês kontaratos pezos); kontos was a c. 3.74 m long (cavalry) spear that could be used for both thrusting and throwing.

targeteer or light-armed slinger (*peltastês ê sfendonêtês psilos*); the 10th cent. AD infantry peltast seems to have been a javelin thrower.

archer (*psilos toxotês*)

horseman with a spear (*kaballarios kontaratos*)

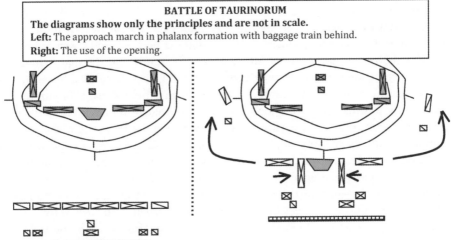

BATTLE OF TAURINORUM
The diagrams show only the principles and are not in scale.
Left: The approach march in phalanx formation with baggage train behind.
Right: The use of the opening.

Interpolation of Aelian, Devine ed. 40.1–6, Dain ed. E1–5).[262] The aim was to frustrate the attack of the enemy *clibanarii* by giving them an opening to charge into. When the *clibanarii* complied (the open space tempted both horses and men) and foolishly charged into the opening, the two phalanxes of the *antistomos difalangia* charged forward and killed them all to a man with clubs and iron maces. It is possible that Constantine had also posted a reserve force in front of the charging formation to block their route of retreat. When the *clibanarii* had been butchered the rest of Maxentius' army fled in complete disarray, but the people of Turin closed the gates with the result that Constantine's army butchered the fugitives.

Battle of Brixia in late August, and Battle and Siege of Verona in September

As a result of these victories, Milan and the rest of the towns in the North-Central plains of Italy surrendered to Constantine. Constantine's strategy was to win over enemies with a policy of clemency, and this brought results. Constantine marched to Milan where he was welcomed. He stayed there for a while. He was in no hurry, because he wanted to give his fleet time to blockade the enemy ports so that the populace in Rome would start to starve before he marched there.

Constantine continued his march against Maxentius' NE armies in late summer only after he had rested his men. He needed to neutralize them before he could move against the city of Rome. Constantine's cavalry vanguard met, charged and easily defeated a large elite cavalry contingent blocking the road near Brixia (Brescia), the remnants of which fled back to Verona. Verona was held by the *PP* Ruricius Pompeianus. Pompeianus knew that his forces suffered from poor morale and it is also probable that he was outnumbered as well. Consequently, he decided to prevent the enemy from crossing the River Adage. Constantine answered by using the classic strategy of sending part of his army across at a point farther away that had been left unguarded by the enemy. Pompeianus withdrew inside the city, but when Constantine attempted to surround the city from two sides, Pompeianus sallied out. The sally failed miserably, but enabled Pompeianus to slip past the approaching forces.

Pompeianus was not ready to give up, but collected a relief army. When this force was approaching, Constantine decided not to abandon the siege, but left a part of his army to continue the siege while he himself advanced with the rest against the approaching enemy.

When one combines the circumstances in which Constantine's led his army against the relief army with Roman combat doctrine, one can conclude that Constantine's initial battle array was likely to be a double phalanx. He needed to march fast and could not therefore protect his rear with a line of slow moving wagons. However, when Constantine approached the enemy force and could see that the numerically superior enemy force outflanked him, he ordered the army to extend its width by having the front line march to the flanks and by advancing the second phalanx forward. As I noted in my article, the series of commands for the first line to divide itself in the middle would have been 'Spearward face! March!' (*Ad conto clina, Move*) and 'Shieldward face! March!' (*Ad scuto clina, Move*), and simply 'March!' (*Move*) for the second line. It is also possible that the reserves would have been used to make a wedge in the middle.

Nixon and Rodgers (p.309 with n.65) interpret the text differently. They consider that Constantine's array was reinforced by depth, and that the widening of the front would have been done by ordering the ranks to spread out. Their interpretation is plausible, but in my opinion the use of a real double line was meant in this case (no baggage) and that it was the front of the array that was spread out to give room for the second line. The method they suggest, which was to make the line wider by having every second man in each file to march forward to thin the line, would have taken too long to accomplish. We should not forget that the Strategikon instructed that the approach march was to be conducted in open order with file depths of four men because it would have taken way too long to open up and spread out the deep formation. (See Syvänne, 2004, 201–211, 243–4 (partially revised ed. pp. 202–212, 244–5).) The resulting 'grand tactical formation' is one of the variants of the *epikampios emprosthia* formation (see Syvänne; with Vegetius 3.20, the fourth and fifth formations). It should be noted that the use of the reserves or light infantry to extend the length of the front line would have been a more typical solution and safer (Aelian 29.4/6, 31.2; Asclepiodotus 6), but in this instance Constantine's choice allowed him to outflank his enemy's wings immediately without giving them chance to extend their own line. The attached diagram of the battle (not in scale) is borrowed from my article.

Left: Constantine's cavalry wings charge to gain time for the infantry manoeuvre. It is likely that the relief army had baggage train accompanying it, and therefore I have reconstructed their array as a single phalanx.

Right: The frontline marches to the wings to encircle the enemy and the second line marches forward. The flank reserves would have protected the inner flanks of the split up first line. Eventually these two units would have been arrayed between the split up 1st line and the advanced 2nd line to form the one continuous lengthened phalanx. The centre reserves may have been used to form an infantry wedge or deep array in the middle for the breaking up of the enemy array.

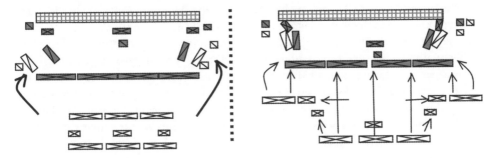

Constantine led his cavalry forward to the attack into the midst of the enemy in person. Constantine thrust himself into the densest throng of the horse and opened a path through it, which means that he broke through one of the enemy cavalry wings, probably the right. In the meantime the other wing achieved a similar result on the other flank. Constantine's purpose was to protect the manoeuvre of his infantry phalanx. The panegyrics claim that Constantine and his cavalry routed the enemy without much in the way of input by the infantry, but we may suspect with a good reason that the lengthened infantry line must also have contributed to the success by outflanking the enemy phalanx after Constantine and his cavalry wings had driven away their cavalry protection. In short, Constantine had put his life on the line to encourage his troops and it had paid off handsomely. Pompeianus was killed and his army annihilated. Constantine, however, would have continued to pursue the fleeing enemy had his officers not forcibly restricted him. They did not want Constantine to take needless personal risks. The victorious Constantine returned to continue the siege. The death and defeat of Pompeianus caused the surrender of Aquileia, Verona and the rest of the north eastern cities.

The Battle of the Milvian Bridge on 28 October 312

Now, the route lay open for an attack on Rome. It is probable that by now Maxentius had too few troops left to defend the territory between the Po and Rome. It is also probable that prior to this Constantine's navy had occupied the ports of Rome and cut off the corn supply. The same forces could also threaten Maxentius' rear if Maxentius decided to march north to meet Constantine in battle. Consequently, Maxentius resorted to the use of the same defensive strategy that had brought him victory twice before, which was based on the defensive strength of the walls of Rome and bribery of the besiegers.

In addition to this, the previous victories had caused many superstitious persons to believe that Maxentius was a powerful sorcerer, and it is probable that he also cultivated this reputation purposefully with continuous pagan ceremonies. The Christian sources make this abundantly clear. It was the superstitious fear of Maxentius' spells that frightened his enemies senseless and emboldened his own army. Constantine had been aware of this problem from the very start of his campaign. He knew that he had to find a way to assure his own men that they too had divine protection which negated Maxentius' spells. It is also very probable that Constantine had already converted to Christianity and was contemplating the way in which he could publicly confess his belief while also reassuring his men. At first, he had prayed to the 'Highest God' to help his cause. However, en route to Rome, he claimed that he and his army saw in the sky a cross and the message 'Conquer by This', and then he had a dream in which Christ appeared to him.

There are two possible explanations for this. Firstly, it is possible that as a Christian (or as a person who was still vacillating in his beliefs) who was under great stress, he really believed that he had seen the miraculous sign and as a result of his own conviction managed to convince others around him of the truth of the sight. Or, it is possible that as a Christian convert who needed to encourage his men, he exploited their superstition and managed to convince them that they had seen a miracle sent by a God who would grant the men a victory.

We know that when Constantine reached Rome, Constantine was ready to confess his Christian beliefs publicly, as a sign of which he ordered his soldiers to carry the 'sign of the cross', the Chi-Rho, on their shields. It was to serve as a talisman against the evil spells of Maxentius. The night before the battle Constantine ordered a new imperial battle standard, the *Labarum*, to be made. This standard was then paraded around the army in the morning so that they could paint the same sign on their shields. In an age of superstition, Constantine's strong belief in the help of Christ is certain to have uplifted the fighting spirit of his army. Thanks to Constantine's foresight, the men were no longer frightened by the 'evil eye' and black magic. We should not underestimate the effect of the supernatural on the fighting spirit of the ancient armies.

All in all, in my opinion it is more likely that the entire episode with signs in the sky and supernatural dreams were premeditated actions with which Constantine wanted to reassure his men and with which he intended to convert his soldiers to Christianity. The chosen symbol for the *Labarum*, the *Chi-Rho*, was suitably ambiguous for his pagan followers to accept, which does suggest premeditation and political concerns. Had Constantine wanted to act unambiguously he could have used the plain cross as a symbol just like the later Crusaders did. Most importantly for Constantine and his men, he could prove that God had so far been on his side. The best proofs of this were the defeats already suffered by Maxentius' armies.

Religious aspects aside, Constantine's position was actually very strong. He had a string of successes behind him, on top of which his enemy had made himself hated. The taxes Maxentius had levied on Italians and Romans, as well as his personal brutality, his cruelty, his human sacrifices and most of all the raping of noble women, had made him hated. The populace had not forgotten that Maxentius had crushed the food riots with bloodshed. Constantine's agents inside the city were not slow in exploiting this in their propaganda.[263] Furthermore, the naval blockade had by now caused famine and unrest which made it impossible for Maxentius to attempt to prolong the conflict in the same manner as he had done previously. Had he stayed inside the walls, the populace would have opened the gates.

Consequently, Maxentius led his army out against the attacker. Maxentius had previously demolished the Milvian Bridge, as a result of which he was now forced to build a pontoon bridge of boats and planks to the place where it had stood. Maxentius arrayed his army with its back against the Tiber. Maxentius was essentially using the classic stratagem of desperate commanders when they wanted to force their unwilling men to fight to the death. Constantine did not attempt to prevent the foe, because it was advantageous for him that the enemy fight a pitched battle. Constantine simply arrayed his phalanx opposite the enemy, and then ordered the cavalry wings to charge. Once again Constantine encouraged his men by putting his own life on the line. He led the cavalry charge. Nazarius (Pan.4.29.5) states that Constantine wore a very distinct dress (helmet glittering with gems, and golden shield and armour) in this battle so that all could recognize him. The admiring panegyrist tells us that Constantine protected himself ably against enemy missiles and sword blows during the fighting, and that the 'beam' of his spear threw down his opponents, after which his horse always leaped up and crushed the downed opponents underfoot. This account clearly proves that Constantine's personal equipment consisted of armour, helmet, shield and spear, and that he used his spear/ lance to unhorse his enemies whilst his horse was trained to trample the men underfoot. It is no wonder that the men loved Constantine. He was a superb horseman and fighter, who had an equally well-trained warhorse. When one combines this piece of information with the great numbers of tombstones which show Roman horses trampling enemies, one can conclude that the Romans probably trained their horses to trample opponents underfoot.

The battle scenes in the Arch of Constantine imply that at least important sections of Constantine's cavalry fought without armour, which does suggest the use of a very fast charge in order to avoid having to spend time under enemy archery fire. Constantine either lacked the money to equip his men or he dispensed with armour in order to increase the speed of his armies on the march and in battle. When we remember that Constantine recruited large numbers of Germans to serve as infantry (later *auxilia palatina*) and as cavalry (*scholae* etc.) this is by no means surprising. There was therefore a great contrast between Constantine's lightly equipped elite force and Maxentius' heavily armoured army. In phalanx warfare it was not necessary to equip every man with armour. It was quite enough to equip only the two front ranks with full set of arms and armour, and it

1) *Labarum* (Constantine' standard with the letters of Christ/*Christos*, *Chi Rho*) and the standard bearer of the 50 men strong *Labarum* Guard unit. I have also given the bearer the talismanic shield even though in practise the standard bearer probably did not use the shield on horseback. The three circles represent Constantine and two of his sons and probably dates from a later period. 2) Constantine's lightly equipped cavalry. 3) Member of Constantine's lightly-equipped German *Auxilia* (*Palatina*) *Cornuti*. Source: the Arch of Constantine. The shields in the arch do not include the cross. The reason may be that the crosses were painted over the sculptures or that the German auxiliaries did not use the cross because the symbols in their shields were already talismans. (Source: the Arch of Constantine/ Syvanne 2006)

was the front rank men, the best fighters of the phalanx, who usually decided the winner in a melee situation.

However, in the case of Constantine's army not even all of the front rankers appear to have had armour, because there were significant numbers of tribal auxiliary units and new elite Germanic *auxilia* present. In fact, it is probable that the lack of armour actually improved their warrior fighting spirit. They could show their bravado as 'berserks'. We should remember that this was not a new practice. One only needs to remember the almost-naked Germanic auxiliaries on Trajan's Column. Furthermore, the use of armour was not always even recommended. The Strategikon instructed the footmen to dispense with their long spears, helmets and armour in difficult wooded terrain, and adopt lighter equipment (smaller shields, javelins etc.) more suited to the situation. In sum, the soldiers could vary their clothes, equipment and arms according to the terrain, enemy and weather, and Constantine's army was not worse off for being less well equipped than Maxentius' army. Most importantly, Constantine's army had better morale and fighting sprit than his opponent's army. The illustrations (based on Constantine Arch) from my article (slightly altered) are included only to demonstrate how little armour Constantine's soldiers wore.

After Constantius had routed Maxentius' cavalry wings he gave his infantry phalanx the order to attack. The defeat of Maxentius' cavalry effectively decided the battle, and it is therefore not surprising that Maxentius' Italian and Roman soldiers purposefully avoided the taking of any risks. They did not have any love for the tyrant and could expect to be pardoned. However, the foreign troops, the Praetorians and the Germanic bodyguards fought bravely because they could not expect any mercy and were therefore either trampled by Constantine's cavalry or killed by the infantry. The bravery of the foreigners and the intervention of Maxentius' bodyguards enabled Maxentius' cavalry to regroup, at least temporarily. In fact, Zosimus claims that there was hope left for Maxentius as long as his Horse Guards (the German *Equites Singulares Augusti* and the Praetorian Horse) and cavalry stood firm.[264] However, the orderly infantry attack by Constantine's forces from the front supported by cavalry from the flanks made all resistance futile. When Maxentius' other reserve units failed to give support, the situation became hopeless. His army collapsed and fled towards the river. Most of the Praetorians fell where they stood while the panicked Maxentius, with his routed Guard cavalry, rushed on to the bridge of ships, with the result that it collapsed under the immense weight of the fugitives. Maxentius fell from his horse and was drowned. The attached illustrations from my article show the principal events of the battle.

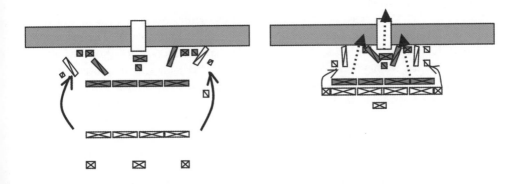

Maxentius' corpse was sought out before his head was cut off, placed on a pole, and then paraded before the people of the city. The populace rejoiced at the death of the tyrant and the victory of Constantine. Constantine lived up to his reputation for clemency. He did not enter the city immediately, but waited for the next day so that the soldiers would not enter the city before they had calmed down.

Constantine secures his position through astute policies of clemency and reform

Constantine calmed the senators and populace with a calculated show of clemency. Constantine punished only the most vehement supporters of Maxentius, disbanded the Praetorian and Germanic Horse Guards that had supported the tyrant, recalled exiles, restored property confiscated by the tyrant, and annulled Maxentius' decisions that were not 'rightful'. After the abolition of the Praetorians, the powers of the Praetorian Prefect were restricted to the area he controlled so that he acted as superior to the vicars of the dioceses. He no longer had any official command of military units even if he retained control over their supply. We should not, however, make the mistake of thinking that the official administrative organization would have been always followed. There were to be several powerful praetorian prefects that had de facto control over military units, and sometimes the emperor also appointed them to command of some military forces. Strong personalities could always exercise power that exceeded their official powers. The surviving enemy soldiers were also given a chance to redeem themselves. They were transferred to frontier duty on the Rhine. The navy was sent to secure Africa. Constantine had followed the same kind of policy of clemency in civil war as Julius Caesar before him and with at least equal success. The only affront he made was that as a Christian emperor he did not make the customary sacrifices to Jupiter when he entered Rome.

Constantine adopted the same policies as Maxentius had followed towards the Senate. He claimed to restore its ancient authority and once again allowed its members to attain high positions in the imperial court. In other words, the positions that were previously regarded as belonging only to the equestrians were now opened up for the senators. Constantine's policies effectively removed the distinction between senators and equestrians and this would eventually also be recognized in law. The Senate rewarded Constantine with the title of senior Augustus.[265]

After the introduction of Christianity into his army on 28 October 312 Constantine promoted the cause of Christianity in every way imaginable. His new huge statue at Rome held the *Labarum* in its hand. He also started to legislate in favour of Christianity immediately. He wrote a letter in his and Licinius' name to Maximinus in which he ordered Maximinus to stop the persecution of Christians immediately. The restoration of properties to Christians was speeded up and he provided money to bishops to build or rebuild churches. Money was also made available for charitable Christian organizations. The poor, orphans and widows were all given access to Christian charities paid by the emperor. He improved the legal position of the Church, the priests were given exemption from taxation, and other legislation with a Christian flavour was also introduced. However, at this stage Constantine still did not make a full-scale attack against paganism. He only forbade private divination, but still allowed public divination to continue in the presence of magistrates. Constantine appears to have actually favoured gladiatorial games as a form of punishment, and forbade the games to please the Christians only in 325, but in practice the games continued. The result of this policy was the emergence of the charioteer hooligans grouped as Blue and Green factions.[266] This favoured position of Christianity affected the army directly because when an ever increasing number of the populace converted to Christianity, the number of Christian recruits increased as well.

In addition to this, the emperor introduced Christian symbols into his court and most importantly into his army. Thanks to the thematic arrangement of the topics in Eusebius' Life of Constantine it is difficult to discern the exact time for many of Constantine's reforms and this problem also encompasses the introduction of many Christian elements into the military. On the basis of the order in which Eusebius (Vita 4.18.2–21) presents his material it would seem that Constantine introduced the day of rest on Sunday (Sun Day) for his army after 324, but in light of other evidence the year 312/3 seems likelier. It is clear that by the 320s Constantine's army was full of Christians and the prayer Constantine introduced for his army was also used by Licinius in 313. It is notable that the day devoted to the worship of the Sun was now converted for Christian purposes.

Christian soldiers were allowed free-time to attend the church while the non-believers were marched to an open place to recite prayers for God. This essentially introduced Christian ceremony in place of the pagan one, but this was probably not too great a difficulty for the pagans who could see such a ceremony as simply ritual. What is notable, however, is that the Christians were given a day free while the pagans were drilled. This must have served as a positive encouragement for the soldiers to convert at least superficially so that they would obtain a day of rest. This posed no problem for the vast majority of soldiers, because most Roman soldiers were indifferent towards religion and just followed the lead taken by their superiors. Their principal sources of motivation were the military life and prospects of booty. Theodoret also claimed that Constantine introduced Christian chaplains into the army, which in my opinion has been unnecessarily suspected on the grounds that there is no other evidence for this: it is quite clear that some sort of chaplains had to be in existence to perform the Christian services instituted for the 'believers'.[267]

We should not forget, however, that Constantine did not stop following the old Roman military traditions overnight. Several of those old pagan forms like shouts in unison of 'May gods protect the emperor!' continued to be practised as late as 326 (Lee, 2007, 183). Constantine also continued to hold the position of High Priest of the Roman pagan religion as Pontifex Maximus and appointed other pontifices. In this capacity Constantine undoubtedly could preside over pagan ceremonies when necessary and learn of the possible threats to his person through the soothsayers/astrologers acting as informers.

It is still clear that the numbers of Christians increased significantly as the fourth century progressed and the religious convictions of the soldiers grew with it. According to Eusebius (3.59), the Church of Antioch was divided into two, with the result that the army was also divided into two factions, and this would have resulted in bloodshed had not Constantine intervened. Since Constantine visited Antioch only in 324 it is clear that his own personal Comitatus and Protectores consisted largely of Christians by the time he defeated Licinius. This does suggest the probability that the abovementioned positive measures for Christian service were already taken in 312/3. Despite this, it is clear that throughout the fourth century there were, generally speaking, less Christians in the Western portion of the empire, partially thanks to the persistence of pagan beliefs in less urbanized areas and partially to the recruitment of pagan tribesmen into the army. In contrast, the numbers of Christians among the population and in the army in the East were greater and only increased further when Constantine chose to remain in the East with his elite Christian army. The greatest impetus to the Christianization of the Eastern forces came as a result of Constantius II's policy of favouring Christians in his administration (see later).[268]

The public conversion of Constantine to Christianity also brought with itself a series of dilemmas. The Christians were far from united in their beliefs and Constantine was immediately faced with the problem of the Donatists in Africa. Constantine decided in favour of the party that had won the position of bishop, but the problem did not go away. Donatus and his supporters refused to give up. Eventually Constantine ordered his army to interfere, with the result that in 317 the Donatists gained their first martyrs when the soldiers and mob attacked their churches. The local military commanders continued a policy of repression after this, which was ended only in 321. At that time a new war with Licinius began to seem inevitable and Constantine decided that it was time to stop persecuting Donatists so that he could claim to act as the protector of all Christians. All Donatist exiles were recalled and given freedom to worship. The end result was that the Donatists dominated the African church despite the support Catholics received from the state. The conflicts between the Christians also made it necessary for Constantine to convene the Council of Nicaea in 325, which he attended in person.[269] Henceforth it was necessary for emperors to possess quite a deep understanding of Christian doctrine in order to be able to act as the ultimate judges in religious matters. According to the law, the Church decided its own doctrinal issues without the intervention of the emperor, but this was merely a façade.

Monotheism triumphant

Constantine left Rome in January 313 and Licinius left Carnuntum in the beginning of February for a joint meeting of the emperors at Milan. The alliance was now finally sealed with the marriage of Licinius and Constantine's sister. The emperors also planned their future operations, and Constantine seems to have given Licinius a detailed account of the use of Christianity to defeat Maxentius. They also issued the Edict of Milan, which ensured religious freedom for Christians, and Constantine also advised Licinius to use the same methods as he had to encourage his troops.

This was sorely needed, because Maximinus had finally managed to bring to a successful conclusion his Armenian war and was fast marching against Licinius. Maximinus seems to have reached Asia Minor while Licinius was still at Milan. He had 70,000 men, but his main strategy was to win over the soldiers of Licinius by bribing them. He crossed the straits and offered terms for the defenders of Byzantium, but in vain. He ordered an assault, but it was repulsed. The garrison surrendered after a siege of eleven days. After this, he moved against Heraclea (Perinthus), which also surrendered after a siege lasting only a few days. When Maximinus then continued his journey for a distance of eighteen miles from Heraclea, his scouts informed him that Licinius and his army were at a distance of eighteen miles (evidently just south of the River Ergina) blocking his way forward. The two short sieges had bought Licinius enough time to collect an army of only 30,000 men from the scattered armies of the Danube. When the small size of the enemy army was brought to Maximinus' attention he was naturally more than eager to advance immediately.

The Battle of the Plain of Ergenus, 30 April 313: Licinius vs. Maximinus.

Licinius followed Constantine's example to the letter. He too saw a dream about an angel that told him to seek aid from the 'Highest God'. Maximinus was the first to array his forces ready for combat on the Plain of Ergenus. This gave Licinius the chance of adapting his battle plans to suit the situation.

Licinius continued to follow Constantine's example and ordered his men to put down their shields, remove their helmets, and then stretch out their hands to the heaven while the officers and emperor recited a common prayer to the Supreme God three times. After this, the soldiers armed themselves. This both encouraged the men and showed their superior fighting spirit to their enemies. Then the two emperors advanced before their troops and had a futile parley.

When the negotiations had ended, the Licinians grasped the initiative and attacked impetuously. It is probable that the numerically inferior Licinian army refused either a single wing or both wings so that they could concentrate their attack against only one spot of the enemy line, but unfortunately we do not know what tactic they used because Lactantius does not give any details of the array. It is also possible that the Lactantians could have used the wedge array in the centre, but as stated we don't know the details. What is certain, however, is that the show of confidence shown both before the battle and now in the attack demoralized Maximinus' men. They fled without attempting any resistance. Maximinus tried to rally his men by galloping along the lines, while also making every effort to bribe the attacking enemies – but all in vain. He was forced to flee. Licinius enrolled the survivors into his own troops and then dispersed them in several different garrisons.

In the meanwhile Maximinus reached Nicomedia on 2 May, after which he continued his flight all the way up to the Cilician Gates, where he intended to stop Licinius. When Licinius' men forced their way through, Maximinus fled to Tarsus where he killed himself. Licinius exploited his victory by ordering Galerius' son Candidianus and Valeria, the daughter of Diocletian, to be put to death together with Severus' son Severianus so that there would not be any potential dynastic competitors with him in the East.

Stratagem in Gaul, 313

In the meanwhile, Constantine appears to have waited for the results of the Battle of Ergenus on 30 April before moving into Gaul. It is actually possible that the stratagem in Gaul mentioned by the Latin Panegyrics (12.21.5–24.2 and 4.18.1–6) was in truth the arrival of Constantine's army from the south only after the Franks had already invaded in the winter of 312/13, but I have given the panegyrics the benefit of the doubt and accepted their version.

According to the panegyrics, when Constantine learnt of the impending invasion of the Franks, he rushed to the border, but then to his dismay he found that the enemy was now unwilling to invade. However, Constantine was determined not to let the opportunity slip by and decided to lure the Franks to the Roman side of the Rhine. In order to achieve this, with the bulk of his forces he marched south. He left only a skeleton force behind with orders to engage the enemy only after the enemy had dispersed to plunder so that they could be destroyed piecemeal. When the enemy obliged, Constantine blocked their route of retreat with a fleet of ships and disembarked his army on the opposite bank to devastate the homes of the Franks.[270] In sum, thanks to the foresight of Constantine Roman civilians had taken refuge inside fortresses and his generals could fight a guerrilla campaign against the invaders, while on the opposite bank of the Rhine the Romans faced only a mass of helpless civilians to butcher.

Just like before Constantine continued his policy of terror against neighbours and had all Frankish prisoners slaughtered in the amphitheatre. Constantine clearly liked this form of punishment despite being a Christian ruler. The Franks had been taught a lesson they could not immediately forget. This invasion was a huge disaster for the Franks and it took a long time for them to recover fully, but this did not prevent them from making still another attempt in the following year.

In late 313 Constantine made a brief expedition to Britain, and his presence is attested at Treves on 1 June 314 and at the Council of Arles which opened on 1 August 314 (Barnes, 65). In late 314 Constantine achieved a series of victories over the Franks and Alamanni along the Rhine which were celebrated in imperial coinage. Constantine spent the winter of 314/5 at Treves and then moved to Rome to celebrate his *decennalia*, which once again gave him a chance to reward his troops with a donative. Constantine remained at Rome from July until 27 September, after which he passed the winter of 315/6 at Treves. Constantine spent the summer of 316 in the south of Gaul and prepared for a lightning campaign against Licinius. While he was there his wife Fausta gave birth to a son at Arles on 7 August 316. The official cause of war was the attempted murder of Constantine by Licinius.

Licinius' Wars from late 313 to 316

The extant titles prove that Licinius fought a campaign against the Persians in Cappadocia, Adiabene, Media and Armenia either in late 313 or in 314. His old friend Trdat seems to have eagerly sought alliance with him, which unsurprisingly spelled disaster for the Persians. Licinius' positive attitude towards Christianity made the rapprochement possible. A council of bishops was convened at Caesarea in 314 to consecrate Gregory as Patriarch of Armenia. The alliance between Rome and Armenia effectively secured Mesopotamia for the Romans.

It was also then that Licinius made a real coup on his Arabian frontier.[271] The Christian king of Hira, Imru al-Qays, seems to have become a Federate of the Roman Empire. The reason for the change of loyalties seems to be the fact that Imru had converted to Christianity and the new regime of Constantine and Licinius promised him advantages. There are several pieces of evidence for the conclusion of the *foedus* in 314: firstly, from an inscription of Namara we know that he had become a Federate by 328; secondly, the

Persians were too weak to protect the Lakhmids and the Lakhmids consequently needed new allies; and thirdly, there is an inscription set up by Flavius Terentianus, the *praeses* of Mauretania, in 318/19 which includes the title *Arabicus* for Constantine.[272] The threat posed by Licinius' army at a time when no help from Persia would be forthcoming must have tilted the balance in favour of them becoming Roman Federates. It is in fact quite probable that the desertion of the Christian rulers Trdat and Imru to the Roman side tilted the balance in favour of Licinius.

Now the Romans had a truly powerful monarch to protect their desert frontier. In 328 in his epitaph Imru titled himself the King of all of the Arabs and held sway at least over the Arabs of Iraq, Azd, Nizar, Ma'add and had campaigned as far as Najran, which was located deep in Himyar territory. Soon after achieving Federate status Imru's possessions seem to have encompassed at least the Syrian Desert, Hijaz, Bahrain and the lands of the Mudar, Ma'aad, and Yamana. The lands of the Kinda lay just outside his territory and within the Himyarite sphere of influence. In short, after concluding the *foedus* Imru was able to extend his domains to cover at least the central and southern federate tribes.

Imru's fears of Persian action in 313/4 proved unfounded because the Persian magnates and priests were at loggerheads with each other. The Persian troops, the conscripts, were apparently kept along distant frontiers (evidently in the east) in a sorry state at a time when their families were facing hardships, with the result that the army was in a mutinous state. The bulk of the Persian magnates consisted of the Parthian (or Saka-Parthian) nobles whose territories bordered the north, north-east and south-east, with the result that most of the Persian forces were naturally used against the 'Turks' (Kushans? and/or the Chionitai?) in this situation. The other borders were predictably neglected, hence the Arabic incursions. According to Tabari (i.837), Shapur (or more likely his advisors) cleverly defused the time-bomb created by the mutinous forces posted in Central Asia by giving everyone who so wished permission to return to their families. The men who stayed in their posts were promised rewards and the men who returned were allowed to stay with their families until recalled to complete their service. This must have happened in about 313/4. This meant that the Persian armies remained on the defensive until about c. 325/6. This also meant that in about 315 Imru was able to conquer the client kingdom of Bahrain/Bahrayn from the Persians, and then with their naval assets he was able to occupy significant portions of Fars/Persis around Ardashir Khurrah. In other words, Imru took control of Bushihr, the principal Persian commercial port in the area.

Christianity had also gained ground in Mesopotamia, Iran, India, Central Asia and China. Ctesiphon had got its first bishop, Mar Papa, already in 291. He was later promoted to be patriarch of Persia and the entire east in 324 so that he could act as their representative towards the western Church. The position had been coveted by archdeacon Semon, whose parents were very close to the King of Kings, but Papa managed to calm the situation by making Semon his successor. The Christians also managed to bribe the commander of the elite guards in Ctesiphon to stop the persecution that apparently took place after Constantine had become sole ruler.[273] Regardless, Constantine's adoption of Christianity as state religion in 324 changed the situation forever. Henceforth being an orthodox Roman Christian would be seen as tantamount to treason by the Persians, regardless of the periodical cessation of persecution that could result, for example, from bribery – as shown above.

In 315 Licinius was forced to return to the Balkans to fight a campaign against the Goths. After Licinius had won, he rebuilt the city of Tropaeum Traiani, probably in an effort to present himself as the new Trajan. This obviously begs the question whether he had conquered territory north of the Danube and was responsible for some sections of the so-called 'Giant's Furrow' ditch. In that same year Licinius' wife gave birth to a son and Licinius could look forward to creating a dynasty.

… And Then There Was One: Constantine vs. Licinius: the First War (See Maps Section)

In my opinion there is no reason to suspect the official reason for the war which was the attempted murder of Constantine by Licinius, because the incidental evidence backs it up. According to this official version Licinius employed Senecio, a *dux* on the Danube frontier, to persuade his brother senator Bessianus (married to Constantine's half-sister Anastasia) to murder Constantine. The plot was evidently uncovered by Constantine's secret service. When Bessianus was confronted with the evidence, he confessed and was duly executed. Senecio fled to Licinius and when Constantine demanded the extradition of Senecio. Licinius refused and this became the *casus belli*. This case had also other consequences: all of those who had been supporters or friends of Bessianus were purged or exiled.

The Battle of Cibalae, 8 October 316

This time there was no chance of Constantine surprising his enemy entirely, but true to his nature Constantine attacked immediately at a time when his enemy was not expecting it (he was at Verona on 29 September and campaigns were usually not fought after that) with the forces he had at hand just like Julius Caesar had when he crossed the Rubicon in 49 BC. Constantine had with him only 20,000 cavalry and infantry, but all of these forces consisted of elite units. It is probable that this was part of Constantine's overall plan. Had he assembled more men in the north of Italy he would have given a warning to his enemy. Now Licinius' spies could report back that Constantine was not preparing a campaign for the autumn. As a result of this, Constantine was able to pit his crack troops against whatever Licinius had with him at his headquarters and nearby. The surprised Licinius managed to collect in haste 35,000 cavalry and infantry. In other words, Licinius had the quantitative advantage, Constantine had the qualitative advantage.

Licinius established his headquarters near the town of Cibalae (Vincovci) on 8 October 316 and waited for the arrival of his enemy. In other words, Licinius chose the battlefield. The fact that Licinius chose a good defensive position speaks volumes. It proves that he did not feel any confidence in the ability of his troops to defeat Constantine, even though he had almost twice as many men. When Licinius learnt that Constantine was close by, he deployed his army on the plain below so that the hill and the town protected the rear of his army against possible outflanking attempts, but he did not stop at this. Licinius followed Roman military doctrine to the letter and also placed his marching camp and baggage train behind the army. The reason for this conclusion is that Zosimus claims that the Licinians abandoned their cattle, pack animals and all other equipment when they fled after the battle.

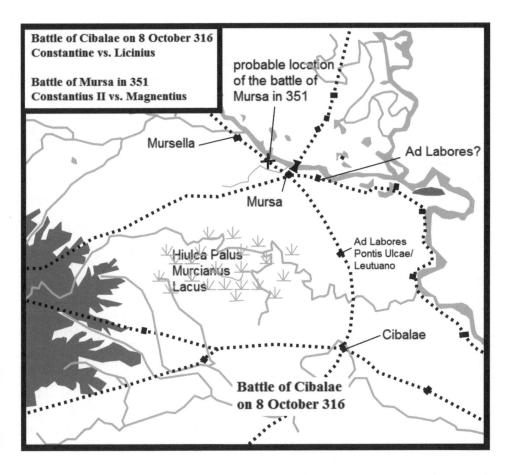

Battle of Cibalae on 8 October 316
Constantine vs. Licinius

Battle of Mursa in 351
Constantius II vs. Magnentius

probable location
of the battle of
Mursa in 351

Mursella

Ad Labores?

Mursa

Hiulca Palus
Murcianus
Lacus

Ad Labores
Pontis Ulcae/
Leutuano

Cibalae

Battle of Cibalae
on 8 October 316

Constantine faced a problem, because the only road that led to the plain was narrow and had a marsh lying alongside it. Constantine's solution was to deploy his cavalry in front and attack immediately with these to buy time for his infantry to reach the scene unhindered and deploy for battle. It is very unfortunate that Zosimus fails to give any details of the cavalry combat, but we can make the educated guess that Constantine conducted a prolonged and successful cavalry skirmish in which the javelin- and spear-armed units performed skirmishing in single files that charged forward and the other types of units charged and retreated in turn. It is probable that after this had continued as long as was necessary to secure the deployment of the infantry Constantine withdrew his cavalry to the flanks of his infantry.

However, it is possible that Eusebius (Vita 2.6–11) actually describes this battle, and not the Battle of Chrysopolis in 324 as is usually thought. If this is the case, then Licinius attacked first with his cavalry when Constantine's cavalry emerged from the narrows. This would make sense because it would have been in Licinius' interest to attack immediately with his elite cavalry (he had *clibanarii* and bodyguard units) before Constantine could deploy his forces. This attack, however, failed and Constantine was able to defeat him (in cavalry combat). Eusebius' account states that Licinius repeated his attack after this, which would imply the regrouping of the forces and the use of cavalry reserves. According to Eusebius, in the course of the battle Constantine had noticed that the section which had the *Labarum* was always successful (i.e. where he and the *Labarum* were). The reason was that the enemy could see the arrival of the reserves from the approach of the banner. Consequently, he gave the *Labarum* a special guard of fifty men chosen from the ranks of his personal guardsmen and sent these men with the *Labarum* wherever there was a unit in difficulties.

Eusebius then goes on to claim that when Constantine's forces had proved successful, he gave the order for his men to advance in good order. The men who formed the forefront of Licinius' army did not resist but surrendered at the emperor's feet. This would suggest that Constantine's right wing had defeated Licinius' left cavalry wing. However, according to Eusebius, the others – the reserves and infantry phalanx – refused to surrender and stood their ground. As a result of this, Constantine ordered his men to attack, with the result that they too were routed. When Licinius saw this he panicked and fled. According to Eusebius, Constantine did not pursue the fugitive hard out of pity for him.

According to Zosimus' version of the events this battle was among the hardest fought battles in history. He states that after both armies had exhausted their arrows, they continued the fight with a prolonged exchange of thrown spears and javelins. As a result, the battle lasted from the morning till the night, and was only decided when the right wing (undoubtedly consisting of cavalry) under the personal command of Constantine crushed the left wing of Licinius. According to this version, it was then that Licinius mounted his horse and fled, and, as a result of his flight, the army also panicked and fled. In essence, therefore, there is no contradiction between the accounts of Eusebius and Zosimus. According to Origo, this defeat had been very costly for Licinius for he lost 20,000 foot soldiers and part of his mailed cavalry (i.e. the *clibanarii*). In other words, Constantine's more manoeuvrable horsemen had once again proved themselves in combat against the more heavily-equipped but less-mobile cavalry. It is also notable that Zosimus' account proves that Constantine's troops did not attack the well-ordered enemy forces until they had sufficiently reduced the morale of the enemy by missiles. It is probable that Constantine's forces were able to do that because the Licinians were unwilling to leave their good defensive positions. In other words, the fact that Licinius had been able to pick and choose the best locale (in his opinion) for the battle contributed to his defeat. It is also notable that the battle had once again been decided by the cavalry charge conducted by Constantine and his *Labarum* guard. At the head of his forces, in his dashing uniform, he was like a fourth-century Alexander the Great. The diagrams from my article represent the principal stages of the battle.

The Battle of Campus Ardiensis, January 317

As noted above, Licinius managed to flee together with some of his cavalry. In order to prevent pursuit, he demolished all of the bridges behind him. When Licinius reached Sirmium, he was joined by his wife, son, and treasury. He continued his flight to Serdica, where he met Valens, who had assembled a large army at Hadrianopolis. In order to secure Valens' loyalty Licinius proclaimed him *Augustus*. Constantine, however, was not slow in following. He is attested to be at Serdica on 4–8 December. When he reached Philippolis, also in December, he was met by Licinius' ambassadors who offered

The Battle of Cibalae

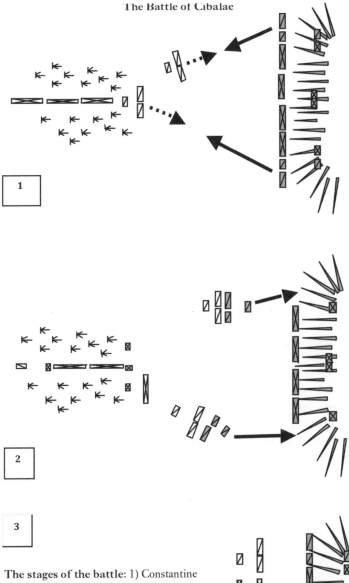

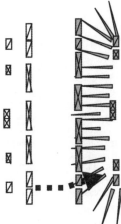

The stages of the battle: 1) Constantine marches to the plain and attacks with cavalry; 2) The Licinian cavalry attacks, but is forced to retreat back to the safety of the infantry phalanx, while Constantine's infantry deploy for combat; 3) After a prolonged exchange of missiles, Constantine leads a cavalry charge up the hill and defeats the enemy.

negotiations. Constantine refused to listen, continued his march, and caught up with his adversary at Campus Ardiensis near Hadrianopolis in January 317. Zosimus claims that Constantine had previously sent 5,000 horsemen to pursue Licinius, but that these had lost their way. This is patently false. In truth, Constantine had sent these 5,000 horsemen by a circuitous route to attack the enemy from behind. It seems probable that in this case the pagan Zosimus or his pagan source just could not stomach the tactical genius of Constantine and claimed incorrectly that Constantine's men had lost their way.

The Licinians were once again unwilling to leave their defensive position, which meant that the Constantinians again resorted to the use of a prolonged softening of the enemy with missile fire, which was responded to in kind by the Licinians. The missile engagement lasted as long as the supply of arrows. After this, the Constantinians advanced and started a brutal melee with spears and short swords. Now that Constantine's men had tied the enemy formation in place so that it could no longer manoeuvre, the 5,000 cavalry appeared on a hill behind Licinius. The timing was impeccable. However, the Licinians did not panic, but fought bravely against them, which means that Valens' infantry was able to form a double front and then double phalanx against the attackers. This speaks volumes about the quality of the forces under Valens and also of his generalship abilities. Zosimus' hostile account claims that the battle ended in a stalemate after both sides had suffered great losses, following which the armies separated. The Origo retains a corrective to this version. In truth, Constantine's army forced Licinius' men to retreat and it was only the darkness of the night that saved the Licinians. (See map taken from my article.)

Now Constantine believed that he had won the war and made the greatest mistake of his career. Constantine let the enemy escape and continued his march straight towards the city of Byzantium. However, Licinius and Valens had foreseen this. They turned aside to Beroea and cut off Constantine's route of retreat. In this situation Constantine felt compelled to accept Licinius' peace proposal. The negotiations lasted for a while, in the course of which Constantine was able to march back to Serdica in February. The terms of the agreement stipulated that Licinius recognized Constantine as his superior, and gave Constantine the Dioceses of Pannoniae and Moesiae. Constantine had also demanded that Licinius was to execute Valens, and Licinius felt compelled to agree to this in

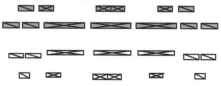

The Battle of Campus Ardiensis:
1) Constantine sends 5,000 horsemen to encircle the enemy; 2) Constantine purposefully delays the attack. The battle begins with a long exchange of missile attacks; 3) Constantine orders a general attack along the front to tie up the enemy forces so that his ambushers would have better chances of defeating the enemy. However, Valens' infantry responded by forming a double front (and then double phalanx). The Licinian infantry gave way only after the darkness gave them the opportunity to flee in relative safety. 4) The retreat appears to have been done in a comparatively orderly manner under the able leadership of Valens. It is likely that he commanded the left wing while the right was under the command of Licinius himself. It is more than likely that the attack of Constantine's cavalry was directed against the left wing. The importance of Valens' leadership is shown by the fact that the only time that Licinius was able to frustrate Constantine's manoeuvres occurred when Valens was at hand to assist him.

return for peace. This was a wise policy move for both parties to make. The removal of Valens secured the entire East for Licinius, while Constantine eliminated Licinius' best commander. The treaty was concluded at Serdica on 1 March 317.

The Cold War from 317 to 324: the Setting of the Stage (See Maps Section)

Both parties to the contract knew that the stalemate was only temporary and that both sides would eventually have to continue the unfinished war. After the conclusion of the peace, Constantine appointed his sons Crispus and Constantine II (Constantinus) as Caesars (note that the earliest date for the three-headed version of the *Labarum* is after 317). Similarly, he appointed Licinius' son as Caesar so that he ranked in the hierarchy between the sons of Constantine. This reorganization meant that if the elderly Licinius died, Crispus as eldest Caesar would succeed as Augustus of the East so that the end result would be once again a Tetrarchy.

Licinius transferred his capital to Nicomedia and soon after this started to purge Christians from his army and administration because he rightly feared their loyalty. However, he still tried to find a middle road between complete persecution and toleration of Christianity and ended up not pleasing anyone. The first step Licinius took was to expel Christians from the imperial palace. His aim was undoubtedly to remove potential spies and assassins from his immediate entourage. His next step was to force all members of the imperial administration and army to sacrifice to the gods or resign. He also legislated against Christians by forbidding Christian assemblies and councils of bishops, cancelled the tax advantages of the priests instituted by Constantine, and the governors were once again allowed to punish Christians and so forth. Unsurprisingly, Constantine eventually responded by issuing a law that promised punishment to anyone who had forced Christians to sacrifice to the gods on 25 December 323 (a symbolically important date).

Licinius is also said to have started to rape virgins and married women of the nobility and to have his men indulge themselves in the same activities. It would be easy to consider this as a stock accusation used by the sources against the so-called tyrants.[274] However, there may be 'good psychological reasons' for his behaviour. Firstly, it is possible that Licinius may have wanted to insult his wife and through her Constantine. Secondly, such wanton lusts are quite common among men who consider that they have nothing to lose. Thirdly, Licinius may have wanted to make his soldiers his co-criminals while also satisfying their carnal desires. Fourthly, considering Licinius' monetary needs, he may have indulged in the same kind of robbery as Maximian before him.

Both emperors had already started to make preparations for the eventual war in earnest in 321 by amassing money to increase the size of the army. The breach between the emperors was now apparent because both nominated their own consuls. It was also the year when the empire-wide census was conducted to reassess the tax base. Licinius fleeced his subjects particularly hard with many new innovations in an effort to collect money, which did add money to his coffers but angered important sections of society. In direct contrast, Constantine made the census fairer and lowered the liturgies and taxes. Similarly, when Licinius removed from retired soldiers their exemption from liturgies and taxes, Constantine restored these. There was a clear difference in their approach.

Licinius' only thought was to fill the coffers so that he could increase his military build-up, while Constantine sought to endear himself to wide sections of society to obtain their support, or at least their neutrality. In short, Constantine attempted to make himself appear as the only defender of the soldiers, taxpayers, and Christians. This was a very wise policy. It made his soldiers fight eagerly for him, while it made Licinius' men less eager to fight on his behalf.[275]

In the meantime, Constantine had made Serdica his de facto capital while Sirmium served as his second base of operations. Even though Constantine made no pretence about his favouritism of Christianity, he was still wise enough to show his respect towards Greek philosophy, culture and inheritance, all of which benefited from his patronage. He also showered favours on high ranking pagans. In consequence of this, he was elected as 'Hoplite General of Athens', which received in return a free annual supply of grain. As a consequence of this, Licinius' favouritism of paganism did not cause the Western pagans to transfer their allegiance to his side.

The Caesar Crispus (born c. 305) had taken up his residence at Treves and was given his own imperial administration. It is probable that the choice of the experienced Junius Bassus as Crispus' *PP* was made by Constantine because his son was still young and needed an experienced hand to guide him. The same must be true of other military appointments. The purpose was to help Crispus develop the necessary skills to manage the imperial administration and to lead armies in combat. Consequently, it is probable that the Romans initiated the two wars along the Rhine that took place between 319 and 323: Crispus' victorious campaigns against the Franks in 319 and against the Alamanni in 323 must have been part of his schooling. It was only then that his military apprenticeship was over. He was now a full-blooded warrior general – just in time to take part in his father's war against Licinius. It is quite possible that the reason why Constantine did not attack Licinius already in 318 was that he wanted to prepare his son to lead part of the army that he would assemble for the task. He knew that he could trust his flesh and blood with a large command. Crispus had also been given a wife who gave birth to a daughter in October 322 and was pregnant again in 324. Unbeknownst to the Romans in about 320 there also took place a momentous event in India that would change the course of history in Central Asia. It was then that Chandragupta 1 (ca.320–325?) started the rise of the Guptas in India, which would eventually lead to conflict with Sasanian Persia.

In 321 or 322 Constantine faced troubles of his own. The 'Iazygian' Sarmatians (opposite Valeria) invaded Pannonia, which required a response. Consequently, in 322 Constantine led in person a retaliatory campaign against them. The Sarmatians were duly defeated and forced to make a peace. It is possible that Constantine started the reinforcement or building of the so-called Devil's Dyke at this time. After this, Constantine started full-scale and massive preparations for war against Licinius, but Licinius struck first by using proxies. In that same year an embassy arrived from Persia to Constantine evidently with a peace proposal (Barnes, 1981, 72). This secured the Eastern frontier so that Constantine could not be claimed to have caused a disaster if he moved against Licinius. The relationship between the Christian Trdat and Licinius had also become sour thanks to Licinius' policies, which meant that no help would be forthcoming for Licinius from Armenia.

In 323 Licinius purposefully withdrew the troops protecting the Gothic bank, as a result of which the Tervingian Goths and Sarmatians led by Rausimundus/Rausimond invaded Roman territory and advanced against Constantine. According to Origo (21), Constantine was at the time at Thessalonica, which suggests that he was already engaged in the building of the naval base for his invasion of Licinius' territories. The identity of the attackers is contested. The name of the leader and location suggests the involvement of the Goths – Origo 21 in fact claims that they were Goths – but other sources name the attackers as Sarmatians. Thanks to the fact that the area from the Danube to the Caucasus included several Sarmatian, Gothic and other tribes, in the absence of detailed narratives it is impossible to be certain which group or groups were involved. However, the details in Constantine Porphyrogenitus' and Zosimus' texts suggest strongly that the invaders consisted of the Sarmatians of the Bosporan Kingdom, even if Zosimus calls the attackers 'Scythians'. Since we know that the Greuthungi Goths were the overlords of a huge tribal confederacy (although at this time the Heruls were probably not part of it – see later), it is possible to postulate that by this time the Bosporan Kingdom may have been ruled by a Gothic prince married to a Sarmatian princess. It is quite probable that the crushing defeat of Sauromatus (the Sarmatian ruler of Bosporus) in 285 had weakened the kingdom to such an extent that the Goths had managed to reassert their supremacy in the region. It is notable that archaeology proves that there was a Germanic presence in the Crimea at this time.

In sum, I suggest that the invaders consisted of the Goths and Sarmatians of the Bosporan kingdom under their Gothic ruler. It is possible that the ruler belonged to the Baltha of the Tervingi, even if he still recognized the Greuthungi as overlords, because that would have enabled him to conduct a joint operation with the Tervingi against the Romans and would have allowed him passage through the Tervingian territories. This would explain why it was possible to call the attackers Goths and Sarmatians. However, it is possible that the invasion was actually conducted by a Bosporan fleet because Zosimus claims that the Sarmatians crossed the Danube on ships.

It is quite clear that Licinius' purpose was to fight a war by proxy against Constantine to weaken him before he launched his own attack. On 28 April 323 Constantine also enacted a law according to which all those found to have collaborated with the barbarians would be burned to death – which can be seen to implicate Licinius too. According to Constantine Porphyrogenitus (*De administrando imperio* 53.1ff.), it was then that Constantine the Great remembered his father's strategy against the Sarmatians and used the Chersonites against these 'Scythians' in like manner. (See the events of 285.) Constantine's purpose was clearly to save his own forces and also fight through proxies, which also enabled him to deny having overstepped his authority. Consequently, the Chersonites once again prepared their military wagons carrying *cheirobolistrai*, (hand-ballistae), but this time they marched to the Danube, crossed it, formed a battle array, and defeated the Scythian cavalry. Constantine showed his gratitude by paying 1,000 Chersonites to serve as an *arithmos* of *ballistroi*. Constantine Porphyrogenitus also noted why Cherson could always be controlled by the 'Byzantines'. They, and therefore also the Late Romans, could always control the city of Cherson by cutting sea trade to the city. (See the illustrations in Chapter 2.)

It is probable that this is the same war as described by Zosimus (2.21). Zosimus claims that the Sarmatians who lived near Lake Maeotis (i.e. the Sarmatians of the Bosporan Kingdom) under their king Rausimundus sailed across the Danube and then initially fought with success against Constantine (this success may actually have consisted of the advance through the undefended territories of Licinius) and then attacked a strongly garrisoned town protected by a stone wall which was topped with a wooden palisade. He also claims that the Sarmatians then set alight the wooden part of the wall, but regardless of this the defenders managed to keep the enemy at bay by throwing down on them missiles and stones. It was then that Constantine arrived and fell on the attackers from the rear. Rausimundus lost most of his army, fled across the Danube and then to a thick wooded hill, but Constantine followed. He attacked again and Rausimundus and many of his men lost their lives and a lot of captives were taken. If one attempts to combine the accounts, it is possible that Constantine and the Chersonites engaged separate enemy divisions. The 'Sarmatian' survivors were distributed to different cities to discourage the possibility of revolt.

As I suggested in my article (Slingshot, 2006), the most likely interpretation for the above is that the first encounter(s) between Constantine and the Goths-Sarmatians had ended in Roman defeat(s) or at least in strategic withdrawal and use of guerrilla warfare. It is also clear that Constantine must have sent an urgent plea to the Chersonites to assist him almost immediately after he had learnt of the invasion, or even in advance for the Chersonites to be able to participate in timely fashion. This implies that he must have known the purpose of Licinius from the very start and may also have had spies inside Licinius' administration, for example in the staff of Licinius' wife. It is also clear that Constantine's defensive organization was not designed to meet this type of threat. The expectation would have been that Licinius would stop such invasions in Thrace. It is also probable that the core of Constantine's expeditionary reserves consisted of lightly-equipped German auxiliaries, which would not have been well-suited for use against the Gothic and Sarmatian heavy cavalry and their mounted archers. Firstly, Constantine did not possess enough horsemen with which to engage the enemy without the support of the infantry. Secondly, the use of infantry made Constantine's forces slower than the enemy. Thirdly, the lightly-equipped *auxilia* were more vulnerable against the mounted archers than the legions. Consequently, it seems probable that Constantine let his frontier armies use guerrilla warfare until the lack of victuals (populace and cattle would have been evacuated inside the cities) would force the enemy to attempt to besiege a location with a food storage. This in turn tied the enemy to the spot, allowing Constantine to rush to the scene.

The Chersonites were clearly used in a diversionary role and also to block the enemy's route of retreat. Furthermore, it is likely that they were also used against the families of the Sarmatians, as they had been used in 285. According to Barnes (1981, 76) fighting was recorded to have taken place at Campona, on the River Margus, and at Bononia, all of which were inside Constantine's territory. If the fighting took place along this wide front, then the 'Iazygian Sarmatians' would have also participated in the action. However, it is equally possible that the fighting that was recorded to have taken place at Campona belonged to the previous year. What is clear, however, is that the invaders did not manage to penetrate deep into Constantine's territory from the Danube before being pushed back.

In sum, Constantine had once again proved himself to be a superb military leader who knew how to respond to any kind of threat facing his forces. If possible, this endeared him to the troops even more. This is by no means surprising considering his wealth of military experience. In this case, Constantine had once again used the most efficient combination of ways to deal with the threat of the steppe cavalry. Most importantly, Constantine realized that in order to achieve a decisive victory he needed to deny the enemy cavalry the possibility of retreat. He accomplished this objective by: 1) first luring the enemy to besiege a fixed position (a city in Moesia?) after which he attacked them from behind (undoubtedly with the cavalry placed in the van and infantry following behind); and 2) catching the enemy between two forces, the Chersonites and Romans.

This campaign also proves once again the effectiveness of the salvoes of the carriage-mounted ballistae and crossbows against the heavy cavalry of the Goths and Sarmatians. It is not known whether the Romans had employed their ballistae-carts (they had definitely used those in pitched battles, note especially Trajan's Column) as moving wagon laagers, but if they had not done that before, it is certain that they started to do that from this date onwards. The hiring of the Chersonites to act as *ballistarii* makes it certain that the tactics that they had employed were now copied by the Romans. In fact, it is probable that the units of *ballistarii* that appear for the first time precisely during the reign of Constantine are a reflection of the adoption of the wagon laagers by specialist units.

The Crusade against Licinius (See Maps Section)

Constantine's war against the Sarmatians provided the *casus belli* for the emperors, because Constantine had been forced to march his army through the Thracian Diocese in pursuit. Licinius hypocritically protested, which only gave the senior emperor Constantine the excuse he needed. Both prepared for war.[276]

Constantine the Great had assessed the needs of such a campaign and had come to the conclusion that a forward naval base was needed. Consequently, Constantine went to Thessalonica where he supervised the building of military harbour. (See also above.) At the same time he gave orders for his son and naval officers to assemble a fleet at Piraeus in Athens and for his other generals the order to assemble the field army at Thessalonica. Constantine spent part of the winter at Sirmium and probably reorganized the armed force in the area before returning to Thessalonica in the spring.

According to figures given by Zosimus, Constantine the Great had 200 'thirties' (thirty oars; the figures of the seamen actually suggest fifties), more than 2,000 transport ships, 120,000 infantry, 10,000 seamen, and 10,000 cavalry for his war against Licinius. According to Zosimus (2.22.3), Constantine's fleet consisted mostly of Greeks, which would mean that Constantine had left the bulk of his other fleets behind at their stations and had instead built a new fleet for this campaign. The probable reason for this is that Constantine intended to exploit the local knowledge of the Greek crews to his advantage.

Licinius assembled his army at Hadrianopolis and his navy apparently at the port of Ajax. He had 350 triremes, 150,000 infantry, and 15,000 cavalry. Licinius' fleet included 80 triremes from Egypt; 80 triremes from Phoenicia; 60 triremes from the Ionians and

Dorians; 30 triremes from the Cyprians; 20 triremes from the Carians; 30 triremes from the Bithynians; and 50 triremes from the Africans (the withdrawn Libyan Fleet?).

Constantine ordered the fleet to proceed from Piraeus to Thessalonica. Licinius apparently chose to remain at Hadrianopolis and allowed Constantine to march unopposed down the Via Egnatia along the coast, after which Constantine turned north towards his enemy. Considering the fact that Licinius' medium-to-large warships required sizable crews, it is probable that Constantine's forces outnumbered him. It was not safe for Constantine to advance directly to Byzantium, because that would have left Licinius with his army behind him. Consequently, Constantine's goal was to defeat his enemy's field army first and only then advance against the strategic city. Licinius chose to deploy his army in a defensive position along the River Margos to block Constantine's route of advance. This was typical of him. Instead of taking the offensive, he gave the initiative to Constantine.

As regards the figures given by Zosimus, these are usually taken to be exaggerations, but if one takes into account all the facts, the figures are realistic. Constantine's forces constituted only about 35 per cent of the forces available to him and perhaps about the same of Licinius' forces (Licinius seems to have increased his army significantly through heavy taxes). The navies alone would have demanded huge numbers of men on board to make them battle ready.

The Battle of Hadrianopolis, 3–4 July 324

When Constantine marched his own field army towards Adrianople (Hadrianopolis) and occupied the opposite bank of the Hebrus River, Licinius stretched his massive force along the bank to block the crossing points of the river from the mountain to the city. Constantine resorted to the age old stratagem, which had been used, for example, by Alexander the Great. Constantine deployed his army in front of the enemy and brought wood from the mountain as if he were to attempt to build a bridge across. After this, he led a selected force of 5,000 infantry and archers, and 800 horsemen to another location and then hid them behind a wooded hill.[277] According to Zosimus, Constantine took a mere twelve horsemen with him and crossed the river to see if it was fordable and attacked the enemy. If true, this must mean the initial reconnaissance operation in the course of which he and the twelve horsemen surprised the enemy guards which gave the chance for his bridgehead force to cross. The rest of the army was apparently then marched to the scene. As usual, Constantine's manoeuvre took Licinius by complete surprise. Licinius' army fled to the mountain, allowing Constantine's entire army to cross the river.

Once again Licinius took defensive positions and let the enemy take the initiative. His army did indeed possess a good defensive position on the slopes, as a result of which his men initially managed to push Constantine's forces downhill. However, as usual, when Constantine saw his troops faltering, he sent his special *Labarum* Guard to encourage those in distress, with the result that the situation was stabilized.

According to Origo (34), Constantine eventually won thanks to his good fortune (the psychological impact of the *Labarum*?) and the better discipline of his army. However, this time Constantine was himself wounded in the thigh, which is no wonder considering his tendency to lead his men from the front. According to Zosimus, Licinius' losses were heavy. About 30,000 lost their lives, and many must have been wounded. The rest surrendered at daybreak. Licinius fled with the few survivors to Byzantium.

The Siege of Byzantium and Naval Battle of the Hellespont, 324

Now Licinius decided to lessen the ardour of his enemy by resorting to the use of the walls of Byzantium and the wooden walls of his fleet. He sent all those troops that were not needed in the defence of Byzantium to Asia. The fleet was ordered to block any attempts by Constantine's fleet to sail through the Hellespont to Byzantium. In other words, once again Licinius gave the initiative to the enemy. Had he been a good naval commander, he would have realized that it would have been in his interest to attempt to defeat Constantine's fleet in the open seas rather than fight in the narrow straits.

While Constantine prepared to besiege Byzantium, he sent orders for his son Crispus, who was at least in nominal command of the fleet, to break the blockade in the Hellespont and to join him in Byzantium. Constantine seems to have inherited from his father Constantius I a navy that was led by very competent admirals. Notably, these very same commanders had already distinguished themselves in the operations against Italy and Africa in 312. It goes without saying that it is likely that these unnamed admirals were in charge of the operations and Crispus, who lacked naval experience, acted merely as a figurehead.

Crispus, or rather his admirals, showed their better understanding of naval warfare by choosing only 80 'thirties' (or 'fifties'?) for the engagement at Hellespont, while Abantus, Licinius' admiral, foolishly chose 200 triremes. It seems probable that Constantine's admirals retained the rest of the ships behind as an emergency reserve if Licinius' fleet somehow managed to break through. The greater understanding of the circumstances by Constantine's officers is probably a reflection of the fact that his admirals had actual combat experience while Licinius' admirals did not. As things progressed, the straits proved too narrow for the 200 triremes, which only got in the way of each other. In contrast, the smaller numbers of more agile 'thirties' were able to maintain their good order, as a result of which they managed to sink a great number of the larger ships.

Even though Constantine's fleet sank large numbers of enemy galleys, they had still not managed to fight their way through. Consequently, at nightfall Constantine's ships were anchored at Eleus (Elaious) in Thrace while Licinius' ships were anchored at the Port of Ajax. On the following day, Abantus initially decided to take advantage of a strong north wind and therefore arrayed his fleet for combat. However, it was now that he realized that Constantine's admirals had brought the rest of their galleys to the scene. Consequently, Abantus hesitated and made no move, with the result that at about midday the wind turned and the opportunity for attack was lost, and, even worse, the strong south wind proved too powerful for his fleet. Most of it was thrown against the shore. Abantus lost 150 ships and 5,000 men and was forced to flee with 4 ships. This was a huge disaster and decided the outcome of the war.

Thanks to the disaster, caused by gross incompetence, Constantine's fleet was now free to continue its journey, bring in the necessary supplies for Constantine's army, and to blockade the city of Byzantium. Constantine built a mound as high as the wall, and placed on it a wooden siege tower to give his other troops covering fire from above.

The rest of the men brought the battering rams and other siege engines into position to start their work. It was then that Licinius understood that the fall of the city would be inevitable. He had no other alternative than to sail across the Sea of Marmara, if he wanted to keep his hopes alive. Constantine's strategic and tactical genius, and luck, had once again overcome all obstacles. He was a person who realized the value of the fleet and the use of joint combined arms operations. He had employed fleets in almost all of his military campaigns along the rivers and seas in one form or another. Thanks to their naval experience Constantine and his admirals also knew the value of smaller galleys in narrow places and they also knew how to save their ships from strong winds – unlike Licinius' men.

The Battle of Chrysopolis/Chalcedon, 18 September 324

Once again Licinius attempted to regroup his men in defensive positions along the Hellespont, Propontis and Bosphorus. He guarded the Bosphorus in person by taking position opposite Byzantium at Chalcedon with the Gothic mercenaries under Alica. Licinius appointed his Master of Offices Martianus to the rank of Augustus and sent him to Lampsacus to protect the Hellespont. According to Zosimus, Constantine intended to bypass the enemy, as he had done so many times before, but he feared that the Bithynian coast near the Sacred Promontory would be inaccessible to his transport ships. As a result, he gave the order to build galleys and swift sailing skiffs suitable for the mission. This proved that his staff included persons who knew what types of ships were needed and also knew how to build them. After the new fleet was ready, Constantine and most of his army sailed to the Sacred Promontory, located at the mouth of the Black Sea. After disembarkation Constantine deployed his army in formation and advanced against his foe. Licinius had been able to observe the sailing of the enemy fleet, as a result of which he had immediately recalled Martianus from Lampsacus. The armies met at Chrysopolis on 18 September 324.

Licinius' position was hopeless, despite the fact that he had probably managed to collect additional forces as Constantine had built the new fleet. On top of this, Licinius had also apparently developed a superstitious fear of the *Labarum*. He is claimed to have issued an order for his officers not to look at it. The officers were also told to avoid fighting against it. If there is any truth to these claims, then these orders alone would have caused a defeat. Whatever the reason, Constantine won the battle with a single vigorous charge. Origo claims that the Licinians lost 25,000 men while the rest fled, while Zosimus claims that scarcely 30,000 out of 130,000 survived the battle. If Zosimus' figures are correct, then Licinius would have been able to collect another huge army only to lose it again, with the result that the overall losses would have been well over 100,000 men. In my opinion, Origo's figures are to be preferred in this case. If Licinius had lost 30,000 dead at Hadrianopolis, 5,000 at Hellespont, and 25,000 at Chrysopolis, the overall losses in dead would have been 60,000 in addition to which would have come the huge numbers of wounded. Thanks to the huge size of the Late Roman army at this stage, this did not endanger the borders – as we shall see.

The survivors of the battle surrendered to Constantine next day when they saw the latter's legions approaching in Liburnian galleys. In other words, Constantine's navy had once again coordinated its operations with the land forces. As I noted in the article (Slingshot, 2006), the presence of Constantine's navy makes it possible that he had used its naval artillery to protect his right flank. If he did not use it that way, then he must have planned to force the enemy army against the sea and his navy so that its route of retreat would be cut off. When the news of Licinius' defeat spread, Byzantium and Chalcedon opened their gates to the victor. Licinius fled to Nicomedia, and sent his wife to beg for mercy. Constantine promised to spare him and Martinianus as well, but soon after their surrender he had both of them killed. The civil war was finally over and there was only one master of the entire Roman Empire left.

Constantine the Great: Christian Reformer

Constantine's Christian Empire and His Reforms

Constantine's victory over Licinius enabled him to move decisively against the pagans. He instituted a purge of Licinius' supporters which effectively consisted of the most powerful pagans in the East. He forbade the making of sacrifices before the start of official business, the erection of cult statues, the consultation of oracles, the use of divination, and the making of sacrifices to the pagan gods. He ordered his financial officials to confiscate all valuables from the pagan temples to the treasury, and closed some of the most offensive (to the Christians that is) pagan cult-centres. He established the Christian Church as the official state religion and ordered that the governors and financial officials were to cooperate with the Christian bishops in the building of churches and in the conversion of buildings for Christian use.[278]

In the meanwhile, however, in about 324, a Persian prince named Hormizd/Hormisdas, the eldest son of Hormizd II, managed to flee from prison with the help of his wife (Zos. 2.27). He had fled to the Armenian king Trdat who was his friend and from there to Licinius. Hormizd, who was a famed javelin thrower, proved very useful as a military commander and advisor for the Romans under Constantine and his successors.

Unsurprisingly, the old friendship between Trdat and Licinius had grown cold. According to Moses (2.88), Licinius was an old man who dyed his hair, lusted after Glaphyra despite being married, persecuted Christians, and killed St. Basil, as a result of which Trdat knew that Constantine would soon attack Licinius. Consequently, Trdat had remained aloof, had not supported Licinius, and had waited for the opportunity to conclude a treaty with Constantine. Indeed, very soon after his victory over Licinius, Constantine appears to have received ambassadors from Trdat begging for peace. According to Agathangelos (873–5), after having learnt of Constantine's victories Trdat had held a council in which the matter was discussed, following which he went to meet Constantine in person. Unsurprisingly, Trdat's entourage included the bishops Gregory, Aristakes, and Albianos. He also took with him the four *vitaxae* and the great prince Angl, the *aspet*/coronet, the *sparapet*, the prince of Mokk, the prince of Siwnik, the prince of Rshtunik, the prince of Malkhazdom, the prince prefect of Shahapivan, and the master of the court, and with many other magnates and 70,000 chosen troops he marched to Ayrarat from the city of Valarshapat, and then passed into Greek territory. If the meeting between Constantine and Trdat actually took place, then it must have happened on the border between September 324 and January 325, and if Agathangelos' information regarding the composition of Trdat's embassy is accurate, one of his purposes must have been to demonstrate the entire might of Armenia, together with the bishops, so that Constantine would realize that it was in his interest to conclude a treaty with Armenia. Regardless, it is still clear that Agathangelos' account also includes legendary material which I have not included here.

Of great importance is also the referral in Moses (2.89) to the events of 325. Moses claims that when Constantine asked Trdat together with St. Gregory to take part in the Council of Nicaea which he had called to settle Church matters, Trdat refused because he had heard that Shapur had concluded an alliance with the 'King of India' and 'Khagan of the East'. This means that Shapur had managed to end the war against the 'Turks' mentioned by Tabari (i.836), which is also to be connected with the presence of Persian troops in garrison duty far away from their homes (i.837–8). We do not know who the 'King of India' was because there were several rulers in India and Central Asia that could fit the description, but the Indian connection is very important because very soon after this Metrodorus (see below) arrived from India bearing gifts to Constantine, clearly with the mission of provoking the emperor to declare war on Persia. It would be interesting to know whether this person arrived from the kingdom that had concluded the alliance with Persia or from its competitor. It would also be interesting to know whether this had any connection with the rise of the mighty Indian warrior king and conqueror Samudragupta (c. 325–376/380) who became ruler of the Guptas in about 325. We know that he immediately launched a series of campaigns that forged a huge empire, with far reaching consequences to the detriment of the Sasanians.

This incident also shows that Trdat had relatively well-working intelligence apparatus inside Persia, as a result of which he was ready for a possible Persian invasion. But then his operatives made a mistake. When Shapur launched his campaign against Arab invaders in 325 and the Arabs of Arabia in 326, rather than against Armenia, Trdat's agents made the wrong conclusion that Armenia would be safe for a while. Considering the fact that one of Trdat's nobles betrayed him, it is possible that he had fed this disinformation to him. On the basis of Trdat's subsequent visit to meet Constantine (according to the legend all the way to Rome) in about 326/7, it seems probable that he believed Armenia to be safe (Moses 2.84; Agathangelos 874–80).

Shapur's campaign against the Arabs was actually directed against the Roman Federate Imru. He chose 1,000 elite Asavaran horsemen and with these attacked the Arabs who occupied part of Fars. After Shapur had reconqured Fars, he embarked an unknown number of troops on ships, probably at Bushihr, and then crossed the sea and made a landing in the territory of Bahrayn, after which he marched through it killing everyone encountered until he reached Hajar. He renewed the general butchery there and marched to Yamama (evidently along the main caravan route) and killed everyone encountered. While he marched, his forces filled up and blocked all water springs and cisterns along the route. After this, Shapur marched to Medina (evidently still along the main caravan route), where the Persians once again renewed their killing spree. From there he marched to Bakr and Taghlib, which lay between Persia and Roman Syria. Some of the tribesmen were killed, but prisoners were also taken. The water sources were once again filled. This implies that Shapur had now defeated Imru and had forced him to flee to Roman territory. I would date this final stage of the Arabian campaign to the year 327, when Shapur also defeated Constantine (see below). Shapur exploited his victory by transferring various Arabic tribes from one place to another in an effort to take control of the region.[279]

The conversion of Iberia and its alliance with Rome must have taken place very soon after the renewal of the alliance between Armenia and Rome. In fact, we can definitely date the conversion to the period between 325 and 327 on the basis of a dream sequence in the Georgian Chronicles. According to the dream sequence, the Persians had been in the land of Saba 'yesterday', and had arrived in Iberia with a great army, pillaged the city after an earthquake, and had captured Mirian. However, then after all had awakened, they all found out that it had only been a dream. I would suggest that this refers to an actual event, namely to the Persian invasion that would have followed after Shapur's Arabian campaign and Constantine's defeat in about 327. The withdrawal of the Persians and the reinstatement of Mirian as a ruler would have happened after Trdat had defeated the 'northerners' (allies of Persia – see later). King Mirian had already converted and sent envoys to Constantine before the date of the dream sequence, which means that his own conversion took place in about 325/6. However, since the official conversion of the nobles and populace took place only after Constantine's envoys arrived (after the dream sequence), it appears probable that the official conversion of the entire Iberian nation took place in 328. The conversion of the king had resulted from the persistence of St. Nino and her women followers of Mary Magdalene, who had already managed to convert the queen Nana, and most importantly from the victory of Constantine over Licinius. Before this, Mirian had even contemplated a massacre of Christians to please Licinius.[280]

On the basis of the above, I would suggest that the alliance between Constantine and Mirian took place very shortly after the alliance between Constantine and Trdat, probably already in late 324 or early 325, but the sending of the official Roman delegation of priests etc. took place later, after the victory over the Persians in 327.

It is clear that Constantine's self-confidence had grown immensely thanks to his victory and that he saw himself as the protector of Christians everywhere, and he may also have seen himself as a new Christian Trajan, conqueror of both Dacia and Persia, with a mission to conquer the surrounding territories for Christ. He appears to have sent an outwardly courteous letter to Shapur very shortly after October 324 in which he made a veiled threat to Shapur by claiming the right to protect the Christians in Persia. After his victory over Licinius and his alliances with Armenia and possibly already with Iberia, Constantine's position vis-à-vis Persia was very strong because Shapur was still in the middle of his campaign against the Arabs. This very real threat brought a swift response from the Persians who dispatched an embassy bearing gifts and asking for a peace. Constantine answered in the affirmative and the nations concluded a peace, but thanks to the devious efforts of one Christian man this peace was not to last.[281]

On November 324 Constantine took the fateful move of founding the city of Constantinople (Konstantinopolis) on the place where Byzantium stood. He wanted a new entirely Christian city to be his capital instead of the pagan Rome or Diocletian's capital Nicomedia. The conquest of the eastern portion of the Empire and the founding of the new capital also meant the beginning of the process of restructuring of the administration of the Empire. (See Maps Section.) Unfortunately, we do not know many of the necessary details, but one of Constantine's first steps must have been the reorganization of the naval forces.

From later sources we know that the city of Constantinople had its own Imperial Fleet, which must mean that Constantine posted a significant part of his invasion fleet and captured enemy fleet in Byzantium/Constantinople, with probable detachments also in Nicomedia and Cyzicus. On the basis of Constantine's military operations on the Red Sea and Indian Ocean, it is also clear that he must have kept the *Classis Alexandrina* in operation and may even have reinforced it. The same seems also to be true of the other earlier fleets in existence in the east. For example, from Procopius (*Wars* 3.11.13ff.) we learn that the bulk of the invasion fleet of 500 cargo ships with 30,000 sailors that sailed to North Africa in 533 consisted of Egyptians, Ionians and to a lesser extent of Cilicians, all of whom were placed under *archêgos* (prefect of the Alexandrian Fleet?) Kalônymos of Alexandria.

The fleet also had 92 single-banked and fully-decked dromons in which there were 2,000 Byzantine rowers/soldiers. These are likely to have belonged to the Numeri (Arithmos/ Arithmoi/Noumera) I have postulated (2011b) to have been marines of the Imperial Fleet. It is important to understand that the 2,000 Byzantines in the dromons were only part of the total crew and that the rest consisted of the abovementioned Egyptians, Ionians, and Cilicians. If the dromons were fifty-oared as seems likely, the 'Byzantines' rowed only 20 or 40 dromons, which leaves 52 or 72 dromons as detachments from Egypt, Ionia, and Cilicia. The Byzantine dromons would also have been a detachment and not the entire strength of the Imperial Navy. One can easily recognize the *Classis Alexandrina* in the Egyptians, and the *Classis Syriaca* in the Cilicians, but the Ionians pose a problem. Perhaps the best guess for that would be that an Ionian Fleet was created by Diocletian.

All of these fleets would have naturally still fallen under the jurisdiction of the commanders of the land forces. In the case of the river fleets the immediate commanders above the prefects of the fleets were the local dukes, as can be seen from the Notitia Dignitatum, but in the case of the open sea fleets the situation is more complicated. In the case of the western portion of the Empire, the *Mag.Eq.* commanded the fleets in the 370s and the *Mag.Ped.* after 395, but even in that case it is probable that the situation would have fluctuated according to the situation and wishes of the emperor. For the East the situation is even more complicated, because the required section of the ND is missing. Later evidence suggests that the eastern fleets were commanded by the *magistri praesentales*, but unfortunately it is not clear how these two men divided their responsibilities, and which officer/official was the acting admiral of the Imperial Fleet in Constantinople (proconsul?).[282]

As noted above, Constantine also issued an Edict in 324/5 which prohibited sacrifice in pagan temples. At the same time he also appointed special *comites* to confiscate the gold, silver and precious stones stored away in the temples with which he rewarded his loyal supporters and supported the Church. The most distasteful temples and shrines to the Christian morals were destroyed altogether. These included shrines of Afrodite and the sacred prostitutes of these temples were forbidden to practise their trade. Unsurprisingly, the confiscation of temple gold and their closing in particular was criticized by pagan authors later in the fourth century. However, surprisingly they did not criticize the action itself but its economic consequences, which do lend credence to their claims. According to the anonymous author of the DRB (1–2), Constantine's extravagant grants of gold to the powerful had led to the destruction of the poorer classes who were held down by force. In other words, the rich had managed to rob the property of the poor through legal and illegal means thanks to their riches and their official standing. This in turn had caused the poor to lose all loyalty towards the state and had caused the downtrodden to turn to brigandage. The same treatise (3–4) also criticized the corrupt practices of the workers of the mints and the greed of the governors. The governors exploited their position to extort extra money for themselves on top of all regular taxes (*annona*, recruits, money meant for the building of walls, tax arrears) while their subordinates did the same. In short, the poor were forced to pay ever more for the upkeep of the enlarged army and administration, which naturally weakened their loyalty towards the state. These criticisms have undoubtedly a basis on truth, but all the same it is probable that the grievances are exaggerated by the mainly pagan authors.

Libanius' Oration 49 clarifies how the system operated in practice. The richest and most powerful consisted of two classes of people who could also belong to the same families. Firstly, there were the rich members of the imperial administration with plentiful money, and secondly there were the rich city councillors (*principales*). These two classes of people could benefit from the troubles of the other rich persons, middle class and poor. Libanius states that when Constantine had died just before the Persian war, this caused serious troubles for the city councils in the east. The most powerful of the city councillors could decide and force the other poorer members of the city councils to bear the entire responsibility for the support of the war effort. When those who were sent to the Tigris could not cover their costs, they had to sell their family property to pay for the shortfall in taxes. The auctioned properties were then bought by the members of the imperial administration or by the *principales*.

In the case of Antioch this had meant that whereas there had been about 1,200 rich families in the city in the 320s there were only 12 super-rich left by the 380s. These super-rich were unwilling to accept any new councillors into the council so that they could run the city and its tax gathering as they wished, and the corrupt imperial authorities were not interested in correcting this as long as the state coffers and army got their taxes and the authorities their bribes. This meant that the remaining billionaires were unwilling to commit any more money than was absolutely necessary for the upkeep of the theatres, roads, baths, walls etc., with the result that these were in ruins in many places. The only places that were well kept were the houses and estates of the rich. In essence the billionaires could decide who would pay what with the result that they themselves could avoid having to pay any significant amount of money, or supply conscripts or produce, and when necessary they could also bribe the authorities. This meant that the tax burden fell ever more heavily on the poorer members of the society while the rich got richer and the infrastructure of the cities fell apart. The obvious problem with this was that the entire tax burden fell on those who could least afford it. This, together with corruption, meant that in the course of the next forty years the taxes would be doubled for those who still paid them (Themistius Or. 8.113). In light of this it is not that surprising that after 363 the emperors resorted to the use of fake accusations to obtain money from the rich, but this was nothing new.

According to Libanius, this was true in every city, and one may therefore presume that the city councils close to the warzones in the west had similar problems. At the same time, everyone was unwilling to become a councillor because they knew that this would mean that their property would soon be auctioned off to enrich the rich, with the result that they too bribed the authorities and judges so that they would not be forced to become decurions. Women also shunned those who were under the threat of becoming decurions, with the result that such men joined the army and immediately got married. The army was not the only way to avoid this duty. The imperial administration also offered similar immunity. However, the problem was recognized and successive emperors legislated against this and also forced those who had served in such a position to fulfil their duties after retirement or alternatively forced their children to do that. The only problem with this was that the rampant corruption made the enforcement less than effective.

In terms of defence, this meant that the populace got increasingly demoralized as the century progressed, the numbers of bandits increased, the roads were not maintained, and the city walls were not repaired. However, the army and administration still got their equipment, salaries and victuals. Furthermore, the situation was not quite as bleak at it appears at first sight. When there was a threat of enemy invasion, the city councillors and populace usually worked together to repair the walls and prepare the cities for the possible siege, and this usually proved sufficient. The actual threat of death made even the rich willing to share the costs of defence. Most importantly, the problems did not really begin during the reign of Constantine, because the populace still possessed enough money for the taxes to be doubled by c.364, which means that the problems are exaggerated. The above account also makes it clear that the problems resulted mainly from the continuous state of war between Rome and Persia, which was very costly. Furthermore, as I will make clear later, the inflation brought by the release of the temple gold into the economy actually caused the economy to grow. It is also clear that the principal reason for the many difficulties was corruption, which actually became rampant only after the reign of Constantius II. Most of the authors who presented the complaints mentioned above actually wrote at a time when it was safer to critizise Constantine and Constantius rather than their successors.

At the Council of Nicaea Constantine decreed that the decisions of the Church Councils were divinely inspired and legally binding on the governors of the provinces. This implies that the pronouncements of the Councils were legally binding to all secular authorities including even the emperors. Since the civilian and military authorities had the duty of upholding the law, they also had the duty of enforcing the decisions taken by the Councils. As is obvious, in practice the emperor could choose not to abide by any such decisions and/or could coerce the decision he wanted from the Council. In this case the result was the Nicene Creed. Similarly, the local authorities often had their own political agendas and religious convictions that affected their willingness to enforce decisions made by the Councils or emperors. Constantine's decision was momentous. Before this, the ultimate authority in all disputes had been the emperor. This meant that henceforth the military would be used to support either the Nicene Creed or the Arian Creed depending upon the religious policy of the emperor and the councils. The battle between the different religious views lasted until the reign of Theodosius, who finally settled the matter in favour of the Nicene Creed.[283]

This was not even the whole extent of the Constantinian revolution. The bishops received the right to act as judges in disputes between Christians; and they started to act as imperial ambassadors in missions of the greatest political importance, because the conversion of neighbours became one of the most important goals of the Empire. In a letter dated to 23 September 355, Constantius II stated that the imperial law forbade the trying of bishops in secular courts, and that they could be tried only by their peers. According to Barnes (1993, 174), this practice was already in use during the reign of Constantine with the result that bishops started to form coalitions amongst themselves, which can be seen as religious parties, that promoted the ambitions of their members. In essence, the bishops were considered to be above the law and, regardless of the crime, could only be condemned to be deposed and exiled by their peers, and not be tortured and executed. Of course, in practice, the situation was more complex, but the very strong legal position of the bishops meant that whoever wanted to encroach their legal rights had to take into account the possible consequences.[284]

The skilled bishops who had strong local bonds and were good agitators could now field strong influence on local and imperial authorities through their loyal supporters. In due course of time, the importance of the bishops only grew as they were often members of the local upper classes and men who could stir up trouble against anyone who opposed them. Eventually, the bishops became the most important authorities in several cities so that they could even take over the leadership of military operations from their legitimate commanders – and even when they did not do this, they could have a decisive role in the upkeep of morale against the enemy. After all, local commanders had already become accustomed to following the orders of bishops in enforcing their will against their 'heretic' co-religionists.

Either in 325 or 326 Constantine also reformed the entire civilian and military administration to follow the system that he had apparently used in the West. In some cases this meant only the change of names, but in the case of the fiscal system this meant a real reform. Henceforth, the provinces were controlled by three parallel administrations, the Praetorian Prefecture, the *Comes* of the Sacred Largesse, and the *Comes res privata*, undoubtedly to ensure that none of those got too powerful (Bohec, 2005, 209). Constantine also created the office of imperial *Quaestor*, who prepared legislation and wrote responses to the petitions and letters sent to the emperor. In fact, this office is the only one for which the evidence is certain that it was created by Constantine. The dioceses and provinces remained largely the same, except that some adjustments were made to the status, the borders, and that names were changed and a new office of *comes* (exact duties unknown) was created for the diocese. The reform of the Eastern military meant the removal of part of the frontier forces into the *Comitatenses*, which were billeted in cities. This naturally caused dissatisfaction among those who were forced to share their homes with the soldiers. (See the introduction.) However, the great military successes of Constantine's reign and that of his sons prove that the army was highly disciplined and effective and that the new tax system brought enough money into the state coffers to pay for the expanded military and for the fortification programs undertaken everywhere, especially by Constantius II.[285]

Constantine renamed the *Consilium* (Council) to the *Consistorium* (Consistory, later the 'Sacred Consistory') and may have been responsible for its new official structure. It was the most important organ of the state. It was the place in which almost all of the important decisions of state were made. It was a true Council of the State. Its permanent members consisted of the *Mag. Off.* , *Quaestor*, and the two counts of the finances: the *Comes Sacrarum Largitonum*, and the *Comes Rei Privatae*. When the council discussed military or diplomatic matters the *magistri militum* were invited to take part, together with anyone else considered necessary. When it discussed matters that concerned legal questions or provinces, the *PP*, together with anyone whose presence could be useful was invited to attend. In addition, as before, the council could include friends of the emperor who did not have any official position in the administration. In essence, these persons were rich friends of the ruler who advised him in important matters at their own pleasure. As a result, these private persons wielded considerable power behind the scenes.

The members of the Consistory were ranked into three categories: permanent members, those who attended regularly, and honorary members. The official activities of the Consistory consisted of: 1) military matters (revolts, military campaigns, diplomacy, conspiracies, military organization, strategy etc.); 2) religious matters (discussions of religious policy); 3) the nomination of dignitaries (for example the *Protectores* were appointed before the Consistory); and 4) the receiving of ambassadors from foreign powers, the Senate, the army, cities, etc. Depending upon the situation, the council invited the necessary staff and experts to attend the meeting. The Consistory also included special staff consisting of the *silentiarii* and decurions (ensured silence in the palace when the Consistory was in session), *admissionales* (invited and introduced 'guests'), and *a secretis* (secretaries of the Consistory). It was expected that the emperor would make his decisions on the basis of the advice given by the council, but in practice anyone who had personal influence with the emperor could affect his decisions. These included his wife, relatives, friends and the eunuchs of the bedchamber.[286]

Constantine also continued the fortification program throughout the empire to protect the borders and cities. The tetrarchs had already been able to move from the 'elastic defence' to the safer defensive strategy of shallow defence in depth. Constantine basically created an even deeper zone of defensive depth. The enlarged *Comitatenses* were placed under *comites*. The billeting of the troops in the cities eased the provisioning of the troops and lowered costs. However, Constantine's strategy was not based solely on defence, even if he built fortifications and defensive structures into the interior and along the frontiers. In truth, he favoured the taking of the offensive at every opportunity and pushed the borders forward where possible.

The creation of the larger field armies facilitated the taking of the offensive against an enemy. The aggressive policies were also a reflection of Constantine's personality. His 'grand strategy' was based upon the combination of defence in depth, the use of pre-emptive strikes, and outright opportunistic invasions to annex new territories. His goal was also to terrorize the neighbours into obedience, and/or to convert them into Christian allies.

Indeed, Constantine's conversion to Christianity had far reaching consequences for imperial foreign policy. Constantine represented himself as the defender of the faithful. Now the conversion of the ruler of a people or tribe and his subjects into Christianity also meant the automatic joining of the religious community led by the Roman emperor. Therefore, Constantine instituted an active policy to convert all the neighbouring peoples. He acted as the protector of those who had already converted. This also created

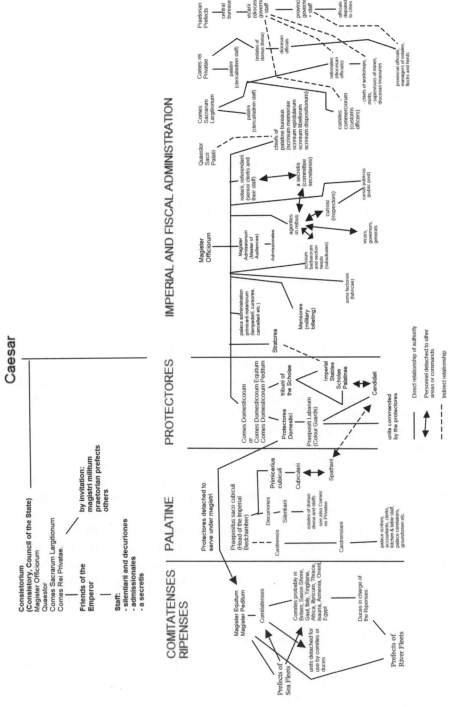

the convenient excuse for Constantine to interfere in the affairs of foreign peoples if they did not respect the rights of Christians. The allies, whether Christian or otherwise, formed buffer zones around his empire.

Constantine, and after him his successors, used the *agentes in rebus* (postal couriers, inspectors, special operative etc.) as well as the *notarii* (secretaries), as his secret agents. These formed his civilian secret service. The notarii appear to have served in this capacity already during the reign of Aurelian (Cizek, 197-8). In addition, just like his predecessors, he continued to use the *Protectores Domestici* and *Protectores* as his special operatives, spies, intelligence officers and assassins. These formed the military side of his secret service/ intelligence gathering organization. In addition to these, he, just like other emperors, could use any person he considered loyal and trustworthy for any mission he thought wise.

Constantine also made a number of financial reforms to finance his policies. The most important of these was the creation of the stable new gold coin solidus which proved to be a boost for the economy. According to Zosimus 2.38, Constantine instituted a new tax called *collatio lustralis* or *chrysargyron* on the merchants, shopkeepers and even to prostitutes which was paid in four-year-cycles. The aim was probably to make it easier to pay the donatives. This was seen very oppressive even though it produced very little income. In 327 Constantine forced the senators to become praetors with the duty to pay the expensive games. In addition to this, Constantine instituted a new progressive land tax on the senators (rates two *folles*, four *folles*, eight *folles*) called *collatio glebalis* or *follis*. In practice, the tax produced very little income. It is also probable that Constantine appropriated to the treasury the local customs and other dues from the cities, which made the decurions liable to pay more taxes. See Jones 1.107-110.

The appended diagram presents the resulting overall administrative structure of the empire. As noted, it proved highly efficient in the collection of taxes and can therefore be said to have been a great success, despite what the pagan critics claim. It is based on diagrams of Delmaire and Haldon (2008) and probably includes elements that were introduced only later. It doesn't include the new temporary offices of *Censor* and *Patricius* created by Constantine for his half-brothers. The principal problem that we have is that we do not possess firm evidence to date all of the changes that took place between c.211 and 395. It is also probable that the diagram includes many things that were actually introduced during the latter half of the third century by the soldier emperors or by the Tetrarchs. As noted earlier, it is probable that Constantius I was actually already serving as (*Tribunus et*) *Magister Officiorum* as early as 285. However, the diagram should still give readers a good overall picture of the administration which is useful background information for the titles mentioned in the following narrative. Readers should bear in mind, however, that the actual power structure was not and is not necessarily the same as the official one. It was and it is possible for some persons to wield power far in excess of their official standing.

Personal and Dynastic Disaster

During 326 a disaster struck from an unexpected corner. Constantine's wife Fausta accused Crispus of having attempted to rape her. It was claimed that Fausta had lusted after Crispus, who had turned down these advances. In truth, the dynastic policies of Fausta may have influenced her account. The removal of Crispus would secure the throne for her sons. She must have known Constantine's harsh view of adultery and incest. Consequently, Constantine acted more in anger than with good judgement and ordered an investigation, as a result of which his gifted eldest son Crispus was executed and his friends either executed or exiled. Unfortunately, we do not know whether this official version is true, but I have here given it a benefit of doubt. On 15 July Constantine entered Rome to celebrate his twenty years on the throne, which enabled him to bribe his armies with a donative at the expense of the upper classes. It was then that Constantine met his mother Helena, who mourned for the loss of Crispus. It is probable, as Barnes (1981, 220–221) suggests, that Helena told Constantine the truth of the matter, as a result of which Constantine confronted Fausta. After the meeting, Fausta was led to the hot bath and the water was heated up to boil her alive. After this, at least one of those who had been previously exiled was recalled, which suggests that Crispus and his friends had been wrongfully accused and that Fausta had been killed as a result. Readers should keep in mind that by the standards of the day, the punishment through boiling was not harsher than usually exacted on persons who were considered traitors and in this case Fausta had caused Constantine to execute his gifted eldest son. Indeed, according to Constantine's legislation traitors who betrayed their country to the enemy were roasted alive. The punishments were meant to scare and terrorize people.

This left him with three underage successors. Consequently, Constantine had to come up with a temporary administrative structure. The system he instituted was built upon the rotation of several praetorian prefects between himself and his sons, Constantine II and Constantius II, from 326 until 333/4. These included: Iunius Bassus 14; Aemilianus 3; L. Papius Pacatianus 2; Evagrius 2; Flavius Constantius 2 (exceptionally only once *PP* of Italy from 326–7); and Fl. Ablabius 4 (for all, see PLRE1). These men seem to have held the actual power in their respective areas when they accompanied the underage Caesars. This would also seem to imply some kind of control over the military machine in their area of jurisdiction, even if the actual military operations were conducted by the members of the military establishment. The likely purpose with the rotation of these persons between the prefectures was to ensure that they would not develop too strong ties with the military and administration of any particular area. In short, there were three praetorian prefects in existence until Constantine created a special prefecture for the whole of Africa in 333, and then added a new *PP* for Constans Caesar (his son) in 334 and another for Dalmatius Caesar (his nephew) in 336. At that time, in 336, there were altogether six praetorian prefects in existence, one for Constantine I, one for Africa, one for Constantine II, one for Constantius II, one for Constans, and one for Dalmatius. It is not known whether all of these 'emperors' also possessed all of the other parts of the imperial administration and how the African prefecture, without any Caesar, was organized.

Persian and Egyptian Wars, 327 (See Map 327–336)

According to Kedrenos, Constantine received a guest called Metrodorus from the east in the twenty-first year of his rule, that is in 326/7.[287] Metrodorus was a Persian and Christian who had studied under Indian Brahmins and had then received gifts from the local ruler to present to the Roman Emperor. When Metrodorus met Constantine, he presented the gifts and claimed incorrectly that other gifts had been sent overland but these had been confiscated by the Persians. Metrodorus' intention was clearly to incite war between the superpowers. Constantine became incensed and sent an angry letter to Shapur demanding the return of the gifts. Shapur, however, was apparently already planning to continue his war against the Roman Federate Arabs as well as against their Roman backers (see above), and did not even bother to answer. He also began a persecution of Christians in the course of which 18,000 were killed. The granting of a place of refuge for Hormizd as well as the alliances between the Christian rulers of Rome, Armenia, and the Lakhmids, undoubtedly made the devout Zoroastrian Shapur II quite hostile towards Christians. Shapur's haughtiness and the persecution of Christians angered Constantine even more and he declared war. Constantine had made a fateful decision. Henceforth he would act as protector of the faithful Christians everywhere and the spread of Christianity and protection of Christians would become one of the goals of Roman diplomacy and warfare.[288] This leaves open the motive of Metrodorus. Had he only personal motives (protection of Christians?), or had he been sent to provoke war between Rome and Persia by the Indians because Shapur's campaign against the Arabs threatened the trade route between India and Rome? The last alternative seems the likeliest.

I would suggest that we should date Constantine's first Persian war mentioned by Kedrenos and Malalas to the year 327. As noted above, the immediate reason for the conflict appears to have been the 'lie' of Metrodorus. According to Kedrenos, Constantine first suffered a defeat, but then collected a new army and defeated the Persians. I would suggest that the first defeat refers to Shapur II's campaign against Roman territories in about 327, as a result of which Imru was forced to flee to Roman territory, where he died in 328. I would also suggest that for his Persian campaigns Constantine collected forces from all over the East, including Egypt, with the result that the Nubians and Blemmyes revolted, making it necessary to conduct the campaign mentioned by Blemyomachia (see below). This first Persian campaign would have taken place between 27 February (when Constantine is attested at Thessalonica) and 11 June (when Constantine is attested at Constantinople).[289] The defeat forced Constantine to regroup his forces and go to Constantinople to gather reinforcements from Europe. After he had gathered the men, Constantine marched against the Persians in Mesopotamia (?) and from there continued his journey to Egypt, where he crushed the Nubians and possibly also the Blemmyes. This campaign would have taken place between 30 July (at Nicomedia) and December 327/January 328 or 1 March 328 (when Constantine attended the church council at Nicomedia).[290]

This same war can also be connected with the simultaneous Persian campaign against Armenia and Iberia (see above and below). According to Moses (2.84–7), these events took place soon after Trdat arrived from the West where he had met Constantine and had then supposedly travelled to 'Rome'. There is a strong possibility that this is some kind of distorted memory of Trdat's visit to Constantinople. The Persians had made a plan for a multipronged attack against the Armenians and Iberians in 327, which involved the revolt of Sluk Slkuni in Armenia, the use of northern nomads in conjunction with the Albanians against both Iberia and Armenia, and an attack by the Persian main army under Shapur, which would move from Persian territory and unite with the northerners. The plan, however, failed thanks to the lies of Metrodorus, who convinced Constantine to declare war on the Persians. It was this that delayed Persian operations in the north and enabled Trdat to engage the northerners separately. However, considering the situation, it is possible to speculate that Constantine may actually have quite purposefully engaged the Persians with inadequate forces for the very reason that he could buy time for Trdat to deal with the revolt and the northerners. There was definitely a chance for the two rulers to discuss their plans because the Armenian tradition does suggest that Trdat was with Constantine at the time the northerners and Persians invaded.

The Persian plan started with the assassination of *Hazarapet* Awtay Amatuni by Sluk Slkunik, undoubtedly with the intention of paralyzing the Armenian realm just before the invasion. However, since the revolt and invasion began before the arrival of the Persians, Trdat decided to move fast. He advanced first against the rebel who had taken refuge in his castle called Olakan on the mountain of Sim. The enemy position, however, proved too strong to begin a siege, as a result of which Trdat promised the possession of the Slkuni family domains to whoever managed to bring the head of Sluk. 'Mamgon', a member of the Armenianized Chinese Mamikonean family, promised to achieve this through a stratagem. He pretended to desert Trdat while the latter moved against the invaders from Albania.

Trdat met the enemy on the Plain of Gargar northeast of the Lake Sevan. He was clearly outnumbered because his attack was directed against the enemy centre. However, his cavalry charge met with success and he was able to cut the enemy force in two. The enemy leader, the King of the Basilk (Hunno-Bulgarians?), threw a lasso around Trdat from the left shoulder to the right armpit (Trdat had raised his sword for a cut). Since arrows proved useless against Trdat's chainmail armour and he was unable to pull the king from his horse, the King grasped the horse's chest. Trdat proved too fast for the King. Trdat cut him in half, together with the head and reins of his horse. The death of the King crushed enemy morale and they panicked and fled. Trdat pursued the nomads all the way across the Derbend Pass and took hostages in return for peace. It was Trdat's victory over the northerners that brought about the release of the Iberian King, who now at the latest became the subject and client of the Armenian king. Meanwhile, Mamgon had managed to kill Sluk by shooting him in the back during a hunt, after which he had gained possession of the fort with a speedy commando attack. The victory over the northerners, however, had come with a great cost. The *Sparapet* Artavazd Mamikonean and many princes had been killed in the battle together with a significant proportion of the Armenian forces.

After this, Trdat assembled together all of the forces of the north for a campaign against Shapur. He appointed Vache Mamikonean his father's successor as *Sparapet*; Bagarat the *Aspet* as general of the Western Gate; Mirian, the prince/king of Iberia and *Vitaxa* of Gugark as general of the Northern Gate; Vahan Amatuni as general of the Eastern Gate; and Manachihr, prince of Rshtunik as general of the Southern Gate. Of note is the fact that Mirian, King of Iberia, was also an Armenian noble and general. According to Moses, Trdat trusted him because he was a Christian. Mirian was also in great personal debt to Trdat because Trdat had saved him and his realm from the northerners. Having already suffered terribly, Trdat did not dare to challenge Shapur alone and waited for the arrival of the Roman forces (under Constantine) that had attacked Assyria, defeated Shapur in battle, and pillaged the land. It was only then that Trdat, together with the

Romans, invaded the north of Persia. He and the Romans were greeted by glad tidings when Kamsar of the Karin Pahlav deserted to the Armenian side. This weakened the Persian defences further and Trdat (together with Constantine) was able to conquer Ecbatana. He left his second-in-command (Vache?) and governors there and returned back to Armenia together with Kamsar and his men. Kamsar Karin became the ancestor of the Kamsakaran Noble House. The forces left at Ecbatana were obviously withdrawn back to Armenia after the peace was concluded.

It is no wonder than in this situation Shapur II was ready to agree to a peace treaty as a result of which the Persians sent Hormisdas' wife to the Romans. Despite the fact that the Armenians had gained territory and the Romans client kingdoms, the peace treaty still appears to have been a face saving compromise for Shapur. The Persians handed all of the Lakhmid territories back to the Lakhmids, now the clients of Rome, and in return the Romans stopped their trade embargo of iron and once again started to sell it to the Persians. This had far reaching consequences that Constantine probably did not foresee, because he clearly did not see any advantage in equipping his own men as heavily as the Persians. In contrast, Shapur II saw advantage in encasing his army, especially its cavalry, in full armour. In consequence, the bulk of his rebuilt armed forces came to consist of the *clibanarii* (so fully armoured that they needed no shields).

As noted above, there is a strong possibility that there was also a war against the Blemmyes during the reign of Constantine, if one dates the fragments of Blemyomachia to this era. Unfortunately, the only sources for this war are the fragments of Blemyomachia that do not provide any other clues to the date of the war except that it was conducted under a Roman general called Germanus who had just returned from a Persian war. Consequently, the suggested dates for this conflict range from the reigns of Aurelian, Probus, Diocletian, Constantine the Great, Theodosius II, Valentinian III (his *magister militum vacans* was named Germanus), Marcianus, to even Justinian (his nephew was named Germanus). So far the most convincing date has been the one suggested by Enrico Livrea, who dates it to about 421–423, but I would suggest that it is more likely that the war actually took place during the reign of Constantine the Great and I will in the following discussion present the case in support of this date.[291]

There were clearly troubles in the area during Constantine's reign, the best example of which are the campaigns of the Aksumites in the area, who were undoubtedly acting in the interest of both in securing the trade routes. According to the extant fragments (Select Papyri III, pp.588–603; Blemyomachia), the local Roman commander (*Dux*?) Germanus had previously marched to fight against the Persians as a result of which the Blemmyes had invaded. The locals had sent urgent calls of help to the *Dux* who had responded by returning (the emperor had probably given him the order to return, or he had been forced to return immediately before reaching the assembly point). The fragments describe only the use of cavalry against the Blemmye infantry (employed both javelins and bows), but due to the fragmentary nature of the evidence one cannot fully exclude the presence of Roman infantry nor the presence of some Blemmye horsemen. Germanus used his cavalry to great effect. Being fully armoured, he led the charge of his spear-armed cavalry in person, and broke through the dense enemy ranks while the rest of his cavalry encircled the enemy. The fugitives on foot were pursued up to their fenced encampment, which included their tents and families. The Romans encircled the camp and charged.

Led by their commander, the Romans wielded their swords and spears to deadly effect. The tents and fences were broken and burned, and prisoners taken. The women were put on one side and the young warriors on the other. Those who managed to flee the carnage were pursued up to the Nile or rocks and hills. The Romans aquired plenty of booty. In other words, the Roman cavalry achieved a complete and overwhelming victory over the Blemmye raiders.

The current order of the fragments would also suggest that the commander with his troops would have left the scene for the second time to take part in Constantine's second victorious campaign against the Persians (or less likely Germanus simply continued his arrested march north to join Constantine for the first campaign), which the Blemmyes (and/or Nubians?) once again exploited by invading. The new invasion was once again crushed in like fashion but this time probably by Constantine in person (see above and below) since he seems to have also conducted a campaign in the area. If the order of fragments is correct – which is uncertain because these later fragments could equally well be placed first, suggesting only a single campaign – then the sequence of events would fit perfectly to the reign of Constantine. His reign saw two Persian campaigns before May 328.

The above also sheds additional light onto Eusebius' (Vita 1.8.2–4, 4.7) claim that Constantine extended the borders as far as the Blemmyes and Aethiopians (Aksumites). He maintains that Constantine did not attempt to go beyond that because he did not want to over-extend his forces. Instead, Constantine chose to illuminate the ends of the inhabited earth with true religion. In other words, the implication is that the conversion of Ethiopia occurred now. Unfortunately, he fails to mention when Constantine undertook this campaign. In my opinion the likeliest date for this would be in 327. This date receives support from the need to secure Egypt amidst the Persian and Blemmye wars.

Unfortunately, Eusebius also fails to mention the enemy against whom the campaign was led, but fortunately it is easy to see that the enemies were probably the Blemmyes rather than the Nubians. Constantine's campaign appears to have been a great success. The Blemmyes and Aksumites were subjected to tribute paying status (Eusebius Vita 4.7). If the campaign took place in late 327, the Aksumites were under the rule of the caretaker government led by the Christian 'prime minister' Frumentius, of Roman origin (a former slave), and the mother of the King of Kings Ezana. Both nations, the Blemmye and Aksumites, sent embassies to Constantine and offered their friendship and Constantine responded by sending missionaries, who had managed to convert the Aksumite king of kings by 333. Both nations also chose to send tribute to the emperor at a later occasion (probably in 336/7). However, I would suggest that the actual status of Ezana was that of allied king, and that the treaty between the rulers confirmed the Aksumite King of Kings as the Federate ruler of the Nubians, Blemmyes, Meroe, and the coastal areas of Arabia, with the purpose of securing the trade routes. This conjecture receives support from the fact that Ezana subsequently conducted campaigns in these areas whenever the trade routes were threatened. It is probable that this secured the trade route with the Indian King represented by Metrodorus, and it is possible that Constantine's war with Persia had been undertaken quite purposefully. In short, while Imru and his successor secured the land trade routes from Arabia, it was Ezana who secured the Red Sea and Nile trade routes. When discussing the wars between Rome and Persia it is also important to understand that some of these were actually conducted by their allies against each other, with the tacit support of one or both, while the empires were nominally at peace.

Constantine in the Footsteps of Trajan: Dacia (See Map 327–336)

After having successfully concluded his eastern wars, Constantine moved west to teach his eldest surviving son military skills. He needed to groom his successors in military skills. Constantine's route of march took him from Nicomedia (1 March 328), via Serdica (18 May) and Oescus (5 July, where he ordered a bridge to be built) to Treves (27 Sept), after which he, in the company of his son Constantine II (11 yrs), conducted a successful campaign against the Alamanni in 328. The war was continued under the nominal command of his son, but in truth by the experienced officers until c.331 (Le Bohec, 2006, 34).

In preparation for his forthcoming war on the Danube, Constantine had also given the order to build a bridge (length 2,437m) across the Danube between Oescus and Sicida and had a fortress built at Daphne in 328. He also improved the 'ferry' and road networks in the area. The bridge was built in imitation of Trajan, whose architect Apollodorus had similarly built a huge stone bridge over the Danube as a manifest signal of Roman power to all tribes in the area. Constantine had also given orders for camps and cities to be built on the other side of the Danube as forward staging posts and assembly areas for his planned campaign. Consequently, in 329 Constantine led his armies across the Danube and defeated the Goths. As a result, he was able to reoccupy part of the Dacian territory lost by Aurelian. The empire was back on the offensive. Constantine was celebrated as a new Trajan. As I noted in my article (Slingshot, 2006), Constantine was now fast expanding the empire by acquiring new buffer zones for the heartland. After the conclusion of the campaign, Constantine reorganized the border defences to reflect the new situation.

In the meantime, the Goths had learnt from their previous defeat that it was not wise to attack Constantine's territories, as a result of which they directed their invasions against other barbarians. Consequently, they now turned their predatory eyes towards Transylvania, where traces of their existence have been detected by archaeologists. This inevitably led to a conflict with the Sarmatians who were allies of Rome in 331/332. The Tervingi Goths defeated the Sarmatians. However, in the midst of their joy there was one sad piece of news for the Goths. One of their war leaders (probably the king of the Tervingi) called Vidigoia met his death because of the 'cunning of the Sarmatians' near the River Tisza (Wolfram, 1990, 61).

The joy of the Goths was short-lived. Constantine I had recalled his son Constantine II (15 yrs) from Gaul and now sent him against the homeland of the Tervingi in 332. The Tervingi were utterly crushed, but at some point in time 500 Taifali horsemen managed to inflict large numbers of casualties on Constantine I's personal following, as a result of which Constantine was forced to flee. Zosimus claims that the Taifali actually killed most of Constantine's army, but this is a patent lie as can be seen from the figures involved. However, it is entirely plausible that the Taifali could have surprised and killed most of Constantine's personal retinue when his army had spread out after a victory, and that he and his bodyguards would have been acting too carelessly as a result. What is certain is that the Romans crushed the Taifali and transferred large numbers of them to

Phrygia, where they subsequently revolted. The rest of the Tervingi who had invaded Sarmatian territory were starving thanks to the fact that they had been placed between the Sarmatians and Romans. They could no longer return to their homes. The Tervingi Goths are said to have lost almost 100,000 men, women and children as a result of starvation and frost. In this emergency the Tervingi chose Ariaric as their leader and thereby he probably became the first Judge (*Iudex*, *Kindins*) of the Tervingi. Ariaric made the only sensible decision in the circumstances and negotiated a *foedus* with Constantine. Ariaric gave his own son Aoric (father of Athanaric) as hostage and received victuals in exchange. The treaty meant that henceforth the Goths would provide *Foederati* for the Romans whenever required. According to Jordanes, the Goths were required to furnish 40,000 warriors for use against other tribes.[292] If Vidigoia is to be identified as King of the Tervingi from the House of Baltha, it is easy to see why the Tervingi nobility would choose to overthrow their kings and choose a Judge. The Goths valued military success above all else and the House of Baltha had failed.

The creation of the office of *Iudex* meant the de facto separation of the Gothic realm into two major groupings, the Greuthungi ruled by King Geberich, and the Tervingi under Ariaric. It is in fact possible that one of the goals of Constantine had always been to divide the Gothic Empire and if this was the case he was successful. The Tervingi did not help the Greuthungi in 336. However, the Goths did cooperate against the Romans in 369 and against the Huns in about 375, but by then the Romans had already broken the *foedus* and had thereby released the Tervingi from their vows of loyalty. The Tervingi were therefore treaty-bound to the House of Constantine until 367 while the Greuthungi were not.

I agree with Whittaker's assessment (185–6) that it is probable that the so-called *Brazda lui Novac* (the furrow of Novac the giant, 'Giant's Furrow') with a length of about 300km was probably built by the Romans earlier, but was now reused by Constantine to mark the border of his conquests. The best proof for this are the extant ruins of a new Roman fort built at Piotroasa/Pictroasele at the end of the ditch during the reign of Constantine, but which was subsequently used by Gothic warriors (Kazanski, 1991, 502–509). I would suggest that Constantine's original plan was to push the frontier this far, but that either he or his successor Constantius II decided to leave the territories to the Goths in return for their service as Federates, the former being the likelier alternative because the Goths remembered Constantine the Great with such warmth.

In 333/4 the Greuthungi Goths made a retaliatory attack on behalf of their brethren against the Sarmatians for their actions in 332 (Jord. Get. 113–5). This time the Goths were successful, because Constantine did not attack them from behind. The Sarmatian Agaragantes (Free Sarmatians) knew that Constantine would not attack and had armed their subjects, the Limigantes (Unfree Sarmatians), with weapons, but still suffered defeat in 333/4. This resulted in the uprising of the Limigantes against their overlords. The 'slaves' in their turn defeated the Agaragantes with the result that one part of them fled to the Vandals-Victufali for safety while most of them fled to Roman territory, where Constantine settled them as Federates in 334. At the same time Constantine appears to have defeated the Limigantes as a result of which he was able to claim the title *Sarmaticus Maximus*.[293]

According to Jordanes (Get 113–5), Geberich engaged the Vandal king Visimar on the bank of the river Maris(os), which suggests that the latter may have attempted to use the river as a defence. This also suggests that the Goths had pursued the fleeing Sarmatians. The battle raged on equal terms until the Vandal king together with the bulk of his forces died, after which the remaining Vandals fled. The remnants of this army collected their families and asked Constantine to settle them in Pannonia. Permission was granted and they served the Romans evidently as Federates for about sixty years, until Stilicho summoned them and sent to Gaul. It is difficult to know what Jordanes meant by 'Pannonia' because there is no evidence for the presence of large numbers of Federate Vandals on Roman territory. However, if he meant that these Vandals migrated together with the Sarmatians into Roman territory or the barbarian portion of Pannonia north of the Danube then that is plausible. As noted, at the same time the Romans transferred altogether 300,000 Sarmatian fugitives into Thrace, Scythia, Macedonia and Italy (Origo 1.6.31).

I agree with Whittaker (176–178) that we should connect the building or at least the reinforcement of the massive Devil's Dyke, which consisted of 700 kilometres of earth ditches, with Constantine the Great's campaigns against the Sarmatians in 322 and 334.[294] In other words, I would suggest that the Romans considered the territory between the Danube and the so-called Devil's Dyke to be part of the Roman Empire in such a manner that the people(s) inhabiting it, who were mainly the Sarmatians, were Roman *Foederati* and therefore also under Roman protection (see also the reign of Constantius II).

The Conversion of Ethiopia and the Roman Trade Network

According to the traditional dating of the reign of the Aksumite king Ezana, he reached maturity in about 327/8 after which the native Roman 'prime minister' of Ethiopia Frumentius resigned and travelled to Alexandria where he reported the situation to the patriarch Athanasius and stated that Aksum needed a bishop. (See above.) The patriarch suggested that this person should be none other than Frumentius, who already knew the country. Consequently, Frumentius was appointed to the post and returned to Ethiopia. This created a precedent according to which the patriarch of Alexandria would appoint an Egyptian Copt as bishop of Ethiopia. When Ezana then converted to Christianity, undoubtedly at the instigation of Frumentius, the precedent set by Frumentius' appointment suited the King of Kings, because the Egyptian Copts were foreigners and therefore entirely dependent upon the support of the ruler.

The alliance between Rome and Aksum proved to be mutually beneficial. The inscriptions suggest that the king of kings Ezana conducted a series of campaigns against those who threatened the trade routes to the Roman Empire. He fought against the Blemmyes and Meroe (evidently after they had revolted against their subordinated status) probably in 328/9 and conducted a maritime campaign from Leuke Kome to the land of the Sabateans (that is, Himyarite Kingdom) as a result of which the Arabs and 'Kinaidokolpitas' were subjected to tribute paying status.[295] The latter campaign occurred at some point in time between c. 329–32. Ezana's campaign had two consequences: 1) it subjected the coastal areas to tribute paying status and secured communications; and 2) it weakened the Himyarites, which enabled the federate king of Hira to reassert its power in central Arabia. In short, Ezana secured land and sea communications between India, Africa, Arabia, Aksum and Rome. The conversion of the Aksumite King of Kings Ezana to Christianity sealed the alliance, after which Ezana conducted further campaigns as an ally against those who threatened their commercial routes. One of the fruits of the abovementioned campaign against Yemen was also the sending of high ranking hostages by the Yemenis, Omanis and Dibans to the Roman emperor, which basically proves that the Roman fleet aided Ezana in his Red Sea campaign that also included a naval campaign all the way up to the mouth of the Persian Gulf and India.[296] The probable purpose of this naval operation on the Indian Ocean was to establish a direct link with the Indian ruler who had sent Metrodorus. On the basis of this it is clear that the Aksumite Kingdom and its subjects from the Red Sea and Arabia up to the Maldives were Roman tribute-paying clients with a duty to provide hostages. The task of securing these domains lay with Ezana who even before his conversion in 333 was forced (DAE 9: refers to tr. by Munro-Hay) to conduct a campaign in Arabia against the Agwezat tribe (Hadramawt?) in Arabia, because they had failed to stick to their part of the treaty.

The inscription DAE 11 (and another version of the same) proves that the Aksumite King of Kings Ezana conducted a campaign against the Kasu and Noba when he had already converted to Christianity. This campaign took place either in 349, 355, or 360 (Hatke, Chapter 4.5, esp. p.95). The inscription also proves that Ezana considered himself to be the ruler of Aksum, Himayar, Raydan, Saba, Salhin, Tsiuamo, Beja (Blemmyes), and of Kasu, which also supports an early date for this campaign. The Kasu meant the territories of the former Kingdom of Kush, which now consisted of Meroe (the successor Kingdom of Kush), and the Noba meant the Nubian Kingdoms of Nobatia, Makuria, and Alwa. The immediate reason for the campaign was that the Nubians had revolted and attacked other tribes under Ezana's protection three times, and had then twice robbed Ezana's envoys that he had sent to admonish them. The same revolt naturally threatened the trade routes to the interior of Africa and therefore Ezana's campaign also served Roman interests in the area. He defeated the Nubians twice at the ford of Kemalke and then at the confluence of White and Blue Niles, after which he conducted two separate campaigns against the Nubians of Alwa in which he spread his army into several separate columns. On the basis of this the campaign may have lasted two years, but as a result the trade route was secured. The Romans were well served by their Christian allies.

Armenia Falls into Anarchy

Probably in about 330–2 a momentous event happened in Armenia. The pagan magnates, who had refused to convert to Christianity, poisoned King Trdat. Persian involvement can also be suspected. Constantine and the Christians had now lost their staunchest ally in the east, which spelled problems.

In 332/3 Caesar Constans (about 12–13 yrs) received the title *Persicus Maximus* which implies that Constans' generals had conducted a successful campaign of some kind against Persia (Le Bohec, 2006, 34), but there is no other evidence to back this up. Had the Romans invaded Persia to protect Armenia?

Trdat was succeeded by his son Khosrov, but Khosrov was unable to assert his rule over the magnates and client states. Armenia was in a state of anarchy. The pagans, in collusion with the adulterous queen, attempted to murder the high-priest, but in the end this was not carried through. This begs the question what was Khosrov's role in this? Considering the lack of Roman support for Khosrov (at least after 333) it is possible that the Romans suspected Khosrov of having killed his father and of being a pagan. Then, two of the great houses of Armenia, the Manawazean and Ordruni, started to fight against each other and when the king attempted to reconcile them they started to pillage the king's domains. As a result, the king sent his *sparapet* Vache Mamikonean against them. Mamikonean duly quelled the revolt, but this was not the whole extent of the trouble facing Khosrov. There is a possibility that Constantine finally broke his alliance with Armenia in 335 when he appointed his nephew Hannibalianus as ruler of Pontus and Armenia – unless this meant Roman Armenia. At least that would explain why the Romans failed to help Khosrov against his enemies. If there is any truth in Moses' assertion that the queen was hostile towards the Christians, there also exists the possibility that this policy change in Armenia had caused Constantine to change his policies.[297]

In about 335/6 Sanesan/Sanatruk, the Arsacid ruler of Mazkutk (Massagetae?) and/or Aluank (Alans), in collusion with the Albanians, decided to take advantage of the situation and assembled a force of nomads – including the 'Honk' (Huns?), as well as the Caucasian mountaineers – and invaded in an attempt to take over Armenia as 'rightful successor' to the throne.[298] Of note is that his army not only included cavalry but also club-bearers on foot that were highly efficient against the Armenian cataphracts. Even if the Romans would have wanted to assist the Armenians at this time, they could not have because Constantine was fighting against the Goths and his son Constantius against the Persians. At the same time as Sanatruk began his quest for the Armenian throne, the *Vitaxa* of Aljnik, Bakur, revolted in order to become independent. In order to achieve this he sought help from the Persians (Moses 3.4). The revolt of Aljnik is important from two points of view. It was part of the Roman Empire even if its ruler was a vassal of the Armenian king. It is very probable that the Persians had supported Sanesan's invasion from the very start and that Shapur's overall invasion plan for 336 actually consisted of two invasions, one under Narses to support Bakur, the *Vitaxa* of Aljnik, the other under Sanesan. (See below.)

Thanks to the Armenian civil war Sanesan's invasion met with success. The invaders pillaged Armenia as far as the Roman border, and the king had to take refuge in the stronghold of Dariwnk with Vartanes, the Chief-Bishop of Armenia, while in 337 Vache went to meet Constantius, the new ruler of the East, who following the murder of Hannibalianus had changed Rome's policies. Just before that in 336 or 337 the refugee *Vitaxa* of Aljnik had received an army from the Persians to take back his own domains from the Romans. Consequently, it is not surprising that Constantius was more than willing to dispatch a Roman army under Antiochus to assist Khosrov in 338. (See later.)

Constantine's Dynastic Plans and Reform of the Administration[299]

In about 326 Constantine had recalled his exiled half-brothers Flavius Dalmatius and Julius Constantius. He made them ordinary consuls and revived for them the special titles *censor* and *patricius*, both of which were used in a new sense. In 333 Constantine made his youngest son Constans Caesar and at the same time Dalmatius was appointed as *Censor*. Dalmatius resided at Antioch and performed wide ranging duties as a sort of vice regent of the East. As *Censor* Dalmatius ranked above the Praetorian Prefect but was still below a Caesar. In 334 Constantine appointed Fl. Optatus, who had probably married his relative, as the first *Patricius*. Once again this title ranked above that of *PP* but was below that of Caesar. The half-brother Constantius was in his turn made *Patricius* in 335. Constantine appointed Dalmatius' son Dalmatius as Caesar on 18 Sept. 335, which meant the recreation of the Tetrarchy, except that Africa was still ruled by the *PP* of Africa. The rest of the provinces were divided between the four emperors. Constantine II was given Britain, Gaul and Spain (PP Saturninus 9 then Tiberianus 4); Constans was given Italy and the Pannonian Diocese (PP Pacatianus 2); Dalmatius was given the dioceses of Moesia and Thrace (PP Maximus 49); and Constantius was given the Diocese of Oriens (PP Ablabius). In addition, Constantine arranged dynastic marriages. For example, Constantius married his cousin, the sister of the future emperor Julian.

Towards the end of his reign Constantine's religious policies caused revolts. Firstly, the pagans revolted under Calocaerus, the 'keeper of the imperial camels', in Cyprus in about 335. This revolt was quickly crushed by the *Censor* Dalmatius. Constantine had also started to persecute Jews and had introduced legislation against them. This caused Jewish zealots to attempt to seize Jerusalem and rebuild the temple (note also the events under Julian's reign), but this revolt was crushed with equal ease. There also appears to have been an assassination attempt against Constantine by a member of his bodyguards which was found out in time.

The Campaigns of 336 (See Map 327–336)

Constantine appears to have planned to complete his conquest of Dacia, after which he meant to start his campaign against Persia with the intention of conquering it once and for all. The former campaign was probably at least in part undertaken to punish the Greuthungi Goths for their previous campaigns against the Sarmatians and Vandals. Constantine clearly saw himself as a Christian equivalent of Trajan. He was a warrior emperor who would retake Dacia and Persia at least up to the Persian Gulf – as Trajan had done briefly. Consequently, Constantine again led his armies across the Danube in the spring of 336. The Goths and their allies were defeated, Constantine was hailed as *Dacicus Maximus*, and Dacia was re-established as a Roman province. It is possible that Geberich, the king of the Greuthungi, who had previously led the campaign against Constantine's allies, was killed in this campaign. Jordanes laconically states that Geberich died soon after having defeated the Vandals in 334 and was succeeded by Hermanaric. This would not be the only occasion in which Jordanes would have hidden unwelcome Gothic defeat. In the meanwhile, however, dark clouds had appeared on the horizon.

In about 336 the Taifali who had been posted to Phrygia as Federates revolted, but were duly crushed by the *stratelates* (i.e. *magister*) Ursus, who was sent to the scene by Constantine (Barnes, 1981, p.398, n.17).

As noted above, in 336 the Armenian situation boiled over and caused renewed conflict between Rome and Persia. When Constantine was preoccupied with his ongoing campaign against the Goths, Shapur decided to take advantage of the situation. As a result of his very thorough preparations, Shapur was confident that he would win, especially because the Emperor was unable to commit the main Roman army against him, but he miscalculated. Constantine sent his son Constantius to take command of the operations.

327-336

War against the Alamanni
- Constantine I with Constantine II in 328
- Constantine II 329-331

Constantine I defeats the Limigantes in 334 and receives 300,000 Agragantes and Vandals inside Roman territory to serve as Federates

- Constantine I crosses the Danube at Oescus and defeats the Tervingi Goths in 329
- Constantine I and II defeat the Tervingi Goths and Taifali in 332
- Constantine I defeats the Greuthungi Goths and conquers Dacia in 336

Devil's Dyke

Giant's Furrow

- Tervingi attack the Sarmatians in 332, defeat them, but are defeated by Romans and forced to sign a *foedus*.
- Greuthungi attack the Agragantes and Vandals and defeat them.
- Limigantes defeat the Agragantes in a civil war in c. 333/4

'Constans' defeats the Persians in 332/3

Constantius II suffers minor setbacks in a war against Persian invaders and then annihilates the Persian army at Narasara near Amida in 336

X

Northerners and Persians capture Iberia and its king in 327

Romans and Armenians advance deep into Persian territory and force Shapur to sign a peace

Sluk assassinates the Hazarapet probably in the capital and then withdraws to Olakan

Olakan

Trdat besieges Sluk and advances against the invaders and defeats them in the spring/summer of 327

Constantine defeats Shapur in late 327 and joins forces with Trdat

Ecbatana

Shapur moves north after his Arabian campaign and defeats Constantine in early 327

Constantine marches fast to Egypt after having defeated the Persians

Roman and Aksumite joint operations on the Red Sea and Indian Ocean in c. 328-333

ASORESTAN (ASSYRIA)

- Germanus defeats the Blemmyes in the spring/summer of 327.
- Constantine defeats the Nubians and Blemmyes in the winter of 327/8 and forces the Aksumites to convert into Christianity in 328

Carpi

Angles
Saxons
Frisii

0   100   200   300   400   500 Miles
0   200   400   600   800 km

Consequently, the Persians under Narses (prince or magnate?) launched their invasion of Armenia and Mesopotamia with the support of the *Vitaxa* of Aljnik and captured Amida. The Persians had been planning and preparing for this for a long time. The previous peace agreement had enabled Shapur to rebuild his strength. He had amassed stockpiles of money, siege equipment, men, arms and elephants. He had also used Constantine's readiness to sell iron to the Persians well. His troops were better equipped than any of their predecessors. At least half of his cavalry forces appear to have consisted of the Asvaran/ Savaran *clibanarii/cataphracti*. Besides their bows, arrows, and swords, each of them also had a long *contus*-spear that they used with a two-handed grip.[300] The most interesting point, however, concerns the information that Libanius (Or. 59.69) gives regarding horse-armour. He states that whereas previously the horses had been protected only by head and chest bronze plates, Shapur's cavalry was protected from the crown to the hooves in chain mail. Figuratively speaking the men were therefore armoured from their heads to their feet and their horses from the crown to the tip of the hooves in fine mail armour. Only the eyes and mouth were left without defences. I would suggest that the real difference between the *cataphracts* (partial plate or scale armours for the front) and the *clibanarii* (chain mail etc. for the entire horse) lay in the amount and type of armour carried by the horses, but that as time passed the distinction between the two became blurred.

Constantine dispatched his son Caesar Constantius II (19 yrs) to take charge of the eastern front. At first Constantius suffered a series of minor setbacks, probably under his generals, at Amida and Constantia (Festus 27), but then he managed to force the enemy to a battle at Narasara (probably Nararra, thirteen Roman miles east of Amida) in which the Persians were annihilated and Narses killed. The location suggests that the Romans had manoeuvred themselves behind the Persians to block their route of retreat. After this, Constantius rebuilt Amida and added strong walls and towers and mural artillery to its defences, and founded a new fortified town called Antinopolis/Constantia (or Tella/ Constantina) to serve as a place of refuge for the local population.[301]

The Rise of Hermanaric

As stated, at some point in time soon after 334 the ruler of the Greuthungi died and was succeeded by the greatest Gothic king of all time: Hermanaric. He seems to have followed the same policy as two well known first-century Germanic kings, Maroboduus and Vannius, before him. He did not threaten the Roman Empire with any military action and directed his attention towards other barbarian nations. It is possible that this policy was supported by the Romans, just as it had been during the first century, and it is possible that just like before the Romans then turned against him (in 367 and 375) when he had achieved too much power. In my opinion, it is actually probable that Hermanaric had been installed on the throne by Constantine. However, since there is no concrete evidence for this, it is best to assume that Hermanaric just chose the wisest course and avoided conflict with Rome.

Hermanaric was able to create a huge empire as a result of which he was called Alexander the Great of the Goths. According to Jordanes, Hermanaric conquered first the Golhtascytha,[302] Thiudos,[303] Inaunxis, Vasinabroncae, Merens (Mari?; NE of Moscow), Mordens (Mordva/Mordvians, east of Moscow), Imniscaris, Roga (Rugi?), Tadzans,

Athaul, Navego (Narova?), Bubegenae, and Coldae (Koltta/Kola?). In other words, Hermanaric seems to have conquered most of the territory up to the Volga and Kama Rivers, and thereby gained control of the fur trade and possibly also control of the northern portions of the Silk Road. After this, Hermanaric subdued the last remaining free Heruli to the south east.

I would suggest that the Romans and Hermaneric actually cooperated in the crushing of the Heruls. Then Hermanaric attacked the Venethi Slavs (Venethi, Antes, Sclaveni) near modern Poland and the Aesti (Eesti, Estonians) and gained control of the coasts of the Baltic with its amber trade. The fact that Hermanaric directed his attention towards the north and north-east meant that the Romans would not have to worry about the Gothic menace before 376.[304] Hermanaric's strategy seems to have been to take possession of the fur and amber trade routes as well as the northernmost section of the Silk Road. In fact the continuous state of war between Rome and Persia between 336 and 363 must have worked to Hermanaric's great advantage and brought great wealth to the Goths as they controlled the northern trade route to the east.

Despite lack of any concrete evidence I would suggest that a splinter group of the Xiongnu (Huns) must have created a new Xiongnu Empire in Central Asia towards the middle of the third century that lasted until the late 330s. The existence of such a Central Asian Empire during the third century and its conquests in the western steppes from the 240s until 260s would explain the mass migration of the Goths against the Roman Empire during the late 260s. Furthermore, the existence of such a Xiongnu/ Hun Empire would explain why the various clearly separate ethnic groups were known as Huns/Xiongnus. These included the 'real Huns' (mostly Mongols, but included also Turks, Iranians, Ugrians, and Slavs) that advanced against Europe, the Hepthalites (White Huns, Alkhons, mostly European features) that attacked Iran and India, the Kidarite Huns (Kidarites, Kushans, European features) that attacked Iran, and the Chionitai (Hyôn, Huns, European features) that attacked Iran. Indeed, it is practically necessary to postulate the existence of such an empire to explain the use of the term Hun/Xiongnu for the various different ethnic groups, tribes and tribal coalitions. The earlier Xiongnu Empire cannot explain this variance, because, for example, the Kidarites/Kushans had been in the area from the second century BC. The vast spread of archaeological finds associated with the Huns in Eurasia would also support the existence of a vast empire at some point in time. The existence of such an empire would also explain why the Greuthungi Goths under Geberich moved towards the Sarmatians and Hasdingi Vandals in c.332 rather than towards the north or east. The fall of this Xiongnu/Hun Empire would also explain why Hermanaric was able to conquer such vast tracts of land in the east and north as he did between about 340–365. In fact, it is even possible that Hermanaric may have caused the fall of the Hun Empire, but it is still likelier that the Huns had been defeated by the Ruanruan ('Real Avars', either Mongols or Turks), which in turn eventually led to the creation of the Avar Empire that was to eventually succumb to the 'Turks'. The pressure created by Hermanaric's advance to the east also explains why the Chionitai attacked Persia in the early 350s, which in its turn eased pressure against the Roman Eastern border. On the other hand, one may also speculate that Hermanaric's advance against the Venethi could have caused a domino effect in Europe that pushed tribes westward against the Roman borders in the 360s and early 370s. In sum, there is plenty of circumstantial evidence to suggest the existence of a third century Xiongnu/Hun Empire, which must have consisted of various Ugrian, Mongol, Turkish, and Iranian groups of Central Asia.

The Death of Constantine

Encouraged by his own unblemished military record, Constantine planned to conduct a military campaign against Persia in 337. His nephew Hannibalianus was designated as future ruler of Persia. Constantine's Arab Federates spearheaded the operation and captured numerous peoples from the 'Assyrians' that they sold as slaves. Constantine sailed in a trireme and made a stop at Soteriopolis/Pythia to enjoy the hot-springs. According to one story, probably spread by Constantius II and his supporters later, he drank there a poisonous drug mixed by his half-brothers after which he reached Nicomedia – where he fell ill and then after a long illness died in May. As a reflection of Constantine's favouritism of the Arian Creed during his last years in power, it was the 'Arian' Eusebius who baptized the Emperor on his deathbed on 22 May 337. His son Constantius had managed to hurry from Antioch to be beside his father when he died. Just like Julius Caesar, Constantine had died before he could fulfil his dreams of further conquest. However, as we have already seen, his plans were truly grandiose in scale but clearly not unachievable had he been in charge.

Constantine the Great as General and Emperor

As I noted in my article years ago (Slingshot, 2006), Constantine the Great was the consummate soldier of the age. He was probably the greatest military commander Rome had produced since Probus and he was certainly the greatest military commander of the fourth century if one judges his career on the basis of his successes. However, he had not achieved this success alone. He was blessed with excellent senior officers and admirals, and the first-rate military machine that he had inherited from his father. Regardless, we should still remember that it was Constantine who made all of the final decisions. A poor or mediocre emperor and military commander would not have achieved what he did and could have ruined everything.

Constantine knew how to raise the morale of his men and how to maintain their loyalty with various means at his disposal, which included camaraderie with the soldiers, use of religious and political propaganda, the rewarding of the men, the maintenance of discipline, and so forth. Constantine planned his military operations meticulously and carried them out swiftly and efficiently. Constantine clearly followed the historical examples set out by Alexander the Great, Julius Caesar, and Trajan. Constantine preferred to decide wars and battles through the use of relatively small numbers of elite forces in rapidly-performed campaigns. The use of masses of regular but less efficient soldiers would have only slowed him down. It was wiser to use the forces he had at hand rather than betray his plans through prolonged military preparations. However, when the situation did not allow this and he was forced to rely on the use of a massive army, as happened in 324, he and his staff were also up to this task. They clearly knew how to plan such a massive campaign, and how to coordinate the logistics and movements of the separate armies and fleets. Constantine could also lead truly massive armies without losing control.

It is also important to understand that Constantine's successes owed a lot to his skilful use of the fleets. It can be said with a good reason that without the wise use of his naval assets, he would have been unable to win his wars against the Franks, Maximian, Maxentius, and Licinius. However, even though the sources fail to mention the presence of fleets on other occasions, we can postulate their presence in the theatre of war whenever it was conducted close to the sea or near rivers. Constantine knew how to use each and every asset he had at his disposal and he knew how to exploit political propaganda and religion to undermine the enemy's willingness to fight.

Constantine and his staff possessed an expert knowledge of every field of military activity. Constantine was also unsurpassed as a tactician, diplomat and plotter. He knew how to strike the right balance between clemency and cruelty in a civil war. He knew that it was more advantageous to show clemency and only punish the 'ringleaders' of the enemy.

He defeated the Picts, Franks, Alamanni, Sarmatians, Bosporans, Goths, Taifali, and the mighty Persians in pitched battles, and also many Roman emperors and generals who were considered to be masters of their trade. Maximian was known for his tactical skills; Maxentius and his generals had defeated Severus and Galerius through the use of the walls of Rome; and Licinius had had a long and very successful military career behind him and had, for example, defeated Maximinus on the plain of Egrenus in 313 with less than half the troops the enemy had.

This comparison with enemies, if anything, should reveal the scope of Constantine's achievement. Constantine knew how to deploy his army for pitched battles and for sieges in the most advantageous way. He knew what were the weaknesses and strengths of any tactical system he faced and how to counter those with the strengths his army possessed. Constantine knew how to exploit any kind of terrain to his advantage, and how to circumvent the enemy's advantageous defensive position through manoeuvres, ruses, religious propaganda, and personal example. This does not mean that Constantine would not have suffered setbacks. It is very rare for any military leader to achieve a constant string of successes, but in the end Constantine was always able to rectify the situation, regroup his forces and win.

What is particularly notable about Constantine's battle tactics is that his cavalry, especially those grouped around the *Labarum*, usually decided battles. This does suggest the probability that most of the battles were decided by Constantine's elite *Scholae* and what is striking about this is that Constantine seems to have preferred to equip his cavalry with lighter equipment in order to increase its mobility on the battlefield. In essence, he practised the same principles as were later used by Frederic the Great's 'heavy cavalry'. The cavalry did not have to be equipped with heavy armour for it to be heavy cavalry. What was decisive was the way in which it was used, and the lightness of equipment improved mobility and improved the endurance of the troops and horses. As we shall see, there was a clear difference of opinion regarding the preferential type of cavalry between Constantine I and son Constantius II. The latter preferred to equip his cavalry as *clibanarii* to improve its ability to withstand showers of Persian arrows, but we should not forget that Constantine had also faced the Persians many times: there was obviously a clear difference of opinion between the two. It is difficult to be certain who was correct, because the cavalry of both performed extremely well.

In combat Constantine knew how to encourage his men with personal example and when to stay behind to direct the reserves. In general he seems to have struck the right balance between these two extremes. However, on occasion he seems to have been carried away by his eagerness to lead the decisive cavalry charge in person. This is the only thing that can be criticized. The taking of constant personal risks could have ended in disaster, but on the plus side his personal heroism and example endeared him to the troops. On the other hand, the results speak for themselves. In order for any military commander to be successful he needed to be lucky, and Constantine was certainly lucky. He was wounded only once. Constantine acted as a sort of latter-day Alexander the Great who always led the decisive cavalry charge, with the difference that after he had led his cavalry forward, he usually retreated back behind his cavalry wing because the sources show him giving orders to the infantry and to his *Labarum* Guard: he was clearly behind his army. This means that in practice Constantine acted as traditional Roman generals were expected.

What is also striking is Constantine's level of knowledge of the enemy plans, troop disposals, and activities. It is clear that Constantine operated an effective intelligence organization consisting of 'civilian' and military spies. His supporters inside enemy territories also effectively undermined the position of his imperial rivals. It is probable that most of these supporters/spies/agent provocateurs consisted of Christians. At least it is clear that Licinius believed this to be the case. In fact, there is reason to believe that the Christians formed a similar source of information both at home and abroad for Constantine, as the augurs and astrologers had for the *Pontifex Maximus*. As emperor and de facto head of the Church, Constantine could learn everything that was transmitted to the bishops in his entourage.

The most important legacies of Constantine were his adoption of Christianity as a state religion and the transferral of troops away from the frontiers into the interior to form the *Comitatenses*. The former changed the entire history of mankind and was also to form an instrumental part of Roman internal and external policies during the fourth century – and it also gave the emperors a suitable excuse to start 'just wars' against those who persecuted the Christians. The latter reform created the highly effective field forces of the early-fourth century that achieved so many successes during the reign of Constantine and his immediate successors. As we shall see, Constantine's reforms were not responsible for what happened after the death of Constantius II.

In sum, as I have noted before, Constantine the Great truly earned his title the Great as a general and emperor. He was the only ruler of the fourth century that truly deserved to be called great.

Chapter Six

The Sons of Constantine

Constantius Massacres his Cousins and Uncles, 337

Constantine's last wishes regarding his succession are not know, but the imperial organization does suggest the possibility that Constantine II (eldest, born out of wedlock in Feb 317) and Constantius II (born 17 Aug 317) could have been designated as *Augusti* while Constans (born probably in 320) and Dalmatius the Younger (date of birth unknown) would have served as their *Caesars*. It is impossible to know what Constantine's plans were because Constantius II could have easily distorted his father's last wishes to his own benefit. Constantius was beside his father at the time of his death (Julian Or. 1.16C-D). Then there is the problem whether Constantine had died as a result of a plot hatched by his half-brothers and the *PP* Ablabius. Whatever the truth, such stories were certainly spread by Constantius and believed by the army at large. Furthermore, even if the faction consisting of Ablabius, and Constantine's half-brothers and nephews had not murdered Constantine, there was still a very strong possibility that they would attempt to oust and kill Constantine's biological sons. Consequently, the 19-year old Constantius II, who was the only one of the brothers close to the scene, had to act quickly and decisively. When his relatives and their supporters assembled for a funeral at Constantinople in June, Constantius had already secured the support of the army and was therefore able to use the soldiers to murder his uncles, cousins, Ablabius and all their supporters. Only Gallus and Julian were left alive, probably because Constantius was married to their sister. It is possible or even probable that the support of *Magister* Ursus and *Comes* Polemius had been instrumental for the success of Constantius against his cousins and they were therefore rewarded with consulships in 338 (Barnes, 1981, 262).

After this, Constantius was forced to fight a brief defensive campaign against the Sarmatians (probably the Limigantes), who had exploited the situation by invading. The probable reason for this invasion was that the death of the emperor had made the previous treaties void and the Sarmatians either wanted to improve their terms by a demonstration of military strength, or they just wanted to exploit the opportunity in order to obtain their full freedom and possibly land from Dacia. The Sarmatian invaders were duly defeated. Then in about September Constantius met his two brothers in Pannonia to discuss the division of the empire. In this meeting Constantius and Constans allied themselves against their half-brother Constantine and 'outvoted' him in the division of territories. Constantius kept control of the East and gained possession of Constantinople and Thrace. Constans added Moesia to his domains, but Constantine was left with his old domains. Constantine II was the eldest of the three and was not happy with the result. Thanks to the Persian invasion Constantius was also forced to make concessions to his brothers. The churchmen in exile were allowed to return to the East.[305]

This division of Constantine's inheritance came to dominate the administrative structures of the entire Empire for the rest of the century. Each of the sons had their own separate armies and civilian administrations, *magistri*, praetorian prefects, etc. The related map describes the situation in 345 (the date when the *PP* of Illyricum is first attested), but may date from c.337.

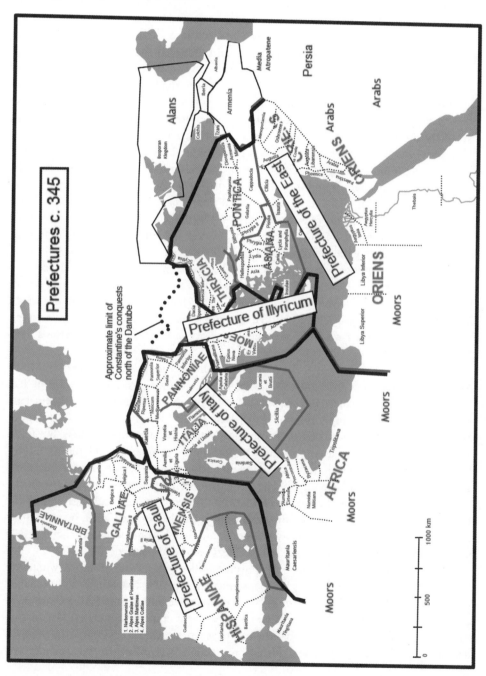

Constantine (Constantinus) II, Constans, Constantius II, 337–340

Constantine II, the eldest of the brothers, was dissatisfied with the division of the Empire but decided to bide his time. He sent repeated demands to Constans to hand Italy and Africa over to him but to no avail. He vented his anger against his half-brother Constantius in particular by freeing the Trinitarian Bishop Athanasius, who had been exiled by their father, in an effort to cause him trouble. Since it took three years for Constantine to start his campaign against Constans in a situation in which Constans was fighting against the Sarmatians and Constantius against the Persians, it is probable that Constantine II also faced troubles of his own in Gaul and/or Britain. The death of Constantine the Great had annulled all treaties between the Romans and their Federates with the result that the first order of things for each of the emperors was to renew those either through negotiations or with demonstrations of force. I would suggest that at least part of the problems facing the brothers in 337 was caused by this.

The first thing Constans had to do was to continue the war against the Sarmatians. The Sarmatians undoubtedly calculated that the young and inexperienced emperor, who could not expect any help from his brothers, would be vulnerable. In this situation it was fortunate for Constans that the Goths renewed their treaty with Constantius II. They had easier pickings in the north and the steppes. The divisions of the resources between the brothers meant that Constans did not have enough men at his disposal to defeat the invaders immediately with the result that the war dragged on until the 350s. On top of this, Constans was later forced to fight against the Alamanni, Franks, Picts and Scots.

The Arab Federates also showed their dissatisfaction towards the favouritism of Arians that the late emperor Constantine had shown during his last years by revolting, which Constantius managed to pacify by returning the Orthodox bishops back to their sees. As a result, Constantius was able to renew the treaty of alliance with the various Arab chieftains in 337/8.[306]

In the beginning of his reign, the Arian Constantius was prepared to be conciliatory towards the Orthodox Christians in order to secure his own position, but after he had secured his position, he was ready to show his public support for the Arians and persecute the Orthodox/Catholic supporters of the Nicene Creed. The staunchest supporters of the Nicene Creed did indeed consider Constantius to be an Arian in his beliefs, but it can be guessed from his later attempt to find a compromise through the 'Homoean Creed' that in his own mind he favoured reconciliation between the religious groups even if his opponents didn't see it that way.[307] The principal cause of disagreement between the Arians and Catholics was that the Arians wouldn't accept the use and meaning of the terms of 'from the essence' and 'of the same essence' in the Nicene Creed, because these terms were not in the Bible. Basically, the both sides had become so entrenched in their positions that any reconciliation was impossible. (See the Appendix.)

Constantius interfered heavily in Church politics and favoured those whom he considered to have similar ideas as he. Consequently, it is clear that when the Council of Antioch in 338/9 (with the emperor present) condemned and deposed Athanasius once again from his Alexandrian Church, it was done with the emperor's approval. Athanasius and his supporters, however, proved unwilling to accept the decision. Athanasius grouped together his Christian supporters for his protection. According to Athanasius' own version, the Arian *Praefectus Aegypti* Philargius responded by arming gangs of pagans, Jews, and thugs with swords and clubs in support of the new bishop Gregory and sent them to attack the Christians in their churches. Sozomen (2.6) notes also the presence of Arian Christians among the gang. Regardless, it is still clear that most of the attackers were not Christians, let alone local Christian soldiers. They could not be trusted to carry out the orders. A general mayhem resulted. The main church was burned, some nuns raped, monks beaten, scriptures burned and so forth, after which the new Arian bishop Gregory entered the city. After this, the gang attacked Athanasius and his supporters who had occupied the other main church of the city. In the end, Athanasius chose to flee by ship to Rome. What is notable is that the imperial authorities proved unable to stop the flight of the bishop even though they tried to control access to the harbour. The Christian bishops clearly had important contacts inside the administration that were willing to lend a hand, and wielded considerable power to cause urban unrest.[308]

This was a sign of things to come. In order to promote his Christian views Constantius II was forced to resort to the use of the army throughout his reign. There were to be problems in Constantinople (342–4), in Alexandria (339, 356, 357, 358/9), and in Paphlagonia (358/9). The success of these operations proved ephemeral and short-lived. The Nicene Creed could not be rooted out and by the end of the century its dominance was clear. It is notable that in several instances the forces of Constantius included significant numbers of pagans that could be more readily used against the Christians.

Constantius' preference of Christians, especially the Arian Christians, over the pagans can also be detected in his appointments to the positions of consuls and praetorian prefects. Constantius appointed only one pagan as ordinary consul during his entire reign, in 355 as a reward for his dynastic loyalty. Similarly, he appointed only one pagan as praetorian prefect of the East. In short, he showed clear favouritism towards Arian Christians in all his important appointments. Regardless, Constantius like all emperors of the fourth century, tolerated pagan soldiers and pagan officers, if for no other reason than because it was necessary. The army included so significant a number of pagans that it was next to impossible to purge them. Similarly, the fanatically pagan Julian was forced to keep Christian generals in office.[309]

First Siege of Nisibis in 337

But in the meantime, in 337 Shapur II had attempted to exploit the situation by launching a pre-emptive invasion which was directed against Nisibis, the bullwark of Rome. At the time Constantius was still preoccupied with the problems of succession and was able to reach Antioch only after Shapur had already invaded. Shapur appears to have been able to defeat the local Roman forces, after which he besieged Nisibis.

The Persians used all kinds of war engines, towers, palisades, embankments and undermining in the course of the siege, but the best idea they came up with was to use the Nymphius River as a battering ram. They built a dam to block the river and then released the waters with the result that the wall collapsed in two places, where the river entered the city and where it left it. The Persians, however, were unable to exploit the situation immediately because of the flooding. The local bishop Jacob had an important role in the upkeep of the morale of the defenders. The Romans used the period of inactivity well and built new walls during the following night, but the decisive thing was the sudden appearance of swarms of insects that made the elephants, horses and men ill and mad. The Persian elephants in particular could not bear the mosquitoes and gnats. Many Persians lost their lives. It is not known whether this resulted from the presence of pools of water or whether the Romans were practising a form of biological warfare.[310] The official Christian propaganda claimed that the insects appeared as a result of the prayers of the local bishop. Shapur instead attributed it to the presence of the Emperor after he mistakenly believed that he saw someone (a bishop?) in imperial attire on the wall. He accused his spies of incompetence, but in the end they managed to convince him that Constantius was still at Antioch. After the battle of Narasara even the mentioning of the name of Constantius made the Persians tremble.

Consequently, when it was announced that Constantius II was on his way to the scene, Shapur had no alternative than to retreat without accomplishing his goal. When Constantius reached the scene of operations, he was unable to catch the Persian ruler because his entire force had made haste to avoid having to fight another battle against the feared Emperor.

The East after the Siege of Nisibis

Meanwhile, Shapur's intelligence operatives had not been idle. They had learnt that the Persian Christians had warned the Romans in advance of Shapur's forthcoming invasion as a result of which Constantius was able to reach the scene of operations in a 'timely fashion'. Naturally enough, the result of all this was the beginning of the persecution of Christians in Persia. The Christians indeed appear to have acted as spies just as their enemies accused. The close contact between the bishop of Nisibis and the Persian bishops was well known, as was the embassy of Christians to the new emperor Constantius II. The magi were given orders to destroy the Churches and to kill the Christians. This stage did not last long. Some of the magi failed to follow the unreasonable order and Shapur also had second thoughts. He needed money to sustain the war when there was no quick victory in sight. Consequently, in 340 he doubled the head tax of the Christians, most of whom were wealthy merchants and artisans, and ordered that only those who refused to submit were to be killed and their property confiscated. However, the change of heart did not include the bishops, metropolitans, deacons or anyone connected with the Church hierarchy who were all rounded up, tortured, interrogated and then executed by the religious police. The persecution intensified even further during subsequent years.[311] This policy had several consequences. The Persian king undoubtedly filled his war chest and stopped the information flow from his kingdom, but he did this at the cost of losing a very productive class of citizens that could have provided him with more taxes in the long run. It also weakened his position in the India trade.

Constantius was unable to begin the invasion of Persia proper in 338 probably because part of the Roman army was used to install a new king on the Armenian throne and to crush the revolt of Aljnik. The rest were needed for the defence of Mesopotamia and Arabia.

Constantius reversed his father's policies regarding Armenia (Hannibalianus was a thing of the past). As noted before, when Sanesan/Sanatruk had attacked Armenia with

Persian support, probably in 336, Khosrov had taken refuge at the fortress of Dariwnk and had dispatched Vache Mamikonean to beg help from the Romans. According to Faustos (3.7) when Vache returned (in 338?) from 'Greek' territory, he attacked the camp of the enemy at Mt. Tzugloukh (Clu Gluch, 'Bull's Head' near Oshakan) at dawn and put them to flight with his Armenian feudal forces. This means that the relief army had now freed Khosrov from the siege. Another possibility is that there was another Mt. Tzuglough somewhere east of Dariwnk because that sequence of events would make more sense than the traditional locale for the battle south-east of Oshakan. The remnants of the defeated forces fled to the city of Valarshapat. It is clear that Faustos has ignored Roman participation. From Julian (Or. 1.20D–21.A) we know that Constantius had helped the Armenian ruler to gain control of his country in about 338. Consequently, it is certain that Moses (3.5–6) is correct when he stated that the Roman 'Palace Prefect' Antiochus made Khosrov king and then established the same military organization (four military zones plus the royal army under the *sparapet*) in place as had existed under Trdat. In other words, Antiochus reappointed Bagarat the *Aspet* as general of the Western Gate; Mirian, the prince/king of Iberia and *Vitaxa* of Gugark as general of the Northern Gate; Vahan Amatuni as general of the Eastern Gate; and Manachihr, prince of Rshtunik as general of the Southern Gate. Of particular importance is the position of the King of Iberia as a noble and general of Armenia. It is clear that Iberia was still a client state of Armenia. It is probable that the Antiochus in question is Julius Antiochus (PLRE1 Antiochus 15) who was *Praefectus Vigilum* between 313 and 319 and had now evidently been promoted as *Mag.Off.* Considering the difficulty of the task, it is probable that the Roman army consisted at least of 35,000–40,000 men, if not more.

According to Faustos, after the surprise attack against the enemy camp Vache (or rather Antiochus) led his army down to the plain of the district of Ayrarat. Note that this makes more sense if there was another Bull's Head east of Dawink. After this, Vache (i.e. Antiochus) attacked the enemy at Valarshapat and forced them to flee to the fortress of Oshakan. There the armies fought still another battle in which Sanesan was defeated and then pursued all the way up to the country of Paytarakan. According to Faustos, the head of Sanesan was brought to the king. According to Moses' version, after having reorganized the Armenian kingdom it was Antiochus who advanced together with the Armenians (the northern army with a paper strength of 18,500 knights and the western army with a paper strength of 23,500) against Sanatruk (i.e. Sanesan) in Paytarakan. That is, there was probably a short pause in the campaign after the enemy had been forced to flee from Oshakan. The overall size of the combined Roman and Armenian forces advancing against Paytarakan was probably at least 50,000–60,000 men. According to this version, Sanesan chose not to fight, but put a Persian garrison inside the city and then continued his flight to Persian territory. The Roman troops pillaged the rebel territories and then returned back home and left the war in Armenian hands.

In the meanwhile, a second operation under Manachihr (Southern Gate and the Cilician Army) was launched against the rebel Bakur and his Persian helpers in Assyria (Moses 3.7). Bakur was killed in battle and his son taken captive. According to Moses, Manachihr brought back many captives, including Christian deacons, from the territory of Nisibis. Considering the locale, it would seem strange if Manachihr's forces were not supported by the Romans, just like the other Armenian army in Paytarakan was, but in this case Moses doesn't specifically mention these. The domains of the *Vitaxa* of Aljnik belonged to the Romans, which means that he had not only revolted against his feudal lord, but also against the Romans. Indeed, in my opinion the referral to the Cilician Army by Moses should be seen to mean the Roman field army posted in the region, which may also mean that the actual command of the operation was in Roman hands as it was with the other army.

Whatever the truth, it is still clear that the Armenians were acting as Roman allies and effectively secured the approaches to Nisibis with the victory they achieved. According to Faustos' version (3.9), Bakur's revolt and the Persian forces were defeated by Khosrov's forces which consisted of the forces of Korduk, Great Copk, Copk, Siwnik, Hashteank, Basean and others. The Armenian army (with the Roman Field Army of Cilicia) facing the united forces of Aljnik (perhaps about 15,000–20,000) and Persians (perhaps about 20,000–30,000) must have therefore consisted at least of about 40,000 men. Khosrov appears to have kept the royal army in reserve to oppose other possible invasions by Persians and/or northerners. Khosrov was effectively fighting on behalf of the Romans with very sizable forces when he crushed this revolt and invasion.

In the short term, the support of Khosrov proved to be a wise policy move. It secured for Constantius the support of the Armenians against the Persians for a period of about seven to eight years. It is therefore not at all surprising that Constantius also adopted an aggressive strategy against Persia from about 338 until 344. Roman help did not end Khosrov's troubles, however. After the Roman forces had withdrawn, the Persians invaded Armenia. Khosrov made the mistake of ordering Databay/Databe, the *nahapet* of the Bznuni, to collect irregular levies and take the elite-contingent with him and then block the enemy's route. Databe betrayed his army to the Persian princes and delivered it to be ambushed. The Persians killed 40,000 men while the rest fled. Now Khosrov gave command of the army to Vache who led the remaining 30,000 men against the invaders and defeated the Persians at Arest on the shore of L.Van. Faustos (3.8) as usual states that the Persians were defeated in their camp, but this is a misunderstanding of the Persian battle tactics, which involved the use of the camp directly behind the cavalry line. In truth, the Armenian cavalry overran the Persian cavalry and their infantry forces and captured the camp. After this Khosrov the Small entrusted his forces only to two commanders Vache Mamikonean (*Sparapet*) and Vahan Amatuni (commander of the East Gate: Moses 3.9), and kept the rest of the magnates at court so that he could keep an eye on them. This was not the end of the war, however. It continued unabated until about 345.

Around 338/9, after Constantius had gathered enough money and provisions through extra taxes, built riverboats for use as pontoon bridges and transports, collected enough horsemen to match the Persian cavalry, conscripted new troops, and had retrained his army, he started to conduct yearly raids across the border. Constantius conquered and pillaged a number of forts, towns and cities, but he did not make the mistake of penetrating too deeply into enemy territory by bypassing enemy fortifications as Julian later did. In the course of the next decade Constantius built safe harbours for Antioch to facilitate the transport of supplies, arms and troops. Antioch became his base of operations as well as his headquarters. During the winters he rested his army and planned the next summer's operations and during every summer he then put the plans into practice. At the same time he strengthened the fortifications so that the enemy could not exploit his absence from some sector of the border. His only purpose was to attempt to force the enemy to fight a decisive pitched battle of the kind they had foolishly fought in 336, but with no result because the enemy fled whenever they heard that they faced the emperor and his elite forces. Constantius knew that he had to destroy the enemy's main field army first in order to be able to invade the enemy territory unhindered so that he could conquer the plentiful enemy fortresses without having to fear enemy relief armies.

Of particular interest is the fact that Shapur's heavy cavalry had made such an impression upon Constantius that despite his victory over them at Narasara he decided to imitate it. He equipped his cavalry with similar equipment so that both the rider and horse were fully armoured with chain mail from head to foot – even the face was covered by a metal mask – and the hands were covered with flexible fine mail 'mittens'. The last mentioned detail doesn't mean that the Romans would have been unable to use bows, because the Persians were using similar equipment with bows.[312]

The West, 340

In 340 Constantine II decided to wrest the control of Italy and Africa from his half-brother, which he considered to be his by birthright. He was the eldest of the brothers. When in 340 Constantine learnt that his brother, who was at Naissus in 'Dacia', was facing problems in overcoming the Sarmatians, he hatched a plot. Naissus undoubtedly served as Constans' headquarters for a campaign in Dacia proper. Constantine convinced his brother Constans that he intended to send reinforcements to him, or alternatively that he intended to send reinforcements for Constantius through Constans' territory (Fox, 224). As a result, Constantine was able to march his army across the Alps unmolested and launch a surprise invasion, but Constans acted quickly when he realized his mistake. He immediately dispatched a vanguard (evidently cavalry) under his generals to secure Aquileia, while he would follow behind them with the main army. When the generals came face-to-face with Constantine II near Aquilea, they placed part of their forces in ambush and advanced forward with the rest in order to feign a flight. Constantine with his cavalry swallowed the bait and set out in pursuit, with the result that the ambushers managed to surround them all. Constantine II and his cavalry were annihilated leaving Constans as the sole ruler of two-thirds of the Empire.[313] Thanks to the troubles he was facing in the East Constantius had no other alternative than to accept what had happened, but Constans was not coy about showing his strengthened position vis-à-vis his brother.

We do not know when the Romans lost 're-conquered' Dacia, but the year 340 seems the likeliest alternative because it was in that year that Constans was forced to withdraw his campaign army from the field against his brother and then march to Gaul to secure his brother's former possessions. After this, Constans was constantly moving from one front to another against the invaders with little chance of attempting a reconquest of the lost territories.

Constans and Constantius II, 340–350

West

After his victory Constans appears to have retained most of the administrative system as it was so that the offices that had been created for or by Constantine II were kept in existence. This means that each of the separate prefectures became effectively local governments in the absence of the Emperor. Constantius' response to the enlargement of Constans' domains and power was to create a separate Senate with traditional magistracies for the city of Constantinople in 340. His purpose was to stress his equal standing with his brother.[314]

In the field of military organization there is a possibility that Constans created a new supreme commander for the entire army called the *Magister Equitum et Peditum* while he retained the other magisterial offices in existence. A possible proof of this is that the Theodosian Code (7.1.2, 8.7.3) includes references to the existence of an office called *magister equitum et peditum* (or *magister militum*) for the year 349, which suggests the possibility that an office which combined both cavalry and infantry had been created to act as commander-in-chief for the entire army. It is of course also possible that the *magistri* had simply received this new title because in practice both commanded both arms of service anyway, or that some later copyist has updated the text. Still another alternative is that the title referred to the existence of honorary *magistri vacantes* that could also actually serve as *magistri in actu positi/administratores*.[315] However, the first alternative appears likelier because in 363 (see the second book in the series) one of the first actions of the new emperor Jovian was to appoint his father-in-law Lucillianus as *Magister Equitum et Peditum*, which does suggest that he would have acted as a commander-in-chief of all forces in the west. The date when this office was first created is not known. Possible dates for such would be after Constans I had absorbed Constantine II's army in 340, or when the brothers divided the empire in 337, or even during the last years of Constantine's rule to separate his *magistri* from those of his sons. The honorary *magistri* were probably only created during the reign of Jovian.

In 341 and 342 Constans was fighting against the Franks.[316] The withdrawal of forces from Gaul by Constantine II for his campaign against Constans had created a power vacuum that the Franks had exploited. Defeated, the Franks were forced to sign a treaty. Circumstantial evidence also suggests that Constantine II had similarly drawn reinforcements from Britain for his campaign in Italy or that Constans had drawn reinforcements from there for his campaign against the Franks, with the result that the Picts and Scots had invaded in 341/2. The situation became so acute in late-342 that it required Constans' personal attention in the middle of winter. He left Milan in December (he is attested in Milan on 4 December, 342) and reached Bononia by 25 January, 343, which means that he crossed the Channel in the middle of winter.

Circumstantial evidence suggests that Constans' British visit was a success. On the basis of archaeological evidence it has also been suggested that he initiated major re-fortification projects throughout Britain. Most of this work consisted of repairs to the damaged fortifications, or of the remodelling of the town walls, or of the adding of external towers. In most cases it is impossible to date the work, because from this date onwards the defences were either constantly improved or repairs were made to those that had suffered damage. It is also probable that he conducted treaties with the enemy tribes that secured the frontiers at least for a while. In addition, according to Ammianus Constans also created an organization called the *Arcani/Areani* who conducted espionage operations among the tribes bordering the Empire.[317] On the basis of their involvement in the great barbarian conspiracy of 367 it is likely that the *Arcani* consisted of native barbarians who were used to spy on their fellows.

At some point in time between 340 and 345 there were also religious troubles in Africa. The local *Comes* massacred large numbers of Donatists, creating large numbers of martyrs for them. In 347 Constans sent two legates to investigate the situation in Africa, but since these two legates were staunch Catholics a new round of massacres, confiscations and exiles ensued. In general, Constans left the Church to govern itself, but as a staunch supporter of the Nicene Creed he intervened against the Donatists.

At that moment the Donatists were joined by the so-called Circumcellians (after *circumcella*) who were landless poor who simply sought social justice in the name of the God. Now even the Donatists were prepared to call the army to their assistance and the army complied with brutality. The Circumcellians responded to the assault with mass suicides. This did not end the dissention. The greatest years of the Donatist Church still lay in the future.[318] Consequently, the African Church was badly divided and this definitely did not help the central government, as it preoccupied its representatives with quite trivial matters.

We know precious little about the military events and policies of Constans for the next seven years. We know the names of some of the locations he visited and that he oppressed his subjects like an intolerable tyrant and that he made himself hated with his homosexual extravagances – on top of which he did not marry and procreate successors. He is said to have bought or taken as hostages handsome young barbarians, who then, in return for sexual favours, were allowed to mistreat his subjects at their whim. The reference to the hostages suggests that Constans had not been idle during these seven years, but fought several wars despite the claims that Constans was only devoted to the joys of hunting in the company of his boyfriends and catamites – unless of course 'hostages' is a reference to Constans' predatory sexual behaviour.[319] Libanius' Panegyric (Or. 59) makes it clear that Constans was a robust, tireless warrior and hunter, who spent all his days in manly pursuits like fighting and hunting.

Constans returned to Gaul in the spring of 343 and was still at Trier in June 343 where he interviewed Athanasius. Constans intervened on behalf of Athanasius and sent a message to his brother Constantius that he should reinstate him, but with no results. We do not know what Constans did in Gaul, but it seems probable that he at least strengthened the defences and paraded his forces near the border to make certain that the Franks would keep their side of the bargain. In the meantime, the Sarmatians appear to have invaded Illyricum during the winter of 343–4, which suggests the possibility that Constans may have created the post of *PP* of Illyricum as a response in about 345 (Harries, 191) – a creation of some importance – but it is possible that it had been created earlier, for example for Dalmatius Caesar in 335. Consequently, Constans marched to Pannonia where he is attested in the autumn of 344. It is likely that he fought another campaign there after which he once again returned to Gaul, where he is attested at Trier on 15 May, 345 and at Cologne in June/July. The locations suggest that at least some of the Frankish tribes had not respected their treaty, with the result that Constans was once again forced to fight a campaign against the Franks. On 5 March, 346 Constans was once again back at Sirmium, which means that the Sarmatian problem had persisted while he had been in Gaul. The war against the Sarmatians, and possibly also against other tribes in the area like the Quadi, who usually operated together with the Sarmatians, and possibly also with the Hasding Vandals who were their neighbours, appears to have continued until the death of Constans. This means that Constans campaigned against them in person at least in 346 and 349, after which the war was continued by the *Mag. Ped.* Vetranio. At the time of Constans' death in 350 the war against the 'Scythians' in Pannonia was definitely being conducted on behalf of Constans by the veteran commander Vetranio and one may make the educated guess that he and other similarly loyal commanders had performed comparable service on Constans' behalf whenever he was not present in person. Constans clearly travelled frantically between the fronts, accompanied only by his most intimate entourage and bodyguards, and took charge of the operations when necessary.

We also know that the name of Constans put fear in the hearts of the Alamanni decades after the fact, which means that he probably conducted a very bloody campaign against them at some point in time between 346 and 349. The fact that he is attested to have been at Caesena in Italy already on 23 May, 346 does suggest that he had returned from

Sirmium (5 March) in a hurry, probably to fight against the Alamanni. He is known to have been at Milan on 17 June, 348, which suggests that he probably conducted a very memorable and successful campaign against the Alamanni between 346 and 348. It has also been suggested that Constans had concentrated the bulk of his forces on the Danube frontier just prior to his murder (Harries, 221), but the location of his murder does rather suggest that he had been improving the defences against the Alamanni while also making certain that the Alamanni would not break their treaty. The fact that troops had been transferred from Illyria (see later) to Gaul bespeaks rather of continuing troubles.

The fact that Constans possessed two-thirds of the Empire and had achieved a number of important military successes made him arrogant in ecclesiastical matters. He was a staunch believer in the Nicene Creed and was not afraid to show it. This resulted in conflict with Constantius, who no longer felt it necessary to court the opinion of the Orthodox clergy. As noted above the Arians dominated the Council of Antioch in 339 and had deposed Athanasius. Constantius' men did manage to throw out Athanasius from Alexandria, but they faced at least as bad difficulties in Constantinople. In 341 the populace placed the orthodox Paulus back in office as Patriarch of Constantinople. Next year Constantius sent his *Mag.Eq.* Hermogenes to expel Paulus, with the result that Hermogenes was killed in a riot. Consequently, in 343 Constantius was forced to take his army to the capital in the middle of the Persians war and exile Paulus to Singara. In 343/4 there was a quarrel between the Western and Eastern bishops at Serdica, but Constans ignored it and tried to force his brother to follow the majority decision and restore the exiled Orthodox bishops and punish their enemies. In 345 Constans went so far as to threaten Constantius with military action. Constantius backed down. The most famous of the refugees who returned was Athanasius. The situation had now reached the point in which a different interpretation of the Christian Doctrine could be a *casus belli* between brothers. This was not a healthy situation, but in the end the brothers chose not to fight against each other.

In contrast, in 349 Constantius felt strong enough to challenge his brother. The Council of Antioch once again deposed Athanasius in the expectation that Constantius would enforce the decision. However, this time the situation was not ripe. Magnentius' usurpation changed the state of affairs, and Constantius kept Athanasius in office in order not to stir up trouble in Egypt while he faced civil war.

Constans' slavish behaviour towards his favourites and arrogance naturally angered many people, but it was the *Comes Rerum Privatarum* Marcellinus, and the *protector* and *Comes* Magnus Magnentius (I would suggest that he was *Comes Domesticorum Peditum*), the commander of both the *Ioviani* and *Herculiani*, who formed the actual plot to kill the tyrant. The usurpers were in daily contact with the emperor and they could no longer tolerate the behaviour of Constans and his toy-boys.

When the court resided at Augustodunum, Marcellinus called the most important officers together to celebrate his son's birthday (Zon 13.6: Magnentius' pretended birthday) on 18 January, 350, while Magnentius hid imperial costume and guardsmen in a bedroom. When Magnentius emerged in full imperial attire accompanied by his guardsmen, he either convinced or forced the officers present to join the revolt. This was an audacious thing to do because, according to Julian (Or. 1.34), Magnus Magnentius was of barbarian origin (Saxon father and Frank mother, or according to another source

British father and Frank mother, the former alternative being the more likely). At one point in time Constans had saved Magnentius from being murdered by soldiers. Magnentius was clearly very ungrateful towards his benefactor. It is also clear that the conspirators had very little support among the military. Constans had proved himself a very able military commander and therefore this usurpation proved to be a particularly great disaster for the Roman Empire. It not only removed an able warrior emperor, but it also unleashed a period of serious military trouble resulting from both the ensuing civil war and its consequences.

Following his 'elevation', Magnentius sent his men to kill the emperor. The assassins, led by Gaiso, accomplished their mission and killed some of Constans' boyfriends too. After this, Magnentius fabricated letters in Constans' name, summoned Constans' loyal supporters to the court and had them ambushed and killed. Similarly, he put away, on the grounds of mere suspicion, some of the officers who had attended the banquet.

When report of the usurpation was spread around, the army and soldiers of Gaul 'eagerly' joined the usurper's cause because there were none left to oppose it, and this also included the Illyrian cavalry that had been sent to reinforce the army in Gaul.[320] The fact that there were reinforcements from Illyria also speaks for the existence of troubles in Gaul in 349.

As we shall see Magnentius' usurpation was by no means well received among the Italian aristocrats and among the Illyrian army. Magnentius also needed to secure the support of the army and its officers and he needed money to accomplish this. Consequently, he levied an extra property tax of 50 per cent (of the regular tax) and auctioned off the imperial estates.

East

As noted above, in 340 Constantius was in no position to challenge his brother Constans. He was preoccupied with his ongoing war against Shapur. We have actually one clue dated to the year 340 for the size and quality of Constantius' field army during his campaigns against the Persians, as well as for his strategy. This is the so-called Itinerary of Alexander (*Itinerarium Alexandri*), which may have been written by Constantius' courtier and *Comes* Flavius Julius Valerius Alexander Polemius. He was a very prominent person and apparently an ardent supporter of Constantius for he was consul in 338. The Itinerary is dedicated to Constantius and in the extant manuscript tradition it is united with the Latin version of the 'Alexander Romance' to act as a sort of historical counterbalance for the less reliable fictious Romance. The author's intention was to include the itineraries of both Alexander and Trajan with an eye for the forthcoming operations against the Persians. It is notable that both emperors sought to engage the Persians in pitched battles in the open. In other words, it foresaw that Constantius would launch an offensive campaign against the Persians like Alexander and Trajan. Unfortunately, the extant text breaks up immediately after the death of Alexander so we are only left with a summary of Alexander's campaign, which is mostly based on Arrian. We can only suppose that the account of Trajan's campaign would also have been based on Arrian. The extant Itinerary portrays Alexander's good and bad qualities realistically and thereby offers advice on what to imitate and what to avoid. Of particular note is the indirect advice to allow free speech for friends, so that these could keep the ruler from making mistakes, and not to let power go to the head.[321] For what it is worth, Constantius indeed seems to have avoided Alexander's excesses, but it may have been a personality issue more than a conscientious decision.

As noted above, the Itinerary can also be used to indicate the probable size and quality of Constantius' field army in about 340. According to the Itinerary (Mai 8, 13; Volkmann 4–5), Constantius' army had as many men as Alexander's army, but was better trained. The text also states that Alexander's army and by implication Constantius' was not large in numbers, but it was very powerful and highly mobile thanks to its good training. The Itinerary (Mai 23, 51–8; Volkmann, 13, 23–4) also includes two clues to the size of Constantius' army. At the battle of Issus the Persians supposedly had 600,000 men while the Macedonians had a mere twentieth of this: that is, the Macedonians would have had about 30,000 men. One may perhaps consider this to have been an approximation and emend this to follow Arrian, which the author summarizes so that the Macedonians had more than 30,000 infantry and more than 5,000 cavalry. Secondly, at the battle of Gaugamela/Arbela Alexander had 40,000 infantry and 7,000 cavalry. This means that the Roman army envisaged by the author, which was not large but was extremely well-trained, had between 30,000 and 47,000 men. It is impossible to know which figure Polemius had in mind when comparing the sizes of the armies, but at least this does give some sort of basis for further educated speculation. The use of Alexander and Trajan as examples implies that the goal was nothing less than the conquest of Persia, at least up to the Persian Gulf if not up to India.

Between 340 and 343 Constantius continued his previously adopted strategy. He attempted to force the Persians into a decisive battle by leading his armies across the Tigris. The crossing of the river was done by using mobile pontoon bridges that could then be broken into pieces and reassembled as needed. This procedure made it possible for the Romans to invade any sector they chose quickly, but they were still not quick enough to catch the enemy unprepared. The Persians avoided open battles and resorted to the use of guerrilla warfare. The situation remained the same until about 343. It was then that Constantius was able to capture Adiabene and transport its entire population to Roman territory.[322] It is also possible that Constantius fortified Bezabde at this time to serve as a bulwark against the Persians. This campaign finally brought a Persian response.

In 344 Shapur raised levies, assembled feudal forces, and even collected women to act as suttlers for the army. In addition, he strengthened his army with the forces of his tributory nations and foreign mercenaries. His army included foot archers, slingers, 'hoplites', mounted archers, regular cavalry, and cataphract cavalry. This massive preparation did not go unnoticed by Roman spies and Constantius was aware of every move the Persians made. The Roman scouts gave a detailed and accurate report of enemy movements near Nineveh as a result of which the emperor decided to lure the enemy across the Tigris in order to attack Singara. He ordered his frontier troops to retreat so that the enemy would feel confident to cross the river. The Persians built three pontoon bridges and crossed the river in good order, after which they built a fortified camp (which included water cisterns) on the rough terrain at Eleia that favoured defence and the use of archery. Shapur's aim was clearly to cut off the Romans' supply route.

The Battle of Singara, 344[323]

Shapur placed his infantry archers and javelin men on the walls and peaks of the hills and the cataphract cavalry in front of the wall. The rest of the cavalry advanced against the Romans in an attempt to lure the Romans to follow them up to the camp. The intention was to tire the Romans with a long march before the battle and then use the archery of the foot archers and cataphracts, plus the rough terrain and fortified camp, to bring the Romans to a halt, after which the cataphracts would then trample the Romans under their hooves with a frontal charge. Consequently, when the armies came face-to-face, the Persian cavalry feigned flight. Constantius tried to convince the troops to postpone fighting, but in vain. The men were overconfident. The Romans pursued the Persian *hippotoxotai* for about 18.5km (Julian) or 30km (Libanius) up to their camp and within the range of the arrows. On the basis of Libanius' numbers the Romans were at Singara and the Persians had cut off their lines of communication to the west. Whenever the Persian cavalry reached higher ground during their retreat, they halted and shot showers of arrows at their pursuers. Even though this is not mentioned, it is probable that the Roman marching formation was a hollow square, suited to the open terrain, in which the footmen used the tortoise order to withstand the enemy volleys of arrows.

When the Romans reached the Persian camp close to the evening, the men were tired and thirsty. Constantius ordered his troops to halt but in vain. The elite fighters, the club-bearers/mace-bearers, trained to engage the *clibanarii*, burst forward in open order, followed by at least the first line of the 'hoplites'. The emperor had no other alternative than to attempt to salvage the situation as best he could. Fortunately for him, he still managed to keep most of his men (three flanks of the square?) behind so that he was able to use them as a reserve. At about this time Shapur wanted to observe the Roman army in person. He ordered his own 'hoplites' to form a tortoise array for him to climb up on. The sight horrified Shapur. He realized that the Romans had brought a huge army to the scene of operations, with the implication that the Romans outnumbered his own forces. He left his son, the crown prince, in charge of the army and the fighting retreat, while he himself fled to the Tigris, but the Romans would not allow the Persian to flee unhindered.

The tactic adopted by the Roman club-bearers was simple but effective. Each club-bearer advanced at a run towards one charging Persian *clibanarii* opposite him and sidestepped (or jumped) at the last moment to avoid the enemy *contus* and horse (if the men faced the *clibanarii* from the left, then they also deflected the *contus* with their shield) and then struck the rider with their club/mace on the temple as he passed by and thereby knocked him off his horse. In order for this technique to be effective the Roman clubmen would have been trained to coordinate their movements so that they would not jump at each other. My own personal guess is that some of the club-bearers would have struck the horse's temple rather than the rider, as this would have been even easier to do. What is clear is that these club-bearers were extraordinarily brave men who were expert martial artists, gymnasts and athletes, but we should keep in mind that the use of club-bearers was not peculiar to the fourth century: for example, there are several scenes on Trajan's Column where there are German club-bearers (note also the Sarmatian cataphracts). Similarly, club-bearers decided the Battle of Emesa in favour of Aurelian, and the Battle of Turin for Constantine.

The Romans tore down the battlements, plundered the tents, and killed. The panicked Persians fled. The brave crown prince was captured and then later brutally tortured and killed. By now the Romans were utterly exhausted. When the Romans saw the water cisterns prepared by the Persians they stopped their pursuit and started to quench their thirst. As a result, the Persians were able to regroup just when the night fell. At that moment, the Romans inside the camp made a fateful mistake. They used torches to light their way around with the result that the Persians were able to shoot a series of deadly volleys of arrows accurately at them from the hills and from behind the camp with the result that most of the Romans inside were either killed or wounded within seconds. The Romans were on the brink of defeat. There were three things that saved them: 1) The Persians did not know the deadly results of their archery attack; 2) Constantius was up to the task and sent his reserves forward to save his men; and 3) Constantine's veterans possessed extraordinary bravery. Consequently, the tired legionaries made one last desperate attack and drove the enemy off the field. In the morning, the remaining Persians withdrew. This was a Pyrrhic victory if there ever was one. The Romans had suffered a frightful number of casualties, but so had the Persians. On top of it, the Persians had lost their crown prince, and the women and treasures of the camp. Consequently, when Shapur had crossed the Tigris and torn down the bridges behind him, he vented his anger by executing many of his senior officers as befitted an eastern tyrant. Shapur's unfortunate officers served as scapegoats for the defeat.

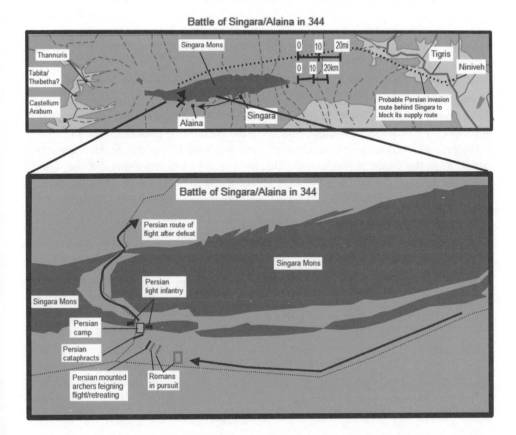

Battle of Singara/Alaina in 344

The opponents of Constantius accused the emperor of failure and claimed that the battle had been a defeat, but this is unfair. There is no doubt that the enemy had suffered the greater number of casualties. Furthermore, Shapur had lost his heir to the crown, his treasury and camp, and had been forced to flee back across the border. Regardless, the losses on both sides were such that neither side risked a major battle for the next six years – raids continued, but neither was willing to take any major risks. Henceforth, Constantius' strategy was to defend Roman territory successfully with as little risk as possible by resorting to the use of fortified positions. His aim was to achieve a peace with Persia that would maintain the status quo. However, the Persians were never ready to conclude a permanent or even semi-permanent peace unless in the process they regained possession of Mesopotamia and Armenia, which they regarded as their own. They could be forced to conclude peace treaties, but they would always restart hostilities in order to regain those at the first possible opportunity.

The course of this battle also suggests that the field army that Constantius led consisted of true elite troops that possessed extraordinary fighting spirit and morale. Despite their long march, and lack of food and drink, the soldiers defeated the Persians with one furious charge, and even when they had suffered horrendous numbers of casualties their morale did not succumb. Instead, they made still another attack and drove the enemy off the field. Constantius could be proud of his men despite their disobedience at the beginning of the battle. As we shall see, they won all of their pitched battles.

Constantius' Wars, 344–350

The sources for the war between the Battle of Singara and the Third Siege of Nisibis are very scarce and confused.[324] According to Festus, there were nine major pitched battles/ sieges during Constantius' reign, but he also includes the events that took place during the reign of his father in the same list. Constantius was present only on two of those and the rest were fought by his generals. Festus claims that the empire suffered grievously at the 'battles' of Sisara, Singara, 2nd Singara with Constantius present, Sicgara (Singara? or Bezabde which is missing from the list), Constantia (in 336) and at Amida when it was captured. At the battle of Narasara in 336 the Romans were victorious and they would have been at the night Battle at Eleia (or Hileia or Alaina) near Singara had the soldiers obeyed the emperor. It is clear that Festus' 2nd Singara and the Battle at Eleia are one and the same battle and that the second battle in which Constantius was present in person was the Battle of Narasara, which leaves open the question when the battles of Sisara, 1st Singara and Sicgara (probably Singara) took place.

We know that in about 346/7 Shapur besieged Nisibis for the second time, with equally poor results as before, and Constantius was definitely at Nisibis in May, 345, probably making certain that its defences were in order. It is feasible that he may also have considered the possibility of making an incursion into Persian territory. It is possible to shed additional light on these events from Armenian sources. Moses (3.9–11) mentions that at some point in time during his nine-year-long reign (338–347) the Armenian king Khosrov concluded a peace with the Persians and started to pay them tribute. I would suggest that we should place this change of policy to the year 345/6 and connect it with the support given by Arshak/Arsaces (then only a prince and not yet king as claimed by Faustos 4.20, and clearly in command of the Southern Gate and about 20,000 men) for the Persians in front of Nisibis, which must have taken place during the second siege of Nisibis in 346/7 rather than in 350. It is clear that this is still another instance in which Faustos has misplaced events. According to Faustos, the Armenians defeated the Romans who had encamped before the city. I would suggest that the Romans in question were actually encamped at Sisara and had acted as a defensive bulwark/holding force against enemy forces approaching from the Tigris.

In my opinion, it is probable that we should also connect the 'defeat' of Constantius and the flight of Constantius with a small body of companions to the frontier post of Hibiuta mentioned by Sabinianus of Nisibis in 363 (Amm. 25.9.3) with this same event. Since we know that Constantius was present in person in only two major battles (Narasara and Singara), it is probable that the Persians (in truth the Armenians) defeated Constantius' general at Sisara and then evidently surprised the emperor and his retinue en route there with the result that Constantius was forced to flee in panic. The Armenian betrayal would have come as a surprise to the Romans. The event must have taken place near Nisibis, because it was a resident of that city who mentioned it. However, the defeat in question cannot have been significant. Had it been, Constantius' enemies would have surely made more of it. Instead, all mention that the Persians suffered far greater casualties in all of their sieges of Nisibis than the Romans.

However, the cooperation between the Armenians and Persians proved short, because the Persians had double-crossed the Armenians. Shapur had instigated an invasion of 20,000 'northerners' under Sanatruk against the Armenians at the time when their army was helping the Persians against Nisibis. Moses (3.9) claims that the enemy defeated the remnants of the Northern Gate (undoubtedly strengthened with Iberians) under Mirian, because Khosrov was at the time fighting in the land of Tsopk (Sophanene) with the bulk of the Northern Forces, which means that he was attacking Roman territory (with Amida as the target?) from another direction while Arshak (Khosrov's grandson) was operating near Nisibis. Mirian/Mihran was killed in the debacle, and the invaders moved towards Valarshapat. The GC (p.144) claims that Mirian died of old age, but this is not believable. The author of the GC was at pains to hide Armenian dominance over Iberia at this time and has probably purposefully created fables around the facts. However, before the invaders could penetrate any deeper, the Western and Eastern Gates, respectively under the *Aspet* Bagarat and Vahan Amatuni, defeated them at Awshakan. After this, these forces and the bulk of the Royal Army appear to have been placed under Vache.

Moses (3.10–11) claims that it was then that Khosrov realized that the Persians were assisting his enemies, allied himself with the Romans and was given in return a Roman army to assist him. He also gave his son Tiran as hostage to the Romans. However, in this context Moses has failed to mention the crushing defeat of the Armenian forces by the Persians that happened after the defeat of the northerners. Faustos (3.11) mentions a hard fought battle between the Persians and Armenians in which the Armenian commander-in-chief Vache and many nobles died which in my opinion suggests that the Armenians had suffered a terrible defeat. It was this that actually brought about the alliance between the Armenians and Romans. In other words, I connect the flight of the Armenians from Roman territory to have resulted from the invasions of the northerners and Persians. The threat of a complete takeover of Armenia by the Persians also explains why the Romans so readily gave help to the Armenians despite their previous betrayal and invasion of Roman territory. The only Armenian armies left in existence were those with the king and Arshak and it is probable that it was this force that was then united with the Romans and defeated the Persian invaders in Armenia, while the other Persian Corps was defeated in front of Nisibis by its defenders.

The appointment of Garjoyl Malkhaz Khorkhoruni as the new commander of the Northern Gate suggests that the Armenians lost control of Iberia at this time and this is confirmed by the GC (p.146). According to the GC (p.143), the Armenians did not accept Mirian's son Bakar as his successor because they wanted to make the son of Trdat's daughter their king, as a result of which Bakar fled to Persia. The Persians gave Bakar an army with which he defeated the Armenians at Jawaxet/Javaxeti. The Romans didn't give any help to the Armenians, because Bakar had previously been held hostage by the Romans and was therefore considered loyal towards them. Indeed, Bakar asked the Romans to mediate between himself and the Armenians. This proved successful and Bakar became the ruler of Iberia with the support of both the Romans and Persians. Regardless of this, the Iberian Church still remained subordinated to the Armenian one.

It was soon after this, in about 347, that Khosrov died and Arshavir Kamsakaran, the acting commander of the Armenian army, took Tiran to get Constantius' approval – which Constantius duly granted – and Tiran was sent back to Armenia (Moses 3.10–11). Tiran's son Trdat and his family were given as hostages. There is nothing surprising regarding the short length of Khosrov's rule. His father had been about 80 years old when he died. The opportunistic ruler of Persia immediately exploited the death of the ruler of Armenia and sent an army to conquer it. The Persians managed to penetrate almost as far as the Roman border before they were annihilated by Arshavir Kamsakaran's army on the Plain of Mrul (north-east of Satala), which this time consisted of the entire Army of Armenia. The location suggests that the Armenians may have received some Roman support and we should not forget that there was also a Roman army permanently assisting the Armenians at this time.

In about 348 the Persians besieged the city of Singara, but with very poor results. Two recently-formed legions, the *Praeventores* and *Superventores* under their *Comes* Aelianus, made a surprise attack against the Persian camp at night and butchered the sleeping Persian besiegers. The fact that the legions consisted of recruits does indeed suggest that after the battle of Singara Constantius had been forced to recruit new forces. The war had now become a war of attrition in which both sides resorted to the use of tit for tat raids and shallow invasions against cities, towns and forts close to the border. It is therefore not surprising that Constantius continued to strengthen the defences (especially in Mesopotamia) throughout the 340s.[325]

One very significant facet of Constantius' overall strategy was the spreading of Christianity among his neighbours. The obvious idea was to make them part of the wider Christian Community led by the Roman Christian Emperor. Consequently, Constantius (or his father) had dispatched Ulfilas and other priests to convert the Tervingi Goths. The idea was to make their alliance more secure. Christianity was also less bellicose as a religion than the Nordic and Germanic religions and therefore bound to weaken the Germanic tribes, at least in the short run. We do not know whether this had been done with the approval of Constans, but that seems very unlikely because Ulfilas was Arian. The Goths naturally perceived the purpose, as a result of which the anti-Roman faction led by Athanaric exiled Ulfilas and most of his followers, but this did not take place without the shedding of blood. However, in the long run Constantius' effort had far reaching consequences. It was thanks to this that most of the Germanic peoples became Arians.

In the short run, the expulsion of Ulfilas and his followers led to their settlement in the Nikopolis area (Nicopolis ad Istrum) and to the creation of 'numerous and unwarlike *Gothi Minores*', as well as to the temporary breakup of the *foedus* between the nations. It seems probable that the Tervingian raids across the frozen Danube that are recorded to have taken place at about this time are connected with these events. The internal divisions created by the prosetylizing among the Tervingi led to a rising of the traditionalist pagans against their pro-Roman brethren as well as their foreign supporters. Consequently, it is actually possible that Constantius' policy provoked a hostile reaction unforeseen by him.[326] Another possibility is that the raids across the border occurred when Constans was murdered, which could have been seen to have ended the *foedus*. Regardless of the exact timing of these events, it is clear that these took place while the emperor was still fighting against the Persians, as a result of which he appeased the Goths enough so that the *foedus* could be revived. It seems probable that it was at that time that the Romans gave up to the Goths at least part of their possessions on the other side of the Danube, that is, most of the area between the Danube and Giant's Furrow excepting the bank of the Danube.

Constantius and Magnentius (350–353)

Magnentius Secures his Position

As noted above, Magnus Magnentius had usurped power in early 350. When news of this spread, Constantia, Constantius' sister, persuaded Constans' *Magister Militum* Vetranio to declare himself emperor on 1 March, 350 as a pre-emptive measure against the usurper. Constantius, who was at Edessa, immediately recognized Vetranio as Emperor, and apparently sent money – and possibly also troops – to support him against the 'Scythians'. Magnentius was unable to react immediately, because he had to secure his own position first in Gaul. As usurper his first order of things was to gather enough money to pay /bribe his troops and supporters, but the measures that he took to accomplish this obviously did not endear the new government to the rich and powerful in Gaul.

After Magnentius had managed to collect a sizable army consisting of the troops from Spain and Gaul and Federates consisting mainly of Franks and Saxons, his fellow tribesmen, he invaded Italy in April-May. I would suggest that very soon after this Magnentius managed to capture the passes running through the Julian Alps by deceiving the *Comes* Actus/Acacius (same as Acacius 4 in PLRE1?) into believing that the troops that were approaching were loyal to Vetranio(?) (Amm. 31.11.3), but then the troubles in his rear (usurpation and barbarian invasions, see below) caused him to abandon the idea of invading Pannonia. As a result, Magnentius decided to attempt to form an alliance with Vetranio against Constantius.

The barbarian Magnentius had managed to secure Italy for himself, but not the support of its upper classes. Nepotianus, son of Constantius' half-sister Eutropia, seized his opportunity, collected a group of irregulars, declared himself emperor on 3 June and advanced against Magnentius' *PP* Anicetus who was at Rome. Anicetus armed some citizens and marched against Nepotianus, but these were butchered by Nepotianus' men. Anicetus fled inside the city and shut the gates. Magnentius, however, was close by, and dispatched his *Mag. Off.* Marcellinus with professional troops against Nepotianus with the result that Nepotianus and his supporters were all killed only a couple of days after their initial victory. It was now at the latest that those who opposed the usurper fled to Constantius. These men included a significant proportion of the Roman Senate. Parts of the *Classes Misenatium* and *Ravennatum* also deserted to Constantius' side (Julian Or. 1.38, 1.48.B).

In this difficult situation Magnentius still needed to secure North Africa and its grain supply for Rome before making an attempt to move into Pannonia and the desertion of the Italian Fleets did not help the situation, but he still seems to have been able to do that by the end of the year. In the same winter Magnentius also appointed his brother Decentius as Caesar to take charge of the threatened Rhine frontier.

Constantius' Response

Constantius' situation was unenviable. He still faced a powerful enemy right across the border that had spent the previous year assembling a new army for a major invasion. The first thing Constantius did was to begin to make plans for the war against the usurper while still attempting to secure the eastern border with as few men as possible. He made certain that every fort, town and city was secured with fortifications, supplies and garrisoned, and appointed Lucillianus to take charge of the war in the east in his absence, with headquarters at Nisibis. Constantius also formed alliances with the Alamanni and Franks against the usurper who had emptied the Rhine frontier of troops when he had invaded Italy. It seems probable that the Frankish tribe(s) who allied themselves with Constantius had some sort of tribal hatred against the Franks that supported Magnentius. The first invasions of Gaul by both tribal groupings had already occurred in 350, but the major operations started only in 351. In 352 Chnodomarius, one of the Alamannic kings, defeated Caesar Decentius, Magnentius' brother, and now the border lay open for the barbarian invasions. By the end of 353 the Franks and Alamanni were in control of the entire Rhine Valley, and Constantius faced the unenviable task of clearing it.[327] It is clear that whatever Constantius had promised in writing to the tribal chieftains, he did not intend to keep his promises. He had done that under duress only in order to secure their support against the usurper.

The fact that Constantius did not attempt to relieve the city of Nisibis in 350 proves that he clearly did not want to commit his imperial reserves to combat in this situation. Regardless, it is still certain that he lingered in the area just in case his personal attention was needed. He wanted to be certain that the safety measures he had made – the supplying of the fortifications with both men and victuals – would prove to be sufficient to secure the border before marching to the west to crush the revolt.

The Third Siege of Nisibis, 350[328]

Shapur exploited Constantius' troubles by launching an invasion in late-350, the primary objective of which was the capture of the city of Nisibis. It is also probable that he was able to capture the Armenian king Tiran at about the same time. (See later.)

Shapur had once again collected a huge army consisting of the Persian feudal levies, allies, elephants, and masses of civilian conscripts. Julian's Panegyric (Or. 2.63Aff.) makes clear that most of Shapur's army consisted of the Parthian feudal levies and Indians, which means that Shapur's armies had suffered so many casualties in the course of his prolonged war against Constantius that he had been forced to transfer forces from the north-east and east to the west. This had left those frontiers weakly defended, which the enemies of Persia were not slow to exploit. The fact that Constantius failed to bring any relief to the city of Nisibis suggests that he had already transferred significant proportion of his troops to Thrace, probably to protect the city of Constantinople. Julian also notes that it was Constantius who had finished the building of new walls for the city, and its safety was undoubtedly very high on Constantius' agenda.

This time Shapur decided to make a lake around Nisibis by enclosing it with dykes. The Persians employed a huge rampart to overlook the wall and boats with siege-engines on the artificial lake. The defenders, under the spirited leadership of Lucillianus, used a number of methods invented by Archimedes to repulse all enemy attacks. They hurled fire and fire-darts, hauled up many of the ships, and shattered others by stone-throwers that discharged stones that could weigh seven Attic talents (181 kg). We do not know whether the stone-throwers were torsion engines or trebuchets (the necessary knowledge to build these had existed since Archimedes' day), because both could deliver the same loads. Then the dykes suddenly collapsed as a result of shoddy work and the water flowed out and with it went about 45m of the wall of Nisibis. Shapur ordered those responsible for the building of the dykes executed.

This time Shapur did not repeat the same mistake he had made during the first siege of Nisibis and ordered his army to attack immediately. He placed in the first line his *thorakoforoi* (=*clibanarii*) and *hippotoxotai*, behind them the rest of the horsemen, and behind the cavalry he placed his Indian elephants at regular intervals and between them the 'hoplites'. We do not know whether the *thorakoforoi* and *hippotoxotai* were deployed in the same units (*thorakoforoi* forming the front ranks and the *hippotoxotai* the rear), or whether they were deployed side by side (the *hippotoxotai* as rhomboids and *thorakoforoi* as either rectangles, wedges or rhomboids). Notably, each of the Indian elephants had an iron tower with archers and javelin-throwers. These were the best war elephants available. Behind the entire throng sat Shapur on a throne placed on an artificial hill.

The Romans blocked the gap with a phalanx of soldiers and placed a mixed force of civilians and soldiers on the walls. The Persians were so confident of their success that they did not bother to use their bows, but confidently galloped at full speed but with the result that the entire throng became stuck in the mud that had been left in the place of the former moat. The Romans ran forward to kill those stuck in the mud while the rest hurled stones and missiles. The Persian attack had failed. Shapur responded by sending forward the elephants and infantry, but they succumbed under a rain of stones and arrows. The wounded elephants rampaged, and under their feet the last semblance of order within the ranks dissolved. After this Shapur sent his foot archers into combat, with the divisions (*moirai*) being rotated to keep up a continuous fire against the defenders so that they would not be able to build a new wall, but to no avail. The Romans built a new wall in one-and-a-half days behind the protective cover provided by the 'hoplite' phalanx.

The Persians did not yet give up. They abandoned the siege only after they had lost thousands of men to hunger and combat. Shapur had no other alternative, because it was then that he learnt of the invasions of his Central Asian and Indian domains. Zonaras claims that the invaders were Massagetae, but see below. The siege had lasted for four months and Shapur had lost 20,000 men (Zon. 13.7). Shapur used as scapegoats those satraps who had advised him to start this invasion. They were duly executed in true eastern fashion.

After Shapur had retreated, Constantius sent aid to Nisibis. His defensive strategy in the East was based on the holding of fortified places with a minimum of forces while he campaigned in the West. Fortunately for him, for the next few years the Persians had other things on their mind than attempting to invade Roman territory. The Chionitai and Euseni/Cuseni (Kushans or Guptas) were troubling Central Asia.[329] I would suggest that the Euseni were actually the Indian Guptas under their gifted leader Samudragupta whose career spanned the years 325 to 375/381, during which he conquered most of India. The Saka satraps of Sind, who were nominally under the Sasanians, and the Kushans also recognized his suzerainty, which means that he had conquered significant portions of Sasanian possessions in the east. It was therefore not at all surprising that he received the name of *Sarva-rājo-chchhettā*, 'exterminator of all kings', and I would date his western and northern campaigns to the 350s.[330] Of particular note is the subsequent large-scale use of elephants by the Sasanians, which does suggest some kind of agreement with the Guptas. It is therefore quite probable that Shapur's campaigns in the 350s were fought against the Guptas rather than against the Kushans. Considering the subsequent events, it is also probable that Shapur managed to convince the Chionitai to change sides, as a result of which he managed to negotiate a truce in the east. What is certain, however, is that the Sasanians had not won, but had merely achieved a stalemate, because the Saka satraps remained subjects of Samudragupta. It is likely that Shapur had made a deal similar to that of Seleukos I (312–281 BC). In return for a large numbers of elephants, Shapur would have ceded territory.

Of particular note is also the fact that the king of Ceylon/Sri Lanka recognized Samudragupta's suzerainty, which together with Samudragupta's conquests of the Saka satrapies meant that the control of the Indian branch of the Silk and Spice Routes passed into his hands. This meant that the Persians had lost their stranglehold on those, with the result that the Romans and Indians could now bypass them – as undoubtedly happened as a result of the hostilities between the Guptas and Sasanians. The only thorn in the side of Constantius was the ruler of Hira, who changed his allegiance to the Persian side in about 352/3. (See below.)

War against Magnentius: Stage 1[331] (See Maps Section)

Meanwhile, Constantius had made truly massive preparations for the forthcoming war. He had assembled more than 1,200 ships in Constantinople (Julian Or. 1.42C-D). The size of this fleet implies an army of about 100,000 men, which seems to have been divided into at least two fleets and army corps. Unfortunately, Julian fails to state what Constantius did with these. It is probable that one part of this fleet was used to support Constantius' own army operating in the Balkans, but it appears probable that at least one portion was dispatched to the Po and still another part to Egypt, where Constantius was assembling a fleet for use against Carthage, Sicily and Italy.[332] The obvious purpose of the buildup of the latter fleet was to deny the African corn supply to the enemy and to attack the enemy's flank.

The first order of things was to secure Vetranio's army for use against Magnentius. Contrary to what some other ancient sources claim, it is quite clear that Zosimus was right when he stated that Vetranio sided with Constantius. All of his supposedly friendly gestures towards Magnentius were just meant to fool Magnentius. Consequently, when Constantius reached the scene of operations, the 'two' emperors met each other at Serdica from where they marched together to Naissus. Note that 'both' emperors with their forces were making their way towards the enemy! At Naissus Constantius mounted a platform and gave an inspiring speech before the assembled troops (already bribed by Constantius' representatives) who then duly acclaimed him as the sole emperor on 25 December 350, the Birthday of Christ. The 'deceived' Vetranio was stripped off his purple and then given a pension on an estate in Bithynia. He had served his emperor well. According to Julian (Or. 2.77.B), Constantius had won to his side myriads of hoplites, 20,000 horseman, and the most warlike Federates (ethnê).

In the winter, the emperor seems to have received faulty intelligence (a rumour?) that Shapur was planning to invade. This was undoubtedly based on the preparations for war that Shapur was making against his enemies in the east. It was on the basis of this that Constantius decided to appoint his cousin Gallus as Caesar of the East and arranged for him to marry his sister Constantia. Barbatio was appointed as Gallus' Com. Dom. and guardian, and Lucillianus was rewarded for his successful defence of Nisibis with the title Com. Dom. and headquartered at Constantinople. The career soldier Ursicinus was appointed as Mag. Eq. with headquarters at Nisibis. Constantius left other henchmen of his to keep an eye on Gallus. Gallus was appointed as Caesar on 31 March 351. According to an inscription dated to the year 356, there existed at least one unit that was divided into seniores and iuniores. This suggests the possibility that Constantius may have divided at least one of his units so that Gallus had been given one half, or at least that the iuniores were a detachment of the seniores that was formed into a new unit and that this practice was continuously followed during the fourth century when soldiers were detached from their mother units (LeBohec, 2006, 189). However, see also Chapter 3.

Vetranio's removal changed Magnentius' strategy. He decided to take the initiative and forestall Constantius by invading the Balkans in person in 351. When Constantius' army was making its way to Italy, Magnentius set up an ambush in the valley near Atrans into which Constantius' unsuspecting scouts foolishly fell and were wiped out. Constantius beat a hasty retreat, which Julian claims to have been a feigned retreat to lure the usurper to a suitable place for cavalry combat. Constantius had no intention of being caught in a valley. In the meanwhile, Magnentius bypassed Constantius and marched straight towards Siscia (evidently from Emona) with the intention of marching from there to Sirmium, where he intended to engage Constantius in a decisive battle. Constantius sent his trusted friend Philippus as a spy to Magnentius' camp with the pretence that he was discussing terms of peace. The usurper foolishly let Philippus make a speech to the army, which almost cost him his life because Philippus came close creating a mutiny and it was with great difficulty that Magnentius and his henchmen managed to calm the troops.

By now Magnentius had learnt Philippus' real purpose. He was taken prisoner and later killed. Then the Frank Silvanus and large numbers of infantry deserted Magnentius and joined Constantius. This was a bad blow. Constantius was now aware of what the enemy was planning. He informed the garrison of Siscia of the imminent approach of the enemy. The defenders of Siscia performed well. When Magnentius arrived, they shot and killed all those who attempted to cross the Savus (Sava) either by swimming or via the bridge. The attackers suffered considerable loss of life and when Constantius arrived on the scene Magnentius' position was becoming untenable. Magnentius then challenged Constantius to a battle and stated that he would not cross the Savus unless allowed. Constantius decided to allow this in an effort to lure Magnentius to the plain in front of Cibalae/Cibalis where his father had fought against Licinius and therefore marched there, but when Magnentius had crossed the river he turned back and took Siscia with the first attack.

After this, Magnentius chose the southern route which bypassed Cibalae and then pillaged and plundered his way up to Sirmium, but this time the defenders foiled all his attempts. Balked, Magnentius decided to try his luck against Mursa (undoubtedly bypassing Cibalae via Malata and Teutoburgium), but once again failed to take the city. Magnentius did not have any siege equipment and was therefore at a loss what to do until he heard that Constantius was coming to the rescue. Now he had a chance to engage his arch-rival in battle. Magnentius once again decided to use an ambush. He placed four phalanxes of Gauls (four legions?) inside an old stadium/circus just outside the city, which was overgrown with woods. The defenders of Mursa saw this and sent a warning to Constantius which gave him a chance to ambush the ambushers. Constantius sent the tribunes (*taxiarchs*) Scodilo (*tribunus scutariorum*) and Manadus with the best infantry and archers to the scene. They closed all the doors and mounted the steps above and shot and killed all inside. When Magnentius' plan failed he marshalled his army for combat.

The Battle of Mursa, 28 September 351[333] (See the Map of the area in Chapter 5)
Magnentius was simply foolish to decide to engage Constantius because he was heavily outnumbered with his 36,000 men against Constantius' 80,000 men (Zon. 13.8). Magnentius' second mistake was to fight the battle in the open terrain that favoured Constantius, who possessed both numerical superiority and superior numbers of higher-grade cavalry forces, while the rebel's army consisted of the elite Gallic legions, *auxilia palatinae*, and of the Franks, Saxons, and other tribal units. It seems probable that the battle was fought somewhere west or north-west of Mursa, because the above-mentioned incident makes it clear that Constantius' forces had advanced very close to the city prior to the battle. If Magnentius had deployed his forces east of the city he would have faced the possibility of the defenders attacking his rear.

Neither side rested their flank against the Drava River but both deployed their cavalry on the wings and infantry on the centre. It is probable that Constantius' fleet patrolled the river (Mursa was a naval base). Constantius deployed his archers and slingers behind the 'hoplite' phalanx, and the cavalry was apparently deployed so that the *thorakoforoi* (cataphracts/*clibanarii*) cavalry were deployed next to the infantry on both sides. The *thorakoforoi* of Constantius were so fully armored (both man and the horse) with cuirass and chain mail, chain-mail mittens, greaves, metal masks and helmets that the men did not need shields (Julian Or.1.37C-D, Or.2.57.B-C; Amm. 16.10.8). These men also appear to have carried bows just like their Persian models, but their primary combat mode was still the cavalry charge in such a manner that the rear ranks supported the attack with archery volleys. After (or behind) these, Constantius posted other cavalry in plentiful numbers, consisting of the shield-bearing horsemen (*aspidoforoi, scutarii*), and the mounted archers. My interpretation is that Julian meant that the shield-bearers were posted next to the *thorakoforoi* rather than behind them because Julian claimed that the infantry in the centre supported the cavalry on the wings. It is of course possible that Constantius did hide the shield-bearers and archers behind his *thorakoforoi* so that these could suddenly outflank the enemy cavalry, but Julian doesn't mention this.

Julian also claims that the usurper had deployed his line wrongly from the start, but unfortunately fails to specify what he meant. It is possible that this referred to the fact that Constantius' left wing outflanked Magnentius' wing, with the implication that Magnentius should have perhaps used double phalanx or some other formation that protected the flank. The indication, however, is that Magnetius deployed his phalanx eight deep (plus four ranks of light infantry) to make it longer while Constantius deployed his phalanx sixteen deep (plus eight ranks of light infantry) to increase its weight in attack. It is also unfortunate that Julian fails to give any indication on how both sides deployed their reserves.

The battle began with the cavalry charge of Constantius' wings. When Magnentius, who was evidently on the right wing saw that Constantius' left wing outflanked his right wing and that Constantius' cavalry maintained the momentum of their charge, he fled and left his hipparch (*Mag.Eq.*), chiliarchs, and taxiarchs to continue the fight. The usurper's men renewed the fight, so part of Magnentius' cavalry dismounted while his infantry renewed the battle by the units (*kata lochous*) – or rather half-files – by forming a new front towards the rear.[334] In other words, the Gallic infantry formed an *amfistomos/ orbis* (double front) and then probably the double phalanx, because it is unlikely that Constantius' cavalry that had outflanked them could have prevented the disciplined infantry from doing that. This would also have enabled some of the usurper's horsemen to remain mounted between the phalanxes, as seems to have happened. After this, the Gallic infantry and the dismounted and mounted cavalry fought fiercely against the emperor's forces until nightfall. The Gallic forces simply refused to surrender and some footmen even threw away their shields and rushed with sword in hand against the emperor's men in order to cause maximum damage with their self-sacrifice: in other words, it seems that the usurper's Germans fought as berserks, but the odds were stacked against them. Constantius' cavalry also charged boldly at the enemy ranks and then fought as footmen if their horses fell.

Eventually, the deadly combination of fast-moving mounted archers and *thorakoforoi* brought results after nightfall, because thanks to the darkness some of the defenders began to think that it might be possible to flee unnoticed. The open and level terrain made the pursuit easy for the *thorakoforoi* and *hippotoxotai*. Constantius had clearly deployed his *thorakoforoi* and *hippotoxotai* in separate units side by side, because according to Zosimus the Armenian mounted archers and their commander Menelaus (who fitted three arrows at once to his bow) deserved particular credit for the victory. This Menelaus was killed by Romulus, Magnentius' *Mag.Eq.*, but before this Romulus had himself received a fatal arrow wound from Menelaus. It would seem that Menelaus and his Armenian cavalry probably used one version of the 'Persian shower archery' technique to wreak havoc in the enemy ranks that eventually disordered it completely. After this, Magnentius' men attempted to flee in two directions. One part of the army fled to the river and they were butchered, while the rest fled to their camp. Some of the latter managed to find safety in the darkness of the night. Constantius' army kept up the pursuit and took the enemy camp with its slaves and baggage by assault. The battle had been a huge disaster for the Romans. According to Zonaras (13.8), Constantius lost about 30,000 dead and about 24,000 men were killed from the usurper's army. Marcellinus, the usurper's commander, was missing-in-action and his body was never found.

Period authors considered this Pyrrhic victory of Constantius to have been a huge disaster for the Roman Empire, and they were right. The Romans had lost 54,000 men killed and many others wounded. The casualty figures are comparable with those of Cannae and Adrianople. However, just like after Cannae, the Roman Empire showed a great ability to make a comeback. The losses had been replaced within a year, which proves the vitality of the Empire at the time. Constantius and Constans had kept the Empire in good shape. We should not forget that the Late Roman army was a professional army, unlike the conscript army of the Punic Wars. It was more time-consuming and costlier to train the conscripts from scratch for the professional army than it was to replace the losses from the reserves of already trained conscripts after Cannae, but it was done. One may presume, however, that in this case existing garrison forces were transferred to the field army while the new conscripts were used to replace them. It is in fact possible that some of the so-called *Pseudo-Comitatenses* and *Seniores/iuniores* of the ND were created as a result of this. We should not forget, however, that the transferral to a new category was not a one-way street. In practice the different categories of troops could be used for a great variety of purposes. The *Comitatenses* could be used to bolster the frontier defences as garrison troops and still maintain their higher status, and the frontier troops could be used as field forces when needed. Once a unit was promoted, it kept the new higher position with its privileges – unless it was later demoted or disbanded.

The Final Showdown, 352–353 (See the Maps Section and below)
Magnentius had continued his flight all the way to Aquileia, and had placed a strong defensive force in the Julian Alps. Thanks to the very heavy casualties suffered by Constantius' army, he was in no position to continue his march to Italy immediately. Consequently, he let his army rest, gathered new recruits and then reassembled his army in the spring of 352 for the Italian campaign. Before this, however, Constantius had declared a general amnesty to all those who would change sides. This brought tangible results. A fleet with fugitives arrived from Italy and was welcomed by Constantius. The coasts of Italy now lay open to Constantius' fleet.

According to Julian (Or. 1.38.D–39B), Magnentius chose to hide in Aquileia, because the mountains protected it from the Balkans and Italy, and the shoals from an invading fleet. This suggests that the above-mentioned fleet that Constantius had assembled in Egypt had already taken Carthage and was making its way via Sicily into Italy, and that the fleet (Italian Fleets?) that subsequently attacked along the River Po had already started its voyage there, with the purpose of forcing the usurper to retreat from the Julian Alps, a possibility that didn't materialize thanks to the defensive strength of Aquileia.

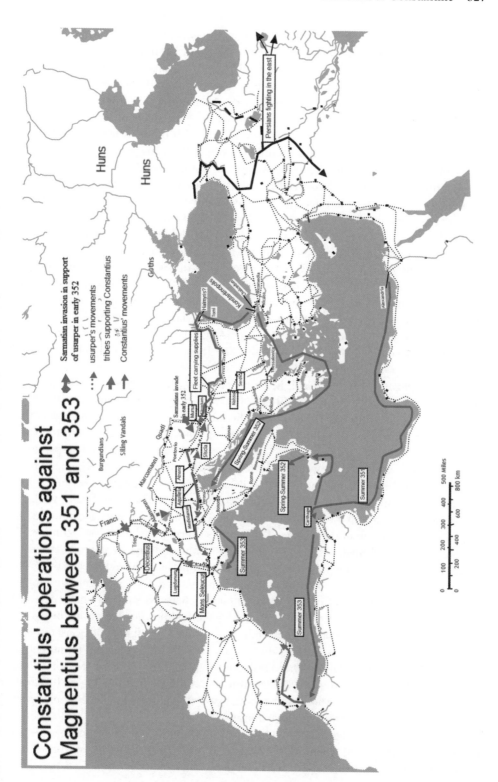

Constantius' operations against Magnentius between 351 and 353

Sarmatian invasion in support of usurper in early 352

usurper's movements

tribes supporting Constantius

Constantius' movements

Huns

Huns

Goths

Burgundians

Siling Vandals

Franci

Decentius

Trier

Lugdunum

Mons Seleucus

Marcomanni

Quadi

Sarmatians invade in early 352

Mursa

Poetovio

Siscia

Aquileia

Alban

Spring-Summer 352

Rome

Summer 353

Summer 353

Spring-Summer 352

Summer 351

Carthage

Alexandria

Fleet carrying supplies

Haemus?

Tomi

Constantinople

Persians fighting in the east

0   100   200   300   400   500 Miles
0   200   400   600   800 km

When Constantius was ready to begin the next stage of his campaign a sudden invasion of the Sarmatians forced him to delay the operation until August. The invaders were duly defeated and Constantius assumed the title *Sarmaticus Maximus*.[335] I would suggest that the Sarmatian invasion had been brought about by Magnentius – that is, just as Constantius had promised rewards for the Alamanni if they invaded Magnentius' territory, Magnentius had undoubtedly promised the Sarmatians rewards for attacking Constantius. The Alamanni had defeated Magnentius' brother in battle and diverted crucial resources that could have been used elsewhere. This suggests that the Alamanni were considerably more effective as allies for Constantius than the Sarmatians were for Magnentius, or perhaps we should rather say that Constantius was the better general. As we shall see, Constantius defeated the Sarmatians and Alamanni with equal ease. In the meanwhile, Magnentius had also dispatched a special operative to Antioch to assassinate Gallus, but the plot was unconvered when the agent talked too freely (Zon. 13.8).

According to Julian, when Constantius was finally able to launch his invasion of Italy, Constantius discovered (via his scouts) an unknown path past the enemy defenders, and then sent a *moira* (2,000–3,000?) consisting of selected 'hoplites' (legionaries) behind the enemy during the night. When Constantius learnt that his men had reached their destination, he led his army forward and defeated Magnentius' garrison. The news was brought to the usurper when he was attending a horse-race just before noon. He immediately abandoned the town and Italy. The Italian garrisons duly changed their loyalty to the legitimate emperor.

When Magnentius reached Gaul, he launched a campaign of terror to keep loyalties from wavering and once again foolishly put his trust in the impregnability of the Alps. Once more Constantius was either unable (because of the many cities and towns that needed to be secured) or unwilling (because he was very cautious as a general) to march straight after his enemy. Consequently, Constantius again made very careful preparations and with bribes instigated even more of the barbarian tribes across the Rhine to attack Magnentius. As before, Constantius' plan called for the use of combined and joint forces concept so that his fleets were sent to secure both southern Gaul and Spain, while he himself was to march with the main army across the Alps. Indeed Zosimus' account (2.53.3) confirms that as a result of the change of allegiances Constantius' forces had 'conquered' the Mauretanias and Spain (that is, the fleet had 'conquered' the Pyrenees as stated by Julian) probably before mid-July. Meanwhile, Constantius had landed forces in the south of Gaul and had himself forced his way through the Alps by defeating Magnentius' forces at Mons Seleucus. Magnentius fled to Lugdunum, where his soldiers finally deserted him. At some point in time, probably after Magnentius' brother Decentius began his march south to assist his brother, Poemenius also revolted in support of Constantius at Treves.[336] When Magnentius realized that all hope was lost he attempted to murder all his friends and relatives. His brother Desiderius managed to flee, even though he was wounded in the process. After this, Magnentius committed suicide on 10 or 11 August, and his brother Decentius, who was marching to assist him, followed his example on 18 August. Desiderius unsurprisingly gave himself up.

After the usurper had been defeated Constantius set out to purge everyone suspected of being a supporter of Magnentius.[337] Constantius, who spent the winter at Arelate, left the actual purge in the hands of his 'secret service', which included the *notarii, agentes in rebus* and units of bodyguards, but it was the first two that received most of the bad press. Ammianus was a *protector* and therefore unlikely to criticize its members. According to Ammianus, a mere suspicion was treated as sufficient grounds for punishment. He also stated that Constantius grew ever more cruel, violent and suspicious with age. According to Ammianus, he was a paranoid ruler who unleashed his secret services after anyone who could be suspected of having harboured ill will against him. These and similar claims by Ammianus have given Constantius an undeservedly bad reputation. In truth, Constantius had very good reasons for his 'paranoia'. He had indeed faced a series of plots against his life and it is not at all surprising that he took precautions against this. Furthermore, it is only natural for a man to exact vengeance against the murderers of his brother. Gregory Nazianzus' (Or. 4 Against Julian 1.21–42) contrary view of Constantius' character acts as a good corrective to Ammianus' poisonous pen in this case. According to him, Constantius was merciful, just and trusting as a person and ruler. We should not forget that Ammianus' account is coloured by his need to flatter his patron Ursicinus, who in his opinion was unjustly treated by the emperor, but on closer analysis even this is questionable, because Constantius was clearly ready to use Ursicinus' services again and again, despite the contrary views of his advisors.

Depending upon the situation, the range of punishment ranged from execution and torture, to exile and confiscation of property. The most notorious of Constantius' henchmen was the *notarius* Paulus 'the Chain' who was sent to Britain. Paulus did his job with ruthless efficiency, but at the same time he also overstepped his instructions and targeted those who were clearly innocent. This angered the new substitute governor, who protested, with the result that Paulus threatened to associate him with the plotters. This in turn led the desperate governor to attempt to kill Paulus with his sword, and then himself after the attack had failed. After Paulus had accomplished his mission he returned to Constantius with a bunch of prisoners that were then put under torture to find out who their connections and associates were.

At the same time as Constantius launched the purge of Magnentius' supporters or suspected supporters, he also changed his military strategy to that of restoring the frontiers. The Alamanni and Franks had served their purpose and now it was time to push them back over the border and restore the previous status quo. Similarly, it was time to restore order along the Danube, but before Constantius could begin these operations disturbing news arrived from the east.

The East, 351–353 (See Maps Section)

In the East, the new Caesar Gallus had proved himself to be arrogant, cruel and paranoid. On top of it all, his new wife encouraged this behaviour. Instead of doing his job, which was to secure the East against the Persians, Gallus appears to have concentrated upon making everyone in the East obey his wishes. If anyone stated anything contrary, he was put away cruelly. Gallus may have taken part in a campaign in Mesopotamia in 351, and he did suppress a Jewish rebellion in 352 (probably caused by his own actions), but on the whole seems to have concentrated on plotting.[338] He created his own independent network of informers and spies who roamed the streets. His sole priority was the securing of his own position and the gathering of enough support to proclaim himself Augustus.

He even failed to secure an adequate supply of grain for the residents of Antioch. When Constantius learnt of Gallus' actions, he removed from Gallus the regular troops and left him with the command of the 'Schools' of the *palatini, protectores, scutarii* and *gentiles* that served under the loyal *Comes Domesticorum* Barbatio.

The last straw was that Gallus had treated many of Constantius' courtiers arrogantly and had had some of them killed. The fact that Gallus refused to follow Constantius' request, as conveyed by the new *PP* Domitianus, and had had him and his supporters killed was tantamount to treason. Despite the fact that Shapur had marched to the east and had left Nohorades in charge of the war against Rome, the situation was grave enough and should have required imperial attention.

The Isaurians had stopped their banditry and started to wage war against neighbouring provinces. There were two reasons for this: 1) some of the Isaurian raiders who had been taken prisoner had been thrown to the beasts in the amphitheatre of Iconium; and 2) the famine that Gallus had failed to solve drove the Isaurians to despair when winter arrived. The Isaurians descended from their mountains, surprised sailors in their boats (*scaphae*), killed everyone they found, and captured the cargo. The civilian guardsmen near the locale had acted promptly, with the result that the Isaurians were no longer able to capture any merchant vessels. The merchants had been warned to avoid the coast.

Consequently, the Isaurians moved on to Lycaonia, facing Isauria, set up road-blocks, and started to plunder the province. The soldiers who were quartered in the towns of the region naturally sortied out to destroy the Isaurian forces that had spread out to pillage, but with mixed results. The Roman infantry defeated the Isaurians whenever they were able to catch them in the open and level terrain, but whenever they met them in the mountainous parts or the Isaurians were able to flee to the mountains, the gazelle-like Isaurians defeated the Romans with ease, either by using javelins (each carried two to three) from a distance or with rocks. As a result of this, the Romans stopped pursuing the Isaurians up the narrow and pathless tracks and engaged them only on level ground. In response, the Isaurians marched into Pamphylia, which according to Ammianus was strongly garrisoned. Their intention was to surprise the defenders, but they failed. When the Isaurians reached the banks of the River Melas, they were forced to stop for a night. When the sun rose and they intended to cross the river, they learnt that it was too deep to cross on foot. They started to seek fishermen's boats and put together woven rafts. However, while they were doing this, the legions that were wintering at Side marched out, formed a shield-wall on the opposite bank, and killed those daredevils who crossed the river by swimming or in hollowed tree trunks. The frustrated Isaurians were forced to continue their march to the neighbourhood of the town of Laranda. There they managed to find food and after having rested, they started to attack the wealthy villages nearby. However, the Romans had sent some cavalry 'cohorts' to protect these with the result that the Isaurians were once again forced to retreat to the mountains.

When the Isaurians reached their home territory, they summoned the flower of their youth and marched against Palaia. Their purpose was to capture the supplies stored there for the entire Roman army distributed in the area. The position and walls proved too much for the Isaurians. After they had attempted all their tricks, which included mining, their specialty, they retreated on the third day because they lacked victuals.

In desperation, the Isaurians marched against Seleucia, the capital of the province. The Roman *speculatores* reported the approach of the enemy, as a result of which all three legions of the garrison of Seleucia marched out to meet them. The Romans crossed the bridge over the Calycadnus River and deployed for combat. The Isaurians halted, rested their men, and started to advance with a slow pace and with drawn swords. The use of swords signalled to the Romans that the Isaurians were desperate and willing to fight to the death. The Romans changed their order of battle and the men started to strike their *scuta* with their *hastae* in order to stimulate their wrath and scare the enemy. The commanders, however, considered the odds unfavourable because the Isaurians outnumbered them and were desperate. Consequently, they ordered a retreat and led the legions back inside the city. As a result of this, the Isaurians were able to capture some grain boats anchored on the river. The intention had been to resupply the garrison with these supplies, but now the provisions ended up feeding the enemy. By contrast, the defenders had eaten almost all of their supplies. The Romans sent an urgent plea for help to Gallus. It was only then that Gallus reacted and sent the *Comes Orientis* Nebridius to save the legions. He could not dispatch the *Mag. Eq.* Ursicinus to the scene, because he was 'far away', fighting against the Persians – and apparently not without success (Amm. 16.12.69).

When the Isaurians learnt of the imminent arrival of the relief army, they simply fled back to the mountains and scattered. However, the capture of the grain boats appears to have saved their lives and it was mission accomplished for the Isaurian chieftains.

I would also suggest that the capture of Singara by the Persians mentioned by Ammianus took place during Gallus' tenure, at some point in time between 351 and 353. The reason for this conclusion is that if its capture had taken place when Constantius was himself in charge of the operations Ammianus would surely have made more of this failure. Secondly, since we know that the Persians were using siege engines captured from Singara against Amida in 359, but not in 350 against Nisibis, it seems fairly certain that the fall of the city must have happened in the 350s during Gallus' tenure, and possibly when Ursicinus was in charge because the relevant portions of Ammianus' text are missing. Consequently, we can say with very high confidence that Constantius' defence of the Eastern frontier, when he was personally in charge during the 340s, was successful.[339]

In the interim, the Arabs had also raided Roman territory, which is indicative of the desertion of the Arab Federates of Hira to the Persian side. It is very probable that the reason for their change of allegiance was the arrogant behaviour of Gallus (Shahid BAFOC, 79). Tabari claims that Shapur II nominated Imru I's son Amr as ruler, but on the basis of the length of Amr's rule it is clear that this did not happen immediately after his father's death in 328. Furthermore, there is also the complication that Tabari nowhere even mentions the desertion of Imru to the Roman side (attested in his obituary), which makes it possible that all references to Hira's loyalty towards the Sasanians are equally suspect. However, there are other indications that Amr may indeed have changed his allegiance from the Roman side to that of Persia at some point in time during the 350s, the year 352 being the likeliest date.[340] This date receives support from the fact that Ammianus (14.4) mentions an Arabic raid for the year 352/3 and very soon after that we find the Himyarites acting as Roman allies against the Lakhmids of Hira (see below). Consequently, it is likely that it was in about 352 that Shapur II appointed Amr b. Imri Al-Qays, the son of Imru, as governor of Hira and it is also likely that the transferral of the Assanitae/Ghassanids to northeast Arabia, near the Hira and the Euphrates regions, took place at the same time as an insurance policy against the possible revolt of Amr.[341] In other words, I agree with Shahid (BAFOC, 79) that it is probable that the Arab Federates revolted as a result of Gallus' arrogant policies that also caused the Jews' revolt in 351. It would take years for Constantius to repair the damage.

The Arab raiders appear to have been very successful. Ammianus mentions that Serenianus had been the *Dux* whose incompetence had led to the pillage of Celse in Phoenicia. I would suggest that the pillagers had been the former Arab Federates of Rome. Similarly, I would suggest that the first capture of Singara by the Persians had also taken place either in 351 or 352, even if there had also been a failed Persian attempt to take Batne in Oshroene with a surprise attack. In this case, Persian deserters had provided a timely warning.

According to Moses (3.11), the Armenian king Khosrov (to be emended to Tiran) died in the seventeenth year of the reign of Constantius (i.e. in 354) and was succeeded by his son Tiran (to be emended to Arshak). On the basis of the age of Arshak's son Pap at the time Arshak was overthrown, it is clear that Moses' figures cannot be trusted in this case. The figures do tally, however, if we assume that Arshak succeeded his father, as usually assumed, in about 350/1. What happened was that the Persians managed to lure Tiran to Persian territory to negotiate, where he was duly blinded (Moses 3.17). It is probable that Tiran was seeking to establish full independence from Rome by allying with Persia at a time when Constantius was distracted by the usurpation of Magnentius. Tiran may also have felt vulnerable, because he knew that the Romans would lack the resources with which to support him against Persia. The Persians appointed Tiran's son Arshak as his successor and took hostages from all of the leading families. In short, the Romans were now thrown out of Armenia with Persian help. However, the Persians were unable to exploit the situation thanks to the fact that the 'northern nations' had invaded and were threatening Persia's north-east and south-east frontiers (Moses 3.19).

According to Moses, soon after Arshak's accession in about 352/3 Valentinian (that is, Constantius) sent a letter to Arshak but got no reply, but then part of the Armenian nobility – probably with Roman support – revolted against Arshak. This brought about a change in policies. In the third year of Arshak's reign (353/4) Nerses the Great returned to Armenia and became its archbishop. He immediately started a project modelled after the Roman practice. Each province was to have poorhouses similar to Greek hospitals in remote places. Towns and fields were to provide these with fruits of the earth and milk. Lodgings were to be built in every village for travellers, and hospices were to be built for the orphans, aged and poor. The intention was to make people ever more dependent on Christians for their daily needs and thereby tie Armenia more closely to the Roman Empire. This same policy is also being practised today by many religious organizations in Third World countries that lack proper social security. If Nerses did indeed arrive before what happened next, it is clear that he just like the other churchmen of the period served as imperial ambassadors. Indeed I would suggest that it was he who negotiated the conditions of the alliance between Rome and Armenia. According to Moses, Valentinian (Constantius) ordered the Armenian hostages, Trdat and his brother, to be killed and Armenia to be threatened with a Roman army. This supposedly brought about reconciliation, which was negotiated by Nerses, and Arshak started to pay tribute to the Romans. At the same time Constantius returned the remaining hostages. These included Trdat's son Gnel. The alliance was also sealed by a marriage between Olympias (daughter of the former *PP* Ablabius) and Arshak. I would suggest that the killing of Arshak's relatives had been part of the bargain – its precondition. Apparently very soon after this, Arshak had Gnel murdered, after which he married the widow Parandzem, with whom he then sired the future king Pap. In due course of time Parandzem convinced an unnamed unscrupulous priest to poison Olympias in order to replace her as queen.[342]

The Persian response to Arshak's change of allegiance was swift. Ammianus records a Persian invasion of Armenia for the year 355. This figure corresponds neatly with Faustus' (4.21) figure of eight years of peace between Persia and Armenia after the flight of Arshak from Nisibis in 346/7 (rather than from Persia).

My educated guess is that we should identify the Armenian king Arshak with the Iberian king Archil who according to the GC (153ff.) was the son of Trdat (in truth grandson), who married a Greek wife Mariam (claimed as a descendant of Jovian, but in truth Olympia, the daughter of Ablabius), and who declared war against the Persians. The GC (152–3) claims that before this Archil's predecessor 'Mirdat' (i.e Bakur) had simultaneously become an enemy of both the Romans and Persians with the result that the Persians occupied Iberia.[343] Three years after this, at a time when the Persians were fighting in the east (i.e. in about 354), the Iberians exploited their opportunity and made Archil their king, who with the help of the Greeks waged war against the Persians. In other words, the Romans helped Arshak to gain the throne of Iberia as well. In sum, there are too many parallels between the persons and events for this to be a mere coincidence.

However, at some point in time after this (GC, pp.155ff.), Arshak appears to have nominated his son 'Mirdat' as king of Iberia and in this capacity he seems to have fought against the Albanians while the Persian king was fighting against the Indians (Guptas?), Sinds (Saka satraps/Guptas) and Abashes (Habashes/ Aksumites/ Ethiopians/ Himyarites). The Himyarite and Aksumite operations against the Persians and Lakhmids took place after 356 (see below), and the wars on the Central Asian and Indian fronts lasted until the 370s.

Usurpations, Attempted Usurpations, and Wars 354–356 (Map 354–356)

After Magnentius had been crushed, Constantius faced the consequences of his alliance with the Franks and Alamanni. The Rhine frontier had been penetrated at least to the distance of 60km west from the river. Practically all Roman fortifications and towns within those limits had been overrun. Consequently, Constantius prepared to begin operations against the invaders very early in 354 to re-establish the frontiers. The first stage of the plan was to clear up the road between the Rhine and Milan. Constantius assembled his army at Cabillonum, and moved himself from Arelate to Valentia to wage war against the Alamanni kings and brothers Gundomadus and Valomarius. The start of the campaign, however, was delayed by the spring rains that had held-up the transport of supplies from Aquitania. It was very early in spring as there was still snow on the ground. While Constantius was tarrying in Valentia, he received a report through the *protector domesticus* Herculanus of the treasonous behaviour of Gallus. In the meantime the soldiers were becoming restless as a result of inaction and the lack of the necessities of life, and threatened the life of the *PP* Rufinus (brother of Gallus' mother). Rufinus managed to pacify the men and Constantius dispatched his *Praepositus Sacri Cubiculi* Eusebius with plenty of gold to further calm the unrest.

When the supplies finally arrived, Constantius led his army through the snow-covered ground to Augusta Rauricorum (Castrum Rauracense) on the banks of the Rhine. The Alamanni, however, had assembled together in superior numbers to oppose the crossing. When it became apparent that it would be impossible to finish the building of the pontoon bridge under the hail of their missiles, the attempt was halted. Then a local guide pointed out a place where the river could be crossed, but this plan was betrayed to the enemy by some high-ranking Alamanni in Roman service. The fingers pointed towards the *Com. Dom.* Latinus, the *Tribunus Stabuli* (commander of the *stablesiani?*) Agilo, and the *Rector Scutariorum* Scudilo, but no punishment followed. I would suspect that Constantius and the Alamanni had already held secret discussions behind the back of the rest. The news of Gallus' behaviour had undoubtedly made Constantius anxious – note the existence of three *comites domesticorum* at the same time. Constantius appears to have placed one *Com. Dom.* in charge of each group of imperial bodyguards. Then ambassadors arrived from the Alamanni kings suing for peace, and Constantius convinced the troops with a speech that the wisest policy was to grant peace to the enemy.

After this, Constantius marched to Milan, where in secret nightly discussions attended only by his closest friends, he planned how to get rid of Gallus. It was decided to resort to the use of a ruse. First the emperor recalled the *Mag.Eq.* Ursicinus (Ammianus served on his staff as *protector*) and replaced him with the *Comes* Prosper, because it was feared that Ursicinus might attempt to usurp power. After this, Constantius sent Scudilo to Gallus, and it was thanks to his persuasion that the latter agreed to come to Italy. Constantius claimed that Gallus would be put in charge of the war in Gaul. His operatives managed to separate Gallus from all possible military units that might have supported him, with the result that when Gallus reached Poetovio he was duly arrested by the *Com. Dom.* Barbatio and the *agens in rebus* Apodemius. Gallus was interrogated by the *PSC* Eusebius, the *notarius* Pentadius, and the *Tribunus Armaturarum* Mallobaudes, and then beheaded: all of Constantius' security organs were involved in the apprehension and interrogation of Gallus. After this, the emperor launched a purge of all suspected supporters of Gallus. The investigation was conducted by the *notarius* Paulus the 'Chain' and the *rationalis* Mercurius, the 'Count of Dreams'. The suspects included Ursicinus and Julian, but both were acquitted. The latter had made the mistake of meeting with his brother Gallus when he was on his way to the emperor, but the empress Eusebia saved his life.

In Illyricum *agens in rebus* also reported treasonous talk at a dinner-party of the governor of Second Pannonia to the *PP* (of Illyricum?) Rufinus, with the result that the *protector domesticus* Teutomeres was sent to apprehend the culprits. Note that the *agentes in rebus* appear to have reported to the *PP*.

In the West the year 355 began with a double campaign, one led by the *Mag.Ped.* Silvanus against the Franks and one led by the emperor in person against the Lentienses. According to Ammianus, Constantius II declared war on the Lentienses and Raetovarii, two tribes of the Alamanni.[344] The previous year's campaign had clearly not yet fully secured the road between Milan and Rhine. It is clear that Constantius' plan was to keep part of the enemy force tied up in front of him near Campi Canini, while his *Mag.Eq.*

Arbitio, with the stronger part of the army, consisting of the elite cavalry, would march on along the shores of Lake Constance (Brigantia) and clear the area of enemies. The plan was a good one and was to become one of the standard strategies of the East Roman army, but thanks to the carelessness of Arbitio it almost failed.[345] He did not wait for the arrival of his scouts and advanced recklessly and was ambushed. Luckily for the Romans when this happened it was close to nightfall and the horsemen were able to save themselves by scattering. The commander's rashness had been costly, though. Large numbers of men and ten tribunes had been lost. The Romans regrouped next day, and the Alamanni advanced against the Roman camp. The *scutarii* cavalry sallied out, but were driven back by the enemy cavalry *turmae*. The *scutarii* called out their comrades to their assistance. Arbitio hesitated, but three of his cavalry tribunes, Arintheus (second-in-command of the heavy armed bodyguards/*Armaturae*), Seniauchus (tribune of the *Comites Sagittarii*), and Babbo (*Dux* of the *Promoti*) burst out of the camp. These elite units charged at a gallop in scattered irregular formations and defeated the enemy in a series of sharp cavalry skirmishes. The rest of the men followed their example and charged out of the camp to pursue the fleeing foes. The enemy had been defeated only thanks to the bravery of the elite troops and their commanders, and it was because of their bravery that the campaign ended in success. The southern shore of the lake was cleared of enemies and the emperor was able to return in triumph back to Milan.[346]

In the meanwhile the *Mag. Ped.* Silvanus had been at least equally successful against the Franks, but unlike Constantius he seems to have used mainly bribery rather than force to obtain their surrender.[347] Unbeknownst to him his position was also becoming precarious. The clique led by *PP* (of Gaul?) Lampadius and ex-*Comes Cubiculi* Eusebius forged Silvanus' letters so that the letters also implicated the tribunes of the imperial bodyguards. *Rector Gentiles* Malarichus, who was a Frank, was upset and advised that he or his friend should bring Silvanus to court, but Constantius accepted Arbitio's advice, as a result of which Apodemius was dispatched to recall Silvanus. This was a bad decision. Apodemius didn't follow his instructions and moved so slowly that Silvanus learnt of the suspicions raised against him. In addition, the conspirators forged still another letter that implicated Malarichus with Silvanus, but the person who received the letter sent it to Malarichus with the result that he convened all of the Franks, who according to Ammianus at this time were numerous and influential in the palace, to discuss the plot against them. The emperor learnt of the meeting immediately and defused the situation by calling a meeting of his sacred consistory. It was duly found out that the letters had been forged. The *PP* was sacked, but his life was saved thanks to the help of his friends at the palace. Eusebius admitted his guilt on the rack, but the rest were set free. This suggests the possibility that Arbitio or even the emperor may have had a role, and that the scheme was abandoned only after it became apparent that the powerful Frankish block would react violently.

The uncovering of the plot, however, came too late. When Silvanus learnt of the suspicions in desperation he usurped power. Once again the emperor decided to defuse the danger with a ruse and special operatives. Ursicinus was given the mission so that he could exonerate himself of all possible guilt in the Gallus affair. He took with him some tribunes and ten *protectores domestici*, all friends and relatives except Ammianus and Verianus, and then travelled to Colonia Agrippina (Cologne) to meet Silvanus. Silvanus foolishly welcomed his old friend. Ursicinus and his entourage managed to bribe the

Bracchiati and *Cornuti* to change sides, with the result that they killed Silvanus. He had worn the purple for only twenty-eight days. Paulus the Chain took charge of the investigations and all real and imagined followers of Silvanus were purged.

In the meanwhile there had been unrest in Rome. The arrest of a charioteer led to rioting, but the quick and decisive action (several persons arrested and exiled) taken by the *PU* Leontius calmed the situation for a while. Then he located, arrested, flogged and exiled the ringleader with the result that the whole city was calmed. Constantius had also tried to make the Western Church follow his wishes with the Council of Milan in the summer, but with unsatisfactory results. His views faced opposition from the pope and others. The hostile pope was removed from office by carrying him away in the middle of the night so that the populace could not rise in his support. This was effective police work by Leontius. No military intervention was needed. In the East, however, the new appointees, the *Mag. Eq.* Prosper (a coward according to Ammianus) and *PP* Musonianus proved incapable to stop the bold Persian raids in 354–355. The Persians targeted both Mesopotamia and Armenia. We should keep in mind, however, that since Ammianus' goal was to flatter his patron Ursicinus in this case we should take his statements with a grain of salt. It is clear that the Persians did not achieve any major successes during this time despite the 'cowardice' of Prosper.

Constantius' Religious Policies, 350–359[348] (See Appendix 1)

Constantius had assumed a conciliatory stance towards the Nicene Creed at the beginning of Magnentius' usurpation for political reasons, but this stance was not to last. The gradual strengthening of Constantius' position resulting from the submission of Vetranio, the defeat of Magnentius at the Battle of Mursa in 351, the conquest of Italy in 352, and the death of the usurper in 353 all enabled Constantius to become progressively more outspoken in his pro-Arian stance. In 351 the Council of Sirmium had once again supported the Arian creed as expounded in the Council of 342 and condemned and deposed the bishops who opposed it, but its decisions were not yet put into effect in full. After his victory, Constantius enforced the decisions of Sirmium by holding Church Councils at Arles (Arelate) in 353/4 and Milan in 355. The orthodox bishops who opposed the decisions of the Council of Sirmium boycotted the councils of Arles and Milan so that they would not be forced to sign the creed. However, the emperor made sure that everyone would sign or be exiled, and by 357 everyone had either signed or been exiled.

Constantius had put the decisions of the Council of Sirmium into effect already in 355 while the Council of Milan was still in session, and then renewed the effort again in 356. As before, in Alexandria and Egypt this meant the use of force. This time even military intervention was needed, first under the *Dux* Syrianus in 356, then under the *Comes* Heraclius in 357, and under *Dux* Sebastianus in 356–358. During this time the size of the army required to suppress the opposition varied from 3,000 to 5,000 men. Athanasius was forced to flee. He spent the next six years in hiding, which once again proves how much support his cause had. Despite their frantic efforts, the imperial authorities could not find Athanasius. On top of this, urban unrest against the new Arian bishop George in 357–9 was so bad that he chose not to enter Alexandria for the next three years: he feared for his life.

In 358/9 Macedonius, the Arian bishop of Constantinople, launched a full scale persecution of Catholics and Novatian heretics in and around Constantinople (for example in Cyzicus, Nicomedia and Eleusius), mainly with the help of his co-religionist fanatics, but he felt that these were insufficient against the Novatians of Mantium in Paphlagonia. Consequently, he asked for and got four *arithmoi* of troops (probably marines) to kill the Novatians. It is difficult to known the size of each *arithmos*, because these could signify any unit of unspecified size, the most likely unit sizes being about 500, or 1,000, or 2,000 men. It is perhaps safest to assume that there were no more than 2,000 or 4,000 men involved. The Novatians were warned of this development and they armed themselves with sickles, axes and whatever could be used as weapons, and marched to meet the soldiers. The civilians suffered numerous casualties, but killed almost all of the soldiers. According to both Socrates and Sozomen, this angered the emperor. Even more importantly, Macedonius made the mistake of removing Constantine's coffin from its resting place without the permission of Constantius because the mausoleum was falling apart. This also resulted in a riot in which the Arians who favoured Macedonius' decision fought against the Catholics who opposed it. Once again great numbers of people died. The killing of soldiers and the unauthorized removal of Constantine's coffin caused Macedonius to fall from favour, and also gave Constantius food for thought. Constantius was about to change his religious policies. Macedonius was also duly deposed by the Council of Seleuceia at the request of the emperor.[349]

Constantius' Foreign Policy in the East, 350–358

Philostorgius (2.6, 3.4–6) has preserved a tradition according to which Constantius sent ambassadors led by Theophilus the 'Indian' to Himyar to convert their king to Christianity and to allow the building of three churches for the Roman trader communities in the area. This happened at some point in time during the 350s, the usual dating for this being the year 356. We should see this mission as part of Constantius' eastern strategy, of which the peace negotiations were only one part. According to Philostorgius, Theophilus led the mission because he was a native of the region from the island of Diva/Divus (a former hostage, see above, the reign of Constantine the Great). Philostorgius claims that Theophilus was successful and managed to convert the Jewish Himyarite king to Christianity. He was also allowed to build the three churches, one in Zafar (Himyarite capital), one in Aden (commercial hub) and one at the mouth of the Persian Gulf (commercial hub), all of which evidently belonged to the Himyarite Kingdom.[350]

On the basis of this we can draw several conclusions. Firstly, the Himyarites had either managed to free themselves from the Aksumite rule, or at least that they had managed to gain considerable autonomy. The evidence suggests that the latter is true, especially because the titles suggest that the Aksumite king had higher ranking. Secondly, the likeliest purpose for the Roman embassy was the forming of an alliance with the Himyarites against the Lakhmids and the Persians, as will be made clear below. Thirdly, the alliance was sealed by the at least nominal conversion of the king to the Roman religion. Fourthly, there was a very significant presence of Roman merchants in the Himyar ports (including modern Arab Emirates and Oman) requiring the building of churches for their use.

According to Philostorgius, after having completed his mission in Himyar Theophilus continued his journey to the island of Diva/Dibos, which Shahid locates in the Gulf of Oman, and from there to the other regions of 'India' (in this case this may also mean the actual India).[351] On the other hand, Fiaccadori identifies the Diva with the Maldives, which in this instance makes more sense.[352] According to Philostorgius, Theophilus journeyed from Diva/Greater Arabia to Aksum where he took care of matters, and then returned to Roman territory. Philostorgius states that Constantius showed him great honour but didn't give him his own see. I would suggest that the principal purpose of the trip to Aksum was the securing of an alliance with its ruler Ezana, who may have needed some sort of conciliatory measures and promises by the Romans because they had now granted federate status to the Himyarites, the subjects of Aksum. However, there is more to it than that. It is probable that the Romans fought a war against the Himyarites and Aksumites in the 350s.

According to Symmachus (Or. 1.2), the future emperor Valentinian had at one point in his career carried the Roman *signa* (standards) against the Ethiopians and Indians (Himyarites?). This event is also to be dated to the 350s because Valentinian was born in 321. Despite what Symmachus says, it is obvious that Valentinian did not lead the army, but only took part in the campaign.[353] The big question is, when did this campaign take place? Did it take place before the mission of Theophilus, or during it, or after it? I would suggest that it took place before Theophilus' mission and that his mission was only to ensure that the countries put into effect the peace terms previously agreed. This also means that there must have been a breakup in relations probably resulting from Constantius' religious policies and possible support for the Nubians (e.g. in 348/9). The reasons for the interest shown by the Romans in these areas were manifold. Firstly, there were the commercial advantages to be gained that must have influenced Roman thinking. It is also practically certain that some Roman merchant houses must have lobbied (i.e. bribed) the members of the administration and Constantius to make him improve their trading opportunities with India. Secondly, it was in the interest of the Romans to open up the trade route to India for their merchants and to form trade and military alliances with the Ethiopians, Himyarites and Indians against their rivals the Persians. Both of these needs were mutually beneficial. It was also in the Roman interest to promote Christianity even if Constantius' Arian version failed to gather support.

The Roman military campaign in the area and the diplomatic mission of Theophilus were great successes. Now the Romans regained control of the entire maritime trade network from Egypt to Africa and India. Their allies also blocked easy access from the Persian Gulf to the Sea of Oman. In addition, the Romans were now in a position to threaten the possessions of the Persian Lakhmid allies in Central Arabia by using the Himyarites. In fact, it is very likely that the Romans provided naval support along the Red Sea coastline where needed against the Lakhmids. Considering the previous naval operations, it is also more than likely that at least the Roman merchant ships sailing on those seas aided the locals against the Persians.

But this was not the entire extent of the Roman and Himyarite operations in the area. The Himyarites were busy enlarging their possessions into Bahrayin and Abd al-Qays, which denied the Persians access to the entire Arabian coastline. We have archaeological evidence to support this. According to one Yemeni inscription dated to June 360, the Yemeni armies were at the time fighting in Yamana, in Central Arabia close to ar-Riyad, and in Abd al-Qays. Towards the end of the century, the Himyarites organized these areas under their client Kingdom of the Kinda, who in their turn fought against the Lakhmids of Hira.[354] Consequently, there is at least one certain piece of evidence for the year 360 that supports the interpretation that Constantius was using his allies against the Persians. Constantius' diplomacy in the east was a great success. The embassies that arrived immediately after his death prove this beyond doubt. The Persians were to face constant difficulties in the Persian Gulf and Central Asia for years to come. Constantius' military pressure in combination with religious diplomacy forced Himyar and Aksum to choose their side, and diplomacy helped to gain the support of the Guptas. The Aksumites and Himyarites also raided the Persian coasts as pirates. As a result of this, the Romans controlled the trade route from India via the Red Sea and seriously hindered Persian trade in Arabia and on the Persian Gulf, and thus denied from the Persians an important source of income.

Symmachus (Or. 1.2) also mentions that the future emperor Valentinian took part in a campaign that moved the Pontic frontiers to the kingdoms of Scythia and the Tanais (Don). I would suggest that we should connect this with Hermanaric's campaign against the Heruls who occupied the Don area: that is, I suggest that Hermanaric and the Romans conducted a joint campaign against the Heruls, whose position had become too strong, and that the Roman goal in joining Hermanaric was to improve the position of its Pontic clients. Another possibility is that the campaign was directed against the Caucasian Alans at about the same time as Hermanaric fought against the Heruls. The joint campaign must predate the year 356. In sum, there are reasons to believe that the Romans helped their allies in the area to wrest control of the northernmost portion of the Silk Road away from hostile tribes.

African Backwaters, ca. 355–361

Inscriptions in Tripolitania name two governers for this era, of whom at least one appears to have fought a successful war against the Laguatans. Firstly, there are several inscriptions from Lepcis, Gigthis and the fort of Ras el-Ain that name Flavius Archontius Nilus as *Comes et Praeces Provinciae Tripolitanae* c.AD 355–60. In other words, he combined both military and civilian duties, which does suggest the creation of some kind of special command to solve a military problem. Secondly, there is also an inscription that names Flavius Nepotianus as *Comes et Praeses* at Lepcis. This inscription is usually dated to the years 355–370, but, as Mattingly notes, it seems improbable that this inscription would date from a period after 363.[355] In both cases the unification of civilian and military duties point to the existence of a crisis and in the latter instance the referral to the defeat of the barbarians makes this clear.

In my opinion it is probable that the Laguatan war coincided with the Roman war against the Ethiopians (see above), because a similar set of problems had also taken place during the 290s. The probable reason for the occurrence of such disturbances would have been the disruption of commercial activities caused by the conflict with the Aksumites. The use of two successive governors with similar emergency powers does suggest that the war continued for several years and that at some point in time Nilus was replaced by Nepotianus, who then stopped the hostilities temporarily. However, I would still suggest that Nepotianus' successes must predate the year 362 because when the hostilities restarted in 363 Ammianus implies that there had been peace at least for a while which was then disturbed, and also because the Roman war with the Aksumites should be dated to about 355 or before. It is also possible that similar troubles occurred further west, because the pattern of events for the 290s suggests this. In the absence of any extant inscriptions to prove that, this is only pure speculation on my part.

Constantius and Julian 356–361

Julian Appointed as Caesar in 356 (Map 354–356)

Barbatio was named as Silvanus' successor as *Mag.Ped.* in 356. The practical responsibility of the military operations in the north of Gaul was given to *Mag.Eq.* Marcellus. Before his arrival Ursicinus was in control of operations and after Marcellus' arrival Ursicinus served as his subordinate. Ursicinus appears to have continued Silvanus' policy of bribing the Franks until he was accused of the misuse of public funds. Constantius' goal was not to pay the enemies, but either to drive them out or force them to submit so that the frontier defences could be rebuilt and re-garrisoned. In the short run, this led to the paralysis of all operations and further raiding by enemies. Ursicinus' replacement Marcellus was also not up to the task he had been given, because the Franks managed to capture the strongly fortified city of Colonia Agrippina.

In desperation Constantius came up with the idea of appointing his cousin Julian as Caesar with the responsibility of reconquering Gaul. Julian's only recommendations to the post were his birth and the counsels of Constantius' second wife Eusebia (married since c.353). As noted above, it had also been Eusebia who had shortly before saved Julian's life.

Julian was at least initially expected to act as a figurehead, but as we shall see he desired much more than that. Julian had no prior military experience and had devoted his entire life to philosophical studies, but his study of history had still given him at least a grounding of military knowledge as his future career proves. Had Constantius known the true character of Julian and his secret conversion into an esoteric form of paganism under the tutelage of the philosopher Maximus of Ephesus in 351 it is certain that Julian would have been executed rather than promoted. Libanius (Or. 18.21–27) even implies that in 354 the learned pagans and Julian both started to contemplate the possibility that Julian would become emperor and that he would restore the old gods. Eunapius' Lives of the Sophists also implies the existence of a pagan plot to kill Constantius (Tougher, 38). The central pagan figure in Julian's own entourage was the doctor Oribasius who would certainly have known how to poison someone. Julian's own letter to this Oribasius in 358/9 includes a dream which alludes to the possibility of removing Constantius (Tougher, 39). In other words, there are reasons to believe that these pagan philosophers formed a cabal to obtain the throne for Julian, and Constantius' foolish decision to make Julian Caesar was God-sent, or rather sent by the gods to them. In this context one should pay close attention to Ammianus' statement (21.16.16) that Constantius was too excessively under the influence of his wives. It had been his first wife (sister of Julian and Gallus) who had saved their lives in 337 and it was his second wife Eusebia who first saved Julian's life and then recommended his promotion as Caesar. When we take into account Ammianus' barely hidden disappointment in Julian's performance during the Persian war together with his other criticism of his activities (see the second book in the series), it is possible that Ammianus wanted to hint with this that it was a serious mistake to make Julian Caesar.

Nazianzus' comments (Or. 4 Against Julian 1.34ff.) regarding the promotion of Julian bring to light the questions that all historians think when they ask why Constantius appointed Julian. Unsurprisingly, Nazianzus questions the sanity of Julian's appointment and asks whether one should accuse Constantius of stupidity on the grounds that he had previously killed Gallus and had then appointed Julian, his mortal enemy, as Caesar and had thereby given Julian access to power. He could justify Constantius' foolish decision only on the grounds that Constantius must have considered that the 'kindness' that he had shown to Julian personally would convince him to act honestly and that Constantius considered his own position so strong that Julian could not pose any threat to him.

Julian was duly married to Helena, Constantius' sister, and nominated Caesar on 6 November, 355. On 1 December Julian began his journey. Constantius gave Julian detailed instructions like a teacher regarding everything from campaign plans down to the smallest detail regarding food and manners. Constantius' plan for the year 356 was to use a pincer movement against the barbarians and thereby deny them the possibility of joining forces, and with this action clear up the road on the Roman side of the Rhine up to Cologne. Julian spent the winter at Vienna and ordered the troops to be assembled at Durocortorum for a campaign against the Franks.

In May or June 356 Julian, who had no military experience to speak of, received alarming news amidst his prolonged preparations. The barbarians had taken advantage of Roman inactivity and were already besieging Augustodunum (Autun). Its walls had been weakened by centuries of neglect, but the old veterans had rallied to its defence and kept the barbarians at bay. Julian was forced into action. After having completed preparations, the philosopher led his forces to Augustodunum, which he reached on 24 June. He failed to catch the barbarians. After a meeting of his advisors, Julian decided to emulate Silvanus and use the shortest route via the wooded roads to Durocortorum. In order to accomplish his mission as fast as possible Julian took with him only the *cataphractarii* and *ballistarii* (horse-drawn ballistae carts?), who according to Ammianus were quite unsuited to protect the Caesar. The fact that *ballistarii* were expected to be able to march alongside the cataphracts means that they too must have been mounted. Julian marched to Autosudorum/Autessiodurum (Auxerre) and from there continued his march towards Augustobona (Tricasses, Troyes). En route, barbarian *catervae* began to harrass Julian's marching column with the result that he had to reinforce his flanks and take greater care of the reconnaissance. Whenever he reached open terrain, his forces trampled the enemy, but thanks to their heavy armour his men could not catch those who fled. This clearly means that the barbarians consisted of horsemen. Julian got inside Augustobona only with difficulty because the locals feared the barbarians.

After a short rest Julian continued his march to Durocortorum where the army waited for his arrival. What is notable is that the Frankish bands of marauders roamed freely deep inside Roman Gaul and it was only with difficulty that Julian was able to reach his army. The barbarians were in possession not only of Colonia, but also of Argentoratum (Strasbourg), Brotomagum (Brocomagus, Brumath), Tres Tabernas (Saverne), Salisonem (Saletio, Seltz), Nemetas (Noviomagus, Speyer), Vangionas (Vangiones = Borbotemagus/Worms?), and Mogontiacum (Mainz): that is to say, all the major places between Argentorate and

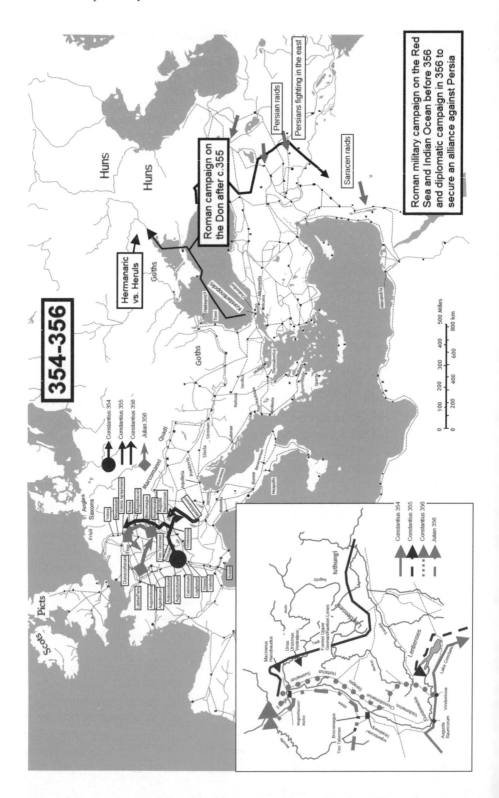

The likeliest two-horned formations are the *epikampios emprosthia* (forward-angled half-square) and *menoeides* (crescent). The illustrations below are taken from the Byzantine Interpolation of Aelian (Burney Codex Folio 20v-21r, pp.40–41). The instruction was to use these against different types of cavalry rhomboids, which may imply that the Alamanni Julian faced consisted of cavalry. These versions of the formation, however, were meant to be used at unit level, but there were also actual 'grand-tactical' versions of these, which were not used solely against cavalry and it was these that were employed in this case. (For the symbols, see Chapter 5.)

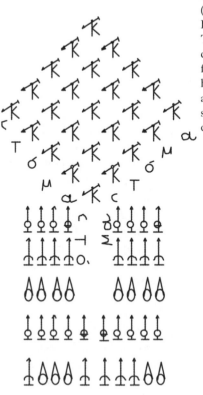

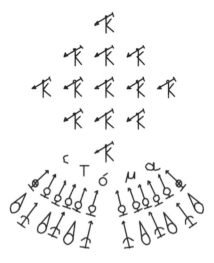

Mogontiacum were in enemy hands. In short, they had overrun the entire Roman defensive system, and now the only Roman goal was to establish the old frontier.

After a meeting of officers, it was decided to engage the Alamanni with dense *agmina* through the Decem Pagi. This plan had undoubtedly been preconceived at Constantius' headquarters and Julian, under the guidance of the officer cadre, was just chosen to put it into effect. Julian's campaign didn't begin well because the day was misty and overcast, which enabled the enemy to go around the Romans and attack two legions bringing up the rear. Only the timely arrival of *auxilia* saved them. Near Brogomagus the Alamanni blocked his way. Julian, or rather Marcellus, arrayed his army in *bicornis*-formation (two-horned), which means either the crescent or the '*epikampios emprosthia*', which were well suited to the terrain. The barbarians were crushed. (See 'Map of Alamannia'.)

In the meanwhile, Constantius had begun his operations against the Alamanni from Raetia. Since Ammianus (16.12.15–16) states that Romans were operating on the other side of the Rhine, it is clear that Constantius' army had marched from the already-pacified areas of Lake Constance and Vindonissa through the mountains to the opposite bank from Argentorate.[356] The purpose of this was to make it impossible for the Alamanni to unite their forces against either corps: that is, Constantius and Julian marched northwards on the opposite banks of the river and prevented the enemy from either uniting or fleeing to the other side. The enemy chose not to fight but fled as best they could. Constantius' campaign was a partial success and resulted in the conclusion of several treaties, but as we shall see their enemies had not yet been cowed into full obedience. They had to be chastised with butchery.

Constantius' campaign lasted until about October, after which he returned to Milan. In the meantime Julian continued his march up to Cologne, which he retook, but it is not known how far north Constantius had marched before his return. According to Ammianus, Julian refortified three places between Mogontiacum (Mainz) and Colonia (Cologne) and overawed the Frankish kings to conclude a peace, after which he went into winter quarters. On the basis that Ammianus is at pains to give all the credit to Julian at the expense of Constantius (Ammianus' villain because of his supposedly unjust treatment of Ursicinus), it appears very probable that Constantius had also continued his march up to Cologne and was actually the person responsible for the conclusion of the peace with the Franks. It would seem strange that Constantius would have tarried around Argentorate until October and not continued his march northwards while Julian continued his march on the opposite bank. Even more importantly, it would make better sense for the Franks to sue for peace if there was a Roman army on the barbarian side of the river and not solely on the Roman side, as was Julian's army. After the conclusion of the campaign, Julian's army was wintered in towns to facilitate its provisioning while he established his own headquarters at Agedincum.

When the Romans had returned to their winter quarters, the Alamanni formed immediately a coalition of seven Alamannic kings led by Chnodomarius. Their compatriots killed Gundomanus and forced Gundomanus' and Vadomarius' tribes to join their united front. Deserters informed the Alamanni of the dispositions of Roman troops, and they took the first opportunity to break the peace and attempt to kill the Caesar whose position was vulnerable. Contrary to their expectation, however, Julian managed to defend himself for about a month in early-357 after which the Alamanni gave up.

Julian accused Marcellus, whose forces were stationed 'nearby' (at Durocortum), of neglect of duty because he had made no attempt to rescue Julian. Marcellus accused Julian of having greater designs than remaining Caesar. Constantius should have believed him, but instead of this, he supported his cousin and duly removed Marcellus from office, sending Severus as his replacement. This means that Julian had managed to get rid of the officer who did not trust him and showed too much independence. Ursicinus was also ordered to go to Sirmium. In the meanwhile, the unscrupulous persons in Constantius' court exploited his fear of conspiracies and accused Arbitio, a man who had risen through the ranks to the very top, of contemplating usurpation, but Arbitio was cleared of all charges. At this time all sorts of accusations and innuendo were spread around, as was natural in the aftermath of real conspiracies (Magnentius, Gallus, Silvanus), and as a result many people died in all corners of the Empire, but not the one who should have. Some of the persons around Constantius managed to convince him that Julian would stay loyal. Regardless, there was now an atmosphere of suspicion and fear all around the empire among the members of the upper classes.

The old wars remained unsolved and new ones emerged. In the winter of 356–7, the 'Suebi' (the Iuthungi?) invaded Raetia, the Quadi invaded Valeria, and the Sarmatians

Upper Moesia and Lower Pannonia. The enemies were exploiting the absence of troops. The emperor and his elite field army were required to be present everywhere. The Persian war also continued unabated, with raids across the borders. It was then that the *PP* Musonianus and Duke of Mesopotamia Cassianus, after they had learnt that Shapur was in the remotest corners of his empire, initiated a project to bring about peace with Persia. They convinced the Persian commander/spy master Tamsapor to convey their message to Shapur, who was fighting against the Chionitae and Euseni (the Guptas?). At the same time the Romans also appear to have scored a number of significant successes against the Persian invaders that led them to stop their raids in 357 (Amm. 17.5.1).

Operations Continue around 357 (Map 357–359)

In early 357 Constantius made his famous visit to Rome after which he marched to the Balkans to take care of operations there. Before his departure, he had formulated a campaign plan according to which the Roman armies under Barbatio and Julian were to destroy the Alamanni with a pincer movement, clearly on the hostile side of the Rhine so that overall command was in the hands of Barbatio. Barbatio had 25,000 men (Libanius: 30,000, which probably includes non-combatants) and Julian had 13,000 men at the Battle of Argentorate (Libanius: 15,000, which probably includes non-combatants), but the original size of his army must have been significantly larger (ca. 20,000?) as he garrisoned several forts before the battle. The two commanders were at odds from the very start. Barbatio was the man who had arrested Gallus. When the *Laeti* (surrendered tribesmen settled within Roman borders as soldiers), who had become bandits, noted the wide separation between the armies, they exploited the opportunity by attacking Lugdunum. It was then that Julian departed from the planned joint operation for the first time. He dispatched three cavalry units to intercept the raiders. Now that Julian's subordinate was the more malleable Severus, he had no intention of following the plan. At this time, Barbatio's tribune Cella accused Julian's tribunes Bainobaudes and Valentian of attempting to tamper with Barbatio's soldiers, with the result that both were cashiered. The former, however, refused to accept it and joined Julian's army once again. Valentinian had personal reasons to hate Constantius because he had confiscated the property of his father.

After this, instead of crossing the Rhine and acting as the second pincer Julian claimed to need seven ships to cross the river. Ammianus claims that Barbatio burned the ships so that Julian could not cross, and Libanius (Or. 18.49–51) claims that Constantius had ordered Barbatio not to join up with Julian but then contradicts himself by stating that the Alamanni had destroyed Barbatio's bridge with which he had intended to bring Julian's army to the same side of the river. These claims are pure nonsense because after Barbatio had later left the scene Julian crossed the river without any difficulty. What actually happened was that when Julian should have crossed the river at Mainz, he actually marched along the friendly side of the river against the Alamanni – who were actually considered friendly – and targeted them. The local Alamanni unsurprisingly fled to the woods and islands with the result that Julian sent the abovementioned Bainobaudes with the *Cornuti auxilia* to surprise those who had fled to the islands. The *Cornuti* strode and swam on their shields to the first island and killed all of the men, women and children, and then took their boats and did the same to a great number of places. Had Julian wanted to cross the river, he could have built a bridge with the help of these boats. I would suggest that it was now that Barbatio reached Julian's position on the opposite shore and attempted to force Julian to come across by building a bridge, which Julian's saboteurs (the 'Alamanni') duly destroyed with logs sent downriver. After this Julian decided to rebuild and garrison the fortress of Tres Tabernae. His only priority was to make it impossible for the *Laeti* and others to use the pass in the mountains, instead of the actual objective of destroying the Alamanni kings. It was then that Barbatio had had enough. The fact that Julian had stayed on the other side of the river had meant that the Alamanni had managed to join their forces, which in turn meant that his way forward would be difficult. Barbatio turned around and retreated in good order despite constant harassment by the natives until he reached the crossing point opposite Rauraricorum. Thanks to the enemy presence he was forced to abandon most of his baggage train so that his army could get across. After this, he conducted his army to its winter quarters and returned to the court to make an official complaint about Julian's behaviour. Ammianus claims that Barbatio had suffered a major defeat, but this is clearly untrue.

The Battle of Argentoratum/Argentorate, 357

Now the seven united Alamannic kings were free to move against Julian, which they duly did. In the meantime Julian had marched his army back north – which the Alamanni interpreted as a sign of fear, and crossed the river before marching towards Argentorate. When the news of this was brought to Julian, he marched his army back in battle formation so that his cavalry was placed on his open right flank. He made a forced march of 21 miles, after which the men were both tired and hungry. Despite this, the men were eager for battle because in the previous year the enemy had refused to engage them in combat. The Praetorian Prefect Florentianus urged Julian to follow their wishes.

The approach of the Roman army was noted by the Alamannic scouts who were located on a small hill near the bank of the Rhine. The Romans captured one infantryman for interrogation, after which the Roman leadership reconnoitred the terrain in person. They saw that the enemy was in the process of arraying themselves for combat and forming up in several infantry wedges (three to five) on the plain. The situation appeared favourable because the Alamanni could now be engaged in the open terrain that favoured the Romans.

The 'High Kings' ('*exelciores ante alios reges*') of the Alamanni, the brothers Chonodomarius and Serapio, led the army so that the former was in command of the left wing, and the latter of the right. Below them served five kings (*reges*), ten 'princes' (*reguli*), nobles (*optimates*) and 35,000 warriors (*armati*). The barbarian army consisted of both the Alamanni and tribal mercenaries. The centre was apparently placed under the five kings, all of whom dismounted to encourage their men. The Alamanni placed an ambush on their right wing in the riverbed and on their left they placed their cavalry, amongst whom they intermingled light-armed infantry for use against the vulnerable steeds of the Roman *clibanarii/cataphractarii*. According to Ammianus (16.12.22), the mixing of footmen among the Germanic cavalry allowed the footmen to sneak low and attack the horses' (evidently unprotected) sides unseen. The implication of this description is that these cataphract horses wore only frontal armour, but it is impossible to assume any difference between the *clibanarii* and *cataphractarii* on the basis of this because Ammianus uses the terms interchangeably. On top of this, Ammianus' description of this cavalry type here suggests that these *clibanarii/cataphracti* used shields and *hasta*-spears, which would make them separate from the *clibanarii* of Constantius II described elsewhere that did not require shields and whose horses were more fully armoured. It is in fact possible that there was a difference between Constantius II's *clibanarii* (more fully armoured and no shield) and the former cataphracts that used shields and whose horses wore only frontal armour, but that Ammianus used the terms inaccurately either to show disrespect to Constantius' reform (his new cavalry was not really different from the older cataphracts), or just out of carelessness.

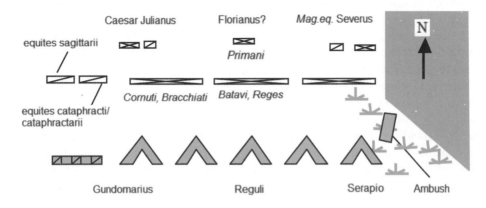

The Roman elite *auxilia palatina* infantry was deployed as a phalanx in front, with reserve palatine legions on the flanks and middle. Contrary to popular belief, the Romans did not use two lines. In fact, even Ammianus notes (16.12.34) that Julian placed most of his army in the first line. There was no need for the use of two lines because the Romans descended from a hill. The cavalry kept its place on the right. Severus commanded the left wing and Julian the right. Ammianus doesn't mention any commander for the centre, but it is probable that someone (perhaps Florentianus) served as such. We do not possess exact figures for each arm of service, but a good guess is that there were probably about 2,500–3,000 horsemen (mostly elite *scholae*) and about 10,000–11,500 footmen. It is probable that the depth of the phalanx was only eight men to make the length of the Roman line equal to that of the enemy. The Roman plan appears to have been to outflank the enemy's left wing.

After having completed their deployment for combat, the Romans began their advance, but then all of a sudden Severus halted his troops because he suspected an ambush. Julian galloped to the scene and it is possible that the left wing was reinforced at this time. The battle began with the typical exchange of volleys of missiles, against which the Roman infantry defended itself with the tortoise array. The Alamanni didn't wait for the Romans to act, but immediately charged against the Roman cavalry. As a result of this, at first only the wings came into contact with each other with differing outcomes. While the experienced Severus defeated his opponents, the Roman cavalry performed less well. It was forced to flee to the bosom of the infantry. The reason for the flight of the *cataphracti equites* was that their leader (*rector*) was wounded, which caused the rest of the men to panic. Had he been leading his men from the front as the apex of a wedge formation? At least that would explain why his men had seen his wounding and fall. In those places where the infantry of both sides fought each other the most skilled of the Germans forced the Romans backward by bending their knees and by pushing shield-boss to shield-boss.

The Roman right wing formed a shield wall towards their exposed right, while the flight of the cavalry was stopped by Julian and his bodyguards. The horsemen could detect Julian from his Purple *Draco*. However, it was not Julian alone who had stopped the flight. The presence of infantry reserves behind also blocked the most direct route of retreat. In fact, the cataphracts almost trampled under their hooves the infantry reserves, before the example of Julian and one tribune of the *turmae* (implies light cavalry, but could also have been used figuratively) managed to convince the cavalry to regroup.

In the meantime, the Alamanni attacked the exposed Roman right. The first response of the *Cornuti* and *Bracchiati* was to shout their slowly rising battle-cry, the *barritus*, to scare the enemy, but to no avail. Then both sides used their missiles and the Alamanni advanced to close quarters and almost overwhelmed the outflanked Romans. The situation was saved by the Batavians and the Reges, who brought help to them. The most likely location for the units would be in the middle, because the presence of the cavalry behind the *Cornuti* and *Bracchiati* would have made it difficult for the reserves to move forward. The Batavians and Reges would have first formed the double-front array and then sent the rear half of four ranks to assist their comrades. While the front ranks fought with swords, the rear ranks of both sides continued to pepper the enemy with javelins (*spicula* and *verruta*). At this point it would seem as if Ammianus would resort to the use of commonplaces by claiming that the combatants were evenly matched because the Alamanni were stronger and taller while the Romans were more disciplined. This was only partially true now that the Roman armies included large numbers of Germans. However, there still appears to have been a real height difference between the forces, but it didn't result from the physical characteristics of the combatants – but rather from the different fighting methods with the sword. The Germans appear to have stood more upright to deliver sword-cuts against the shield wall from the above while the Romans bent their knees, to obtain better cover from their shield wall and better balance, and rather used their swords for stabbing.

The bringing of help by the Batavians and Reges saved the right, but it dangerously weakened the centre of the formation, which the Alamanni exploited immediately by sending forth a *globus* consisting of the elite *optimates* who were followed up by the other tribesmen. The Romans countered this by using the hollow wedge (scissors) technique. The Romans opened up the centre and admitted the enemy in so that the *Primani* legion acted as the bottom of the hollow wedge in the tower formation. The tower (*turres*) was a military formation, but it is not known what it was. It is possible that it was a deep column (*orthe falanx*) that acted like a wall against the enemy (in this case the bottom of the hollow wedge), or it is possible that it was a hollow wedge itself used to receive the enemy attack, or even *epikampios emprosthia*. The fact that the enemy faced only one reserve unit, the *Primani*, proves that the Romans had not used a double phalanx. The outflanked Alamanni panicked and started to flee with the Romans following. The bodies left behind hindered the flight and it was easy for the Romans to massacre the fugitives

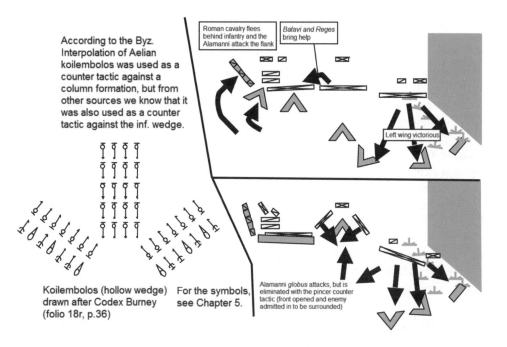

According to the Byz. Interpolation of Aelian koilembolos was used as a counter tactic against a column formation, but from other sources we know that it was also used as a counter tactic against the inf. wedge.

Roman cavalry flees behind infantry and the Alamanni attack the flank

Batavi and Reges bring help

Left wing victorious

Koilembolos (hollow wedge) drawn after Codex Burney (folio 18r, p.36)

For the symbols, see Chapter 5.

Alamanni *globus* attacks, but is eliminated with the pincer counter tactic (front opened and enemy admitted in to be surrounded)

in the centre. Now the panic became universal and the Romans pursued the enemy up to the river, where they killed the helpless fugitives with missiles. Some of the fugitives fled towards their camp which lay to the south, but most of these were killed too.

There is one problem with the above description, which is that many of the details would also fit a cavalry attack by the Alamanni. For example, the *globus* could also mean an irregular throng of cavalry; the *optimates* were usually mounted; and the opening up of the infantry phalanx was not used only against an infantry wedge, but also to admit enemy cavalry through to be butchered by the infantry clubmen posted behind (in tower-array?). However, since Ammianus' account states in no uncertain terms that the Alamannic centre consisted of foot, on balance it is safest to assume that the *optimates* must also have been footmen arrayed as a wedge.

The Romans lost 243 soldiers and four '*rectores*' (i.e. tribunes) which suitably included Bainobaudes. Chonodomarius was captured and sent to Constantius, who duly exiled him to Italy (for possible later use), where he died of old age. The soldiers hailed Julian as Augustus, but he wisely declined the 'honour'. Was this Julian's rehearsal for the future? Did he and his supporters test the terrain in advance? People do not shout in unison as if of one mind without someone taking the lead! It is clear that someone acted as agent provocateur among the soldiers. This was a great victory that made Julian's reputation.

Conclusion of the Campaign Season, 357 (See Maps Section and Map 357–359)

After the battle Julian made an ersatz camp on the spot so that the army was protected by numerous rows of *scutum*-shields, which I interpret to mean that three spears were crisscrossed (and tied) so that one of those pointed towards the 'enemy' and that it was against this structure that the shields were then rested to form a wall bristling with spears. After this, Julian returned to Tres Tabernae and from there he sent all the booty and captives to Mediomatrici (Divodurum), while he himself went to Mogontiacum to build a bridge for the crossing of the Rhine. Julian clearly had no difficulty in bridging the river if he wanted to. He invaded the territory held by 'three kings'. The enemy sued for peace, but this was just a ruse according to a deserter. Julian dispatched 800 men on small boats behind the enemy. The enemy fled and the Romans were free to loot and pillage until once again a deserter informed Julian that the enemy had placed an ambush behind felled trees. The Romans retreated and repaired an old fortress and placed a temporary garrison in it. Now the three kings sued for peace in earnest and Julian granted to them a peace lasting for ten months.

I would suggest that it was after his 'three king' campaign that Julian met the charismatic Charietto. According to Zosimus, at some point in time before the appointment of Julian a bulky barbarian with the name Charietto had spent some time with the Treveri (just east of Mogontiacum) and had come to the conclusion that he had to do something against the invaders. He decided to defend the towns, but since he had no legal permission to do this, he acted undercover. Initially, he started to kill the enemy alone through subterfuge. He killed as many of the enemy as he could in the forests in the middle of the night and then brought the heads for the townspeople to wonder at. In the morning all the enemy could see were the headless corpses amidst them. The barbarians were naturally scared beyond reason, despite the fact that the actual damage was slight. Other 'robbers' soon joined Charietto to form a sizable paramilitary force. It was then that Charietto went to meet Julian. Charietto managed to convince Julian that the regular army was not well suited to counter-guerrilla warfare, while his band of daredevils was. Julian agreed and reinforced Charietto's army with some Salii Franks. It is not known when this happened, but the winter of 356/7 stands as the likeliest date. Julian's hopes were not in vain, because Charietto soon achieved a very significant success with his unorthodox tactics. He managed to capture the son of the King of the 'Quadi' (a mistake for the Alamanni) with the result that the king sued for peace.[357] Since Charietto operated near the Treveri, I would suggest that the king who sued for peace in 358 was Suomarius (see later).

After this, Julian returned to winter quarters, but en route Severus fell on 600 Frankish invaders who had exploited the absence of Roman armies. Julian decided to engage them, but the Franks fled to two strongholds which they managed to hold for fifty-four days in December and January before hunger forced them to surrender. The Frankish relief army was already marching to the rescue, but was then forced to return home empty handed.

Meanwhile, Constantius had continued his attempts to conclude a peace with Persia. His hopes were high, because the Persians had been forced to stop their raiding against Roman territory. They had suffered too heavy losses and Shapur was still in the east. Shapur, however, interpreted the asking for peace as a sign of weakness and became swelled with pride. He demanded both Armenia and Mesopotamia in return for peace. Constantius did not give up, but continued his efforts of achieving peace. He sent two new embassies in the course of the next year, but in vain. Shapur had won or at least had achieved a situation in which he had managed to turn the Chionitai into his allies and mercenaries. Constantius' alternate goal was to delay Shapur's preparations so that he could launch an invasion of Persian territory.

Wars against the 'West Germans', 358–359[358] (See Maps Section and Map 357–359)

During the winter Julian prevented his *PP* Florentianus from carrying out his duties, which included the gathering of extraordinary taxes. Julian's goal was to endear himself with the governing classes of Gaul. Governors who had looted were also treated leniently. It was Julian's order not to gather the extraordinary taxes, which was the reason why his soldiers had not received their donative or their salaries, and not the ill-will of Constantius as claimed by Ammianus (see later). Julian endeared himself to his men also by other means. He allowed them to pillage, loot and rape (that is, no punishments were given). Eventually Julian's liberality with the taxes was to lead to a huge mess. After he gained the throne, he abolished several taxes and lowered others, which in combination with his liberality to his friends resulted in huge public debt by the end of his rule that his successors inherited (see the second book in the series). It is likely that Julian followed the same policy in 358 and borrowed the money to maintain his army.

Amidst all this, the Alamannic Iuthungi launched an unexpectedly-serious invasion of Raetia and, contrary to their usual practice, also besieged towns. Constantius dispatched Barbatio with a large army to deal with them. According to Ammianus, the 'cowardly' Barbatio managed to crush the enemy so that only a small number of them managed to flee. Ammianus claims that Barbatio achieved his victory only thanks to his skills as an orator: allegedly, Barbatio encouraged the troops with a superb speech. This is clearly rubbish. There was nothing cowardly about Barbatio, and his victory was at least comparable to that achieved by Julian at Argentorate. Furthermore, ancient military theory stressed the importance of being able to encourage the soldiers at the right moments to superhuman feats through rhetorical skills. If one judges Barbatio according to this standard, he was a superb commander. However, since we know that Ammianus was biased against the competitors of Ursicinus, it is clear that Barbatio was a good general judged by any standard.

Barbatio seems to have continued this campaign until 359, and it was then that he received from his wife an indiscreet, hysterical and compromising letter in which she stated that she feared that he would abandon her after he became emperor. When this letter was brought to Arbitio's hands and then given to Constantius, it was more than enough to secure the beheading of both Barbatio and his wife. Ursicinus was appointed as his successor. Had the letter of Barbatio's wife been forged?

Julian spent the winter of 357/8 at his winter quarters in Paris making plans for a retaliatory campaign against the Salii Franks. He was anxious to begin the campaign, but could not do so because he had to wait for the arrival of grain from Aquitania which was possible only after the mild summer season had arrived. However, since he didn't want to wait until then, Julian prepared twenty-days' rations of hardtack (*bucellatum*) from the winter rations that he had at hand. Consequently, he began his campaign in May with the intention of ending it within twenty days. When the Romans reached the Tungri (a tribe of the Salii), the Tungri sent envoys to ask for peace. Julian fooled them and sent them back so that Severus could follow in their footsteps. The Romans achieved a complete surprise and the enemy surrendered. On the basis of the locale, the Tungri were clearly a Federate tribe that had revolted. The Chamavi (evidently also Federates) had also asked for peace and Julian treated them in like manner, killing part, and capturing some. Somewhat later the survivors begged for mercy and obtained it. The goal of this operation appears to have been to open the mouth of the Rhine for future grain shipments from Britain (Julian, Letter to the Athenians, 297Dff.). Florentius and Constantius had recommended the paying of money to the Franks (as possibly required by the treaty), but Julian had decided otherwise. He didn't have the money!

After this, Julian restored three fortresses on the River Mosa (Meuse) and left part of the remaining seventeen-days' provisions in them to support the garrisons he implanted. This would suggest that Julian had accomplished all of the above in a mere three days, but obviously this is not the case. He had undoubtedly obtained additional provisions from the tribes that he had looted. However, now Julian made a serious mistake. He assumed that his soldiers would be able to live off the land. The crops were not yet ripe and supplies could no longer be obtained from enemies. This caused the soldiers to mutiny. They insulted their commander by calling him an Asiatic, a Greekling etc. As Ammianus notes, the soldiers had good reasons for their complaints. They had not received their donative, nor pay and now not even their rations. It was Julian's goal to make the soldiers unhappy with Constantius and it suited him that the soldiers didn't receive their money. He claimed that Constantius had withheld the money, even though it was thanks to his own irresponsible fiscal policies that there was no money to be delivered. The *notarius* Gaudentius (a former *agens in rebus*), who was assigned to Julian's staff as a spy, duly informed Constantius that Julian sometimes gave money from his own pockets in an effort to gain the soldiers' goodwill. Julian, however, was well aware of Gaudentius' role and therefore able to hide the most important facts from him.

After Julian had managed to calm the men with words, he built a pontoon bridge and led them across the Rhine so that they could obtain food. This time the object of the attack was the Confederacy of the Alamanni. According to Ammianus, the *Mag.Eq.* Severus started to act in a cowardly manner, possibly because he foresaw his own death, and supposedly bribed the scouts to claim that they did not know the terrain. In response, the cavalry formed the van and advanced really slowly, contrary to the wishes of Julian. However, it was thanks to this slow advance that the *rex* Suomarius was able to come to meet the Romans in person and sue for peace. He was granted this on condition that Roman captives would be returned and the army was to be provisioned by his subjects. I would suggest that the reason why Severus had advanced slowly was because he knew that Charietto, who was accompanying the army, had captured Suomarius' son as hostage. In the circumstances it would have been extremely foolish to attack him as demanded by Julian. Ammianus' need to please his audience may have once again crept into his text. It is unfortunate that Ammianus doesn't mention the cause of Severus' death, because he appears to have indeed died in the course of this campaign and was succeeded by Lupicinus (PLRE1 Severus 8). Perhaps Julian had him murdered, because there was a clear tendency for all those who had acted against his wishes to be removed from office or die from poison.

Now the Romans moved against the *Rex* Hortarius. Since the Romans lacked guides, Julian dispatched the *Tribunus Scutariorum* Nestica and Charietto to catch a prisoner. They captured a young man who acted as their guide, but their route was blocked by a barricade of felled trees. With the help of the same man, the Romans bypassed it and attacked the undefended homes and fields of the tribe. The angry Romans pillaged, killed, destroyed, burned and captured. Hortarius begged for mercy, but acted dishonestly by trying to keep some of the Roman captives, after which Julian took hostages and forced the king to hand them over. Since the Romans had destroyed much of the crop, they didn't require that Hortarius provide them with supplies, but with carts and timber for the rebuilding of Roman towns and farms. After this, the Caesar led his army to its winter quarters.

On the basis of the above, it is probable that Julian intended to obtain from the enemy those resources that he could no longer obtain through taxation. In order to succeed, the policy obviously required constant military successes and tribes to plunder. According to Ammianus, when Julian's report reached Constantius' court, Julian was disparaged by Constantius' courtiers as a timid and unpractical pedant, which only reflected their envy of his achievements. There is undoubtedly a germ of truth in this, but as noted above Ammianus has undeservedly blamed the professional soldier Severus for cowardice while extolling Julian. On the basis of Ammianus' own account, it is clear that the inexperienced and impatient Julian had not paid enough attention to the supply situation and it is also clear that he almost attacked an Alamannic king who was about to surrender anyway. Severus was clearly the more sensible of the two. He had been forced to attack the Alamanni, because his army lacked supplies. Therefore, on closer inspection Julian's so-called military credentials for the year 358 were not that impressive and it is therefore not at all surprising that these were derided.

Julian's campaign in 359, however, proves that he was a good student who learnt from his past mistakes. This year's campaign was based upon the use of unorthodox warfare, subterfuge, assassinations, and commando operations. His plan was to subject the remaining tribes to his will and weaken Constantius' grip on these very same tribes. However, before he embarked on this well-planned campaign, Julian had not forgotten to endear himself further with the ruling classes of Gaul.

Before beginning his campaign, Julian sent secretly the *tribunus vacans* Hariobaudes to meet Hortarius and discuss his plan of assassinating the enemy leadership with the help of Hortarius. Then, Julian assembled his forces and marched to rebuild a number of destroyed cities, forts and granaries with the help of his men. Now Julian was wise enough to begin his campaign only after the grain had ripened and only after having transported grain in 600 ships from Britain. Julian rebuilt Castra Herculis, Quadriburgium, Tricensima, Novesium, Bonna, Antennacum, and Vinco. He filled the granaries with the grain brought from Britain. The wagon loads of building material sent by the treaty-bound Alamannic kings enabled Julian to build the forts at a minimum cost to the exchequer. Ammianus even claims that Julian was able to convince the barbarian *auxilia* to join in the building. Considering Julian's underlying motives, it is possible that he had claimed that this order had come from Constantius. Ammianus states that it was at Vinco that Florentius appeared unexpectedly, bringing with him forces and provisions. If Julian really had not expected Florentius' arrival, as claimed by Ammianus, it is clear that Florentius had saved Julian once again from the making of a grave mistake. Since Julian had been forced to leave a garrison and grain in each rebuilt fortification, it is clear that he would have run out of both by the time he actually started his real campaign, which happened next.

Meanwhile, the Alamanni kings had learnt of Julian's planned campaign and had demanded that Suomarius should protect the opposing bank against the Romans. Suomarius maintained that he could not do that alone with the result that the others brought their forces into his territory opposite Mogontiacum. Suomarius, however, remained secretly loyal to the Romans. When the enemy army appeared on the opposite bank, Florentius and the new *Mag.Eq.* Lupicinus, who were unaware of Julian's stratagem, demanded that they build a bridge and attack. Julian opposed on the grounds that this would force Suomarius to join the enemy. In order to lure the enemy to follow, Julian then started to march southwards, supposedly in an effort to find a better place to build a bridge across the river. When the army reached its next marching camp, Julian finally confided with Lupicinus and told him of the plans. He ordered loyal tribunes to collect 300 *expediti* (in this case probably light-armed troops). These were embarked on 40 *lusoriae naves* (scouting boats) and ordered to go downstream quietly. In the meantime, Hortarius had invited the other kings to a banquet, undoubtedly as agreed with Hariobaudes. When these left the feast on the third watch, they encountered the 300 Romans who had disembarked. Unfortunately for the Romans the plan didn't work. Thanks to the darkness and fast horses, the nobility managed to flee. The Romans managed to kill only the servants and squires who were following on foot. After this the panicked Alamannic leaders fled without attempting to find out how many Romans had crossed, with the result that the Romans were able to build their bridge unhindered. The Romans marched through Hortarius' lands without causing any damage and then started to burn and pillage when they reached his neighbour's lands. When the Romans reached the border between the Alamanni and Burgundians, they planned to continue the campaign against Macrianus and Hariobaudes, however before this could happen both sued for peace. Both were granted peace on terms.

Vadomarius soon followed, coming with a letter of protection written by Constantius. He was welcomed, but Vadomarius was not given any reply on behalf of those (Urius, Ursicinus, Vestralpus) whom he represented as a middleman. Ammianus claims that Julian's reason for this was that the Alamanni were untrustworthy. The real reason must have been that Julian wanted to undermine Constantius' standing among the Alamannic chieftains as their protector. The Alamanni were to be allowed to receive protection only from Julian, so that Constantius would be unable to use the Alamanni in the future against him. Consequently, Julian attacked them, burned their harvests and houses, killed or captured their people, until they sought peace from him and him alone. Julian had now proved that Constantius could not protect the natives.

Constantius vs. the Sarmatians and Quadi, 358–359[359] (See Maps Section and Map 357–359)

Meanwhile, Constantius had wintered at Sirmium between October 357 and 3 March 358. He was planning to exact revenge against the Quadi and Sarmatians who had exploited the absence of major field forces in Pannonia, Valeria and Moesia. To add insult to injury, the very same tribes also invaded the Pannonias and Second Moesia in detached 'wedges' during the winter of 357/8 when Constantius had already reached the scene. According to Ammianus, the Quadi and Sarmatians fought in a similar manner to bandits. They had *loricae* made of horn scales, used sturdy and obedient geldings well-suited to ambushes, and were armed with bows and long *hastae* (the Sarmatian *Contus*). (See Chapter 2.) Having three centuries of warfare with the Sarmatians behind them, the Romans knew how to oppose the Sarmatians.

Constantius started his well-prepared campaign in April 358 when the Danube was still flooding from the melted snow and ice. This did not prevent operations. The Romans had chosen the most suitable places for the building of a bridge over the decks of ships. The first part of Constantius' campaign was a two-pronged attack launched simultaneously from two directions against the Sarmatian Limigantes (the former slaves of the Agaragantes). The main army advanced under Constantius from Second Pannonia and the other army from Valeria under an unknown general.

The Sarmatians attempted to prevent the building of the bridges with showers of missiles (probably mostly arrows), but no Romans were lost in the building or crossing of the river (Amm. 17.18.28). Despite the opposition, Constantius had still managed to surprise the Sarmatians with his early invasion, as a result of which the enemy was unable to assemble together to oppose the attack. The use of the two-pronged offensive only added to the confusion among the enemy. Consequently, the Sarmatians attempted to flee, but Ammianus claims that the Romans managed to kill most of their enemies thanks to the speed of their invasion. The survivors fled to the Carpathian Mountains. On 21–23 June Constantius was back in Sirmium, but by 27 June he was already at Mursa, evidently en route to fight the Quadi.[360]

According to Ammianus, the Quadi came to the assistance of the Sarmatians. The Quadi army included as allies one group of the Free *Agaragantes* and one splinter group of *Agaragantes* as a subjugated client tribe. The two Roman divisions had by now united under the emperor, as a result of which the Quadi and their allies were crushed with ease and forced to flee. As a result, the Roman army marched to the lands of the Quadi in dense wedge formations suited to marching in such conditions.

The Free Sarmatians under the young *regulus* (minor king) Zizais and the Quadi decided to sue for peace. The Romans controlled the order and way in which these were allowed to approach the emperor to beg for mercy. The first to approach was the young *regulus* Zizais who fell flat on his face, cried, begged for mercy, and obtained it. Zizais had demonstrated the type of humility that was expected by the Romans, and he was soon rewarded for this. After his basement, Zisais was told to get up. He gave the signal for his men to throw their shields and javelins to the ground and to stretch their hands with prayers. The weaponry suggests German influence upon the Sarmatians.

The Sarmatian *subreguli* (sub-kings) Rumo, Zinafer, Fragiledus, and the *optimates* (nobles) also received merciful treatment. They handed over all Roman prisoners and gave hostages. The next group of supplicants were the *regulus* Araharius of the Quadi and the *optimate* Usafer of the Agregantes. The emperor feared that these two tribes could cause trouble, and therefore divided them into two groups. Constantius asked Araharius to present the case of the Quadi first, and when their appearance was not suitably humble, the emperor ordered them to send hostages in advance of the petition. After they had received an amnesty, the emperor ordered the Sarmatians under Usafer forward. When Araharius protested that the amnesty given to him also included his subjects, he was told that the Sarmatians were henceforth under the Roman protection and not subjects of the

Quadi. According to Ammianus, several other peoples with their kings also submitted, but unfortunately he fails to name them. In order to break up the alliance structures that had led to the invasion of Roman territories, Constantius reversed the policies of his father and transferred the Agaragantes of Usafer and Zizais back to their former domains and appointed the suitably humble Zizais as their *rex*.

After this, Constantius established his headquarters at Brigetio and attacked the remaining tribes of the Quadi with equal vigour, assaulting the heart of the enemy country. The *regulus* Vitrodorus, son of the *rex* Viduarius (that is, there had been one king before), the *subregulus* Agilimundus, the *optimates*, and the *iudices* (judges) duly submitted to the emperor.

In the meantime, in August 358 a series of earthquakes, accompanied by at least one tsunami, hit Asia, Macedonia, and Pontus and devastated numerous cities. The most notable casualty was the city of Nicomedia on 24 August. It was hit by a combination of earthquake, tsunami and a landslide caused by the earthquake. Much of the city was levelled. This obviously meant that the tax income from these areas was severely hit, limiting Constantius' options in the coming years: for example, it made it more difficult for him to raise new units, which in turn must have been at least one of the reasons why he subsequently ordered Julian to send him reinforcements from the West.

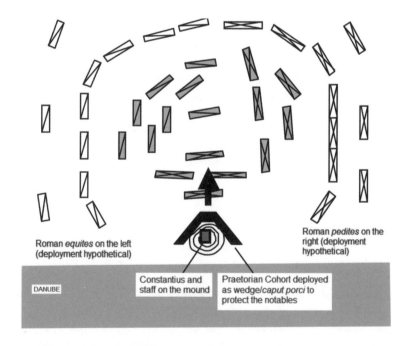

Roman *equites* on the left (deployment hypothetical)

Roman *pedites* on the right (deployment hypothetical)

DANUBE

Constantius and staff on the mound

Praetorian Cohort deployed as wedge/*caput porci* to protect the notables

Constantius continued his unfinished campaign against the Limigantes in the spring of 359. His plan was to transfer them to some remote locale so that they could no longer invade Roman territory. He sent an order for the Limigantes to come to their bank of the river (Danube?) to present their case. According to Ammianus, the Limigantes' purpose was to attack the emperor in the midst of the negotiations and the emperor, who was suspicious of their motives, had made preparations against this. When the Limigantes had reached the location and were not showing the necessary humility, the emperor had his *agmina* (divisions) surround the enemy. (See the attached illustration.) The emperor stood directly in front of the enemy on a mound protected by his '*cohors praetoria*', which was apparently formed into a wedge (*cuneus, caput porci*) to cover the front and flanks of the mound from the very start. Unfortunately, it is practically impossible to know what unit Ammianus meant by the Praetorian Cohort, perhaps the dismounted of the *Scholae* or *Protectores Domestici*, or just a chosen unit from among the palatine units. The Roman cavalry was posted on the left and the infantry on the right, probably because of the requirements of the terrain. The Limigantes purposefully and constantly threw their shields a long distance forward so that they could advance inconspicuously towards the emperor, before the men picked their shields up, raised the standards, formed themselves into a mass, and attacked Constantius. The Praetorian Cohort charged as a wedge and scattered the enemy in front while the infantry on the right crushed the enemy *catervae* and the cavalry on the left the cavalry *turmae*. The barbarians fought furiously and according to Ammianus not a single one of them asked for mercy or dropped their weapons. The massacre of the Limigantes lasted half-an-hour and not one was left alive. We should remember that this is the Roman version, and it is possible that Constantius' plan had been all along to ambush any enemy who would be foolish enough to come to negotiate.

After this, the Romans attacked the civilian population. The soldiers destroyed and burned the humble cots, huts, and sturdy timber houses, and butchered the inhabitants with no regard for age or sex. Those who fled the burning houses faced steel, and of those who managed to dive into the neighbouring river (probably the Parthissus or one of the many other rivers nearby) most died by drowning while others were pierced by javelins. Next the Romans used a commando operation against the Sarmatian Amicenses on the opposite bank. The Romans placed *expediti velites* (light-armed without baggage) on the native boats and rowed to the hiding places of the Sarmatians in the swamps and rivers. When the natives saw their own boats approaching rowed in their distinctive manner (paddled?), they were fooled into believing that their fellows approached until the gleam of the weapons betrayed the Romans. Then the natives took to their heels and fled to the marshy places, but to no avail because the Romans followed them and killed and killed until almost everyone had died.

The Romans now moved against the Sarmatian Picenses in the Carpathians, but since the Picentes had already learnt of what had happened and were prepared to fight, the Romans resorted to the use of Free Sarmatians and Taifali to subject the Picenses to attack from all directions. The Romans attacked from Moesia, the Taifali from their own lands, and the Free Sarmatians from the opposite direction. In this situation, the Limigantes Picenses called an assembly of the tribal elders, which decided that they should surrender to the Romans. Consequently, the Romans granted a safe-conduct. The extended families of the Limigantes descended from the mountains to the plains to be transported to the location chosen by the emperor for them, somewhere between the northern Parthissus and Carpathians.

Constantius wintered in Sirmium from about October 358 to March 359, but while still there he learnt to his horror that the Limigantes had abandoned their homes and were marching towards Valeria and then along the river with the intention of crossing into Pannonia while the Danube was still frozen.[361] He collected his army and marched opposite the Limigantes to keep an eye on the situation. Constantius was eager for action. He knew that his men were eager for action as well because they expected similarly abundant booty as they had got the previous year and also because his Prefect of Illyricum Anatolius had managed to gather enough supplies for a campaign well ahead of time. According to Ammianus, Anatolius was the most skilled manager of the northern provinces of the century. He corrected all abuses and even lowered the taxes. Constantius sent two tribunes with interpreters to enquire why the Limigantes had left their new homes contrary to the agreement. The Limigantes presented a number of excuses, and then begged the emperor to let them cross the river and become Roman subjects. Constantius was glad to hear the tidings. He admitted them all because the new group of child-bearing populace would produce much needed recruits for the Roman army, which in turn would enable him to pocket the conscript-taxes in gold for other uses.

Constantius had a rampart and tribunal built near Acimincum to receive the fugitives, and ordered some *expediti* legionaries (probably lightly-equipped) to patrol the river on ships near the banks with the *agrimensor* (field-measurer) Innocentius, who had suggested this safety measure. Innocentius and the legionaries were to attack the Limigantes from behind if they showed any signs of disorder. The appointment of Innocentius to be acting commander of the legions and river fleet shows how self-assured legitimate emperors like Constantius could appoint anyone who they wished to act as military commanders. They didn't need to take into account the wishes of the top brass, because they did not owe their position to them. Compare this with the later reigns of Valentinian and Valens.

The Limigantes were aware of the presence of the legionaries behind them, but still chose to double-cross the Romans. This time the otherwise so-cautious Constantius had not taken adequate safety measures. His army was not fully deployed and most of them did not wear armour. On top of it all, he had taken position right in front of the enemy army on the mound/tribunal in the company of only a few attendants. When he was preparing to receive the Limigantes with mild rebuke and open arms, one of them shouted 'Marha, Marha!', which was their war-cry.[362] The Limigantes raised their banner and ran towards the emperor. The mob ran to the mound, missiles were flying and the barbarians were already on the mound with drawn swords and javelins, when Constantius mounted his horse and galloped away. He was able to escape only because he wore undistinguished clothes so that he did not look like a *comes* (general) or *miles* (soldier). Those of his attendants who were trying to gain time for Constantius to escape were either killed or trampled by the swallowing mass of men. Constantius had first-rate bodyguards!

When the soldiers saw their emperor in danger, they burst forward as one furious mass of men. The imperial bodyguards, the *Scholae*, appear to have been the first to reach the scene because the *Tribunus Scutariorum* Cella was the first to rush into the middle of the Sarmatians. The price of his bravery was a glorious death as befitted a bodyguard. The Romans had no time to don armour, or equip themselves fully. They immediately rushed forward to save their emperor and in the process wiped out the entire enemy force. Even those who attempted to surrender were cut down with repeated strikes. After everyone had been cut to pieces, the trumpets sounded a recall and it was after this that the situation was evaluated. It was then that the Romans found out that some of their men had also died either because they had been trampled underfoot by their own men during the violent attack or because the enemy had wounded them on their unprotected (non-armoured) sides.

This battle is a good example of the importance of psychology of masses in combat. The Limigantes had spent all their internal fury and energy during their mad charge against the emperor, and when they suddenly faced the Roman counter attack they were out of breath and therefore unable to regain their internal strength for another fight. In contrast, the Romans were in a state of mass psychosis. They were angered by the barbarian betrayal and by the barbarian attack against their beloved leader. Consequently, the Roman army ran and galloped furiously at the enemy without any semblance of order and killed and killed until their fury was sated with rivers of blood and piles of mutilated corpses. In other words, in this instance the Romans possessed what is often called 'barbarian fury', which is no surprise considering the numbers of barbarians in their service. However, this fury was (and is) not limited to the barbarians. Almost all humans have an inner ability to turn into furious madmen when angered and when this happens the object of this fury usually becomes immediately frightened, as happened to the Limigantes. Humans are animals and have animal reactions. When the Limigantes in their tired state saw the wild Roman attack they instinctively understood with their inner animal instincts that all resistance would be futile. There would be just one mad charge and everyone would be cut to pieces. The rigorous Roman military training and the use of tight combat formations were intended to counter this human instinct, but the instinct is (and was) still there underneath the rough military surface, despite all the effort that the military put into training. It is this that causes even elite units to panic and flee when the circumstances for this are right, and it was this that sometimes made the furious barbarian charge so successful.

This butchery stands as still another indication of the superb quality of Constantius' field army. The previous instances (for example at Singara and Mursa) have already suggested that Constantius' field army possessed an exceptionally high fighting spirit and morale, and this battle makes the case for that conclusion even stronger. It is clear that Constantius had a superb army and it is very doubtful that Julian could have withstood the fury of this army had Constantius lived long enough to punish the traitor. Readers should also note the great difference in the outcome of the revolt of the armed Limigantes against Constantius and the revolt of the Tervingi Goths against Valens' corrupt and effeminate representatives in 376. When the Romans handled the situation at least adequately (in this case the precautions were by no means adequate), by posting enough elite troops to the scene, the barbarians, even when armed, posed no real risk for the Romans.

After this, Constantius organized the defences in the area and returned to Sirmium by 22 May (Barnes, 1993, 223). There he assessed the situation and came to the conclusion that he needed to go to Constantinople in order to be closer to the Persian frontier so that he could remedy the situation after the loss of Amida (see below) by dispatching reinforcements and then by following later in person. Constantius was definitely at Constantinople by 11 December (Barnes, 1993, 223). At the same time, he also received reports from the oracle of Abydum in Thebais that several important persons had made inquiries regarding who would be emperor. (Note how the oracles reported to the Pontifex.) Constantius took these kinds of inquiries very seriously and the investigation was delegated to the *notarius* Paulus the Chain and the *Comes Orientis* Modestus, because the *PP* of *Oriens* Hermogenes of Pontus was considered too mild. The investigators sent Simplicius, former prefect and consul, and Parnasius, ex-prefect of Egypt, into exile, but acquitted several philosophers. Ammianus considered the acts committed by the persons who were convicted of making improper questions to the oracles as not worth conviction, but it is still clear that when such high ranking men were making such inquiries they could also attempt to form an actual plot against the emperor. What is notable about this is the inclusion of philosophers in the list of suspects. There are strong reasons to suspect that several philosophers were working together as a sort of cabal in an effort to promote Julian's career, and they did not stop their activities even after Julian had died. In this context the referrals to the suspected use of poison or magic to harm the Christian emperors Valentinian and Valens stand out most clearly. Was this Ammianus' way to implicate the philosophers as poisoners acting on behalf of Julian? There seems to have been a strange connection between the users of black magic and poison at least until the modern era.

On 1 November, 359 Constantius also issued an Edict (CTh. 1.9.1–2) to his *Mag.Off.* to conduct an investigation of the *agentes in rebus* and purge all those of office who were of unworthy birth or of bad character. Note, however, that it is possible that the wording could have been used as a code which the *Mag.Off.* understood, but we do not. This does suggest a problem with the secret service in charge of reading the mail just at the time when Julian's cabal was moving to usurp power. This suggests two possibilities: firstly, it is possible that Constantius just wanted to get rid of the bad apples (those who misused their position); and secondly, it is possible that he had heard reports that some of the *agentes in rebus* were disloyal and had not reported the activities of Julian's friends (for example, the *PP* Florentius had warned Constantius of this). If the former is true, then the organization had grown inefficient and Constantius was just trying to reform it. In this case it is possible that the inefficiency of the organization had given the pagan plotters their chance to exchange messages in code without fear of exposure, or that Constantius had just chosen a really bad time to reform this part of the security system. The removal of staff could have caused some suspicious letters to pass through. If the second is true, then Constantius was aware that his security apparatus had been infiltrated by disloyal pagans.

Constantius' Homoean Creed, 359–360[363] (See Appendix)

In about 358/9, Constantius appears to have analyzed the extent of the opposition against his religious policies, as a result of which he came to the conclusion that an attempt had to be made to reconcile the Orthodox/Catholics with the Arians. This decision coincides with the resurgence of the Persian threat and may have been one of its results. The result was the decisions taken at the Councils of Ariminum and Seleucia in 359. Constantius attempted to steer clear of controversy by avoiding technical religious terms in the redrafted creed, but this satisfied neither the Catholics nor the Arians. Regardless, Constantius had forced his will on the bishops through coercion by the end of 359 and had the new Homoean Creed confirmed at the Council of seventy-two bishops at Constantinople in January 360. The problem with this was that Constantius forced the recalcitrant western bishops to sign the new creed just before Julian usurped power in the West. This enabled Julian to gather support from the Western Church with promises of religious freedom. Julian also appears to have already issued an edict that allowed the exiled bishops to return in 360. In fact, the bishops of the West met at Paris and denounced the Homoean creed during 360.

Ammianus (21.16.18) makes an important point regarding the quarrels over matters of Christian dogma during the reign of Constantius when he notes that thanks to these the bishops were constantly travelling from one place to another on public post horses with the result that Constantius had effectively destroyed the courier-service. Ammianus may indeed have a point in this case, because the bishops not only went to the major councils, but also held local councils and meetings yearly. Ammianus doesn't give any examples of the dire consequences resulting from this, but it is easy to see that, for example, when churchmen were attending the meeting at Seleuceia in 359, at a time when the Persians were about to invade or had already invaded, some couriers who had reached certain courier-stations could not find any spare horses because the bishops and their staff had taken them. In short, the constant use of post horses by bishops hindered military operations. The use of trains by the Nazis to transport the Jews, leftists and others to concentration camps stands as a good modern example of similar misuse of public transport to the detriment of military operations, even if in the latter case it caused even greater damage than with the Roman courier service.

The Persian Invasion, 359[364] (See Maps Section and Map 357–359)

In the course of the year 358 Constantius continued his futile peace negotiations with Persia. Shapur II was set on invading and there was nothing that could change this. Prosper, Spectatus, and Eustathius had met Shapur II at Ctesiphon after he had returned from the east, but they returned empty-handed, just like the previous embassies. Constantius dispatched still another set of ambassadors, the *Comes* Lucillianus with the *notarius* Procopius (the future usurper/emperor), to negotiate in 358. They reached the King of Kings apparently in very late 358 or early 359, in time to witness Shapur's last preparations for the invasion.

Meanwhile, the Persians had made a real coup when the Roman *protector* Antoninus defected to their side. Antoninus had started as a rich merchant, then moved on to become *rationarius* (supply officer) of the *Dux* of Mesopotamia, and had finally ended up as a *protector domesticus*. The reason for his defection appears to have been that he had had business dealings with some powerful high ranking men at the court that had caused them financial loss in the form of taxes. Antoninus was forced to bear the entire loss himself because the examiners naturally favoured the higher-ranking men. In this case, the abuse of power proved most unfortunate for the Romans. As *protector* Antoninus had access to all records of troop strengths, transferral of troops, supply of provisions, and quantity of arms because the administration of the entire East was handled from the Imperial Court in Illyricum. Antoninus bought a farm by the Tigris so that he could travel inconspicuously to the border in the winter of 358/9. Antoninus managed to establish contact with the local Persian governor Tamsapor, whom he already knew as an intelligence officer. Tamsapor appears to have acted as some kind of Spy-Master of the Persian western frontier. Tamsapor helped Antoninus and his family across the border and dispatched them to Shapur, who welcomed them with open arms. Now the Persians knew each and every detail there was to know about Roman defensive arrangements and could plan their campaign accordingly.

In the winter of 358/9 court intrigue also caused another unfortunate consequence for the defence of the East. According to Ammianus, Constantius relied in particular on the advice of the eunuch Eusebius, the *Praepositi Cubiculi*, who essentially acted as a sort of prime minister. Unfortunately, Eusebius was prone to take bribes to further the careers of those who were willing to pay, and according to Ammianus his superior Ursicinus was one of those very few who didn't. Consequently, Eusebius convinced Constantius to recall Ursicinus from the East and appoint him as Barbatio's successor as *Mag.Ped.*: that is, Ursicinus was essentially demoted and succeeded by Sabinianus, who according to Ammianus was cultivated and rich, but completely unsuited to assume the magisterial rank because he did not have the necessary experience. Constantius actually appears to have been aware of this, because the first thing he did when he learnt that the Persians were about to launch an invasion (evidently detected from the preparations that went on during the winter: Amm. 28.6.4) was to send Ursicinus back to take charge of the actual defence of Mesopotamia.

When the new order arrived, Ursicinus and Ammianus returned to meet Sabinianus, who would act as their superior. There they learnt from scouts and deserters that the Persians were about to launch their invasion. Consequently, Ursicinus and Ammianus travelled to Nisibis to prepare its defences for a siege. While they were there, smoke and fires were seen from the Tigris past Castra Maurorum, which indicated that the enemy had already sent their advance guard and raiders across the river. Ursicinus and Ammianus left the city in haste so that their route of retreat would not be cut off. The Persians were clearly following a tactic in which fast moving cavalry forces preceded the main army, conducted intelligence gathering, and prevented the movement of messengers and troop transferrals and the evacuation of civilians and provisions. In addition, they caused chaos and mayhem among the defenders by their speed of movement. En route, Ammianus was almost captured by the Persians when he helped a local boy to reach safety. When the Persians learnt that Ursicinus was fleeing, they set out in pursuit but failed to catch him.

When Ursicinus and Ammianus were riding towards Amida, they received a cryptic letter from Procopius (hidden in a sword and written with a cipher) in which he stated Shapur's goals. However, Ursicinus was not satisfied with the state of intelligence and therefore dispatched the *protector* Ammianus with one centurion of tried loyalty to the satrap of Corduene (double-agent in Roman service). The role of the *protectores* as staff and military intelligence officers is quite obvious. Ammianus was now acting as a spy. The satrap sent Ammianus with one guide to spy upon the Persians. The guide took them to a mountainous spot where they could observe the terrain for a distance of up to fifty miles. After having waited for two days, on the morning of the third Ammianus could observe Shapur leading his army from the front and close by on the left Grumbates, the king of the Chionitae, and on the right the king of the Albani. After them followed the other leaders, and behind them the army. When Ammianus had observed that the kings had passed Nineveh and had taken omens in the middle of the river crossing at Anzaba, he came to the conclusion that it would take probably more than three days for the entire army to cross. Ammianus returned immediately.

After Ammianus had briefed his superior, Ursicinus sent messengers to the *Dux* of Mesopotamia Cassianus, and to Euphronius, the *rector* (governor) of the same province, with orders to force the peasants and their flocks to safer locations, to abandon Carrhae because its fortifications were too weak, and to set the plains on fire to deny the enemy fodder. The operation was performed with due diligence and the fires were spread throughout the dry plains, with the result that many wild animals like lions died too. At the same time Ursicinus sent tribunes with *protectores* (implies the presence of imperial bodyguards) to protect the bank of the Euphrates. The crucial role of the *protectores* in the defence of the empire is quite obvious. The whole bank was protected by troops, towers and sharpened stakes, and field-artillery (*tormenta*) was placed to protect those places which were not protected by the currents of the river. According to Ammianus, while Ursicinus was busy making these preparations, Sabinianus spent his time in aimlessness by watching his men perform the Pyrrhic dance at Edessa. Ammianus is clearly unfair towards Sabinianus. The Pyrrhic dance was a form of military training. Sabinianus was clearly training his army for combat as any good general was expected to and had also posted himself in forward position in Edessa.

In the meantime the kings had bypassed Nisibis in order to penetrate deeper into Roman territory, as advised by Antoninus. The Persians avoided the burning plains and marched along the grassy valleys of the mountains and thereby made the Roman scorched-earth policy ineffective. When the Persians reached Bebase (unknown, possibly later Dara), which was at a distance of 100 miles (about 150km) from Constantina, they halted there because they learnt from their scouts that the Euphrates was flooding as a result of the melted snow and therefore couldn't be forded. This means that Ursicinus' defensive plan of using the river to block the enemy advance had succeeded. Ammianus' distances, however, are mistaken. Shapur was marching along the road from Nisibis to Constantina and evidently halted somewhere before the crossroads at Monokarton (c.72 km from Constantina and 65km from Nisibis). The Persians held a council of war in which Antoninus advised them to turn right and march through the regions that the Romans had not scorched. His advice was accepted, and he led the army towards the garrison camps of Barzalo (possibly Barsalium?) and Claudias (unknown, probably near Barsalium) where the river was fordable.

When the Roman scouts informed Ursicinus of the change in Persian plans, he decided to go from Amida to Samosata and cross the Euphrates there and break up the bridges at Zeugma and Capersana. When the Roman horsemen had started their journey, they learnt to their horror that the Persians had already managed to cut off their route of retreat. The reason for this was that the two understrength *turmae* of cavalry sent from Illyricum consisting of about 700 horsemen had failed to perform their guard duty. Since they had feared night attack, they had withdrawn from the roads in the evening, even though, as Ammianus notes, they should have doubled their efforts during the night. The Persians had observed this, bypassed the guards unobserved with 20,000 horse, and advanced north. The shining of their armour betrayed their approach, with the result that Ursicinus and his horsemen froze where they stood. The Persians advanced as two lines so that the *cursores* (runners, light cavalry) appear to have formed the vanguard and the cataphracts the second line. The Roman cavalry was similarly deployed in two lines (Amm. 28.8.7: the second line up the hill). At first the Romans could see only the Persian vanguard led by Antoninus. Ursicinus ordered his men to stay still because the enemy possessed a clear numerical superiority. Regardless, some Romans charged at the enemy with predictable results. After this Antoninus approached Ursicinus for a brief discussion, the purpose of which was clearly to make the Romans stay in place a little longer. It was then that the Romans posted in the rear on the higher part of the hill saw the approach of the Persian cataphracts, with the result that all Romans panicked and scattered in flight. The Persian *cursores* charged and became intermingled with the fleeing Romans. Ursicinus was saved by the speed of his horse and managed to flee to Edessa. Ammianus and many others managed to gallop to the walls of Amida, where they crowded against the wall and waited until sunrise when they were let in through a postern gate. The city was full of refugees and merchants who had come for the annual fair.

The Siege of Amida, 359[365] (See Maps Section, Map 357–359, and City Map)

The city had been fortified and supplied with mural artillery by Constantius in about 336, and now his efforts bore fruit. The city was approachable only from its northern and western sections. The other sections were protected by escarpment, and the basaltic bedrock protected it from mining. It also had an abundant supply of water. We do not know what type of walls there were at the time because the extant remains date from the reign of Valens and his successors. These walls, however, are 8–12 metres high and 3–5 metres thick. There are 4 main gates and 82 towers, and the length of the circuit is 5km. The strongest defensive structures were naturally placed to cover the vulnerable sections.[366] In my opinion, it is likely that the original walls would have been similar in scope. (See the accompanying Map.)

According to Ammianus, the regular garrison consisted of the *Legio Parthica V* and of a *turma* of native (*indigenae*) cavalry. This garrison had been reinforced by six other legions (*Magnentiaci*, *Decentiaci*, *Legio XXX*, *Legio X Fortenses*, *Superventores*, and *Praeventores*) that had managed to reach the city before the Persians. The *Magnentiaci* and *Decentiaci* were Magnentius' former legions that Constantius had 'exiled' to the East while the *Superventores* and *Praeventores* (both under the *Comes* Aelianus) had been raised by Constantius, probably after 344. In addition, most of the elite *Comites Sagittarii* had taken refuge in the city alongside Ammianus. Altogether there were 20,000 soldiers, men, women and children in the city, of whom perhaps 8,000–14,000 were soldiers. The Romans were heavily outnumbered for the attacking force of Persians and their allies consisted of 100,000 men. Despite the odds the Romans were clearly expecting that the strengthened garrison would be able to defend the city because the walls evened out the odds.

Shapur marched from Bebase (later Dara?) through Horce (Horren), Meiacarire, and Charcha. However, when Shapur was near the fortresses Reman (unknown) and Busan (unknown), he learnt from deserters that people had brought their wealth there and that the beautiful wife of Craugausius of Nisibis was also there. Consequently, Shapur conquered these places and treated the captives courteously. His intention was to use the wife as a bargaining chip.

After this, Shapur marched to Amida despite the fact that the original plan was to bypass it and penetrate deeper into Roman territory as advised by Antoninus. Shapur rode in front of his whole army and then approached the gates in the company of his escort and signalled that he wanted to negotiate. When the Romans recognized him, they started to shoot arrows and other missiles, but they missed him thanks to the dust raised by the horses. Shapur was enraged and wanted to abandon the invasion plan and attack the city.

In my opinion, one may actually question the validity of the original plan to penetrate deep into Roman territory as suggested by Antoninus. If Shapur had marched across the Euphrates into Asia Minor he would have taken the risk of having his route of retreat cut off by the Roman field army posted at Edessa, and it is probable that he could have faced a similarly difficult retreat back home as Julian would face in 363. Consequently, it is possible that, luckily for him, Shapur actually made the right decision in anger when he stopped to besiege Amida and chose not to penetrate any deeper. Regardless, the original plan, as well as Julian's subsequent campaign, prove that there existed a school of thought both in Rome and Persia which favoured the taking of greater risks and which favoured the use of offensives deep into enemy territory, but which actually did not take into account the presence of vast numbers of fortified cities, towns and fortresses everywhere along the invasion route, and the presence of field armies that could be used to harass the invaders. In truth, in order for such a plan to succeed, the invader would have had to destroy the enemy's field army in a pitched battle in its entirety first and only then make a deeper penetration of enemy territory. Constantius understood this.

After his generals had calmed him down, Shapur decided to send another envoy on the next day to demand the surrender of the city. He sent the king of the Chionitae Grumbates forwards, but when the Chionitae came close enough a Roman sharpshooter killed Grumbates' son with a ballista dart. The Chionitae fled, but then returned when they realized that the Romans could carry off the corpse. The Romans sallied out. The Chionitae managed to take the body off the field at nightfall only after a prolonged battle. Both sides agreed to a seven day truce during which the Chionitae could mourn the dead prince and burn him on a funeral pyre.

After the Persians had rested two more days, they sent a large force to destroy the cultivated fields that the Romans had not burned thanks to the negligence of Ursicinus. The Persians surrounded the entire city with a line of shields five ranks deep (or, rather figuratively speaking, by the Persians and four allied nations). The Chionitae were placed opposite the eastern wall, the Gelani opposite the southern wall, the Albani opposite the northern wall, the Segestani (Sacae) with the elephants opposite the western wall, and the Persians in reserve. After the Persians had deployed around the city, they stood still until nightfall and then retired.

Next day, Grumbates ceremoniously threw a bloodstained *hasta* on the ground which signalled the beginning of the attack. The Persians (or rather their allies) charged forward and were met by a murderous barrage of darts, arrows, stones and javelins, while the Persians responded with showers of arrows and missiles shot from the artillery pieces they had captured from Singara. The defenders conserved their strength by working in relays.

The attack continued until nightfall, before it started afresh in the morning and once again lasted until nightfall, and so it continued until the constant toil and sleeplessness started to affect the defenders. Eventually the besieged were also hit by a plague as a result of the maggot-infested bodies scattered in the streets. The plague oddly stopped ten days after it had started when light showers cleared the air. In the meantime, Ursicinus had demanded that Sabinianus gather together all his lightly-armed troops with the purpose of starting to harass the besiegers, which Sabinianus considered dangerous and contrary to his orders, which stated that he was to conserve his men. Constantius could not help because he was still fighting against the Sarmatians. In addition, Sabinianus also faced another problem in the form of an Isaurian revolt behind his lines of communication (see later). In a sense both commanders were right. It is clear that Sabinianus' army was heavily outnumbered and it would have been unwise for him to risk a battle in the open with the Persians. On the other hand, Ursicinus was also right in that Sabinianus should

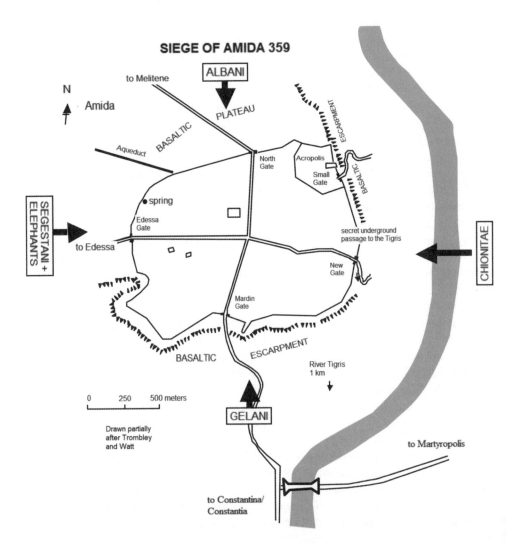

SIEGE OF AMIDA 359

have at least attempted to assist the besieged by means of a guerrilla campaign that didn't endanger the entire army. With the troops at his disposal Ursicinus was unable to achieve anything.

The Persians built sheds, mantlets, siege mounds, and iron-fronted towers each with a ballista on the top. While the Persians were doing this, the skirmishing with slingers and archers continued non-stop. It was then that the two Magnetian legions demanded that they be permitted to sally out into the open as they had previously done. According to Ammianus, these legions could only fight in the open field, and were totally unsuited to fighting from the walls. They could not use the artillery or build walls and their reckless sallies against the builders of the mound had been utterly useless and had only endangered the defence of the city. Consequently, the officers had barred the gates and forbidden them to make any more sallies. On the eastern side of the city (Ammianus mistakenly has southern) there was a secret tunnel from a tower down to the Tigris from which the defenders could bring additional water to the city. This tunnel was unguarded. A deserter from Amida led seventy Persian elite archers from the king's bodyguard to the tower in the middle of the night. In the morning these men displayed a cloak which was a signal for the Persians to begin the attack with scaling ladders. The Romans posted to defend the eastern wall divided their forces. Some defended the walls against the attackers while others attacked the Persians on the tower. The Romans moved five lighter ballistae against the tower and started a murderously rapid fire as a result of which the tower was cleared quickly and easily. All of the Persians were either killed or wounded or chose to jump to their death. The rapid rate of fire and the penetrative power of the darts (even two killed at a time) suggest the use of exceptionally-powerful repeating ballistae. After the mission was accomplished, the ballistae were returned to their original positions and the defenders felt more confident in their ability to defend the city.

On the following morning the Romans saw that the Persians were bringing captives to their camp from the fortress of Ziata, which they had captured, and this was not the end of Persian pillaging. They also seized and burned several other forts in the area and brought thousands of captives to their camp. The Gallic legions could not bear this sight and threatened to kill their tribunes and the general if they were not let out. The officers had no other alternative than to allow this, but on condition that they would attack such a spot in the enemy line which was not much further than a bowshot away from the city. The Gauls charged out with swords and axes in hand, surprised the outposts and outer guards of the camp who were sleeping, but were then forced to halt when they faced the enraged Persians coming at them from all directions. The Gauls faced them stoutly, but were eventually forced to flee back inside. The *tormenta* (torsion artillery) protected the flight by shooting 'blanks' (i.e no missiles), the noise of which frightened the Persians in the darkness. The Gauls had lost 400 men.

In the interim, the Persian infantry had built two mounds to a great height which the defenders opposed with a counter-mound built almost to the same height. The Persians brought forward their iron-clad towers, on top of which they had placed the ballistae to clear the walls of defenders. Shapur next sent forward his Persian iron-clad footmen protected either by penthouses or shields. When these came within bowshot, the Roman artillery broke their formations apart with the result that the attackers assumed open order and were killed even more easily. Even the cataphracts were forced to flee. However, the Roman victory had come at a great cost. The ballistae mounted on the Persian siege towers had killed a huge number of defenders. Consequently, the Romans spent the following night in devising plans on how to counter them. It was decided to place scorpions (onagers) against the towers. While these were being put in place, the Sacae began an attack with elephants. The Roman counter tactic proved effective and the round stones shot by the iron-armed scorpions broke down the towers while the elephants were routed by shooting firebrands at them. Note the use of iron arms in the onagers! The Romans also managed to burn the siege works with the result that Shapur rushed forward to fight like a common soldier, which was unheard of according to Ammianus, but could not save the day.

Next morning the Persians attempted to attack the city by using their mounds, as a result of which the Romans brought more earth on the inside to equal the height of the enemy mounds. This together with the mass of men standing on the mound proved too much for the groundwork. The mound collapsed forward and fell over the wall and filled up the gap between the wall and enemy mound and thereby created a causeway for the enemy to enter the city. The Persians rushed in and the Romans poured from all around to oppose them, but the Persians defeated the outnumbered and shocked defenders in a hard hand-to-hand combat with swords and burst into the city. The Persians slaughtered all they came across and the streets overflowed with corpses. Regardless, when night fell there were still large numbers of Roman soldiers fighting back, which enabled the historian Ammianus to hide with two others and then escape through a postern gate during the night. They managed to find their way to the Euphrates, but when they saw some Roman horsemen being pursued by Persian cavalry, they fled through the thickets, woods and mountains to Melitene, from which they returned to Antioch.

Meanwhile, the Persians had hanged the *Comes* Aelianus and all the tribunes. Persian deserters were also carefully searched for and killed. The paymasters of the *magistri equites*, Iacobus and Caesius, together with all of the *protectores* were taken prisoner so that these could be interrogated. Amida was a gateway to Asia Minor, but it was now too late in the year to continue the campaign. Winter was approaching and Shapur decided to retreat. The presence of the Roman field army in Edessa behind Shapur's lines of communication must also have played its role, alongside the casualties suffered so far. It was time to retreat.

The wife of Craugasius sent a message to her husband in which she begged him to follow. When Craugasius answered in the affirmative, Tamsapor (clearly the Spy-Chief), asked Shapur to grant him an asylum. In the meanwhile, the sudden arrival and departure of a foreigner had aroused suspicions against Craugasius. When the *Dux* Cassianus and other important officials threatened Craugasius, he, fearing a charge of treason, pretended to marry another woman (it was presumed that his wife had died) and was allowed to go outside the city to attend the marriage ceremonies, as a result of which he was able to flee at full gallop to a *globus* of Persians waiting for him. He was received by Tamsapor, who then took him to see the king who accorded Craugasius a rank just below Antoninus.

The siege of Amida had lasted for 73 days and had cost 30,000 casualties for the Persians. The figure appears to be approximately accurate, as it is based on the calculation made by the Roman *tribunus* and *notarius* Discenes after the siege. In addition to these we should obviously add the wounded Persians who survived the siege, but who could still have become maimed for life. The fact that the Persian army possessed medical services makes

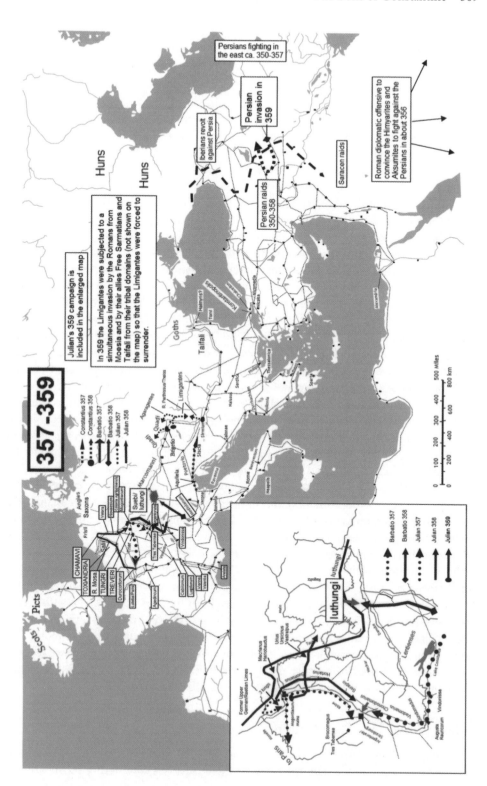

it likely that quite a few of the wounded would have survived. According to Ammianus (19.9.9), Shapur was greatly disturbed by this because he had always lost more men in sieges and battles against the Romans. The several sieges of Nisibis and Singara had been particularly costly. In this way Ammianus inadvertently admits that Constantius had also defeated Shapur near Singara in 344. It should be noted that Shapur had not suffered grievous damage this time because the bulk of the casualties would have been borne by the allies. Consequently, after having recruited more men, he was able to renew the offensive in the following year.

When the news of the fall of Amida was brought to the emperor, he ordered an investigation (Amm. 20.2). Ammianus states that the judges *Mag. Eq.* Arbitio and *Mag. Off.* Florentius, in fear of Eusebius, rejected all evidence against Sabinianus and concentrated on trivial matters with the result that Ursicinus lost his temper. He stated that his case could be examined only by Constantius and that as long as Constantius trusted his eunuchs, nobody, not even the emperor with his elite forces, would be able to prevent the destruction of Mesopotamia. When this outburst was brought to the emperor's attention, he retired Ursicinus and replaced him with Agilo, former tribune of the *Gentiles* and *Scutarii*. This investigation brings to light several interesting matters. There were simultaneously three *magistri equitum*, the highest ranking (*in praesenti*) Arbitio under Constantius, Lupicinus under Julian, and Sabinianus in the East. However, as far as we know there was only one *Mag. Ped.* , Ursicinus. Eusebius was clearly the de facto prime minister of the empire. The highest ranking officers continued to be selected from the ranks of the bodyguards. And, finally, Constantius was not the cruel and vindictive tyrant Ammianus makes him out to be. Constantius was quite ready to let Ursicinus retire.

As noted above, the Persians were not the only problem the Romans were facing in the East. The Isaurians either exploited the situation or acted in collusion with the invaders and besieged the city of Seleucia, and at the same time harassed other neighbours by bypassing the guard-posts and then fleeing to the mountains before their opponents could catch them. As a result, Constantius appointed Lauricius in charge of putting down the revolt. In order to achieve this in the most efficient way he was simultaneously appointed as *Comes* and *Rector* (governor) of Isauria. This proved to be a happy decision for he quickly suppressed the revolt with the use of threats rather than by force and as long as he remained in charge of the province, there was peace.[367]

In 359 while Constantius was back in Constantinople, he decided to increase its importance even further by creating the office of Urban Prefect of the city. Traditionally, only Rome had had an Urban Prefect, but henceforth the New Rome had one too. This office was considered the second most important in the Empire, directly after the Praetorian Prefect, and was so ranked in the Notitia Dignitatum. The fact that Constantinople was now the only city in the Empire in which the emperor was constantly in residence secured it also the most prestige. In contrast, the Western emperors changed their place of residence constantly, even if their courts were usually located in Trier and/or Milan.

Julian Shows His True Colours[368]

According to Ammianus, the Picts and Scots invaded north of Britain apparently in very late 359. He doesn't state the cause of the attack, but considering Julian's recent extraordinary confiscation of grain from Britain in 359 it is quite reasonable to suspect that some of the locals could have asked the barbarians to come to help them against Julian's officials. It is quite clear that Julian's measure of shipping grain from Britain for his army was not the usual method, because in all other instances Ammianus stated that the grain was brought from Aquitania. This must have caused plenty of anger in Britain. Ammianus states that Julian, who was passing the winter in Paris, feared to go across the sea because he was supposedly apprehensive that the Alamanni would invade if he left. Consequently, Julian dispatched the *Magister Armorum* Lupicinus with the Heruli, the Batavi, and two *numeri* of Moesians to settle the matters. This is likely to be rubbish. There are two likely reasons for Julian's action. Firstly, he feared to sail in the middle of winter. Secondly, he wanted to remove a general potentially loyal to Constantius from Gaul so that he could usurp power.

Consequently, Lupicinus advanced in the middle of winter to Bononia (Boulogne), crossed the Channel to Rutupias (Richborough) when the wind was favourable, and went to London to assess the situation and then take action. According to Ammianus, Lupicinus was a warlike man and skilled in military matters, but at the same time greedy and cruel, that is to say dishonest. Lupicinus appears to have been successful despite being 'corrupt'.

In the meanwhile, amidst his eastern troubles Constantius had received disturbing news regarding Julian's actions. The reports sent by the *PP* Florentius appear to have accused Julian of bad faith with very good reason. Constantius chose not to confront the question openly, but sent the *tribunus* and *notarius* Decentius to take away from Julian his *auxilia*, the *Heruli*, *Batavi*, *Celtae*, and *Petulantes*, together with 300 picked men from each of the other *numeri*, for Constantius' eastern campaign. The aim was clearly to remove, with a suitable excuse, those units from Julian that were potentially the most loyal to him, but it is also probable that Constantius needed good quality soldiers for his eastern campaign. These were to be taken to the East by the *Mag.Ped.* Lupicinus, because Constantius was unaware that he had been sent to Britain. This proves that Lupicinus was considered to be loyal and trustworthy. In addition, Constantius ordered that the *Tribunus Stabuli* Sintula was to choose the best fighters of the *Scutarii* (*Schola Scutariorum*) and *Gentiles* (*Schola Gentilium*) and then lead them in person to the emperor.

At first Julian appeared as if he would follow the order and only complained that the volunteers who had joined the army would not accept being led away from the Rhine frontier. Decentius didn't pay any attention, but chose the troops and went on his way. Ammianus claims that Julian was worried over how to proceed and therefore asked Florentius, who was at Vienna to obtain supplies, to return. Ammianus claims that Florentius was aware of the possible troubles and therefore chose to remain at Vienna, and then asserts that it was thanks to the absence of Lupicinus and Florentius that Julian decided to assemble his army. This is untrue. Julian's aim was undoubtedly to arrest Florentius and the latter understood the threat. However, it is still probable that if both men and their troops had been present, Julian would not have been able to usurp power.

After this, Julian's agent placed a letter in the camp of the *Petulantes* in which the soldiers supposedly voiced their grievances against the transfer, and when the letter was brought to Julian he found the complaints reasonable but still ordered the *Petulantes* with their families to the Orient. However, he gave the men the privilege of using the wagons of the postal service. Ammianus claims that it was Decentius who suggested that the soldiers would march via Paris where Julian stayed. This suggests two possibilities: Decentius was either a fool or Julian had bribed him. Julian met the men in the suburbs and then invited the officers to dinner. In this manner Julian tested the loyalty of the officers before making his next move, which was to give them orders on how to proceed. When the night came, these officers duly incited the men to a revolt, hailed Julian as Augustus and raised him on a shield. Julian in his turn promised each man a pound of silver and five gold coins. When Sintula heard of these developments he returned to Paris: he had obviously been tarrying on the road waiting for this.

Since Julian and his henchmen feared the reaction of Lupicinus, because according to Ammianus he was proud and arrogant and could therefore cause trouble, they dispatched a *notarius* to Bononia to prevent anyone from crossing the Channel. The precaution proved effective: Lupicinus turned back and was duly apprehended by Julian's men. Julian appointed Gomoarius as Lupicinus' successor. Florentius, however, was quicker. When he learnt of Julian's usurpation, he fled immediately to Constantius and even left his family behind. Florentius accused Julian as a traitor. Julian, however, responded with clemency and sent his family to him, because his intention was to win over followers while also keeping up the façade of friendship with Constantius.

Julian's position was not yet strong enough to challenge Constantius. It was for this reason that Julian sent an embassy led by the *Mag. Off.* Pentadius and *Praepositus Cubiculi* Eutherius to Constantius to inform him of events and to present Julian's excuses for what had happened. They found Constantius at Caesarea in Cappadocia on his way to the eastern front. Constantius was already well aware of what had happened from Decentius and from those *cubicularii* who had delivered to Julian part of his yearly income. Constantius only became angered when the envoys presented Julian's case. Julian claimed that the soldiers had forced him to become Augustus and promised that he would send Spanish horses for Constantius' chariots, and those of the *Laeti*, *Gentiles* and *Scutarii* who would volunteer. He also promised to accept Constantius' nomination for the position of Praetorian Prefect, but wanted to keep for himself the right to nominate the other officials, officers and bodyguards. Julian claimed that he could not send the *auxilia palatina* units because these were needed to pacify the barbarians of the Rhine frontier. In addition, Ammianus states that Julian also sent a secret letter to Constantius, but he did not know its contents and if he knew he would not disclose it. The subsequent events make it clear that Julian promised that he would maintain peace and would not attack Constantius. Constantius sent the ambassadors back without any answer.

After having pondered the situation for a long time, Constantius decided to treat Julian's usurpation as if nothing had happened and continued his march against the Persians. Constantius knew that Julian's position was weak. Julian did not possess enough men to threaten his position seriously. Consequently, Constantius simply sent his *Quaestor* Leonas to Gaul to declare that Constantius would not accept Julian as Augustus. He also appointed Julian's *Quaestor* Nebridius as Julian's new *PP* and the *notarius* Felix as his new *Mag. Off.*, and also made other similar appointments. Constantius' aim was to show his own confidence and to cause dissent among those whom Julian would possibly refuse to promote as ordered. Julian accepted the appointment of Nebridius, but not the others. Instead, he made his own appointments, the most significant of which was the promotion of Anatolius to the position of *Mag. Off.*, which does suggest that Julian considered him more trustworthy than Pentadius. Regardless, Julian still maintained the outward look of friendship towards Constantius and sent envoys to him to announce his continued loyalty and the actions he had taken or would take. In fact, Julian even appears to have sent the *Laeti* to the East as he had promised (Amm. 21.13.16). Julian confirms this in his Letter to the Athenians (280C-D) in which he referred to the sending of reinforcements (both elite and less good infantry) to Constantius.

After this, Julian began his campaign against the Franks by marching to Germania II. He crossed the Rhine near the city of Tricensima (modern Kellen) and attacked the Attuarii Franks, who according to Ammianus were in the habit of raiding Gaul. He caught the Franks unawares, as a result of which he managed to force them to beg for peace, which he granted. Julian returned across on the double and examined and strengthened the defences up to Rauracos. He fortified the places that the barbarians had previously destroyed and then marched via Vesontio to Vienna, where he passed the winter of 360/1 and made plans for the future. He undoubtedly wanted to make sure that there would not be any trouble caused by the former subordinates of Florentius in Vienna.

The Persian War, 360[369]

After having reinforced his army with equipment, men, supplies and arms, Shapur decided to exploit the absence of Constantius by invading early. Thanks to the fact that Constantius' preparations had been delayed by the worrisome news he had received from Gaul, Shapur had plenty of time to act before Constantius would reach the front. Shapur was unaware what the cause of the delay was but he used the intervening time well. This time, however, Shapur had changed his strategy. He no longer aimed to penetrate deep into Roman territory as Antoninus had suggested. It would have been very risky for him to penetrate deep this time because this time he would have eventually faced the elite Roman field army under Constantius himself. Now Shapur aimed only to destroy the key border fortresses of the Romans both south and north of Nisibis, and with this in mind he had taken with him heavier siege equipment than previously. He wanted to avoid Nisibis for two reasons. He had never had any success against this city and on top of this the Roman Eastern field army had now been stationed inside it.

The Siege of Singara, Early 360[370]

Shapur's first target was Singara, which he had already taken once before with the help of a huge battering ram after two failed and costly attempts. The defenders knew of the approaching storm, closed the gates, collected stones, and positioned the *tormenta* (torsion-artillery).

The city was defended by two legions, *Flavia I* (c. 2,000 men?) and *Parthica I* (c. 2,000 men?) and by significant numbers of natives and some cavalrymen who had taken refuge there thanks to the speed of the Persian invasion. According to Ammianus, the Romans were unable to bring aid to the defenders because most of the Roman forces had been posted to defend Nisibis, which was too far off. He claims that nobody had ever been able to bring help to Singara because the surrounding country consisted of dry desert.

This sounds like an excuse for the failure of Ursicinus to help the city in 351/3. He also states that Singara had been fortified to act as a forward guardpost against sudden enemy invasions. In his opinion this had been detrimental because the Persians had conquered the place 'several' times. Ammianus' account is once again very biased. In light of his comments, it is clear that Constantius in 344 and the Persians on several occasions had achieved very significant logistical feats when they campaigned in the area, which proves that it was by no means impossible to do that. As regards the Roman decision to fortify Singara, Ammianus is at fault once again. The fact that the Persians attacked the city again and again despite their terrible losses proves that it was a thorn in their side, and the fact that they suffered far more casualties in attacking Singara than the Romans in defending it proves that Singara served its purpose really well.

When Shapur reached Singara, he sent his *optimates* (grandees) forward to convince the defenders to give up, but in vain. Next morning Shapur ordered his army to assault the city from every direction. Some brought ladders, others war-engines, others *vinea* (penthouses) and *plutei* (mantlets), and still others tried to undermine the foundations of the walls. The townsmen responded by shooting stones and missiles. The assault continued for several days without any result. This situation lasted until the Persians had managed to assemble the exceptionally-strong battering ram that had previously breached the city wall.

Towards the evening (so that the Romans could not use their artillery as effectively as during the daytime) the Persians brought the battering ram against the very same round tower that they had previously brought down with it. The Romans concentrated their forces opposite this very same spot and shot firebrands and fire darts, and threw torches at it in an effort to burn it. In addition, both sides continuously employed showers of arrows against the enemy personnel to force the other side to leave their battle stations. According to Ammianus, everything was in vain because the ram soon penetrated the joints between the stones, which were still moist and therefore weak. This implies that the tower had been rebuilt only recently, which means that the city was probably left ungarrisoned for several years after its first fall. The tower fell and the Persians rushed in. They killed only a small number of defenders, because the majority surrendered and were transported to the faraway corners of Persia.

Siege of Bezabde, Summer 360[371]

After this, Shapur 'turned right' and marched obliquely against the city of Bezabde, and avoided going near the city of Nisibis. This probably means that Shapur retreated back and marched northwards via the road that ended between Castra and Bezabde. Shapur's intention was also not to penetrate too deep into Roman territory for fear of facing Constantius' palatine forces. However, Constantius' march was delayed by the news of Julian's usurpation while he was still at Caesarea. It was only after he had decided that he would move against the Persians that he continued his march. In the meantime, however, Shapur had placed Bezabde under siege. According to Ammianus, Bezabde was a very strong fortress placed on a hill, which was protected by a double wall on the side where it was vulnerable. It was defended by *Flavia II*, *Armeniaca II*, *Parthica II*, and

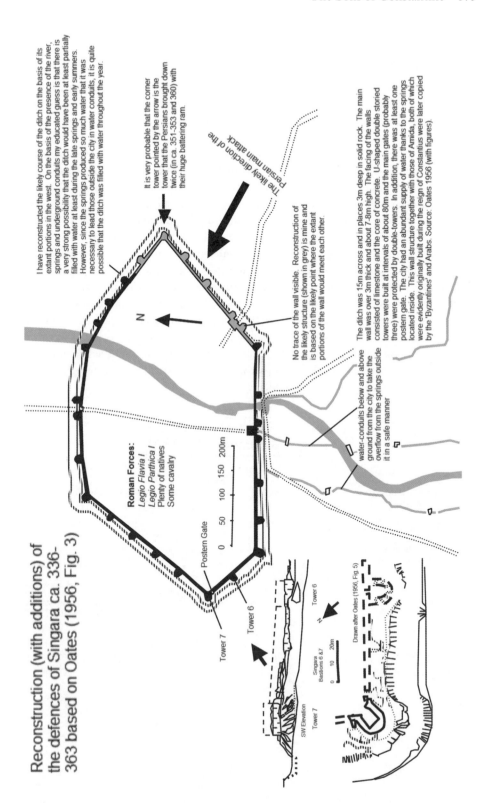

Reconstruction (with additions) of the defences of Singara ca. 336-363 based on Oates (1956, Fig. 3)

I have reconstructed the likely course of the ditch on the basis of its extant portions in the west. On the basis of the presence of the river, springs and underground conduits my educated guess is that there is a very strong possibility that the ditch would have been at least partially filled with water at least during the late springs and early summers. However, since the springs produced so much water that it was necessary to lead those outside the city in water conduits, it is quite possible that the ditch was filled with water throughout the year.

It is very probable that the corner tower pointed by the arrow is the tower that the Persians brought down twice (in ca. 351-353 and 360) with their huge battering ram.

The likely direction of the Persian main attack.

No trace of the wall visible. Reconstruction of the likely structure (shown in grey) is mine and is based on the likely point where the extant portions of the wall would meet each other.

Roman Forces:
Legio Flavia I
Legio Parthica I
Plenty of natives
Some cavalry

0   50   100   150   200m

Postern Gate

water-conduits below and above ground from the city to take the overflow from the springs outside it in a safe manner

The ditch was 15m across and in places 3m deep in solid rock. The main wall was over 3m thick and about 7-8m high. The facing of the walls consisted of limestone and the core of concrete. U-shaped double storied towers were built at intervals of about 80m and the main gates (probably three) were protected by double-towers. In addition, there was at least one postern gate. The city had an abundant supply of water thanks to the springs located inside. This wall structure together with those of Amida, both of which were evidently originally built during the reign of Constantius were later copied by the 'Byzantines' and Arabs. Source: Oates 1956 (with figures).

Tower 7

Tower 6

Tower 6

SW Elevation
Tower 7

Singara
Bastions 6 & 7

0   10   20m

Drawn after Oates (1956, Fig. 5)

great numbers of local Zabdiceni archers. This would probably mean about 4,000–6,000 legionaries and perhaps the same number of locals.

At first the *Shahanshah* rode around the city with his cataphract cavalry to reconnoitre the defences, but when he reached the edge of the trenches he was met by a hail of missiles shot from ballistae and bows. His men, however, formed a tortoise of shields for his protection and helped him to flee. This proves that the Persian cataphracts also carried shields. Then the king sent heralds to urge the defenders to surrender. They were let close by the defenders only because they were protected by prisoners taken at Singara who now acted as human shields for the heralds, but the Romans did not give any response, as a result of which the heralds eventually retreated in frustration.

The Persians began their attack with an assault. They advanced under the protective fire of their archers, some carrying ladders while others carried osiers to fill up the ditch. Ammianus claims that both sides suffered equal losses. The clouds of Persian arrows supposedly found their targets among the Romans because they were forced to crowd together. This seems improbable, because the Persians in the open were easier targets than the Romans. Ammianus claims that combat continued with the same results for the next two days until the chief priest of the local Christians was allowed to go and negotiate with Shapur. Ammianus claims that the priest's mission was to tell Shapur to go home. However, he also maintained that some Romans suspected the priest of having told Shapur which parts of the city to attack because it was after this that the Persians started to target those sections of the defences that were insecure thanks to the decay. Ammianus considered these suspicions unfounded.

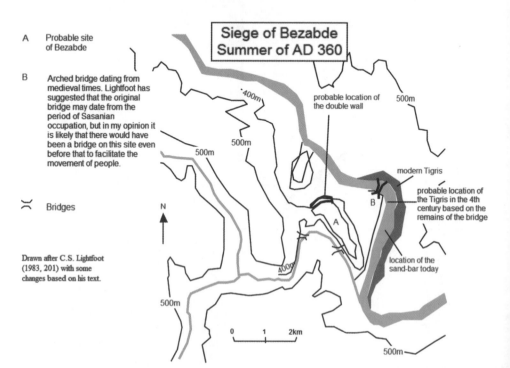

A   Probable site
    of Bezabde

B   Arched bridge dating from
    medieval times. Lightfoot has
    suggested that the original
    bridge may date from the
    period of Sasanian
    occupation, but in my opinion it
    is likely that there would have
    been a bridge on this site even
    before that to facilitate the
    movement of people.

≍   Bridges

Drawn after C.S. Lightfoot
(1983, 201) with some
changes based on his text.

**Siege of Bezabde
Summer of AD 360**

probable location of
the double wall

modern Tigris

probable location of
the Tigris in the 4th
century based on the
remains of the bridge

location of the
sand-bar today

400m   500m

500m

500m

N

500m

0   1   2km

500m

By now the Persians had managed to assemble their rams, which they brought forward despite the difficulty of the operation. The defenders responded with ballistae, scorpions (*onagri*), arrows and stones thrown by hand. The fiery darts, and the stones and wicker baskets (fire-bombs filled with pitch and bitumen) shot by the scorpions kept the Persians at bay, but this only encouraged them to try even harder. Eventually, at a great cost in lives, the Persians managed to bring their biggest ram, covered with wet bulls' hides, against a weakened tower. Its beak dug into the joints between the stones and brought the tower down. Since Ammianus states that the Persians rushed forward into the town after this, it is clear that the attack had not been made against the section with the double wall. The defenders, however, did not give up but fought with drawn swords at close quarters with the attackers, yet eventually the Persians pushed their way through thanks to their overwhelmingly superior numbers. The angry Persians vented their anger by butchering everyone regardless of age or sex, and took as spoils everything even remotely valuable.

Shapur had wished to take Bezabde for a long time, as a result of which he now repaired the destroyed sections of the walls, stored supplies inside, and chose elite troops of high birth to act as its garrison. Shapur knew that the Romans would attempt to retake this fortress because of its strategic position. Lightfoot (190) has aptly summarized the strategic importance of Bezabde as follows: 1) it was strategically situated to control Zabdicene; 2) it blocked the way to Arzanene and Sophanene, as well as the strategic passes that led through the Taurus mountains into central Armenia; and 3) it could serve as a forward base of operations for the Romans into Corduene, and may have been used for this purpose during the 340s.

Shapur exploited the absence of Constantius by moving further inland along the Tigris towards Amida. En route to Virta he captured some small and insignificant fortresses, but Virta's well-positioned and prepared ancient defences with salient angles frustrated every effort Shapur made. He used promises, embankments and all kinds of siege engines, before he had to give up. I would suggest that the immediate cause of Shapur's flight was that he had learnt that Constantius had finally made up his mind to move against the Persians and that he had already reached Melitene or Lacotena. (See below.)

Constantius' Defensive and Offensive Operations against Shapur, 360[372] (See Maps Section)

During the winter of 359/360 Constantius had assembled new recruits and arms, had brought the legions to full strength with young recruits, and had asked the Scythians (that is, the Goths) to contribute auxiliaries so that he could march with them from Thrace in late spring (Amm. 20.8.1). Of particular note is Ammianus' statement in this context that the steadiness of these legions in action during oriental campaigns had brought several notable successes in the past: in other words, he admits that Constantius' legions had proved themselves in combat against the Persians! Of note is also the fact that Constantius asked the Goths to contribute a contingent of their superb lancers to the war. In this Constantius and his staff were following a well-trodden path. The Romans had been using the Gothic lancers against the Parthians/Persians at least from the reign of Caracalla onwards, because their effectiveness was well-known.

After having decided to treat Julian's usurpation as a bad joke, Constantius continued his march against the Persians. However, before moving against the invader Constantius called Arshak (Arsaces), the King of Armenia, to meet him in Caesarea. He had heard that the Persian king had attempted to influence Arshak to abandon his alliance with Rome through deception and threats and wanted to secure his ongoing loyalty. The Armenian king swore that he would be forever loyal because he was in personal debt to Constantius for his kindness. Constantius rewarded the king for his continued loyalty and sent him back to Armenia. After the loss of Bezabde, it was particularly important for Constantius to secure the loyalty of the Armenian king because the Persian ruler was now in a position to threaten Armenia from still another direction. Arshak must have been somewhere close by with his army for him to have been able to arrive on such a short notice.

Constantius marched against the Persian invaders finally in late-July or early-August. Constantius' itinerary consisted of Melitene, Lacotena, Samosata, and Edessa, where he arrived either in late-August or September. It is obvious from the selection of the route that Constantius' intention was to march directly against Shapur if he continued his march towards Amida. The same route also makes certain that when Constantius learnt that Shapur had withdrawn he could change his route of march towards Edessa, where he probably joined forces with the Eastern Field Army previously posted at Nisibis. According to Ammianus, Constantius stayed at Edessa for a long time waiting for the arrival of reinforcements and supplies from all quarters. After 21 September, Constantius left Edessa and marched to Amida. He surveyed the damage and wept when he saw the piles of ashes. Regardless of the cost, the city was rebuilt.

Constantius continued his march from there to Bezabde, where he built a fortified camp for his army. Then he rode around the city at a safe distance as a result of which he became aware that the Persians had strengthened those points in particular that had been previously weakened through neglect. After this, he offered to let the enemy go, if they would surrender. When the enemy refused, Constantius ordered his legions to assault the town from every side. The soldiers advanced in tortoise-formations and tried to undermine the walls, but when they came close, their shield roofs collapsed under the weight of enemy missiles. The Romans rested for one day during which they built *vimineae* (wicker mantlets). Then the Romans attacked again. The Persian defenders had built a screen/sail of hair-cloth to defend themselves against Roman missiles, and they emerged from behind this screen whenever they needed to counter the Romans. When the Romans brought their sheds close to the walls, the Persians dropped from above great jars, millstones and pieces of columns that crushed the sheds underneath. The Romans continued their futile attempts until on the tenth day they decided to put together the great ram that the Persians had previously used to crush the walls of Antioch in the 250s and had then abandoned at Carrhae, and build mounds for this monster as well as for the smaller rams. While this was going on, both sides employed artillery to great effect. According to Ammianus, many Roman soldiers died needlessly because they had removed their helmets so that the emperor could recognize them. As a result, the expert Persian archers/sharpshooters were able to target their exposed heads.

When the mounds had reached a great height, the Persians attempted to set the mounds and rams on fire with firebrands and darts, but with no results because the timbers were covered with wetted hides and rags, and all places had been coated with alum. Consequently, the Romans were able to push the rams forward against the walls, but the Persians had prepared effective counter-measures. When the giant ram was about to start its operation, the Persians lifted its ram-shaped iron head up from both sides with long ropes and at the same time poured down hot pitch on the device. In addition, they targeted all of the engines with missiles and huge stones. The Romans withdrew their machines. When the Romans had raised their mounds even higher so that the Persians could not use these counter-measures, the Persians made a reckless sally through the gates. They brought with them firebrands and 'iron-baskets' filled with fire (some sort of explosive?). The Persians, however, were forced back inside and when they returned to their walls they were subjected to a relentless bombardment of arrows, slingshots, and fire-darts. Thanks to the presence of the screen and the use of firefighters, the Roman missile attack had little effect on the defenders. Regardless, the defenders' situation was now becoming desperate. As a result, they repeated their sally with even more troops. This time their attack met with greater success and they were able to place the iron-baskets with fire, plus faggots and other fire-kindling devices, on the woodwork of the mounds. The resulting clouds of black smoke engulfed the Romans. Constantius ordered the reserve legions to attack the enemy.

When the men were fighting hand-to-hand, all of a sudden all of the Roman siege-engines, except the great ram, were destroyed by the fires. This does suggest that the Persians were using some sort of explosive/incendiary (possibly proto-gunpowder with low-nitrate or higher nitrate powders, but not yet true gunpowder) in their iron-baskets because these clearly exploded or engulfed everything on fire all of a sudden at the same time. The Romans were able to save the great ram in a half-burned state only thanks to the bravery of the soldiers.

The Romans also appear to have built earthworks/mounds on the other sides which had not been destroyed at the same time as the rams, because on the next day they placed two ballistae on top of every mound that now overtopped the walls. Constantius arrayed his army in a *triplex acies* for the assault of the walls, which in this case probably means they had three columns (one for each mound?) or they attacked from three sides. According to Ammianus, the men had cones on their helmets and some of the men carried ladders. When the Romans noted that the Persians had hidden themselves to avoid being transfixed by the darts of the ballistae, the Romans brought forward a ram against a tower. In addition, they brought forward scaling ladders, mattocks, pickaxes and crowbars. Consequently, the Persians were forced to assume their defensive positions with the result that they started to suffer badly from the effects of ballista fire, which came down on them like on a tight rope: meaning that the Romans were clearly employing rapid fire repeating ballistae. In desperation most of the Persians sallied out of a postern gate. The Persian swordsmen protected those who brought forward concealed fires. The Persians managed to set one of the mounds on fire with coals, as a result of which the Romans were forced to withdraw their ballistae from it. The night put a stop to the fight.

Now the emperor decided to stop the active measures and settled on starving the defenders. It was just too costly to waste men against the desperate defence. However, thanks to the late season the situation became untenable for the Romans. The wet weather made life miserable and when one added to the equation that the winter was fast approaching, the emperor decided that it was wisest to withdraw rather than face the prospect of mutiny of the army. Consequently, Constantius led his army to its winter quarters.

Constantius spent the following winter at Antioch as usual. During his stay Constantius married Faustina, because his beloved Eusebia had died some time before. Faustina became pregnant very soon after this. During all this time Constantius was busy making preparations against the Persians for the coming campaign season. He levied troops from the provinces, called additional reinforcements, and collected clothes, arms, siege-artillery, supplies and money as taxes. Of note is Ammianus' (21.6.6) referral to the siege-artillery (*tormenta*) which had proved particularly effective against the Persians. This suggests that Constantius and his staff had assessed the effectiveness of the various tactics previously used during the siege of Bezabde.

Constantius also sent envoys with gifts (bribes) to the kings and satraps beyond the Tigris in an effort to buy their loyalty. In light of the events that occurred subsequently during Julian's reign it seems probable that Constantius' diplomatic efforts were not only directed to the rulers beyond the Tigris, but also the various Arab kings on the Roman side of the border. Julian's campaign makes it practically certain that the Tanukhids were loyal Roman allies, while the Lakhmids of Hira and the Ghassanids were allies of Persia. The conflict between the Himyarites, who were Roman allies, and the Lakhmids continued into the reign of Julian. Constantius paid particular attention towards Arshak, the King of Armenia, and Meribanes (Mirdat, son of Arshak), the King of Iberia. Constantius never forgot the importance of diplomacy and bribes in warfare. Constantius also appointed the absolutely loyal Florentius as *PP* of Illyricum, because its *PP* had recently died. At the time, Italy was still in Constantius' hands, but the situation was about to change.

We have the first extant piece of evidence for the successful implementation of Constantius' alliance with the Himyarites for the year 360. According to one Yemeni inscription dated to June 360, the Yemeni armies were fighting in Yamana, in Central Arabia close to ar-Riyad, and in Abd al-Qays. These areas were to be organized by the Himyarites under their client Kingdom of the Kinda probably towards the end of the century.[373] The simultaneous referrals to the invasions of the Persian coast by the Aksumites in the Georgian Chronicles (p. 155, during Archil/Arsak's reign while his son Mirdat had taken the throne of Iberia) suggest that the Himyarites were probably fighting as clients of the Kingdom of Aksum and thereby creating a much needed diversion on the Persian Gulf at the time Constantius was fighting against the Persians in Mesopotamia. The same chronicle also mentions the attack of the Indians and Sinds in the east against Persia. As noted above, Constantius had formed alliances with all these peoples during the previous decade and their invasion of Persian territory should be seen to reflect this. Indeed, the first results of this policy would start to yield dividends in the following year, but Julian would high-handedly dismiss these.

Julian the Dragon[374]

As noted above, Julian spent the winter of 360/1 at Vienna. According to Ammianus it was only then that Julian decided to openly oppose Constantius because he feared that he would face the same fate as his brother Gallus, but this is likely to be just Ammianus' justification for Julian's betrayal of Constantius' trust. Vienna was the logistical hub of the Prefecture of Gaul and it is probable that Julian not only wanted to secure the loyalty of the supply officers posted there, but that he also went there to organize the logistical aspects of his forthcoming campaign against Constantius, which needed readjustment from the practices followed previously. He also started to collect additional forces for his campaign against Constantius, which included re-enlisting former disbanded soldiers of Magnentius (Lib. Or. 18.104).

Julian celebrated the quinquennial in grand style as Augustus and then sent the remains of his dead wife Helena to Rome to lie beside the dead wife of his brother. In this context it is interesting to note that Helena was a devout Orthodox Christian and that her death occurred very soon after Julian had usurped power at Paris in 360. She had previously had a miscarriage in about 357, which Ammianus claims to have resulted from Eusebia's potion: Eusebia was childless. Even before this, Helena had given birth to a boy who had died because the umbilical cord had been cut too short. Ammianus fails to give any cause of death for Helena. Ammianus' stories of Eusebia plotting against Helena and Julian seem like a story concocted by Julian. This doesn't correlate with what Ammianus claims about Eusebia before this. It was Eusebia who had recommended Julian and had been behind his promotion and marriage to Helena. One may rather suspect that Julian hated Constantius so intensely that he was behind the deaths of the children and also of Helena, who after all was Constantius' sister and a devout Christian. After his usurpation Julian was definitely in a position to kill Helena so that he could later take a pagan wife of his own choice. It is quite possible or even probable that the pagan Julian would have sought to soothe his brother's manes with the death of Constantius' sister – a sister for a dead brother. The only person near Helena at the times of her misfortunes was Julian and his staff. I would in particular suspect the pagan doctor Oribasius. The almost simultaneous cause of death of Eusebia resulting from wasting away is also unknown. Considering Ammianus' tendentious reporting, it is perhaps possible to suspect that her death may also have been unnatural. In the meantime Julian sought solace from the company of harlots.[375]

Ammianus claims that Julian was now ready to attack Constantius because Gaul was supposedly at peace and because Julian had learnt from 'dreams' that Constantius would die soon. According to Ammianus this had nothing to do with the black magic supposedly practised by Julian, but was based on his sound scientific understanding of the signs sent by the gods. This latter in particular raises the possibility that Julian and his pagan friends had managed to infiltrate Constantius' palace staff with an assassin. (See later.) Since Julian's position was not yet secure, he still publicly pretended to be a Christian in order to gather support from the Nicene Christians against the Arian/Homoean Constantius. Only his most intimate and best friends knew that he was a pagan. Julian was clearly a very skilled actor – a psychopath with great ability to playact his role. He was clearly able to fool most of his observers and supporters.

In the midst of his war preparations, probably in February or March 361, Julian learnt that the Alamanni kings he had previously attacked and 'pacified' had attacked through the Canton of Vadomarius, who was at peace with Romans, and devastated Raetia. In response Julian sent the *Celtae* and *Petulantes* under their *Comes* Libino against the invaders. When Libino reached the town of Sanctio, he saw a number of barbarians in front of him and decided to attack, even though he had only a small army. Unfortunately for him, the Alamanni had posted the bulk of their forces in an ambush in the valleys. Libino attacked at the head of his army and was the first to be killed. The Romans fled headlong after only a few of them had been killed or wounded.

Ammianus claims that according to a rumour (undoubtedly spread by Julian's men) Constantius had ordered Vadomarius, who was considered to be loyal, to break up the peace secretly and cause Julian troubles in Gaul in order to keep him preoccupied. It was supposedly because of this that Vadomarius had allowed the other tribesmen to pass through his territories against Julian. Of note is that no such suspicions were levelled previously against Suomarius by Ammianus, when Suomarius was forced to allow other tribesmen to march against Julian although he had concluded a *foedus* with Julian. The truth must be the opposite. Julian just concocted an excuse to eliminate Constantius' supporter. He could not leave Constantius' loyal ally behind his lines of communication.

Vadomarius had sent a letter to Constantius in which he warned him not to trust the wily Julian. When Julian's guards at the border captured the messenger with the letter, Julian decided to capture Vadomarius with a ruse. He sent his *notarius* (secretary) Philargius to the scene with a sealed note which he was to open only when Vadomarius was on the Roman side of the Rhine. When Vadomarius then crossed the river, because he believed that there was nothing to be feared since he was an ally, he was duly captured at a banquet and then exiled to Spain. Julian could not believe his good luck and immediately exploited the situation by crossing the river at night with only the unencumbered auxiliary forces and surrounded and surprised the enemy. As a result, there was 'peace'.[376]

Now Julian was ready to launch his long-planned lightning campaign against Constantius. His aim was to achieve a surprise. Julian aimed to capture Illyricum and Dacia while the bulk of the regular forces were still in the east with Constantius, and while the Illyrian forces were still spread out in their winter quarters. When Nebridius learnt of Julian's decision to attack Constantius, he showed unprecedented loyalty in a dangerous situation and stated that he could not betray Constantius because he owed everything to his kindness. Julian, like Julius Caesar before him, chose to fight through clemency and therefore allowed Nebridius to leave in safety back to his home. In order to secure his rear Julian appointed Germanianus as the new *PP*, replaced Gomoarius with Nevitta, appointed Jovius as *Quaestor*, made Mamertinus *Comes Sacrarum Lagitionum*, and appointed Dagalaifus as *Com. Dom.* This series of new appointments also proves that Julian could not entirely trust the previous office holders. Of these at least Gomoarius was able to flee to Constantius.

After this, Julian ordered his army to begin its march into Pannonia along the Danube. Being bookwise Julian emulated two of the greatest military leaders of all time: 1) he copied Julius Caesar's lightning attack at the beginning of Civil War in 49 BC by launching his initial offensive with only a small force; and 2) he copied Alexander the Great's (and Caesar's) tactic of dividing his forces into three divisions to spread terror among the enemy and also to make his army appear bigger than it was (Amm. 21.8.2–3). In other words, Julian launched his campaign with the forces he had at hand and ordered the rest to follow behind. Julian ordered Jovinus (*Mag.Eq.*) and Jovius to lead their forces into Italy, while Nevitta was to lead his forces into Raetia. The column under Nevitta and Julian marched to the Danube and boarded boats. Julian's plan was to bypass the usual and well-defended route through the Julian Alps and use the Danube as his highway. He must have assembled ships for this in advance, which proves Julian's premeditation.

However, we should still not make the mistake of believing that Julian's army would have been as small as claimed by Ammianus. He had spent the previous years enrolling additional forces into the army. For example, according to Zosimus (3.8) Julian had enrolled the Salii, and some of the Batavians and Quadi (probably Alamanni), which means that Julian no longer had a field army of a mere 13,000 men plus the garrisons. Regardless, it is still clear that he was heavily outnumbered and outmatched as far as the number and quality of troops is concerned. Constantius also possessed vastly greater numbers of superior quality cavalry. In addition, Constantius had the advantage in the numbers of experienced high-ranking commanders and in the quantity and quality of military equipment, and also possessed mastery of the seas. Julian had clearly taken a huge gamble.

In order to maintain operational security and to speed up his progress Julian chose not to enter any fort or town or city en route. Regardless of these safety measures, the enemy still learnt of the imminent arrival of his forces so that Taurus, the *PP* of Italy, was able to flee across the Julian Alps by using the horses of the public post and to take with him Florentius, the *PP* of Illyricum. Lucillinianus, the *Comes et Magister Equitum* in Illyricum (PLRE1), with his headquarters at Sirmium, also hastily collected together all those troops that he could assemble at a moment's notice, but regardless of this he was caught by surprise. When Julian reached Bononea, at a distance of 19 miles from Sirmium, he disembarked his *expediti*-troops under Dagalaifus to capture Lucillinianus with a commando attack. These forces surprised the commander still asleep in his bed. When he woke up because of the noise he found himself surrounded by Dagalaifus' men. The captive naturally begged for mercy, which was granted. Lucillianus was allowed to retire to Sirmium.

It had taken one surgical strike for Julian to gain possession of the Army of Illyria. Julian and his men were clearly experts in commando-style operations. It is probable that the father of this style of fighting was the abovementioned Charietto and Julian had clearly been a very adept pupil of these tactics. It is quite probable that the capture of Lucillianus is the instance in which Julian's men were equipped in the uniforms of the men they had captured, as a result of which they were admitted inside a fortified city (Lib. Or. 18.111). During this lightning campaign Julian had also used the earlier letters of Constantius in which Constantius had asked the Alamanni to attack during the usurpation of Magnentius (Lib. Or.18.111–113) and possibly also some forged letters to the same effect to convince the garrisons to change sides.

When Julian then boldly marched into Sirmium, he was received with shouts of Augustus and Dominus. He duly rewarded the populace with chariot races on the next day, but by the third he had already started to make preparations for the future. He ordered Nevitta to march to Serdica and take charge of the defence of the Succi Pass against the Army of Thrace. Julian had arrived with too few forces to attempt to move past the pass. The rest of Julian's forces were still en route, converging towards the predetermined assembly point. Having left Nevitta at Succi, Julian returned to Naissus, which possessed a magazine full of supplies, and appointed Sextus Aurelius Victor, the future historian, as governor of Pannonia II. After this, Julian sent a letter to the Roman Senate in which he charged Constantius of various crimes and asked their support. The Senate, however, declared its unanimous support for Constantius. In this case, Ammianus censures Julian for having poor taste and consideration: Julian had criticized Constantine for making innovations and for appointing barbarians as consuls, but did exactly the same.

He appointed the 'boorish' and cruel barbarian Nevitta, together with Mamertinus, as consuls in 362. In my opinion, however, Nevitta certainly deserved his consulship for he had played a crucial role in Julian's successes.

When Julian had conquered Sirmium he had immediately dispatched two legions, a cohort of archers and a *turma* of cavalry to the Rhine frontier, because he could not fully trust Constantius' forces. His fears proved well-founded. When these forces reached Aquileia, they revolted under Nigrinus, a native of Mesopotamia and the tribune of a *turma* of cavalry. Their revolt was supported by two local senators and the populace. Now Julian faced a serious problem. The revolt at Aquileia posed a threat to his line of supply. Consequently, Julian sent an order to Jovinus, who had entered Noricum, to return to Italy immediately to crush the revolt: in other words, Jovinus had by now secured Italy and its navies together with Sicily and had left an army behind with the mission to conquer Africa at the first possible opportunity (Amm. 21.7). Constantius, however, had been quicker and had already secured Africa before those forces could attempt to make a landing. When Constantius had heard of Julian's revolt, one of his first actions had been to send his *notarius* Gaudentius by sea to Africa. The local *Comes* Cretio and the other commanders in Africa immediately assembled their own forces and the allied Mauritanian light-armed troops to guard the shores 'opposite' Aquitania and Italy. The strong forces already posted in Sicily by Julian for the purpose of securing the African grain supply achieved nothing. The fact that Jovinus was not marching through the direct route via Julian Alps but had entered Noricum means that his mission was to collect reinforcements from the forces posted to protect the Danube frontier and then take these forces to Julian. Now these troops, together with those that were still en route from Gaul and probably also from Britain, were directed against the city of Aquileia.

Being a learned man Julian knew that no-one had been able to take Aquileia through force in the past and this proved to be the case this time too. Jovinus' men surrounded the city immediately with 'a double line of shields', which probably means that it was surrounded from both sides of the river. The generals attempted to force the defenders to surrender with this show of military might but in vain. The attackers attempted to undermine the defences underneath their mantlets, but when these were brought below the walls the defenders dropped heavy stones on them: the mantlets were crushed and the exposed attackers were subjected to a hail of missiles. After this, the defenders placed their artillery in suitable places and protected the wall very effectively. The besiegers finally realized that there were no good sites for the location of mines or use of their rams and other siege-engines, as a result of which they resolved to attack from the direction of the river. They decided to build towers higher than the walls on groups of three ships. The idea was that the men on the top would clear the walls of defenders so that the men below could drop their bridges on the walls. The plan failed. When the ships approached the walls, the defenders shot fire-darts and kindling material with the result that the towers were toppled and some of the attackers pierced with darts shot by the mural artillery. The footsoldiers who had taken part in the attack were crushed underneath huge stones. After this, the besiegers attempted to storm the wall by sending their men forward in tortoise-arrays while others carried ladders and still others iron bars to break the gates. The attack failed badly. Some were killed with fire, and some with stones and the rest put to flight with a sudden sally from a postern gate.

Eventually the besiegers gave up and settled on starving the defenders out, but even this turned out badly because the besiegers carried out their duties so badly that the defenders managed to gather supplies from the surrounding fields. The besiegers also attempted to subdue the defenders through thirst. They cut down the aqueduct and then even turned the course of the river, but all in vain because there were wells inside the city. In the end, the siege ended only after the defenders had been informed of the death of Constantius by the *Mag.Ped.* Agilo in person. The defenders were pardoned, except Nigrinus who was convicted by the *PP* Mamertinus as the ringleader of the revolt and burned to death. The two local senators were also convicted of treason and beheaded.

Despite the initial success of Julian's surprise attack, his position was by no means strong. The siege of Aquileia tied up significant numbers of troops that could have been used elsewhere. In addition, when the news of his attack had reached the *Comes* Martianus in Thrace he had immediately assembled the Army of Thrace and had begun to march towards the Pass of Succi. In response Julian had assembled and posted the Illyrian Army to protect the pass, but this was all he could do. In order to regain his momentum, Julian had to wait for the arrival of reinforcements, and even then he was heavily outnumbered and outclassed in the quality of troops.[377] Consequently, it is not surprising that according to Ammianus everyone expected that Constantius would emerge as the victor of the civil war (e.g. Amm. 21.7.3). Julian's forces would have had no chance against the far superior elite forces of Constantius. Julian's position was desperate, and this is also noted by the period author Nazianzus (Or.4 Against Julian 1.47–48). Julian did not have enough high-quality forces to defeat even the Army of Thrace let alone the elite army of Constantius. And, we should also not forget that Julian could not put his full trust in the loyalty of the Army of Illyricum because these men had previously served under Constantius and not under Julian. Julian's only hope was that his assassination plot against Constantius would work out as planned. He had taken a desperate gamble.

Constantius' Persian War, 361[378]

When Constantius learnt of Julian's betrayal, he pondered for a long time whether he should first march against the Persians or whether to march against Julian. After several discussions with his generals, Constantius formulated a plan according to which he would first deal with the Persian threat after which he would conquer both Illyricum and Italy and capture Julian. When Constantius' generals (*duces*) informed him that Persian forces had been assembled under their *Shahanshah* and were approaching the Tigris, he moved out of winter quarters and assembled his army. The rest were left to defend their respective forts, towns, cities and surroundings. The above confirms the sequence in which military intelligence was gathered and disseminated in normal circumstances. The *duces* on the frontiers were in charge of collecting information concerning enemy activity, and after they had collected it they disseminated it to their superiors.

Constantius crossed the Euphrates on a bridge of boats at Capersana and marched to Edessa, which was centrally located, strongly fortified and well supplied with provisions and therefore a suitable location to serve as Constantius' military headquarters. It was also a place where he could await further information regarding the enemy's movements from his scouts.

According to Ammianus (21.13.1–2), Shapur did not dare to cross the Tigris because he waited for a suitable sign from the heaven, which I would interpret in a more rational way that Shapur was aware of the presence of Constantius' field army at Edessa and was therefore hesitating to make his move. In addition, I would suggest that he was also aware that the Indians and Sinds had invaded his eastern possessions and that the Himyarites/Aksumites were raiding his coasts. In these circumstances he could not endanger his field army needlessly. The delay caused Constantius to ponder whether he should again besiege the strategically important Bezabde because he did not think it safe to leave it in Persian hands if he were to march against Julian. On the other hand, he feared that it would be unwise to expose his men to an offensive siege when he was fighting a civil war against Julian. In the end, he decided that the wisest course of action would be to prepare his army to fight a field battle against Shapur's army.

Consequently, Constantius decided to send forward the *Mag.Eq.* Arbitio and *Mag. Ped.* Agilo with strong-enough forces to keep a closer watch on the Tigris frontier. They had orders to retreat immediately after they had observed the enemy cross the river. It is evident that the other purpose of these forward-posted forces was to harass the enemy long enough for Constantius' field army to be able to reach the scene of operations. In short, Constantius' plan was to move his main army to the spot where the enemy attacked. Just like a boxer he was ready to counterpunch immediately after the enemy committed himself. However, this was not easy to achieve because the scouts and deserters brought conflicting information. According to Ammianus, the reason for this was that the King of Kings communicated his plans only to his grandees (*optimates*) and these men were silent and loyal. It is also obvious that the Persians were making feint movements in order to draw the emperor away from the spot where they aimed to cross the river and when they found out that this had not been achieved they tried again.

While this shadow boxing was still going on, Constantius received worrisome news from the West. He learnt that Julian had already captured Italy and Illyricum up to the Succi Pass and was collecting forces for the invasion of Thrace. In these circumstances, Constantius decided that the prudent course of action was to start to send his forces gradually to the Balkans. The generals approved of the plan, and Constantius ordered the forces to proceed as *expediti* (with no baggage train). However, when these arrangements were being made, Constantius received the news that Shapur had withdrawn his entire army because the 'auspices' had not been favourable: in other words, the presence of Constantius and his army close to the border had made the invasion untenable while the distractions created by Constantius' diplomacy had begun to cause troubles. The Persians were well aware that they had lost all their battles and sieges when the emperor had been present in person or nearby. In short, it is clear that the fearsome reputation of Constantius was one of the reasons for the Persian withdrawal from the border. Consequently, Constantius was now free to turn his attention towards the traitor. Had there not been need for this, Constantius would have surely besieged Bezabde and in all probability would have retaken it this time.

Constantius recalled all his forces, except those that were usually posted to protect the eastern border, and prepared his army for the march. When Constantius reached the aptly-named city of Nicopolis, he assembled all the centuries, maniples and cohorts and encouraged his troops with a speech, which the troops duly rewarded by brandishing their *hastae* (this probably implies that the infantry had been equipped with the *hastae* to face the Persian cavalry) and by demanding to be led against the rebel. After this, Constantius ordered the highly experienced and loyal Arbitio to take the *Lanciarii*, *Mattiarii*, and *catervae* of *expediti*-forces (implying barbarian auxiliaries), plus the loyal Gomoarius with the *Laeti*, to the Succi Pass in order to secure its defence until the main army under Constantius could reach it. Meanwhile, Constantius himself went to Antioch.

Constantius' Death[379]

Unfortunately Ammianus fails to mention why Constantius went in person to Antioch even though he could have continued his march more quickly to the Balkans from Nicopolis. Two possible reasons come to mind. Firstly, Antioch served as the main hub of the Roman logistical network in the East and it is therefore probable that Constantius went there to discuss in person with the *PP* of *Oriens* and *Comes Orientis* how to organize the logistical side of the campaign in the Balkans and Italy. Secondly, it is very probable that Constantius would have wanted to see his newlywed and pregnant wife Faustina before embarking upon his next campaign.

According to Ammianus, some persons in Constantius' entourage opposed Constantius' eagerness and speed in setting out against Julian. Should we see in this a cryptic referral to double agents within Constantius' court? Constantius continued his march at the beginning of autumn, and when he reached suburban Hippocephalus, at a distance of three miles from Antioch, he came across a man's corpse whose head had been cut off so that he lay stretched towards the west. The headless corpse pointed towards the setting sun and implied death. The corpse had clearly been placed there by someone who knew the route Constantius would take. The implication is that Julian's collaborators were within Constantius' bodyguards and/or court. There may also be another more sinister reason for the placing of the corpse besides presenting an omen of impending death. It is possible that the corpse had belonged to a diseased man and its purpose was to contaminate the air nearby with bacteria. The Romans were certainly aware of the use of corpses and other means of spreading illnesses as a result of which this is therefore a distinct possibility.[380] The subsequent law of Julian (CTh 9.17.5) in which he forbade the carrying of corpses during funeral processions in daytime because of the risk of spreading diseases, does, in my opinion, imply that it is possible that this was the precise way in which a disease was administered to Constantius. I would also suggest that the likely perpetrator of such an operation would have been the conjuror and philosopher Maximus himself and/or his followers. However, it is still possible that the corpse was just meant to instil a fear of pagan magic among those who saw it and that the real poisoning/contamination of the food and/or drink was done by someone belonging to Constantius' staff or by someone else (like the governor of Cilicia, Constantius' host at Tarsus and Julian's friend) who was in a position to give Constantius something to drink/eat. This is the likeliest alternative.

Constantius paid very little attention to the corpse, and continued his journey. When he reached Tarsus he was taken by a slight fever, but still decided to continue his march to

Mopsucrenae [Ma(m)psoukrenai] situated at the foot of Mt. Taurus. He rested there for a night, but when he intended to continue his journey next morning he could not because the fever had become so intense that he could barely be touched. The doctors did their best, but on 5 October, 361 (to be emended to 3 November according to Barnes, 1993, 224) he breathed his last breath. At the time of his death Constantius was 45 years old and had ruled for 25 years after the death of his father.

Constantius' death was considered to be natural, and it may well have been, but the positioning of the corpse in Antioch (by the theurgian henchmen of Maximus?) and the fact that nobody else is mentioned to have suffered from the fever strongly suggests the possibility that Constantius had been administered poison/bacteria. As noted above, the likeliest candidates as the killers of Constantius are the cultists of the philosopher Maximus and/or Celsus, the *Praeses* (governor) of Cilicia, who was Julian's personal friend and a fellow student of Libanius. Another possibility is that the poison/bacteria was administered to Constantius by someone within the imperial household as Nazianzus (Or. 4, Against Julian, 1.47–48) suspected. In this case the likeliest suspect would be some eunuch who had been bribed. Julian's subsequent decision to expel all eunuchs from the palace does lend some support for this theory. According to Ammianus (22.1.1–2), when just before Constantius' death Julian needed reassurance, Aprunculus, a Gallic orator (and undoubtedly a follower of Maximus' theurgy like Julian), supposedly foretold to Julian exactly what would happen as a result of the inspection of a liver. Note also that Julian is said to have presented to those who were suspicious about the news of Constantius' death earlier 'oracles' fetched from one of his chests which had foretold exactly what would happen (Lib. Or. 18.118). If there is any truth to these stories, they do suggest some kind of foreknowledge of what would happen that can have resulted only from the knowledge of a plot to kill Constantius with poison or bacteria, either in Antioch or in Tarsus of Cilicia. This same was also suspected by Nazianzus, who stated that if Constantius had been killed by demons as claimed by Julian and other pagans, then Julian too must have died in the hands of demons and not by human hand.

The whole court went into mourning, after which the highest ranking men started to ponder what to do. After some men had been asked in vain for their willingness to become emperors, Eusebius suggested that Julian should be made emperor, because he was already too near for others to usurp power. According to Ammianus (21.15.4), Eusebius made the suggestion because of his guilty conscience, that is, because of his role in the death of Gallus, but if this was really the case, he miscalculated badly. Ammianus' referral to guilt can also mean that Eusebius had had a role in the death of the emperor (had he been bribed?), but in light of the extant evidence this seems unlikely. On the other hand, if he had been, he was clearly in a position to murder the emperor and the purpose of his subsequent execution would have been to cover this up.

According to Ammianus, a rumour claimed that before his death Constantius had designated Julian as his successor and had written a testament to him. This sounds like a story concocted by Julian's supporters, but cannot entirely be ruled out because at the time of his death Constantius could have considered it the best option to leave the empire to his relative. Constantius' wife, however, was pregnant at the time of his death and subsequently gave birth to a posthumous daughter who was later married to Gratian.

Assessment of Constantius II, the Conscientious Ruler[381]

Constantius had performed his role well. He had been a conscientious ruler who had enhanced his power through imperial protocol. In other words, he had made himself the object of awe in order to be able to rule more efficiently. According to Ammianus, Constantius had not enlarged the administrative bureaucracy, and had not allowed the military high command to assume too much power. In short, he had not added to the cost of maintaining the bureaucracy. He had maintained a strict separation of civilian and military offices. In particular, he had prevented the military from interfering in civilian matters. Under his rule, the praetorian prefects were still the highest ranking officials in the Empire. In addition, Ammianus claims that during Constantius' reign nobody was appointed to any high position in the palace unless he had served for ten years and was thoroughly tested. Ammianus also praises the fact that military men were rarely appointed to hold civilian magistracy and that only men with military experience were appointed to command soldiers. In short, Constantius usually appointed only proven men to high positions. He was well-educated but Ammianus claims that Constantius was still not a good speaker or writer. This is clearly unfair, because we know that Constantius was clearly able to inflame the passions of soldiers for combat with his speeches.

Ammianus also praises Constantius' chaste behaviour, temperate manner of life, moderation in eating and drinking, and notes that Constantius was also able to bear sleep deprivation when required. Most of all, he was a good rider, javelin-thrower and excelled in particular in mounted archery. He was also expert in all the exercises required from footmen. These qualities and skills undoubtedly endeared Constantius to the troops. He could survive on very little food and sleep and fight as well as any man in the army. Constantius was their comrade-in-arms. Under Constans (gay) and Constantius II (chaste) it was also no longer acceptable for the emperors to rape women (Lib. Or. 59.157–8). This change in imperial practice undoubtedly had very positive internal security implications during their reign and afterwards. There were now no high ranking men eager to kill the emperors because these had violated their women.

There is no doubt that Constantius was probably not among the greatest military leaders of all ages, but he was certainly a very competent one, the best of his era. He never lost a major battle and suffered only minor setbacks in his lifelong war against the Persians. It is also absolutely certain that Constantius possessed superb forces that were willing to fight to the death on his behalf and not lose their morale even in the most trying of circumstances – as the battles of Singara and Mursa attest. It can be said with good reason that when Constantius could not out-general his enemies, it was his elite army that won the day for him. As a military leader Constantius was usually extremely cautious and careful. He always made very thorough preparations before embarking on any campaign.

Initially Constantius' strategy against Persia was to take the offensive. He aimed to force the enemy to fight a decisive battle in the open, but on his own terms so that he could then conquer the Persian territories. We should remember that it was not his will to fight the battle at Singara in 344, the way his soldiers did. Regardless, the battle of Singara still formed a watershed in Constantius' thinking. After this Constantius' goal was to force the Persians to sign a peace treaty in which they would recognize the status quo. He aimed to achieve this through a combination of defensive warfare, alliances and diplomacy.

Constantius' particular specialty was to let the Persians attack his well-fortified cities and forts with huge forces, while he himself kept his elite forces in reserve. The purpose of this strategy was to let the Persian enemy, who possessed numerical superiority, hit his head uselessly against the walls. Even when victorious, the Persians always lost tens of thousands of soldiers, while the Romans lost at most only a few thousand soldiers plus the civilians inside, and even with the civilians included in the body-count, the Persians always lost more men. In addition, Constantius was also an adept user of diplomacy, through which he managed to gain allies against foreign and domestic enemies, which forced his enemies to divide their forces. On top of that, Constantius was also a skilled user of unorthodox warfare as his many special operations prove. Constantius' cautious strategy was a very cost-effective way to conduct war, even if it was inglorious in the eyes of some. However, it is very likely that Constantius was planning to change his strategy towards the end of his life. He had launched a combined military, religious and diplomatic effort in the 350s to bring about a grand alliance of his neighbours against the Persians. The ambassadors from all these nations arrived at Constantinople in early 362 to meet Constantius, only to find that he had died and had been replaced by a young man who scorned all foreign help. In contrast, Constantius' strategy in the West was the restoration of the status quo before the usurpation of Magnentius. It was not wise to fight several major wars simultaneously, as Constantius fully well knew.

Ammianus accused Constantius (22.4.6–8) of having allowed military discipline to become too lax. His examples speak volumes on Ammianus' own bias. According to him, the soldiers were no longer using stone beds, but feather mattresses and folding couches. Their cups were no longer earthenware cups but made of valuable metals. On top of it all, some men had been able to buy houses of marble. Ammianus also accused the soldiers of too good a knowledge of the value of gems and gold. He also claimed that the soldiers treated their countrymen in a high-handed fashion and were cowardly when fighting against the enemy. Libanius (Or. 18.206) also confirms that Constantius' soldiers were well-equipped, which proves that their officers had not stolen their money and which demonstrates that under Constantius military discipline was still kept and corrupt officers rare.

As is obvious, Ammianus' and Libanius' accounts are highly tendentious. The luxuries did not make the soldiers weak as, for example, Julius Caesar knew full well. In his opinion, the soldiers fought better when they were protecting their own property. The examples of the beds also prove that the Romans had developed suitable transportable beds for field use, which must have made life much easier. In fact, Ammianus' claims can be used as proof that Constantius maintained military discipline exceptionally well. He clearly did not allow the officers to cook up the roster books and extort their men. In addition, the examples prove that Constantius' men had managed to gather sizable booty from their enemies thanks to the many military successes of Constantius. There is a clear contrast between the well-to-do soldiers of Constantius' day and the wretched poor of Theodosius' day – could it be that Ammianus criticized the problems of the latter half of the century by highlighting this?

It is clear that Constantius left Julian with superbly-trained and highly-disciplined armed forces, in which cases of corruption were an exception rather than a rule. The same was clearly not true of the civil service, even though the level of corruption was still apparently at such a degree that it did not cause any serious problems. Ammianus points out the case of the eunuch Eusebius and there is no doubt that this man was corrupt to the bone, but that doesn't mean that the system would not have worked well enough, because Constantius did not rely on Eusebius alone but used various advisors, as the council meetings prove. According to the *Expositio Totius Mundi et Gentium*, during the reign of Constantius the bulk of the eastern recruits came from Galatia, Thrace, Lesser Armenia (mounted archers), and possibly also from Phrygia (which produced brave men), while most of the members of the imperial court came from Pontus, Paphlagonia, Galatia and Cappadocia. The same treatise also states that Gaul produced a large army of courageous men for the Western Emperor. This implies that the vast majority of the imperial staff and forces still consisted of natives, which ensured stability.

The taxes were apparently doubled between 325 and 361 but this cannot be used as evidence for widespread corruption because the information Ammianus provides states otherwise. The standard complaint of the Roman pagans was that the upper class (who were immune from service as decurions thanks to their service in the military or court) created by Constantine the Great amassed most of the wealth with the result that the taxes for the rest increased. This is only partially true (see the second book in the series). It is clear that at least part of the blame for the increased taxation belongs to the opportunities the increased size of the administration offered for patronage (i.e. corruption), but the two principal reasons for the increase in taxation were the costly war against Persia and the inflation created by the influx of gold after Constantine's favourites put the gold of the temples into circulation. Unlike usually assumed, the last mentioned was not detrimental to the economy when there was enough bullion to mint coins. On the contrary, in order for the economy to grow it has to be accompanied by a sufficiently robust inflation (in a modern society perhaps about 5–8 per cent per year). In short, the population growth attested for this period together with the inflation and growing economy created circumstances in which it was possible for Constantius to replace the men he had lost, for example, at Mursa without any real problems. He could fill up the ranks with new recruits even though he was simultaneously facing an usurpation and a Sarmatian invasion! In short, it was not the reforms of Constantine or the policies of Constantius II that created the problems the Romans were facing later in the century as claimed by the pagan writers. It was the cumulative result of the policies followed by the successors of Constantius II.

Ammianus accuses Constantius of uncalled for cruelty, and of the appointment of merciless judges to conduct veritable inquisitions of people. Once again this is extremely unfair. Constantius was surrounded by enemies and would-be-usurpers, and it is not at all surprising that Constantius purged his relatives in 337, launched another purge of his brother's killers after 353, and then eliminated Gallus, Vetranio and Silvanus. It can even be said with justification that Constantius was not paranoid enough. He foolishly trusted in his wife's judgment of Julian's character and he was also all too ready to forgive Julian's transgressions, and instead should have acted decisively against Julian when his representatives in Gaul suggested it for the first time. It is in fact quite probable that Ammianus also implied the same with his several contrary comments that he inserted in the text. As noted before, it seems unlikely that so intelligent a person as Ammianus would have mistakenly placed evidence to the contrary here and there in his text unless he wanted to say something that was not allowed in the political atmosphere of the times. As noted before, the hostile comments regarding Constantius were probably meant to please Ursicinus and the courts of Theodosius I and Valentinian II.

The reason why Constantius had promoted his cousins as Caesars had more to do with imperial succession and misplaced trust in relatives than with the defensive needs of the empire. Constantius had believed that the presence of a figurehead Caesar could prevent usurpation by some high ranking general. The fact that neither Ursicinus nor Lucillianus usurped the power in the East while Constantius was away proves that in actual fact he would have had far less to fear from his generals than from his relatives. As regards Constantius' promotion of Julian, it is quite possible that he did this because he felt remorse for having ordered the killing of Julian's father and brother. It is also possible that he just felt that women were better judges of character than men and therefore foolishly trusted their advice. Indeed, in my opinion Constantius' greatest failing was that he trusted a man he should not have. It was this that cost him his life. The cost of these failures proved also to be immense for the Roman Empire. Julian was not a competent ruler and he left the Empire in a state of complete disarray when he died. This in turn caused the rise of the military mafia in the second half of the century, which worsened military discipline and resulted in unprecedented corruption in all levels of the society. However, it should be stressed that the problems of the latter-half of the fourth century were not the inheritance of Constantius. They were the result of Julian's mismanagement of the Empire and military, and of the relative weakness of his successors vis-à-vis the top brass. (See the next book in the series for a full analysis of these.)

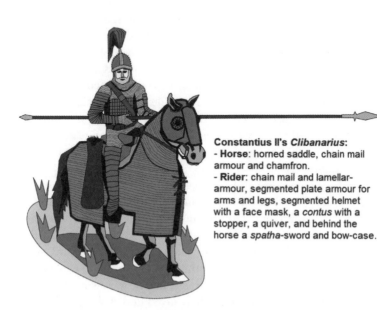

Constantius II's *Clibanarius*:
- **Horse**: horned saddle, chain mail armour and chamfron.
- **Rider**: chain mail and lamellar-armour, segmented plate armour for arms and legs, segmented helmet with a face mask, a *contus* with a stopper, a quiver, and behind the horse a *spatha*-sword and bow-case.

Constantius II (Kertch Missioriorum)

Note the stoppers/crossbars in Constantius' spear. I have made the upper portion purposefully more visible than it is in the *missoriorum*. The intention was to draw the spear back after it had hit its target and then reuse it again as a thrusting weapon. The stoppers may also imply the use of the horse's impetus in lancing so that the entire weight of the horse would impact the enemy, but only for the length of the blade. The use of the stoppers also enabled the fighter to keep the enemy at 'spear distance' away, which meant that the enemy could not use weapons that were shorter than the spear (e.g. the sword) against the wielder of the spear. Considering the fact that the spear was intended to be used on horseback, it must have been longer than the one shown in the illustration. The use of the stallion also suggests the use of its aggression to make the cavalry charge more effective.

– it is probable that the shield shown below Constantius' horse is his own shield, which proves that pointed shield-bosses were already in use. Pointed shield-bosses were particularly useful for shield bashing against opponents.

– note the *Chi-Rho* shield-emblem of the bodyguard, as well as the use of a spear that was clearly not meant to be a thrusting weapon as was Constantius' spear. This suggests that the infantry spear was meant to be equally usable as a thrusting weapon and as a javelin. The infantryman did not necessarily need the stoppers/crossbars because his thrust was less likely to penetrate the enemy as deep as the horseman's spear, which had behind it the weight of the moving horse. Incidentally, this also proves that the cavalrymen were able to use the impact of the horse in attack.

– note also the footwear worn by Constantius and his bodyguard.

Christian Controversies[382]

C onstantine's purpose was to solve the conflicts within the Christian community by calling together the Council of Nicaea in 325, but it failed to solve them and only launched another series of conflicts within the Church. The principal area of disagreement was the exact relationship of God the Father with his 'son' Jesus within the Godhead (i.e. the so-called Holy Trinity), because there was the problem of how to fit Jesus into the picture when there was supposedly only one God. The Council decided to incorporate the term *homousios* (of the same being or substance) to the official creed (i.e. the Father, Son and Godhead were of the same substance), which the so-called Arians, the followers of Arius, did not accept. Unfortunately, the exact beliefs of these Arians are not known with certainty today for two reasons. Firstly, Arius changed his opinions in the course of his career, and secondly because the hostile sources group all kinds of variant beliefs under the Arian heresy. Arius was duly excommunicated and the Nicene Creed remained the official creed until the death of Constantine. The followers of this Nicaean Creed (the 'Catholics' and 'Orthodox') can be called the 'Homousians' because they accepted the term *homousios*. Thanks to his charisma Athanasius of Alexandria became the leading proponent of this group. The doctrine of this group was later further refined by Basil of Caesarea, Gregory of Nazianzus, and Gregory of Nyssa.

However, during his last years Constantine had himself started to lean in his opinions towards those former supporters of Arius like Eusebius of Nicomedia who tried to find the middle ground between the views. The Nicaeans, however, considered these views also to be Arian and therefore heretical. After Constantine's death Constantius II changed the official policy in its entirety and adopted this middle-of-the-ground approach, which was still considered Arian by its opponents. The supporters of this school of thought, promoted by Eusebius of Nicomedia, were known as the Homoeans and their leading lights were the bishops Acacius of Caesarea and Eudoxius of Constantinople. They thought that the term *homousios* only confused the meaning and persons of the Trinity, and therefore considered the various definitions of the term useless. This policy was obviously followed only in the East until the conquest of the West by Constantius II changed the situation. It was after this that Constantius decided to find a middle ground between the Eastern Eusebian views and the Nicene Creed followed in the West by adopting the so-called Homoean Creed both in the East and West in 359, dropping altogether the controversial *homousios* from the creed, but the death of Constantius very soon after this changed the situation once again.

In addition to these, there were also two other major schools of thought. Firstly, there was a group of so-called 'Homoueusians' (*homoiousioi*) who believed that the persons of the Trinity were of 'similar' (*homois*) but not of the 'same' or 'identical' substance. This movement was therefore also a compromise movement. It did not accept Arius' views and accepted the term *homousios*, but left the exact differences between the Father and Son unanswered. The movement began after 341 under the leadership of Basil of Ancyra and can be considered similar in purpose to Constantius' decision to drop the term *homousios* from the creed. In other words, their purpose was to find some common ground under which all Christians could unite. During the 350s there emerged the new and even more radical Neo-Arians, the 'Anomoeans', under the leadership of Aetius and Eunomius, who wanted to separate the Son from the Father: that is, the persons of the Trinity were separate and therefore 'unlike' (*an-homoios*). However, the members of this group were ready to accept the compromise of dropping the term *homousios* from the creed when Constantius demanded this.

In addition to these there were several other smaller schools of thought that were also considered heretical. These included the followers of Mary of Magdalene, whose role in the conversion of Armenia and Georgia should merit greater attention than I have given here. Most of these schools of thought were considered heretical then and now, and are nowadays grouped together as Gnostics because most of them claimed that it was possible to reach Heaven only through access to secret knowledge. I have not discussed these in the text for the reason that their importance from the point of view of military history was not significant. However, from the point of view of the history of ideas and religion, these merit further research.

In this context it should be noted that for most modern readers like myself the above-mentioned conflicts over the meaning of the word *homousios* seem quite unimportant and trivial, but from the point of view of religious doctrine this was not so. It was and is a problem for a monotheist religion to explain the exact role of Jesus in the equation, and it was therefore of utmost importance for the members of the Church to explain the apparent discrepancies between Jesus the man and Son of God, and the monotheistic religion. The question involves even more problems (for example, the meanings of "Son of God" in Greek and Hebrew) than I have discussed above, but this is not the place to discuss those and I will leave that to historians of religion and theologians. The existence of several different Christian Churches today is the best evidence for the difficulties of the doctrinal issues. As an example, when I asked from a friend of mine, who is a Lutheran priest, why the Churches cannot find any common ground under which they could unite to become one universal Church, his answer was that as a priest he could not, with good conscience, teach the wrong Christian doctrine (i.e. a compromise doctrine) because that would cause his followers to end up in hell. In short, the differences between the Christian doctrines were and are too great even today for any attempt to find common ground, and the situation must have been even worse when the official doctrine was being formulated in the fourth century.

Bibliography

Primary Sources:

Most of the primary sources (e.g. Ambrose, Ammianus, Eusebius, Jerome, Zosimus, Zonaras, Philostrogius, Rufinus, Socrates, Sozomen, Theodoret, Julian, DRB, Kedrenos, Vegetius, various Armenian sources etc.) are now available on the web either as old editions and translations or as html documents. Good places to start seeking these are Bedrosian's Armenian Resources, the Internet Archive, Google Books, and the Tertullian Project. Whenever possible I have used Loeb or Budé editions and translations, excepting when I have been writing in such locations where I have not had access to my books or library. The following list (Select Primary Sources) refers only to those modern editions/translations that I have cited in the text or notes.

Select Primary Sources and Translations
Aelian (Aelianus/Ailianos), Tactica, ed. H. Köchly and W. Rüstow, *Griechische Kriegschritsteller 2.1*, Leipzig 1855; translation with Byzantine Interpolation of Aelian by A.M. Devine, 'Aelian's Manual of Hellenistic Military Tactics: A New Translation from the Greek with an Introduction', in *AW* 19 (1989), 31–64. Latest edition and translation by C. Matthew, *The Tactics of Aelian*, Barnsley; Edition of Byzantine Interpolation of Aelian by A. Dain, *Histoire du texte d'Élien le Tacticien*, Paris, 1946. Illustrations of the Byzantine Interpolation in this book redrawn from *Codex Burney 108*.
Ammianus, *Ammianus Marcellinus*, ed., and tr. J.C. Rolfe. Loeb 3 Vols.
Arab Archery (1945), tr. N.A. Faris and R.P. Elmer. Princeton.
Arrian, *Periplus ponti Euxini*, ed. and tr. by A. Liddle. Bristol 2003. *Tactica, Flavius Arrianus, techne taktika (Tactical Handbook) and ektaxis kata alanon (The Expedition Against the Alans)*, tr. and ed. J.G. DeVoto, Chicago (1993).
al-Baladhuri, *The Origins of the Islamic State*, 2 vols., tr. by P.K. Hitti. London (1916).
Blemyomachia, *Anonymi fortasse Olympiodori Thebani Blemyomachia (P.Berol.5003)*, ed. Henricus Livrea (Enrico Livrea) Meisenheim am Glan (1978); *Select Papyri III* (1941), ed. and tr. by D.L. Page. Loeb.
Byzantine Interpolation of Aelian, see Aelian.
Constantine Porphyrogenitus, *Three Treatises on Imperial Military Expeditions*, intr., ed. tr., and com. by J. F. Haldon, CFHB 28. Wien (1990).
Chinese Archery, tr. and commentary Stephen Selby. Hong Kong 2000.
Contribution a l'étude de l'archerie musulmane (1968), tr. A. Boudot-Lamotte. Damas (Damascus).
De Rebus Bellicis (DRB), *Anónimo Sobre Asuntos Militares*, ed. Álavaro Sánchez-Ostiz. Navarra; *Anonymi auctoris de Rebus Bellicis*, ed. R. Ireland. Leipzig; *De rebus bellicis. Part 2: the text*. ed. R. Ireland. Oxford; Tompson E. A., *A Roman Reformer and Inventor*. Oxford 1952; *Anonymi De rebus bellicis liber*, ed. R. Schneider. Berlin 1908.
Faustus, *The Epic Histories Attributed to Pawstos Buzand*, tr. N. Garsoïan. Cambridge 1989.
Georgian Chronicles, *Rewriting Caucasian History. The Medieval Armenian Adaptation of the Georgian Chronicles. The Original Georgian Texts and The Armenian Adaptation*, tr. R.W. Thomson. Oxford 1996.

Hadrian's Speech at Lambaesis in 128 AD, Michael P. Speidel, *Emperor Hadrian's speeches to the African Army – a new Text*, Mainz 2006.

Heather P. and Matthews J. (1991/2010), *The Goths in the Fourth Century*. Liverpool.

Heather P. and Moncur D. (2001), *Politics, Philosophy, and Empire in the Fourth Century: Select Orations of Themistius*. Liverpool.

Itinerarium Alexandri, ed. A. Mai (Milan 1817); ed. H. Volkmann. Landschule (1871); English tr. by I. Davies, 'Alexander's Itinerary', in *AHB* (1998), 29–54.

Julian1 = The Emperor Julian. Panegyric and Polemic, (2nd ed. 1989) ed. S.N.C. Lieu. Liverpool (a useful collection of translated sources).

Julian2 = *Julian the Apostate*, ed. and com. S. Tougher. Edinburgh (2007).

Julius Africanus, Kestoi, *Les 'Cestes' de Julius Africanus*, ed. and tr. by J.-R. Vieillefond. Paris (1970).

Kedrenos/Cedrenus, *Georgii Cedreni Historiarum Compedium*, ed. I. Bekker, CSHB. Bonn (1838) and in PG (fragments also translated in Zonaras/Banich).

al-Kindi, *Medieval Islamic Swords and Swordmaking: Kindi's treatise 'On swords and their kinds'*, R.G. Hoyland and B. Gilmour (Oxford 2006).

Letter of Tansar (Tosar), *The Letter of Tansar*, tr. by M. Boyce, Roma 1968 (notes refer to the numbers given in the margins); 'Lettre de Tansar à Jasnaf roi de Tabaristan', tr. by M. Darmesteter, *Journal Asiatique* 1894, 562–555.

Lydus, John, *De magistratibus, Ioannes Lydus On Powers or The Magistracies of the Roman State*, ed. and tr. by A.C. Bandy. Philadelphia (1983).

Mirkhond, French tr. by A.I.S. De Sacy in *Mémoires sur diverses antiquités de la Perse, et sur les médaillons des rois de la dynastie des Sassanides*. Paris (1713).

Moses Khorenatsi, *History of the Armenians*, tr. R.W. Thomson. Cambridge and London (1978)

Munyatu'l-Ghuzat. A 14th-Century Mamluk-Kipchak Military Treatise (1989), tr. by Kurtuluş Östopçu. Harvard.

Nizam al-Mulk, *Siaysat-nama, The Book of Government or Rules for Kings*, tr. by H. Darke. New Haven (1960).

Panegyrici Latini, In Praise of Later Roman Emperors, The Panegyrici Latini, Introduction, Translation and Historical Commentary with the Latin Text, R.A.B. Mynors, C.E.V. Nixon and Barbara Saylor Rodgers. Berkeley, Los Angeles, Oxford (1994).

Philostorgius, *Church History*, tr. by P.R. Amidon. Atlanta (2007).

Pseudo-Hyginus, *Pseudo-Hygin. des fortifications du camp*, ed. M. Lenoir. Paris (2002).

Rees R. (2004), *Diocletian and the Tetrarchy*. Edinburgh (a useful collection of sources).

REF1 = *The Roman Eastern Frontier and the Persian Wars (AD 226–363)*. Eds. M.H. Dodgeon and S.N.C. Lieu. London and New York (1991). A useful collection of sources.

REF2 = *The Roman Eastern Frontier and the Persian Wars. Part II AD 363–630*. Eds. G. Greatrex and S.N.C. Lieu. London and New York (2002). A useful collection of sources.

Rufinus, *The Church History of Rufinus of Aquileia*, tr. by P.R. Amidon. New York, Oxford 1997.

Saracen Archery. (1970), tr. J.D. Latham and W.F. Patterson. London.

Strategikon, *Das Strategikon des Maurikios*, ed. G.T. Dennis, German tr. by E. Gamillscheg. Vienna 1981; *Maurice's Strategikon*, tr. by G.T. Dennis. Philadelphia 1984.

Sylloge tacticorum quae olim 'Inedita Leonis tactica' dicebatur, (c. AD 904 – my opinion; commonly dated to c.950) ed. Alphonse Dain, Paris (1938).

Symeon, Magistros, *Symeonis Magistri et Logothete Chronicon*, ed. S. Walhgren CFHB. Berlin 2006, and earlier editions in the 19th century CSHB and PG (fragments also translated in Zonaras/Bancich).

Tabari, *The History of al-Tabari. Vol. V. The Sasanids, the Byzantines, the Lakhmids, and Yemen*. tr. by C.E. Bosworth. New York 1999.

Tafrij, Muslim Manual of War being Tafrij al-Kurub fi Tadbir al-Hurub by Umar ibn Ibrahim al-Awasial-Ansari, edited and translated by George T. Scanlon, Cairo (1961).

Zonaras, (2009), *The History of Zonaras from Alexander Severus to the Death of Theodosius the Great*, tr. by T.M. Banchich and E.N. Lance. Intr. and comm. by T.M. Banchich. London and New York. Greek txt: PG and CSHB both available from the web.

Zosimus, *Zosimus. A New History*. (1990), tr. by R.T. Ridley. Melbourne; *Nea Historia*, tr. and ed. Paschoud. Budé Paris. 4 Vols. (older English tr. available from the web).

Secondary Sources

Adontz N. (1970), *Armenia in the Period of Justinian. The Political Conditions Based on the Naxarar System*, tr. by N.G. Garsoïan. Lisbon.

Aitchison N. (2003), *The Picts and the Scots at War*. Stroud.

Alcock L. (1971/1989), *Arthur's Britain. History and Archaeology AD 367–634*. London.

D'Amato R. (2009), *Imperial Roman Naval Forces 31 BC–AD 500*. Oxford.

Aquileia. *Città di frontiera. Fondazione Aquileia* (a fragment available as a PDF on the web).

Argüín A.R.M. (2011), *El ejército Romano en campaña. De Septimio Severo a Diocleciano (193–305 D.C.)*. Sevilla.

Ayvazyan A. (2012), *The Armenian Military in the Byzantine Empire. Conflict and Alliance under Justinian and Maurice*. Alfortville.

—— (2007), *The Cornerstones of Armenian Identity: The Language, Army and State*. Yerevan, in Armenian.

—— 2010–2012 exchange of e-mails.

Barker P. (4th ed., 1981), *Armies and Enemies of Imperial Rome*. A Wargames Research Group Publication.

Barnes, T.D. (1976), "Imperial Campaigns, A.D. 285–311", in *Phoenix 30* (1976), 174–193.

—— (1981), *Constantine and Eusebius*. Cambridge and London.

—— (1982), *The New Empire of Diocletian and Constantine*. Cambridge and London.

—— (1985), "Constantine and the Christians of Persia", in *JRS* 75, 126–136.

—— (1993), *Athanasius and Constantius*. Cambridge and London.

—— (2011), *Constantine*. Wiley-Blackwell.

Barrington Atlas of the Greek and Roman World (2000). Ed. R.J.A. Talbert. Princeton.

Beeston A.F.L. (1976), *Warfare in Ancient South Arabia (2nd.-3rd. centuries A.D.)*. London.

Benabou M. (1976), *la résistance africaine à la romanisation*. Paris.

Bishop M.C. & Coulston J.C.N (2006 2nd ed.), *Roman Military Equipment From the Punic Wars to the Fall of Rome*. Oxford.

Bivar (1972), "Cavalry equipment & tactics on Euphrates". DOP.

Boak A.E.R. (1915), "The Roman *Magistri* in the Civil and Military Service of the Empire", in *Harvard Studies in Classical Philology* 26, 73–164.

Bounegru O. and Zahariade M. (1996), *Les Forces Navales du Bas Danube et de la Mer Noire aux Ier-VIe Siècles*. Oxford.

Braund D. (1994), *Georgia in Antiquity. A History of Colchis and Transcaucasian Iberia 550 BC – AD 562*. Oxford.

Breeze D.J. (2011), *The Frontiers of Imperial Rome*. Barnsley.

Brzezinski & Mielczarek (2002), *The Sarmatians*. Oxford.

Brulet R. (1995), 'La sépulture du roi Childéric à Tournai et le site funéraire', in *La noblesse romaine et les chefs barbares du IIIe au VIIe siècle*, ed. by F. Vallet and M. Kazanski, 309–326.

Burgess R. (2008), 'The summer of blood: The "Great Massacre" of 337 and the promotion of the sons of Constantine', *DOP 62*, 5–51.

Burstein S. (2009), *Ancient African Civilizations Kush and Axum*. Princeton.

Calwell, C.E. (1906), *Small Wars*. London.

Cascarino G. and Sansilvestri C. (2009/2010), *L'esercito Romano. Armamento e organizzazione. Vol. III: Dal III secolo alla fine dell'impero d'occidente*. il Cerchio Città di Castello.

Casey P.J. (1977), "Carausius and Allectus – Rulers in Gaul?", in *Britannia* 8, 283–301.

Casson L. (1995), *Ships and Seamanship in the Ancient World*. Baltimore and London.

Charles, Michael B., "The Rise of the Sassanian Elephant Corps: Elephants and the Later Roman Empire," in *Iranica Antiqua* XLII, 2007, 301–346.

Cizek E. (2004), *l'empereur Aurélien et son temps*. Paris.

Coello T. (1996), *Unit Sizes in the Late Roman Army*. Oxford.

Courtois Ch. (1939), "Les politiques navales de l'Empire romain", in *Revue historique*, 17–47 and 225–259.

Coulston J.C.N. (2002), "Arms and armour of the Late Roman Army", in D. Nicolle ed., *A Companion to Medieval Arms and Armour*. Woolbridge, 3–24.

—— (1986), 'Roman, Parthian and Sassanid tactical developments', in P. Freeman and D.L. Kennedy (eds.), *The Defence of the Roman and Byzantine East*, BAR. Int. Ser. 394. Oxford, 59–75.

Cowan, Ross, (2003), *Imperial Roman Legionary* 161-284 AD. Oxford 2003.

Crumlin-Pedersen O. (1997), 'Large and small warships of the North', in *Military Aspects of Scandinavian Society in a European Perspective, AD 1–1300*, ed. by A. Nørgård Jørgensen and B.L. Clausen. Kopenhagen, 184–194.

Dani A.H. and Litvinsky B.A., "The Kushano-Sasanian Kingdom", in *HCCA3*, 103–118.

Dani A.H., "Eastern Kushans and Kidarites in Gandhara and Kashmir", in *HCCA3*, 163–176.

Daryaee T. (2009), *Sasanian Persia. The Rise and Fall of an Empire*. London and New York.

Dawson T. (2007), " 'Fit for the task': equipment sizes and the transmission of military lore, sixth to tenth centuries", in *BMGS* 31.1, 1–12.

Delmaire R. (1995), *Les institutions de bas-empire romain de Constantin à Justinien*. Paris.

Depeyrot G. (2008), *Légions romaines en campagne. La colonne Trajane*. Paris.

—— (2011), *les Légions face aux Barbares. La colonne de marc Aurèle*. Paris.

Dodgeon M.H. and Lieu S.N.C (1991), See REF1.

DRB1 = De Rebus Bellicis, Part 1 Aspects of the Rebus Bellicis, ed. M.W.C. Hassal, Part 2 de rebus bellicis: ed. R. Ireland, BAR Int.Ser. 63, 1979.

Drinkwater J.F. (2007), *The Alamanni and Rome 213–496*. Oxford.

Durdík J (1961), *Hussitisches Heerwesen*. Berlin.

Escher K. *Les Burgondes Ier-Vie siècles apr. J.-C.* Paris.

Farrokh K. (2007), *Shadows in the Desert*. Oxford.

—— (2005), *Sassanian Elite Cavalry AD 224–642*. Oxford.

Fox Lane R.J. (1997), "The Itinerary of Alexander: Constantius to Julian", in *CQ*, 239–252.

Frank R.I. (1969), *Scholae Palatinae*. Rome.

Frézouls E. (1980), "Rome et la Maurétanie Tingitane: un constat d'échec", in *Antiquités africaines 16*, 65–93.

Froehner W. (1865), *La colonne Trajane*. Paris.

Fuhrmann C.J. (2012), *Policing the Roman Empire*. Oxford.

Gall, H. von (1990), *Das Reiterkampfbild in der Iranischen und Iranisch Beeinflussten Kunst Parthischer und Sasanidischer Zeit*, Berlin.

Garsoïan, N. (1998/2004), "The Aršakuni Dynasty (A.D. 12–[180]-428)", in *Armenian People from Ancient to Modern Times. Vol 1*. ed. R.G. Hovannisian. New York, pp. 63–94.

Goodchild R.C. (1952), "Mapping Roman Libya", in *The Geographical Journal* 118.2, 142–152.

—— (1953), "The Roman and Byzantine Limes in Cyrenaica", in the *JRS* 43, 65–76.

Greatrex G., Elton H., and Burgess R. (2005), "Urbicius' Epitedeuma: an edition, translation and commentary", in *BZ* 98, 35–74.

Grignaschi M. (1966), "Quelques specimens de la literature sassanide conserves dans les biobliothèques d'Istanbul", in *JA 254*, 1966, 1–45.

Haldon J. (2008), 'Structures and Administration', in *The Oxford Handbook of Byzantine Studies*, eds. E. Jeffreys, J. Haldon, and R. Cormack, 539–553.

—— (1984), *Byzantine Praetorians*. Bonn.

Handy M. (2009), *Die Severer und das Heer*. Berlin.

Hassall M.W.C. (1979), 'The Inventions', in DRB1, 77–91.

Harries J. (2012), *Imperial Rome AD 284 to 363*. Edinburgh.

Hatke G. (2013), *Aksum and Nubia: Warfare, Commerce, and Political Fictions in Ancient Northeast Africa*. New York.

Haywood, John, *Dark Age Naval Power. A Reassessment of Frankish and Anglo-Saxon Seafaring Activity*, London and New York 1991.

HCCA2 = *History of civilizations of Central Asia Vol. II. The development of sedentary and nomadic civilizations 700 B.C. to A.D. 250*. Ed. J. Harmatta, Co-eds. B.N. Puri and G.F. Etemadi. Delhi.

HCCA3 = *History of civilizations of Central Asia Vol. III. The crossroads of civilizations A.D. 250 to 750* (1999), Ed. B.A. Litvinsky. Co-eds. Zhang Guang-da and R. Shabani Samghabadi. Delhi.

Heath I. (2nd ed., 1980), *Armies of the Dark Ages 600–1066*. A Wargames Research Group Publication.

Heather P. (1996), *The Goths*. Oxford.

Heidorn L.A. (1997), "The Horses of Kush", in *Journal of Near Eastern Studies* 56.2, 105–114.

Herrnándes F.D. (2010/2011), *Los Godos desde sus origines Bálticos has Alarico I*. Spain.

Hopwood K. (1981), 'Policing the Hinterland: Rough Cilicia and Isauria', in *Armies and Frontiers in Roman and Byzantine Anatolia*, ed. S. Mitchell, BAR. Int. 156, pp. 173–181.

Hourani G.F. (1995), *Arab Seafaring. Expanded Edition*. Princeton.

Hoyland R.G. (2001), *Arabia and Arabs from the Bronze Age to the Coming of Islam*. London and New York.

Isaac B.H. (1990), *The Limits of Empire: the Roman Army in the East*. Oxford.

James Edward (1988), *The Franks*. Oxford.

James Elisabeth (2012), *Constantine the Great. Warlord of Rome*. Barnsley.

Jones A.H.M. (1964/1986), *The Later Roman Empire 284–602*. Oxford.

Kazanski M & Mastykova A. (2003), *Les peoples du Caucase du Nord. Le déput de l'histoire (Ier – VIIe siècle apr. J.-C.)*. Paris.

Kazanski M. (1991), 'La défense de la frontiére au bas-empire', *TM 11*, 487–526.

Keys D. (2004), "Kingdom of the Sands", in Archaeology, 24–29 (accessed as html).

Kirwan L.P. (1957), "Rome beyond the Southern Egyptian Frontier", in *The Geographical Journal* 123.1,13–19.

Kistler, J. M. (2006), *War Elephants*. Westport Connecticut and London.

Kouznetzov V. and Lebedynsky I. (2005), *Les Alains*. Paris.

Kreucher G. (2003), *Der Kaiser Marcus Aurelius Probus und seine Zeit*. Historia Einzelschriften 174. Stuttgart.

Law B.C.C. (1967), "The Garamantes and Trans-Saharan Enterprise in Classical Times", in *The Journal of African History 8.2*, 181–200.

Lebedynsky I. (2010), *Sarmates et Alains face à Rome, Ier-Ve siècles*. Clermont-Ferrant.

—— (2007), *Les Nomades*. Paris.

—— (2002) *Les Sarmates*. Paris.

—— (2001), *Armes et guerriers barbares au temps des grandes invasions*. Paris.

Le Bohec, Yann (2009), *L'armée romaine dans la tourmente*. Rocher.

—— (2006), *L'armée romaine sous le Bas-Empire*. Paris.

—— (2005), *Histoire de l'Afrique romaine*. Paris.

—— (1994/2000), *The Imperial Roman Army*. London and New York.

Lee A.D. (2007), *War in Late Antiquity. A Social History*. Malden, Oxford, Carlton.

Lenoir, See Pseudo-Hyginus.

Lenski N. (2007), "Two Sieges of Amida (AD 359 and 502–503) and the Experience of Combat in the Late Roman East", in Lewin & Pellegrini, 219–236.

Lewin A.S and P. Pellegrini (2007) eds., with the aid of Z.T. Fiema and S. Janniard. *The Late Roman Army in the Near East from Diocletian to the Arab Conquest*. Oxford.

Lewin A.S. (1994), "The Organization of a Roman Territory: the southern section of provincial Arabia", in *The Roman and Byzantine Army in the East*, ed. E. Dabrowa. Cracow.

Liebeschuetz J.H.W.G. (2007), 'Warlords and Landlords', in *A Companion to the Roman Army*. Ed. P. Erdkamp. Malden, Oxford, Carlton, 479–494.

—— (1990), *Barbarians and Bishops*. Oxford.

Lightfoot C.S. (1983), "The Site of Roman Bezabde", in *Armies and Frontiers in Roman and Byzantine Anatolia*, ed. S. Mitchell, BAR. Int. 156, pp. 189–204 (maps 201–202).

Luttwak, Edward N. (1976/1979), *The Grand Strategy of the Roman Empire From the First Century A.D. to the Third*, Baltimore and London.

Maailmanhistoria 2 (1917), Helsinki Tietokirja-Osakeyhtiö Porvoo.

McGrail S. (1983/2006), *Ancient Boats and Ships*. Princes Risborough.

Mattesini S. (2006), *Les Légions Romaines. L'armament à travers mille and d'histoire*. Rome.

Mattingly D.J. and Hitchner R.B. (1995), "Roman Africa: An Archaeological Review", in *JRS 85*, 165–213.

Mattingly D.J. (2003), 'Historical Summary', in *The Archaeology of Fazzān. Vol. 1, Synthesis*, ed. D.J. Mattingly. London (2003), 75–106.

—— (1995), *Tripolitania*. London.

—— (1983), "The Laguatan: A Libyan Tribal Confederation in the Late Roman Empire", in *Libyan Studies 14*, 96–108.

Mayor A. (2003), *Greek Fire, Poison Arrows & Scorpion Bombs*. Woodstock, London, New York.

Maxfield V. A. (2000), "The Deployment of the Roman Auxilia in Upper Egypt and the Eastern Desert during the Principate", in eds. G. Alföldy, B. Dobson, W. Eck, *Kaiser, Heer und Gesellschaft in der Römischen Kaizerzeit*. Stuttgart, 407–442.

Mielczarek M. (1999), *The Army of the Bosporan Kingdom*. Lodz.

Morrison J.S. (1996), *Greek and Roman Warships 399–30 B.C. with contributions by J.F. Coates*. Oxford.

Mukherjee, B.N. (1988), *The Rise and Fall of the Kushana Empire*. Calcutta.

Nicolle D. (1991/2001), *Rome's Enemies 5. The Desert Frontier*. Oxford.

—— (1982), *The Armies of Islam 7th–11th Centuries*. Oxford.

Nixon and Rodgers, see Panegyrici Latini.

Odahl C.M. (2004), *Constantine and the Christian Empire*. London and New York 2004.

Oorthuys J. (2011), "Marines and mariners. Deciphering the structure of the fleets", in *AW V.5*, 16–21.

Petrikovits von H. (1971), "Fortifications in the North-Western Roman Empire from the Third to the Fifth Centuries AD", in *JRS* 61, 178–218.

PIPLA = Persia's Imperial Power in Late Antiquity. *The Great Wall of Gorgan and Frontier Lanscapes of Sasanian Iran*. Eds. E.W. Sauer, H.O. Rekavandi, T.J. Wilkinson and J. Nokandeh. Oxford and Oakville 2013.

Pitassi M. (2011), *Roman Warships*. Woodbridge and Rochester.

—— (2009), *The Navies of Rome*. Woodbridge and Rochester.

PLRE1, (1971/2006), *The Prosopography of the Later Roman Empire*, A.H.M. Jones, J.R. Martindale & J. Morris. Volume 1 A.D. 260–395. Cambridge.

PLRE2, (1980/2011), *The Prosopography of the Later Roman Empire*, J.R. Martindale. Cambridge.

Pourshariati P. (2008), *Decline and Fall of the Sasanian Empire*. London and New York.

Pryor J.H. and Jeffreys E.M (2006), *The Age of the Dromon. The Byzantine Navy ca 500–1204*. Leiden and Boston.

Puri, B.N., "The Kushans", in *HCCA2*, 247–263.

Rance P. (2003) "Elephants in Warfare in Late Antiquity", in *Acta Antiqua, Academiae Scientiarum Hungaricae 43*, Budapest 2003, 355–384.

—— (2004), 'The Fulcum, the Late Roman and Byzantine Testudo: the Germanization of Roman Infantry Tactics?', in GRBS 44, 265–326.

Rankov B. (1995), "Fleets of the Early Roman Empire, 31 BC–AD 324", in *The Age of Galley*, Ed. R. Gardiner, Consultant Ed. J. Morrison. London, 78–85.

Raychaudhuri H. (2006), *Political History of Ancient India. Commentary by B.N. Mukherjee*. New Delhi.

Rebuffat R. (1998), "L'armée de Maurétanie Tingitane", in *Mélanges de l'École française de Rome. Antiquité 110*, 193–242.

Reddé M. (1986), *Mare Nostrum*. Paris and Rome.

Reinach, Salomon, (1909), *Repertoire de reliefs grecs et romains*. Easiest to access at The McMaster Paper Collection. Paper 96. http://digitalcommons.mcmaster.ca/mcmastercollection/96.

Robin C. (1991), "Cités, royaumes et empires de l'Arabie avant l'Islam", in *Revue de monde musulman et de la Mediterranée* 61, 45–54.

—— (1996), "le royaume hujride, dit «royaume de Kinda», entre Himyar et Byzance", in *Comptes-rendus des séances de l'Akadémie des Inscriptions et Belles-Lettres, 140e année, N. 2*, 665–714.

Sandhu, Gurcharn Singh Major General (2000), *A Military History of Ancient India*. New Delhi, Mumbai, Hyderabad.

Salway P. (2001), *A History of Roman Britain*. Oxford.

Scanlon, see Tafrij.

Schippmann K. (2001), *Ancient South Arabia*. Princeton.

Schmitt O. (1994), "Die *Buccellarii*", in *Tyche 9*, 147–174.

Scullard, H.H. (1974), *The Elephant in the Greek and Roman World*. London.

Shahbazi, S., "Army", in *EI²* (web, updated Aug. 12, 2011).

Shahid I. *BAFOC*, (1984), *Byzantium and the Arabs in the Fourth Century*.

Shaw B.D. (1986), "Autonomy and tribute: mountain and plain in Mauretania Tingitana", in *Revue de l'Occident musulman et de la Méditerranée 41–42*, 66–89.

Sheldon, R.S. (2005), *Intelligence Activities in Ancient Rome*. Milton Park and New York.

Sherwin-White A.N. (1973), "The Tabula of Basana and the Constitutio Antoniana", in *JRS 63*, 86–98.

Sidnell P. (2006), *Warhorse. Cavalry in Ancient Warfare*. London and New York.

Skupniewicz P. (2011), "Sassanid society and the army it spawned. King, knights and pawns", in *AW* 5.3, 14–19.

—— (2008), "Late Rome's Nemesis. Sassanian armoured cavalry", in *AW* 1.4, 22–27.

Smith R. L. (2003), "What Happened to the Ancient Libyans? Chasing Sources across the Sahara from Herodotus to Ibn Khaldun", in *Journal of World History*, 459–500.

Speidel, M. P. (2006), *Emperor Hadrian's speeches to the African Army – a new Text*. Mainz.

—— (2004), *Ancient Germanic Warriors*. New York and London.

—— (1994), *Riding for Caesar*. London.

—— (1992c) "Maxentius and his *Equites Singulares*," in Speidel, M.P., *Roman Army Studies Vol 2*, Mavors 8, Stuttgart, 279–289.

—— (1992b), "The Later Roman Field Army and the Guard of the High Empire", in *Roman Army Studies 2*. 379–384. Stuttgart.

—— (1992a), "Nubia's Roman Garrison", in *Roman Army Studies 2*. 240–274. Stuttgart.

—— (1975), "The Rise of Ethnic Units in the Roman Imperial Army", in *ANWR* II.3, 202–231.

Starr C.G. (2nd ed. 1960), *The Roman Imperial Navy 31 B.C.–A.D. 324*. London.

—— (1943), "Coastal Defense in the Roman World", in *The American Journal of Philology*, 56–70.

Strobel K. (2007), "Strategy and Army Structure between Septimius Severus and Constantine the Great", in ed. P. Erdkamp, *A Companion to the Roman Army*. Malden, Oxford, Carlton, 267–285.

Sumner G. (2009), *Roman Military Dress*. Stroud.

Suny R.G. (2nd ed. 1994), *The Making of the Georgian Nation*. Bloomington and Indianapolis.

Syvanne (Syvänne/Syvaenne) I. (2011c), Presentations: *Germanicus' Wars AD 13–16* at Kalkriese and at King of Prussia, USA.

—— (2011b), "East Roman Cavalry Warfare and Tactics", 3 Parts in *Slingshot* 2011–2012.

—— (2011a), "The Reign of Decius", in *Slingshot 276*, 2–8.

—— (2010b), "Dragón versus dromón: el día del juicio, julio de 1043", in *Desperta Ferro 6*, 32–39.

—— (2010a), "El sistema military godo", in *Desperta Ferro 1*.

—— (2009–2010), "The Battle of Magnesia", in *Saga Newsletter 121*, 25–77; 'Macedonian Art of War', in *Saga Newsletter 123*, 31–99, 2010.

—— (2009), "The Battle of Melitene in AD 576", in *Saga Newsletter* 120, 32–64.

—— (2008), "The New Cavalry Formations of the Sylloge Tacticorum, AD 904", in *Saga Newsletter* 112, 2008, 36ff.

—— (2006), "The Late Roman Art of War: the Reign of Constantine the Great", *Slingshot* 247.

—— (2006, Water) "Water Supply in the Late Roman Army", in Environmental History of Water, eds. P.S. Juuti, T.S. Katko and H.S. Vuorinen. London, pp. 69–91.

—— (2004), *The Age of Hippotoxotai.* Tampere.

Taylor J. (2003), "Traditional Arab sailing ships", Webpage *British-Yemeni Society* (al-bab.com) accessed 07.06.2012.

Tougher = see Julian2 above.

Treadgold W. (1995), *Byzantium and Its Army.* Stanford.

Trombley F.R. and Watt J.W. (2000), *The Chronicle of Pseudo-Joshua the Stylite.* Liverpool.

Villeneuve F. (2007), "L'armée romaine en mer Rouge et autour de pa mer Rouge aux IIème siècles apr. J.-C.: à propos de deux inscriptions latines découvertes sur l'archipel Farasan", in *The Late Roman Army in the Near East from Diocletian to the Arab Conquest*, Eds. A.S. Lewin and P. Pellegrini with the aid of Z.T. Fiema and S. Janniard. Oxford. pp 13–27.

Wagner P. (2002), *Pictish Warrior AD 297–841.* Oxford.

Welsby D.A. (2002). *The Medieval Kingdoms of Nubia.* British Museum, London.

—— (1998), *The Kingdom of Kush.* Princeton.

Wescher C. (1867), *Poliorcétique des grecs.* Paris.

Wheeler E.L. (1979), 'The Legion as Phalanx', Chiron 9, 303-18.

—— (2004), 'The Legion as Phalanx in the Late Empire 1-2: in L'Armée romaine de Diocletian à Valentinien 1er', eds. Y. Le Bohec and C. Wolf. Lyon, 309-58; and in REMA 1, 147-175.

Whittaker C.R. (1994), *Frontiers of the Roman Empire.* Baltimore and London.

Wiesehöfer, J. (2001), *Ancient Persia.* London and New York.

Wilkes J.J. (2005), "The Roman Danube: An Archaeological Survey", in *JRS* 95, 124–225.

Williams, Stephen (1985), *Diocletian and the Roman Recovery*, New York.

Wolfram H., (1990), *History of the Goths.* Berkeley, Los Angeles, London.

—— (2005), *The Roman Empire and Its Germanic Peoples.* Berkeley, Los Angeles, London.

Wright J. K., (1927) "Northern Arabia. The Explorations of Alois Musil", in *The Geographical Review 17.2*, 177–206.

Yule P. and Robin C. (2005–2006), "Himyarite Knights, Infantrymen and Hunters", in *Arabia 3*, pp.261–271, figs. 157–169, pp.358–363.

Zahariade M. (2011), "Workhorses of the Imperial navy. The Roman provincial fleets", in *AW V.5*, 22–26.

Zeimal, E.V. "Kidarite Kingdom in Central Asia", in *HCCA3*, 119–133.

Notes

Chapter 1

1. Bohec's books on the Roman military are highly recommended. Note, however, that my reconstruction differs from his in some places.
2. For fuller details, see the indispensable Luttwak. Luttwak has made some generalizations that do not stand closer scrutiny, but at the time it was published his work broke new ground and is still very valuable for the many insights it includes. I recommend it highly.
3. I will discuss this in greater detail in a forthcoming study of the campaigns of Germanicus, which is based on my research papers presented at Kalkriese in 2011 and at Historicon 2011.
4. The discussion between Agrippa and Maecenas in Dio gives a good summary of the risks and benefits. Even if the exact words may be fictitious, as suggested by the vast majority of modern historians, it is still clear that such a discussion must have taken place. However, I would not consider it improbable that Dio actually may even record the words accurately, as he may have had access to some source that had preserved the exchange of words. It is no coincidence that the military man Agrippa favoured the use of masses of conscripts while the spy-master Maecenas favoured the use of professional soldiers. It had been the masses of well motivated soldiers that had enabled Rome to defeat all its enemies and to create its empire, but it would have been fraught with risks to keep the population at arms if one wanted to rule the empire as a dictator, as Maecenas recognized.
5. The usual mistake is to assign legions only 120 (= 128) horsemen on the basis of Josephus' statement that 120 horsemen accompanied each legion in the marching formation in 67 AD. In truth, Josephus does not really say anything about the size of the actual cavalry component of each legion, but refers only to the horsemen accompanying each legion in the marching formation. Josephus does state that there were other horsemen in front and rear and it is easy to see that when one includes these in the numbers the likely strength of the legionary cavalry was still the traditional 512 horsemen. I have discussed these things in three research papers, which will be published later.
6. The manuscripts offer three different totals: 730, 732, and 736. Vegetius 2.6 gives the 1st milliarian cohort 132 *equites loricati* (4 x *turmae* of 32 armoured horsemen and 4 decurions) and the second to tenth cohorts 66 *equites* each (2 x 32 and 2 decurions) making altogether 730 or 732 or 736 (22 x 32 *equites* and 22 decurions plus officers etc.), but the numbers add up to only 726 (704 + 22 decurions). At the time when the Strategikon (1.4–5, 3.1–4) was written there was 1 tribune, 1 ilarch, 1 hekatontarch, 1 standard-bearer, 1 trumpeter, and 1 cape bearer per 310-man cavalry *tagma/bandon* (in practice the size varied from 200–400 men). This suggests that there may have been cavalry commanders (hekantontarchs, ilarchs/centurions, vicars) for each c.100-cavalryman unit (3 x 32 + 3 decurions = 99 + 1 hekantontarch = 100) and for each c.300 men one tribune/duke (who seconded as commander of 100 men). With the addition of the three other supernumerary officers, we have 303 men and when one takes into account the possibility that the tribune and *vexillum* may have had a special flag guard, this would explain the missing seven men from the figure of 310 horsemen, but this would not correlate with Vegetius' figures. It is obviously possible that practices had changed or that the figure of 310 men took into account the practice of making the *tagmata/banda* to be of different sizes. Regardless, if one wants to speculate and adds the

seven centurions to the figure of 726 (22 x 32 + 22 decurions) it adds up to 733 horsemen and if one adds the standard-bearer, trumpeter and cape-bearer it adds up to the figure of 736 men, which is to be found in one of the manuscripts. In addition, I would suggest that there was also the possibility that the tribune was the legionary cavalry commander, the equivalent of the prefect of the *auxiliary ala quingeraria* of 512 men (plus 16 decurions + *vexillum*, trumpet, cape-bearer). As can be seen from the above, the figures do add up when the unit in question was either 512 or 704 men strong. On the basis of this, I would suggest that the extra standard-bearer, trumpeter and cape-bearer were always added to the legionary cavalry unit that was at least 200 strong, the actual strength varying depending upon the time period, and that each unit that had over c.500 men also had a special supernumerary officer (prefect or tribune) to lead it. I would also suggest that the organization of the auxiliary and legionary cavalries resembled each other and that we should also add centurions to the organization chart of the auxiliary cavalry.

7. See for example Bohec, 2000, 19–67.
8. See: Le Bohec (2000, 20ff.); Speidel (1994).
9. For additional details see esp. Sheldon (esp. 141ff.) and my forthcoming analysis of the role of *Pontifex Maximus*.
10. This chapter is based on the outstanding studies of Bishop & Coulston (199ff.); Cascarino & Sansilvestri (119ff.); Arguin (159ff.); and Coulston (2002), with some additions made by the author, which means that I alone bear the responsibility for the mistakes when I depart from their interpretation of evidence. For Roman military dress, see also the chapters dealing with the later Roman period in Sumner (2009).
11. For a discussion of the various spear lengths in the sources, see Dawson.
12. Infantry club-bearers (*khoranapakh/choranapakh*) were also used by the Persians and the Mazkutk against the Armenians, which indicates the use of similar tactics to those used by the Romans, for example under the emperor Aurelian against the Palmyrenes. See BP 3.7, 3.20, Garsoian Index p.575. It seems probable that this tactic had been copied from the Romans because this system had been used by the Romans at least since the time of Trajan.
13. This chapter is based on Syvänne, 2004, 2011–2012. See also my forthcoming books dealing with cavalry warfare of the fifth and sixth centuries.
14. For an excellent overview of the Column of Trajan (and Aurelius), see Depeyrot.
15. The diagram of the 'Italian Drill Array' in the Strategikon presents a cavalry army of approx. 30,000 horsemen (see Syvänne, 2004, 2011c). What is notable is that this figure also tallies with the figure of 30,000 horsemen that Phil Sidnell (280) suggests to have been the approx. strength of Gallienus' cavalry corps. See also Chapter 3.
16. I will include a full analysis of the different kinds of hollow squares in use and the different tactical variations in their use (the square could be used in several different ways) in the second book in the series (year 361–395). For further info regarding infantry tactics, see also Syvanne (2004), Wheeler and Rance (2004).
17. For additional info, see Lee, 2007, 95ff.
18. This chapter is based on Bishop & Coulston (233–240) Cascarino & Sansilvestri (119ff.) and Lee (2007, 89–94), excepting the discussion of the quality of the equipment.
19. This chapter is based on the excellent book by Lee (2007) with some very slight modifications.
20. The following is based on Lee, 2007, 163ff.; Le Bohec, 2006, 177ff.
21. E.g. Hassall (1979, 82, 93) has noted that the description bears resemblance to the *ballista fulminalis* in the DRB (see illustration in the second book in the series and in Chapter 2), but is still so difficult that his and Marsden's translations of the text are different.
22. Zahariade (2011), D'Amato (2009) and Rankov provide good introductions, but for fuller and more detailed analyses and discussion of the fleets, see Reddé (highly recommended) together with Pitassi (2009, 2011), Bounegru and Zahariade (Danubian Fleets), and Starr. Most of the following is based on the analysis of Reddé. If my view differs from his or from the

views of the others, it is noted as 'I consider', or 'I think', or 'In my opinion', etc. Oorthuys' analysis of the marines and mariners has also been found useful and together with Reddé's observations has caused me to develop the latter's theory regarding the correspondence of naval and land rankings further. For the river and sea frontiers as defensive systems, see also Breeze.

23. For these early measures, see Starr (1943).

24. For the fleets of the Danube, see the standard work by Bounegru & Zahariade together with Zahariede's 2011 introduction into provincial fleets.

25. For the existence of a fleet in Constantinople not mentioned by the ND, see Reddé, 590–592.

26. For further comments regarding the sea frontier of the Saxon shore, see Breeze (153–158) and Reddé.

27. For the use of naval and military terminology, and their correspondence with each other or lack thereof, see esp. Oorthuys (2011) and Reddé (522ff.). Oorthuys supports the existence of two separate hierarchies: one naval hierarchy for the rowers and sailors (mariners) commanded by trierarchs; and another for marines (soldiers) with a normal military hierarchy. Reddé discusses the various theories presented and then gives his support to the theory that there was only one hierarchy. I subscribe to this theory and develop it further. Since Oorthuys' theory is quite attractive, I will here present the reasons for opposing that. Oorthuys J. (2011), 21: '...the *milites* that referred to a *centuria* were the marines of the fleets. When they referred to a ship as well, they indicated what ship they were (temporarily) attached to.' The reason for Oorthuys' conclusion is that, for example, one inscription proves that a naval *centurio* was in command of a group of soldiers that were divided over several ships when serving at sea. In the inscription mentioned one group of soldiers was under its own *centurio* (trireme Providentia) and the other under an *optio* (trireme Tigris) or a *suboptio* (Liber Pater) or *suboptio* (Salus). On the basis of this it is not necessary to postulate two separate hierarchies. It is still quite possible that the two *suboptiones* were also *trierarchi* (captains) of the ships with lesser rank and that the *optio* and *centurio* were also captains of their respective ships, but in such manner that the *centurio* was also the *navarchus* in charge of all four ships, and the *optio* probably in charge of two ships (his own plus one of the *suboptiones*).

28. Starr (36–38) notes that the duties of the *subpraefectus* are obscure and compares the position with that of the tribune in the legion suggesting that *subpraefectus* served as an administrative aide to the prefect, just like the tribunes served for the legate. Pitassi (e.g. 2009, 318) also suggests administrative duties.

29. The *navarchus* was originally the captain of a ship and the *trierarchus* the captain of a trireme, but the former had come to mean admirals and the latter captains as early as the Hellenistic epoch.

30. Reddé, 541–542.

31. Some modern scholars such as myself equate these centurions with the *nauarchi*, while others consider them to be commanders of marines on board the ship, for example Pitassi. None besides myself seems to equate the *optiones* and *suboptiones* with captains of smaller vessels.

32. Reddé, 538.

33. Based on Reddé, 522ff.; Rankov, 79–80; D'Amato, 8–11; Pitassi, 2009, 318–319. It should be noted that their views are slightly different from each other and that I have also made my own changes to the list.

34. Reddé, 550–554.

35. See also my article in DF 6. Note however that I have changed my opinion regarding the oar arrangement. For alternative reconstructions of period Roman warships from the 3rd to 6th centuries, see esp. Pitassi (2011, 134ff.). For the ships of the Roman Republic, see Morrison. For the Roman ships in general, see also Casson (Roman navy 141–154).

36. For further information regarding Syrianos, see Syvänne 2004.

37. There is a definite reference to 150 rowers on the upper deck and 50 on the lower (and 25 oars per side and bank) in Leo the Wise's Naumachika 8–9 and Ouranos' Peri Thalassomachias 7–8. See also Pryor & Jeffreys, 255.

38. Veg. 4.43: '… quia navalis pugna tranguillo committitur mari liburnarumque moles non ventorum fiatibus sed remorum pulsu adversarios percutit rostris [ram/bow] eorumque rursum impetus [ramming] vitat…'. See also Syvänne, 2004.

39. Reference to the use of a spur-bow in Pitassi (2011, fig. 91) and Pryor &Jeffreys (2006, 134ff.).

40. In fact, Pryor (e.g. 2006, 134ff.) seems to have been the first historian to suggest the adoption of the spur instead of the ram by the Late Romans, and in my opinion this is at least partially correct. The bow-structure was no longer exactly the same as it had been when the only purpose of the ram was to puncture a hole below the waterline.

41. For example there are two illustrations included in Pryor & Jeffreys (figs. 12, 24), not noted by them, that clearly imply the existence of an underwater ram. Regardless, Pryor is still correct that the spur-bow would have been the principal system in use.

42. See Pollux (written during the reign of Commodus; 3 masts akateios, epidromos, dolôn) with Syvanne (2010b). Pryor & Jeffreys (p.240) analyze the interdependence between Pollux and the Anon. 10th century naval treatise.

43. See Pitassi, 2011, fig. 92 with his comments.

44. Pryor & Jeffreys (247–248) opposes this interpretation. They interpret the small sails to be storm sails.

45. Veg. 4.44–46.

46. The latter two alternatives are not mentioned by Vegetius.

47. Veg. 4.37ff.

48. For a fuller discussion of naval tactics, see Syvänne, 2004.

49. Description of the diekplous and periplous summarized and borrowed from Pitassi 2009, 14–16.

50. See also Syvänne, 2004.

51. The following (including the transliteration and translations of the terms) is mainly based on the outstanding studies of Fuhrmann (Civilian Policing, esp. 21–87) and Isaac (1990). Even though I may disagree in places, and the following text contains additional material not included by either of them, I have still based my account on their conclusions and recommend their books wholeheartedly for anyone interested in the policing of the empire. As far as policing of the empire is concerned their books complement each other. It should be noted that contrary to Isaac I consider the fortresses of the strata Diocletiana to be defensive in purpose (besides their other possible uses: administrative, police stations, road safety etc.) and not meant to prevent only nomadic banditry. The fact that the forts were not placed on the best defensive locations is not conclusive in light of the opposition. The military fortresses were placed to protect oases and springs with the purpose of denying the enemy access to the water sources. Thanks to the very poor offensive siege skills of the Bedouins this worked equally well against Bedouin raiders as well as against any large scale invasion by a confederacy of Bedouin tribes. The Romans had clearly analyzed the type of threat they were facing and used the most appropriate defensive structures to meet that threat. In my opinion it is also clear that the Romans did use the defence in depth approach in practice when they also fortified places in the interior and billeted troops in the cities. The narratives prove quite clearly that the Romans could withdraw the population inside the fortified places and allow the enemy to penetrate deeper if the enemy force was too powerful to be defeated near the border. Furthermore, even in those cases where the principal garrisons were placed along the frontiers with connecting road(s), it was possible to use the depth of the defensive zone against the invader. The fortifications in the interior prevented the enemy from taking those places outright with the result that the frontier forces could be assembled and used against the enemy either as a relief army or when the enemy was attempting to withdraw in frustration.

52. Isaac, 1990, 172ff.
53. Isaac, 1990, 172ff.
54. This and the following is based on Fuhrmann.
55. Hopwood.

Chapter 2

56. The following discussion is based especially on the studies of Aitchison, Alcock and Wagner, and to a lesser extent on Barker (41–2, 123–7) and Heath (77–80). However, the reader is reminded that there are still some minor differences of opinion between our interpretations.
57. For further information, see esp. Aitchison and Wagner together with Barker (41–2, 123–7) and Heath (77–80); Alcock, 270ff..
58. See Alcock, 93, 253–4; And esp. Aitchison, 111–129.
59. Alcock, 93, 253–70, 314ff.; Heath, 13–15, 41, 79–80; Barker, 41–3, 113–6; Allen.
60. For building techniques and uses of the Roman coastal forts, see Fields, 2006 with Aithison, Wagner, and Haywood.
61. The following is based on Syvänne (2004) with additional references to sources and secondary literature; Syvanne (2004, 2010a) and the narrative portions of this book; Lebedynsky (2001). For additional details concerning the Strategikon, see Syvänne, 2004. Other sources are mentioned in the footnotes.
62. This division follows that adopted by Lebedynsky, but the Saxons and Heruls could also be included among the Scandinavians.
63. See Speidel (2004) for the tribal behaviour patterns of the Germanic peoples.
64. This chapter is heavily indebted to Haywood as the references show, but still includes several conclusions of mine.
65. This is pure speculation in this case, but the Saxons may have followed the same initiation rites as their neighbouring Heruls in which the young males were required to kill an enemy before being released from the duty of being the female in a homosexual relationship with the adult male warriors. In this context it should be noted that despite being also married, the names of the Saxon war leaders, the brothers Hengist (stallion) and Horsa (mare) may imply their sexual orientation. Among the Danish Vikings it was shameful to be the female half in a homosexual relationship, but not necessarily to be the male half. See The Saga of the Jómsvikings 15, tr. p. 75 by Hollander, the insult: '… I challenge Sigvaldi to do battle with us unless he is an arrant coward and has the heart of a she-animal rather than that of a man'. In fact, the whole Jómsviking warrior band may have followed similar practices, because the presence of females in the fort was strictly forbidden.
66. The actual conquest of Britain was later achieved only in stages as a result of small numbers of warriors under Hengist and Horsa in three ships being first invited to the island followed by the settlement of larger numbers of warriors and civilians after the chieftains had already achieved a stable foothold on the island.
67. The following is based on my interpretation provided on the Saxon ships by Haywood (62ff), Beowulf and The Saga of the Jómsvikings. For the different types of ships in use, see also McGrail.
68. See: Underwood; Harrison; Alcock, esp. 327ff.
69. The following discussion is partly based on the studies of James and Haywood. The discussion of Frankish naval matters is indebted to Haywood's analysis. Consequently, for additional information regarding the Franks, see James and Haywood together with Syvänne, 2004. However, my interpretation differs from theirs in one major instance: I date the emergence of the Frankish confederation to the second century AD. In addition, I provide a new analysis of the Frankish military.
70. Haywood, 27–8.

71. I.e. I agree with Drinkwater's (2007, 56ff.) translation/interpretation of the key text/ inscription that the Iuthungi are likely to have been the 'Young Ones' that had separated from the Semnones, rather than a new name for the Semnones.

72. The Suebic confederacy had undoubtedly been similarly created through conquest by some warrior leader and his retinue.

73. For a fuller discussion of origins, see Katalin.

74. For the archaeological finds, see Katalin.

75. The following account is based on Syvänne (2004; 2010). Hernández' analysis of the Gothic military (147–191) is also a must read. For a fuller discussion, see esp. Syvanne 2010.

76. See also Wolfram, 1990, 97.

77. Note Procopius' (Wars 5.16.11) referral to the Gothic army of 150,000 in front of Rome consisting of both infantry and cavalry. According to him, most of the men and horses were equipped with armour. This suggests that the Goths always used their monetary resources for the equipping of their men and horses with armour. The same must already have been true during the third and fourth centuries, when there was also a clear tendency to increase the amount of armour among the Roman and Persian cavalry forces.

78. For additional information, see Syvänne, 2004. The Romans copied their sword from the Heruls.

79. The behaviour of the Heruli males brings up an ancient and modern taboo, namely the sexual needs of the males in the absence of women. In some modern armies the problem has been solved through the use of prostitutes, which was also one of the standard solutions in the Roman armies. This is not PC in today's public climate and therefore it is not mentioned even if it is common knowledge. The other way of obtaining a temporary release, masturbation, is also considered a taboo and not usually mentioned publicly. As far as I know, modern armies do not provide hiding places for masturbation, but try to prevent its occurrence. But in truth it still happens as anyone who has been in an army knows. In the case of the Heruli, the warriors solved the problem of seeking a temporary release and ecstasy through sex with younger males and asses. This obviously implies that the young males could not obtain a temporary release through copulation with other males. Consequently, it is possible that they masturbated or resorted to using asses. However, it is possible that adult males tried to prevent this from happening, because it would have made the youths more than eager to prove themselves in combat. As abhorrent as it sounds today, we should also not forget that one of the 'French-benefits' for period warriors was the raping of enemy prisoners.

80. The following account relies heavily on Kouznetzov & Lebedynsky; Lebedynsky (2001, 35–49, 109ff.; 2002; 2007, 60–75; 2010); Brzezinski and Miekzarek; and my interpretation of the Strategikon and events post 270.

81. It is possible that the eastern half of the Aorsi are the Yentsai of the Chinese chronicles (between the Caspian and Black Sea) that were supposedly able to put in the field 100,000 trained mounted archers.

82. See Syvanne, 2011b.

83. The following analysis of the army of the Bosporan Kingdom is based on Mielczarek, 1999, 79ff. However, the reader should beware that it also contains my own conclusions especially as regards the use of the war-wagons/crossbows (already mentioned in my dissertation in 2004 and in an article in 2006) and the military balance and Roman deployment in the area after c. 271.

84. If the occupying force (or allied force) self imposes such rules of conduct as western powers have been doing in the past three to four decades, the defeat of mountaineers/guerrillas becomes yet more difficult, even with the help of modern weapons. Of course, in a modern democratic society, where the granting of voting rights to women in the first half of the 20th century has brought softer and more humane values to the forefront of politics (most of the voters are women) and where the mass media cries foul if any war crimes are committed, it

is practically impossible to win such wars without outsourcing the use of violence to locals. The use of violence and terror in the name of national interest (i.e. the prevention of greater evils) is no longer an option unless public opinion is somehow desensitized to violence and killing. This was not a problem for the Romans or Persians.

85. I owe big thanks for Dr. Ayvazyan for reading, commenting and correcting this chapter and its preface. However, he should not be held responsible for any remaining mistakes. Those are my fault alone.

86. Anak means Evil and is not a real name, but a later Armenian name for the killer. The Surens, who were originally Saka chieftains from Sakastan/Sistan, were related to the Arsacid House through marriages and were therefore, just like the other Parthian princely families, called Pahlaw. At one point in time, a cadet line of the Surens appears to have established itself in Fars/Persis so that they were called Suren Parsig. I will discuss the reasons for the dating of the murder of Khosrov to the years 256–257 and not to its traditional date 252–253 in a separate forthcoming study.

87. The discussion of the society is primarily based on: Garsoïan (2004, 75–81); Faustus/ Garsoïan Appendix 3; Comments of Ayvazyan in e-mail. Note, however, that my discussion still contains some suggestions and conclusions which are at variance from the commonly accepted versions.

88. For the various Armenian technical terms, see Faustus/Garsoïan Appendix 3. Note, however, that my discussion contains my own suggestions and conclusions. According to Faustus/Garsoïan (531–532), the office of *hazarapet* was at one point in time also held by Vahan Amatuni and after the fall of the Arsacids the importance of the office grew under the Persians so that it came to signify the position of *wuzurg framadar*.

89. For the various Armenian technical terms, see Faustus/Garsoïan Appendix 3. Note, however, that my discussion contains my own suggestions and conclusions.

90. It has been suggested that the *senekapet* was a royal swordbearer (Faustus/Garsoïan, 557), which in my opinion may suggest a personal bodyguard/spy master in charge of spying and money with the duty of protecting the queen too.

91. For the list of technical terms, see Faustus/Garsoïan, App. 3. The chief executioner may have been the equivalent of the Persian jailer attested in the SKZ: *zindakapet* (Phl. zen = weapon, Phl. zindag = living + Arm. pet = chief), which may signify some sort of police/ security officer in charge of important prisoners (spy master?).

92. Note that the Shakashen refers to the Sakas. Just like most of the eastern portions of the Northern Gate this area was heavily contested between Albania and Armenia and the Armenians lost it in 387. In my opinion the existence of this Shakashen/Sakastan in Armenia supports Moses' version of Armenian history (2.2–3) according to which the area was already conquered by the Parthians during the reign of Mihridates after c.130 BC. According to this version Arshak made his brother Valarshak king of Armenia. I would tie up this event with the campaign of Sam (of the Saka Suren Family) mentioned by the Shahname of Ferdowsi.

93. I owe this to Dr. Ayvazyan's comment (for further info, see his *The Cornerstones of Armenian Identity: The Language, Army and State*, Yerevan 2007 in Armenian, 114–116).

94. See also Syvanne, 2004 with Elishe (148–9) and Faustus/Garsoïan (App. 3). In the 4th century, according to Nicolle (1992, 34), the Armenians also employed special mountain troops and used iron hooks to scale walls.

95. For the use of these terms, see Faustus/Garsoïan, 514. The practice appears to have been the same among both the Armenians and Persians.

96. For one of the latest assessments of Armenian military doctrine (esp. during the 6th century), see the outstanding study by Ayvazyan (esp. 13–85).

97. See Ayvazyan, esp. 55–80. It is probable that the 'Mamikonean tactics' described by him were also used by the Mamikoneans at least from the 3rd century onwards.

98. See Syvänne, 2004 with Lazar (Bedrosian's tr. p.253).

99. See Syvänne, 2004.

100. The Byzantine Interpolated Aelian (Devine 45.1–45.2; Dain J1–2) notes that the rhombus array was made of mounted archers in the Armenian and Parthian fashion. It is also unlikely to be a coincidence that the Gotha Ms. and Nihayat Sul (early 14th century Mamluk military treatises/compilations consisting of the Sasanian treatises, Persian/Arab translations of Aelian, and later additions), includes only rhombus and square/oblong formations as cavalry unit orders. The use of the rhombus array persisted in the area at least until the advent of the Ottoman Turks and their irregular arrays. I have suggested this in several presentations and articles, but I will present a more fully argued case later.

101. That is, I do not see any compelling evidence to contradict the traditional version presented by the Armenian sources that there were only one Khosrov and one Trdat.

102. I.e. I agree with Dr. Armen Ayvazyan's (exchange of e-mails) view of what would have best served Roman interests in the area. For further information regarding the strategic position of Armenia in the area, see his newest book, *The Armenian Military in the Byzantine Empire*, with further references therein. I discuss the reasons for this conclusion in greater detail in the text and in the forthcoming book dealing with the later military history.

103. Iberia/Kartli forms the eastern part of modern Georgia, the western portion being Colchis/Lazica with the Apsilians and Abasgians etc. It should be noted that some parts of modern Georgia do not want to be part of that state. The reasons for this situation lie in the history of the various nations and tribes. I have mistakenly sometimes labelled the Iberians as Lazi in my monograph/dissertation the Age of Hippotoxotai. A more accurate rendering would have either been Iberian and Lazi in the right places or the use of the generic Georgian to mean both the Lazi and Iberians.

104. See Suny 15ff. Additional general information regarding ancient Georgia, see Suny (3–27) and Braund (esp. 238ff). Note, however, that my account differs in several places from theirs.

105. Originally there appears to have been only seven principalities each ruled by a magnate appointed by the king: Shida Kartli, Kakheti, Khunami, Samswilde, Tsunda/Cunda, Cholarzene/Klarjeti, and Odzrkhe/Ojrhe.

106. GC pp. 34–36, 65, 67 with Suny.

107. GC, pp.34–36, 62–63, 65, 67, 73, 81–83, 129–130, 139–140, 146, 201–202.

108. GC e.g. pp. 40–41, 47–48, 168–171. Names and titles from Suny.

109. Hardly plausible in light of the figures given by Leonti Mroveli.

110. GC pp. 165–166, 173–174.

111. Under Khosrov the Great, the King of Armenia, the united forces of Iberia, Armenia, Albania and the northern nomads held their own against the Sasanians from c. 224 until the murder of Khosrov in c. 256.

112. In 1989 there were 123,000 Adyghes and 51,000 Tcherkesses (Kazanski & Mastykova, 8).

113. Of note is the fact that almost the same description can be found from Olaus Magnus' History of the Northern Peoples (ca. 1555). According to him, the 15th and 16th century Russians were following exactly the same practices as these Black Sea pirates, namely that they used 20- or 25-man boats that the Russians were in the habit of carrying into the forests and woods if needed. This obviously brings to mind the possibility of literary borrowing, but there are still several facts that speak for the authenticity of Olaus' account: 1) the Vikings, Russians and Finns are known to have used these kinds of longboats; and 2) the accounts differ in details (i.e. there is information in Olaus that can only refer to local conditions in the north).

114. The Borani were either a local tribe or some Germanic or Slavic or Sarmatian tribe that belonged to the Gothic Confederacy. For further info regarding these peoples and their history, see in particular Kazanski & Mastykova, 48–56.

115. For further information regarding these mountain peoples, see Kazanski & Mastykova, esp 48–56. For the Massagetae/Maskoutes, see Lebedynsky, 2007, 91–96. The numbers of men

are my own educated conservative guesses. It is likely that the overall numbers of arms-bearing male (and female) population would have been greater.

116. Strabo 11.5.6 with Syvänne, 2004.

117. It took 250,000 men for the Russians to conquer the north of Caucasus in the 19th century, and one cannot say that the Russian wars against the Chechens after 1996 would have been easy either. In the end the Russians decided to resort to the use of a local warlord, just like the ancient superpowers had.

118. The following chapter on society is mainly based on Daryaee's (2009) and Wiesehöfer's outstanding books, but also includes conclusions of my own taken from my forthcoming study of the Sasanian military.

119. I have here followed Daryaee's division of society and not the usual division suggested by other researchers consisting of: 1) the priests, 2) the warriors, 3) the bureaucrats (*disheran*), and 4) the common people (peasants *vastrjoshan* and artisans/workmen *hutukhshan*).

120. See Pourshariati's outstanding study of the importance of the Parthian nobles and their military forces within Sasanian society.

121. Based on Wiesehöfer, Daryaee, Purshariati and my own conclusions (i.e. the former do not bear any responsibility for my possible mistakes).

122. Wiesehöfer, 171ff.; with Pourshariati.

123. Garsoïan, Faustus, 530. According to Garsoïan (Faustus, 550), *nuirakapet* (Arm. master of ceremonies, Parth. *nivedag*) was commander of the royal bodyguard and a hereditary position in the family of the Zik. I.e. the researchers do not agree which offices and titles implied what.

124. The following subchapters on military are based on Syvänne (2004 with further references to sources therein) together with a gist of my forthcoming study of Persian military history. For references to secondary literature and sources, see Syvänne, 2004. However, my analysis of the military hierarchy and rankings is based on Shahbazi (2011) and once again on Daryaee, and Wiesehöfer. Skupniewicz's article (2011) also provides a useful summary of the Sasanian military structures and problems involved when attempting to interpret the material. Coulston's (1986) article on the tactical developments in the area remains a useful summary, and is also highly recommended. The latest archaeological evidence (PIPLA, 303–381, esp. 370; 593ff.) regarding the Sasanian campaign bases (i.e. not the garrisons, but campaign bases behind the walls) in the Gurgan area (early 6th century) confirms that the Sasanian field armies could easily reach the figure of 45,000/50,000 men, and possibly even up to 100,000/130,000 men.

125. See Grignaschi, p.24, p.42 n.76 with Shahbazi, 2011. I have also added additional translations from the glossary of Arabic military terms in Scanlon (123–130). Note also that according to Scanlon the *sahib al-liqa* or *sahib al-liwa* can also mean standard-bearer, flag-officer or flag-commander.

126. For a fuller discussion of the equipment used by the Sasanian cavalry, see Farrokh (2005, 2007); Skupniewicz (2008).

127. For different views regarding the Sasanian elephants, see: Syvänne (2004); Rance (2003); Charles; Scullard; Kistler.

128. Daryaee, 2009, 46–7.

129. For the use of Rhomboids by the Persians, see my forthcoming study of the battle of al-Qadisyaah. The formation with 13 ranks was the rhombus.

130. Aelian's 113 men are to be emended to 128. Being an armchair philosopher/theorist he has made the mistake of assuming that the array was an exact rhombus while still noting the sizes of cavalry units being 64 (wedge), 128 (rhombus), 256 etc. while still noting that the wedge was one half of the rhomboid. Note the earlier usage of the rhombus by the Parthians, which finds confirmation also in Justin's (41.2) figures. Justin claims that Mark Antony faced 50,000 horsemen that were led by 400 men, which means that each leader commanded 125 men to be rounded up to the figure of 128 required by the rhomboids. Note also that the 8th

century fighting tactic of the Muslims in the so-called *karadis*-formation (plural for the sing. *kardus* of 128 men) means that they had restarted using the old rhomboid formation. The use of rhomboids was particularly useful for cavalry units deployed on the flanks as it gave them an ability to face attacks from all directions. For earlier use of the rhomboids by the Dahae (Parthians were originally part of the Dahae confederacy) in the Seleucid armies, see Syvanne, 2009–2010 (due to be republished on the web).

131. The arrow-guide with its short darts appears to have been invented by the Sasanians for use against the Turkish multilayered shields only later in the fifth (or sixth) century. See Arab Archery, 125–126 with Syvänne, 2004.

132. For archery during the reigns of Ardashir and Shapur, see: Contribution a l'étude…, pp.46–47 (archery fell into decline after Ardashir and Shapur); Hajiabad Inscription praising Shapur's archery skills (available at Sasanika); Bivar, 1972, 284; Saracen Archery, pp.37–39, p.200. For further details of various archery techniques, see Arab Archery; Saracen Archery; Contribution a l'étude de l'archerie musulmane; Bivar, 1972; and Syvänne, 2004 with further references.

133. One cannot stress enough the importance of successive/shower shooting for the military history of the world as practised and invented by the Parthians and Sasanians. The Sasanian archery techniques and archery manuals served as models for the Muslim armies for years to come and this had an important military role as it enabled the Mamluks to outshoot the Mongols. In comparison, the rapid shooting practised by the Tang Dynasty Chinese (who had copied the technique from the steppes) consisted of the shooting of three shots in rapid succession (Chinese Archery, 202) while in the aftermath of the Mongolian Yuan Dynasty, during the Ming Dynasty, the Chinese considered the shooting of two arrows in rapid succession to be shower shooting (Chinese Archery, 272, 303). This post-Yuan Dynasty Chinese version that had been copied from the steppe nomads consisted of the taking of two arrows simultaneously in the right hand. The Chinese also used only two different types of locks: the Chinese (for infantry shooting with more punching power) and the Nomadic (for rapid shooting with weaker power). I would suggest that this form of shower shooting had been copied from the Mongols and the earlier one from the Turks, but as can be seen both pale in comparison with the Sasanian versions.

134. For the great variety of two-handed spear/lance techniques, see Munuyatu'l-Ghuzat, which provides a good overview of the several possible ways of placing the hands, even if it dates from the 14th century. The Sasanian reliefs (some of which are included here as line drawings) also give a good indication of such variants.

135. Just how efficient the internal security apparatus led by the head of the post (Postmaster) was expected to be can be learnt from Nizam al-Mulk's Siaysat-nama. According to him, the ancient system of agents and informers used by the kings of the age of ignorance (i.e. before Islam) and caliphs of Islam was so efficient that even if anyone wrongly took so much as a chicken or a bag of straw from another the king would know about it and have the offender punished. The kings were expected to appoint informers to keep an eye on everyone, but with the caveat that these informers were expected to be men who were completely above suspicion and self-interest. These men were directly responsible only to the king and no-one else, and they were expected to receive their monthly salaries regularly from the treasury. The king was expected to know of every event that took place and to take the appropriate measures (rewards, punishments, and commendations as needed). See Nizam (pp. 66–67, tr. by Darke).

136. The Late-Roman intelligence apparatus was similarly organized. See my forthcoming entry on the *agentes in rebus*.

137. Herodotus' (1.114) account of the young Cyrus the Great proves that there was just one 'King's Eye' during the Achaemenid era and not several, as often assumed on the basis of Xenophon's Cyropaedia (9.2.10–12). According to Herodotus, Cyrus appointed his friends so that some were to be his builders of houses, some his bodyguard, one to be King's Eye,

and still another his postal master. The implication is that there were separate offices of the Commander of the Bodyguard (chiliarch), King's Eye, and Postal Master, which also means that Postal Master was not the spy-master.

138. Mirkhond, 281.

139. See also Lewin's (1994) and Shahid's (*BAFOC*) analyses. See Wright's quotations of Musil's views (esp. 178–180) for the propensity of the Bedouins for booty and the state of anarchy before the rise of the Saudis. The Turkish frontier posts in the area could not control them. The Bedouins had no respect for life and sought booty merely for the sake of the thrill. For them fighting was just a sport. The situation must have been quite similar during Roman times.

140. See Shahid *BAFOC*, 381ff.

141. See Shahid *BAFOC*, 381ff.; Robin 1996.

142. See Shahid *BAFOC*, 381ff.

143. Lewin, 1994.

144. The following account of the Yemeni builds upon the information provided by Robin (1996, 2005–3006), plus Munro-Hay, Schippmann, and Beeston. However, the reader should be aware that my reconstruction is in places at variance with them, even if still indebted.

145. The following is based on Schippmann (87–90), Beeston , Hourani, Nicolle (1982, illustration of the Himyarite Formation p.5; 2001, 14–16), Yule and Robin, together with my own analysis of the sources.

146. Al-Kindi belonged to the Kinda tribe as the name implies. He was a 9th century Muslim philosopher who wrote a treatise on Swords.

147. For the dhows, see Hourani, 87ff; Green (89–91, 106–109); Taylor (2003). The shipping of elephants: Claudian, On Stilicho's Consulship 3.349ff. The purpose of Claudian's referral to the shipments of elephants was to belittle the fact that Stilicho did not have access to Indian elephants, but only to the smaller Libyan ones. Indeed, besides providing the Romans with silk and spices, it is also important to note that the sea route to India also gave them access to Indian elephants.

148. For the Roman garrison in Nubia, see Speidel (1992a, esp. 270) and for the deployment of Auxilia in Upper Egypt and Eastern Desert, see Maxfield (2000).

149. SHA Aur. 32.2–3, 41.10; SHA Firmus etc. 3–6; SHA Firmus etc. 7–11. The Arabs of Firmus would have been the Palmyrenes. Aurelian also appears to have punished the Egyptians for their disloyalty with extra taxes (additional boatmen on the Nile and Tiber to increase the grain supply, and taxes on produce etc.): SHA Aur. 35.1, 45.1, 47. This caused ever more troubles in Egypt. The support given by the Aksumites for the rebel caused a serious rift in the relationship.

150. The poor relationship between the Palmyrenes and Sasanians undoubtedly affected adversely the caravan network controlled by the former, leading to the conclusion of peace by Zenobia in c.271 with the Persians and to the attempt to increase maritime trade via the Red Sea.

151. Eventually Frumentius became treasurer and secretary, and Aedesius cupbearer of the ruler. On his deathbed the king (Ousanas?) gave the men their freedom, but his wife who had been put in charge of an infant son Ezena, managed to convince both of them to stay, and Frumentius was effectively in charge of the government. After Ezena had grown up, both returned to Roman territory in c. 328. For further details, see the reign of Constantine the Great.

152. Based mainly on Welsby, 1998, 39–40.

153. Welsby, 1998, 39–50; Nicolle, 1991, 10–11.

154. Strabo 6.22–24, 7.1.53–54; Pliny 6.35; Kirwan (1957, 17).

155. Ptolemy Geography 1.8.1–7; Kirwan (1957, 17). David Keys suggests the possibility that the four-month campaign was led by Maternus in AD 90 in the company of the Garamantian ruler to Lake Chad on the northeastern borders of Nigeria to capture slaves.

156. Nowadays there are only few white (grey) rhinoceroses left in the south of Sudan and north of Kenya, but in antiquity it is quite possible that there were rhinos as far north as perhaps Kosti and Sennar or even up to the junction of the White and Blue Niles at Khartoum.
157. See in particular the works of Burstein, Munro-Hay and Welsby.
158. For additional details, see: Syvänne, 2004; Welsby, 2002, esp. 16–20; Nicolle, 1991, 10–12; Speidel, 2004, 160. Further references to sources in Syvänne. Of particular note is Heliodorus' novel (9.16–18): Blemmye heavy infantry horse-stabbers advanced in front of the army against the Persian cataphracts, and then ducked underneath and stabbed the bellies of the horses.
159. The following is based on Welsby (1998, 2002) and Nicolle (1991) with Syvänne 2004. Most of the analysis of the military equipment and organization is indebted to Welsby.
160. The section on military organization owes most of its information to Welsby, but the speculative conclusions drawn from this material are my own.
161. For further information, see Munro-Hay, esp. Chapter 11.
162. Burstein 109–111.
163. The Aksumites used both Greek and Ge'ez as their official languages.
164. The DAE 8 inscription mentions the use of four armies on a campaign, which may suggest the use of four arms of service (infantry, cavalry, elephants, chariots) similar to that of India, or obviously four separate columns. If chariots were also used, these undoubtedly served only as commanders' transport vehicles, just as they were still used in Roman and Persian armies.
165. Most of the following is based on Syvänne (2004) and Mattingly (1983; 1995, 171ff.) and Le Bohec (2005).
166. For the dual citizenship and legal status of tribesmen with Roman citizenship, see Sherwin-White (1973) and Brett & Fentress, 50ff.
167. Nicolle (1991/2001, 6–7); Syvänne, 2004; Mattingly, 1983.
168. For a fuller discussion of the frontiers, see Breeze, 82–84, 126–129, 139–143.
169. Mattingly and Hitchner, 175.
170. This chapter builds upon the outstanding research articles and books of Mattingly (1983; 1995, 171ff.; 2003).
171. Based on Mattingly, 1995, 2003, and Keys' interview of Mattingly.
172. Mattingly, 2003; Keys.
173. Law; Reference to camels in Smith (493) and Mattingly. The North Africans appear to have domesticated the camel possibly in the second millennium BC.
174. Law (193); Mattingly 2003. Possible instances usefully collected by Mattingly, 2003.
175. The following is based on Shaw, Frézouls, Rebuffat, Breeze (143), Benabou (229–231, 238–240).
176. It is quite possible that Silius in his poem uses information he has heard of the various tribes and peoples, and mixes them and facts and fantasy quite freely. Therefore there is a possibility that he may have heard someone mention the mobility of the infantry of the Autololes, but whose homeland he has located in the wrong place. Also of note is the fact that Silius mentions in the same context the Macea, who may actually have been the Macenites, the neighbours of the Autololes in Mauritania. However, it is not impossible that the Autololes would have migrated west, because practically all tribal movements progressed in that direction.

Chapter 3
177. The changes in tactics can readily be detected from Arrian's *Tactica* and *Acies contra Alanos* as well as from the extant fragments of Hadrian's speech held at Lambaesis in 128 AD. For a fuller discussion of the latter, see Speidel 2006.
178. The comparative unattractiveness of naval service noted by Reddé (618), which obviously also holds true of the auxiliaries in general.

179. Problems of piracy during Alexander's reign mentioned by Reddé, 605–606.
180. See Syvanne, 2011a-b.
181. Haywood, 44ff.
182. Le Bohec, 2009, 171–173: i.e. this war was already fought when Valerian was in power. Its likely causes were the too-low esteem of Roman arms after Decius' demise, as well as the probable withdrawal of auxiliary forces from North Africa to fight on other fronts. The religious policies of Decius and Valerian may also have had an effect as, for example, the local Jewish Berbers may have felt that to be oppressive.
183. The referral to the *tagmata* (with the implication that the cavalry units were used in a similar way as the Byzantine *tagmata* of Constantinople, as a central elite reserve) is in Kedrenos/ Cedrenus p.454.6–10, Symeon 80.3, p.101, and in Zonaras/Banich, (translation with commentary on p.110).
184. Also noted by Sidnell, 274, 280.
185. *Aspidoforoi* = *skoutatoi* = *scutati* = *scutum*-shield-bearers (large round or oblong shields).
186. In 1975 (226–228) Speidel suggested that Caracalla created the institution of the *protectores* and that these consisted of his barbarian cavalry (*Leones*). In 1994 (131) Speidel suggested that the 300 *speculatores* came to be called *protectores*. In 1992b Speidel suggested that the *equites singulares Augusti* became first the *equites promoti dominorum nostrorum* under Diocletian and then the *comites seniores* by the time of the ND, which precludes the *protectores/domestici*. Strobel (274) suggests that the *equites singularis Augusti* came to be called *protectores Augusti* by the early-fourth century. In general for the *protectores/protectores domestici*, see Frank and Haldon (1984, 130–136).
187. It should be noted that the Ioviani and Herculiani legions were not necessarily created by the Illyrian emperors Diocletian and Maximianus. The fact that these legions originated in Illyria can actually be seen as evidence that they were raised by Gallienus at the same time as the *equites Dalmatae* and that these legions were given the honorary titles only later by the two emperors as a form of thanks for their loyalty. In my opinion it is difficult to see how these two emperors would have raised two green legions to become their elite strike force.
188. Trdat was the son of Khosrov the Great who had repeatedly defeated the Sasanians until they managed to assassinate him in about 253–257. There followed a short period during which the Armenians acknowledged Persia as their overlords, but the situation did not satisfy Shapur I, who invaded Armenia in about 259/60 after having defeated Valerian. It was then that Trdat, who was still only a child, was taken to safety at the house of Licinius.
189. The conquest of Palmyra was facilitated either by the recent demise of Shapur I and the period of unrest following this (Narses, the king of the Sakas, challenged the order of succession and had to be placated with the position of the Great King of Armenia), or by Hormizd's war against the Haitalites (=Hepthalites) or Sogdians (Thalibi, pp. 498–499), or by the possible contest between Narses the Great King and Wahram after Hormizd's death in 272–273(?). Unfortunately, it is impossible to say which of these it was that eased the conquest as the exact dating of the lengths of the reigns of Sasanian kings is impossible due to the poor state of the available evidence. The different suggestions for the date of the death of Shapur usually vary from 270 to 272, but even earlier and later dates have been suggested. What is certain, however, is that the recurrent problems in the east as well as the problems associated with the advent of each new ruler meant that the Persians could not effectively oppose Roman invasions from ca.272 until ca.293.
190. See Barnes, 2011, 37–38.
191. Lewin (2007), 245.
192. SHA Aur. 33.4; Kirwan (1972b, 458).
193. i.e. I agree with Kazanski & Mastykova (52–53) that it is likely that the Goths had been invited by the Romans.

194. The principal sources for Probus' reign are the SHA, Zos., and Zon. For the life and career of Probus with a discussion of the problems of the sources, see esp. Kreucher. My account of Probus' military campaigns differs somewhat from his, but I still recommend his book wholeheartedly as the best overall account of Probus' career. The sequence of events of Probus' reign is among the most difficult in the annals of Roman history to reconstruct and the reader is advised to take into account that many other reconstructions are almost (in my opinion) as plausible as mine.

195. The letter is included only in the notoriously-unreliable SHA.

196. Zosimus 1.63–64; SHA Tac. 13–14; Zonaras 12.28–29 (with additional references to other sources in Banchich et al. 125ff.).

197. The Georgian Chronicles (78–80), which has mixed Mihran/Mirian (supposedly the king of Georgia and son of Shapur) with Shapur's brother Mihrshah and Shapur's sons Hormizd and Narses with each other, also provides its own version of the events. According to this text, when Mihran/Mirian was 40-years-old, his father (Shapur), the Persian king died. Mihran's younger brother, the legitimate son of the king, Bartam (in truth Hormizd who was succeeded by his brother Bahram/Wahram) was chosen king. If one disregards the reference to the death of the father Shapur, then it is possible to think that the event took place after the death of Hormizd. However, Mihran (i.e. Narses) was unwilling to give up that easily. Mihran (i.e. Narses with Mihran?) assembled his army and marched towards Ctesiphon. His brother marched against him. The armies came face to face near Nisibis. The elders and rulers of provinces (marzpans) wanted to solve the question through mediation. An agreement was reached in which Bartam kept his throne, while Mihran/Narses was given Jaziret, Half of Sam and Atrapatakan (in truth Narses was made the Great King of Armenia with the expectation that he would succeed Hormizd). The GC also claims that while Mirian (and Narses) was preoccupied with the succession struggle the Ossetes (Alans), Perosh and Kavtia exploited his absence and had devastated Kartli (the heart of Iberia). Consequently, Narses invaded/raided Ossetia, which meant that Armenia was open for invasion at the time.

198. See Kazanski & Mastykova, 52–53.

199. Agathangelos 43–47; SHA Prob. 18.2.

200. The title *Persicus Maximus* has been found on a papyrus dated 21 October, 279. For this and an analysis of Probus' Persian campaign, as well as of the possible role of Tiridates in these events, see also Kreucher (158–161).

201. The eastward and southward movement of the Turks after ca.230 could easily be explained by the simultaneous southeast movement of the Goths and Heruls that destroyed the Alan hegemony of the western steppes. The first indications of this Turkish eastward movement can be read from Moses' referral to the invasion by the Khagan Vzurg and his defeat by Perozomat somewhere in Khurasan in the 230's. This in turn would have caused the Turks or Huns to turn their attention back to the Caucasus and the steppes still under the Alans.

202. According to Moses 2.91–92, Gregory the Great's son Aristakes returned from the Council of Nikaia (325) in the 47th year of Trdat's rule, which would mean that Trdat took the crown in 278. Aristakes died on the 52nd year of Trdat's rule (330) and his son Vartanes succeeded on the 54th year of Trdat's rule (332), which would mean that Trdat ruled at least until 332 before being poisoned. However, Faustos (3.3) claims that Vartanes succeeded as patriarch only during the reign of Khosrov. If one tries to reconcile these then it can be presumed that Trdat was murdered on his 52nd year of rule which was followed up by two years of anarchy, which would mean that Trdat was killed on 332. Unfortunately, this is not certain as Moses' and Faustos' accounts also diverge on subsequent details, the former (3.2–6) claiming that the rise of Khosrov to succeed his father with Roman help occurred during the reign of Constantius II, while the latter mentions no Roman help and states that the event took place during Constantine's reign.

Chapter 4

203. The following reconstruction and dating of events during the Diarchy and Tetrarchy is heavily indebted to T.D. Barnes' (1976, 1981, 1982) outstanding studies. His books are compulsory reading for this era. Williams' (1981) biography of Diocletian has also been consulted with profit. I have also found very useful the following collections of translated sources: REF1; Rees. Regardless of the fact that the following reconstruction is indebted to the above, the readers should be aware that I have sometimes adopted conclusions (and have not always noted those) at variance with them (e.g. regarding the dating of events in Armenia and the role of the imperial bodyguards) for which I only bear the responsibility. The sources used consist of the extant inscriptions and works of art as well as of the extant histories, Church histories and panegyrics (SHA, Origo, Eutropius, Aurelius Victor, Zosimus, Zonaras, Procopius, Panegyrici Latini, Victor, Lactantius, Eusebius, Agathangelos, Faustus etc.) most of which do admittedly have a bias in favour of Constantius, Constantine and Christianity. Regardless of this, I am very much inclined to accept Barnes' positive stance regarding the veracity of the Christian sources – and this includes even Lactantius, whose account has been too easily dismissed as mere Christian propaganda. The pagan sources are not more reliable than the Christian ones! Both are just as biased. Most of Lactantius' so-called suspect information can be verified from other sources: for example, as will be made clear, there is plenty of evidence for Maximian's poor handling of the finances that also caused internal dissent against the ruler. Similarly, it is clear that Maximian's sexual behaviour (the raping of hostages etc.) caused troubles with the Franks and Alamanni. There is no doubt about this because the sources are quite unanimous regarding Maximian's sexual behaviour, which included the raping of anyone who was unfortunate enough to catch his attention. I have not noted which source I have used except in such cases that require additional justification. Most of the extant narrative evidence consists of only about thirty pages and can easily be consulted e.g. from Rees, and doesn't therefore require the use of footnotes for each and every statement.
204. For a fuller discussion of the different alternatives, see Reddé, 623ff. Note, however, that my reconstruction differs in some details from that adopted by him.
205. These Heruli were the western branch of the divided nation, probably located somewhere in what is today south of Jutland in Denmark or in the area just south or south-west of it, while the eastern Heruls were living on the Black Sea coast near the River Don.
206. Pan.Lat 10.4.3–5.4.
207. Williams is of the opinion that Maximian was appointed as Augustus only after Carausius had usurped, because Maximian needed to have as high a rank as the usurper. However, I have here chosen to follow Barnes' dating.
208. See for example the analysis of Casey who supports the theory of the conquest of NE Gaul by Carausius in 290.
209. Pan.Lat 10.6.1–7.7.
210. Note, however, that Bohec (2006, 70) is of the opinion that Diocletian used two types of legions, the old about 5,000 strong legions and newer legions with the strength of only about 1,000 men. I am inclined to accept the traditional size for Diocletian's legions on the basis of Malalas' (esp. the referral to the use of legionary detachments as reserves behind the garrisons), Zosimus' and Vegetius' statements.
211. The referral to the use of only 2,000–2,500 legionary bases and to the rotation of the troops in Arguin (2011, 143).
212. The *Ioviani* and *Herculiani* were not new legions, but old ones that were merely renamed.
213. The date and base of the legion in Arguin (2011, 144).
214. Arguin (2011, 144–145).

215. i.e. note that it is likely that this office was already created during the 3rd century and not between 284–320. Constantius had been a governor of Dalmatia would not have been demoted to serve as a mere tribune.
216. Barnes (1981, 6; 182, 50–51).
217. See Barnes (1982, 125–126) on why Constantius should be considered to have been Maximian's *PP* in 288–293.
218. For the existence of the fleet that may have been transferred from Pevensey to the continent, see Reddé, 626ff.
219. I have followed here the timeline of Barnes. For the terms *laeti* and *foederati*, see the Intro.
220. It is not known when the fleets were divided among the *duces*. Reddé dates the creation of the smaller fleets to the reign of Constantine, but in my opinion Diocletian's reign seems a stronger candidate because he demonstrated a tendency to create smaller administrative entities (for example, the provinces were multiplied). See also Chapter 3.
221. That is, I agree with William's (44) assessment of Maximian, but disagree with him on the reliability of the accusations levelled at Maximian regarding Maximian's sexual behaviour.
222. See, for example, Sextus 39.17ff.; Eutropius 9.27.; Anon. Epitome 39.10–12; despite his accusation of greed against Diocletian, Lactantius still admits that he had constant budget surpluses (7.5) in contrast to Maximian (8.1–6).
223. Williams, 75.
224. Summary of the different views in Nixon and Rodgers, 112.
225. See Treadgold's calculations (1995, Chapter Pay) based on the known salary figures from the reign of Theophilus.
226. This is inaccurate. Justinian had more men than that. Agathias just like Procopius criticized him of abolishing the *limitanei* by not paying them salaries for a while.
227. For a fuller discussion of the different views, see Reddé, 623ff.
228. I have made this educated guess on the basis that in 373 at least one fleet served under the *Magister Equitum* and by the end of the fourth century the seagoing fleets served under the *Magister Peditum*. This suggests a pattern according to which the fleets were assigned to the highest ranking military commander in the hierarchy.
229. Reddé, 631ff.
230. It is not known whether the name was still the *Classis Nova Libyca* because the last probable referral to the Fleet dates from the years ca. 246–248 (Reddé, 566–7).
231. Reddé, 604.
232. Bohec, 2006, 71, 81–2.
233. Barnes 1981, 10.
234. Nixon and Rodgers, 115–116; Barnes 1981, 17.
235. Nixon and Rodgers, 115.
236. Evidence collected in Barnes, 1982, 56, 63.
237. The following is based on: Barnes 1981, 16; Eichholz; with some additions by me.
238. Summary of the evidence in Haywood (2nd ed.), 61–2.
239. For the use of the family name *Iulii* as well as for the periodical unity of the Baquates and Bavares, see Sherwin-White. The *Iulii* were Baquate kings or *principes* that had Roman citizenship and who had formed a treaty with Rome. In other words, the Baquates were Roman *foederati* who appear to have successfully united the Bavares and Quinquegentani into their tribal confederacy.
240. The following is based on my interpretation of Agathangelos 123ff. I re-date the conversion of Armenia to an earlier era, because in my opinion the previous researchers have been misled to date the event to the year 303 on the basis of the fact that it was only then that the Tetrarchs started their persecution of Christians. Trdat's persecution of the Christians clearly pre-dates that. It is in fact quite easy to date Trdat's conversion on the basis of how long Gregory

languished in prison (13 or 15 yrs) before being released after the crowning of Trdat that took place in about 278/9+13/15 = 291/2 – 293/4.

241. The following is based on Leonti Mroveli: The Conversion of Kartli by Nino in the GC pp.84ff.; Faustos (pp.238ff.); and Rufinus 10.11. The fact that Rufinus had heard the story straight from the Iberian/Georgian prince Bacurius makes it quite believable.

242. The inscription can be accessed from the Sasanika website.

243. The following reconstruction of the campaigns against Persia and against Egyptian usurpers follows closely Barnes' reconstructed timetable except in the timing of the Persian campaign against Armenia. Other reconstructions are also plausible.

244. This and the following are based on Procop. Wars 1.19.27–37.

245. REF1, 125ff.

246. Bohec 2005, 191–192.

247. Tr. by Nixon and Rodgers, 225.

248. Lee, 2007, 180–1.

249. Schippmann, 63; Hoyland, 50.

250. This and the following discussion of the persecution follows closely Barnes' interpretation, but also includes some departures from his views.

251. I have here followed the dating given by Barnes (1981, 64), as in most cases.

252. Date and place in Barnes, 1981, 56.

253. Libanius 19.13, 20.17–20; PLRE1 Eugenius 1.

254. Barnes, 1981, 56. Barnes suggests that Diocletian may have fought alone (if he fought a campaign in the Balkans in 304), but it would be strange if Diocletian would have conducted the campaign without the participation of Galerius.

255. Bohec, 2006, 71; Coello, 12–13 (discusses several different theories).

Chapter 5

256. The following is based on my article 'The Late Roman Art of War: the Reign of Constantine the Great' in *Slingshot*, the outstanding studies of Barnes (1981, 1982), and some new material so that this chapter is an enlarged and improved (hopefully) version of my article. In most cases, however, I have used Barnes only to date the various events (for which his studies are indispensable), except when I note it in the text. I also recommend highly Odahl's biography of Constantine, which I used with great profit when making the above mentioned article. In the following narrative I refer to the original sources only in such cases where there is a particular need to back up my argument or when those are not included in my article. If one wants to look which sources I have used in other cases I refer the reader to the footnotes in my article. For the persons mentioned, see PLRE1. For the latest biography of Constantine see Elizabeth James, but not used in this study.

257. The evidence for this is included in the second book in the series.

258. Sources collected in REF 144–45.

259. Barnes, 1981, 33; Odahl, 92–3.

260. Barnes, 1981, 35–37.

261. Sources collected in REF 144–45.

262. Contrary to the often stated claim Constantine did not use the hollow wedge/scissors formation, which was a counter tactic against an infantry wedge, but the opening up of the formation which was used against cavalry wedge.

263. It is very probable that Constantine had agents inside the city that may have used similar cryptographic means as Publius Optatianus Porfyrius to exchange messages. He sent a poem to Constantine after the fall of Maxentius in the form of a *technopaegnion* in which the message was hidden with different ink colours and patterns. See Barnes, 1981, 47–8.

264. For the *Equites Singulares Augusti* and the Praetorian horse, see M.P. Speidel (1992c).

265. Barnes, 1981, 45ff.

266. Barnes, 1981, 45ff.
267. Lee, 2007, 176ff.
268. Lee, 2007, 176ff.
269. Bernes, 1981, 53–61.
270. Odahl interprets the stratagem differently. In his view, the generals hid their forces near or on the banks of the Rhine and then both they and the fleet of Constantine defeated them whilst they tried to cross the river. I would suggest that Constantine would have had to withdraw his army quite far away in order to make his stratagem believable. The Frankish scouts would have detected the concealed Romans too soon if the latter would have used the methods suggested by Odahl.
271. The other possibility is that this desertion took place in 317 as suggested by Shahid (BAFOC) on the basis of the *Arabicus* inscription by Constantine's governor. However, I have here chosen to follow Barnes, because the war against Persia in 313/4 would seem to be the likeliest date for the desertion.
272. The various pieces of evidence are collected by Shahid (*BAFOC*), but our reconstructions differ significantly in details. Regardless, all reconstructions of Arab federates, including mine, are indebted to Shahid.
273. Chron. Arb. 10–11.
274. Barnes, 1981, 69.
275. Barnes, 1981, 69–70.
276. The principal sources are Zosimus, Origo and Eusebius' Vita. See also Odahl, 174ff; Reddé, M., Mare Nostrum, Paris (1986), 347–8; Syvänne, 2004, 2006.
277. Is this to be taken to be representative of the strength of a legion belonging to the *Comitatus* (now a Palatine legion) that he had inherited from his father? The figures of 5,000 foot and 800 (726 plus supernumeraries) horse are quite close to the standard sized legion that I postulated for Diocletian on the basis of Vegetius.
278. Eusebius Vita 2.44ff.; Barnes (1985), 130–1.
279. Tabari i. 838–839.
280. GC pp.114–133.
281. Eusebius Vita 4.8; Barnes, 1985, 131–2. Note, however, that my reconstruction differs from Barnes' in this case.
282. In 515, the Imperial Fleet was under the command of the two *magistri praesentales*, but when these refused to command it, another person was chosen instead. See vols. 2 and 4.
283. See Barnes., 1993, 165ff.; Lee, 2007, 198ff.
284. See esp. Barnes 1981, 1993 (useful summary of the relationship between the Church and Emperor from 325 to 361, 165–175).
285. For the administrative structures of the empire, see Delmaire and Jones (321ff.).
286. Delmaire, 29–45, Jones, 335ff. I have here chosen to follow Delmaire.
287. There are useful translations and commentaries regarding the wars in the east in REF1, 143ff.
288. i.e. I date the politicisation of Christianity by Constantine to an earlier period than Barnes (1985).
289. Dates in Barnes, 1982, 77.
290. Dates in Barnes ,1982, 77.
291. Enrico Livrea (Blemyomachia, 23–31) suggests that the so-called Blemyomachia was written by Olympiodorus of Thebes and that it describes a local war conducted by Germanus who is to be indentified as *magister militum vacans* of Theodosius II in the war against the Vandals in 441.
292. Jordanes Get. 21–22, 111–115; Wolfram, 1990, 61–2.
293. Wolfram, 1990, 62–63; Barnes, 250.

294. It should be noted that the maps of the different studies place the ditches in slightly different places, which is reflected also in the accompanying map of the Balkans, which includes two variants in one map. Consequently, I cannot vouch for the accuracy of the locations shown on this map without making a field trip to the locations in person.

295. i.e. I date the so-called *Monumenta Adulitanum* to the reign of Ezana.

296. Philostorgius (2.6, 3.4–5) mentions the sending of Theophilus the 'Indian' from the Yemeni territory (island of Dibos/Divus) as hostage during the reign of Constantine the Great. Shahid (BAFOC 97–99) identifies the island of Dibos with the Diba of the Gulf of Oman but the Maledives have also been suggested, which suggests strongly that the Roman fleets were operating in conjunction with the Aksumites in conquering Yemen. Shahid also suggests that the Roman fleets were operating in the area, but on their own.

297. Faustos 3.1ff.; Moses 3.1ff.

298. Kazanski & Mastykova (57–58) interpret Moses' list of invaders to include the Caucasian Egersvanes (Svanes) and Gogours (Gargarees/Gerrhi). The sources for the following are: Faustos 3.1ff.; Moses 3.1ff.; Julian Or. 1.18D-19A, 1.20D-21A. This suggests the existence of a large Kingdom of Alans, 'Massagetae' and Albanians under Sanatruk.

299. This chapter is based on Barnes, 1981, 252–253.

300. The introduction of the super-heavy cavalry is also noted by Farrokh (2007, 200).

301. REF1, 154ff.

302. May mean the Koltta Lappalaiset = Skolts. The Koltta is sometimes pronounced as Koltha. Today Koltta is approximately the area encompassing the Lapland of modern Finland, Norway and the Kola Peninsula of Russia. If the Goltha-Scythians really mean the nomadic Laps, then Hermanaric would have subdued all of the tribes up to the Barents Sea, which does sound too good to be true. However, when one takes into account the conquest of Siberia by really small forces of Cossacks and the conquest of America by the Conquistadores, this is not that far fetched. It is quite plausible that Hermanaric could have sent some small forces (the equivalents of Cossacks) up north to reduce the tribes encountered to tribute-paying status. The opposition wouldn't have been that significant. The different tribes could probably field only hundreds of men, and in the case of the Tshuudi/Hämäläiset/Tavastians, probably not more than about 2,000–3,000. We shouldn't make the mistake of considering the peoples of the north to have been out of touch with peoples south of them. For example we possess archaeological evidence for direct contacts between the Sasanians, Finns and Swedes for the sixth and seventh centuries, and the fur-route from the north also extended as far north as modern Finland.

303. May mean the Tshuudi/Chud (can also mean all Finns in Russian), which according to some historians meant the Finnish tribe of Häme (Tavastians) which was in possession of the Novgorod area until about 700s and not to the 3rd century as Holtke.

304. Jordanes, Getica 23.

Chapter 6

305. Barnes 1993, 34–5, 219.

306. Shahid, BAFOC, 74ff., 527–29.

307. If the reader is interested in the various nuances between the different Christian doctrines, the roles of Eusebius and Athasius, and the religious policies of the emperors between ca. 284 and 371, I highly recommend the reading of Barnes' outstanding studies (1981, 1993, 2011), and Heather and Matthew's summary 127ff.. This and the following discussion of Constantius' religious policies and his relationship with Athanasius is based on Barnes' 1993 study of their careers, even when not referred to in the following notes.

308. Barnes, 1993, 47–8.

309. Barnes, 1993, 167; Lee, 2007, 193ff.

310. See Mayor for instances of the use of biological warfare during antiquity.

311. Chron. Arb. 11–12.
312. A very useful summary of the sources for Constantius' eastern wars in REF1, 164ff. Libanius' Or. 59, Julian's (Or. 1 and Or. 2) panegyrics of Constantius, Ammianus' History (after c. 354) fill in the missing pieces of evidence. The reader is referred to these. I will refer to these only when I consider it necessary.
313. Zon. 13.5; Zos. 2.41.
314. Salway, 256ff.
315. For the terms, see Boak, 141.
316. Barnes (1993, 224–5) has conveniently collected all the evidence for Constans' movements between 337–350. Some of the same evidence can also be found from Seeck 4 Suppl.
317. Salway, 256ff.
318. Bohec 2005, 199.
319. Zos. 2.42; Vict. 41.23–4; Eutropius 10.9.3; Zon. 13.5–6.
320. Zos. 2.42; Zon. 13.5–6.
321. For a fuller discussion, see Fox, 1997.
322. REF1, 176ff.
323. For the battle, see: Libanius 59.99–120; Julian, Or. 1.22D-25B. Sources collected in REF1 181–190.
324. Once again the sources for the following eastern events are usefully collected in REF1 (188ff.) while Constantius' attested movements are usefully collected by Barnes (1993, 220). It should be noted that my reconstruction doesn't agree with Barnes in all details.
325. Faustos 3.21 confuses this battle with that of Galerius in 298.
326. Wolfram, 1990, 63.
327. Drinkwater, (2007) 200ff.
328. Siege: Julian (Or. 1.27.A-29A; 2.62.Bff.) with REF1 (164–171, 191–207) and Heliodorus (9.1–11).
329. For the Chionitai and Kidarites, see Lebedynsky (2007) and Zeimal. We possess too few pieces of evidence for the events that took place in Central Asia, as a result of which the origins of these tribes are contested. Consequently, some researchers consider the tribes to be separate, while others (e.g. Zeimal) equate the Chionites with the Kidarites on the basis of Priscus (Huns who are Kidarites). For the Kushans, see Raychaudhuri; Lebedynsky (2007); Dani; Dani and Litvinsky; Mukherjee; Puri. For the Gupta military, see Sandhu.
330. Raghuvança Canto 4 (pp.28–36) claims that Raghu (who is probably to be identified with Samudragupta rather than with Chandragupta II) conquered India and then defeated the Persians, Hunas (Huns), Kambodjas, and peoples of Himalaya and south of Himalaya. His army is said to have consisted of the traditional four arms of service: elephants, cavalry, chariots and infantry. Of note is the use of cataphracted elephants clad in mail as well as the marching formation in which the cataphracted elephants were placed in front as a bulwark behind which marched chariots, horses, and infantry. The elephants cleared the roads and made rivers fordable. For additional info regarding Samudragupta, see Raychaudhuri pp.470–487. I will discuss the military organization and tactics of the Gupta in a forthcoming study.
331. The following is primarily based on Julian Or 1–2 and Zos. 44.1ff.
332. Julian Or.1.40C-D mentions that a fleet was gathered in Egypt against Carthage, but it would not have sailed from Italy as the emended text would have it, but to Italy from Carthage. It would not make any sense to collect an invasion fleet against Italy in Egypt when Greece was in Constantius' hands. Julian also mentions naval operations (Or. 2.74C) against Carthage, Sicily and the mouth of the Po, as well as the conquest of the Pyrenees/Cottian Alps (Or. 1.40C, 2.78C) with amphibious operations. The operation against the Po must have been conducted by a separate fleet from that of Carthage/Sicily, and the operations behind the Cottian Alps and to the Pyrenees belong to the last phase of the campaign.

333. Based on Julian Or. 1.29A–49A, 2.55.C–60C; Zosimus 2.50–53; Zonaras 13.8; Syvänne, 2004.
334. Julian 1.36B–D, 2.59C–60A.
335. Barnes 1993, 105–106, 221, 314.
336. Barnes 1993, 105.
337. After this, the information is primarily based upon the extant books of Ammianus unless otherwise stated. I have not included long analyses why I have in some cases chosen not to follow Ammianus' version of events. In most cases, however, the reasons are very obvious and caused by the unfair bias of Ammianus against certain persons. Regardless, Ammianus is by far the best, most impartial and knowledgeable of the sources that we possess, and it is a great regret that his earlier books are lost.
338. Gallus' movements in Barnes 1993, 226.
339. Once again sources usefully collected in REF1, 188ff.
340. Tabari (i.845–46) states that Shapur II appointed Imru's son Amr as governor of Hira and states that he remained in office for the remainder of Shapur's reign (309–379), the whole of Ardashir's (II, 379–383) and part of Shapur's (III, 383–388) reign, for a total of 30 years.
341. Shahid (*BAFOC*, 120–121) places the transferral to an earlier period. The Ghassanids originated in the south of Arabia and migrated north during the third century, ending up near Hira at some point in time. In the fifth they deserted the Persians and became the dominant Roman allied group in the sixth century.
342. Moses 3.19ff.
343. Note that the GC confused several Mirdats with each other.
344. There is a lacuna in Ammianus, but the missing tribe must be the neighbours of the Lentienses, which means that the likeliest candidates are the Raetovarii (men of Raetia) and the Iuthungi further away.
345. See Syvänne, 2004 (strategy vs. Slavs).
346. See Amm. 15.4 with Syvänne, 2004.
347. Drinkwater 2007, 212–3.
348. The following is based on: Barnes 1993, with useful summary 165ff.; Lee, 2007, 198ff.
349. Soc 4.15; Soz. 4.21.
350. See Shahid, BAFOC, 96–100.
351. See Shahid, BAFOC, 96–100.
352. Philostorgius/Amidon, p.41, n.8.
353. PLRE1 (Gratianus1; Valentianus7) dates this campaign to the 320s or 330s so that he would have accompanied his father, but there are two problems with this. Firstly, he cannot have carried the '*signa*' that young. Secondly, his father was *Comes rei Castrensis per Africam*, which belonged to the western half of the empire (i.e. he would have campaigned with the help of the Garamantes on an area under Licinius' jurisdiction). I favour the 350s because Valentinian was then old enough to be a tribune who could have led a unit or units in combat. However, if Gratianus had indeed conducted a campaign this must have happened in 327/8 with the support of the Garamantes.
354. Rubin, 1996, 693.
355. Mattingly, 1995, 176–177.
356. I have accepted here Drinkwater's (2007, 223) suggestion regarding the route, but depart from it in suggesting that Constantius and Julian marched on the opposite sides of the river northwards.
357. Zos. 3.7.
358. The following is mainly based on Amm. 17.2.1ff.
359. The following is mostly based on Amm. 17.12.1ff., 19.11.
360. The locations of Constantius in Barnes, 1993, 223.
361. Dating, Barnes, 1993, 223.

362. For a Finn this war-cry brings to mind 'murha, murha' (or 'murhaa, murhaa' = 'murder, murder' or 'kill, kill'), but obviously the meaning in the Sarmatian dialect of Iranian must have been different.
363. The following is based on Barnes 1993, with a useful summary at the end; and Heather/Matthews, 127ff..
364. The following is based on Amm. 28.4.1ff.
365. The siege of Amida is based on Amm. 18.91.ff., 20.2; Lenski, 2007.
366. Lenski, 2007.
367. Amm. 19.13.
368. The following is mainly based on Amm. 20.1.1ff.
369. Based mostly on Amm. 20.6.1ff.
370. Based on Amm. 20.6 and analysis of the accompanying map of the locale.
371. Based on Amm. 20.7 with Lightfoot's assessment of the likely locale.
372. Based mostly on Amm. 20.11.1ff.
373. Rubin, 1996, 693.
374. The following is mostly based on Amm. 21.2.1ff. with 15.8.3, 15.8.18, 16.10.18, 21.1.5, 25.4.2. For the persons mentioned, see also PLRE1.
375. Ammianus (22.14.3) with the 2nd book in the series.
376. See also Drinkwater's (2007, 255ff.) perceptive comments regarding this incident.
377. Amm. 21.7.1–5, 21.12.21–22.
378. Amm. 21.7, 21.13.1ff.
379. Amm. 21.15.
380. For further discussion of the Roman methods of spreading illnesses, see Julius Africanus (*Kestoi* 1.2.49–136 with comments of Viellefond), Mayor and Syvänne, (2006 water).
381. Ammianus includes a useful summary of the good and bad qualities of Constantius on which the following is partly based, but my assessment will depart from some of his claims.

Appendix
382. The following is mostly based on the very useful summary of the Christian schools of thought in Heather/Matthews, 127ff.

Index